Society

Jeffrey Otto
HM51. M165?

did I get this
for a
sociology class
at SEC in
1995?

This book is offered to teachers of sociology in the hope that it will help our students understand their place in today's society and, more broadly, in tomorrow's world.

John J. Macionis

Society
The Basics

John J. Macionis
Kenyon College

Prentice Hall, Upper Saddle River, NJ 07458

Library of Congress Cataloging-in-Publication Data

Macionis, John J.
    Society: the basics / John J. Macionis. — 3rd ed.
      p. cm.
    Includes bibliographical references and index.
    ISBN 0-13-435819-8 (pbk.). — ISBN 0-13-437906-3 (pbk. : annotated
instructor's ed.)
    1. Sociology.   I. Title.
HM51.M1657   1995
301—dc20   95-2839
                         CIP

Acquisitions Editor: Nancy Roberts
Editorial Director: Charlyce Jones Owen
Development Editor-in-Chief: Susanna Lesan
Development Editor: Diana Drew
Production Editor: Barbara Reilly
Marketing Director: Lauren Ward
Marketing Manager: Kris Kleinsmith
Copy Editor: Amy Macionis
Editorial Assistant: Pat Naturale
Buyer: Mary Ann Gloriande
Design Director: Anne Bonanno Nieglos
Interior Design: Amy Rosen
Cover Design: Thomas Nery
Cover Art: Woodie Long, *Pop the Whip.* 18" × 24". Painted on Arches Water Color Paper using acrylic paints.
Photo Editor: Melinda Reo
Photo Research: Barbara Salz

©1996, 1994, 1992 by Prentice-Hall, Inc.
Simon & Schuster / A Viacom Company
Upper Saddle River, New Jersey 07458

Printed in the United States of America
10 9 8 7 6 5 4 3 2 1

ISBN 0-13-435819-8

Prentice-Hall International (UK) Limited, *London*
Prentice-Hall of Australia Pty. Limited, *Sydney*
Prentice-Hall Canada Inc., *Toronto*
Prentice-Hall Hispanoamericana, S.A., *Mexico*
Prentice-Hall of India Private Limited, *New Delhi*
Prentice-Hall of Japan, Inc., *Tokyo*
Simon & Schuster Asia Pte. Ltd., *Singapore*
Editora Prentice-Hall do Brasil, Ltda., *Rio de Janeiro*

Printed on Recycled Paper

Brief Contents

Contents

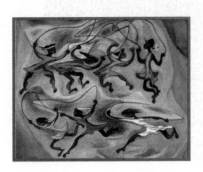

1

Sociology: Perspective, Theory, and Method 1

2

Culture 29

3

Socialization: From Infancy to Old Age 57

4

Social Interaction in Everyday Life 81

5

Groups and Organizations 103

6

Deviance   127

7

Social Stratification   155

8

Global Stratification   187

9

Race and Ethnicity   211

10

Sex and Gender   237

11

Economics and Politics   263

12

Family and Religion   297

14
Population and Urbanization   363

15
The Natural Environment   389

16
Social Change: Modernity and Postmodernity 411

GLOBAL MAPS: WINDOWS ON THE WORLD

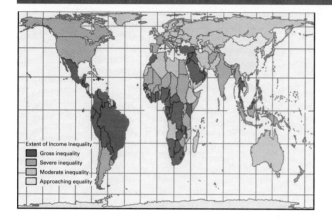

NATIONAL MAPS: SEEING OURSELVES

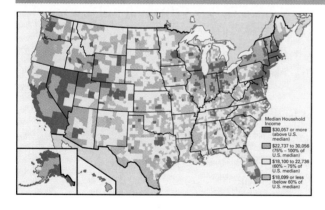

Boxes

GLOBAL SOCIOLOGY

Preface

Across the United States, the number of students studying sociology is increasing rapidly, with almost 1 million men and women per year enrolling in the introductory course alone. Why this swell of interest in sociology? History provides a clue: Just as the rapid changes linked to industrialization stimulated the development of sociology a century ago, the transformations wrought by the emerging postindustrial society are exciting sociological thinking as this century draws to a close.

In the United States, the development of new information technology (coupled with the marked decline of traditional industries) is reshaping the workplace—changing the location and even our conception of work. And, around the world, a single global economy now connects nations the way the burgeoning national economy linked cities a century ago. Change wrought by this process of globalization is rippling through the world's political systems, challenging educators everywhere to rethink their curricula, and setting off waves of migration, especially to the United States. Even the stunning cultural diversity that has long fascinated and frustrated humankind may now be eroding as communications technology—from satellite transmissions to facsimile machines—draws members of thousands of world societies into a global conversation.

Against this backdrop of ongoing change, we are proud to offer the third edition of *Society: The Basics.* This new edition of *Society*—by far the most popular brief text available—is thoroughly revised, refreshed with new features, topics, and images, yet retains its authoritative and inviting voice. Indeed, as daily electronic mail messages from students across the country (and around the world) testify, *Society* is not only good sociology, it is plain fun to read.

Society: The Basics is derived from *Sociology,* fifth edition, which more instructors choose for their students than any other sociology text. Yet this brief edition—sixteen chapters presenting the essentials of sociology in a trim, paperback edition—is favored by colleagues who teach at "quarter" schools, wish to supplement a text with additional readings, or are concerned about minimizing the cost of student texts.

Society: The Basics was not the first brief text in sociology, but it is distinctive. Most brief texts are the cut-down versions of longer books (with scissors wielded as often by editors as by authors). Such "cut-and-paste" books may be attractively priced, but typically they do not earn the loyalty of instructors, who try them for a term only to return to more comprehensive books. By contrast, *Society: The Basics* is the product of extensive *rewriting* by the author. This is why it reads smoothly and seamlessly. Just as important, the author has retained in this brief format each and every major topic found in the longer, hardcover version. There are no holes in the coverage; the presentations are simply more focused and direct, providing fundamentals without frills. We hope that short-text users will conclude that, in this case, less is truly more.

The Organization of This Text

This text carries students through the discipline's basic ideas, insights, and research in sixteen logically organized chapters. Chapter 1 ("Sociology: Perspective, Theory, and Method") explains how sociology's distinctive point of view illuminates the world in a new and exciting way. In addition, the first chapter presents major theoretical approaches and explains the key methods sociologists use to test and refine their thinking.

The next five chapters examine core sociological concepts. Chapter 2 ("Culture") explains how and why our species has created fascinating and variable ways of life around the world. Chapter 3 ("Socialization: From Infancy to Old Age") investigates how people the world over cultivate their humanity as they learn to participate in society. While highlighting the importance of the early years to the socialization process, this chapter describes significant transformations that occur over the entire life course, including old age. Chapter 4 ("Social Interaction in Everyday Life") presents a micro-level look at how people construct the daily realities that we so often take for granted. Chapter 5 ("Groups and Organizations") focuses on social groups, within which we have many of our most meaningful experiences. It also investigates the expansion of formal organization and suggests some of the problems of living in a bureaucratic age. Chapter 6 ("Deviance") analyzes how the routine operation of society promotes deviance as well as conformity.

The next four chapters provide more coverage of social inequality than is found in any other brief text. Chapter 7 ("Social Stratification") introduces basic concepts that describe the variety of social hierarchy throughout history and around the world. The chapter then highlights dimensions of social difference in the United States today. Chapter 8 ("Global Stratification") is a unique chapter that demonstrates this text's commitment to global education by analyzing contemporary social stratification in the world as a whole. This chapter analyzes inequities of wealth and power among all nations and various world regions.

Society: The Basics also provides full-chapter coverage of two additional dimensions of social difference. Chapter 9 ("Race and Ethnicity") explores racial and ethnic diversity in the United States, as well as the social rankings accorded to racial and ethnic categories of our population. Chapter 10 ("Sex and Gender") describes patterns of human sexuality and explains how societies transform the biological facts of sex into systems of gender stratification.

Next are three chapters that survey social institutions. Chapter 11 ("Economics and Politics") explains how the Industrial Revolution transformed the Western world, contrasts capitalist and socialist economic models, and investigates how economic systems are linked to a society's distribution of power. This chapter also contains coverage of the military and important issues of war and peace.

Chapter 12 ("Family and Religion") spotlights two institutions central to the organization and symbolism of social life. The chapter begins by focusing on the variety of families in the United States, making frequent comparisons to kinship systems in other parts of the world. Basic elements of religious life are discussed next, with an overview of recent religious trends.

Chapter 13 ("Education and Medicine") examines two institutions that have gained importance in the modern world. The historical emergence of schooling is addressed first, noting many ways in which educational systems are linked to other social institutions. Like education, medicine has become a central institution during the last century. The chapter concludes by explaining the distinctive strategies various countries—including the United States—employ to promote public health.

The final three chapters of the text focus on important dimensions of social change. Chapter 14 ("Population and Urbanization") spotlights the growth of population and the swelling of cities in the United States and, especially, in poor nations of the world. Chapter 15 ("The Natural Environment") introduces a new and important area of sociological study to brief texts, explaining ecological trends and exploring links between the state of the natural world and patterns of social organization. Finally, Chapter 16 ("Social Change: Modernity and Postmodernity") summarizes major theories of social change, looks at how people forge social movements to encourage or to resist change, points up various benefits and liabilities of modern social patterns, and highlights the recent emergence of a "postmodern" way of life.

Continuity: Established Features of *Society: The Basics*

Although brief texts have much in common, they are not the same. The extraordinary popularity of *Society: The Basics* results from a combination of a dozen popular features.

Emphasis on Social Diversity. A key principle guided the crafting of *Society: The Basics*. First, this text acknowledges the diversity of today's students—who are an unprecedented mix of people of African, Hispanic, Asian, European, and Native-American heritage; women and men; and older learners as well as traditional students in their teens and twenties. This text is broadly inclusive of all people in its content, language, and tone, reflecting the author's own twenty-five years of teaching in diverse academic settings, including large universities, small colleges, community colleges, and even a prison and a police academy. From these experiences, I have learned that inclusiveness is good sociology because a text that acknowledges *all* categories of students provides more learning for *each* by portraying the rich variety of U.S. society.

A Global Focus. *Society: The Basics* analyzes the structure and trends of U.S. society in global context. That is, this text not only reveals how individual lives are shaped by placement in one society, but offers the extended reach of showing how U.S. society is itself affected by our country's position in the world as a whole. Global sophistication is all too rare among today's students. After all, of 12 million U.S. college students, only 50,000—less than 1 percent—have first-hand experience studying abroad. (This number pales in comparison to the 350,000 foreign students currently studying in the United States.)

This text, which reflects not only global research but the author's own experiences in dozens of countries, truly brings the world to student readers. *Society: The Basics* does so as it links social patterns in the United States to processes and trends around the globe. Various chapters explain, for example, how our own way of life is prompting the development of a global culture, and how the increasingly global economy is generating more pronounced economic inequality in this country. This world-wide emphasis in no way lessens the text's focus on the United States; on the contrary, it provides a richer and more accurate understanding of our society.

Emphasis on Critical Thinking. Critical-thinking skills include the ability to challenge common assumptions, formulate questions, identify and weigh appropriate evidence, and reach reasoned conclusions. This text empowers students to discover as well as to learn, to seek out contradictions as well as to formulate consistent arguments, and to forge connections among the various dimensions of social life.

Unsurpassed Writing Style. Equally important, this text offers a writing style widely praised by students and faculty alike as elegant and engaging. *Society: The Basics* is an inviting text that encourages students to read—even beyond their assignments.

Intriguing Chapter Openings. The engaging vignettes that begin each chapter have been a popular feature of earlier editions. These openings—which highlight current research (such as Deborah Tannen's best-selling analysis of how gender shapes interpersonal communication) or contemporary issues (for instance, the "family values" debate)—spark the interest of the reader as they introduce important ideas. For this edition, six of the vignettes are new.

Instructive and Engaging Examples. Readers consistently praise this text for offering high-quality examples and illustrations that enhance clarity because they are meaningful to students. On every page, class-tested examples and illustrations give life to concepts and theories and demonstrate to students the value of applying sociology to their everyday lives.

Inclusive Focus on Women and Men. Few brief texts devote a full chapter to the important concepts of sex and gender. *Society: The Basics* does this and more by "mainstreaming" gender into *every* chapter. This text explains that gender not only affects our answers about how society works but also shapes the way we frame questions in the first place.

Theoretically Clear and Balanced. This text makes theory easy. The discipline's major theoretical approaches are introduced in Chapter 1 and are reapplied systematically in later chapters. In addition to the social-conflict, structural-functional, and symbolic-interaction paradigms, chapters incorporate social-exchange analysis, ethnomethodology, sociobiology, and cultural ecology.

Recent Sociological Research. *Society: The Basics* blends classic sociological statements with the latest research as reported in leading publications in the field. Hundreds of new studies are included in the third edition; on average, more than three-fourths of each chapter's citations are of articles and books published since 1980. As in earlier editions, the statistical data are the most recent available, typically from the 1990 census or newer sources.

Learning Aids. This text has specific features to help students learn. Each chapter begins with a **topic outline** that shows readers at a glance that chapter's content and organization. Throughout the text, **key concepts**, identified by boldfaced type, are each followed by *a precise, italicized definition*. An alphabetical listing of key concepts and definitions appears at the end of each chapter, and a complete **glossary** is found at the end of the book. Each chapter also contains a numbered **summary** to assist students in reviewing material and assessing their understanding. Every chapter concludes with four **critical-thinking questions**—new to the third edition—that provoke student reflection about important issues.

Outstanding Images: Photography and Fine Art. The author has searched extensively for the finest images of the human condition and thoughtfully developed a unique program of photography and artwork. Not only are images of extraordinary quality, but they represent photographs and paintings by artists of various social backgrounds and historical periods. In addition to widely celebrated art by George Tooker and Vincent Van Gogh, for example, this edition has paintings by African-American artists Jacob Lawrence and Henry Ossawa Tanner, Hispanic artists Frank Romero and Diego Rivera, folk artists including

Grandma Moses, and the Australian painter and feminist Sally Swain.

Thought-Provoking Theme Boxes. Although boxes are common to introductory texts, *Society: The Basics* provides a wealth of uncommonly good boxes. Each chapter typically contains two boxes, which fall into five types that strengthen the central themes of the text. *Social Diversity* boxes focus on multicultural issues and enhance the voices of people of color and women. *Global Sociology* boxes provoke readers to think about their own way of life by examining the fascinating cultural diversity found in our world. *Critical Thinking* boxes teach students to ask sociological questions about their surroundings and help them to evaluate important, controversial issues. *Sociology of Everyday Life* boxes show that, far from being detached from daily routines, many of sociology's most important insights involve familiar, everyday experiences. Finally, *Social Policy* boxes, new to this edition, highlight the application of sociological theory and research to today's pressing problems and political debates.

Innovation: Changes in *Society: The Basics,* Third Edition

Each new edition of *Society: The Basics* has broken new ground by introducing new material and innovative features. A revision raises high expectations, and, after two years of work guided by the generous suggestions of faculty and students, we are confident that no one will be disappointed. Here is a summary of the innovations that define the third edition.

An Unparalleled Map Program. The last edition of *Society: The Basics* introduced "**Window on the World**" global maps to the brief text market. This series of nineteen global maps, four of them new to this edition, are truly sociological maps that present, in global perspective, important patterns such as income disparity, favored languages, the extent of prostitution, permitted marriage forms, the degree of political freedom, the incidence of HIV infection, the extent of the world's rain forests, and a host of other issues. **Windows on the World** use a new, non-Eurocentric projection, devised by cartographer Arno Peters, that accurately portrays the relative size of all the continents.

The third edition also presents a new series of seventeen "**Seeing Ourselves**" U.S. maps; data

provided for the 3,014 counties in the United States include suicide rates, median household income, labor force participation, college attendance, divorce rates, most widespread religious affiliations, air quality, and, as a measure of popular culture, where most of the Elvis fans live.

Each **Seeing Ourselves** map includes an explanatory caption and also poses questions to students to stimulate their critical thinking and appreciation of social forces. A complete listing of both the **Window on the World** global maps and the new **Seeing Ourselves** national maps follows the table of contents.

A New Chapter: "The Natural Environment." The last two decades have witnessed a groundswell of interest in the state of the natural environment. Environmental dynamics is a great concern in the natural sciences; however, as sociologists have long recognized, the state of the physical environment is primarily a matter of how we organize social life. Therefore, *Society: The Basics* (along with the full hardcover version, *Sociology*) proudly offers the first full chapter on the natural environment to be found in an introductory textbook.

Chapter 15, "The Natural Environment," takes a decidedly sociological look at environmental issues, explaining how changing technology, population increase, and cultural notions about the desirability of "growth" affect humanity's consumption of resources and generate various problems of pollution. While highlighting issues of special concern in the United States, this new chapter also discusses how and why environmental patterns are necessarily global in scope.

New "Looking Ahead" Conclusions. Concerns about the well-being of the U.S. population and rapid change around the world have prompted speculation about the future. Although social scientists have a relatively poor track record in terms of specific predictions, we can report current trends and likely directions of future developments. Nine of the chapters in this edition of *Society: The Basics*—beginning with Chapter 8 ("Global Stratification") through the end of the text—now conclude with thought-provoking "Looking Ahead" sections.

New Topics. *Society: The Basics* offers topic coverage that is unparalleled among short texts. The third edition is now even stronger, with more global material, better coverage of social diversity issues, and dozens of new or expanded discussions of timely issues. Here is a partial listing, by chapter, of new material:

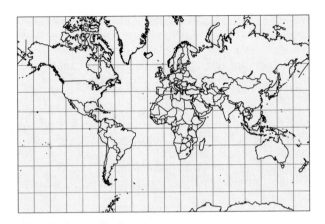 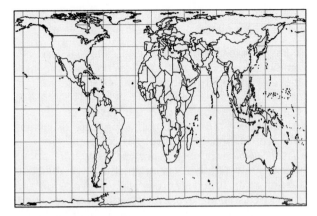

All maps distort reality, since they portray a three-dimensional world in two dimensions. Most of us are familiar with the Mercator projection (devised by the Flemish mapmaker Gerhardus Mercator, 1512–1594), which accurately presents the shape of countries (a vital concern to early seafaring navigators). But Mercator maps like the one at left distort the size of land masses (more so the farther they lie from the equator), thereby exaggerating the dimensions of Europe and North America. The Peters projection, at right, is used in this text because it accurately displays the size of all nations.

Chapter 1: New opening, a statistical look at the "global village"; a greatly expanded discussion of the importance of global perspective, including a new Global Map displaying world economic development; new National Map showing suicide rates across the United States; new Social Diversity box on conducting research with Hispanics; new discussion of feminist research methods.

Chapter 2: New section speculating on the question "A Global Culture?"; new discussion of "high culture" versus "popular culture"; new National Map on the many languages of U.S. children; new graph on U.S. immigration; new Global Sociology box on reading gestures across cultures.

Chapter 3: New presentation of Lawrence Kohlberg's research on moral development; new section highlighting Carol Gilligan's analysis of gender and social development; new Social Policy box on elder-care responsibilities of the "sandwich generation"; new discussion of the politics of the Hollywood elite; new National Maps tracing people's proclivity toward either television-watching or newspaper-reading.

Chapter 4: New opening, a demonstration of how gender undermines effective communication; new Social Diversity box on Deborah Tannen's research on gender and communication; new National Map profiling Elvis fans.

Chapter 5: New opening plus in-depth coverage of the McDonaldization of U.S. society; new National Map showing where people are most likely to file lawsuits; new discussion of the gender and racial composition of U.S. executives.

Chapter 6: New discussion of hate crimes, including a new Social Policy box on the topic; new National Map showing states that have enacted hate-crime legislation.

Chapter 7: An update on South Africa's struggle for racial equality; new Social Policy box on child poverty in the United States; new line art illustration showing attitudes toward government policy to lessen income disparity in global perspective; new National Map on median income across the United States.

Chapter 8: New pie chart showing the distribution of world income; two new Global Sociology boxes, one on infanticide and sexual slavery in poor societies and the second on the effects of modernization on women in Bangladesh; new Global Map showing median age at death for the world's countries; new map depicting Africa's colonial history; new "Looking Ahead" conclusion.

Chapter 9: New opening, a reflection on the continuing turmoil in the former Yugoslavia; updated Social Diversity box and new National Map focusing on the "minority-majority"; new "Looking Ahead" conclusion.

Chapter 10: New opening, an assessment of the "beauty myth"; expanded discussion of sexual orientations; new Global Sociology box on opposition to patriarchy in Botswana; new National Map showing regional support for feminism; new "Looking Ahead" conclusion.

Chapter 11: Expanded coverage of the emerging global economy and global political forces; new National Map on labor force participation across the United States; two new Global Sociology boxes, one on Singapore's "soft authoritarianism" and a second on alleged war-crimes in the former Yugoslavia; new "Looking Ahead" conclusion.

Chapter 12: New Social Policy box on childcare; expanded discussions of grandparenting and gay parenting; new National Map on divorce; new chart showing the relative importance of romantic love in global perspective; a new estimate of the religiosity of U.S. adults; new Global Sociology box on the changing face of religion in Great Britain; new National Map showing the religious diversity of the United States; new "Looking Ahead" conclusion.

Chapter 13: Expanded discussion of school choice; new Social Policy box on illiteracy; new National Map showing rates of college attendance for all U.S. counties; new discussion of eating disorders; new pie chart identifying sources of transmission of HIV in the United States; new Global Sociology box on health problems in Africa caused by poverty; new "Looking Ahead" conclusion.

Chapter 14: Expanded coverage of demographic transition theory; new Global Sociology box contrasting birth control policies in the two Chinas; new National Map that reveals where members of the baby boom generation have chosen to live; new "Looking Ahead" conclusion.

Chapter 15: Completely new chapter on the natural environment featuring a National Map on air quality, a Global Map showing the world's rain forests, a Global Sociology box on how hamburger consumption in the United States affects the rain forest in Costa Rica, and a new Social Policy box on recycling; new "Looking Ahead" conclusion.

Chapter 16: New Global Sociology box on the world's disappearing cultures; new discussion of postmodernity; new Critical Thinking box on U.S. cultural decline;

new National Map showing where most migration in the United States occurs; new Global Map on life expectancy; new "Looking Ahead" conclusion.

The Latest Statistical Data. From beginning to end, this text makes use of the most recent statistical data available. In every case, we employ data from the 1990 census or newer sources, in some instances for 1993 and even 1994. Moreover, this revision is informed by hundreds of new research findings, with three-fourths of each chapter's citations referring to material published since 1980. This revision also illustrates concepts and theories with examples from recent current events familiar to faculty and students alike.

A Word About Language. This text's commitment to representing the social diversity of the United States and the world carries with it the responsibility for thoughtful use of language. In most cases, we prefer the terms *African American* and *person of color* to the word *black*. We use the terms *Hispanic* and *Latino* to designate people of Spanish descent. Most tables and figures refer to "Hispanics" because the U.S. Census Bureau employs this term in collecting statistical data about our population.

Students should realize, however, that many individuals do not describe themselves using these terms. Although the term "Hispanic" is commonly used in the eastern part of the United States, and "Latino" and the feminine form "Latina" are widely heard in the West, across our country people of Spanish descent identify with a particular ancestral nation, whether it be Argentina, Mexico, some other Latin American country, or Spain or Portugal in Europe.

The same holds for Asian Americans. Although this term is a useful shorthand in sociological analysis, most people of Asian descent think of themselves in terms of a specific country of origin (say, Japan, the Philippines, Taiwan, or Vietnam).

In this text, the term "Native American" refers to descendants of the inhabitants of the Americas, including the Hawaiian Islands. Here again, however, most people in this broad category identify with their historical society (for example, Cherokee, Hopi, or Zuni). The term "American Indian" designates only those Native Americans who live in the continental United States, not including Native peoples living in Alaska or Hawaii.

Learning to think globally also leads us to use language more carefully. This text avoids the word "American"—which literally designates two continents—to refer to just the United States. Thus, for example, the "American economy" is more correctly termed the "U.S. economy." This convention may seem a small point, but it implies the significant recognition that we in this country represent only one society (albeit a very important one) in the Americas.

Supplements

Society: The Basics, third edition, is the heart of a comprehensive learning package that includes an unsurpassed range of proven instructional aids. John Macionis has supervised the development of all of the supplements, ensuring their quality and compatibility with the text. No other brief text offers so much high-quality material that will truly enhance teaching and learning.

The Annotated Instructor's Edition. Faculty can request *Society: The Basics* in an annotated instructor's edition (AIE). The AIE is a complete student text annotated by the author with additional material. Annotations have won praise from instructors because of how well they enrich class presentations. Margin notes include summaries of research findings, statistics from the United States or other nations, insightful quotations, information illustrating patterns of social diversity in the United States, and high-quality survey data from the National Opinion Research Center's (NORC) General Social Survey.

Data File. This is the "instructor's manual" that is of interest even to those who have never used one before. The *Data File* provides far more than detailed chapter outlines and discussion questions; it contains statistical profiles of the United States and other nations, summaries of important developments and significant research, and supplemental lecture material for every chapter of the text. The *Data File* has been prepared by Stephen W. Beach (Kentucky Wesleyan College) and John J. Macionis, and is also available in DOS format.

Test Item File. A revised test item file for this edition has been prepared by Edward Kick, University of Utah. This file is available in both printed and computerized form. The file contains 1600 items—100 per chapter—in multiple choice, true/false, and essay formats. Questions are identified as either simple "recall" items or more complex "inferential" issues; the answers to all questions are page-referenced to the text. *Prentice Hall Custom Test* is a test generator and classroom management system designed to provide maximum flexibility in producing and grading tests and quizzes. It is available in both DOS and Macintosh formats. Prentice Hall also provides a test preparation service to users of this text that is as easy as one call to our toll-free 800 number.

Core Test Item File, 2/e. This general test item file consists of over 600 additional test questions appropriate for introductory sociology courses. All of the questions have been class tested, and an item analysis is available for every question.

Social Survey Software. This is the supplement that is changing the way instructors teach and students learn. *STUDENT CHIP Social Survey Software* is an easy yet powerful program that allows users to investigate U.S. society and other nations of the world by calling on the best source of survey data available, the General Social Survey. John J. Macionis and Jere Bruner (Oberlin College) have transformed 260 GSS items into CHIP data sets keyed to the chapters of *Society: The Basics*. Jere W. Bruner and Karen Lynch Frederick (Saint Anselm College) have written a helpful *Instructor's Manual* as well as an easy-to-understand *Social Survey Software Student Manual* that leads students through multivariate analysis of attitudes and reported behavior by sex, race, occupation, level of income and education, and a host of other variables. *Social Survey Software*, which investigators can now operate either by keyboard or mouse, also has a new graphing feature. The *STUDENT CHIP* microcomputer program, developed by James A. Davis (Harvard University), is available in both DOS and MacIntosh formats.

The New York Times Supplement. *The New York Times* and Prentice Hall are sponsoring *Themes of the Times*, a program designed to enhance student access to current information relevant to the classroom.

Through this program, the core subject matter provided in the text is supplemented by a collection of timely articles from one of the world's most distinguished newspapers, *The New York Times*. These articles demonstrate the vital, ongoing connection between what is learned in the classroom and what is happening in the world around us.

To enjoy the wealth of information of *The New York Times* daily, a reduced subscription rate is available. For information, call toll-free: 1-800-631-1222.

Prentice Hall and *The New York Times* are proud to co-sponsor *Themes of the Times*. We hope it will make the reading of both textbooks and newspapers a more dynamic, involving process.

Seeing Ourselves: Classic, Contemporary, and Cross-Cultural Readings in Sociology, 3/e. Create a powerful teaching package by combining this text with the new, third edition of sociology's most popular anthology, *Seeing Ourselves*, edited by John J. Macionis and Nijole V. Benokraitis (University of Baltimore). Better than ever, *Seeing Ourselves*, third edition, now has seventy-five selections, thirty-one new to this edition. Instructors relish this reader's unique format: Clusters of readings—from classic works to well-rounded looks at contemporary issues and cross-cultural comparisons—correspond to each major topic in *Society: The Basics*, third edition.

The **classics** (twenty-nine in all) now include selections by Emile Durkheim, Karl Marx, George Herbert Mead, Max Weber, Georg Simmel, Ferdinand Toennies, Margaret Mead, C. Wright Mills, W. E. B. Du Bois, Mirra Komarovsky, Jessie Bernard, and others.

The **contemporary** readings (twenty-four) range from Shulamit Reinharz on feminist research and Dianne Herman pointing out the cultural roots of sexual violence to William Bennett's contention that the United States is entering a period of cultural decline, Deborah Tannen's insights on why the two sexes often talk past each other, Sally Helgesen on the competitive edge women bring to the corporate world, Robert Reich's investigation of the domestic consequences of the global economy, William Julius Wilson's account of the ghetto underclass, William O'Hare's profile of affluent Latinos, Naomi Wolf on the "beauty myth," Betty Friedan's views on aging, James Woods on homosexuality in the workplace, Catharine MacKinnon's analysis of pornography as a power issue, Lester Brown's survey of the state of the world's environment, and Robert Bellah's thoughts on the difficulty of finding a sense of meaningful participation in modern society.

Cross-cultural selections (twenty-two) include well-known works such as "The Nacirema" by Horace Miner, "India's Sacred Cow" by Marvin Harris, and "The Amish: A Small Society" by John Hostetler. Other cross-cultural articles explore particular issues and problems: how race and class affect socialization, ways in which advertising depicts people of various backgrounds, differences between Japanese corporations and their U.S. counterparts, global patterns of crime, the staggering burden of African poverty, varying cultural attitudes toward homosexuality, traditional arranged marriage in India, Islam's view of women, academic achievement among Southeast Asian immigrants, how the AIDS epidemic is ravaging other continents, and the plight of indigenous peoples worldwide. *Seeing*

Ourselves is a low-cost resource that provides exceptional quality and flexibility for instructors seeking to supplement reading assignments in the text with primary sources.

Media Supplements

ABC News/Prentice Hall Video Library for Sociology Series I, II, III (Issues in Sociology), IV (Global Culturalism), V (Issues in Diversity), and VI. Video is the most dynamic supplement you can use to enhance a class. But the quality of the video material and how well it relates to your course still make all the difference. Prentice Hall and ABC News are now working together to bring you the best and most comprehensive video ancillaries available in the college market.

Through its wide variety of award-winning programs—*Nightline, Business World, On Business, This Week with David Brinkley, World News Tonight,* and *The Health Show*—ABC offers a resource for feature and documentary-style videos related to the chapters in *Society: The Basics,* third edition. The programs have extremely high production quality, present substantial content, and are hosted by well-versed, well-known anchors.

Prentice Hall and its authors and editors provide the benefit of having selected videos and topics that will work well with this course and text and include notes on how to use them in the classroom. An excellent video guide in the *Data File* carefully and completely integrates the videos into your lecture. The guide has a synopsis of each video showing its relation to the chapter and discussion questions to help students focus on how concepts and theories apply to real-life situations.

Prentice Hall Images in Sociology: Laser Videodisc, Series II. Newly updated, *Images in Sociology* presents illustrations both from within the text and from outside sources in an integrated framework appropriate for classroom use. These images include maps, graphs, diagrams, and other illustrations, as well as video segments taken from the *ABC News/Prentice Hall Video Library for Sociology.* See your local Prentice Hall representative for details on how to preview this videodisc.

Multimedia Study Guide. Created using Authorware, the highly acclaimed multimedia programming tool, **The Multimedia Study Guide** is an interactive software program that allows students to test themselves on concepts presented in the text. Multiple choice, true/false, and fill-in-the-blank questions integrate graphics from the text in a colorful, visually appealing format. Students receive immediate feedback, including hints and page references to the text. Chapter objectives, a glossary, and a statistical summary results provide additional pedagogical support.
Windows (ISBN: 0-13-437815-6)
Macintosh (ISBN: 0-13-437807-5)

PowerPoint Presentation Manager for Introductory Sociology. Liven your classroom lectures with multimedia presentations! The **PowerPoint Presentation Manager** combines graphics and text in a colorful format to help you convey sociological principles in a new and exciting way. The **PowerPoint Presentation Manager** is a collection of lectures created in PowerPoint, an easy-to-use software program that is widely available. It provides two 40-minute lectures on each of 23 topics typically covered in an introductory sociology course. These lectures, 46 in total, are suitable for classroom presentation but can be customized for individual instructors' use.
Windows (ISBN: 0-13-437799-0)

Other supplements available to aid in classroom teaching are:

> *Prentice Hall Color Transparencies: Sociology Series III*
> *Instructor's Guide to Prentice Hall Color Transparencies: Sociology Series III*
> *Film/Video Guide: Prentice Hall Introductory Sociology, Fifth Edition*
> *Study Guide*
> *Critical Thinking Audiocassette Tape*

In Appreciation

The conventional practice of designating a single author obscures the efforts of dozens of women and men that have resulted in *Society: The Basics*, third edition. Nancy Roberts, editor-in-chief at Prentice Hall, long-time colleague and valued friend, has contributed enthusiasm, support, and sound advice throughout the revision process. Susanna Lesan, developmental editor-in-chief at Prentice Hall, has played a vital role in the development of this text since its first edition, with day-to-day responsibility for coordinating and supervising the editorial process. I also have a large debt to the members of the Prentice Hall sales staff, the men and women who have given this text such remarkable support over the years. Thanks, especially, to Lauren Ward and Kris Kleinsmith, who direct our marketing campaign. I also offer heartfelt thanks to Pat Naturale, Sharon Chambliss, Charlyce Jones Owen, Will Ethridge, and Phil Miller for all that they have done to make this text what it is today.

The production of *Society: The Basics*, third edition, was supervised by Barbara Reilly, who appreciates the fact that a book is nothing more than a million details. Keeping track of each and every one has consumed her time and energy over the past year, and she has done an extraordinary job. The interior design of the book is the creative work of Lorraine Mullaney. Final page layout was the responsibility of Lithokraft II, of Columbus, Ohio, in collaboration with Barbara Reilly and the author. Copy editing of the manuscript was provided by Diana Drew and Amy Marsh Macionis; at each stage of the production process, Amy also made a significant contribution to maintaining the high quality of this book by checking manuscript for editorial accuracy. The author and Susanna Lesan generated ideas for the photography and fine art program; Barbara Salz and Joelle Burrows each did a wonderful job of researching materials under the supervision of Melinda Reo, photo editor. Skillful research by Carol Singer, librarian at the National Agricultural Library in Washington, D.C., is responsible for keeping the statistical data in this text up to date.

It goes without saying that every colleague knows more about some topics covered in this book than the author does. For that reason, I am grateful to the hundreds of faculty and students who have written to me to offer comments and suggestions. More formally, I want to acknowledge the following people who have reviewed some or all of this manuscript:

Paul B. Brezina, County College of Morris
William Brindle, Monroe Community College
Robert E. Clark, Midwestern State University
Lovberta A. Cross, Shelby State Community College
F. Kurt Cylke, State University of New York at Geneseo
Lynda Dodgen, North Harris College
Dana Dunn, University of Texas at Arlington
Lawrence G. Felice, Baylor University
Kenneth Fidel, DePaul University

Craig J. Forsyth, University of Southwestern Louisiana

Robin Franck, Southwestern College

Louis J. Gesualdi, St. John's University

Michael Goslin, Tallahassee Community College

Larry J. Halford, Washburn University

Wanda Kaluza, Camden County College

Allan O. Kirkpatrick, Riverside Community College

William C. Kuehn, Castleton State College

Michael G. Lacy, Colorado State University

Eric Lichten, Long Island University, C.W. Post College

Martha Loustaunau, New Mexico State University

Joan Lovensheimer, Butler County Community College

James M. Madden, DePauw University

Kooros Mahmoudi, Northern Arizona University

Ruben Martinez, Colorado University at Colorado Springs

Gustave G. Nelson, Berkshire Community College

Barry S. Perlman, Community College of Philadelphia

Marvin Pippert, Roanoke College

Lauren Pivnick, Monroe Community College

Adrian Rapp, North Harris College

Harriett Romo, Southwest Texas State University

Leslie Wang, University of Toledo Community and Technical College

J. David Wemhaner, Tulsa Junior College-Metro

My gratitude also goes to many other colleagues for sharing their wisdom in ways that have improved this book: Doug Adams (The Ohio State University), Kip Armstrong (Bloomsburg University), Rose Arnault (Fort Hays State University), Philip Berg (University of Wisconsin, La Crosse), Bill Brindle (Monroe Community College), John R. Brouillette (Colorado State University), Karen Campbell (Vanderbilt University), Gerry Cox (South Dakota School of Mines and Technology), James A. Davis (Harvard University), Keith Doubt (Northeast Missouri State University), Helen Rose Fuchs Ebaugh (University of Houston), Heather Fitz Gibbon (The College of Wooster), Kevin Fitzpatrick (University of Alabama-Birmingham), Dona C. Fletcher (Sinclair Community College), Charles Frazier (University of Florida), Karen Lynch Frederick (Saint Anselm College), Jarvis Gamble (Owen's Technical College), L. Tucker Gibson (Trinity University), Steven Goldberg (City College, City University of New York), Charlotte Gotwald (York College of Pennsylvania), Jeffrey Hahn (Mount Union College), Dean Haledjian (Northern Virginia Community College), Peter Hruschka (Ohio Northern University), Glenna Huls (Camden County College), Jeanne Humble (Lexington Community College), Harry Humphries (Pittsburg State University), Cynthia Imanaka (Seattle Central Community College), Patricia Johnson (Houston Community College), Ed Kain (Southwestern University), Paul Kamolnick (Eastern Tennessee State University), Irwin Kantor (Middlesex County College), Thomas Korllos (Kent State University), Rita Krasnow (Virginia Western Community College), Donald Kraybill (Elizabethtown College), Michael Levine (Kenyon College), George Lowe (Texas Tech University), Don Luidens (Hope College), Larry Lyon (Baylor University), Li-Chen Ma (Lamar University), Meredith McGuire (Trinity College), Dan McMurry (Middle-Tennessee State University), Errol Magidson (Richard J. Daley College), Alan Mazur (Syracuse University), Jack Melhorn (Emporia State University), Ken Miller (Drake University), Richard Miller (Navarro College), Alfred Montalvo (Emporia State University), Joe Morolla (Virginia Commonwealth University), Craig Nauman (Madison Area Technical College), Toby Parcel (The Ohio State University), Anne Peterson (Columbus State Community College), Dudley Posten, Jr. (Texas A & M University), Daniel Quinn (Adrian College), Nevel Razak (Fort Hays State College), Virginia Reynolds (Indiana University of Pennsylvania), Laurel Richardson (The Ohio State University), Ellen Rosengarten (Sinclair Community College), Howard Schneiderman (Lafayette College), Ray Scupin (Linderwood College), Harry Sherer (Irvine Valley College), Walt Shirley (Sinclair Community College), Glen Sims (Glendale Community College), Verta Taylor (The Ohio State University), Len Tompos (Lorain County Community College), Christopher Vanderpool (Michigan State University), Marilyn Wilmeth (Iowa University), Wayne S. Wooden (California State Polytechnic University), Stuart Wright (Lamar University), Dan Yutze (Taylor University), Wayne Zapatek (Tarrant County Community College), and Frank Zulke (Harold Washington College).

Thank you, one and all.

Jon J. Macionis

Chapter

1

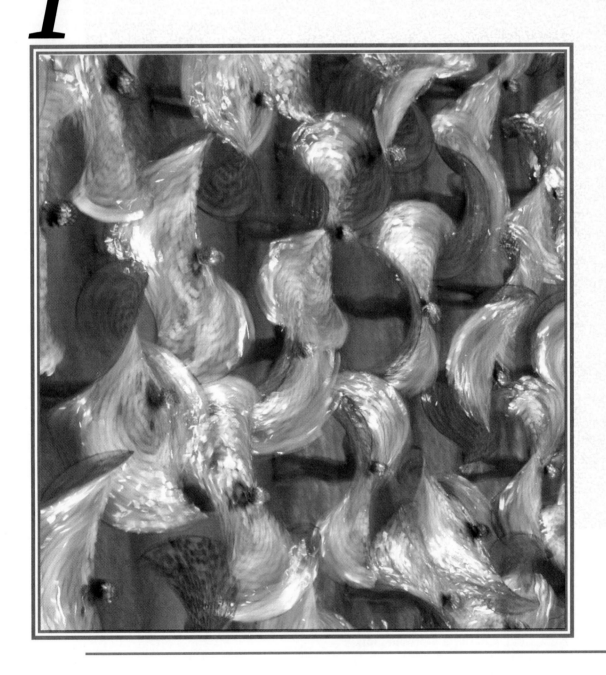

Sociology: Perspective, Theory, and Method

Chapter Outline

*M*ore than 5.5 billion people live on the planet we call Earth, in cities and across the countryside of 191 nations. But imagine this vast world magically reduced to a single village of 1,000 people. If we were to pay a visit to this "global village," we could quickly learn a great deal about our own, much larger world. A survey of the village population would reveal more than half (575) of the inhabitants to be Asians, including 200 people from the People's Republic of China. Next, in terms of numbers, we would find 130 Africans, 125 Europeans, and 100 Latin Americans. North Americans—including people from the United States, Canada, and Mexico—would account for just 65 villagers.

A longer stay in this village might afford the opportunity for careful study of its way of life and yield some startling conclusions: The people are very productive, generating a seemingly endless array of goods and services for sale. Yet most of the inhabitants can do no more than look at such treasures, since half of the village's total income is earned by just 120 individuals.

Food is the village's greatest concern. Every year, village workers produce more than enough food to feed everyone; even so, 500 villagers—including most of the children—are poorly nourished and typically go to sleep hungry. The 200 worst-off residents lack food and safe drinking water, rendering them unable to work and vulnerable to life-threatening diseases.

The village contains many splendid homes. But while the richest 60 families enjoy luxurious surroundings with every convenience, about 600 of their neighbors live in shanty housing that offers neither comfort nor safety.

Villagers can boast of their community's many schools, including numerous colleges and universities. But while 75 of the village inhabitants have completed a college degree (and a few even have doctorates), 700 of the village's people can neither read nor write.[1]

Finally, over its history, the people of this "global village" have attained notable achievements

in the arts and sciences. They have imaginatively solved one after another of the problems that confront them, taming nature and (for those who can afford to) gaining the capacity to travel farther and more quickly with each passing generation. But these people have also learned that their growing ability to shape their surroundings comes at a high price: More than ever before, the deterioration of the physical environment threatens their well-being. And, perhaps most important, the village population remains fractured by many proud divisions based on nationality, religion, language, and skin color. Almost constant fighting disrupts the peace of the community; its people have yet to devise a means by which to control conflict before it explodes into war and bloodshed.

No topic of study is more fascinating than humanity itself. As this chapter explains, poets and philosophers have explored the human condition since the beginning of time; more recently, a wide range of disciplines—from anthropology to zoology—has emerged, each offering particular insights into the human drama. But the richest perspective of all comes from *sociology*, which explains and ties together the many dimensions of human life both here and around the world.

The Sociological Perspective

Sociology is *the scientific study of human social activity.* At the heart of this discipline is a distinctive point of view that we will now describe.

Seeing the General in the Particular

Peter Berger (1963) characterizes the sociological perspective as *seeing the general in the particular.* This means that sociologists observe general patterns in the behavior of particular individuals. While acknowledging that each individual is unique, in other words, we also recognize that social forces shape us into various *kinds* of people who feel, think, and act in distinctive ways.

---

[1]These data are based on research by the World Development Forum (April 15, 1990) and calculations by the author.

We can easily grasp the power of society over the individual by imagining how different our lives would be had we been born in place of any of these children from, respectively, Bolivia, India, Guatemala, Botswana, the People's Republic of China, and South Africa.

Every society places individuals into categories based on age (say, as children or elderly people), sex (as women or men), class (as rich or poor), as well as race and cultural background. To think sociologically is to realize how our particular life experiences are molded by the general categories into which we happen to fall.

Seeing the world sociologically, for example, makes us aware of the importance of gender. As Chapter 10 ("Sex and Gender") points out, every society attaches certain meanings to each sex; our society, for example, accords women and men different kinds of work and family responsibilities. Gender even affects the ways men and women express themselves, creating differences that sometimes make simply talking to one another difficult and frustrating.

Seeing the Strange in the Familiar

To beginners, the sociological perspective amounts to *seeing the strange in the familiar*. This does not mean that sociologists focus on the bizarre elements of society; rather, sociology asks us to give up the familiar idea that human behavior is simply a matter of what people *decide* to do, in favor of the initially strange notion that society guides our thoughts and deeds.

For individualistic North Americans, learning to "see" how society affects us may take a bit of practice. Consider the seemingly personal matter of deciding to change one's name, a practice especially common among celebrities in the United States. But are the names famous people use a matter of personal choice or are social forces at work? The box reveals a

The Name Game: Social Forces and Personal Choice

On July 4, 1918, twins were born to Abe and Becky Friedman in Sioux City, Iowa. They named the first to arrive Esther Pauline Friedman; her sister they named Pauline Esther Friedman. As adults, however, these two women changed their names, and people all over the country now know them as Ann Landers and Abigail ("Dear Abby") Van Buren.

At first glance, a name change may seem to be just a matter of personal preference. But using the sociological perspective, we see that most people who make this change adopt *English-sounding* names. Why? Because our society has long accorded high social prestige to people of Anglo-Saxon background. How many of these well-known

people can you identify from their original names? Looking at the list as a whole, can you see "the general in the particular"?

1. Cherilyn Sarkisian
2. Frank Casteluccio
3. Cheryl Stoppelmoor
4. Robert Allen Zimmerman
5. Larry Zeigler
6. Nathan Birnbaum
7. Paul Rubenfeld
8. George Kyriakou Panayiotou
9. Annie Mae Bullock
10. Patricia Andrejewski
11. Malden Sekulovich
12. Jerome Silberman
13. Bernadette Lazzara
14. Karen Ziegler
15. Ramon Estevez
16. Henry John Deutschendorf, Jr.
17. Allen Stewart Konigsberg
18. Patsy McClenny
19. Jacob Cohen
20. William Claude Dukenfield
21. Lee Yuen Kam
22. Raquel Tejada
23. Frederick Austerlitz
24. Sophia Scicoloni

1. Cher; 2. Frankie Valli; 3. Cheryl Ladd; 4. Bob Dylan; 5. Larry King; 6. George Burns; 7. Pee Wee Herman; 8. George Michael; 9. Tina Turner; 10. Pat Benatar; 11. Karl Malden; 12. Gene Wilder; 13. Bernadette Peters; 14. Karen Black; 15. Martin Sheen; 16. John Denver; 17. Woody Allen; 18. Morgan Fairchild; 19. Rodney Dangerfield; 20. W. C. Fields; 21. Bruce Lee; 22. Raquel Welch; 23. Fred Astaire; 24. Sophia Loren

general pattern in people's particular choices about their names.

Seeing Individuality in Social Context

Sociological insights challenge common sense by revealing how human behavior is not as individualistic as we may think. For most of us, daily living carries a heavy load of personal responsibility, so that we pat ourselves on the back when we enjoy success and kick ourselves when things go wrong. Proud of our individuality, even in painful times we resist the idea that we act in socially patterned ways.

Consider the issue of suicide. Nothing could be more personal than taking one's own life. Yet Emile Durkheim (1858–1917), a pioneer of sociology, was able to perceive social forces at work even in the apparent isolation of the ultimate self-destructive act.

Durkheim discovered that records of suicide in and around his native France clearly showed that some categories of people were more likely than others to take their own lives. Specifically, Durkheim found, men, Protestants, wealthy people, and the unmarried

each had much higher suicide rates than did women, Catholics and Jews, the poor, and married people. Durkheim explained this pattern by reasoning that suicide rates varied according to people's degree of *social integration*. Low suicide rates characterized categories of people with strong social ties; high suicide rates, by contrast, marked more individualistic, socially isolated people.

In puzzling over the meaning of his findings, Durkheim noted that men's greater autonomy in the male-oriented societies of his day translated into a higher suicide rate for men than for women. Likewise, individualistic Protestants were more likely to take their lives than were Catholics and Jews, who shared stronger social bonds. And just as wealth conferred independence on the better-off, single people maintained more tenuous social ties than their married peers: In both cases, less-binding social relationships put both rich people and singles at greater risk of suicide.

Statistical evidence suggests that Durkheim's analysis remains correct even today. Figure 1–1 shows 1991 suicide rates for four categories of the U.S. population. There were 13.3 recorded suicides for every 100,000 white people, almost twice the rate among

African Americans (6.7). Also, for both races, suicide is more common among men than among women. White men (21.7) are four times more likely than white women (5.2) to take their own lives. Among African Americans, the rate for men (12.1) is six times that for women (1.9). Following Durkheim's argument, we conclude that the higher suicide rate among whites and men is due to their greater affluence and autonomy, which insulate them from others. By contrast, the lower rate among women and people of color stems from their typically stronger social ties. In sum, suicide rates (and rates of all kinds when it comes to human behavior) reveal general social patterns, not just the actions of particular individuals.

Yet some situations stimulate sociological insights for everyone. For example, when we encounter people who differ from us, it prompts us to wonder why others think and act as they do. As we interact with people of social backgrounds that initially seem strange, we grasp the power of society to influence our lives and find ourselves easing into the role of sociologist.

By the same token, sociological thinking is familiar to people our society tends to label as "different." Those who experience *social marginality*—that is, being viewed as "outsiders"—on a routine basis typically gain a keen awareness of how society operates. No African American, for example, lives for long in the United States without learning how much of an impact race has on our lives. But because white people are the dominant majority, they think about race only from time to time and often imagine that race affects only black people rather than themselves as well.

Finally, U.S. sociologist C. Wright Mills (1959) pointed out that social disruption also sparks sociological thinking. When, for example, the Great Depression of the 1930s threw one-fourth of the labor force out of a job, unemployed workers could not help but see general social forces at work in their particular lives. Rather than claiming, "Something is wrong with me; I can't find work," they were likely to say, "The economy has collapsed! There are no jobs to be found!"

The 1960s was another decade of change that enhanced sociological awareness in the United States. The civil rights, women's liberation, and antiwar movements each highlighted ways in which political, economic, military, and technological elements of "the system" set the contours of people's lives. Just as important, sociological thinking often fosters social change. The more we learn about the operation of "the system," the more we may wish to change it. An introduction to sociology, then, helps us to understand—and perhaps to reshape—the world around us.

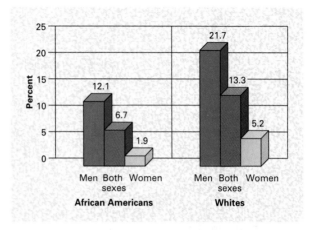

FIGURE 1–1   Rate of Death by Suicide, by Race and Sex, for the United States

Rates indicate the number of deaths by suicide for every 100,000 people in each category for 1991.

Source: U.S. National Center for Health Statistics (1993).

The Importance of Global Perspective

In recent years, many academic disciplines including sociology have incorporated a **global perspective,** *a view of the larger world and our society's place in it.* How does sociology promote a global perspective?

First, global awareness is a logical extension of the sociological perspective. Sociology's basic insight is that our placement in society profoundly affects our individual experiences. It stands to reason, then, that the position of our society in the larger world system also affects everyone in the United States. As the opening paragraphs of this chapter suggest, members of the "global village" are far from equal; some nations (including the United States) are dozens of times more productive than others.

Global Map 1–1 illustrates the relative economic development of the world. The world's **most-developed countries** are *industrial nations that are relatively rich.*[2] These affluent nations include the United States and Canada, most of Western Europe, and also Japan and Australia. Taken together, some three dozen societies produce the lion's share of the world's goods and services and control most of the world's wealth. Individuals in these countries enjoy a high material

[2]This edition of the text no longer employs the terms "First World," "Second World," and "Third World." Chapter 8 ("Global Stratification") details reasons for this change and provides a full discussion of world social inequality.

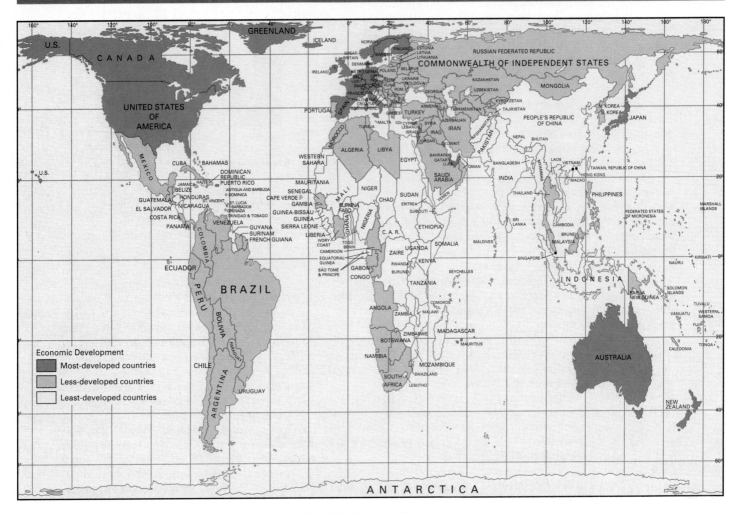

GLOBAL MAP 1–1   Economic Development in Global Perspective*

Most-developed countries—including the United States, Canada, most of the nations of Western Europe, Australia, and Japan—employ industrial technology to provide their people, on average, with material plenty. *Less-developed countries*—found throughout Latin America, Eastern Europe, and the former Soviet Union—have limited industrial capacity and offer their people a standard of living that, while about average for the world as a whole, is far below that familiar to most people in the United States. A significant share of people in these societies has minimal housing and an inadequate diet. In the *least-developed countries* of the world, poverty is severe and widespread. Although small numbers of elites live very well, the majority of people in these poorest nations struggle to survive on a small fraction of the income common in the United States.

*Note: This map uses data from the World Bank and the United Nations. Most-developed countries had 1992 per capita gross domestic product (GDP) of at least $8,000. Many are far richer than this, however; the figure for the United States stands at $22,130. Less-developed countries had a per capita GDP ranging from $2,500 to $8,000. The least-developed countries of the word had a per capita GDP below $2,500. Figures used here reflect the new United Nations "purchasing power parities" system. This calculation avoids distortion caused by exchange rates when changing all currencies to U.S. dollars. Instead, the data reflect the local purchasing power of each currency.

Source: Prepared by the author using data from the *World Development Report* (The World Bank, 1994). Map projection from *Peters Atlas of the World* (1990).

One important reason to gain a global understanding is that familiar problems such as poverty are far more serious in many societies of the world than they are in the United States. So poor is the east African nation of Somalia, that this child has less than a fifty-fifty chance to grow to adulthood.

standard of living, not because they are particularly bright or exceptionally hard-working, but because they had the good fortune to be born in an affluent region of the world.

In a second category of societies are the world's **less-developed countries,** which are *nations characterized by limited industrialization and moderate-to-low personal income.* Individuals living in any of these roughly one hundred nations—which include the countries of the former Soviet Union and (farther down the income scale) most of Latin America—are more likely to reside in rural villages than in cities, to pedal bicycles or ride animals rather than drive automobiles, and to receive only a few years of schooling. Most less-developed countries also have pronounced social inequality so that a significant proportion of the population lacks safe housing and adequate nutrition.

Finally, almost half of the world's people live in the fifty **least-developed countries,** *nations with little industrialization in which severe poverty is the rule.* As Global Map 1–1 shows, most of the poorest countries in the world are in Africa and Asia. While a small number of people in each of these nations is rich, the majority confront the burden of surviving each day with poor housing, unsafe water, too little food, little or no sanitation, and, all too often, little opportunity to improve their lives. Again, these people live on the edge of survival not because of any personal shortcoming, but because of the social organization of their societies and the larger world.

Chapter 8 ("Global Stratification") details the causes and consequences of global wealth and poverty. But every chapter of this text incorporates elements of

life in the world beyond our own borders. Why? Here are three reasons that global thinking is an important component of the sociological perspective.

1. **Societies all over the world are increasingly interconnected, making traditional distinctions between "us" and "them" less and less valid.** For most of our history as a nation, we in the United States have been remarkably indifferent to the world around us. Separated from Europe and Asia by vast oceans, we have taken only passing note of our neighbors to the north (Canada) and south (Mexico and other Latin-American nations). In recent decades, however, the United States and the rest of the world have become linked as never before. Jet aircraft—some traveling faster than sound—allow people to traverse continents in hours, while new electronic devices transmit pictures, sounds, and written documents around the globe in seconds.

   One consequence of these new technologies is that people all over the world now share many tastes in music, clothing, and food. With their economic clout, most-developed nations such as the United States cast a long shadow over the rest of the world: Members of other societies eagerly gobble up our hamburgers, dance to rock-and-roll music, and, more and more, speak the English language.

   But as we have projected our way of life onto much of the world, the larger world has entered our society in myriad ways. The United States now attracts as many immigrants each year as during the heyday of the Great Immigration a century ago, and we are quick to adopt many of the sights, smells, sounds, and tastes of the rest of the world as our own. All this, of course, has enhanced the racial and cultural diversity of our country.

Besides sharing patterns of living, people the world over now participate in a global economy. Hundreds of independent economic systems, circumscribed by national borders, have been replaced by large corporations that manufacture and market goods throughout the world, and financial markets, linked by satellite communication, operate around the clock. In a global economy, a New York stock trader monitors developments in the financial markets in Tokyo and Hong Kong, just as a Kansas wheat farmer notes the price of grain in the former Soviet republic of Georgia.

In short, economic activity has leaped beyond political borders. Businesses in the United States have invested hundreds of billions of dollars abroad, while foreign economic interests have invested trillions of dollars here in the United States. The importance of global awareness for today's students goes right to the "bottom line," with eight out of ten new U.S. jobs involving some kind of international trade (Council on International Educational Exchange, 1988).

2. **A global perspective is important because many human problems that we face in the United States are far more serious elsewhere.** As Chapter 7 ("Social Stratification") points out, our country counts more than 30 million people among the poor. But Chapter 8 ("Global Stratification") goes on to explain that the problem of poverty is both more widespread and more severe throughout Latin America, Africa, and Asia. Similarly, the social standing of women relative to men is especially low in poor societies of the world.

Then, too, some problems—such as degradation of the natural environment—are inherently global in scope. As Chapter 15 ("The Natural Environment") demonstrates, the world is a single ecosystem in which the action (or inaction) of each nation has implications for all others.

3. **Thinking globally is important because studying other societies is an excellent way to learn more about ourselves.** We can hardly consider the life of a young woman growing up in Saudi Arabia or a man living in the African nation of Botswana without thinking about what it means to live in the United States. Making these comparisons

often leads to unexpected lessons. Chapter 8 ("Global Stratification") takes us on a visit to a squatter settlement in Madras, India, for example. There we find that, despite their desperate lack of basic material comforts, people benefit from the love and support of family members. Such patterns prompt us to wonder why poverty in the United States so often involves isolation and anger, and even whether material things—so crucial to our concept of a "rich" life—are the best way to gauge human well-being.

In sum, the question is not whether we should study ourselves or people who live elsewhere. In a world increasingly linked with each passing year, we can understand our society only to the extent that we comprehend our nation's place in the larger world (Macionis, 1993).

The Origins of Sociology

Like individual "choices," historical events rarely just happen; they are typically products of powerful social forces. So it was with sociology itself.

Although people have mused about society since the beginning of human history, sociology is one of the youngest academic disciplines—far younger than history, physics, or economics. Only in 1838 did the French social thinker Auguste Comte apply the term "sociology" to a new way of looking at the world.

Science and Sociology

The nature of society held the attention of virtually all the brilliant thinkers of the ancient world, including the Chinese philosopher K'ung Fu-tzu or Confucius (551–479 B.C.E.) and the Greek philosophers Plato (427–347 B.C.E.) and Aristotle (384–322 B.C.E.).[3] In the centuries that followed, the Roman emperor Marcus Aurelius (121–180), the medieval writer Christine de Pizan (c. 1363–1431), and the English playwright William Shakespeare (1564–1616) all reflected on the state of human society.

---

[3]Throughout this text, the abbreviation B.C.E. designates "before the common era." This terminology is used in place of the traditional B.C. ("before Christ") in recognition of the religious plurality of our society. Similarly, the abbreviation C.E. ("common era") appears instead of the traditional A.D. (anno Domini, or "in the year of our Lord").

This medieval drawing conveys the mix of apprehension and excitement with which early scientists began to question conventional understandings of the universe. Early sociologists, too, challenged many ideas that people had long taken for granted, explaining that society is neither fixed by God's will nor by human nature. On the contrary, Comte and other sociological pioneers claimed, society is a system that we can study scientifically and, based on what we learn, act deliberately to improve.

Yet these philosophers were more interested in envisioning the "ideal" society than they were in analyzing society as it really was. In creating their new discipline, pioneers Auguste Comte, Emile Durkheim, and others reversed these priorities. Although they remained concerned with how human society could be improved, their major goal was to understand how society actually operates.

Comte (1975; orig. 1851–54) identified three stages in the historical emergence of scientific sociology. During the earliest *theological stage,* prior to the end of the medieval era in Europe, people adopted a religious view that society expressed God's will. With the Renaissance, this theological approach gave way to what Comte called the *metaphysical stage* in which people saw society as the product of natural forces. For instance, the English philosopher Thomas Hobbes (1588–1679) suggested that society was guided primarily by selfish human nature. What Comte heralded as the final, *scientific stage* gained momentum with the discoveries of scientists such as the Polish astronomer Nicolaus Copernicus (1473–1543), the Italian astronomer and physicist Galileo (1564–1642), and the English physicist and mathematician Isaac Newton (1642–1727). Comte was quick to embrace **positivism,** *a path to understanding based on science.* As a positivist, Comte believed that he could discern the inherent, underlying order of society just as physical scientists had found the natural world to operate according to gravity and other identifiable principles.

Sociology emerged as an academic discipline in the United States at the beginning of this century, strongly influenced by Comte's ideas. Even today, most sociologists agree that science is a crucial element of sociology. But since Comte's time, we have learned that human behavior is often far more complex than events in the natural world. That is, human beings are much less predictable than physical objects. We are creatures with imagination and spontaneity whose behavior can never be fully explained by any rigid "laws of society."

Social Change and Sociology

Changes in seventeenth- and eighteenth-century Europe propelled the development of sociology. As the social ground trembled under their feet, people understandably focused their attention on society.

Industrial technology. First came new technology—including steam power harnessed to large machines—that produced a factory-based, industrial economy. In the Middle Ages, most people in Europe tilled fields near their homes or engaged in small-scale *manufacturing* (derived from Latin meaning "to make by hand"). But by the middle of the eighteenth century, instead of laboring at home or in tightly knit groups, workers became part of a large and anonymous industrial labor force, toiling for strangers who owned the factories. This change in the system of production prompted a rapid breakdown of traditions that had guided small communities for centuries.

Urban growth. Second, as factories sprouted up across England and the European continent, cities grew to unprecedented size. English industrialists were quick to turn farmland into grazing pastures for sheep—the source of wool for the textile mills. This so-called enclosure movement pushed countless tenant farmers from the countryside toward cities in search of work in the new factories. Soon the small settlement of the medieval world was eclipsed by the towering industrial metropolis that churned with strangers. Widespread social problems—including pollution, crime, and homelessness—further stimulated development of the sociological perspective.

Political change. A third change occurred in political thought. By the sixteenth century, every kind of tradition had come under spirited attack. In the writings of Thomas Hobbes (1588–1679), John Locke (1632–1704), and Adam Smith (1723–1790), we find less concern with moral obligations than with self-interest. Indeed, the key words in the new political climate—*liberty* and *rights*—highlighted not the group but the individual. Echoing the thoughts of Locke, our own Declaration of Independence clearly spells out that each citizen has "certain unalienable rights," including "life, liberty, and the pursuit of happiness."

The political revolution in France that began soon afterward, in 1789, sparked an even more dramatic break with political and social traditions. As he surveyed his own country after the French Revolution, the French social and political thinker Alexis de Tocqueville (1805–1859) exaggerated only slightly when he asserted that the changes we have described amounted to "nothing short of the regeneration of the whole human race" (1955:13; orig. 1856). The new industrial economy, enormous cities, and fresh political ideas combined to draw attention to society; not surprisingly, the discipline of sociology flowered in precisely those countries—France, Germany, and England—where change was greatest.

Individual sociologists reacted differently to the new social order then, just as they respond differently to society today. Although Auguste Comte celebrated the birth of scientific sociology, he feared that rapid change would erode tradition and uproot long-established communities. Comte took a conservative turn, seeking a rebirth of traditional family, community, and morality. By contrast, German social critic Karl Marx (1818–1883) despised tradition, but neither could he condone emerging society's concentration of wealth in the hands of an elite while the masses faced only hunger and misery. Thus Marx argued for further change.

Although they differed sharply in their assessments of changing social conditions, Comte and Marx were both pioneers in the movement that established sociology as an academic discipline. The sociological perspective animates the work of each, showing that people's lives are framed by the social forces at work in a particular time and place.

Sociological Theory

The task of weaving isolated observations into understanding brings us to another dimension of sociology: theory. A **theory** is *a statement of how and why specific facts are related.* Emile Durkheim, for example, constructed a theory following his observation that specific categories of people prone to suicide (men, Protestants, the wealthy, and the unmarried) were those with low social integration.

Of course, sociologists do not imagine that their theories are set in stone; on the contrary, we refine theory as new evidence becomes available, just as all scientists do. National Map 1–1, which displays the suicide rates for the fifty states today, offers an opportunity to do some theorizing.

In building theory, sociologists face a number of choices. What issues should we choose to study? How should we link facts together? In answering these questions, sociologists look to one or more general frameworks, or theoretical paradigms (Kuhn, 1970). A **theoretical paradigm** is *a set of fundamental assumptions that guides thinking and research.* Three major paradigms in sociology are the structural-functional paradigm, the social-conflict paradigm, and the symbolic-interaction paradigm.

The Structural-Functional Paradigm

The **structural-functional paradigm** is *a framework for building theory based on the assumption that society is a complex system whose parts work together to promote stability.* As its name suggests, this paradigm leads us, first, to see society as composed of **social structure,** meaning *a relatively stable pattern of social behavior.* Social structure is what gives shape to family life, behavior in the workplace, or the dynamics of a college classroom. Second, this paradigm focuses on each

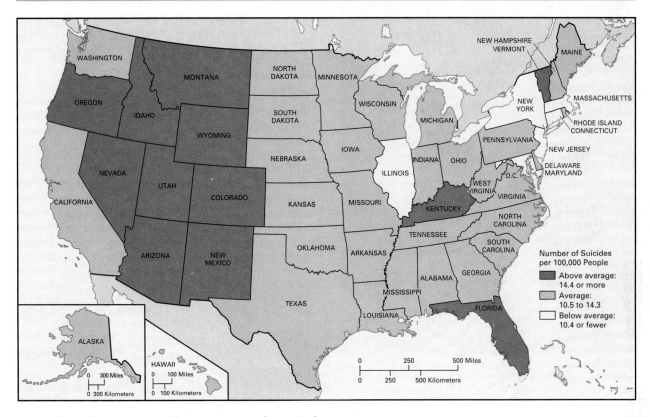

NATIONAL MAP 1–1 Suicide Rates Across the United States

This map identifies states in which suicide rates are particularly high, average, or unusually low. Look for patterns in the map. High suicide rates are common to the mountain states in which population is low and people live far apart from one another. Low suicide rates, by contrast, characterize states that are more densely populated. Do these data support or contradict Durkheim's theory of suicide? Why?

Source: Prepared by the author using data from the 1990 decennial census.

structure's **social function,** or *consequences of a social pattern for the operation of society as a whole.* All social patterns—whether we are thinking of family life or a simple handshake—function to help society persist, at least in its present form.

The structural-functional paradigm owes much to the ideas of Auguste Comte, who sought to promote social integration during a time of dramatic change. Emile Durkheim, who continued sociological research in France, also based his work on this approach. A third architect of the structural-functional orientation was the English sociologist Herbert Spencer (1820–1903),

who compared society with the human body. As the skeleton, muscles, and various internal organs of the body each contribute to the survival of the human organism, Spencer maintained, so do social structures work together to keep society operating. This approach, then, leads sociologists to identify various social structures and investigate the functions of each one.

The work of Robert K. Merton, a contemporary U.S. sociologist, has refined the structural-functional approach by showing that any social structure usually has many functions, some more obvious than others. The **manifest functions** of a social structure refer to

The spirit of the structural-functional paradigm is conveyed by the painting *I and the Village,* completed in 1911 by Russian-American artist Marc Chagall (1881–1985). Here, recalling the tightly integrated Russian villages of his youth, Chagall conveys the essential unity of human beings who share a social setting; he also suggests that human society is bound up with the natural world.

Marc Chagall, *I and the Village,* 1911. Oil on canvas, 63 5/8 x 59 5/8 inches. The Museum of Modern Art, New York. Mrs. Simon Guggenheim Fund.

consequences both recognized and intended by people in the society. **Latent functions,** by contrast, are *consequences that are largely unrecognized and unintended.* Our increasing reliance on automobiles during this century has had both kinds of consequences. The manifest functions of cars range from transporting people and goods to serving as status symbols that say something about a person's taste and bank account. Because automobiles allow people to travel in relative isolation, they also have the latent function of reinforcing our cultural emphasis on privacy and personal autonomy.

Merton makes a further point: It is unlikely that *all* the effects of a social structure will be positive. He uses the term **social dysfunctions** to designate

undesirable consequences of any social pattern for the operation of society. One of the dysfunctions of our society's reliance on some 200 million motor vehicles, highlighted in Chapter 15 ("The Natural Environment"), is to diminish air quality, especially in large cities. No doubt, too, easy travel made possible by cars has eroded the strength of traditional families and local neighborhoods.

Critical evaluation. The structural-functional paradigm highlights how a society operates as an integrated system. But by focusing attention on societal unity, this theoretical approach tends to overlook divisions based on social class, race, ethnicity, and gender and to downplay how such divisions can generate tension and conflict. In addition, the structural-functional emphasis on stability tends to minimize the importance of social change. Overall, then, this paradigm takes a conservative stance toward society. As a critical response to this approach, another theoretical orientation in sociology has emerged: the social-conflict paradigm.

The Social-Conflict Paradigm

The **social-conflict paradigm** is *a framework for building theory based on the assumption that society is a complex system characterized by inequality and conflict that generate social change.* This orientation complements the structural-functional paradigm by highlighting not integration but division based on social inequality. Guided by this paradigm, sociologists investigate how factors such as race, ethnicity, gender, and age are linked to the unequal distribution of wealth, schooling, power, and prestige. Therefore, rather than identifying how social patterns work to promote the functioning of society as a whole, this approach concentrates on how these patterns benefit some people to the detriment of others.

Social-conflict theorists view society as an arena in which conflict arises from the incompatible interests of various categories of people. Not surprisingly, dominant categories—the rich in relation to the poor, whites in relation to people of color, and men in relation to women—typically protect their privileges by supporting the status quo. Those with fewer advantages commonly counter those efforts by attempting to increase their share of social resources.

To illustrate, Chapter 13 ("Education and Medicine") details how secondary schools in the United States prepare some students for college and emphasize vocational training for others. A structural-functional analysis might lead us to ask how society benefits from providing different types of schooling to students of differing academic abilities. The social-conflict paradigm offers the contrasting insight that "tracking" confers privileges on some students that it denies to others, so that schools operate to perpetuate social inequality.

Research guided by the social-conflict paradigm has shown that schools place students in college-preparatory tracks not just based on their intelligence but because of the privileged background of their families. Once they have earned a college degree, most of these young people enter occupations that confer both prestige and high income. By contrast, schools generally fill vocational tracks with students from modest backgrounds, sometimes with little regard for their academic potential. They receive no preparation for college, and thus, like their parents before them, they typically find jobs that offer little prestige and low income. In both cases, the social standing of one generation is passed on to another, and this practice is justified in terms of alleged individual merit (Bowles & Gintis, 1976; Oakes, 1982, 1985).

Finally, many sociologists who embrace the social-conflict paradigm attempt not only to understand society but to reduce social inequality. This was the central goal of Karl Marx, a social thinker who had little patience with those who sought to use science only to understand how society works. In a well-known declaration (inscribed on his monument in London's Highgate Cemetery), Marx asserted: "The philosophers have only interpreted the world, in various ways; the point, however, is to change it."

Critical evaluation. Because the social-conflict paradigm highlights power struggles, it gives little attention to social unity based on functional interdependence and shared values. In addition, say critics, the social-conflict approach advocates explicitly political

---

People whose gender or race put them at the margins of their society also contributed to the development of sociology. Harriet Martineau (1802–1876) (left), born to a rich English family, established her reputation as a sociologist with studies of slavery, factory laws, and women's rights. In the United States, Jane Addams (1860–1933) (middle) was a social worker active on behalf of poor immigrants. In 1889, Addams founded Hull House, a Chicago settlement house, where she engaged intellectuals and immigrants alike in discussions of the pressing problems of her day. Her contribution to the welfare of others earned Addams a Nobel Peace Prize in 1931. William Edward Burghardt Du Bois (1868–1963) (right) was a bright child born to a poor Massachusetts family. He managed to enter Fisk University in Nashville and then Harvard, becoming the first person of color to earn a doctorate there. He is known for his study of the African-American community in Philadelphia at the turn of the century. Like Martineau and Addams, Du Bois argued for linking research to human needs.

goals in its drive for a more egalitarian society, thereby giving up the claim to scientific objectivity. Supporters of this paradigm counter that *all* theoretical orientations in sociology have political consequences, albeit different ones.

Both the structural-functional and social-conflict paradigms envision society in broad, abstract terms, which sometimes seem quite distant from everyday experience. Thus, sociologists also employ a third theoretical paradigm, which views society more in terms of situational interaction. We now turn to this third approach.

The Symbolic-Interaction Paradigm

Both the structural-functional and social-conflict paradigms share a **macro-level orientation,** meaning *a concern with large-scale patterns that characterize society as a whole.* They take in the big picture, rather like investigating a city from high above in a helicopter, noting where pedestrians congregate or observing the striking contrasts between rich and poor neighborhoods. The symbolic-interaction paradigm takes a different tack by providing a **micro-level orientation,** meaning *a concern with small-scale patterns of social interaction in specific settings.* Exploring urban life in this way occurs at street level, observing face-to-face interaction in public parks or how individuals respond to homeless people. The **symbolic-interaction paradigm,** then, is *a framework for building theory based on the view that society is the product of the everyday interactions of individuals.*

How do millions of people weave their lives together into the drama of society? One answer, examined in detail in Chapter 2 ("Culture"), is that we become linked to each other through the common meanings we attach to everyday events and experiences. Sociologists guided by this paradigm view society as a complex mosaic of understandings that emerges from the process of interaction itself.

The symbolic-interaction paradigm rests, in part, on the work of Max Weber (1864–1920), a German sociologist who emphasized the need to understand a setting from the point of view of the people in it. On this foundation, others have constructed a number of specific approaches to learning about social life. Chapter 3 ("Socialization: From Infancy to Old Age") discusses the ideas of George Herbert Mead (1863–1931), who traced the roots of human personality to social experience. Chapter 4 ("Social Interaction in Everyday Life") presents the work of Erving Goffman (1922–1982), whose *dramaturgical analysis* reveals how human beings resemble actors on a stage as they deliberately foster certain impressions in the minds of others. Other contemporary sociologists, including George Homans and Peter Blau, have developed *social-exchange analysis.* In their view, social interaction proceeds according to what each person stands to gain (and lose). In the process of courtship, for example, individuals seek mates who offer them at least as much—in terms of physical attractiveness, intelligence, and social prestige—as they offer in return.

Critical evaluation. The symbolic-interaction paradigm helps to overcome a limitation typical of macro-level approaches to understanding society. Without denying the reality of broad patterns such as "the family" and "social inequality," we must remember that society basically amounts to *people interacting with one another.* In essence, this micro-approach attempts to convey more of how individuals actually experience society.

Table 1–1 summarizes the distinctive features of the three theoretical paradigms. One paradigm may be more useful than another in a given situation, since each leads us to ask different kinds of questions. But, taken together, the three provide a more complete understanding of social life. The box on pages 16–17 illustrates how the structural-functional paradigm, the social-conflict paradigm, and the symbolic-interaction paradigm combine to produce a comprehensive analysis of sports.

Scientific Sociology

Refinements in sociological theory come from research. Spurred on by their curiosity, sociologists ask questions about how and why we behave as we do. To answer these questions, researchers rely on **science,** *a logical system that derives knowledge from direct, systematic observation.* Scientific knowledge, therefore, is based on *empirical evidence,* which means facts we are able to verify with our senses.

Sociological research often reveals that what we accept as "common sense" is not entirely true. Here are three examples of widely held attitudes that are contradicted by scientific evidence.

1. **Differences in the behavior of women and men are "human nature."** Sociological investigation shows us that what we call "human nature" is largely the product of the society in which we are raised. Further, researchers have discovered

TABLE 1–1 The Three Major Theoretical Paradigms: A Summary

Theoretical Paradigm	Orientation	Image of Society	Core Questions
Structural-functional	Macro-level	A system of interrelated parts that is relatively stable based on widespread consensus as to what is morally desirable; each part has functional consequences for the operation of society as a whole	How is society integrated? What are the major parts of society? How are these parts interrelated? What are the consequences of each for the operation of society?
Social-conflict	Macro-level	A system characterized by social inequality; each part of society benefits some categories of people more than others; conflict-based social inequality promotes social change	How is society divided? What are major patterns of social inequality? How do some categories of people attempt to protect their privileges? How do other categories of people challenge the status quo?
Symbolic-interaction	Micro-level	An ongoing process of social interaction in specific settings based on symbolic communications; individual perceptions of reality are variable and changing	How is society experienced? How do human beings interact to create, sustain, and change social patterns? How do individuals attempt to shape the reality perceived by others? How does individual behavior change from one situation to another?

that definitions of "feminine" and "masculine" vary significantly from one society to another (see Chapter 10, "Sex and Gender").

2. **The United States is a middle-class society in which most people are more or less equal.** In fact, the richest 5 percent controls half of the country's wealth, while about half the population has virtually no wealth at all. Chapter 7 ("Social Stratification") provides details.

3. **People marry because they are in love.** It may come as a surprise to many, but research confirms that most marriages worldwide have little to do with love. In addition, as Chapter 12 ("Family and Religion") explains, we can safely predict that most people in the United States will fall in love with someone of similar social background.

As these examples indicate, the sociological perspective—carried forward in scientific research—turns up unexpected facts and can help us to evaluate critically a wide range of information we encounter every day.

Concepts, Variables, and Measurement

A crucial element of science is the **concept**, *an abstract idea that represents some aspect of the world, inevitably in a somewhat simplified form.* Sociologists use concepts to label key dimensions of social life, including "religion" and "the economy," and to categorize individuals in terms of their "gender," "race," or "social class."

A **variable** consists of *a concept whose value changes from case to case.* The familiar variable known as "price" varies from item to item in a supermarket. In a similar way, the concept of "social class" varies as we describe people as "upper class," "middle class," "working class," or "lower class."

Measurement means *determining the value of a variable in a specific case.* We can measure a variable as easily as stepping on a scale to discover our weight. Measuring sociological variables, however, can be more difficult. A sociologist might assess social class, for example, by asking about someone's income, occupation, or education. But these three measures may yield inconsistent results.

An important rule holds that researchers must *operationalize* all variables, that is, they must specify exactly what is to be measured in each case. In measuring social class, for example, researchers must decide precisely what aspect of social class is being measured (income? education? occupational prestige?) and report this decision along with their findings.

A related issue arises when sociologists seek to report measurements of an entire category of people on a variable like income. It would be tedious and confusing to report the income of many people

Sports: Playing the Theory Game

To people in the United States, sports seem indispensable to life. With almost everyone engaging in sports to at least some degree, the field has evolved into a multibillion-dollar industry. What insights can we glean from the three theoretical paradigms as we look at this familiar element of life?

A structural-functional approach directs attention to the functions of sports for society as a whole. Manifest functions include providing recreation, offering a relatively harmless way to "let off steam," and contributing to the physical fitness of the population. Sports have important latent functions as well, from fostering social relationships, to generating tens of thousands of jobs, to celebrating competition, achievement, and success—ideas central to our way of life (Spates, 1976a; Coakley, 1990).

Sports have dysfunctional consequences as well. For example, colleges and universities intent on fielding winning teams sometimes recruit students for their athletic ability rather than their academic aptitude. This can pull down the academic standards of the school and may leave the athletes themselves little time to concentrate on anything but their sport.

A social-conflict analysis begins by pointing out that sports are closely related to patterns of social inequality. Some sports— tennis, swimming, golf, and skiing— are expensive, so participation is largely limited to the well-to-do. By contrast, football, baseball, and basketball are accessible to people of all income levels. In short, the games

The painting *Strike*, by contemporary African-American artist Jacob Lawrence, suggests that baseball is more than mere diversion and entertainment. Like all sports, baseball provides valuable lessons about how members of our society expect one another to think and to behave.

Jacob Lawrence, *Strike*, 1949. Tempera on masonite, 20 x 24 inches. The Howard University Gallery of Art (Permanent Collection), Washington, D.C.

individually; therefore, sociologists employ one or more *descriptive statistics* to specify what is "average" for the category as a whole. The most commonly used statistics are the *mean* (the arithmetic average of all measures, obtained by adding them up and dividing by the number of cases), the *median* (the score that divides a distribution in half or, more simply, the middle case), and the *mode* (the single score that appears most often). The median is used throughout this text.

Reliability and validity. Beyond carefully operationalizing variables, useful measurement also depends on reliability and validity. **Reliability** refers to *consistency in measurement*. If, for example, two measures of a people play are not simply a matter of choice but also reflect their social standing.

In the United States, sports are oriented primarily toward males. The first modern Olympic Games held in 1896, for example, excluded women from competition and, until recently, even Little League teams barred girls in most parts of the country. Such discrimination has been defended by unfounded notions that women lack athletic ability or that women athletes risk losing their femininity. Thus our society encourages men to be athletes while conferring on women the role of attentive observers and cheerleaders. More women now play professional sports than ever before, yet they continue to take a back seat to men, particularly in sports that yield the greatest earnings and social prestige.

Our society long excluded people of color as well from professional sports. Major League Baseball first admitted African-American players when Jackie Robinson broke the "color line" in 1947. By 1993, African Americans (12 percent of the U.S. population) accounted for 17 percent of Major League Baseball players, 68 percent of National Football League (NFL) players, and 77 percent of National Basketball Association (NBA) players (Center for the Study of Sport in Society, 1993).

The increasing proportion of people of African descent in professional sports reflects the fact that individual athletic performances cannot be diminished by white prejudice. Moreover, some African Americans make a particular effort to excel in athletics where they perceive greater opportunity than in other careers (Steele, 1990).

In recent years, African-American athletes have earned higher salaries, on average, than white players. But racial discrimination taints professional sports in the United States because almost all managers, head coaches, and owners of sports teams are still white.

Taking a wider view, who benefits most from professional sports? Although millions of fans follow their teams, the vast earnings sports generate are controlled by the small number of people (predominantly white men) for whom teams are income-producing property. Thus sports in the United States are bound up with inequalities based on gender, race, and economic power.

Turning to the symbolic-interaction paradigm, sports form a complex and changing pattern of interaction. Although play is guided by the players' assigned positions and by the rules of the game, any contest is also spontaneous and unpredictable. Moreover, each player looks at the game from a unique perspective, with some thriving in competitive situations while others perform badly under pressure (Coakley, 1986).

The behavior of any player also changes over time. Rookies, for example, may feel quite self-conscious during the first few games in the big leagues. In time, however, most develop a more comfortable sense of team membership. This process of coming to feel at home in professional sports was slow and painful for Jackie Robinson, who was only too aware that many white players, and millions of white fans, resented his presence in Major League Baseball (Tygiel, 1983). Eventually, however, his outstanding ability and his confident and cooperative manner won him the respect of the entire nation.

Although each of these paradigms differs in its approach to sports, none is more correct than the others. Applied to any issue, the different theoretical paradigms draw out fascinating debates and engaging controversies; the richest sociology, therefore, emerges from using all three.

community's religious attitudes produce different values, we suspect that one or both of them is not reliable.

Even consistent results, however, may not be valid. **Validity** refers to *measuring exactly what one intends to measure.* Say that you are interested in assessing how religious people are. You decide to do this by asking how often your respondents attend religious services. But does engaging in worship necessarily mean than someone is religious? Probably not, since people engage in such rituals for any number of reasons, not all of them religious; some devout believers, on the other hand, avoid organized religion entirely. Thus, even when a measure yields consistent results (having reliability), it can still miss the real, intended

There are many kinds of truth. *The Emergence of the Clowns* by U.S. artist Roxanne Swentzell presents the story of creation according to the Santa Clara Pueblo. Life began, they believe, when four clowns emerged onto the earth's surface, each facing in a different direction. All of the world's people have creation beliefs of some kind (including the Biblical accounts in Genesis). As members of a scientific society, we sometimes dismiss such stories as "myth" (from Greek, meaning "story"). Whether or not they are entirely factual, they do convey basic truths about the way in which each society searches for human origins and struggles to find meaning in the universe. It is science, not "myth," that is powerless to address such questions of meaning.

Roxanne Swentzell, *The Emergence of the Clowns*, 1988. Coiled and scraped clay: 48 x 48 x 23 inches. The Collection of the Heard Museum, Phoenix, Arizona.

target (lacking validity). Because poor measurement undermines scientific precision, researchers must always pay close attention to reliability and validity.

Correlation and Cause

We gain insights about the social world as we begin to link variables together. **Correlation** means *a relationship between two (or more) variables*; in simple terms, we notice that when one variable changes so does the other. Ideally, sociological research seeks to understand not only *what* changes but also *why*. More useful than

merely noting correlation, then, is mapping out **cause and effect**, which means that *a change in one variable is caused by change in another*. As we noted earlier, Emile Durkheim explained varying suicide rates for categories of people in terms of their corresponding degrees of social integration. In cause-and-effect relationships, we designate one factor as the *independent variable* (in this case, the degree of social integration), which means that it is the variable that causes the change. The *dependent variable* (here, the suicide rate) is the variable that is changed. Understanding cause and effect is valuable because it allows researchers to use what they do know to *predict* what they don't.

However, just because two variables change together does not necessarily mean that they have a cause-and-effect relationship. To take a simple case, more cars are stolen during months when the sale of ice cream rises, but there is no direct link between these two facts. Sociologists call such a correlation *spurious*, or "false," because it is not based on cause and effect. Variables often display spurious correlation because both are affected by some third factor. In this case, rising temperatures increase auto thefts because people leave car windows open, just as warm weather encourages them to indulge in ice cream.

Researchers untangle cases of spurious correlation by utilizing scientific *control* to neutralize the effect of one variable so that the relationships among other variables can be clearly discerned. In our example, we might control the effects of temperature by studying auto thefts and ice cream consumption only on, say, very hot days; doing so, no doubt, would reveal little of the original correlation.

In short, to conclude that variables are linked by cause and effect, we must demonstrate (1) that the two variables are correlated; (2) that the independent (or causal) variable precedes the dependent variable in time; and (3) that there is no evidence suggesting the correlation is spurious due to the effects of some third variable.

The Ideal of Objectivity

Another standard of sound scientific study is *objectivity*, or personal neutrality, in conducting research. The ideal of purely objective inquiry would allow the facts to speak for themselves rather than being filtered through the personal values and biases of the researcher. In reality, of course, researchers can never achieve complete neutrality. But carefully adhering to the logic of scientific research will maximize objectivity.

A basic lesson of social research is that people react to being observed. Researchers can never be sure just how this will occur, however; some people bcome highly animated when they are the object of attention, while others become shy. In neither case does the researcher witness natural behavior.

The influential German sociologist Max Weber conceded that research is *value-relevant*, since personal values play a part in sociologists' selection of topics of study. But once their investigation is under way, he continued, researchers should strive to be *value-free* in their observations and analysis. That is, they should be dispassionately concerned with discovering truth *as it is* rather than as they think *it should be*. This difference, for Weber, sets science apart from politics. Researchers (but not politicians) must cultivate an open-minded readiness to accept the results of their work, whatever they might be.

Although widely supported, Weber's views are subject to two kinds of criticism. First, *researchers must always interpret their data*. No scientist's data speak for themselves; sociologists always face the task of constructing meaning from the facts they have gathered. Moreover, the best research springs from a lively sociological imagination as well as careful attention to the scientific method. Science, after all, is basically a series of procedures, like a recipe used in cooking. Just as it takes more than a good recipe to make a great chef, so scientific procedures never, by themselves, yield a great sociologist. In this sense, sociology involves a good measure of art as well as science (Nisbet, 1970).

A second criticism of Weber's goal of value-free research holds that *all research is political* since all knowledge has implications for the way society is organized (Gouldner, 1970a, 1970b). But if sociologists cannot escape being political, this argument goes, they do have a choice about *which* values are worth supporting. This viewpoint is not limited to sociologists of any one political stripe, but it predominates among social-conflict theorists. As we noted earlier, it was Karl Marx who questioned the merit of understanding the world without making an effort to change it (1972:109; orig. 1845).

Research and Gender

In recent years, sociologists have become increasingly aware that research is affected by *gender*, the relative social standing of women and men. In the view of Margrit Eichler (1988), sound research can fall victim to four problems involving gender.

1. **Androcentricity.** Androcentricity (*andro* is the Greek word for "male"; *centricity* refers to "being centered on") means approaching an issue from a male perspective. This problem arises, for instance, when a researcher assumes that men are heads of households and directs questions to them, thereby ignoring the views of women. The parallel problem, *gynocentricity*—looking at the world from a female perspective—limits sociological investigation as well, although this occurs less frequently in our male-dominated society.

2. **Overgeneralizing.** Historically, sociologists have used data obtained from men as the basis for claims about all people. This poses problems, for

instance, when a researcher gathers information about a corporation from male officials and generalizes about the entire corporate culture. Overgeneralizing also occurs when a researcher investigating child-rearing practices collects data only from mothers and proceeds from there to offer conclusions about "parenthood."

3. **Gender blindness.** Sometimes research completely ignores the variable of gender, giving rise to another bias. For example, researchers looking into social isolation among elderly people in the United States would be remiss if they overlooked the fact that the majority of elderly men live with spouses while most elderly women live alone or with other relatives.

4. **Double standards.** Researchers should avoid evaluating people's attitudes or behaviors according to their sex. A double standard emerges when researchers treat rambunctious behavior on the part of males simply as a case of "boys being boys" while viewing the same actions by females as instances of "loose morals."

5. **Gender interference.** Beyond Eichler's list, gender also affects research to the extent that subjects react to the sex of the investigator. For instance, while conducting research in Sicily, Maureen Giovannini (1992) reported that many men, guided by local traditions, responded to her as a *woman* rather than in the sex-neutral sense of a *researcher*. Their response prevented her from engaging in activities (such as private conversations with men) that locals deemed inappropriate for single women.

Nothing stated here should discourage researchers from focusing on one sex or the other. But researchers—and others who read their work—must think critically about how gender can, and often does, influence the process of sociological investigation.

Feminist Research

Some researchers have gone further, forging explicitly feminist methods of research. As yet, there exists no hard-and-fast definition of feminist research methods. But virtually all its adherents (1) advocate that feminist research should focus on the condition of women in society and (2) take as a given that women's general experience involves subordination. Thus feminist research rejects Weber's value-free orientation in favor of being overtly political.

Moreover, proponents of feminist research maintain that, whatever specific research techniques one chooses, feminist research challenges conventional science itself as a masculine form of knowledge. Why? Because, for example, conventional science demands detachment on the part of the researcher; feminists, by contrast, argue for a sense of sympathetic understanding between investigator and subject. In addition, conventional science places the researcher in charge of the investigation, deciding in advance what issues will be raised and how they will be discussed. Feminist researchers favor a less structured approach to gathering information so that participants in research are free to offer their own ideas on their own terms (Stanley & Wise, 1983; Nielsen, 1990; Stanley, 1990; Reinharz, 1992).

Is feminist research less science than political activism, as conventional sociologists charge? The feminist response, echoing our earlier discussion of social-conflict research, is that research and politics are and should be fused. But, whatever side one takes in this debate, notice that Weber's traditional separation of science and politics now stands alongside a counterargument that merges these two dimensions.

Research Ethics

Research directly affects subjects—for better or ill. The American Sociological Association—the major professional association of sociologists in North America—recognized this fact by establishing guidelines that protect the rights, privacy, and safety of anyone involved in a research project. One major guideline is that sociologists must terminate any research, however valuable its prospective results, if they suspect that they are placing subjects at risk. In addition, all subjects in research are entitled to full anonymity, even if sociologists come under legal pressure to release confidential information.

An additional guideline states that sociologists should tell subjects the precise purpose of their research and disclose their organizational affiliations. They should also note their sources of funding in published research.

Finally, upon completing their work, researchers should report their findings in full, with a complete description of how the study was conducted. Researchers should also provide all possible interpretations of their data and point out limitations of their conclusions (American Sociological Association, 1984).

Special ethical considerations apply to research abroad. Before beginning study in other countries, investigators should become familiar with that society, understanding what people *there* are likely to perceive as a violation of privacy or a source of personal danger. Moreover, in a multicultural society such as the United States, the same rule applies to studying people from backgrounds different from our own. The box on page 22 offers some tips about how outsiders can effectively and sensitively study Hispanic communities.

Research Methods

A **research method** is *a strategy for systematically carrying out research.* Here we introduce four commonly used methods of sociological investigation: experiments, surveys, participant observation, and use of existing sources. None is better or worse than any other. Just as a carpenter selects a particular tool for a particular task, distinctive strengths and weaknesses make each method suitable for specific kinds of research.

The Experiment

Research conducted by **experiment** *investigates cause-and-effect relationships under highly controlled conditions.* Experiments typically test a specific *hypothesis,* that is, an unverified statement of a relationship between two (or more) variables. A hypothesis is really an educated guess about how variables are linked. An experimenter gathers empirical evidence in three steps: (1) measuring the dependent variable; (2) altering the independent variable; and (3) measuring the dependent variable again to see what, if any, change has occurred. Based on this evidence, the investigator can then accept or reject the research hypothesis.

Successful experiments depend on careful control of all factors that might affect what is being measured. Such control is easiest in a laboratory, an artificial setting specially constructed for this purpose. But experiments in an everyday location—"in the field" as sociologists say—have the advantage of allowing researchers to observe subjects in their natural settings.

The Survey

A **survey** is *a research method in which subjects respond to a series of statements or questions in a questionnaire or an interview.* The most widely used of all research

Feminist research is not concerned simply with studying the social standing of women. It also transforms scientific research so that an investigator assumes a posture of social parity with others, working cooperatively toward solving their common problems.

methods, the survey is particularly well suited to studying what cannot be observed directly, such as political attitudes or religious beliefs.

A survey targets some *population.* Research measuring people's years of schooling, for example, might focus on the adults living in a particular housing complex. Sometimes every adult in the country comprises the survey population, as in the familiar polls taken during political campaigns. Since contacting a large number of people requires vast resources, most researchers target a *sample,* a much smaller number of cases selected to represent the entire population. National surveys generally provide accurate estimates based on samples of only fifteen hundred people.

Selecting subjects, however, is only the first step in carrying out a survey. The next stage involves a specific plan for asking questions and recording answers. The most common way to do this is by using a *questionnaire,* a series of written questions or items to which subjects respond. Usually the researcher offers a series of responses to each item and asks the subject to select only one (similar to a multiple-choice examination). Sometimes, though, a researcher may want subjects to respond freely as a way of teasing out shades of opinion. Of course, this free-form approach means that the researcher later has to make sense out of what can be a bewildering array of answers.

In an *interview,* a researcher personally administers a series of questions or items to respondents,

Conducting Research With Hispanics

In a racially, ethnically, and religiously diverse society, sociological investigators will inevitably confront people of varied backgrounds. Learning—in advance—some of the distinctive traits of any category of people being studied can both facilitate the research and ensure that no hard feelings remain when the work is completed.

Gerardo Marín and Barbara VanOss Marín (1991) have compiled several useful tips for investigators who plan to conduct research with Hispanic Americans.

1. **Be careful with terms.** The term "Hispanic" is a label of convenience used by the U.S. Census Bureau. Few people of Spanish descent think of themselves as "Hispanic" or "Latino"; most identify with a particular country (generally, with a nation of Latin America such as Cuba or Argentina, or with Spain).

2. **Anticipate unfamiliar interpersonal dynamics.** By and large, the United States is a nation of individualistic, competitive people. Many Hispanic Americans, by contrast, have a more collective orientation. The Maríns note that Hispanics tend to favor harmonious relations; some subjects, therefore, may appear to agree with a researcher's statement out of politeness more than conviction.

3. **Anticipate different family dynamics.** Generally speaking, Hispanic cultures have strong family loyalties. Asking subjects to reveal information about another family member may make them uncomfortable or even angry. The Maríns add that a researcher's request to speak privately with a Hispanic woman in the home may provoke suspicion or outright disapproval from her husband or father.

4. **Expect cultural differences.** Hispanics, the Maríns explain, tend to be more concerned with the quality of relationships

Researchers must always remain respectful of subjects and mindful of their well-being. In part, this means investigators must become familiar—well ahead of time—with the cultural patterns of those they wish to study.

than with simply getting a job done. A non-Hispanic researcher, concerned about delaying a family's dinner with questions, may rush through an interview with a Hispanic family, only to have that action perceived as rude rather than polite by people used to proceeding at a more relaxed pace. Finally, the Maríns explain, people of Spanish descent typically maintain closer physical contact than many non-Hispanics do. Researchers, therefore, can seem "standoffish" to others, who wonder why they have seated themselves across the room. Researchers, in turn, may inaccurately view Hispanics as "pushy" when they move closer than the non-Hispanic researcher may find comfortable.

Keep in mind that Hispanics differ among themselves just as people in every other category do. But general patterns distinguish Hispanic communities in the United States, and researchers must take these into account when carrying out their work. The challenge of conducting research in this country is great, indeed, since differences of the kind noted here apply to hundreds of distinctive categories of people that make up our multicultural society.

thereby overcoming one problem typical of the questionnaire method, that is, the failure of subjects to return the questionnaire forms to the researcher. A further difference is that participants in interviews have considerable freedom to respond any way they wish.

Researchers often ask follow-up questions, both to probe a bit more deeply and to clarify the subject's answers. In doing this, however, a researcher must guard against influencing the subject even in subtle ways, such as raising an eyebrow as the subject offers an answer.

Researchers typically present the results of surveys in the form of tables. The box on page 24 shows the results of one survey along with tips about how to read tables efficiently.

Participant Observation

Participant observation is *a method in which researchers systematically observe people while joining in their routine activities.* This method allows researchers to study social life in its natural setting, from a gambling casino to a religious seminary. Cultural anthropologists, who make wide use of participant observation to study other societies, call this approach "fieldwork."

Researchers often begin with few specific hypotheses, since they may not be sure what the important questions will turn out to be. Compared to experiments and surveys, then, participant observation has few hard and fast rules. Flexibility can be an advantage, however, since investigators frequently must adapt to unexpected circumstances in an unfamiliar environment. Initially, researchers concentrate on working their way into some setting without intruding—and thereby altering—the routine behavior of others. In time, general impressions lead to a broad explanation of a way of life.

As its name suggests, participant observation has two facets. On the one hand, gaining an insider's viewpoint depends on becoming a participant in the setting—"hanging out" with others for months or even years, attempting to act, think, and even feel the way they do. On the other hand, the researcher must maintain the role of "observer," standing back from the action and applying the sociological perspective to social patterns that others take for granted.

Because the personal impressions of individual researchers play such a central role, critics point to the difficulty of replication and claim that participant observation lacks scientific rigor. Yet its personal orientation is also a strength; where a visible team of sociologists administering a formal survey might disrupt a setting, a sensitive participant-observer can often gain considerable insight into people's natural behavior.

Existing Sources

Each of the methods of conducting sociological investigation described so far involves researchers collecting their own data. In many cases, however, sociologists

The exotic often excites the sociological imagination. Participant observation is well suited for exploring an unfamiliar setting such as this urban neighborhood in India. But research abroad demands extensive preparation. To begin, investigators must acquire necessary language skills, and they need to gain at least a basic understanding of the new culture. To minimize these difficulties, researchers often study communities with which they have at least some previous experience.

draw from existing sources, analyzing data collected by others.

The most widely used data are gathered by government agencies such as the Bureau of the Census. Data about other nations in the world are found in various publications of the United Nations and the World Bank. A wide range of such information is as near as the college library.

Drawing on available data saves time and money that otherwise would be needed to assemble information from scratch. This method holds great appeal to sociologists with low budgets; in addition, the quality of data may turn out to be better than what many researchers could hope to obtain on their own.

Table Reading: Some Tips

A table provides a great deal of information in a small amount of space, so learning to read tables can increase your reading efficiency. When you spot a table, look first at the title to see what information it contains. The title indicates that Table 1–2 reports the sexual activity of couples in the United States, broken down by various categories of people. Here, sexual activity is described in terms of three other variables: (1) the type of relationship (married couples, cohabiting heterosexual couples, and homosexual couples); (2) the duration of the relationship (under 2 years, between 2 and 10 years, over 10 years); and (3) the sex of the respondent (female or male).

These three variables form the three major parts of the table, with six categories of people found within each part. For each category, the proportion reporting sexual activity outside of the relationship is noted. The "yes" and "no" responses add up to 100 percent.

Looking at the first part of the table, 13 percent of women married for less than two years reported extra-relational sexual activity, while 87 percent reported no such activity. For women married between two and ten years, the corresponding figures were 22 percent and 78 percent; the percentages hold for women married for more than ten years. Comparable data are presented for other categories of people as well.

What do these data tell us? First, generally speaking, the longer a couple has been together, the more likely partners are to have extra-relational sex. Second, women are more likely than men to remain monogamous. Third, cohabiting heterosexual partners are less likely to remain monogamous than married people are. Note, too, that the pattern among homosexual couples differs sharply by sex: Gay men are far more likely to report nonmonogamy than are lesbian partners.

Finally, a critical reader should try to assess the overall quality of the research. Important clues include the background of the researchers themselves (are they sociologists? newspaper reporters?), as well as bibliographic information (was the research published by a respected journal? by a group with some vested interest in the topic?). In short, the results are only as good as the overall quality of the research.

TABLE 1–2 Sexual Activity Among U.S. Couples, by Type of Relationship, Duration of Relationship, and Sex of Respondent

Married Couples				*Cohabiting Heterosexual Couples*				*Homosexual Couples*			
Reported Sexual Activity Outside Relationship				Reported Sexual Activity Outside Relationship				Reported Sexual Activity Outside Relationship			
Years Together	Females		Males		Years Together	Females		Males		Years Together	Females		Males	
	Yes	No	Yes	No		Yes	No	Yes	No		Yes	No	Yes	No
Under 2	13%	87%	15%	85%	Under 2	20%	80%	21%	79%	Under 2	15%	85%	66%	34%
2–10	22	78	23	77	2–10	42	58	47	53	2–10	38	62	89	11
Over 10	22	78	30	70	Over 10*	no data		no data		Over 10	43	57	94	6

*Too few cohabiting couples had been together for more than ten years.

Source: Adapted from Philip Blumstein and Pepper Schwartz, *American Couples* (New York: William Morrow, 1983), p. 276. © 1983 by Philip Blumstein and Pepper W. Schwartz. Adapted by permission of William Morrow & Co.

Still, existing sources have their drawbacks. For one thing, data may not be available in the specific form a researcher may be looking for. Moreover, one may have difficulty assessing the accuracy of existing data. The World Bank, for example, must rely on various world governments to provide data about their populations.

Characteristics of the four major methods of sociological investigation we have introduced are summarized in Table 1–3.

TABLE 1–3 Four Research Methods: A Summary

Method	Application	Advantages	Limitations
Experiment	For explanatory research that specifies relationships among variables; generates quantitative data	Provides greatest ability to specify cause-and-effect relationships; replication of research is relatively easy	Laboratory settings have artificial quality; unless research environment is carefully controlled, results may be biased
Survey	For gathering information about issues that cannot be directly observed, such as attitudes and values; useful for descriptive and explanatory research; generates quantitative or qualitative data	Sampling allows surveys of large populations using questionnaires; interviews provide in-depth responses	Questionnaires must be carefully prepared and may produce low return rate; interviews are expensive and time consuming
Participant observation	For exploratory and descriptive study of people in a "natural" setting; generates qualitative data	Allows study of "natural" behavior; usually inexpensive	Time consuming; replication of research is difficult; researcher must balance roles of participant and observer
Existing sources	For exploratory, descriptive, or explanatory research whenever suitable data are available	Saves time and expense of data collection; makes historical research possible	Researcher has no control over bias in data; data may be unsuitable for current research

Ten Steps in Sociological Investigation

The following ten steps serve as guidelines for carrying out research projects in sociology.

1. **Define the topic you wish to investigate.** Ideas for social research can be found everywhere, if you remain curious and observe the world around you using the sociological perspective.

2. **Find out what has already been written about the topic.** Spend enough time in the library to learn how others have investigated the topic. In looking over earlier research, be mindful of problems that have come up before.

3. **Assess the requirements for carrying out the research.** What resources are needed to support your research? How much time is necessary? Can you work alone? What sources of funding are available to support the research?

4. **Specify the questions you are going to ask.** Is your plan to explore an unfamiliar social setting? To describe some category of people? To investigate cause-and-effect links among variables? If your study is exploratory, identify general questions that will guide your work. If it is descriptive, specify the population and the characteristics of interest. If your study is explanatory, state the hypothesis to be tested and carefully operationalize each variable.

5. **Consider the ethical issues involved.** Can you promise anonymity to the subjects? If so, how can you ensure that it will be maintained? How can you design the study to minimize the chances for harm to subjects?

6. **Choose the research method.** Consider all major research strategies—as well as innovative combinations of approaches—before deciding how to proceed. The preferred method depends on the kinds of questions you are asking as well as the resources available to support your research.

7. **Put the method to work to gather data.** Be sure to record all information accurately and in a way that will make sense to you later (it may be some time before you actually write up the results of your work). Identify sources of bias that might compromise the research.

8. **Interpret the findings.** What answers to the initial questions do the data suggest? Remember that there may be several ways to interpret the results of your study, consistent with different theoretical paradigms. Be alert to how your own personal values or initial expectations affect interpretation.

9. **Prepare a final report indicating what you have learned from the research.** Also, evaluate your own work. What problems arose during the research process? What questions were left unanswered? How might your own biases have affected your conclusions?

10. **Publish your research!**

SUMMARY

1. The sociological perspective reveals that the lives of individuals are shaped by the forces of society. Because our way of life stresses individual choice, sociology can provide a "reality check" on what we view as common sense.

2. Auguste Comte gave sociology its name in 1838. Earlier social thought focused on what society *ought to be*; sociology is based on the use of scientific methods to understand society *as it is*.

3. Sociology emerged as a reaction to the rapid transformation of European societies during the eighteenth and nineteenth centuries. The rise of an industrial economy, the explosive growth of cities, and the emergence of new political ideas combined to weaken tradition and stimulate embrace of the sociological perspective.

4. Theory involves constructing meaning from sociological insights. Theory building is guided by one or more theoretical paradigms.

5. The structural-functional paradigm is a framework for exploring how social structures promote the operation of society. This approach tends to minimize conflict and change.

6. The social-conflict paradigm suggests that social inequality generates conflict and leads to change. This approach downplays the extent of integration and stability in society.

7. In contrast to these two macro-level approaches, the symbolic-interaction paradigm is a micro-level framework for studying the variable understandings people generate in situational interaction.

8. Sociological research employs the logic of science. Scientific facts are based on empirical evidence.

9. Measurement is the process of determining the value of a variable in any specific case. Sound measurement has both reliability and validity.

10. Science seeks to specify the relationships among variables. Ideally, researchers try to identify relationships of cause and effect by which an independent variable causes change in a dependent variable.

11. The scientific ideal is objectivity. Value-free research requires suspending personal values and biases as much as possible. However, some sociologists argue that all research involves political values and that their work should promote desirable social change.

12. Investigators observe ethical guidelines to ensure that research does not compromise the well-being of subjects.

13. An experiment investigates the relationship between two (or more) variables under controlled, laboratory conditions.

14. A survey collects subjects' responses to items in questionnaires and interviews.

15. Participant observation refers to direct study of a social setting for an extended period of time.

16. The use of existing sources is often preferable to collecting one's own data, especially for sociologists with limited research budgets.

KEY CONCEPTS

cause and effect a relationship between two variables in which change in one (the independent variable) causes change in another (the dependent variable)

concept an abstract idea that represents some aspect of the world, inevitably in a somewhat simplified form

correlation a relationship between two (or more) variables

experiment a research method that investigates cause-and-effect relationships under highly controlled conditions

global perspective a view of the larger world and our society's place in it

latent functions the unrecognized and unintended consequences of any social pattern

least-developed countries nations with little industrialization in which severe poverty is the rule

less-developed countries nations characterized by limited industrialization and moderate-to-low personal income

macro-level orientation a concern with large-scale patterns that characterize society as a whole

manifest functions the recognized and intended consequences of any social pattern

measurement the process of determining the value of a variable in a specific case

micro-level orientation a concern with small-scale patterns of social interaction in specific settings

most-developed countries industrial nations that are relatively rich

participant observation a research method in which investigators systematically observe people while joining in their routine activities

positivism a path to understanding based on science

reliability the quality of consistency in measurement

research method a strategy for systematically carrying out research

science a logical system that derives knowledge from direct, systematic observation

social-conflict paradigm a framework for building theory based on the assumption that society is a complex system characterized by inequality and conflict that generate social change

social dysfunction the undesirable consequences of any social pattern for the operation of society

social function the consequences of any social pattern for the operation of society as a whole

social structure any relatively stable pattern of social behavior

sociology the scientific study of human social activity

structural-functional paradigm a framework for building theory based on the assumption that society is a complex system whose parts work together to promote stability

survey a research method in which subjects respond to a series of statements or questions in a questionnaire or interview

symbolic-interaction paradigm a framework for building theory based on the view that society is the product of the everyday interactions of individuals

theoretical paradigm a set of fundamental assumptions that guides thinking and research

theory a statement of how and why specific facts are related

validity the quality of measurement gained by measuring exactly what one intends to measure

variable a concept whose value changes from case to case

CRITICAL-THINKING QUESTIONS

1. In what ways does using the sociological perspective make us seem less in control of our lives? In what ways does it give us greater power over our surroundings?

2. What changes does sociological thinking produce in how you understand your own biography?

3. Provide a sociological explanation of why sociology developed where and when it did.

4. Guided by the discipline's three major theoretical paradigms, what kinds of questions might a sociologist ask about (a) gender, (b) war, (c) humor, and (d) the mass media?

Chapter

2

Culture

A small aluminum motorboat chugged steadily along the muddy Orinoco River, deep within South America's vast tropical rain forest. Anthropologist Napoleon Chagnon was nearing the end of a three-day journey to the home territory of the Yąnomamö, one of the most technologically primitive societies on earth.

Some twelve thousand Yąnomamö live in villages scattered along the border between Venezuela and Brazil. Their way of life could hardly be more different from our own. The Yąnomamö wear few clothes, live without automobiles or electricity, and have no form of writing. Their traditional weapons, used for hunting and warfare, are the bow and arrow. Many have had little contact with outsiders. Thus Chagnon would be as strange to them as they would be to him.

By two o'clock in the afternoon, Chagnon had almost reached his destination. The hot sun made the humid air almost unbearable. The anthropologist's clothes were soaked with perspiration, and his face and hands swelled from the bites of innumerable gnats swarming around him.

Chagnon's heart pounded as the boat slid onto the riverbank near a Yąnomamö village. He heard voices nearby. Chagnon and his guide climbed from the boat and walked toward the sounds, stooping as they pushed their way through the dense undergrowth. Chagnon describes what happened next:

> I looked up and gasped when I saw a dozen burly, naked, sweaty, hideous men staring at us down the shafts of their drawn arrows! Immense wads of green tobacco were stuck between their lower teeth and lips making them look even more hideous, and strands of dark green slime dripped or hung from their nostrils—strands so long that they clung to their [chests] or drizzled down their chins.
>
> My next discovery was that there were a dozen or so vicious, underfed dogs snapping at my legs, circling me as if I were to be their next meal. I just stood there holding my notebook, helpless and pathetic. Then the stench of the decaying vegetation and filth hit me and I almost got sick. I was horrified. What

kind of welcome was this for the person who came here to live with you and learn your way of life, to become friends with you? (1983:10)

Fortunately for Chagnon, the Yąnomamö villagers recognized his guide and lowered their weapons. Reassured that he would survive at least the afternoon, Chagnon was still shaken by his inability to make any sense of the people surrounding him. And this was to be his home for a year and a half! He wondered why he had forsaken physics to study human culture in the first place.

The 5.7 billion people living on earth are members of a single biological species: *Homo sapiens*. Even so, the differences among people the world over can easily overwhelm us. Entering the world of the Yąnomamö, Chagnon experienced a severe case of **culture shock,** *the personal disorientation accompanying exposure to an unfamiliar way of life.* Like most of us, Chagnon had been raised to keep his clothes on, even in hot weather, and to use a handkerchief when his nose was running, especially in front of others. The Yąnomamö clearly had other ideas about how to live. The nudity that embarrassed Chagnon was customary to them. The green slime hanging from their nostrils was caused by inhaling a hallucinogenic drug, a practice common among friends. The "stench" from which Chagnon recoiled in disgust no doubt smelled like "Home Sweet Home" to the inhabitants of that Yąnomamö village.

In short, despite being the same creatures biologically, human beings have very different ideas about what is pleasant and repulsive, polite and rude, beautiful and ugly, right and wrong. This capacity for startling difference is a wonder of our species: the expression of human culture.

What is Culture?

Culture is defined as *the beliefs, values, behavior, and material objects shared by a particular people.* Sociologists distinguish between *nonmaterial culture,* which includes intangible human creations ranging from altruism to zen, and *material culture,* the tangible products of human society, everything from armaments to zippers. The terms *culture* and *society* are sometimes used interchangeably, but their precise

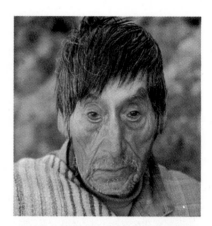

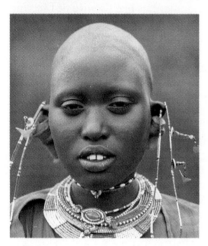

Human beings around the globe create diverse ways of life. Such differences begin with outward appearance: Contrast the women shown here from Iran, Kenya, New Guinea, and Egypt, and the men from Taiwan (Republic of China), Peru, India, and New Guinea. Less obvious, but of even greater importance, are internal differences, since culture also shapes our goals in life, our sense of justice, and even our innermost personal feelings.

meanings are different. Culture is a shared way of life or social heritage. **Society** refers to *people interacting within a limited territory guided by their culture*. Neither society nor culture can exist without the other.

Taken together, cultural elements form broad patterns for living. The way we dress, when and what we eat, and how we enjoy spending our free time are all grounded in culture. Chemists tell us that only ninety-two elements exist naturally on the earth, but sociologists know that the world is home to countless variations of human culture. Our culture infuses life with meaning, setting up standards of success, beauty, and goodness. Culture also shapes our personalities, creating shared orientations that we commonly (yet inaccurately) describe as "human nature." The Yanomamö are fierce and warlike, and they strive to develop these "natural" qualities in their children. The Semai of Malaysia, by contrast, are peace-loving and rarely speak of violence. The cultures of the United States and Japan both stress achievement and hard work; but most members of our society value competition and individualism, while the Japanese place more emphasis on cooperation and self-denying obedience to authority. In short, culture is a blueprint for virtually every dimension of our lives, from the might of enormous corporations to the meaning of a shy smile.

Culture is distinctively human. Every other species of living creatures—from ants to zebras—behaves in uniform ways. To a world traveler, the enormous diversity of humanity contrasts sharply with the behavior of, say, cats, which is everywhere the same. Most living creatures respond to biological forces we call *instincts*, strategies for survival that change only over long periods of time. A few animals—notably chimpanzees and other related primates—have the capacity for basic elements of culture such as using simple tools and teaching these skills to their offspring. But the creative power of people far exceeds that of any other form of life, so that *only humans depend on culture rather than instinct to ensure the survival of their kind* (Harris, 1987).

To understand how this came to be, we must briefly review the history of our species on earth.

Culture and Human Intelligence

In a universe perhaps 15 billion years old, our planet is a relatively young 4.5 billion years of age, and the human species is a wide-eyed infant of only 250,000. Not for a billion years after the earth was formed did life appear on our planet. Much later—some 65 million years ago—our history took a crucial turn with the appearance of the mammals we call primates.

What sets primates apart is their intelligence, based on the largest brains relative to body size of all living creatures. As primates evolved, the human line diverged from that of our closest relatives, the great apes, some 12 million years ago. But our common lineage shows through in traits that humans share with chimpanzees, gorillas, and orangutans: great sociability; affectionate and long-lasting bonds; the ability to walk upright (normal in humans, but less common among other primates); and hands that precisely manipulate objects.

Studying fossil records, scientists conclude that, about 2 million years ago, our distant human ancestors grasped cultural fundamentals like the use of fire, and making tools, weapons, and simple shelters. Although such Stone Age achievements may seem modest, they mark the point at which our forebears embarked on a distinct evolutionary course, making culture the primary strategy for survival. As mental capacity expanded, we became the only species that names itself, and we are appropriately termed *Homo sapiens*, Latin for "thinking person."

Culture, therefore, is an evolutionary strategy for survival that emerged as our ancestors descended from the trees into the tall grasses of central Africa and began to walk upright and hunt in groups. Gradually the biological forces we call instincts were replaced by a more efficient survival scheme: *Human beings gained the mental power to actively fashion the natural environment for themselves*. Ever since, humans have made and remade their worlds in countless ways, which explains today's fascinating (and, as Napoleon Chagnon's experiences show, sometimes disturbing) cultural diversity.

The Components of Culture

Although cultures vary greatly, they all have common components, including language, values, and norms. We shall begin with the one that underlies the rest: symbols.

Symbols

Reality for human beings is not action or feeling but *meaning*. Humans are symbolic creatures; a **symbol** is *anything that carries a particular meaning recognized by people who share culture*. A whistle, a wall of graffiti, a

Travelers know how stressful entering an unfamiliar society can be. Culture shock is one challenge faced by U.S. military personnel when abroad—even on humanitarian missions. This soldier is only too glad to be ending a tour of duty in the African nation of Somalia.

flashing red light, a fist raised in the air—all serve as symbols. We see the human capacity to create and manipulate symbols in the various ways a simple wink of the eye can convey interest, understanding, or insult.

We are so dependent on our culture's symbols that we take them for granted. Often, however, we gain a heightened sense of the importance of a symbol when someone uses it in an unconventional way: for example, when a person in a political demonstration burns a U.S. flag. Entering an unfamiliar culture also reminds us of the power of symbols; culture shock is nothing more than the inability to "read" meaning in one's surroundings. Like Napoleon Chagnon confronting the Yąnomamö, we feel lost, unsure of how to act, and sometimes frightened—a consequence of slipping outside the symbolic system of culture.

The meanings of actions or objects vary from culture to culture. To people in North America, a baseball bat symbolizes sport and relaxation, but the Yąnomamö would probably see it as a well-carved club useful for making war. A dog is a beloved household pet to millions of North Americans but a prized wintertime meal to residents of northern China. Likewise, the cows that India's Hindus revere as sacred are routinely consumed as "quarter-pounders" by hungry people in the United States. Thus symbols bind together individuals of one society but also separate people who live in different societies of the world.

As people of the world interact more and more, we need to remember that behavior that seems normal to us may offend people elsewhere. Women serving in the 1991 Gulf War discovered that simply wearing shorts in an Islamic society like Saudi Arabia is widely condemned as inappropriate. The box on pages 34–35 explains that an innocent gesture for people sharing one culture may provoke an angry response from people who embrace a different cultural system.

Symbolic meanings also vary within a single society. A fur coat, prized by one person as a symbol of success, may represent to another the inhumane treatment of animals. Similarly, the Confederate flag that for one individual embodies regional pride may symbolize to someone else racial oppression.

Language

Language is *a system of symbols that allows people to communicate with one another.* All societies have a spoken language; some, including the Yanomamö, lack a written language and communicate entirely through speech. Written symbols themselves vary: Societies in the Western world write left to right, those in northern Africa and western Asia write right to left, and people in eastern Asia write from top to bottom.

Global Map 2–1 on page 36 shows the regional use of the world's three most widely spoken languages. Chinese is the official language of one-fifth of humanity (more than 1 billion people). English is the mother tongue of about 10 percent (500 million) of the world's people, and Spanish is the official language of 6 percent (300 million) of people worldwide. Notice,

Travelers Beware! The Meaning of Gestures in Other Societies

A young man from Wisconsin is enjoying a summer adventure in the African nation of Nigeria. He stands by the side of a country road, trying to "thumb a ride" to the next town. A truckload of locals approaches; they take one look at him and bring their vehicle to a screeching halt. But they are not about to offer a ride to our hapless visitor; instead, they pile out of the truck, angrily denounce him, rough him up, and leave him, sore and confused, sitting on the ground.

What has happened here? Are Nigerians hostile to foreigners? No, except that, like people everywhere, they don't take kindly to insults. The gesture that the young man from the United States took to mean a request for a ride, Nigerians see as a crude and offensive gesture.

Since much communication involves body language rather than spoken words—especially when we encounter people whose language differs from our own—we need to

be wary of careless gestures that may provoke an angry response. Here are six gestures that seem innocent enough to members of our society but will prompt a stern response from people elsewhere.

Figures (a) and (b) each offend members of Islamic societies. Since Muslims typically perform bathroom hygiene with the left hand, they find the sight of a person eating with that hand, illustrated in Figure (a), to be revolting. Islam also defines

(a)

(b)

(c)

too, that English is becoming a global language that is now spoken as a second tongue in most of the world.

Language not only facilitates communication, it also ensures the continuity of culture. Language—in spoken or written form—is a cultural heritage in coded form, the key to **cultural transmission**, *the process by which one generation passes culture to the next.* Just as our bodies contain the genes of our ancestors, so our words and ideas are rooted in the lives of those who came before us. The power of language, then, lies in giving us access to centuries of accumulated wisdom.

Language skills not only put us in touch with the past, they also unlock the human imagination. Connecting symbols in new ways, we can conceive of life other than as it is. Language distinguishes human beings as creatures aware of our limitations and ultimate mortality, yet able to dream and hope for a future better than the present.

The Sapir-Whorf hypothesis. If the Semai of Malaysia have few words of anger in their language, how do they imagine warfare? Certainly, they cannot do so as readily as the Yanomamö, whose language is rich with terms for fighting. Since language provides what touches the ground as unclean; therefore, to display the bottom of the foot, as in Figure (b), is insulting. In Figure (c) we see the common "A-OK" gesture, by which North Americans express approval and pleasure. In France, however, this symbol conveys the insult "You're worth zero," while Germans take this gesture as a crude word for "rectum." Figure (d) shows the simple curling of a finger, meaning "come here." Malaysians attach the

same meaning to this gesture as we do; but, because they use it exclusively for calling animals, they take offense to being beckoned in this way. Figure (e) pictures the familiar "thumbs up" sign widely employed in North America to mean "Good job!" or "All right!" In Nigeria (as the hapless hitchhiker described earlier learned), and also in Australia, flashing this gesture (especially with a slight upward motion) transmits the insulting message "Up yours!"

Finally, in Figure (f) we interpret the gesture as "Stop!" or "No, thanks." But make this gesture toward a motorist in West Africa and you will probably have a fight on your hands. There it means "You have five fathers" or, more simply, "You bastard!"

Sources: Examples are drawn from Ekman et al. (1984) and Axtell (1991).

(d)

(e)

(f)

the building blocks of reality, linguistic differences mean that members of one culture experience the world differently from those who inhabit another symbolic world.

Edward Sapir and Benjamin Whorf claimed that languages are not just different sets of labels for the same reality (Sapir, 1929, 1949; Whorf, 1956). Rather, each symbolic system is at least partly unique, with words or expressions that have no precise counterpart in another symbolic system. In addition, as multilingual people can attest, a single idea may "feel" different if spoken in Spanish rather than in English or Chinese (Falk, 1987). Formally, then, the **Sapir-Whorf**

hypothesis holds that *we can know the world only in terms of the symbols contained in our language.*

Values

What accounts for the popularity of movie characters like James Bond, Dirty Harry, Rambo, or Thelma and Louise? Each is rugged, suspicious of "the system," and displays unusual abilities and extraordinary personal initiative. Together, they suggest that our culture celebrates an ideal of sturdy individualism, especially among men. Sociologists call such patterns **values,**

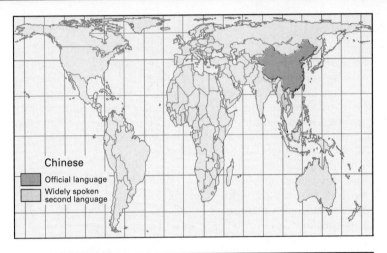

Chinese
■ Official language
□ Widely spoken second language

GLOBAL MAP 2–1
Language in Global Perspective

Chinese (including Mandarin, Cantonese, and dozens of other dialects) is the native tongue of one-fifth of the world's people, almost all of whom live in Asia. More precisely, although all Chinese people read and write with the same characters, they employ any of several dozen dialects. The "official" dialect, taught in schools throughout the People's Republic of China and Taiwan, Republic of China, is Mandarin (the dialect of Beijing, China's historic capital city). Cantonese (the language of Canton, which differs in sound from Mandarin roughly the way French does from Spanish) is the second most common Chinese dialect.

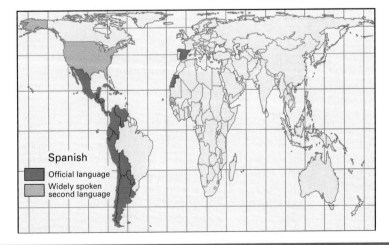

English
■ Official language
□ Widely spoken second language

English is the native tongue or official language in several world regions and has become the preferred second language in most of the world.

Spanish
■ Official language
□ Widely spoken second language

The largest concentration of Spanish speakers is in Latin America and, of course, in Spain. Spanish is also the preferred second language of the United States.

Source: *Peters Atlas of the World* (1990).

culturally defined standards of desirability, goodness, and beauty, which serve as broad guidelines for social living. Values are evaluations and judgments, from the standpoint of the culture, of what ought to be.

Values are broad principles that support **beliefs,** *specific statements that people hold to be true.* While values are abstract standards, in other words, beliefs are specific assertions that people who share a culture consider true. For example, because most U.S. adults share the *value* of roughly equal opportunities for all, they *believe* that a qualified woman could serve as president (NORC, 1993).

Because the United States is a nation of immigrants, few values command the support of everyone. Even so, sociologist Robin Williams (1970) identifies ten values that stand at the core of our culture.

1. **Equal opportunity.** Our sense of fairness dictates that everyone have the opportunity to get ahead. However, due to varying talents and efforts, we do not expect everyone to end up in the same situation. In other words, while not endorsing *equality of condition,* we do embrace *equality of opportunity.*

2. **Achievement and success.** Our way of life encourages competition. In principle, we believe, each person's rewards should reflect personal merit.

3. **Activity and work.** Our heroes, from Olympic skater Kristi Yamaguchi to film's famed archaeologist Indiana Jones, are "doers" who get the job done. Our culture values *action* over *reflection,* and favors working hard to control events over passively accepting one's "fate."

4. **Material comfort.** Success in the United States generally means making money and enjoying what it will buy. Although people sometimes quip that "money won't buy happiness," most eagerly pursue wealth all the same.

5. **Practicality and efficiency.** Just as our way of life values money, so we praise those who solve problems with the least effort. "Building a better mousetrap" represents a cultural goal, especially when done in the most cost-effective way.

6. **Progress.** Members of our society generally believe that the present is better than the past, and that the future will be better still. This value is evident in widespread advertising that hails the "very latest" as the "very best."

7. **Science.** Most members of our society look to scientific experts to improve our lives. We believe

Australian feminist Sally Swain alters a famous artist's painting to make fun of our culture's tendency to ignore the everyday lives of women. The spoof is entitled *Mrs. Chagall Feeds the Baby.*

we are rational people, which probably explains our cultural tendency (especially among men) to devalue emotion and intuition as sources of knowledge.

8. **Democracy and free enterprise.** Members of our society recognize numerous individual rights that cannot be overridden by government. Our political system is based on the ideal of free elections just as we believe that our economy responds to the needs and choices of consumers.

9. **Freedom.** We favor individual initiative over collective conformity. While we acknowledge that everyone has responsibilities to others, we believe that people should be free to act without unreasonable interference from anyone else.

The New "Culture of Victimization"

The Menendez brothers literally blew their parents away with shotguns. However, when they subsequently claimed in court that their father had sexually assaulted them for years, a jury failed to convict them. Lorena Bobbitt severed the penis of her husband, yet won a sympathetic verdict from a jury after explaining that she was a victim of spouse abuse. Colin Ferguson fired ninety rounds of ammunition as he walked through a trainload of commuters in a New York City suburb, killing six and wounding nineteen more; his lawyers argued that his behavior was an expression of rage resulting from long-term racism directed at him as an African American.

Surveying such cases, sociologist Irving Horowitz proclaims the advent of a new "culture of victimization" saying, "Everyone is a victim these days; no one accepts responsibility for anything."

Consider the proliferation of "addictions." No longer limited to the compulsive use of drugs, we now hear about gambling addicts, compulsive overeaters and undereaters, sex addicts, and even people who excuse mounting credit-card debts as a symptom of shopping addiction. Talk shows serve up a steady diet of testimonials from people suffering from alleged new medical or psychological afflictions, and bookstores overflow with manuals to help people come to terms

with conditions ranging from the "Cinderella Complex" and the "Casanova Complex" to "Soap Opera Syndrome." And our courts are ever more clogged with lawsuits driven by the need to blame someone—and sometimes by the desire to collect big money—for the kind of misfortune that we used to accept as part of life.

What's going on here? Is U.S. culture—historically based on the ideal of "rugged individualism" by which people are responsible for whatever befalls them—evolving into a new culture of victimization? Mounting evidence suggests that the answer is yes, and for several reasons. First, members of our society are now more aware (due not just to

Reinforcing "victimization" as an emerging culture, many popular "tell all" television programs feature people who deny personal responsibility for various calamities that have befallen them.

popular talk shows but also to the scholarly work of sociologists) that society itself shapes the lives of everyone. Second, many lawyers now encourage a sense of injustice among clients they hope to shepherd into court. And the number of million-dollar awards in the United States has risen twenty-five fold in the last twenty-five years. Third, there has been a proliferation of special-interest groups that have encouraged what sociologist Amitai Etzioni calls "rights inflation." Beyond the traditional constitutional liberties are many newly claimed rights, including those of hunters (as well as those of animals), the rights of smokers (and nonsmokers), the right of women to control their bodies (and the rights of the unborn), the right to own a gun (and the right to be safe from violence). Competing claims for unmet rights create victims on all sides.

Whether this change will take hold over the long term remains to be seen. But we need to remember that, while a concern with individual rights has helped the United States confront clear cases of injustice, it also has the potential to erode our collective responsibility for one another as members of a cultural system.

Sources: Based on Etzioni (1991) and Taylor (1991).

10. **Racism and group superiority.** People in the United States evaluate others according to their sex, race, ethnicity, and social class. Our culture values males above females, whites above people of color, people with northwestern European backgrounds above those whose ancestors came from other lands, and more privileged people above those who are disadvantaged. Although we describe ourselves as a nation of equals, there is little doubt that some of us are "more equal than others."

Looking over this list, we see that some cultural values contradict others (Lynd, 1967; Bellah et al., 1985). For example, we frequently find ourselves torn between the "me first" attitude of an individualistic, success-at-all-costs way of life and the opposing need to be part of a community. Similarly, we affirm our belief in equality of opportunity only to turn around and promote or degrade others because of their race or sex. Such value conflict inevitably causes strain, leading to awkward balancing acts in our beliefs. Sometimes we decide that one value is more important than another; in other cases, we may simply learn to live with inconsistencies.

Some value inconsistency results from change. New trends may clash with older cultural orientations. For example, what some observers have tagged a new "culture of victimization" now challenges our society's long-time belief in individual responsibility. The box to the left takes a closer look.

Norms

Through values, culture gives shape to ideas. Through norms, on the other hand, culture influences the actions of individuals. **Norms** are *rules by which a society guides the behavior of its members*. William Graham Sumner (1959; orig. 1906), an early U.S. sociologist, coined the term **mores** (pronounced MORE-ays) to refer to *norms that are widely observed and have great moral significance*. Mores, or *taboos*, are exemplified by our society's insistence that adults not engage in sexual relations with children.

But people are more casual about many dimensions of life. Sumner used the term **folkways** to designate *norms about which people allow one another considerable personal discretion*. Examples include codes for dress or polite behavior. A man who does not wear a tie to a formal dinner party may raise an eyebrow for violating folkways or "etiquette." By contrast, were he to arrive at the dinner party wearing *only* a tie, he would be violating cultural mores and inviting more serious sanctions.

Cultural norms, then, steer behavior by defining what is proper and improper. Although we sometimes bristle when others pressure us to conform, we generally embrace norms because, as part of the symbolic road map of culture, they make our encounters with others more predictable.

As we learn—or *internalize*—cultural norms, we build them into our own personalities. This explains the experience of *guilt*—a negative judgment we make

of ourselves for having violated a norm—as well as *shame*—the disturbing acknowledgment of others' disapproval. Only cultural creatures can experience guilt and shame, a fact that writer Mark Twain had in mind when he remarked that human beings "are the only animals that blush . . . or need to."

"Ideal" and "Real" Culture

Values and norms do not describe actual behavior as much as prescribe how members of a society *should* act. We learn to recognize some difference between *ideal culture*, expectations embodied in values and norms, and *real culture*, the patterns that typically occur in everyday life. The vast majority of adults in the United States acknowledge the importance of sexual fidelity in marriage, for example, but at least one-third of married people are sexually unfaithful to their spouses at some point in their marriages. These discrepancies bring to mind the old saying, "Do as I say, not as I do."

High Culture and Popular Culture

In everyday conversation, we usually reserve the term "culture" for sophisticated art forms such as classical literature, music, and dance. We praise film directors, dance choreographers, and college professors as "cultured," because they presumably appreciate the "finer things in life." The term "culture" itself has the same Latin root as the word "cultivate," suggesting that the "cultured" individual has cultivated or refined tastes.

By contrast, we speak less generously of ordinary people, assuming that their cultural patterns are somehow less worthy. In more concrete terms, we are tempted to judge the music of Mozart as "more cultured" than Motown, fine cuisine as better than fish sticks, and polo as more polished than ping pong.

Such judgments rest on the fact that various cultural patterns are not equally accessible to all members of a society (Hall & Neitz, 1993). Sociologists use the shorthand term **high culture**[1] to refer to *cultural patterns that distinguish a society's elite*; **popular culture**, then, designates *cultural patterns widespread among a society's people*.

---

[1]The term "high culture" is derived from the more popular term "highbrow." Influenced by phrenology, the bogus nineteenth-century theory that personality is affected by the shape of the human skull, people a century ago contrasted the praiseworthy tastes of those they termed "highbrows" with the contemptible appetites of others they derided as "lowbrows."

Cultural patterns are not equally accessible to all members of a society. Formal training in technique, color, and composition, for example, is usually necessary in order to gain standing in the "high culture" pursuit of fine art. We reserve the term "folk art" for the work of people—generally of lower social position—who are drawn by their love of art to paint, even though they have no formal training at all. Anna Mary Robertson (Grandma) Moses, the most popular folk artist of this century, began painting while in her seventies. During the next two decades she produced numerous paintings, yarn pictures, and decorative tiles. Her idyllic landscapes, including *Joy Ride*, and interiors celebrate U.S. rural traditions and country life.

Grandma Moses: *Joy Ride.* Copyright © 1991, Grandma Moses Properties Co., New York.

Common sense may suggest that high culture is superior to popular culture. After all, the history schools teach centers on the lives of elites, not those of ordinary women and men. But sociologists are uneasy with this sweeping evaluation, and use the term "culture" to refer to *all* elements of a society's way of life, even while recognizing that cultural patterns vary throughout a population (Gans, 1974).

But is high culture truly superior to popular culture or do we think so merely because its practitioners have more prestige and power? For example, although there is no difference between a violin and a fiddle, we employ the more prestigious designation when the instrument is used by a person of higher position, and the other term when it is played by an individual with lower social standing.

Technology and Culture

The material objects—or *artifacts*—a society creates depend, in part, on its cultural values. The warlike Yąnomamö carefully craft their weapons and prize the poison tips on their arrows. By contrast, our society's embrace of individuality and independence is evident in our long-time love affair with the automobile.

In other words, material culture is shaped by **technology,** *the application of knowledge to the practical tasks of living.* The more complex a society's technology, as

Chapter 15 ("The Natural Environment") explains in detail, the more its members are able to remake the world to their liking.

Gerhard and Jean Lenski (1991) have described *sociocultural evolution,* or historical change in culture caused by technological innovation, in terms of four levels of development.[2] The Lenskis argue that a society's level of technological development determines what cultural ideas and artifacts emerge or are even possible.

Hunting and Gathering

The oldest and most basic productive technology is **hunting and gathering,** *the use of simple tools to hunt animals and gather vegetation.* From the time of our earliest human ancestors until several centuries ago, most people lived in this manner. Today, however, hunting and gathering characterizes only a few societies, including the Kaska Indians of northwest Canada, the Pygmies of central Africa, the Bushmen of southwestern Africa, the Aborigines of Australia, and the Semai of Malaysia. Because their food production strategies are inefficient, hunters and gatherers spend much of their time searching for game and edible plants. Such

---

[2]This account examines only the major types of societies described by the Lenskis; see Lenski, Lenski, & Nolan, 1991.

The members of hunting and gathering societies depend on nature for basic foods and building materials. Pastoral people have a somewhat higher standard of living based on the ability to domesticate animals. Members of agrarian societies use animal power to plow land and for a host of other tasks. People in industrial societies are the most productive of all, utilizing vastly more powerful energy sources; this allows people far greater choice in how they earn a living but also fosters materialism.

societies remain small—generally with no more than several dozen people living in a family-like group. Hunting and gathering bands rove far from one another, since food production requires a large amount of land, and move on as they deplete an area's vegetation or to pursue migratory animals.

Everyone takes part in the search for food, although the very young and the very old contribute only what they can. Women typically gather vegetation—the primary food source in these societies— while men do most of the hunting. Women and men thus have different roles, but they remain relatively equal in social importance (Leacock, 1978).

Hunters and gatherers have few formal leaders. They may recognize one person as a *shaman* who presides over spiritual concerns, but such a position provides no release from the daily responsibility of helping to procure food. Overall, hunting and gathering is a simple and egalitarian way of life.

Limited technology leaves hunters and gatherers vulnerable to the forces of nature. Storms and droughts can easily destroy their food supply, and they have few effective ways to respond to accident or disease. Not surprisingly, therefore, many children die in childhood; as few as half survive to the age of twenty.

Faced with depleted game and vegetation and the encroachment of people with complex technology, hunters and gatherers are fast vanishing from the earth. Fortunately, study of their way of life has already produced valuable information about humanity's sociocultural history and our fundamental ties to the natural world.

Horticulture and Pastoralism

Horticulture, *the use of hand tools to raise crops,* first appeared some ten thousand years ago. The invention of the hoe and the digging stick (used to punch holes in the ground for seeds) initially occurred in fertile regions of the Middle East and southeast Asia, and these tools were in use from Western Europe to China six thousand years ago. Central and South Americans, too, learned to cultivate plants, but rocky soil and mountainous terrain prompted people like the Yanomamö to combine this new technology with traditional hunting and gathering (Fisher, 1979; Chagnon, 1983).

In especially arid regions, societies turned not to raising crops but to **pastoralism,** *the domestication of animals.* In much of the Americas, Africa, the Middle East, and Asia, moreover, societies blended horticulture and pastoralism.

Greater productivity from domesticating plants and animals allows societies to expand to hundreds of members. While pastoral peoples remain nomadic, horticulturalists found permanent settlements. There, a material surplus frees some people from food production to make crafts, engage in trade, or serve as full-time priests. Compared to hunters and gatherers, then, pastoral and horticultural societies are more complex. They are also more hierarchical; wealth is concentrated among a few families who operate as a ruling group.

Hunters and gatherers, who have little control over nature, generally believe that the world is inhabited by spirits. By contrast, pastoral people, with the power to raise plants and animals, typically conceive of God as creator of the world. The pastoral roots of Judaism and Christianity come through in the term "pastor" for some members of the clergy and the common view of God as "shepherd," overseeing the well-being of all.

Agriculture

Further technological advances led to **agriculture,** *large-scale cultivation using plows first drawn by animals.* Agrarian technology first appeared in the Middle East five thousand years ago and gradually spread throughout the world. Distinguished by the invention of the animal-drawn plow, together with the wheel, writing, numbers, and the expanding use of metals, this era has come to be known as "the dawn of civilization" (Lenski, Lenski, & Nolan, 1991:160).

By turning the soil, plows permit land to be farmed for decades, so people live in permanent settlements. Large food surpluses, transported on animal-drawn wagons, allow societies' populations to climb into the millions. Agrarian societies are also marked by extensive productive specialization that requires the exchange of money rather than simple barter. While the development of agrarian technology expanded the range of human opportunities and fueled urban growth, it also rendered social life more and more individualistic and impersonal.

Accompanying agricultural technology is a dramatic increase in social inequality. Historically, most people were serfs (or sometimes slaves) who labored for elites. Without the need to work, the nobility cultivated a "refined" way of life, based on the study of philosophy, art, and literature. At all levels of society, men gained pronounced power and privilege over women.

Technologically simple people live much the same the world over, with minor differences stemming from variations in the natural environment. But agrarian technology, the Lenskis explain, confers sufficient control over the natural world to unleash human creativity, producing marked cultural diversity.

Industry

Industry, a focus of Chapter 11 ("Economics and Politics"), arises as societies replace the muscle power of animals and humans with advanced sources of energy. Formally, **industry** is *the production of goods using sophisticated fuels and machinery.* The introduction of steam-powered machines, beginning in England about 1765, expanded productivity more than ever and transformed cultural patterns in the process.

Agrarian people typically work in or near the home; industry, however, relocates work to factories under the supervision of strangers. Lost in the process of European industrialization were many traditional cultural values and customs that had guided agrarian life for centuries.

As industrialization progresses, the world seems smaller. During the nineteenth century, railroads and steamships revolutionized transportation, moving people farther and faster than ever before. During the twentieth century, additional waves of change followed the invention of the automobile, radio, and television.

Industrial technology has greatly raised living standards for about 15 percent of the world's people (some 850 million individuals). Most of these people pursue formal education because industrial production demands a literate and skilled labor force. Further, as Chapter 7 ("Social Stratification") explains, industrial societies have steadily broadened political rights and achieved some lessening of economic inequality.

Some people deem industrial societies more "advanced" than those that rely on simpler technology. In support of such a judgment, they cite a higher material standard of living, great military power, and an average life expectancy of seventy-five years—almost twice that of the Yanomamö, for example. At the same time, industry fosters pronounced individualism, which, as we have already explained, is a mixed blessing. Then, too, industry has given humankind the power to manipulate the natural environment—perhaps at our peril. And while advanced technology has produced work-reducing devices and seemingly miraculous forms of medical treatment, it has also contributed to unhealthy levels of stress and created weapons capable of destroying in a flash everything that our species has managed to achieve throughout history.

Cultural Diversity

As a nation of immigrants, the United States has never been characterized by a single way of life. Over the last 150 years, more than 60 million immigrants have made this land their home. A century ago, as shown in Figure 2–1, most immigrants hailed from Europe; today, a majority of newcomers arrive from Latin America and Asia.

Subculture

The term **subculture** refers to *cultural patterns that distinguish some segment of a society's population.* Inner-city teens, elderly Polish Americans, "Yankee" New Englanders, as well as race-car drivers and jazz musicians all display subcultural patterns. Rural people sometimes poke fun at the ways of "city slickers," who, in turn, jeer back at their "country cousins." Sexual orientation generates yet another subculture, especially in cities like San Francisco and New York where large numbers of gay men and lesbians live. Moreover, we may participate in several subcultures simultaneously, some of which mean more to us than others.

In global perspective, cultural diversity generally corresponds to ethnicity. In multicultural societies, this diversity often generates conflict. Consider the former nation of Yugoslavia in southeastern Europe in which astounding cultural diversity finally led to civil war. This *one* small country made use of *two* alphabets, embraced

FIGURE 2–1

Recorded Immigration to the United States, by Region of Birth, 1880–1890 and 1980–1990

Source: U.S. Immigration and Naturalization Service (1991).

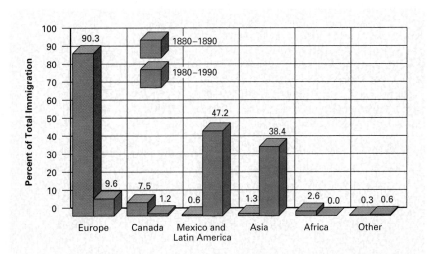

three major religions, spoke *four* major languages, contained *five* major nationalities, was divided into *six* separate republics, and absorbed cultural influences from *seven* other nations with which it shared borders. Is it any wonder that cultural conflict erupted there?

We in the United States historically have taught our children to view this country as a "melting pot" in which many nationalities blend into a single "American" culture. Despite some mixing and "melting" over the decades, however, powerful cultural divisions persist. Moreover, subcultures involve not only *difference* but *hierarchy*. Many of our so-called "dominant" cultural patterns characterize powerful segments of our society, while those we term subcultures are traits of disadvantaged people. This dilemma has sparked a new approach to the study of culture—multiculturalism.

Multiculturalism

In recent years, the United States has been facing up to the challenge of **multiculturalism,** *an educational program recognizing the cultural diversity of the United States and promoting the equality of all cultural traditions.* This movement represents a sharp turn from the past, when our society downplayed cultural diversity, defining the "American way of life" primarily in terms familiar to European (and especially English) immigrants. Today, a spirited debate rages over whether to stress our dominant historical traditions or highlight our cultural diversity.

E Pluribus Unum, the familiar Latin words that appear on each U.S. coin, means "out of many, one." This motto symbolizes not only our national political confederation, but also the ideal of our nation's cultural history—creating a single way of life for immigrants from around the world.

But, from the outset, instead of melting together into a single heritage, subcultures hardened into a hierarchy. At the top were the social patterns of the English founders. Down the pecking order, people of other backgrounds were advised to model themselves after "their betters," so that the "melting" was more accurately a process of Anglicization. So deeply embedded is this cultural hierarchy that historians have focused almost exclusively on the descendants of the English and other Europeans, describing events from their point of view, and pushing to the margins the perspectives and accomplishments of Native Americans, and people of African and Asian descent. Multiculturalists condemn this singular pattern as

Eurocentrism, *the dominance of European (particularly English) cultural patterns.* Molefi Kete Asante, a leading advocate of multiculturalism, argues that like "the fifteenth-century Europeans who could not cease believing that the earth was the center of the universe, many today find it difficult to cease viewing European culture as the center of the social universe" (1988:7).

Few deny that our culture has wide-ranging roots. But multiculturalism is controversial because it asks us to rethink norms and values at the core of our culture. One contested issue involves language. For a decade, Congress has debated a proposal to designate English as the official language of the United States. It has yet to decide the issue, although, by 1991, legislatures in sixteen states had enacted such a directive. To some, "official English" may seem unnecessary, but 30 million U.S. people—more than one in ten—speak a language other than English in their homes. Spanish is our second national language, and U.S. tongues include Italian, German, French, Filipino, Japanese, Korean, and Vietnamese—several hundred languages in all. National Map 2–1 shows where there are large numbers of children growing up in homes in which the first language is not English.

A second controversy turns on how our nation's schools should deal with culture. Two basic positions have emerged from this discussion.

Proponents defend multiculturalism, first, as a way to present a more accurate picture of our nation's *past.* Proposed educational reforms seek, for example, to correct simplistic praise directed at Christopher Columbus and other European explorers by recognizing the tragic impact of the European conquest on the native peoples of this hemisphere. Moreover, a multicultural approach recognizes the achievements of many women and men whose cultural backgrounds up to now have kept them on the sidelines of history.

Second, supporters claim, multiculturalism helps us come to terms with our country's even more diverse *present.* The 1990 census recorded a 50 percent increase in the U.S. Hispanic population, and a doubling of Asian Americans. Some children born in the 1990s may even live to see people of African, Asian, and Hispanic ancestry as a majority of this country's population.

Third, advocates assert that multiculturalism strengthens the academic achievement of African-American children and others who may find little personal relevance in Eurocentric education. A number of more radical educators are calling for **Afrocentrism,** *the dominance of African cultural patterns,* as a corrective for centuries of ignoring the achievements of African societies and African Americans.

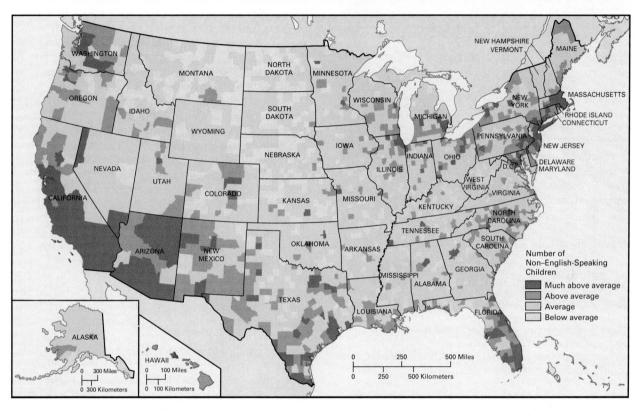

NATIONAL MAP 2–1   Language Diversity Across the United States

According to the 1990 census, 6.3 million children (14 percent of all children aged five through seventeen) speak a language other than English at home. Most of these children are of Hispanic ancestry. These boys and girls are not spread equally throughout the country, however. Children in California, for example, speak more than one hundred languages at home and at school. How would you describe the geographical distribution of these children? What do you think accounts for this pattern?

Source: Adapted from *American Demographics* magazine, April 1993, p. 40. Reprinted with permission. ©1993 *American Demographics* magazine, Ithaca, New York. Data from the 1990 decennial census.

Fourth and finally, champions of multiculturalism view this approach as needed preparation for living in a world in which nations are increasingly interdependent. Multiculturalism, in short, teaches global connectedness.

Multiculturalism has gained favor in recent years but it has provoked its share of criticism as well. What troubles opponents of multiculturalism, first and foremost, is its propensity to fuel the "politics of difference," encouraging people to relate exclusively to their own category rather than identifying with the nation

as a whole. As critics see it, a multicultural approach starts the United States on the road that has led to social collapse in the former Yugoslavia and elsewhere.

Second, critics contend that multiculturalism erodes any claim of universal truth by evaluating ideas according to the race (and sex) of those who present them. Our common humanity, in other words, dissolves into an "African experience," a "European experience," and so on.

Third, critics are skeptical that multiculturalism actually benefits minorities. On the one hand,

As the world's people become increasingly interconnected by communications technology and trade, every society is becoming multicultural. Residents of Mexico City, for example, eagerly consume a wide range of products from the United States. The most popular piñata, in fact, is currently a rendering of television bad-boy Bart Simpson. On the other side of the equation, people in the United States welcome many elements of Mexican culture. To cite one example, members of our society now consume more salsa than ketchup.

multiculturalism seems to demand precisely the kind of racial segregation that our nation has struggled for decades to end. On the other hand, an Afrocentric curriculum may well deny children mainstream knowledge and skills by forcing them to focus on their own cultural background. Historian Arthur Schlesinger, Jr. (1991) puts the matter bluntly: "If a Kleagle of the Ku Klux Klan wanted to use the schools to handicap black Americans, he could hardly come up with anything more effective than the 'Afrocentric' curriculum."

Is there any common ground in this debate? Virtually everyone agrees that we all need to gain greater appreciation of our cultural diversity. But precisely where the balance is to be struck—between the *pluribus* and the *unum*—is likely to remain a divisive issue for some time to come.

Counterculture

Cultural diversity within a society sometimes includes active opposition to some widely shared cultural elements. **Counterculture** refers to *cultural patterns that strongly oppose conventional culture*. People who embrace a counterculture may question the morality of the majority. Not surprisingly, the majority may condemn what they perceive to be wrong and threatening.

Most of us are familiar with the youth-oriented counterculture of the 1960s. Hippies criticized mainstream culture as overly competitive, materialistic, and self-centered. Instead, they favored a collective and cooperative lifestyle in which "being" took precedence over "doing," and the capacity for personal growth—then called "expanded consciousness"—was prized over material possessions like homes and cars. Their disdain for the status quo prompted many hippies to "drop out" of the larger society, establishing countercultural enclaves like the Haight-Ashbury district in San Francisco (Spates, 1976b, 1983).

Countercultural groups still exist, although most maintain a lower profile than in the 1960s. In the United States, the Ku Klux Klan and other white supremacist groups form a counterculture that promotes violence and racial hatred in order to protect what they see as "real American values." In Europe, young "punks" express their contempt for established culture by sporting shaved heads or multicolored hairstyles, black leather clothing, and chains—all intended to offend more conventional members of their societies.

Cultural Change

The Greek philosopher Aristotle observed that "there is nothing permanent except change." Consider, for example, some recent transformations in family life. More women are joining the labor force, and many are delaying marriage and childbearing, or remaining single and having children all the same. The current divorce rate stands at more than twice the level of fifty years ago. And over the last generation, the number of single-parent households has more than doubled so that, adding the effects of divorce, a majority of our nation's children now live with only one parent for some period before they turn eighteen.

Table 2–1 presents another dimension of change, comparing the attitudes of first-year college students in 1968 with those of women and men who matriculated in 1992. Some things have changed only slightly: About the same share of students looks forward to raising a family. But the students of the 1990s seem much more interested in being well off financially, while their counterparts in the late 1960s focused on developing a philosophy of life. (Worth noting is a countertrend during the last five years as young people move away from the materialism of the 1980s.) Interestingly, changes in attitudes generally have been greater among women than among men. This, no doubt, reflects the growing strength of the women's movement in recent decades.

Change in one dimension of a cultural system usually sparks changes in others. Arlie Hochschild (1989:258) points out, "The gender revolution is primarily *caused* by changes in the economy, but people *feel* it in marriage." Such a linkage illustrates the principle of **cultural integration**, *the close relationship among various elements of a cultural system.*

But some parts of a cultural system change more quickly than others. William Ogburn (1964) observed that technology moves quickly, generating new elements of material culture ("test-tube babies," for example), which outpace nonmaterial culture (such as ideas about parenthood). Ogburn called this inconsistency **cultural lag**, *the fact that some cultural elements change more quickly than others, with potentially disruptive results.* In a culture that now has the technical ability to allow one woman to give birth to a child by using another woman's egg, which has been fertilized in a laboratory with the sperm of a total stranger, how are we to apply the traditional terms *motherhood* and *fatherhood?*

Cultural changes are set in motion in three ways. The first is *invention,* the process of creating new cultural elements such as the telephone (1876), the airplane (1903), and the aerosol spray can (1941). The process of invention goes on constantly, as indicated by the thousands of applications received by the U.S. Patent Office each year.

Discovery, a second cause of change, involves recognizing and understanding something already in existence—from a distant star, to the foods of a foreign culture, to the athletic ability of women. Discovery often comes from scientific research, but sometimes it happens by a stroke of luck, as when Marie Curie unintentionally left a "rock" on a piece of photographic paper in 1898 and discovered radium.

The third cause of cultural change, *diffusion,* refers to the spread of objects or ideas from one cultural system to another. Missionaries and anthropologists like Napoleon Chagnon have introduced many cultural elements to the Yąnomamö. Cultural traits have likewise spread from the United States throughout the world: jazz, with its roots deep in the culture of African

TABLE 2–1 Attitudes Among Students Entering U.S. Colleges, 1968 and 1992

		1968*	1992	Change
Life Objectives (Essential or Very Important)				
Develop a philosophy of life	Male	79	44	– 35
	Female	87	47	– 40
Keep up with political affairs	Male	52	41	– 11
	Female	52	37	– 15
Help others in difficulty	Male	50	52	+ 2
	Female	71	72	+ 1
Raise a family	Male	64	69	+ 5
	Female	72	72	0
Be successful in my own business	Male	55	48	– 7
	Female	32	37	+ 5
Be well off financially	Male	51	76	+ 25
	Female	27	71	+ 44

*To allow comparisons, data from the early 1970s rather than 1968 are used for some items.

Sources: Richard G. Braungart and Margaret M. Braungart, "From Yippies to Yuppies: Twenty Years of Freshmen Attitudes," *Public Opinion,* vol. 11, no. 3 (September–October 1988): 53–56; Eric L. Dey, Alexander W. Astin, William S. Korn, and Ellyne R. Riggs, *The American Freshman: National Norms for Fall 1992* (Los Angeles: UCLA Higher Education Research Institute, 1992).

Americans; computers, first built in the mid-1940s in a Philadelphia laboratory; and even the U.S. Constitution, on which several other countries have modeled their political systems.

Diffusion works the other way as well, so that much of what we assume is "American" actually comes from other cultures. Ralph Linton (1937) has pointed out that most of our clothing and furniture, clocks, newspapers, money, and even the English language are derived from other cultures. As the technology of communication and travel makes the world seem smaller, the rate of cultural diffusion increases as well.

Ethnocentrism and Cultural Relativity

A question in the well-known game Trivial Pursuit asks which beverage is the most popular drink in the United States. Milk? Soft drinks? Coffee? The answer is soft drinks, but all the beverages mentioned are popular among members of our culture. If the Masai of eastern Africa were to join the game, however, their answer might well be "Goat blood!" To us, of course, the idea of drinking blood is unnatural, if not downright revolting. But we should keep in mind that drinking cow's milk (which we believe is more healthful than soft drinks or coffee) is intolerable to billions of people the world over, including most Chinese (Harris, 1985).

In a world of many cultures, how do we come to terms with other people's ways of living when they offend our own notions of what is proper? Anthropologists and sociologists caution us against **ethnocentrism,** *the practice of judging another culture by the standards of one's own culture.* Some ethnocentrism is inevitable because our reality is rooted in our own culture. But evaluating an unfamiliar practice without understanding its cultural context can lead to misunderstanding and conflict.

Ethnocentrism is a two-way street, of course. Just as we tend to dismiss those who differ from us, so others may judge us in the same way. Note, for example, that North Americans and Europeans traditionally have called China the "Far East." Such a term has little meaning to the Chinese because "Far East" is an ethnocentric expression for what is far east *of Europe*. But the Chinese, too, place themselves in the center of their world; the Chinese character that designates their nation literally means "central state." Figure 2–2 shows ethnocentrism at work in a "down under" view of the Western Hemisphere.

An alternative to ethnocentrism is **cultural relativism,** *the practice of evaluating any culture by its own standards.* Cultural relativism doesn't come easily, since it requires both understanding unfamiliar values and norms and breaking the grasp of a culture we have known all our lives. Still, the attempt is worth making for reasons of both good will and self-interest. Success in the emerging global economy depends on cultural sensitivity and sophistication. Consider the troubles several corporations had when they translated advertising slogans into Spanish. General Motors learned that sales of its Nova were hampered by a product name that means "Doesn't Go." The phrase "Turn It Loose," used to promote Coors beer, startled customers with words that read "Get the Runs." In Coca-Cola's early attempts to entice the Japanese to buy their soft drink, the company translated the slogan "Coke adds life" into a Japanese phrase that meant "Coke brings your ancestors back from the dead." Even Frank Perdue fell victim to poor marketing: His pitch, "It Takes a Tough Man to Make a Tender Chicken," ended up in Spanish as "It Takes a Sexually Excited Man to Make a Chicken Affectionate" (Westerman, 1989; Helin, 1992).

But cultural relativity can also pose problems. Because virtually every kind of behavior is found somewhere in the world, we need to ask if anything and everything is right just because *somebody* thinks so.

What about the practice among Yąnomamö men of routinely offering their wives to others for sexual encounters and beating women who displease them? Even in the unlikely event that Yąnomamö women accept this sort of treatment, should we argue, citing the relativity of truth, that these practices are right as long as the Yąnomamö themselves think so?

One might imagine, since we are all members of a single human species, that there must be some standards of fair conduct for people everywhere. But which ones? How can we resist imposing our own standards on others? Sociologists have no simple answer to this dilemma, yet in a world where societies confront each other amid ever-present crises like hunger and war, this issue demands careful thought.

A Global Culture?

Today, more than ever before, we observe many of the same cultural patterns the world over. Walking the streets of Seoul (South Korea), Kuala Lumpur (Malaysia), Madras (India), Cairo (Egypt), and Casablanca (Morocco), we find familiar forms of dress, hear well-known pop music, and see advertising for many of the same products we use at home. Recall, too, as noted earlier in Global Map 2–1, that English is rapidly becoming the world's common language. Are we witnessing the birth of a global culture?

The world is still broken up into 191 nation-states and thousands of different societies, each with a distinctive cultural heritage. Yet, societies of the world now have more contact with one another than ever before, as goods, information, and even people travel across national borders.

1. **The global economy: the flow of goods.** The extent of international trade has never been greater. The emerging global economy has spurred cultural diffusion, with many of the same consumer goods (from automobiles to rock music and T-shirts) appearing the world over.

2. **Global communications: the flow of information.** Satellite-based communications now enable people throughout the world to experience— often as they happen—the sights and sounds of events taking place thousands of miles away. Over most of the globe, a person can readily locate a telephone, radio, television, or a facsimile (fax) machine.

3. **Global migration: the flow of people.** As people learn more about the world, they are increasingly

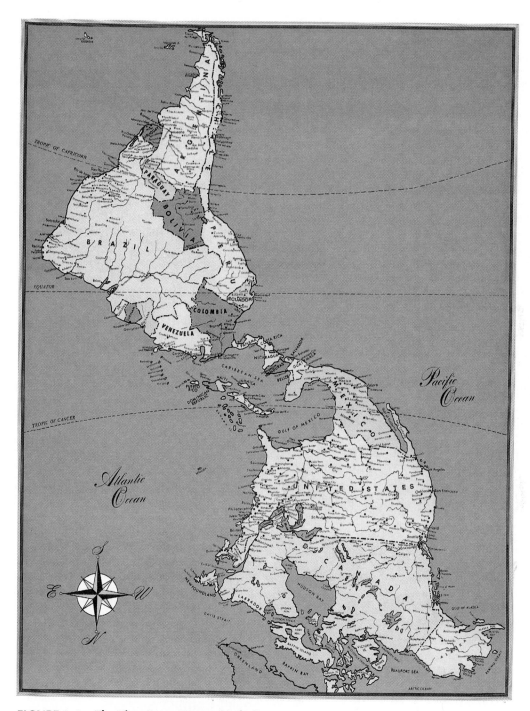

FIGURE 2–2   The View From "Down Under"

North America should be "up" and South America "down," or so we think. But, because we live on a globe, such notions are conventions rather than absolutes. The reason that this map of the Western Hemisphere looks wrong to us is not that it is geographically inaccurate; it simply violates our ethnocentric assumption that the United States should be "above" the rest of the Americas.

likely to move to a place where they imagine life will be better. Transportation, too, is more efficient than ever before. As a result, most nations encompass significant numbers of people born elsewhere (20 million people, about 8 percent of the U.S. population, for example, were born abroad).

Taken together, these changes have forged a global culture, in at least superficial respects. But there are three important limitations to the global culture thesis. First, although urban areas (which are centers of commerce, communications, and people) are now closely linked to one another, most rural villages remain isolated. Chagnon (1992) reports, for example, that there are still a few Yanomamö settlements in Venezuela that have had little or no contact with outsiders. Then, too, the greater economic and military power of North America and Western Europe means that nations in these regions influence the rest of the world more than the other way around.

Second, even assuming that people in poor societies wanted an array of goods and services, few can afford these luxuries. As Chapter 8 ("Global Stratification") explains, intense poverty in much of the world deprives people of even the basic necessities of a safe and secure life.

Third, although many cultural elements have spread throughout the world, people everywhere do not attach the same meanings to them. If we in the United States eagerly embrace, say, a "new" form of African music, we do so on our own terms with little understanding of the music's meaning to its creators. Similarly, as people in other parts of the world adapt objects and ideas from our society, they view these items and concepts through the lens of their own culture (Featherstone, 1990; Hall & Neitz, 1993).

Theoretical Analysis of Culture

Culture is the key to understanding ourselves and the surrounding world. Sociologists, however, have the special task of understanding culture. To comprehend something as complex as culture requires several theoretical approaches.

Structural-Functional Analysis

The structural-functional paradigm depicts culture as a long-term strategy for meeting human needs. This point of view, influenced by the philosophical doctrine of *idealism,* asserts that values lie at the core of a culture (Parsons, 1966; Williams, 1970). Any way of life, then, rests on values that give meaning to life and bind people together. Resting on this foundation, countless individual patterns of thought and action function to perpetuate a cultural system.

Take the Amish, strongly religious people living in Pennsylvania, Ohio, and Indiana, known for their rejection of modern conveniences. An outsider may marvel at the Amish farmer tilling hundreds of acres with horse and plow rather than a tractor. From the Amish point of view, however, dismissing modern technology makes sense because continuous labor is functional for maintaining Amish discipline, binding family members together, and rendering local communities self-sufficient (Hostetler, 1980).

Of course, some Amish traits also have dysfunctional consequences. The practice of "shunning," socially isolating anyone judged to have violated religious mores, reinforces conformity but can also cause a serious rift in the community if people disagree over a matter of proper behavior.

Because cultures are strategies to meet human needs, we might expect to find many common patterns around the world. The term **cultural universals** refers to *traits found in every culture of the world.* Comparing hundreds of cultures, George Murdock (1945) identified dozens of traits common to them all. One cultural universal is the family, which functions everywhere to control sexual reproduction and to oversee the care and upbringing of children. Another example is funeral rites, since people in all societies confront death. Jokes, too, are found in every society, serving as a relatively safe means of relieving stress.

Critical evaluation. Structural-functional analysis has the strength of showing how culture operates to meet human needs. All cultures have much in common, but since there are many ways to meet almost any need, cultures around the world reveal striking diversity.

One limitation of structural-functional thinking is its tendency to highlight a society's dominant cultural patterns, directing less attention to cultural diversity. Moreover, because this approach emphasizes cultural stability, it downplays the importance of change.

Social-Conflict Analysis

The social-conflict paradigm maintains that cultural traits function to the advantage of some more than others. Thus, culture operates as a dynamic arena in which inequality drives an ongoing power struggle.

Why does one set of values rather than another dominate a society? Many conflict theorists, especially Marxists, argue that culture is shaped by a society's system of economic production. "It is not the consciousness of men that determines their existence," Marx asserted, "it is their social existence that determines their consciousness" (1977:4; orig. 1859). In other words, the social-conflict paradigm draws on the philosophical doctrine of *materialism*, which holds that a society's system of material production (such as our own industrial-capitalist economy) exerts a powerful influence over all dimensions of culture. Such a materialist approach contrasts with the idealist leanings of structural-functionalism.

Social-conflict analysis, then, suggests that our competitive and individualistic values reflect our capitalist economy. The culture of capitalism further teaches us to think that the rich and powerful have more talent and discipline than others, and therefore deserve their wealth and privileges. Viewing capitalism as somehow "natural" also discourages efforts to lessen economic disparity in the United States.

Social-conflict analysts claim that strains created by social inequality eventually transform cultural systems. The civil rights movement and the women's movement exemplify the drive for change propelled by disadvantaged categories of people. Both, too, have encountered opposition from defenders of the status quo.

Critical evaluation. The strength of the social-conflict paradigm lies in its suggestion that if cultural systems address human needs, they do so unequally. Put otherwise, the main "function" of many cultural elements is to maintain the dominance of some people over others. This inequity, in turn, promotes change.

However, the social-conflict paradigm falls short by stressing the divisiveness of culture while understating ways in which cultural patterns integrate members of a society. Thus we should consider both social-conflict and structural-functional insights to gain a fuller understanding of culture.

Cultural Ecology

Ecology is a branch of the natural sciences that explores the relationship between a living organism and its natural environment. **Cultural ecology,** then, is *a theoretical paradigm that explores the relationship between human culture and the physical environment.* This paradigm investigates how climate and the availability of natural resources shape cultural patterns.

We tend to think of funerals as an expression of respect for the deceased. The social function of funerals, however, has much more to do with the living. For survivors, funerals reaffirm their sense of unity and continuity in the face of separation and disruption.

Consider the case of India, a nation that contends with widespread hunger and malnutrition. The norms of India's predominantly Hindu culture prohibit the killing of cows, which are considered sacred animals. To North Americans who consume so much beef, this practice is puzzling. Why should Indians refrain from eating beef?

Marvin Harris (1975) points out that cows cost little to raise since they consume grasses of no benefit to humans. And cows produce two vital resources: oxen (their neutered offspring) and manure. Unable to afford the high costs of machinery, Indian farmers depend on oxen to power their plows. From their point of view, killing cows would be as clever as farmers in the United States destroying factories that build tractors. Furthermore, each year India (a nation with little oil, coal, or wood) burns millions of tons of manure as fuel or processes it into building material. In short, the cow's food value is far surpassed by its importance to the overall Indian ecology; these factors, then, underlie the cultural "sacred cow" pattern.

Critical evaluation. Cultural ecology adds to our understanding of the interplay between culture and the natural environment. This approach can reveal how and why specific social patterns arise under particular physical conditions.

However, the physical environment rarely shapes cultural patterns in any simple or direct way. More precisely, the cultural and physical worlds interact, each shaping the other.

Sociobiology

Sociology has maintained a rather uneasy relationship with biology. In part, this friction stems from early and erroneous biological assertions about human behavior—for example, that some categories of people are inherently "better" than others. By the middle of this century, sociologists had demonstrated that culture rather than biology is the major force shaping human behavior.

In recent decades, however, new ideas linking culture to the principles of biological evolution have created **sociobiology,** *a theoretical paradigm that explains cultural patterns in terms of biological forces.* While some sociologists are skeptical of this new paradigm, others think that it may provide useful insights into human culture.

Sociobiology rests on the logic of evolution. In his book *On the Origin of Species,* Charles Darwin (1859) asserted that living organisms change over long periods of time as a result of *natural selection,* a process involving four simple principles. First, all living things live and reproduce within a natural environment. Second, genes, which carry traits of one generation into the next, show some random variation in each species that allows a species to "try out" new life patterns in that environment. Third, this variation enables some organisms to survive better than others and to pass on their advantageous genes to their offspring. Fourth and finally, over thousands of generations, genetic patterns that promote survival and reproduction become dominant. In this way, as biologists say, a species *adapts* to an environment, and dominant traits represent its "nature."

Sociobiologists explain the large number of cultural universals by noting that all humans represent a single biological species. It is our common biology that underlies, for example, the apparently universal "double standard" by which men engage in sexual activity more freely than women do. As sex researcher Alfred Kinsey

put it, "Among all people everywhere in the world, the male is more likely than the female to desire sex with a variety of partners" (quoted in Barash, 1981:49).

We all know that children result from joining a woman's egg with a man's sperm. But the biological significance of a single sperm and a single egg differ dramatically. For healthy men, sperm represents a "renewable resource" produced by the testes throughout most of the life course. A man releases hundreds of millions of sperm in a single ejaculation—technically, enough to fertilize every woman in North America (Barash, 1981:47). A newborn female's ovaries, however, contain her entire lifetime allotment of follicles or immature eggs. Women commonly release just one mature egg cell from their ovaries each month. So, while men are biologically capable of fathering thousands of offspring, women are able to bear a relatively small number of children.

Given this difference, men reproduce their genes most efficiently through a strategy of sexual promiscuity. This strategy, however, opposes the reproductive interests of women. Each of a woman's relatively few pregnancies demands that she carry the child, give birth, and provide care for some time afterward. Thus, efficient reproduction on the part of the woman depends on selecting a man whose qualities will contribute to her child's survival and successful reproduction (Remoff, 1984).

The "double standard" certainly involves more than biology; it is also a product of the historical domination of women by men (Barry, 1983). But sociobiology suggests that this cultural pattern, like many others, has an underlying bio-logic. Simply put, it has developed around the world because of our common biological traits as women and men.

Critical evaluation. Sociobiology has succeeded in generating insights about the biological roots of some cultural patterns. But sociobiology remains controversial for several reasons.

First, some critics fear that sociobiology may revive old arguments that support the domination of one race or sex by another. Defenders respond, however, that sociobiology has no connection to the past pseudoscience of racial superiority. On the contrary, sociobiology serves to unite rather than divide humanity by asserting that we all share a single evolutionary history. The notion that men are superior to women also has no place in sociobiology. Sociobiology does rest on the assumption that men and women differ biologically in some basic ways. But, far from asserting that males are somehow more worthy than females, sociobiology emphasizes how both sexes are vital to human reproduction.

Second, say the critics, despite optimistic predictions by sociobiologists that research will demonstrate the biological roots of human culture, a generation of scholars has yet to reveal that biological forces *determine* human behavior in any strict sense. Rather, abundant evidence supports the conclusion that human behavior is *learned* within a cultural system. The contribution of sociobiology, then, lies in explaining why some cultural patterns are more common than others.

Culture and Human Freedom

How does culture affect human freedom? Culture enhances our capacity to think critically and make choices. But our ability to view the world symbolically also makes possible the experience of alienation, which is unknown to other forms of life. Cultural systems also weigh heavily, binding us in some respects to the past.

This dual character of culture shows through in our society's insistence on competitive achievement, which both encourages us to strive for excellence and isolates us from one another. Moreover, material comforts improve our lives in some ways, yet a preoccupation with things diverts us from the security and satisfaction of close relationships and the spiritual dimension of life. And just as our emphasis on personal freedom ensures privacy and autonomy, our culture often denies us the support of a human community in which to share common problems (Slater, 1976; Bellah et al., 1985).

For better and worse, human beings are cultural creatures, just as ants and bees are prisoners of their biology (Berger, 1967). But there is a crucial difference. The burden of culture is *freedom*, the responsibility to shape the world for ourselves. Testifying to human creativity is the cultural diversity of our own society, and the even greater human variety around the world.

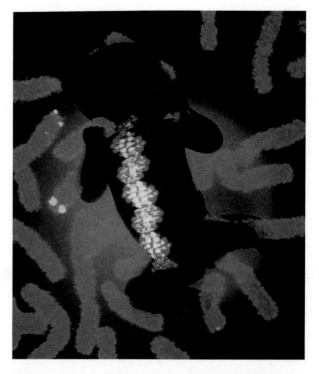

Debate continues about the role of biology in shaping human behavior. The truth is that scientists are only beginning to "map" genetic processes that guide physical development. Present evidence suggests biology can explain some variation in how individuals think and act. But the bigger picture is that our human nature demands that we create culture, and that we learn a way of life through social experience.

Furthermore, far from being static, culture is everchanging. And although it sometimes functions as a constraint, culture also stands as a wellspring of human opportunity. The more we understand the workings of our culture, the greater our ability to use the freedom it confers.

SUMMARY

1. Culture is a way of life shared by members of a society. Several species have limited capacity for culture; only humans rely on culture to survive.

2. As brain size grew over the long course of human evolution, culture steadily replaced biological instincts. Basic elements of culture appeared 2 million years ago; complex civilization emerged only during the last ten thousand years.

3. Culture relies on symbols. Language is the symbolic system by which we pass culture from generation to generation.

4. Values represent general orientations to the world. Beliefs are statements people who share a culture hold to be true. Norms guide specific behavior; mores have greater moral significance than folkways.

5. High culture refers to patterns that distinguish a society's elites; popular culture includes patterns widespread in a society.

6. Culture is shaped by technology. Technological development yields four stages of sociocultural evolution: hunting and gathering, horticulture and pastoralism, agriculture, and industry.

7. Culture involves not only common patterns but also diversity. A subculture is a distinctive set of traits that characterizes a segment of society; a counterculture strongly opposes widely accepted cultural patterns.

8. Multiculturalism refers to efforts to enhance appreciation of cultural diversity.

9. Invention, discovery, and diffusion all generate cultural change. Cultural lag results when some elements of a cultural system change faster than others.

10. Ethnocentrism involves judging others based on standards of our own culture. By contrast, cultural relativism refers to understanding other cultures according to their own standards.

11. Global cultural patterns are emerging as a result of the worldwide flow of goods, information, and people.

12. Structural-functional analysis views culture as a relatively stable system built on core values. Each cultural trait helps to maintain the entire social system.

13. The social-conflict paradigm envisions culture as a dynamic arena of inequality and conflict. Cultural traits typically benefit some categories of people more than others.

14. Cultural ecology studies how culture is shaped by the natural environment. Sociobiology investigates links between culture and our species' evolutionary past.

15. While culture can constrain human needs and ambitions, it provides us with the capacity and freedom to shape and reshape our world.

KEY CONCEPTS

Afrocentrism the dominance of African cultural patterns

agriculture large-scale cultivation using plows first drawn by animals

beliefs specific statements that people hold to be true

counterculture cultural patterns that strongly oppose conventional culture

cultural ecology a theoretical paradigm that explores the relationship between human culture and the physical environment

cultural integration the close relationship among various elements of a cultural system

cultural lag the fact that some cultural elements change more quickly than others, with potentially disruptive consequences

cultural relativism the practice of evaluating any culture by its own standards

cultural transmission the process by which culture is passed from one generation to the next

cultural universals traits found in every culture

culture the beliefs, values, behavior, and material objects shared by a particular people

culture shock the personal disorientation accompanying exposure to an unfamiliar way of life

ethnocentrism the practice of judging another culture by the standards of our own culture

Eurocentrism the dominance of European (especially English) cultural patterns

folkways norms about which people allow one another considerable personal discretion

high culture cultural patterns that distinguish a society's elite

horticulture the use of hand tools to raise crops

hunting and gathering the use of simple tools to hunt animals and gather vegetation

industry the production of goods using sophisticated fuels and machinery

language a system of symbols that allows people to communicate with one another

mores norms that are widely observed and have great moral significance

multiculturalism an educational program recognizing the cultural diversity of the United States and promoting the equality of all cultural traditions

norms rules by which a society guides the behavior of its members

pastoralism the domestication of animals

popular culture cultural patterns widespread among a society's people

Sapir-Whorf hypothesis the assertion that people perceive the world only in terms of the symbols provided by their language

society people interacting within a limited territory guided by their culture

sociobiology a theoretical paradigm that explains cultural patterns in terms of biological forces

subculture cultural patterns that distinguish some segment of a society's population

symbol anything that carries a particular meaning recognized by people who share culture

technology the application of knowledge to the practical tasks of living

values culturally defined standards of desirability, goodness, and beauty that serve as broad guidelines for social life

CRITICAL-THINKING QUESTIONS

1. Discuss the statement "Human nature is culture."

2. How does a schoolroom activity such as a "spelling bee" transmit U.S. cultural values? Identify other common activities that express various cultural values.

3. Why do members of every society tend to be ethnocentric? Point out at least one positive and negative function of ethnocentrism. Do the same with cultural relativism.

4. In what ways does culture constrain us? In what ways does it liberate us?

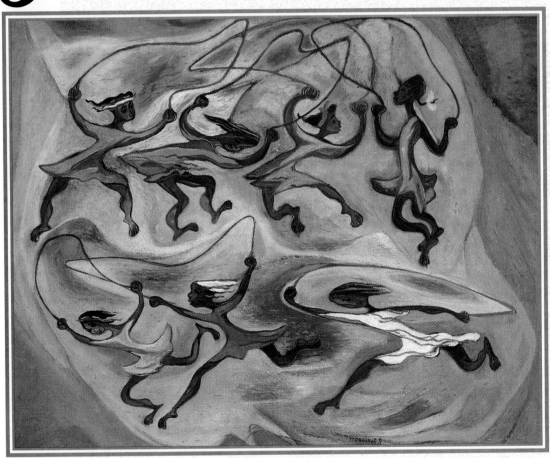

Hale Woodruff, *Girls Skipping*, 1949. Oil on canvas, 24 X 32 inches. Courtesy of Michael Rosenfeld Gallery, New York.

Socialization: From Infancy to Old Age

On a cold winter day in 1938, a concerned social worker drove to a farmhouse in rural Pennsylvania and made a chilling discovery: a five-year-old girl hidden in a second-floor storage room. Anna sat rigidly in a chair with her arms tied above her head. Her limbs were like matchsticks—so thin and frail that she could not use them (Davis, 1940:554).

Anna's mother, an unmarried woman of twenty-six, lived with the child's grandfather. Enraged by his daughter's "illegitimate" motherhood, at first he refused to even have the child in his house. Anna therefore spent the early months of her life in the custody of various welfare agencies. But, because her mother was unable to pay for this care, Anna was returned to the home where she was not wanted.

Because of the grandfather's hostility and the mother's indifference, Anna was placed alone in a room where she received little attention and just enough milk to keep her alive. There she stayed, with virtually no human contact, for five years.

Upon learning of the discovery of Anna, sociologist Kingsley Davis traveled immediately to see the child, who had been taken to a county home. He was appalled that the emaciated girl could not laugh, speak, or even smile. Anna was completely apathetic, as if she were a solitary character in an empty world (Davis, 1940).

The Importance of Social Experience

Here is a deplorable but instructive case of a human being deprived of social contact. Although physically alive, Anna had none of the capabilities associated with full humanity. Anna's story illustrates that, without social experience, an individual develops no capacity for thought, emotion, or meaningful behavior.

Sociologists use the term **socialization** to refer to *the lifelong social experience by which individuals develop their human potential and learn culture.* As Chapter 2 ("Culture") explained, the behavior of other species of life is biologically set; only humans depend on culture for survival. Social experience is also the foundation of **personality,** *a person's fairly consistent patterns of acting, thinking, and feeling.* We construct

personality by drawing on our surroundings, each in our own way. But without social experience, as the case of Anna shows, personality simply does not emerge.

Social experience is as vital for society as it is for individuals. Through the lifelong process of socialization, society transmits culture from one generation to the next.

Nature and Nurture

Virtually helpless at birth, the human infant needs others to provide care and nourishment and to teach patterns of culture. Although Anna's experience makes these facts clear, a century ago most people mistakenly believed that human behavior was solely the product of biology.

Charles Darwin's groundbreaking studies of evolution, conducted in the mid-nineteenth century and described in the last chapter, led most people to think that human behavior was instinctive, simply the "nature" of our species. Such notions are still with us. People sometimes claim, for example, that our economic system reflects "instinctive human competitiveness," that some people are "born criminals," or that women are emotional while men are rational (Witkin-Lanoil, 1984).

People trying to explain cultural diversity also misconstrued Darwin's thinking. After centuries of world exploration and empire building, Western Europeans knew well how different human behavior is around the world. But they attributed unfamiliar practices and beliefs to biology rather than culture. Thus it was an easy—although terribly damaging—step to conclude that members of technologically simple societies were biologically less evolved and, thus, less human. Such a self-serving and ethnocentric view helped justify colonial practices: If native people were not human in the same sense that you were, they could be exploited, even enslaved, without a second thought.

In this century, naturalistic explanations of human behavior came under fire. Psychologist John B. Watson (1878–1958) devised an approach called *behaviorism,* which held that human behavior is not instinctive but learned. Watson rejected the notion that human diversity reflects any evolutionary distinctions claiming, instead, that human behavior is shaped by people's environment. Watson, in short, rooted human behavior in *nurture* rather than nature.

Today, social scientists are cautious about describing *any* human behavior as instinctive. This does

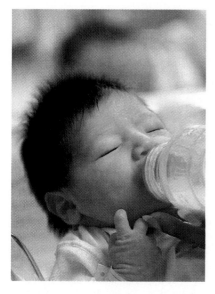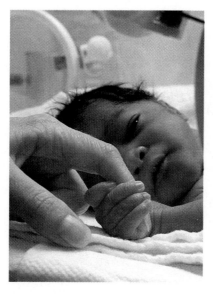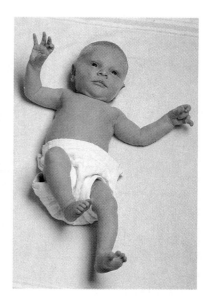

Human infants display various reflexes—biologically based behavior patterns that enhance survival. The sucking reflex, which actually begins before birth, enables the infant to obtain nourishment. The grasping reflex, triggered by placing a finger on the infant's palm causing the hand to close, helps the infant to maintain contact with a parent and, later on, to grasp objects. The Moro reflex, activated by startling the infant, has the infant swinging both arms outward and then bringing them together across the chest. This action, which disappears after several months of life, probably developed among our evolutionary ancestors so that a falling infant could grasp the body hair of a parent.

not mean that biology plays no part in human behavior. Human life, after all, depends on the functioning of the human body. We also know that children often share physical attributes (including height and hair color) with their parents, and that heredity plays a role in the transmission of intelligence, musical and artistic aptitude, and personality characteristics (such as how one reacts to frustration). However, what we do with inherited potential depends on our social experiences (Plomin & Foch, 1980; Goldsmith, 1983). On balance, then, nurture matters much more than nature in shaping human behavior. Or perhaps we should say that, because it is human nature to create and learn culture, nature and nurture stand not in opposition but rather are intertwined.

Social Isolation

For ethical reasons, researchers cannot subject human beings to experimental isolation. But research on the effects of social isolation has been conducted on nonhuman primates.

Research with monkeys. Psychologists Harry and Margaret Harlow (1962) observed rhesus monkeys—whose behavior is in some ways surprisingly similar to that of human beings—in various conditions of social isolation. They found that complete isolation (with adequate nutrition) for a period of even six months was sufficient to cause developmental disturbances. When reintroduced to others of their kind, these monkeys were fearful and defenseless against aggression.

The Harlows also placed infant rhesus monkeys in cages with an artificial "mother" constructed of wire mesh and a wooden head and the nipple of a feeding tube where the breast would be. These monkeys, too, were subsequently unable to interact with others. But when they covered the artificial "mother" with soft terry cloth, the infant monkeys clung to it, deriving some emotional benefit, which reduced developmental harm. The experiment revealed the profound importance of the simple act of cradling an infant.

Finally, the Harlows discovered that, when socially isolated for shorter periods of time (about three months), infant monkeys eventually regained normal emotional patterns after rejoining others. But they

The personalities we develop depend largely on the environment in which we live. When a child's world is shredded by violence, the damage can be profound and lasting. This drawing was made by a young boy living in a low-income neighborhood in south-central Los Angeles, where rioting exploded in 1992. What are the likely effects of such an environment on a child's self-confidence and capacity to form trusting ties to others?

found that longer-term isolation caused irreversible emotional and behavioral damage.

Isolated children. The later development of Anna roughly squares with the Harlows' findings. After her discovery, Anna benefited from extensive social contact and soon showed some improvement. When Kingsley Davis (1940) revisited her after ten days, he noted that she was more alert and displayed some human expression, even smiling with obvious pleasure. Over the next year, as she experienced the humanizing effects of socialization, Anna showed more interest in other people and gradually gained the ability to walk. After a year and a half, she was able to feed herself, walk alone for short distances, and play with toys.

Yet it was apparent that Anna's five years of social isolation had left her permanently damaged. At age eight her mental and social development was still less than that of a normal two-year-old. Only as she approached ten did she begin to use language. Complicating our analysis is the fact that Anna's mother was mentally retarded, so that Anna may have been similarly disadvantaged. The puzzle was never solved, however, because Anna died at age ten of a blood disorder, possibly related to her years of abuse (Davis, 1940).

A second, similar case reveals more about the long-term effects of social isolation. At the same time that Anna was discovered, another girl of the same age was found under strikingly similar circumstances. After more than six years of virtual isolation, this girl—known as Isabelle—revealed the same lack of human responsiveness as Anna (Davis, 1947). Isabelle made more rapid progress than Anna, however. One week after an accelerated program was begun, Isabelle was attempting to speak, and a year and a half later, her vocabulary consisted of almost two thousand words. Psychologists observed Isabelle progress through what is normally six years of development during two years of intensive effort. By the time she was fourteen, Isabelle was attending sixth-grade classes in school, apparently on her way to an approximately normal life.

The fate of Anna and Isabelle demonstrates that social experience is crucial for the development of personality. Human beings are resilient creatures, sometimes able to recover from even the crushing experience of prolonged isolation. But there may well be a point—precisely when is unclear from the small number of cases studied—at which isolation in infancy results in damage, including a reduced capacity for language, that cannot be fully repaired.

Understanding Socialization

Numerous social scientists have explored the complex process of socialization. The following sections summarize five significant contributions.

Sigmund Freud: The Elements of Personality

Sigmund Freud (1856–1939) lived in Vienna at a time when most Europeans thought human behavior was biologically fixed. Trained as a physician, Freud soon turned to the analysis of human personality; his towering achievement was the development of psychoanalysis.

Freud contended that biology plays an important part in the human personality, although not in terms of simple instincts common to other species. He maintained that humans have two basic needs or drives. One, the need for bonding, Freud termed the life instinct, or *eros* (ancient Greece's god of love). The other, an aggressive drive, he called the death instinct, or *thanatos* (derived from Greek meaning "death"). Freud asserted that these opposing forces ignite tension—mostly at the unconscious level—in our personality.

Freud incorporated both basic human drives and the influence of society into a model of personality with three parts: id, ego, and superego. The **id** represents *the human being's basic drives,* which are unconscious and demand immediate satisfaction. (The word *id* is Latin for "it," suggesting the tentative way in which Freud envisioned this aspect of the human mind.) Rooted in our biology, the id is present at birth, making a newborn a bundle of needs that demands attention, touching, and food. But society opposes such a self-centered orientation, so the id's desires inevitably run up against resistance—surely the reason children soon grasp the meaning of "no."

To lessen frustration, a child learns to approach the world more realistically. This is accomplished through the **ego** (Latin for "I"), which represents *a person's conscious efforts to balance innate pleasure-seeking drives with the demands of society.* The ego arises as we gain awareness of our distinct existence and face up to the fact that we cannot have everything we want.

Finally, the human personality develops the **superego** (Latin meaning "above" or "beyond" the ego), which is *the presence of culture within the individual in the form of internalized values and norms.* We experience superego as conscience, which helps us to grasp *why* we cannot have everything we want. First expressed as the awareness of parental control, the superego matures as the child comes to recognize that parents, too, must rein in their desires in response to the cultural system.

A child first encounters the world as a bewildering array of physical sensations. As the superego develops, the child's comprehension extends beyond pleasure and pain to the moral concepts of right and wrong. In other words, an infant initially can feel good only as physical sensation. Later the child can feel good for behaving in culturally appropriate ways and, conversely, feel bad (the experience of guilt) for breaking the rules.

If the ego successfully manages the opposing forces of the id and the superego, a well-adjusted personality develops. If this conflict is not successfully resolved, personality disorders result. Freud believed that conflicts experienced during childhood often linger as an unconscious source of personality problems later on.

Freud called society's efforts to control human drives *repression.* Some repression is inevitable, he claimed, since society must coerce people into looking beyond themselves. *Sublimation,* Freud's term for the compromise between personal drives and the imperatives of society, transforms those selfish drives into more socially acceptable behavior. For example, sexual urges may lead to marriage, and aggression can be released normatively through sports.

Critical evaluation. Freud's work sparked controversy in his own lifetime, since his society vigorously repressed sexuality, and few of Freud's contemporaries were prepared to acknowledge sex as a basic drive. More recent critics of Freud's work argue that his thinking depicts humanity strictly in male terms with a distorted view of women (Donovan & Littenberg, 1982). But Freud's ideas unquestionably have influenced virtually all who subsequently examined the human personality. Of special importance to sociology are his notions that we internalize social norms and that childhood experiences have lasting importance in the socialization process.

Jean Piaget: Cognitive Development

Swiss psychologist Jean Piaget (1896–1980) also stands among the foremost social scientists of this century. His research centered on human *cognition*—how people think and understand. From his early fascination with his own three children—wondering not only what they knew, but *how* they understood the world—Piaget eventually identified four stages of cognitive development.

The first is the **sensorimotor stage,** *the level of development at which individuals experience the world only through sensory contact.* For roughly the first two years of life, in other words, the infant knows the world only by touching, looking, sucking, and listening. Children gain skill at imitating the actions or sounds of others during the sensorimotor stage, but they have no comprehension of symbols. Thus, very young children reason only in the limited sense of direct physical experience.

Second, from about age two to seven is the **preoperational stage,** *the level of development at which individuals first use language and other symbols.* Symbols are the child's doorway into a vast world of meanings extending beyond the immediate senses. At this point, children can appreciate fantasy and fairy tales (Kohlberg & Gilligan, 1971; Skolnick, 1986). But young children attach only specific names and meanings to objects, identifying a particular toy, for example, but not describing toys in general. That is, they cannot yet grasp abstract concepts such as beauty, size, or weight.

In a well-known experiment, Jean Piaget demonstrated that children over the age of seven had entered the concrete operational stage of development because they could recognize that the quantity of liquid remained the same when poured from a wide beaker into a tall one.

In one of his best-known experiments, Piaget placed two identical glasses containing the same amount of water on a table and asked several five- and six-year-olds if the amount in each was the same. They nodded that it was. The children then watched Piaget take one of the glasses and pour its contents into a taller, narrower glass, raising the level of the water. He asked again if each glass held the same amount. The typical five- or six-year-old now insisted that the taller glass held more water. But children over the age of seven, who are able to think more abstractly, realized that the amount of water remained the same.

Next, in Piaget's model, is the **concrete operational stage,** *the level of development at which individuals perceive causal connections in their surroundings.* During this stage, typically corresponding to ages seven through eleven, children begin to understand how and why things happen. They also learn that more than one symbol can be attached to a single event; "Wednesday," for instance, can also be "My birthday!" However, the thinking of children remains centered on concrete events and objects. They may understand that hitting a brother without provocation will bring punishment, but they still fail to appreciate principles of fairness.

The fourth level in Piaget's model is the **formal operational stage,** *the level of development at which individuals think abstractly and imagine.* By about the age of twelve, children can report not only wanting to become, say, a teacher, but they can describe such work as "challenging" and "satisfying." This capacity for abstract thought also allows the child to comprehend metaphors. Hearing the phrase "A penny for your thoughts" might prompt a younger child to think of money, but an older child will recognize a gentle invitation to intimacy.

Critical evaluation. If Freud envisioned human beings as torn by the opposing forces of biology and society, Piaget saw the mind as active and creative so that children steadily gain the ability to shape their own social world. His contribution lies in showing that this capacity unfolds gradually as a result of both biological maturation and increasing social experience.

However, Piaget's theory falls short by failing to recognize that members of all cultures do not necessarily follow these stages in the same time frame. For instance, people living in a traditional, unchanging society may find it impossible to imagine the world being different than it is. Even in our own society, a substantial proportion of adults—especially those exposed to little creative thinking while growing up—never reach the formal operational stage (Kohlberg & Gilligan, 1971).

Lawrence Kohlberg: Moral Development

Lawrence Kohlberg (1981) extended Piaget's work to the issue of moral reasoning, asserting that individuals come to judge situations as right or wrong in predictable stages.

Young children who experience the world in terms of pain and pleasure (Piaget's sensorimotor stage) display the *preconventional* level of moral development. At this point, "rightness" amounts to "what feels good to me."

The *conventional* level of moral development, Kohlberg's second stage, appears among teenagers (corresponding to Piaget's last, formal operational stage). At this point, young people are less self-centered in their moral reasoning, defining right and wrong in terms of what pleases parents and what is consistent with broader cultural norms.

A final stage of moral development, the *postconventional* level, moves individuals beyond the specific norms of their society to ponder abstract ethical principles. At this level, people reflect on the meaning of liberty, freedom, or justice, perhaps criticizing their own society by arguing that what is lawful still may not be right.

Critical evaluation. Kohlberg's work resembles that of Piaget by casting moral development in identifiable stages. But, here again, whether this model applies to people in all societies remains unconfirmed. Then, too, many people in the United States apparently do not reach the postconventional level of moral reasoning, although exactly why remains, at present, an open question.

The greatest limitation of Kohlberg's research, however, is that his subjects were all boys. Thus, Kohlberg commits the research error, described in Chapter 1 ("Sociology: Perspective, Theory, and Method"), of generalizing from the results of his male subjects to all of humanity. This provoked his colleague Carol Gilligan to further investigate how gender affects moral reasoning.

Carol Gilligan: The Gender Factor

Carol Gilligan (1982) was disturbed by the fact that Kohlberg had involved only boys in his research. Therefore, she set out systematically to compare the moral development of females and males and concluded that the two sexes use different forms of moral reasoning. Males, on the one hand, embrace a *justice perspective*, relying on formal rules in reaching a judgment about right and wrong. Boys playing soccer, say, are quick to condemn one of their number for touching the ball with his hands or ignoring a boundary line on the field. Girls, on the other hand, adopt a *care and responsibility perspective*, which leads them to judge a situation with an eye toward personal relationships. In other words, breaking a rule may not be wrong if it is done in an effort to help someone else who is in need.

Worth noting is that Kohlberg treats rule-based male reasoning as morally superior to person-based female thinking. Gilligan counters that we should not set up male standards as norms by which we evaluate everyone. She reminds us that the impersonal application of rules has always been at the heart of men's lives in the workplace. Concern for attachments, by contrast, is more relevant to women's lives as wives, mothers, and caregivers.

Critical evaluation. Gilligan's work both sharpens our understanding of human development and points out the problem of ignoring gender while conducting research.

But what is the source of the differences she documents between females and males? Are they rooted in biology? Or, as Gilligan posits, do they reflect cultural conditioning? If culture underlies these differences,

In her more recent work, Carol Gilligan studied the social development of girls ranging in age from six to eighteen. She concluded that young girls have relatively high self-esteem, but they appear to lose this valuable resource as they move through adolescence. She links this loss to our culture's definition of women as cooperative and deferential to men. Note, too, that as girls move from elementary to secondary school, a greater share of the authority figures with whom they interact are men.

then as the lives of men and women become more alike when it comes to work and child rearing, the moral reasoning of the two sexes should also converge.

George Herbert Mead: The Social Self

What exactly is social experience? George Herbert Mead (1863–1931) spent much of his life answering this vital question. Mead's approach (1962; orig. 1934), called *social behaviorism*, begins by arguing that environment shapes behavior, but goes on to highlight the centrality of symbols to human thought and action.

Mead's central concept is the **self,** *a dimension of personality composed of an individual's self-awareness and self-image.* Mead's genius lay in seeing the self as inseparable from society, a connection explained in a series of steps. First, Mead asserted, the self is absent at birth and develops only through social experience. Mead rejected the view that humans have biological

George Herbert Mead wrote: "No hard-and-fast line can be drawn between our own selves and the selves of others." The painting *Les Réfugiés* by Fateh Al-Moudarres conveys this important idea. Although we tend to think of ourselves as unique individuals, each person's characteristics develop in an ongoing process of interaction with others.

drives (as Freud asserted) or develop only with biological maturation (as Piaget claimed). For Mead, the self gradually arises as the individual comes into contact with others. In the absence of social experience—as isolated children show us—the body grows but no self emerges.

Second, Mead claimed, social experience is *symbolic interaction,* or the exchange of symbols. A wave of the hand, a spoken word, or a broad smile are all symbolic. Thus, while Mead recognized that human behavior is shaped by the environment, he maintained that humans display a unique and powerful capacity for symbolic thought and action. A dog, for example, can learn to respond to a specific stimulus, but the dog attaches no meaning to this behavior. Human beings, by contrast, are as sensitive to intention as we are to action. In short, a dog responds to *what you do,* but a human imagines *what you have in mind* as you do it. Thus one can train a dog to go to the hallway and bring back an umbrella. But, grasping no intention behind the command, a dog unable to find an umbrella would never offer a raincoat instead, as a human being would.

Third, humans comprehend intention by learning to *take the role of the other.* Seeing ourselves from another person's point of view, we can anticipate the other's response to us. In the simple act of throwing a ball, for example, we imagine the other's response—in this case, catching the ball. Based on that projected response, we know how to direct the throw.

Furthermore, how we think of ourselves has a great deal to do with how others think of us. Charles Horton Cooley, one of Mead's colleagues, described others as a social mirror or looking glass in which we imagine ourselves as they see us. Cooley (1964; orig. 1902) used the phrase **looking-glass self** to mean *a conception of self based on the responses of others.* We come to know ourselves, in other words, by how others think and act toward us. We are unlikely to imagine ourselves as, say, trustworthy unless we find that others treat us that way.

Mead's fourth argument is that, as we take the role of another, we become *self-reflective.* The self, then, has a dual nature. As subject, the self initiates action, in creative and spontaneous ways. For simplicity, Mead dubbed this subjective side of the self the *I* (the subjective personal pronoun). The self is also object, as we imagine ourselves from the viewpoint of others. Mead called the objective side of the self the *me* (the objective personal pronoun). Combining the two we distill the essence of social experience: The self initiates interaction (as the I) and simultaneously imagines this action (the me) through taking the role of the other. That is, we initiate behavior that we subsequently guide by "seeing" ourselves through others.

The key to developing the self, then, is gaining sophistication in taking the role of the other. Like Freud and Piaget, Mead thought that early childhood was crucial in this process. However, he did not closely link the development of the self to age. Mead consistently minimized the importance of biological forces, claiming that the complexity of the self simply derived from amassing social experience.

Mead explained that, with limited social experience, infants respond to others only in terms of

The self is able simultaneously to take the role of:	*no one* — no ability to take the role of the other	*one* other in *one* situation	*many* others in *one* situation	*many* others in *many* situations
when:	engaging in imitation	engaging in play	engaging in games	recognizing the "generalized other"...

FIGURE 3–1 Building on Social Experience

George Herbert Mead described the development of the self as the process of gaining social experience. This is largely a matter of taking the role of the other with increasing sophistication.

imitation. That is, they mimic behavior without understanding underlying intentions and, so, they have no self. As children learn to use language and other symbols, the self appears in the form of *play*. Play involves assuming roles modeled on significant people—such as parents—who are sometimes termed *significant others.* Playing "Mommy" or "Daddy," for instance, helps children imagine the world and themselves from a parent's point of view.

Further social experience teaches children to take the roles of several others simultaneously. Able to initiate different actions in response to different others, children move from simple play involving one role to more complex *games* calling for many roles at once.

A final developmental step hinges on children learning to see themselves as society in general does. Figure 3–1 shows how this works as an extension of the ability to engage in play and games. Once children incorporate norms and values into their personalities, they respond to themselves as they imagine *any* other person in *any* situation would. What Mead labeled the *generalized other* refers to widespread cultural norms and values we use as reference points in evaluating ourselves.

The emergence of the self does not conclude the socialization process. Quite the contrary: We change throughout our lives as a result of changing social experiences. Just as important, Mead stressed, social life is *interactional* so that, as society shapes us, we can "act back" on others. As creative beings, Mead concluded, we play a large part in our own socialization.

Critical evaluation. George Herbert Mead pointed out that symbolic interaction is the foundation of both the self and society.

Critics fault Mead for his radically social approach, which recognizes no biological element in the self. In this, he stands apart from Freud (who identified

general drives in the organism) and Piaget (whose stages of development are tied to biological maturation).

Be careful not to confuse Mead's concepts of the I and the me with Freud's terms id and superego. First, Freud rooted the id in the biological organism, while Mead rejected any link between the self and biology (although he never clearly spelled out the origin of the I). Second, Freud's concept of the superego and Mead's concept of the me both reflect the power society wields over our lives, but Freud's superego is locked in continual combat with the id. Mead, however, saw the I and the me working closely and cooperatively together (Meltzer, 1978).

Agents of Socialization

We are affected in at least a small way by every social experience we have. However, several agents of socialization have pronounced importance, as we shall now explain.

The Family

For most people, the family has the greatest impact on socialization. Infants are almost entirely dependent on others, and this responsibility typically falls on family members. Through physical contact and verbal stimulation, parents foster the development of children. At least until the onset of schooling, the family remains the center of a child's world (Riley, Foner, & Waring, 1988).

Not all socialization in the family is intentional. Children also learn from the environment adults unconsciously create. Whether children believe they are strong or weak, smart or stupid, loved or simply

Sociological research indicates that affluent parents tend to encourage creativity in their children while poor parents tend to foster conformity. While this general difference may be valid, parents at all class levels can and do provide loving support and guidance by simply involving themselves in their children's lives. Henry Ossawa Tanner's painting *The Banjo Lesson* stands as a lasting testament to this process.

the intentions and motivations that underlie their children's actions. Working-class parents, by contrast, stress behavioral conformity. With more schooling, Kohn explains, middle-class people usually have jobs that provide more autonomy and encourage the use of imagination. These parents, therefore, try to inspire this same creativity in their children. Working-class parents have less education and are more likely to hold jobs in which they are closely supervised. In turn, they demand obedience and conformity in their children. In many ways, parents teach children to follow in their footsteps, adapting to the constraints or privileges of their inherited social positions.

Schooling

Schooling enlarges children's social world to include people of more diverse social backgrounds. Such experiences heighten children's awareness of their own social identities; as researchers have observed, school children soon begin to form play groups made up of one sex and one race (Lever, 1978; Finkelstein & Haskins, 1983).

Schooling begins with basic skills such as reading, writing, and arithmetic and later includes advanced knowledge that prepares students to assume a specialized role in their complex society. Beyond formal lessons, however, the school's so-called *hidden curriculum* imparts important cultural values. School activities such as spelling bees and sports encourage competition and showcase success. Children also receive countless messages that their society's culture is both practically and morally good.

Family life is based on personal relationships. School presents the new experience of impersonal evaluation of skills such as reading based on standardized tests. Of course, the confidence or anxiety that children develop at home can have a significant impact on how well they perform in school (Belsky, Lerner, & Spanier, 1984).

School is also a child's first experience with rigid formality. The school day is based on a strict time schedule, subjecting students to impersonal regimentation and fostering traits, such as punctuality, required by the large organizations where many students will work later in life.

Finally, schools further socialize young people into culturally approved gender roles. Raphaela Best (1983) notes that, at school, boys engage in more physical activities and spend more time outdoors, while girls tend to be more sedentary, often helping the

tolerated, and whether they believe the world to be trustworthy or dangerous largely depend on the signals they get from their parents.

Parents not only bring children into the physical world, they also place them in society in terms of class, religion, race, and ethnicity. Within several years, these elements of social identity become part of the child's self-concept.

Why is class position important? Of course, affluent parents typically spend far more on their children than parents of modest means do. Moreover, Melvin Kohn (1977) found that middle-class parents tolerate a wide range of behavior and show concern for teacher with various housekeeping chores. Gender differences continue through college as women tend to major in the arts, humanities, or social sciences, while men gravitate toward economics, engineering and computer science, or the natural sciences.

Peer Groups

In school, children discover another new setting for social activity, the **peer group,** defined as *a group whose members have interests, social position, and age in common.* Unlike the family and the school, the peer group allows children to escape the direct supervision of adults. Among their peers, children gain valuable experience in forging social relationships on their own. Peer groups also draw out interests that young people may not share with adults (such as styles of dress and popular music) as well as topics they may not wish to discuss with parents and teachers (such as drugs and sex).

Especially in a rapidly changing society, peer groups often rival parents in influence, and the attitudes of parents and children may be separated by a "generation gap." The importance of peer groups typically peaks during adolescence when young people begin to break away from their families and to think of themselves as responsible adults.

In any country in the world, schooling is a way of teaching the values and attitudes that a society deems important. It is also a means favored by government to instill in children conformity and compliance. Holding portraits of a revered leader, these children in Taiwan participate in a lesson in "political correctness."

Young people in the United States receive mixed messages about sexuality. On the one hand, parents may instruct teens about the need for sexual restraint. On the other hand, peer groups (and also the mass media) often take a more encouraging posture toward sexual experimentation.

Even during adolescence, however, parental influence on children remains strong. While peers may guide short-term choices in dress and music, parents retain more sway over long-term aspirations. For example, one study concluded that parents had more influence than even best friends on young people's educational aspirations (Davies & Kandel, 1981).

Finally, any neighborhood or school operates as a social mosaic composed of numerous peer groups. As Chapter 5 ("Groups and Organizations") explains, members typically perceive their own peer group in positive terms while viewing others negatively. Many peer groups, then, contribute to socialization as individuals conform to one group while opposing others. Moreover, people can be influenced by peer groups they would like to join as much as by those to which they already belong. Such action represents what sociologists call **anticipatory socialization,** *social learning directed toward gaining a desired position.* For instance, a young lawyer who hopes to become a partner in her firm may voice particular views and conduct herself in ways designed to win her acceptance into this exclusive group.

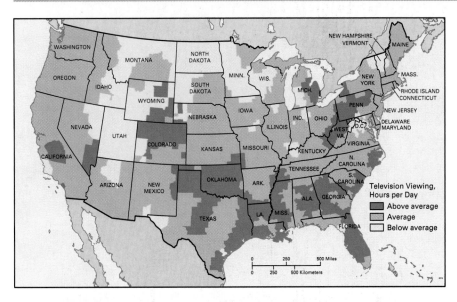

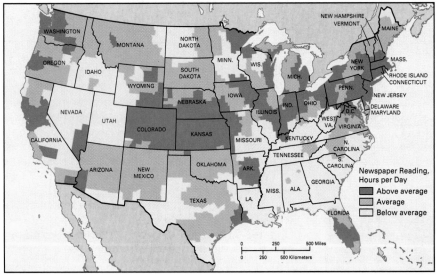

NATIONAL MAP 3–1
**Television Viewing
and Newspaper Reading
Across the United States**

The map on the left identifies U.S. counties in which television watching is above average, average, and below average. The map below provides comparable information for time devoted to reading newspapers. What do you think accounts for the high level of television viewing across much of the South and in rural West Virginia? Does your theory also account for patterns of newspaper reading?

Source: From *American Demographics* magazine, July 1992, p. 54. Reprinted with permission. © 1992 *American Demographics* magazine, Ithaca, New York. Data from Young and Rubicam, San Francisco.

The Mass Media

The **mass media** are *impersonal communications directed to a vast audience.* The term "media" is derived from Latin meaning "middle," indicating that the media serve to connect people. *Mass* media emerged as communications technology (first newspapers then, later, radio and television) spread information on a massive scale.

In the United States, the mass media have an enormous effect on our attitudes and behavior, making them central to socialization. Television, introduced in 1939, is now the dominant mass medium in this country, with about one television set for every person. But people in some regions are more attuned to television, while others favor newspapers: National Map 3–1 provides a graphic comparison.

When Advertising Offends: Another Look at Aunt Jemima

Companies advertise to sell products. However, some ad campaigns offend their audience by portraying certain categories of people in demeaning ways.

A century ago, many whites were uneasy with growing racial and cultural diversity in the United States. Businesses commonly exploited this discomfort by depicting racial and cultural minorities in condescending ways. In 1889, for example, a pancake mix appeared featuring a servant mammy named "Aunt Jemima." Although recently modified, this logo remains on a product that still holds a commanding share of the market. Likewise, the hot cereal "Cream of Wheat" is still symbolized by the African-American chef Rastus, and "Uncle Ben" is familiar to millions of people as a brand name for rice. To many, such caricatures—which, after all, originally represented the black slaves of white people—are insensitive at best.

Changes for the better have occurred in recent decades in all the mass media. The stereotypical Frito Bandito, long familiar to older television viewers, was abandoned by Frito-Lay; the characterization of Latinos as bandits or outlaws, embodied in this bumbling cartoon figure, discredited an entire segment of the population. Other such

images have also disappeared as U.S. businesses recognize and respond to the growing voice and financial power of minorities, who represent a market worth one-half trillion dollars a year. Taken together, Americans of African, Latino and Asian descent represent 20 percent of the population and may constitute a national majority by the end of the next century. And, just as important, the share of the minority population that is affluent is steadily increasing.

In the last ten years U.S. businesses have doubled their spending on advertising aimed at African Americans to about $1 billion annually. The results of this policy shift have been encouraging for the businesses involved—far higher sales—and pleasing to people who have historically found little to like in commercial advertising.

Sources: Based on Westerman (1989) and Simpson (1992).

Today, 98 percent of U.S. households have at least one television set (just 94 percent have telephones); surveys indicate that a television is on in the average household for seven hours a day (U.S. Bureau of the Census, 1994). Children watch television well before they learn to read, and they end up spending more hours in front of a television than they do in school or interacting with parents (Anderson & Lorch, 1983; Singer, 1983; Singer & Singer, 1983).

Comedian Fred Allen once quipped that we call television a "medium" because it is rarely well done. For a variety of reasons, television (like other media) has provoked plenty of criticism. One issue involves alleged bias in television programming. Liberal critics maintain that television shows are conservative since they rarely challenge the status quo (Gans, 1980; Parenti, 1986). For example, television has traditionally portrayed men in positions of power and women as

mothers or subordinates (Cantor & Pingree, 1983; Ang, 1985; Brown, 1990). In addition, although racial and ethnic minorities watch more television than other people, until recently they have been all but absent from programming. Major television producers turned down the 1950s comedy *I Love Lucy*, for example, because it featured Desi Arnaz—a Cuban—in a starring role. The couple formed Desilu studios and produced the show themselves; it became a smash hit.

The number of people of African and Hispanic descent making appearances in all the mass media has increased mainly because advertisers recognize the marketing advantages of appealing to these large segments of U.S. society (Wilson & Gutiérrez, 1985). The box offers a critical look at the problem of media advertising portraying minorities in terms of negative stereotypes.

On the other side of the debate, conservative critics argue that the television and film industries

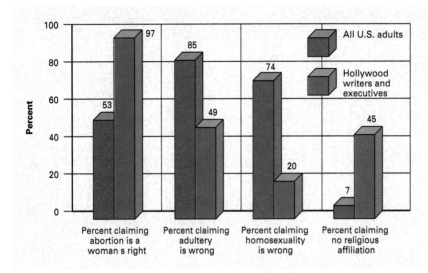

FIGURE 3–2
**The Politics
of the Hollywood Elite**

A recent survey of 104 television
writers and producers shows that, on
four social issues, the Hollywood elite
is far more liberal than U.S. adults
taken as a whole. This discrepancy
suggests why, in the eyes of critics,
Hollywood does not support what
conservatives consider "American
family values."

Sources: The Center for Media and Public
Affairs (1991) and NORC (1992).

constitute a liberal "cultural elite." Figure 3–2 provides the results of one survey of top television writers and producers that supports this contention (Woodward, 1992; Rothman, Powers, & Rothman, 1993).

Television and other mass media have enriched our culture in many respects, bringing into our homes a wide range of entertaining and educational programming. Furthermore, this "window on the world" has enhanced our awareness of diverse cultures and sparked debate on public issues. At the same time, the power of the media—especially television—to shape how we think and act makes the mass media a flashpoint for contrasting views about various social trends.

Public Opinion

Public opinion refers to *the attitudes of a society's people about one or more controversial issues.* The mass media track trends in public attitudes on a host of issues, and there is little doubt that most of us are influenced by what we imagine other people think.

Even so, what "people say" and what is true are far from the same. For example, we are all familiar with common notions that homosexuals are "weird," that noncompetitive men "lack character," and that assertive women are "pushy." Such assertions are value judgments, however, rather than facts. Nonetheless, what people think—or what we *think* they think—affects how we see others and ourselves.

Other agents of socialization, beyond those described here, also play a role in our learning. For most

people in the United States, these include religious organizations, the workplace, and a wide range of social clubs and organizations. As a result, socialization inevitably proceeds inconsistently. In the end, socialization is not a simple learning process but a complex balancing act through which—in the midst of many diverse influences—we try to forge and refine our own distinctive personalities and attitudes.

Socialization and the Life Course

Socialization continues throughout the life course, in childhood, through adolescence and early adulthood, and, finally, into old age. Each stage has distinctive characteristics.

Childhood

In industrial societies, *childhood*—roughly the first twelve years of life—is ideally a time of freedom from adult responsibilities. This has not always been the case, however. Historian Philippe Ariès (1965) explains that, in medieval Europe, as soon as children could survive without constant care, they were expected to fend for themselves. This meant that by age six or seven, poor children worked long and hard, just as adults did. Global Map 3–1 shows that this pattern persists today in poor societies throughout Latin America, Africa, and Asia.

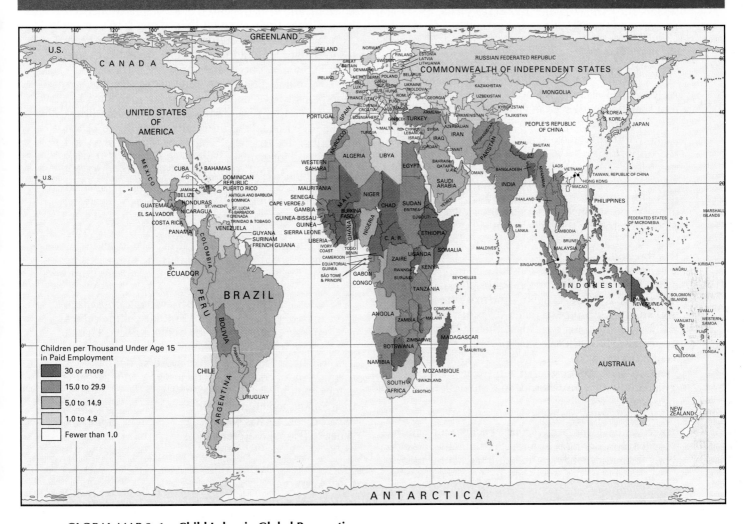

GLOBAL MAP 3–1   Child Labor in Global Perspective

Industrialization has the effect of prolonging childhood and discouraging children from engaging in work and other activities deemed suitable only for adults. Thus child labor is relatively uncommon in the United States and other industrial societies. In less industrialized nations of the world, however, children form a vital economic asset, and they typically begin working as soon as they are able.

Source: *Peters Atlas of the World* (1990).

The notion of children toiling for long hours may be startling because our common sense suggests that youngsters are very different from adults—inexperienced in the ways of the world and biologically immature. But much of this difference is rooted in society, not biology. Because technologically complex societies are more affluent, children can be freed from the burdens of work. In addition, rich societies extend childhood to allow time for young people to learn complex skills required of adults. Thus we define children and adults in contrasting ways, with "irresponsible" children looked after by "responsible" adults (Benedict,

1938). In global perspective, however, this pattern does not always hold true. The traits assigned to childhood—and even whether this stage of life exists at all—are one variable dimension of culture.

Adolescence

As childhood became a distinct stage of life in industrial societies, adolescence emerged as a buffer stage between childhood and adulthood, corresponding roughly to the teenage years. This time of life offers the opportunity to gain independence and learn specialized, adult activities.

We generally associate adolescence with emotional and social turmoil; young people spar with their parents and struggle to develop their own identities. Since adolescence generally begins at the same time as the onset of puberty, we often attribute the conflict of this stage of life to physiological change. However, the shakiness of adolescence also reflects inconsistencies in socialization. For example, adults give adolescents mixed signals about sexuality—the mass media glorify sex, while parents urge restraint. Consider, also, that an eighteen-year-old male may face the adult responsibility of going to war, but he lacks the adult right to drink alcohol. Without denying the role of biological forces, then, we must recognize that adolescence is a time of social contradictions when people are no longer children but not yet adults.

Finally, like all stages of the life course, adolescence varies according to social background. Young people from working-class families commonly move directly from high school to the adult world of work and parenthood. Those from wealthier families, however, typically attend college and perhaps graduate school, extending adolescence into the later twenties and even the thirties (Skolnick, 1992).

Adulthood

Adulthood, which begins between the late teens and early thirties, depending on social background, is typically the period during which most of life's accomplishments occur. Having completed their schooling, people embark on careers and raise families of their own. Personalities are now largely formed, although major crises in adult life—such as unemployment, divorce, or serious illness—may bring about significant changes (Dannefer, 1984).

During early adulthood—until about age forty—young adults learn to manage for themselves a host of day-to-day responsibilities, often juggling conflicting priorities and demands on time from parents, spouse, children, and work (Levinson et al., 1978). Women, especially, face the realization that "doing it all" can be extremely taxing: Our culture confers on them primary responsibility for child rearing and household chores, even if they work outside the home.

By middle adulthood—roughly between the ages of forty and sixty—people begin to sense that marked improvements in life circumstances are less likely. Middle-aged people also become more aware of the fragility of health, something most younger men and women take for granted. Women who have spent many years raising a family can find middle adulthood especially trying. Children have grown up and require less attention, husbands become absorbed in their careers, leaving some women with spaces in their lives that are difficult to fill. Many women who divorce during middle adulthood also confront economic problems (Weitzman, 1985). For all these reasons, an increasing number of women in middle adulthood are returning to school and beginning careers.

Growing older means that everyone must face the reality of physical decline. But our culture makes this prospect more painful for women. Because good looks are defined as more important for women, wrinkles, weight gain, and loss of hair are more traumatic for them. Men, of course, have their own particular difficulties in middle adulthood. Some are disappointed by their limited achievements; others realize that the price of career success has been neglect of family or personal health (Farrell & Rosenberg, 1981; Wolf, 1990).

Old Age

Old age comprises the later years of adulthood and the final stage of life, beginning about the mid-sixties. As Figure 3–3 shows, about one in eight members of our society is over the age of sixty-five, so that the elderly now outnumber teenagers. By 2020, our population beyond the age of fifty will soar by 75 percent, while the number of people under fifty will rise a scant 2 percent (Wolfe, 1991). The "oldest old"—people eighty-five and over—are the fastest-growing segment of our population; their numbers will increase sixfold over the next century.

The "graying of the United States" will have profound consequences for everyone. More people will depend on Social Security and other pension programs, medical facilities will be increasingly burdened, and elderly people will be more prominent in all aspects of

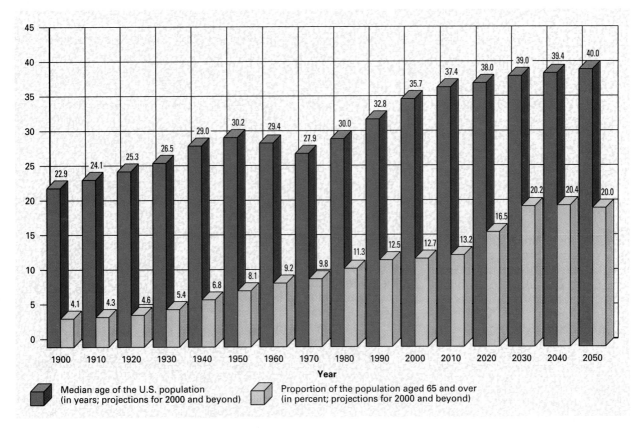

FIGURE 3–3   The Graying of U.S. Society

Source: U.S. Bureau of the Census (1992).

everyday life. Many middle-aged people (especially women) already think of themselves as a "sandwich generation," because they will spend as much time caring for aging parents as they did for their young children. The box on page 74 provides a closer look.

The graying of the United States has sparked the growth of the relatively new field of **gerontology** (from the Greek word *geron*, meaning "old person"), which is *the study of aging and the elderly*. Gerontologists study both the physical and social dimensions of growing old.

Aging and biology.   For most of our population, gray hair, wrinkles, and overall decline in vitality begin in middle age (Colloway & Dollevoet, 1977). After about age fifty, bones become brittle, and falls of little consequence earlier in life can result in disabling injuries that take longer to heal. Moreover, an increasing share of elderly people (more men than women) lose some of their sensory abilities.

Even so, the bigger picture shows that most elderly people are not physically disabled. Only one in ten reports trouble walking, and one in twenty requires the intensive care provided by a hospital or nursing home. No more than 1 percent of the elderly are bedridden. Overall, 71 percent of people over the age of sixty-five assess their health as "good" to "excellent," while 29 percent characterize their condition as "fair" or "poor" (U.S. National Center for Health Statistics, 1994).

Aging and culture.   Culture shapes our understanding of growing old. In preindustrial societies, old age typically confers great influence and respect because the elderly control most land and other wealth, and they bask in their society's respect for wisdom gained over a lifetime (Sheehan, 1976; Hareven, 1982). A preindustrial society, therefore, tends to be a **gerontocracy,** *a form of social organization in which the elderly have the most wealth, power, and privileges.*

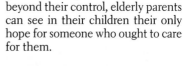

The Sandwich Generation: Who Should Care for Aging Parents?

How can anyone deny that parents who have toiled for their children in their youth, have lost many a good night's sleep when they were ill, have washed their diapers long before they could talk and have spent about a quarter of a century bringing them up and fitting them for life, have the right to be fed by them and respected when they are old?

So asked the Chinese philosopher Lin Yutang centuries ago. This old question is taking on new meaning in the United States as baby boomers become the first generation in our nation's history destined to spend as much time caring for elderly parents as they did for their young children. This challenge has earned them the title of the "sandwich generation," because they face the demands of their children, on the one hand, and those of their aging parents on the other.

Three trends combine to create the sandwich generation. First, *there are now more elderly people.* An explosion of the elderly population is currently under way as people live longer and require greater support and assistance. Second, *adults are having fewer children.* The number of young children in the United States began falling about 1960 as the baby boom came to an end. This downturn in birth rates means that the increasing number of old people will have fewer children to care for them. Third, *more women are in the labor force.* The typical married couple in the United States is now made up of two people who work for pay. Women (in their roles as

daughters and daughters-in-law) historically have been the key providers of support for the elderly. Now that they are working for income, women have less time and energy to do this.

So who should support the elderly? In forging a coherent policy, there are three possibilities: the elderly themselves, the elderly's adult children, and the government. Historically, the U.S. elderly have always taken primary responsibility for their own welfare. But the costs of growing old (inflated by soaring medical expenses and added years of life) threaten the security of even those older women and men who have tried to be self-reliant.

Advocates of a larger role for children, echoing the sentiments of Lin Yutang, point out that family ties involve reciprocity and obligation. Furthermore, the family seems properly suited to provide the emotional support that older people require. As Daniel Callahan states:

In a world of strangers or fleeting casual acquaintances, of distant

government agencies and a society beyond their control, elderly parents can see in their children their only hope for someone who ought to care for them.

But not everyone is convinced that caring for aging parents is a family matter. Our culture does stress the duties of parents toward their young children; but the obligations of children to aging parents are less well defined. Moreover, the growth of government-sponsored social services programs (especially Social Security and Medicare) during the last fifty years has weakened our sense of family responsibility toward the elderly. And many adult children simply do not have the resources—financial or emotional—to handle the caregiving role.

In the future, most elderly people will be able to care for themselves—as they have in the past—without a great deal of help from anyone. But the graying of the United States in the decades ahead means that the costs and responsibilities of supporting the elderly population will rise dramatically. With fewer adult children to meet this need, government involvement in elderly care is bound to expand. Deciding precisely how to assign responsibility for meeting the needs of the elderly will command national attention for decades to come.

Sources: Based on the Institute for Philosophy and Public Policy (1988); also Gelman (1985), Callahan (1987), and Stone, Cafferata, & Sangl (1987).

Industrialization, however, diminishes the social standing of the elderly. Older people commonly live apart from their grown children, and rapid social change renders much of what they have learned obsolete, at least from the point of view of the young. In industrial societies, these factors give rise to **ageism,** *prejudice and discrimination against the elderly.*

For all these reasons, growing old in the United States is a challenging experience. Earlier in life, growing older means entering new roles and taking on fresh responsibilities. Entering old age, however, follows the opposite path: leaving roles that have provided social identity and prestige. Although retirement sometimes fits the common image of restful recreation after years of work, it can also pull men and women out of familiar routines, so that they lose the self-worth derived from work and sometimes suffer outright boredom.

Aging means living with diminished income. Financially, however, the U.S. elderly population is doing better than ever. In 1960, one-third of the elderly were poor; in 1992, this figure had fallen to 13 percent (U.S. Bureau of the Census, 1993). Put otherwise, a generation ago, old age carried the highest risk of poverty; today, childhood holds that unfortunate distinction.

Why the change? For one thing, better health helps today's older people earn more. In addition, pension programs are easing the financial burden on those who have retired. Government policies also play a big part, with more federal spending channeled to the elderly in the form of Social Security and Medicare. Over the last decade, while the income of young people (under twenty-five) has actually fallen by 11 percent, the income of seniors (over sixty-five) has risen by some 20 percent (U.S. Bureau of the Census, 1993).

During the 1980s, median household income fell among young people but rose sharply among those over age sixty-five. This trend could continue in light of the increasing numbers—and political clout—of those age sixty-five and older. A reasonable question, in light of this windfall for the elderly, is whether we should continue to favor the oldest members of our society and risk slighting the youngest—those who now suffer most from poverty.

Death and Dying

To our ancestors, a low standard of living and simple medical technology made death a familiar fact of life. Today, however, about 72 percent of people die after the age of sixty-five. Therefore, even though most senior citizens look forward to decades of life, old age implies the recognition of impending death.

After research observing many dying people, Elisabeth Kübler-Ross (1969) described death as an orderly process involving five stages. Because our culture tends to ignore the reality of death, people's first reaction to the prospect of their demise is usually *denial.* The second stage, *anger,* emerges as the person begins to acknowledge the possibility of death but views it as a gross injustice. In the third stage, anger gives way to *negotiation,* the attitude that one might yet escape death through a bargain struck with God. The fourth stage is *resignation,* often accompanied by psychological depression. Finally, a complete adjustment to death requires *acceptance.* At this point, no longer paralyzed by fear or gloom, the person sets out constructively to make use of whatever time remains.

Today, our society physically isolates dying people. While our ancestors generally died at home, most people now die in impersonal hospitals or rest homes. Even hospitals segregate dying patients in a special part of the building, and hospital morgues are located well out of sight of patients and visitors (Sudnow, 1967; Ariès, 1974).

Thus the historical acceptance of death has been replaced by modern fear and anxiety about dying. No doubt, this has prompted an increase in medical research aimed at prolonging the lives of the elderly. But we may be reaching a turning point. Many elderly people are less fearful of dying than they are of the prospect of being kept alive to no good purpose by high-technology medicine. In short, people want control over their deaths no less than they want control over their lives.

The Life Course: An Overview

This brief examination of the life course leads to two general conclusions. First, although the essential traits of each stage of life—from infancy to old age—are linked to the biological process of aging, they are also socially constructed. For this reason, people in one society may experience a stage of life quite differently from those in another. Second, each phase of the life course presents characteristic problems and transitions that involve learning something new and, in many cases, unlearning what has become familiar.

Keep in mind, too, that the experience of growing older varies according to class, race, ethnicity, and

The infancy of photography in the 1840s was also a time of deadly epidemics in the United States, with between one-third and one-half of children dying before the age of ten. Many grieving parents rushed to capture their dead children on film. The post-mortem photograph, in most cases the only picture ever taken of someone, suggests a far greater acceptance of death during the nineteenth century than is found today. In this century, death has become rare among the young so that dying has been separated from life as a grim reality that people do their best to deny.

gender. Thus, the general patterns we have described are all subject to modification as they apply to various categories of people.

Finally, people's life experiences also vary depending on when, in the history of a society, they were born. A **cohort** is *a category of people with a common characteristic, usually their age.* Age-cohorts are likely to have been influenced by the same major events and thus display similar reactions to particular issues (Riley, Foner, & Waring, 1988). Most of today's college faculty, for example, grew up during an era of economic expansion that fueled optimism about the future, an attitude that is far less characteristic of today's younger and recession-weary college students.

Resocialization: Total Institutions

A final type of socialization, experienced by more than 1 million people in the United States at any given time, involves being confined—often against their will—in prisons or mental hospitals. This is the special world of a **total institution,** *a setting in which individuals are isolated from the rest of society and manipulated by an administrative staff.*

According to Erving Goffman (1961), a total institution controls the full round of daily life, subjecting resident inmates to standardized food, sleeping quarters, and enforcing rigid schedules and rules. The regimentation of a total institution has the goal of **resocialization,** *deliberate socialization intended to radically alter the individual's personality.* Typically, this goal is pursued by depriving inmates of other social experience through walls and fences, barred windows, locked doors, and control of the telephone, mail, and visitors. Cut off in this way, the staff seeks to produce change—or at least compliance.

Resocialization is a two-part process. First, the staff undermines the new inmate's established identity using what Goffman (1961:14) describes as "abasements, degradations, humiliations, and profanations of self." For example, staff members require inmates to surrender clothing and grooming articles normally used to maintain a distinctive appearance. In their place, inmates receive standard-issue items and standardized haircuts that make everyone look alike. The staff also processes new inmates by searching, weighing, fingerprinting, and photographing them, and by issuing them a serial number. Once inside the walls, individuals also give up their privacy: The staff conducts routine surveillance and searches of inmates' living quarters. Taken together, these "mortifications of self" undermine the identity that the inmate brings to the total institution.

The second part of the resocialization process involves efforts by the staff to build a new self by manipulating inmates with rewards and punishments. The privilege of keeping a book or receiving a visitor may seem trivial to the outsider, but in the rigid environment of the total institution, it can be a powerful motivation to conform. In the end, the length of incarceration in a prison or mental hospital often depends on how well an inmate cooperates with the staff.

Resocialization can bring about considerable change in an inmate, but total institutions affect people in different ways. Some inmates may experience "rehabilitation" or "recovery" (meaning change that is officially approved), while others gradually

The demand by guards that new prisoners publicly disrobe is more than a matter of issuing new clothing; such a degrading ritual is also the first stage in the process by which the staff in a total institution attempts to break down an individual's established social identity.

sink into an embittered state. Over a long period of time, the rigidly controlled environment of a total institution may even render some people *institutionalized*, that is, incapable of the independence required for living in the outside world.

Socialization and Human Freedom

Through socialization, society shapes how we think, feel, and act. If society has such power over us, in what sense are we free? This chapter ends with a closer look at this important question.

Children and adults delight in watching the Muppets, stars of television and film. Observing the expressive antics of Kermit the Frog, Miss Piggy, and the rest of the troupe, one almost believes that these puppets are real rather than objects animated from backstage. The sociological perspective suggests that human beings are like puppets: We, too, respond to the backstage guidance of society. Indeed, more so, in that society affects not just our outward behavior but our innermost feelings.

But our analysis of socialization also reveals where the puppet analogy breaks down. Viewing human beings as the puppets of society leads to the trap that Dennis Wrong (1961) has called an "oversocialized" conception of the human being. Wrong reminds us we are biological as well as social creatures, a point emphasized by Sigmund Freud. To the extent that we are imbued with innate human drives or a distinctive temperament, we can never be entirely the puppets of society.

The fact that human beings may be subject to *both* biological and social influences, however, hardly advances the banner of human freedom. Here is where the ideas of George Herbert Mead are of crucial importance. Mead recognized the power of society to act on human beings, but he argued that our spontaneity and creativity (conceptualized in the I) empower us continually to *act back* on society. Therefore, although we sometimes seem to respond like puppets to forces beyond our control, Peter Berger points out that "unlike the puppets, we have the possibility of stopping in our movements, looking up and perceiving the machinery by which we have been moved" (1963:176). Doing this, we can act to change society by, so to speak, pulling back on the strings. And, Berger adds, the more we utilize the sociological perspective to study how the machinery of society works, the freer we become.

SUMMARY

1. Through socialization, social experience makes us fully human and enables each generation to transmit culture to the next.

2. A century ago, people thought human behavior was grounded in biological instinct. Today, however, we recognize that human behavior is mostly a result of nurture rather than nature.

3. Sigmund Freud envisioned the human personality in three parts. The id expresses general, innate human drives; the superego represents internalized cultural values and norms; the ego mediates between the demands of the id and the constraints of the superego.

4. Jean Piaget believed that human development reflects both biological maturation and increasing social experience. He asserted that child development follows four major stages: sensorimotor, preoperational, concrete operational, and formal operational.

5. Lawrence Kohlberg's analysis of moral development holds that individuals first judge rightness in preconventional terms, according to their individual needs. Next, conventional moral reasoning takes account of the attitudes of parents and the norms of the larger society. Finally, postconventional moral reasoning allows for philosophical critique of society itself.

6. Carol Gilligan adds that gender affects moral reasoning. Females, she claims, tend to consider the effect of decisions on relationships, while males rely more on abstract standards of rightness.

7. To George Herbert Mead, social experience nurtures the self, which Mead characterized as partly autonomous (the I) and partly guided by society (the me).

8. Charles Horton Cooley used the term looking-glass self to underscore that the self is influenced by how we think others respond to us.

9. Commonly the first setting of socialization, the family is the greatest influence on a child's attitudes and behavior. Schooling exposes children to social diversity and introduces them to impersonal performance evaluations.

10. Peer groups free children from adult supervision and take on special significance during adolescence. The mass media also shape the socialization process; the average U.S. child now spends more time watching television than attending school. Public opinion plays a role in socialization as well, because popular attitudes influence our individual views and values.

11. Each stage of the life course—from childhood to old age—is, to a significant degree, socially constructed and variable from society to society.

12. People in industrial societies typically die in old age. Acceptance of the inevitability of one's own death is part of socialization for the elderly.

13. Total institutions such as prisons and mental hospitals have the goal of resocialization—significantly changing an inmate's personality.

14. Socialization demonstrates the power of society to shape our thoughts, feelings, and actions. Yet, the relationship between the self and society is a two-way process: Each shapes the other.

KEY CONCEPTS

ageism prejudice and discrimination against the elderly

anticipatory socialization social learning directed toward gaining a desired position

cohort a category of people with a common characteristic, usually their age

concrete operational stage Piaget's term for the level of development at which individuals perceive causal connections in their surroundings

ego Freud's designation of a person's conscious attempts to balance the pleasure-seeking drives of the human organism and the demands of society

formal operational stage Piaget's term for the level of development at which individuals think abstractly and imagine

gerontocracy a form of social organization in which the elderly have the most wealth, power, and privileges

gerontology the study of aging and the elderly

id Freud's designation of the human being's basic drives

looking-glass self Cooley's term referring to a conception of self derived from the responses of others

mass media impersonal communications directed to a vast audience

peer group a group whose members have interests, social position, and age in common

personality a person's fairly consistent patterns of acting, thinking, and feeling

preoperational stage Piaget's term for the level of development at which individuals first use language and other symbols

public opinion the attitudes of people throughout a society about one or more controversial issues

resocialization deliberate socialization intended to radically alter an individual's personality

self George Herbert Mead's term for the dimension of personality composed of an individual's self-awareness and self-image

sensorimotor stage Piaget's term for the level of development at which individuals experience the world only through sensory contact

socialization the lifelong social experience by which individuals develop their human potential and learn culture

superego Freud's designation of the presence of culture within the individual in the form of internalized values and norms

total institution a setting in which individuals are isolated from the rest of society and manipulated by an administrative staff

CRITICAL-THINKING QUESTIONS

1. What do cases of social isolation teach us about the importance of social experience?

2. Describe the "nature-nurture" debate. In what sense do human nature and nurture complement one another?

3. How do the theories of Freud, Piaget, Kohlberg, Gilligan, and Mead build on one another? In what ways do they seem incompatible?

4. Explain how humans living in societies are, and are not, free.

Chapter
4

Social Interaction in Everyday Life

Harold and Sybil are on their way to another couple's home in an unfamiliar section of the city.[1] *They are late, and they're also lost. Harold, who is driving, is getting angrier and angrier the longer he keeps looking for Beechwood Terrace. Sybil, sitting next to him, squirms uncomfortably in her seat. Both realize that the evening is not likely to go well.*

There is more to this everyday situation than meets the eye. Harold and Sybil are lost in more ways than one: They do not understand why they are growing enraged at their predicament and at each other.

Consider the situation, first, from Harold's point of view. Like most men, Harold cannot tolerate becoming lost. The longer he drives around, the more he feels incompetent in handling what should be a simple task. Sybil is seething, too, but for a different reason. She cannot figure out why Harold does not simply pull over and ask someone where Beechwood Terrace is. If she were driving, she fumes to herself, they would have arrived already and would now be comfortably settled with drink in hand.

Why don't men like to ask for directions? Because men value their independence, they are uncomfortable asking for help (and also reluctant to accept it). To ask someone for assistance is an admission of inadequacy and, to make matters worse, it is an acknowledgment that others know something they don't. If it takes Harold a few more minutes to find Beechwood Terrace on his own—and maintain his self-respect in the process—he thinks the bargain is a good one.

If men pursue self-sufficiency and are sensitive to hierarchy, women are more attuned to others and strive for connectedness. Asking for help makes sense to Sybil because, from her point of view, sharing information reinforces social bonds. Requesting directions seems as natural to Sybil as continuing to search on his own appears to Harold. But the two people are unlikely to resolve their situation since neither one understands the other's point of view.

---

[1]This example is based on Tannen (1990:62).

Analyzing examples of everyday life is the focus of this chapter. We begin by presenting many of the building blocks of common experience and continue by exploring the almost magical way in which face-to-face interaction generates reality.

The central concept throughout is **social interaction,** *the process by which people act and react in relation to others.* Social interaction is the key to creating the reality we perceive. And we interact according to particular social guidelines.

Social Structure: A Guide to Everyday Life

Earlier chapters have suggested that, living in a culture that prizes self-reliance, we resist the idea that human behavior is socially patterned. Instead, we emphasize individual responsibility for behavior and highlight the unique elements of our personalities. But behaving in patterned ways does not threaten our individuality. On the contrary, social structure actually promotes our individuality in two key ways.

First, as Chapter 3 ("Socialization: From Infancy to Old Age") explained, in the absence of society, we would never become fully human at all. Second, with no social structure, the world would be disorienting and frightening. After all, entering any unfamiliar setting inhibits us from freely expressing ourselves until we discern what sort of behavior is appropriate. Only after we understand the behavioral rules can we comfortably "act like ourselves."

This is not to deny that social structure also places some constraints on everyday life, since established patterns inevitably discourage the unconventional. In North America, for example, norms and values still press men to be dominant and assertive, while women are expected to adopt a deferential and supportive stance. By pressuring each of us to fit neatly into "feminine" or "masculine" categories, social structure gives us identity at the cost of narrowing our range of thought and action.

Yet social structure *guides* rather than *determines* human behavior. A cello and a saxophone are each designed to make only certain kinds of sounds. Similarly, "fatherhood" is a social structure that calls out certain behavior. Like a musical instrument, however, any social arrangement can be "played" in a wide range of ways.

Since 1619, when Africans first came to these shores, race has served as a powerful ascribed status in the United States. Winslow Homer painted *A Visit From the Old Mistress* in 1876—a decade after the abolition of slavery—as black and white people were taking their first, uncertain steps toward social equality. Ambiguity and awkwardness are outstanding qualities of this portrait of a white woman calling on her former slaves; notice, for instance, the stiffness of the figures and the distance that separates the people of each color. Yet this painting also conveys a certainty that, however long the road ahead, the abolition of slavery has transformed U.S. society fundamentally and forever.

A Visit from the Old Mistress, 1876. Oil on canvas, 18 × 24⅛ (45.7 × 61.3). Unsigned. National Museum of American Art, Smithsonian Institution. Gift of William T. Evans.

Status

One of the basic building blocks of social interaction is **status,** *a recognized social position that an individual occupies.* Sociologists use the term "status" somewhat differently from its everyday meaning of "prestige." In common usage, a bank president has "more status" than a bank teller; sociologically speaking, however, both "president" and "teller" are statuses or social positions in the bank organization.

Every status we hold contributes to our social identity by placing on us responsibilities and expectations that build our relationships with others. In the college classroom, for example, professors and students have distinct, well-defined rights and duties in relation to one another. Similarly, family life ties us to a host of "relations," including mother, father, son, daughter, and so on.

We each simultaneously occupy many statuses. The term **status set** refers to *all the statuses a person holds at a particular time.* A teenage girl is a *daughter* to her parents, a *sister* to her brother, a *friend* to others in her social circle, and a *goalie* to members of her hockey team. Just as status sets branch out in different directions, so they change over the life course. A child turns into a parent, a student becomes a lawyer, and people marry to become husbands and wives, sometimes becoming single again as a result of divorce or death. Joining an organization or finding a job enlarges our status set; retirement or withdrawing from activities diminishes it. Individuals gain and lose dozens of statuses over a lifetime.

Ascribed and Achieved Status

Sociologists analyze statuses in terms of how people attain them. An **ascribed status** is *a social position a person receives at birth or assumes involuntarily later in life.* Examples of statuses ascribed at birth are being a daughter or a Canadian. Statuses ascribed as part of the aging process include becoming a teenager or a senior citizen. All ascribed statuses are matters about which people have little or no choice.

By contrast, an **achieved status** refers to *a social position that a person assumes voluntarily and that reflects a significant measure of personal ability and choice.* Examples of achieved statuses are being an honors student, an Olympic athlete, a wife or husband, or a computer programmer.

Most statuses actually involve a combination of ascription and achievement. That is, people's ascribed statuses influence the statuses they achieve. Children cannot be lawyers, since this status is open only to adults. And adults who complete law school are likely to have been born into relatively privileged families. By the same token, many less desirable statuses, such as criminal or drug addict, are more easily "achieved" by people disadvantaged by ascription.

Master Status

Some statuses are more significant than others. A **master status** is *a social position with exceptional importance for identity, often shaping a person's entire life.*

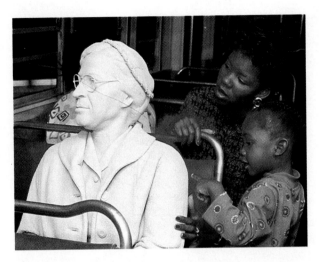

We learn from what we see. Thus each one of us selects others as *role models*, people whose behavior we wish to emulate. The National Civil Rights Museum in Memphis, Tennessee, contains this sculpture of Rosa Parks, a woman of color and a seamstress, who boarded a public bus on December 1, 1955, in Montgomery, Alabama. Although she took her place in the section reserved for African Americans, the driver ordered her to give up her seat to a white man. When she courageously refused, police arrested her. The episode led to the Montgomery Bus Boycott, which lasted for a year and finally brought an end to racial segregation on that city's buses.

A person's occupation is often a master status because it suggests a great deal about someone's education, income, and family background. No doubt, this is why adults typically introduce themselves by stating their occupations along with their names. Similarly, being "a Rockefeller" or "a Kennedy" is enough by itself to push an individual into the limelight.

In a negative sense, serious disease also operates as a master status. Sometimes even lifelong friends shun cancer patients or people with acquired immune deficiency syndrome (AIDS) simply because of their illness. Most societies of the world also limit the opportunities of women, whatever their abilities, so that gender, too, can serve as a master status. Additionally, people with physical disabilities may feel dehumanized because others perceive them as little more than the sum of their handicaps. Many people tend to think of people with disabilities as childlike, asexual, or different in some fundamental sense (Orlansky & Heward, 1981).

Role

Besides status, a second major component of social interaction is **role**, *normative patterns of behavior for those holding a particular status.* Ralph Linton (1937) described a role as the dynamic expression of a status. In short, people *occupy* a status and *perform* a role. The student role, for example, is bound up with responsibilities to professors and other students, as well as entitling the student to devote much time to personal enrichment through academic study.

Cultural norms influence *role expectations*, suggesting how a person with a particular status ought to act. As noted in Chapter 2 ("Culture"), however, real culture only approximates ideal culture, so that actual role performance varies according to an individual's social background and personality.

Like a status, a role is *relational*, organizing our behavior toward other people. The parent's role, for example, is centered on caring for a child. Correspondingly, the role of daughter or son consists largely of obligations toward a parent. Other examples of such role pairs include wives and husbands, baseball pitchers and catchers, physicians and patients, and performers and members of an audience.

The many statuses we hold at one time typically call out an even greater number of roles since any status may lead us to take on several roles in relation to various other people. Robert Merton (1968) introduced the term **role set** to identify *a number of roles attached to a single status.*

Figure 4–1 depicts four statuses of one individual, each linked to a different role set. First, the woman occupies the status of "wife," with a "conjugal role" (serving as confidant and sexual partner) toward her husband, with whom she would share a "domestic role" toward the household. Second, she also holds the status of "mother," with a "maternal role" toward her children and a "civic role" in organizations such as the PTA. Third, as a professor, the "teaching role" is directed toward students, and through the "colleague role" she engages other academics. Fourth, as a researcher, her "laboratory role" yields the data for publications in her role as author.

A global perspective reveals that the key roles people use to define their lives differ significantly from society to society. In agrarian countries, for example, most people work in agriculture and have few of the occupational choices enjoyed by members of industrial societies. Another dimension of difference is housework. As Global Map 4–1 on page 86 shows, especially in poor nations of the world, housework falls heavily on women.

Conflict and Strain

We often find ourselves pulled in different directions by all our obligations at a single point in time. Sociologists use the concept of **role conflict** to refer to *incompatibility among roles corresponding to two or more statuses*. As mothers and fathers who work outside the home can testify, carrying out the demanding roles of parent and breadwinner can sometimes seem all but impossible.

Even the many roles linked to a single status make competing demands on us, sometimes leading to **role strain,** meaning *incompatibility among roles corresponding to a single status*. A plant supervisor may wish to be an approachable friend to other workers. At the same time, however, to ensure worker performance the supervisor may have to resort to occasional discipline, dictating a measure of personal distance. In short, performing the roles of even a single status often requires something of a "balancing act."

One strategy for dealing with role conflict is to "compartmentalize" one's life by performing roles linked to one status at one time and place and carrying out those corresponding to another status later on. The familiar notion of "leaving the job at the office" when returning home illustrates this pattern. Another way to handle such conflict is to define some roles as more important than others. A new mother, for instance, might devote most of her efforts to parenting and put her career on hold, at least for the present. Of course, resolving role conflict in this way depends on being able to afford not to work—an option unavailable to many mothers.

Setting priorities also reduces strain among roles linked to a single status. A father, for example, may decide that maintaining an open relationship with his child is more important than enforcing cultural norms as a disciplinarian.

Role Exit

Recent research has focused on *role exit*, the process by which people disengage from important social roles. Helen Rose Fuchs Ebaugh (1988) began to study role exit as she herself left the life of a Catholic nun to become a university sociologist. Interviewing ex-nuns, ex-doctors, ex-husbands, and ex-alcoholics, Ebaugh identified elements common to the process of "becoming an ex."

According to Ebaugh, the process begins as people experience mounting doubts about their ability

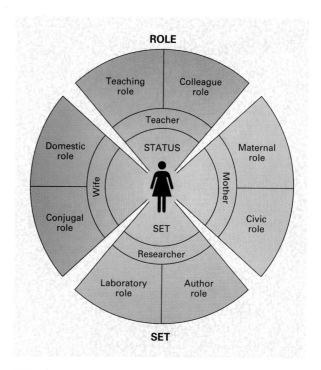

FIGURE 4–1   Status Set and Role Set

or willingness to perform a particular role. As they consider alternatives, they ultimately reach a turning point that leads them in a new direction. In the subsequent "ex-role," they disengage from the previous situation, building a new sense of self marked by changing appearance and behavior (an ex-nun, for example, begins to wear stylish clothing and pursue a social life). "Exes" must also assist others accustomed to dealing with them in an earlier role. Often, too, there is much for the "ex" to learn. Ebaugh reports, for example, that nuns who begin dating after decades in the church are startled to discover that today's sexual norms are quite different from those they knew as teenagers.

The Social Construction of Reality

Some sixty years ago, the Italian playwright Luigi Pirandello created the character of Angelo Baldovino—a brilliant man with a rather checkered past. In the play *The Pleasure of Honesty*, Baldovino enters the fashionable home of the Renni family and introduces himself in a most peculiar way:

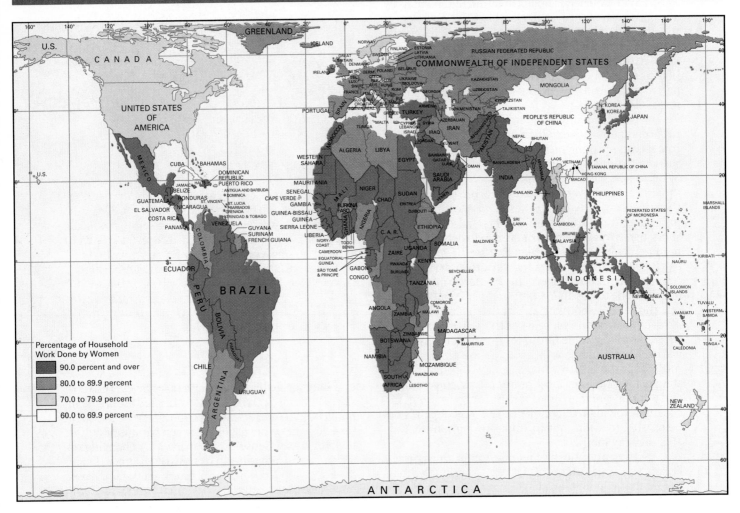

GLOBAL MAP 4–1   Housework in Global Perspective

Throughout the world, a major component of women's routines and identities involves housework. This is especially true in poor societies of Latin America, Africa, and Asia, where women are not typically in the paid labor force. But our society also defines housework and child care as "feminine" activities, even though a majority of U.S. women work outside the home.

Source: *Peters Atlas of the World* (1990); updated by the author.

Inevitably we construct ourselves. Let me explain. I enter this house and immediately I become what I have to become, what I can become: I construct myself. That is, I present myself to you in a form suitable to the relationship I wish to achieve with you. And, of course, you do the same with me.... (1962:157–58)

Pirandello is suggesting that, while situations are guided by status and role, each of us has considerable ability to shape how they unfold. "Reality," that is, is not as fixed as we might think (Berger & Luckmann, 1967).

The phrase **social construction of reality** refers to *the process by which individuals creatively build reality* *through social interaction.* This idea is familiar as the foundation of the symbolic-interaction paradigm in sociology, detailed in Chapter 1 ("Sociology: Perspective, Theory, and Method"). Here, Angelo Baldovino's remark implies that, as an encounter begins, quite a bit of "reality" is not yet clear in anyone's mind. Pirandello's character thus "presents himself" in terms he thinks will suit his purposes. As others do the same, the process of reality construction proceeds.

Given the presence of culture, social interaction typically yields considerable agreement about how to define a situation. But participants rarely have exactly the same perceptions of events. Impressions vary because social interaction draws together people with different purposes and interests, each of whom will seek a different situational outcome.

Another phrase for steering reality in this way is "street smarts." In his biography *Down These Mean Streets,* Piri Thomas recalls moving to a new apartment in Spanish Harlem, which soon brought him into contact with the local street gang. Returning home one evening, young Piri found himself cut off by Waneko, the gang's leader, and a dozen others.

"Whatta ya say, Mr. Johnny Gringo," drawled Waneko.

Think man, I told myself, *think your way out of a stomping. Make it good.* "I hear you 104th Street coolies are supposed to have heart," I said. "I don't know this for sure. You know there's a lot of streets where a whole 'click' is made out of punks who can't fight one guy unless they all jump him for the stomp." I hoped this would push Waneko into giving me a fair one. His expression didn't change.

"Maybe we don't look at it that way."

Crazy, man, I cheer inwardly, *the cabron is falling into my setup. . . .* "I wasn't talking to you," I said. "Where I come from, the pres is president 'cause he got heart when it comes to dealing."

Waneko was starting to look uneasy. He had bit on my worm and felt like a sucker fish. His boys were now light on me. They were no longer so much interested in stomping me as seeing the outcome between Waneko and me. "Yeah," was his reply. . . .

I knew I'd won. Sure, I'd have to fight; but one guy, not ten or fifteen. If I lost, I might still get stomped, and if I won I might get stomped. I took care of this with my next sentence. "I don't know you or your boys," I said, "but they look cool to me. They don't feature as punks."

I had left him out purposely when I said "they." Now his boys were in a separate class. I had cut him off. He would have to fight me on his own, to prove his heart to himself, to his boys, and most important, to his turf. He got away from the stoop and asked, "Fair one, Gringo?" (1967:56–57)

This situation reveals the drama—sometimes subtle, sometimes savage—by which human beings creatively build reality. We all know that there are limits to what even the most skillful personality can achieve. Should a police officer have come upon the fight that ensued between Piri and Waneko, both young men might well have ended up in jail. Clearly, not everyone enters a negotiation with equal standing; the police officer would undoubtedly have had the last word simply because of a status that holds greater power than that of the boys (Molotch & Boden, 1985).

The Thomas Theorem

By displaying his wits and courage, Piri Thomas won acceptance that evening. W. I. Thomas (1966:301; orig. 1931) captured the essence of such events in what is known as the **Thomas theorem:** *Situations that are defined as real become real in their consequences.* In other words, although reality is initially "soft" as it is fashioned, it can become "hard" in its effects. In the case of Piri Thomas, once others defined him as worthy, this young man *became* worthy in the eyes of his new comrades.

Ethnomethodology

We have explained that, as symbolic-interactionists see it, reality is not something "out there"; reality is created by people engaging one another. But how, exactly, do we define reality for ourselves? Answering this question is the objective of *ethnomethodology,* a specialized approach within the symbolic-interaction paradigm.

The term itself has two parts: The Greek *ethno* refers to people; *methodology* designates a set of methods or principles for understanding our surroundings. Combining them makes **ethnomethodology,** *the study of the way people make sense of their everyday surroundings.*

Ethnomethodology was devised in the 1950s by Harold Garfinkel, a sociologist dissatisfied with macro-level views of society as a broad "system" with a life of its own. Garfinkel viewed society as the reality people construct in countless everyday situations. He further assumed that, because any situation is so complex, people interact by taking for granted many ideas about how the world operates.

Think, for a moment, about how much we assume about human behavior when driving onto a freeway. We take for granted that traffic on our side of the road will flow in a particular direction, at a predictable and steady

Cultures frame reality in different ways. This man lay on the street in Bombay, India, for several hours and then quietly died. In the United States, such an event would probably have provoked someone to call the rescue squad. In a poor society in which death on the streets is a fact of everyday life, however, many Indians responded not with alarm but with simple decency by stopping to place incense on his body before continuing on their way.

speed, and that other drivers will display at least some measure of caution and courtesy. Although we may not think very much about these conventions, they are extremely important to us. To see how significant they are, imagine the disruption caused by any driver who violates them.

Garfinkel devised a useful technique for exposing the unacknowledged patterns of everyday life: *Break the rules.* That is, we can tease out how people build reality by deliberately ignoring conventional rules and observing how people respond. Although he never advocated doing this on the highway, Garfinkel (1967) and his students did refuse to "play the game" in less threatening situations. Some students entered stores and insisted on bargaining for items, a strategy that brought to the surface assumptions about how shopping is carried out. Others recruited people into simple games (like tic-tac-toe) only to intentionally flout the rules, which made clear our assumptions about fair play. Still others initiated conversations while slowly moving closer and closer to the other person, which revealed that we generally conform to unspoken rules about the use of space.

The provocative character of ethnomethodology, coupled with its focus on commonplace experiences, has led some sociologists to view it as less-than-serious research. Even so, ethnomethodology has succeeded in drawing out many unnoticed patterns of everyday life.

Reality-Building in Global Perspective

Taking a broader view, people do not build everyday experience "out of thin air," but according to specific interests. Lovers see romance in the night sky, for example, while scientists look at the same stars dotting the heavens as hydrogen atoms fusing into helium. Social background also guides our perceptions so that residents of, say, Spanish Harlem experience the world somewhat differently than people living on Manhattan's affluent East Side. To offer another example, we would not expect people across the United States to embrace the same heroes or to share the same tastes in music. Take the case of Elvis Presley fans: National Map 4–1 shows that followers of "The King" live in particular types of communities.

In global perspective, reality varies even more, so that social experiences common to, say, women in Saudi Arabia would seem unreal to many women in the United States. Similarly, social reality changes over time. People living in Japan a century ago forged social worlds very different from those typical of that nation today.

Because reality is grounded in the surrounding culture, how we interpret any object or action depends on time and place. The meanings people attach to the two sexes, to stages of the life course, or even to the days of the week vary from culture to culture. Supporting this conclusion, JoEllen Shively (1992) screened "western" films to an audience composed of both Anglo and Native-American men. Both groups claimed to enjoy the films but saw different meanings in them. The Anglos interpreted the films as praising rugged individualism and imposing human will on nature. Native Americans, by contrast, saw in the same films a celebration of land and nature apart from any human ambitions.

Finally, how variable around the world are basic human feelings? Do people everywhere respond to situations with the same emotions? Researchers, who have conducted cross-cultural investigations of human

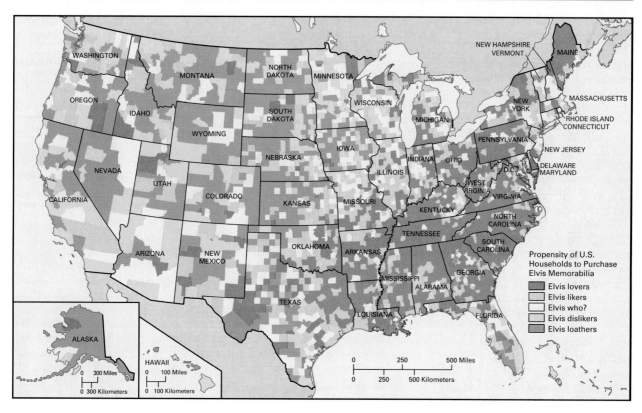

NATIONAL MAP 4–1   Where Are the Elvis Fans?

Thousands of people across the United States belong to fan clubs celebrating the career of Elvis Presley, the first rock and roll superstar. This map identifies counties across the country in which Elvis fans are most likely—and least likely—to live. Examining the map, what can you say about the counties that are home to Elvis fans? In which regions of the nation does Elvis—who died in 1977—live on? Is his following stronger in urban areas or rural locales?

Source: *American Demographics* magazine, August 1993, p. 64. Reprinted with permission. © 1993 *American Demographics* magazine, Ithaca, New York. Data from DICI, Bellaire, Tex.

emotions, conclude that the answer is yes—and no—as the box on pages 90–91 explains.

Dramaturgical Analysis: "The Presentation of Self"

Erving Goffman (1922–1982) argued that people socially constructing reality have much in common with actors performing on a stage. Viewing everyday life like a director scrutinizing the action in a theater, Goffman pioneered **dramaturgical analysis,** *the investigation of social interaction in terms of theatrical performance.*

Dramaturgical analysis offers a fresh look at two now-familiar concepts. In this theoretical scheme, a status mirrors a part in a play, and a role serves as a script, supplying dialogue and action for each character. In any setting, then, each of us is partly the actor, partly the audience. Goffman called the intricate drama of everyday life the **presentation of self,** meaning *ways in which individuals, in various settings, try to create*

Emotions: Are Feelings the Same Everywhere?

On a busy New York sidewalk, a woman reacts angrily to the skateboarder who hurtles past her. Her facial expression, accompanied by a few choice words, broadcasts a strong emotion that any New Yorker can easily recognize. But would an observer from Nigeria, Nicaragua, or New Guinea be able to interpret her emotion? In other words, do people everywhere have similar emotions and express them in the same way?

Paul Ekman (1980) and his colleagues studied emotions in a number of countries—even among members of a small society in New Guinea. From this research, they concluded that basic emotions the world over include anger, fear, disgust, happiness, surprise, and sadness. Moreover, these researchers learned that people everywhere express these feelings using the same distinctive facial gestures. To Ekman, this commonality points to the fact that *what people feel* is essentially universal—and not culturally specific—and the display of emotion is also common to all human beings because it is biologically rooted in our facial features, muscles, and central nervous system.

But Ekman notes three ways in which emotional life does differ in global perspective. First, what *triggers* an emotional response varies from one society to another. Whether a particular situation is defined as an insult (prompting anger), a loss (calling out sadness), or a mystical event (provoking surprise) depends on culture. In other words, although people in various societies share the same range of emotions, they react quite differently to the same event.

Second, people *express* emotions according to the norms of their culture. Every society has its own rules about when, where, and to whom people may exhibit certain emotions. Members of our society, for example, typically approve of emotional expression in the home but consider such behavior out of place at work. Similarly, we expect children to show emotions to parents, although parents are taught to exercise care in the display of emotions in the presence of children.

Third, cultures differ in terms of how people *cope* with emotions. Some societies encourage people to freely express their feelings, while others belittle emotions and demand that their members try to suppress them. Significant gender differences characterize societies in this regard as well. Our culture tends to label emotional expression as feminine, expected of women but interpreted as a sign of weakness among men. In other societies, however, this sex typing of emotions is less pronounced or even reversed.

In sum, people the world over all experience the same six basic emotions. But what sparks a particular emotion, how and where a person expresses it, and how people define emotions in general all vary as matters of culture. In global perspective, therefore, everyday life differs not only in terms of how people think and how they act, but how they infuse their lives with feeling.

Sources: Ekman (1980a, 1980b), Lutz & White (1986), and Lutz (1988).

---

specific impressions in the minds of others. This process, sometimes termed *impression management,* contains several distinctive elements (Goffman, 1959, 1967).

Performances

As we present ourselves to others, we convey information—consciously and unconsciously—about how we wish to be understood. Goffman called these efforts, taken together, a *performance.* A performance includes an individual's dress (costume), objects carried along (props), and tone of voice and gestures (manner). Setting, too, affects a performance. People may joke loudly on the sidewalk, for example, but assume a more reverent manner upon entering a house of worship. Equally important, individuals design settings, such as homes or offices, to evoke desired reactions in others.

Consider, for example, how a physician's office conveys appropriate information to an audience of patients. Physicians enjoy considerable prestige and power in the United States, a fact grasped by patients

To most people in the United States, these expressions convey anger, fear, disgust, happiness, surprise, and sadness. But do people elsewhere in the world define them in the same way? Research suggests that all human beings experience the same basic emotions and display them to others in the same basic ways. But culture plays a part by specifying the situations that trigger one emotion or another.

immediately upon entering the office. First, the physician is nowhere to be seen. Instead, in what Goffman describes as the "front region" of the setting, the patient encounters a receptionist who functions as a gatekeeper, deciding if and when the patient can meet the physician. A quick look around the doctor's waiting room, with patients (often impatiently) waiting to gain entry to the inner sanctum, leaves little doubt that the medical team controls events.

The physician's private office and examination room are the "back region" of the setting. Here the patient confronts a wide range of props, such as medical books and framed degrees, that reinforces the impression that the physician possesses specialized knowledge and deserves deference. In the office, the physician usually remains seated behind a desk—the larger it is, the greater the statement of power—while the patient is provided with only a chair.

The physician's appearance and manner convey still more information. The usual costume of white lab coat may have the practical function of keeping clothes from becoming soiled, but its primary

African-American artist Jacob Lawrence captured the element of drama in everyday experiences in his painting *Vaudeville*. The fact that the words "person" and "mask" are derived from the same Latin root (the word *persona*) raises the intriguing question of whether our public behaviors are authentic or contrived. In most cases, no doubt, they are a little of each.

Jacob Lawrence, Theatre Series, No. 8: *Vaudeville*, 1951. Hirshhorn Museum and Sculpture Garden, Smithsonian Institute, Gift of Joseph H. Hirshhorn, 1966.

function is to let others know at a glance the physician's status. A stethoscope around the neck or a black medical bag in hand serves the same purpose. A doctor's highly technical terminology—occasionally necessary, but frequently mystifying—also emphasizes the hierarchy in the situation. The use of the title "Doctor" by patients who, in turn, are frequently addressed only by their first names also underscores

the physician's dominant position. The overall message of a doctor's performance is clear: "I can help you, but you must allow me to take charge."

Nonverbal Communication

Novelist William Sansom describes the performance of a fictional Mr. Preedy, an English vacationer on a beach in Spain:

> He took care to avoid catching anyone's eye. First, he had to make it clear to those potential companions of his holiday that they were of no concern to him whatsoever. He stared through them, round them, over them—eyes lost in space. The beach might have been empty. If by chance a ball was thrown his way, he looked surprised; then let a smile of amusement light his face (Kindly Preedy), looked around dazed to see that there were people on the beach, tossed it back with a smile to himself and not a smile *at* the people. . . .

> . . . (He) then gathered together his beach-wrap and bag into a neat sand-resistant pile (Methodical and Sensible Preedy), rose slowly to stretch his huge frame (Big-Cat Preedy), and tossed aside his sandals (Carefree Preedy, after all). (1956; cited in Goffman, 1959:4–5)

In this performance, Mr. Preedy offers a great deal of information about himself to anyone caring to observe him. Notice that he does so without uttering a single word. This illustrates the process of **nonverbal communication,** *communication using body movements, gestures, and facial expressions rather than speech.*

Body language, our movements and gestures, conveys much information to others. Facial expressions have special importance to nonverbal communication. Smiling, for example, symbolizes pleasure, although we distinguish between the casual, lighthearted smile of Kindly Preedy on the beach, a smile of embarrassment, and the full, unrestrained smile of self-satisfaction we often associate with "the cat who ate the canary."

Eye contact is another important element of nonverbal communication. Generally, we use eye contact to initiate social interaction. Avoiding the eyes of another, by contrast, discourages communication. Hands, too, speak for us. Common hand gestures within our culture convey, among other things, an insult, a request for a ride, an invitation for someone to join us, or a demand that others stop in their tracks. Gestures also supplement spoken words. Pointing in a menacing way at someone, for example, gives greater emphasis to a word of warning, as shrugging the shoulders adds an air of indifference to the phrase "I don't know," and rapidly waving the arms lends urgency to the single word "Hurry!"

Most nonverbal communication is culture-specific. As noted in Chapter, 2 "Culture," many gestures significant to North Americans mean nothing—or something very different—to members of other societies. For instance, what we call the "A-Okay" gesture with thumb touching forefinger means "You're a zero" to the French and symbolizes a crude word for "rectum" to many Italians (Ekman, Friesen, & Bear, 1984).

Performances may convey mixed messages when an unconscious element of nonverbal communication contradicts our intentional behavior. A teenage boy offers an excuse for coming home late, but his mother begins to doubt his words because he avoids looking her in the eye. The movie star on a television talk show claims that her recent flop at the box office is "no big deal," but the nervous swing of her leg hints at a deeper disappointment. No body gesture directly conveys deceit; however, such inconsistent messages—especially likely when strong emotions are involved—are distinct clues to deception. In much the same way that a lie detector measures subtle physical changes in breathing, pulse rate, perspiration, and blood pressure that signal the stress of telling lies, a trained observer can discern discrepancies in a performance (Ekman, 1985).

Gender and Performances

Because women are socialized to be less assertive than men, they tend to be especially sensitive to nonverbal communication. In fact, gender is a central element in personal performances. Based on the work of Nancy Henley, Mykol Hamilton, and Barrie Thorne (1992), we can extend the conventional discussion of personal performances to spotlight the importance of gender.

Demeanor. Goffman (1967) links *demeanor*—general conduct or deportment—to social power. Simply put, people in positions of power have more personal discretion in how they act. Office behavior such as swearing, removing shoes, or putting feet up on the desk may be appropriate for the boss, but rarely for subordinates. Similarly, powerful people interrupt the performances of others with impunity, while those subject to their power must display deference by becoming silent (Smith-Lovin & Brody, 1989).

For women, who generally occupy positions of minimal power, demeanor is a matter of particular

Women and men use space in different ways, a fact that is reflected in our clothing and demeanor. Because controlling space is a measure of power, men typically take up as much space as they can—even while relaxing—while women try to use as little as possible.

concern. As Chapter 10 ("Sex and Gender") explains, about half of U.S working women perform clerical or service work under the control of supervisors, who are usually men. Women, then, must craft their personal performances more formally than men, and display a greater degree of deference in everyday interaction.

Use of space. How much space does a personal performance require? Here again, power plays a key role, since using more space conveys a nonverbal message of personal importance. Thus, our society has long measured femininity by how little space women occupy (the standard of "daintiness"), while men enhance their masculinity by controlling as much territory as possible.

The concept of **personal space** refers to *the surrounding area over which a person makes some claim to privacy*. In the United States, people generally remain at least two feet apart, maintaining more personal space than members of societies in North Africa, the Middle East, or Japan. Moreover, almost everywhere men readily intrude on the personal space of women. A woman's intrusion into a man's personal space, however, is likely to be construed as a sexual overture. Here again, women have less latitude in everyday interaction than men do.

Staring, smiling, and touching. Eye contact encourages interaction. Women more than men work to sustain eye contact. One exception is *staring*. Men often make women the objects of stares, a practice which reflects both male dominance and men's tendency to define women as sexual objects.

Especially in public places, men often make women the objects of stares and sexual overtures in the form of shouting and whistling. Behavior of this kind—as Ruth Orkin's photograph, *American Girl in Italy*, conveys—is one dimension of male dominance in everyday life that is demeaning and intimidating to women.

Although frequently conveying pleasure, *smiling* can also be a symbol of appeasement or submission. In a male-dominated world, Henley, Hamilton, and Thorne maintain, women smile more than men.

Finally, mutual *touching* generally conveys intimacy and caring. Apart from close relationships, however, touching is generally something men do to women. A male physician touches the shoulder of his female nurse as they examine a report, a young man who has just begun dating touches the back of his woman friend as he guides her across the street, or a male skiing instructor excessively touches his female students. In such examples the touching may evoke little response, but it amounts to a subtle ritual by which men express their dominant position in an assumed hierarchy that subordinates women.

Idealization

Complex motives underlie human behavior. Even so, Goffman suggests, performances tend to *idealize* our intentions. That is, we try to convince others that our actions reflect the higher standards of our culture rather than more self-serving motives.

Idealization is easily illustrated by returning to the world of physicians and patients. In a hospital, physicians engage in a performance commonly described as "making rounds." Entering a hospital room, the physician often stops at the foot of the bed and silently examines the patient's chart. Afterwards, physician and patient briefly converse. In ideal terms, this routine involves a physician making a personal visit to inquire about a patient's condition.

In reality, something less exemplary is usually going on. A physician who sees perhaps thirty-five patients a day may remember little about most of them. Reading the chart gives the physician the opportunity to rediscover the patient's identity and medical problems. Openly acknowledging the impersonality of much medical care would undermine the cultural ideal of the physician as deeply concerned about the welfare of others. Idealizing the physician's role also encourages patients to "follow doctor's orders," which, they assume, are in their own best interest. No doubt this is often the case. But, as Chapter 13 ("Education and Medicine") explains, physicians often prescribe drugs, order tests, admit patients to hospitals, and perform surgery with a keen awareness of what's in it for themselves (Kaplan et al., 1985).

Physicians and other professionals typically idealize their motives for entering their chosen careers as well. They may describe their work as "making a contribution to science," perhaps "answering a calling from God," or "serving the community." Rarely do such people concede the less honorable, although common, motives of seeking the high income, power, and prestige these occupations confer. More generally, we all smile

Hand gestures vary widely from one culture to another. Yet people everywhere define a chuckle, grin, or smirk in response to someone's performance as an indication that one does not take another person seriously. Therefore, the world over, people who cannot restrain their mirth tactfully cover their faces.

and make polite remarks to people we do not like. Such small hypocrisies ease our way through social interactions. Even when we suspect that others are putting on an act, we usually refrain from openly challenging their performance, for reasons that we shall explain next.

Embarrassment and Tact

The presidential candidate enters the room and stumbles over the rug; the eminent professor consistently mispronounces a simple word; the president becomes ill at a state dinner. As carefully as individuals craft their performances, slip-ups of this kind frequently occur. The result is *embarrassment,* or discomfort following a spoiled performance. Goffman describes embarrassment simply as "losing face."

Embarrassment looms as an ever-present danger because, first, idealized performances typically contain some measure of deception. Second, most performances draw on a complex array of elements, any one of which, if badly done, can shatter the intended impression.

A curious fact is how readily an audience overlooks flaws in a performance, thereby sparing another person embarrassment. We discreetly inform a man that his zipper is open (creating some embarrassment), to help him avoid an even greater loss of face. In Hans Christian Andersen's classic fable "The Emperor's New Clothes," the child who blurts out that the emperor is naked tells the truth, but is scolded for being rude.

Members of an audience not only ignore errors in a performance, Goffman explains, they often help

the performer recover from them. *Tact* is a strategy to help another person "save face." After hearing a supposed expert make an embarrassingly stupid remark, for example, people may use tact in a variety of ways. They may ignore the statement, acting as if it were never made. They may laugh, indicating that they dismiss what was said as a joke. Or a listener might gently respond, "I'm sure you didn't mean that," suggesting that the statement will be discounted so as not to destroy the expert's overall performance.

Why is tact so common? Because embarrassment provokes discomfort not simply for the actor but for *everyone.* Just as members of a theater audience feel uneasy when an actor forgets a line, people who observe a social blunder are reminded of how fragile their own performances often are. Socially constructed reality thus functions like a dam holding back a sea of chaotic possibility. Should one person's performance spring a leak, in most cases others tactfully assist in making repairs. Everyone, after all, jointly engages in building reality, and no one wants it to be suddenly swept away.

In sum, Goffman's research shows that, although our behavior may be spontaneous to some degree, we employ many familiar social patterns in our performances. William Shakespeare recognized this fact some four hundred years ago when he wrote:

All the world's a stage,
And all the men and women merely players:
They have their exits and their entrances;
And one man in his time plays many parts . . .
(*As You Like It*, II)

Interaction in Everyday Life: Two Illustrations

We have now examined a number of dimensions of social interaction. The final sections of this chapter illustrate these lessons by focusing on two important, yet quite different, elements of everyday life.

Language: The Gender Issue

As Chapter 2 ("Culture") explains, language is the thread that joins members of a society into the symbolic web we call culture. Language conveys not just *manifest* meaning, or what is explicitly stated, but also *latent* messages about social reality. One latent message involves gender. Language defines men and women differently in at least three ways (Henley, Hamilton, & Thorne, 1992).[2]

Language and power. A young man drives into a gas station, eager to display his new motorcycle, and proudly asks, "Isn't she a beauty?" On the surface, the question has little to do with gender. Yet, why does the fellow use the pronoun "she" rather than "he" to refer to his prized possession?

The answer has to do with power. Some men use language to establish control over their surroundings. That is, a man attaches a female pronoun to a motorcycle, car, yacht, or other object because it reflects *ownership*. Male ownership of female things is part of our culture: Try reversing the pronoun to see how awkward it sounds.

The interplay of power and language comes through clearly in how people are named. Traditionally in the United States, as in many other parts of the world, a woman takes the family name of the man she marries. While few today consider this an explicit statement of a man's ownership of a woman, many think it does reflect male dominance. For this reason, a small but increasing percentage of women now retain their own name (more precisely, the family name obtained from their father) or merge two family names.

Language and value. Language tends to attach greater value to what is defined as masculine. This pattern is deeply rooted in the English language, in ways that few

women or men realize. For instance, the positive adjective "virtuous," meaning "morally worthy" or "excellent," is derived from the Latin word *vir* meaning "man." By contrast, the disparaging adjective "hysterical" comes from the Greek word *hyster*, meaning "uterus."

In many more familiar ways, language also confers different value upon the two sexes. Traditional masculine terms such as "king" or "lord" have retained their positive meaning, while some comparable terms, such as "queen," "madam," or "dame" have now assumed negative connotations. In short, language both mirrors social attitudes and helps perpetuate them.

Language and attention. Language also shapes reality by directing attention to what is masculine. Consider the use of personal pronouns. In the English language, the plural pronoun "they" is gender-neutral, since it refers to both sexes. But the corresponding singular pronouns "he" and "she" specify gender. According to traditional grammatical practice, we use "he" (as well as the possessive "his" and the objective "him") to refer to *all people*. Thus, we assume that the masculine pronoun in the bit of wisdom "He who hesitates is lost" refers to women as well as men. But this practice also reflects the traditional cultural practice of neglecting the lives of women (MacKay, 1983).

The English language has no gender-neutral third-person singular pronoun. In recent years, however, the plural pronoun "they" has gained currency as a singular pronoun ("*Everyone* should do as *they* please"). This usage does violate grammatical rules. Yet, in an age of growing concern over gender-linked bias, English (and other languages) are evolving in response.

Even as our languages evolve, gender issues embedded in language are likely to continue to spark miscommunication between women and men. In the box, Harold and Sybil—whose misadventures finding a friend's home opened this chapter—return to illustrate how the two sexes often seem to be speaking different languages.

Humor: Playing With Reality

Humor plays a vital part in everyday life. Comedians rank among our favorite entertainers, most newspapers contain cartoon pages, and even professors and members of the clergy include humor in their performances. Like many aspects of daily living, however, humor is largely taken for granted. While everyone enjoys a good joke, few people think about what makes something funny or why humor is a part of social life the world over. Many of the ideas developed in this

---

[2]The following sections draw primarily on Henley, Hamilton, & Thorne (1992). Additional material is derived from Thorne, Kramarae, & Henley (1983) and MacKay (1983).

Gender and Language: You Just Don't Understand!

Just as gender-based differences color the way men and women behave when they're lost on the road (think back to Harold and Sybil in the chapter-opening story), these differences also guide our reactions in other everyday situations. Linguistic researcher Deborah Tannen offers the case of what men call "nagging." Consider the following exchange (Adler, 1990:74):

Sybil: "What's wrong, honey?"

Harold: "Nothing . . . ."

Sybil: "Something is bothering you; I can tell."

Harold: "I told you nothing is bothering me. Leave me alone."

Sybil: "But I can see that something is wrong."

Harold: "OK. Just why do you think something is bothering me?"

Sybil: "Well, for one thing, you're bleeding all over your shirt."

Harold: (now irritated): "It doesn't bother me."

Sybil: (losing patience): "WELL, IT SURE IS BOTHERING ME!"

Harold: "I'll go change my shirt."

The problem couples face in communicating is that what one partner *intends* by a comment is not always what the other *hears* in the words. To Sybil, her opening question is an effort at cooperative assistance. She can see that something is wrong with Harold and wants to help solve the problem. But Harold interprets her effort to point out his problem as belittling. Therefore, he denies that anything is wrong and tries to close off the discussion. Sybil, confident that Harold would

be more positive toward her if he just understood that she only wants to be helpful, repeats herself. This sets in motion a vicious cycle in which Harold, thinking his wife is trying to make him feel incapable of looking after himself, responds by digging in his heels. This, in turn, makes his wife all the more sure there is a problem that requires attention. And 'round it goes until somebody loses patience.

In the end, Harold gives in only to the extent that he agrees to change his shirt. But notice that he still refuses to discuss the original problem. Misunderstanding his wife's motives, Harold just wants Sybil to leave him alone. For her part, Sybil fails to understand Harold's view of the situation and walks away thinking that he has been insensitive to her for no good reason.

Sources: Adler (1990) and Tannen (1990).

---

chapter provide insights into the character of humor, as we shall now see.[3]

The foundation of humor. People create humor by deliberately playing with reality; more specifically, they do so by setting up and contrasting incongruous realities. One version of reality is *expected,* because it is consistent with what people usually foresee in some situation. The other reality can be dubbed *unexpected,* since

it is unanticipated and often at odds with cultural norms or values. In simple terms, humor arises when contradiction, ambiguity, and "double meanings" overlay our definitions of some situation. Note how this principle works in these simple pieces of humor:

> The husband quips: "My wife and I have no secrets from each other . . . At least none she knows about."

In this example, the first thought represents a conventional reality. A man claims that he and his wife are close. The second sentence, however, injects an unexpected contradiction.

---

[3]The ideas contained in this discussion are those of the author (1987), except as otherwise noted. The general approach draws on work presented earlier in this chapter, especially the ideas of Erving Goffman.

This simple pattern comes through in the off-hand joking of comedian Woody Allen:

"I'm not afraid to die; I just don't want to be there when it happens."

Or how about one of the many "lawyer jokes" of recent years:

Speaker #1: "How do you know when lawyers are lying?"
Speaker #2: "I don't know, how?"
Speaker #1: "Their lips move . . ."

Here, again, these jokes contain two major elements, a conventional assertion followed by an unconventional one. The more powerful the incongruity between the two definitions of reality, the greater the humor. This explains why comedians strive to strengthen the opposition between contrasting realities by paying careful attention to the precise words they use as well as the timing of each part of the delivery. A joke is "well told" if the comic creates the sharpest possible opposition between the realities, just as a careless performance allows humor to fall flat. Because this opposition often strikes us like a blow to our conventional understanding, the climax of a joke is called the *punch line*.

The dynamics of humor: "Getting it."   Someone who does not understand both the expected and unexpected realities embedded in a joke may complain, "I don't get it." To "get" humor, members of an audience must understand the two realities well enough to perceive their incongruity.

But getting a joke can be more challenging still, because the comic may leave unstated some of the information listeners must grasp. The audience, in other words, must pay attention to the *stated* elements of the joke, figure out the *unstated* elements, and then complete the joke in their own minds. Consider the comment of movie producer Hal Roach upon reaching his one hundredth birthday:

"If I had known I would live to be one hundred, I would have taken better care of myself!"

Here, "getting" the joke depends on realizing that Roach *must* have taken pretty good care of himself since he lived to be one hundred in the first place.

A more complex joke, written on the wall of a college restroom, goes beyond everyday knowledge:

Dyslexics of the World, Untie!

This joke demands more of the audience. One must know, first, that dyslexia is a condition in which people reverse letters; second, one must identify the line as an adaptation of Karl Marx's call to the world's workers to unite; third and finally, one must recognize "untie" as an anagram of "unite," as one might imagine a disgruntled dyslexic person would write it.

Try this one, which requires knowledge of three specialized words:

Speaker #1: "What do you get when you cross an insomniac, an agnostic, and a dyslexic?"
Speaker #2: "I don't know, what?"
Speaker #1: "A person who stays up all night wondering if there is a dog."

Why would an audience be required to make this sort of effort in order to understand a joke? Simply because our enjoyment of a joke is heightened by the pleasure of having been clever enough to complete the puzzle in order to "get it." In addition, "getting" the joke confers on the audience a favored insider status. These insights also explain the frustration that accompanies not getting a joke: anxiety about mental inadequacy coupled with a sense of being excluded from the pleasure shared by others. Not surprisingly, "outsiders" in such a situation may fake "getting" the joke; sometimes, too, others may tactfully explain a joke to them to end their sense of having been left out.

But, as the old saying goes, if a joke has to be explained, it won't be very funny. Besides taking the edge off the language and timing on which the *punch* depends, an explanation relieves the audience of mental involvement, substantially reducing their pleasure.

The topics of humor.   People throughout the world smile and laugh, providing ample evidence that humor is a universal human trait. But, living in diverse cultures, people differ in what they find funny. Musicians frequently perform for receptive audiences around the world, suggesting that music may be the "common language" of humanity. Comedians rarely do this, confirming that humor does not travel well.

What is humorous to the Chinese, then, may be lost on most people in the United States. To some degree, too, the social diversity of our society means that people find humor in different situations. New Englanders, southerners, and westerners have their own brands of humor, as do Latinos and Anglos, fifteen- and forty-year-olds, bankers and construction workers.

For everyone, however, humor deals with topics that lend themselves to double meanings or controversy. For example, the first jokes many of us learned as children concerned what our culture defines as a childhood taboo: sex. The mere mention of "unmentionable acts" or even certain parts of the body can dissolve young faces in laughter.

The controversy inherent in humor often walks a fine line between what is funny and what is considered "sick." During the Middle Ages, the word *humors* (derived from the Latin *humidus*, meaning "moist") referred to a balance of bodily fluids that determined a person's health. Most societies value the ability to take conventional definitions of reality lightly (in other words, having a "sense of humor"). In fact, empirical evidence supports the old saying "Laughter is the best medicine" since maintaining a sense of humor contributes to a person's physical health by decreasing stress (Robinson, 1983; Haig, 1988). At the extreme, however, people who always take conventional reality lightly risk being defined as deviant or even mentally ill (mental hospitals have long been dubbed "funny farms").

Every social group considers some topics too sensitive for humorous treatment. A violation may result in the comedian being admonished for telling a "sick" joke, one that pokes fun at a situation that is expected to be handled with reverence. Some topics, in other words, are "off limits" because people expect them to be understood in only one way. People's religious beliefs, disabilities, or tragic accidents are the stuff of "sick" jokes.

The functions of humor.

From a structural-functional point of view, humor acts as a "safety valve" that allows people to safely express potentially disruptive sentiments. That is, ideas that might be dangerous if taken seriously are framed as lighthearted remarks, as in the case of racial and ethnic jokes. Called to account for a remark that could be viewed as offensive, a person may defuse the situation by simply stating, "I didn't mean anything by that—it was just a joke!" Likewise, rather than taking offense at another's words or actions, a person might use humor as a form of tact, smiling as if to say, "I could be angry at this, but I'll assume you were only kidding."

Like drama and art, humor also allows a society to challenge established ideas and to explore alternatives to the status quo. Sometimes, in fact, humor may actually promote social change by loosening the hold of convention.

Humor and conflict.

While humor holds the potential to liberate those who laugh, it can also be used to oppress others. Men who tell jokes about feminists, for example, are probably voicing some measure of

Because humor involves challenging established social conventions, "outsiders"—particularly ethnic and racial minorities—have always been disproportionately represented among our society's comedians. In her comedy career, Whoopi Goldberg (shown here in the movie, *Sister Act*) has poked fun at virtually every kind of formality and pretense.

hostility toward the feminist social agenda (Benokraitis & Feagin, 1986; Powell & Paton, 1988). Similarly, individuals who poke fun at gay people reveal the tensions that currently surround sexual orientation in the United States.

"Put down" jokes, which make one category of people feel good at the expense of another, are common around the globe. After collecting and analyzing jokes from many societies, Christie Davies (1990) concluded that ethnic conflict is a driving force behind humor virtually everywhere. Typically, these jokes label some disadvantaged category of people as stupid or ridiculous, thereby imputing greater wisdom and skills to those who share the humor. In the United States, Poles have long been the "butt" of jokes, as have Newfoundlanders ("Newfies") in eastern Canada, the Irish in Scotland, the Scots in England, the Sikhs in India, the Hausas in Nigeria, the Tasmanians in Australia, and the Kurds in Iraq.

Disadvantaged people, of course, also make fun of the powerful. Women in the United States have long joked about men, just as African Americans portray whites in humorous ways, and poor people poke fun at the rich. Throughout the world, people target their leaders with humor, and officials in some countries take such jokes seriously enough to vigorously repress them.

The significance of humor, then, is greater than first impressions suggest. Michael Flaherty (1984, 1990) points out that humor amounts to a means of mental escape from a world not entirely to our liking. As long as we maintain a sense of humor, then, we assert our freedom and are never prisoners of society. And, in doing so, we actually do change the world and ourselves just a little.

These very different issues—the impact of gender in our language and humor—are both important dimensions of everyday life. Each demonstrates our power to socially construct a world of meaning and then react to what we have made. Each also demonstrates the value of sociological thinking for understanding—and more actively participating in—this process.

SUMMARY

1. Social life is patterned in various ways. By guiding behavior within culturally approved bounds, social structure helps to make situations more understandable and predictable.

2. A major component of social structure is status. Within an entire status set, a master status has particular significance.

3. In principle, ascribed statuses are involuntary, while achieved statuses are earned. In practice, however, many statuses incorporate elements of both ascription and achievement.

4. Role is the dynamic expression of a status. Like statuses, roles define relationships between people.

5. When roles corresponding to two or more statuses are incompatible, role conflict results. Likewise, incompatibility among various roles linked to a single status causes role strain.

6. The phrase "social construction of reality" conveys the important idea that people build the social world through their interaction.

7. The Thomas theorem states that situations defined as real become real in their consequences.

8. People build social reality using elements of their culture and available social resources.

9. Ethnomethodology explores how people generate their understandings of everyday social situations. This approach sometimes utilizes norm-violation to help identify social conventions that people take for granted.

10. Dramaturgical analysis examines everyday life in terms of elements of theatrical performances.

11. People speak, use body language, and fashion physical settings to assist their performances. Often performers try to idealize underlying intentions.

12. To the extent that they have less social power, women craft their behavior differently than men do.

13. Social behavior carries the ever-present danger of embarrassment. Tact is a helpful response to a "loss of face" by others.

14. Language is a major tool of reality-building. In various ways, language defines women and men in different terms, generally to the advantage of men.

15. Humor is based on the contrast between expected and unexpected social realities. Because comedy is framed by a specific culture, people throughout the world find humor in different situations.

KEY CONCEPTS

achieved status a social position that a person assumes voluntarily and that reflects a significant measure of personal ability and choice

ascribed status a social position that a person receives at birth or assumes involuntarily later in the life course

dramaturgical analysis the investigation of social interaction in terms of theatrical performance

ethnomethodology the study of the way people make sense of their everyday surroundings

master status a social position with exceptional importance for identity, often shaping a person's entire life

nonverbal communication communication using body movements, gestures, and facial expressions rather than speech

personal space the surrounding area over which a person makes some claim to privacy

presentation of self Goffman's term for the ways in which individuals, in various settings, try to create specific impressions in the minds of others

role normative patterns of behavior for those holding a particular status

role conflict incompatibility among roles corresponding to two or more statuses

role set a number of roles attached to a single status

role strain incompatibility among roles corresponding to a single status

social construction of reality the process by which individuals creatively build reality through social interaction

social interaction the process by which people act and react in relation to others

status a recognized social position that an individual occupies

status set all the statuses a person holds at a particular time

Thomas theorem the assertion that situations that are defined as real become real in their consequences

CRITICAL-THINKING QUESTIONS

1. Consider ways in which a physical disability can serve as a master status. How do people commonly characterize, say, a blind person with regard to mental ability? With regard to sexuality?

2. How do people on a first date commonly present themselves and construct reality?

3. Provide several personal experiences that illustrate the validity of the Thomas theorem.

4. Keeping in mind the dramaturgical analysis of a doctor's office found in this chapter, develop a similar analysis of a college classroom. What about a professor's office?

Groups
and
Organizations

Back in 1937, few people paid much attention as a new restaurant opened in Pasadena, California. Yet this small business, owned and operated by Mac and Dick McDonald, would eventually revolutionize the restaurant industry, introducing the concept of "fast food" to our vocabulary and providing an organizational model that countless other businesses and even schools and churches would copy.

The basic formula of the McDonald brothers boiled down to serving food quickly, to large numbers of people, at an attractive price. The McDonalds trained their employees to perform highly specialized jobs, so that one person grilled hamburgers, while others "dressed" them, made french fries, mixed milkshakes, and presented the food to the customer in assembly-line fashion.

As the years went by the single McDonald's restaurant moved to San Bernardino, where, in 1954, events took an unexpected turn when Ray Kroc, a traveling blender and mixer merchant, paid a visit. Kroc was fascinated by the brothers' efficient system and, almost immediately, he saw the potential for a greatly expanded chain of fast-food restaurants. Initially in partnership with the McDonald brothers, Kroc soon set out on his own to become one of the greatest success stories of all time. Today, people in the United States and dozens of countries around the world enjoy food and drinks at almost fifteen thousand McDonald's restaurants.

From a sociological point of view, the success of McDonald's reveals much more than the popularity of hamburgers. Rather, as sociologist George Ritzer (1993) explains, the larger importance of this story lies in the extent to which the principles that guide the operation of McDonald's are coming to dominate social life in the United States as well as the rest of the world.

This chapter will explain how this came to be. We begin with an examination of *social groups,* the clusters of people with whom we interact in much of our daily lives. We then turn to the expanding scope of group life during this century. From a world built on the family, the local neighborhood, and the small business, the structure of our society now turns on the operation of vast businesses and other bureaucracies that sociologists describe as *formal organizations.*

Social Groups

Virtually everyone moves through life with a sense of belonging based on group membership. A **social group** is defined as *two or more people who identify and interact with one another.* As human beings, we continually join together in couples, families, circles of friends, neighborhoods, teams, churches, businesses, clubs, and numerous large organizations. Whatever the form, groups encompass people who share experiences, loyalties, and interests. In short, while maintaining their individuality, the members of social groups also think of themselves as a special "we."

Not every collection of individuals forms a group. People who happen to be at the same place at the same time but do not interact or share a sense of belonging are correctly termed an *aggregate.* Riders on a subway train exemplify an aggregate, not a group. People who have some status in common, such as "mother," "sergeant," "homeowner," or "Roman Catholic" are also not a group but a *category.* While they may be aware of others like themselves, most such people are strangers who never interact.

People in an aggregate or category *could* become a social group, if the right circumstances gave them a common identity and caused them to interact. When a subway train recently crashed beneath the streets of New York City, for example, passengers were prompted by their common plight toward group awareness, helping each other survive the ordeal.

Primary and Secondary Groups

Acquaintances commonly greet one another with a smile and the simple phrase "Hi! How are you?" The response is usually a well-scripted, "Just fine, thanks. How about you?" This answer, of course, is often far from truthful. In fact, providing a detailed account of how you *really* are doing might well prompt the other person to beat a hasty and awkward exit.

Social groups fall into one of two types according to their members' degree of personal concern for each other. According to Charles Horton Cooley, a **primary group** is *a small social group in which relationships are personal and enduring.* Bound together by strong and lasting loyalties, which Cooley termed *primary relationships,* people in primary groups share many activities, spend a great deal of time together, and feel that they know one another well. In short, they display genuine concern for each other's welfare.

The family is the most important primary group in any society.

Cooley called personal and tightly integrated groups *primary* because they are among the first groups we experience in life. In addition, the family and peer groups hold primary importance in the socialization process, shaping attitudes and behavior, conferring social identity, and providing comfort and security. Not surprisingly, then, members of primary groups almost always think of themselves as "we."

Although members of primary groups are dependent on one another, they generally do not think of mutual aid as the reason for the group's existence. Rather, family and friendship groups commonly are composed of people who feel that they "belong" together. Put otherwise, members see a primary group as an end in itself rather than as a means to other ends.

Finally, each member of a primary group shares a special, personal relationship with other group members. Family members and friends are unique people who are not interchangeable with others as is the individual who cashes our check at the bank or drives the cross-town bus. Moreover, bound to one another by emotion and loyalty, kin or close friends generally persist despite periodic conflict.

In contrast to the primary group, the **secondary group** is *a large and impersonal social group based on a specific interest or activity.* Examples of secondary groups include people who work together in an office, enroll in the same college course, live in some neighborhood, or belong to a particular political organization.

In most respects, secondary groups have precisely the opposite characteristics of primary groups. *Secondary relationships* usually involve little personal knowledge of one another and weak emotional ties. Secondary groups vary in duration but are frequently of short term, beginning and ending without particular significance. Students in a college course, for example, may or may not see each other again after the semester ends. Because secondary groups focus on some special interest or activity, members have little chance to develop a concern for one another's overall welfare. In some cases, such as co-workers who share an office, relationships may edge from secondary to primary with the passing of time. But, generally, people in a secondary group do not think of themselves as "we," and the boundary that distinguishes members of secondary groups from nonmembers is far less clear than in primary groups.

While primary relationships have a *personal orientation,* secondary relationships have a *goal orientation.* This does not mean that secondary ties need be

Around the world, families are the most important primary group. In industrial societies, however, numerous friendship groups stand alongside families, joining individuals on the basis of shared interests rather than kinship.

formal and unemotional. On the contrary, social interactions among students, co-workers, and business associates can be enjoyable even if they are rather impersonal. But while primary-group members define each other according to *who* they are, those in secondary groups look to one another for *what* they are, that is, what others can do for them. In secondary groups, we tend to "keep score," mindful of what we offer others and what we receive in return.

The goal orientation of secondary groups encourages members to carefully craft their behavior. In these roles, then, we remain characteristically impersonal and polite. The secondary relationship, therefore, is one in which the question "How are you?" may be asked without really seeking a truthful answer.

The characteristics of primary and secondary groups are summarized in Table 5–1. Using these two ideals as ends of a continuum, we can describe any real group as primary or secondary to some degree. Some family relationships, after all, are more primary than others, and not all business relationships are equally secondary.

In general, primary relationships dominate life in preindustrial societies where strangers stand out in the social landscape. By contrast, secondary ties take precedence in modern, industrial societies, where people are more geographically mobile and assume highly specialized social roles. In today's world, we routinely engage in impersonal, secondary relationships with strangers—people about whom we know very little and may never meet again (Wirth, 1938).

Not all regions of the United States today are equally primary or secondary, however. One indicator of the predominance of secondary ties is a tendency to settle disputes not through personal discussion but by turning to the formal legal system. National Map 5–1 examines the quality of social relationships in the United States by looking at people's willingness to sue each other.

Group Leadership

Social groups vary in the extent to which members recognize leaders, people charged with responsibility to direct the group's activities. Some friendship groups grant one person the clear status of leader; others do not. In families, parents have leadership roles, although husband and wife may disagree about who is really in charge. In many secondary groups, such as corporations, leadership generally involves a formal chain of command.

We tend to think that leaders possess extraordinary personal abilities. But research over several decades suggests that who emerges as a leader has less to do with individuals and more to do with the needs of the group itself (Ridgeway, 1983; Ridgeway & Diekema, 1989). Moreover, two different leadership roles commonly emerge in groups (Bales, 1953; Bales & Slater, 1955).

TABLE 5–1 Primary Groups and Secondary Groups: A Summary

	Primary Group ←→	Secondary Group
Quality of relationships	Personal orientation	Goal orientation
Duration of relationships	Usually long term	Variable; often short term
Breadth of relationships	Broad; usually involving many activities	Narrow; usually involving few activities
Subjective perception of relationships	As ends in themselves	As means to an end
Typical examples	Families; circles of friends	Co-workers; political organizations

Instrumental and expressive leaders. The term **instrumental leaders** refers to *group leaders who emphasize the completion of tasks*. Group members look to instrumental leaders to "get things done." **Expressive leaders,** by contrast, *emphasize collective well-being*. Expressive leaders are concerned less with the performance goals of a group than with providing emotional support to members and minimizing conflict among them.

Because they concentrate on performance, instrumental leaders usually forge secondary relationships with group members. Instrumental leaders give orders and reward or punish people according to their performance. Expressive leaders, however, cultivate more primary relationships. They offer sympathy for a member having a tough time, work to keep the group united, and lighten serious moments with humor. While successful instrumental leaders gain a distant *respect*, expressive leaders generally enjoy more personal *affection*.

In the past, this differentiation of leadership has been linked to gender. In traditional families, for example, cultural norms have bestowed instrumental leadership on men. As fathers and husbands, they have assumed primary responsibility for earning and spending family income, making major decisions affecting the family, and disciplining children. As mothers and wives, women have taken the expressive leadership role, lending emotional support to other members of the family and maintaining peaceful family relationships (Parsons & Bales, 1955). This division of labor partly explains why many children have greater respect for their fathers, but closer personal ties with their mothers (Macionis, 1978). But changes in family life have blurred the gender-linked distinction between leadership roles and, in other settings as well, women and men are assuming both types of leadership roles.

Leadership styles. Decision-making styles also characterize leaders. *Authoritarian leaders* focus on instrumental concerns, make decisions on their own, and demand strict compliance from subordinates. Although this leadership style wins little affection from the group, members may praise an authoritarian leader in a crisis situation requiring immediate decisions and strong group discipline. *Democratic leaders* are more expressive and try to include everyone in the decision-making process. While less successful when a crisis leaves little time for discussion, democratic leaders can otherwise draw on the ideas of all members to forge reflective and imaginative responses

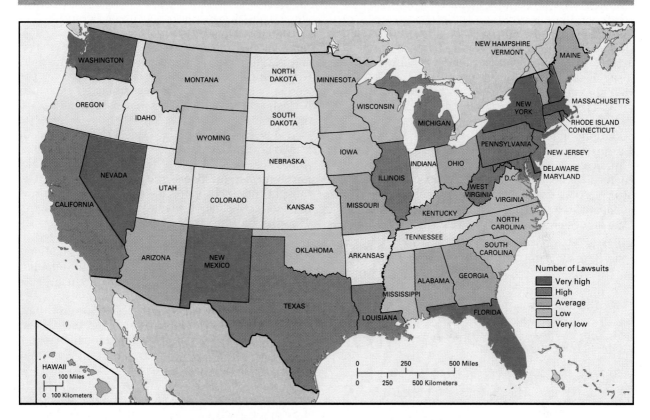

NATIONAL MAP 5–1   The Quality of Relationships: Lawsuits Across the United States

Social conflicts are found everywhere; whether people tend to resolve them informally or resort to legal action, however, varies from state to state. In regions of the country where people's social ties typically are more primary in character, litigation is less common. By contrast, where secondary social ties predominate, people more readily turn to lawyers to settle their differences. Looking at the map, therefore, we can assume that states with high rates of litigation have less personal social ties. What do these states have in common? What traits mark states in which people tend not to sue each other?

Source: Prepared by the author using data from Frum & Wolfe (1994).

to the tasks at hand. *Laissez-faire leaders* (from the French phrase meaning roughly "to leave alone") downplay their position and power, allowing the group to function more or less on its own. Laissez-faire leaders are generally the least effective in promoting group goals. Once again, which leadership style emerges in any particular case depends, in large part, on the needs of the group itself (White & Lippitt, 1953; Ridgeway, 1983).

Group Conformity

Groups influence the behavior of their members, often promoting conformity. Some measure of group conformity provides a secure feeling of belonging; at the extreme, however, group pressure is quite unpleasant. Moreover, even groups of strangers can foster conformity, as a classic experiment by Solomon Asch (1952) showed.

Asch's research. Asch (1952) formed groups of six to eight people, allegedly to study visual perception. He arranged with all but one member of the group to create a situation in which the remaining subject would feel pressure to agree with unreasonable conclusions. Asch asked group members, one at a time, to match a "standard" line, as shown in Figure 5–1 on "Card 1," to one of three lines on "Card 2." Anyone with normal vision could see that the line marked "A" on "Card 2" was the correct choice. Initially, everyone gave correct answers. Then, Asch's secret accomplices began responding incorrectly, leaving the naive subject bewildered. Asch found that more than one-third of subjects placed in this awkward situation chose to conform to the others by answering incorrectly. Many of us apparently are willing to compromise our own judgment to avoid the discomfort of being different from others, even from people we do not know.

Milgram's research. In the early 1960s, Stanley Milgram—a one-time student of Solomon Asch—conducted a controversial conformity experiment of his own. In his initial study, a researcher explained to pairs of people—one of whom was "in" on the experiment—that they were engaging in a study of memory. The naive subject was assigned the role of "teacher" and the insider became the "learner."

The learner sat in a forbidding contraption resembling an electric chair with electrodes attached to one arm. The researcher instructed the teacher to read pairs of words, later repeating each first word and asking the learner to recall the corresponding second word. As mistakes occurred, the researcher instructed the teacher to shock the learner using a "shock generator," a phony but realistic-looking device marked to regulate electric current from 15 volts (labeled "mild shock") to 450 volts (marked "Danger: Severe Shock" and "XXX"). Beginning at the lowest level, the teachers were to increase the shock by 15 volts every time the learner made a mistake. The experimenter explained to the teacher that the shocks were painful but caused no permanent damage.

The results are striking evidence of the ability of leaders to obtain compliance. None of the forty subjects assigned in the role of teacher during the initial research even questioned the procedure before they thought they had applied 300 volts, and twenty-six of the subjects—almost two-thirds—went all the way to 450 volts. In subsequent trials, Milgram's subjects administered "shocks" to people who verbally objected, to those who protested that they had heart conditions, and even to individuals who screamed and then feigned unconsciousness. Not surprisingly, many subjects found the experiment extremely stressful, the source of the controversy ever since. No less disturbing is the implication of Milgram's research that people who commit atrocities against fellow human beings—as some Nazi and Soviet soldiers did during World War II—are more or less typical people who are "just following orders" (Milgram, 1963, 1965; Miller, 1986).

Milgram (1964) then modified his research to see if Solomon Asch had found a high degree of group conformity only because the task of matching lines seemed trivial. What if groups pressured people to administer electrical shocks?

To investigate, he varied the experiment so that a group of three teachers, two of whom were his accomplices, made decisions jointly. Milgram's rule was that each of the three teachers would suggest a shock level when the learner made an error and they would then administer the *lowest* of the three suggestions. This arrangement gave the naive subject the power to lessen the shock level regardless of what the other two teachers suggested.

The accomplices recommended increasing the shock level with each error, placing group pressure on the third member to do the same. Responding to this group pressure, subjects applied voltages three to four times higher than in experiments when they were acting alone. Thus Milgram's research suggests that people are surprisingly likely to follow the directions of not only "legitimate authority figures," but also of groups of ordinary individuals.

FIGURE 5–1   Cards Used in Asch's Experiment in Group Conformity

Source: Asch (1952).

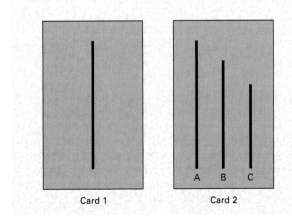

Card 1   Card 2

A   B   C

Janis's research. Even the experts succumb to pressure for group conformity, according to Irving L. Janis (1972, 1989), sometimes producing foreign policy blunders in the process. Janis attributes the failure to foresee the Japanese attack on Pearl Harbor in World War II, the disastrous U.S. plan to invade Cuba in 1961, and our ill-fated involvement in the Vietnam War to group conformity among our highest-ranking political leaders.

We often assume that group "brainstorming" improves decision making. However, Janis explains, rather than examining a problem from many points of view, group members often seek consensus, actually narrowing the range of options. Janis called this process **groupthink,** *group conformity that limits understanding of an issue.* Looking back on the Kennedy administration's decision to invade Cuba—a plan that failed—Arthur Schlesinger, Jr., former adviser to President John Kennedy, confessed guilt "for having kept so quiet during those crucial discussions in the Cabinet Room," but added that the group discouraged anyone from challenging even what seemed to be "nonsense" (Janis, 1972:30, 40).

In many traditional societies, children of the same age forge strong loyalties, generally with members of their own sex. Among the Masai in Kenya, for example, boys born during the same four-year period undergo ritual circumcision together and maintain a group bond throughout their lives.

Reference Groups

Groups play a part in all decision making. A **reference group** is *a social group that serves as a point of reference for making evaluations and decisions.* A young man who imagines his family's response to a woman he is dating is using his family as a reference group. Similarly, a banker who assesses her colleagues' reactions to a new loan policy is using her co-workers as a point of reference.

As these examples suggest, reference groups can be both primary and secondary. And, to the extent that we wish to join some group, the attitudes of those group members can greatly affect our evaluations through the process of *anticipatory socialization,* examined in Chapter 3 ("Socialization: From Infancy to Old Age").

Stouffer's research. Samuel A. Stouffer (1949) conducted a classic study of reference group dynamics during World War II. In a survey, Stouffer asked soldiers to evaluate the chances of promotion for a competent person in their branch of the service. Common sense suggests that soldiers serving in outfits with high promotion rates would be optimistic about future advancement. Yet survey responses revealed just the opposite: Soldiers in branches of the service with low promotion rates thought they had the best chances of getting ahead.

The key to this paradox is that the soldiers measured their progress against specific groups. Those in branches with lower promotion rates compared their advancement with people like themselves; that is, although they had not been promoted, neither had many others, so they did not feel deprived. Soldiers in a service branch with a higher promotion rate, however, could easily think of people who had been promoted sooner or more often than they had. Using these people for reference, even soldiers who had advanced were likely to feel they had come up short. Such soldiers thus voiced more negative attitudes.

The lesson here is that, regardless of our situation in *absolute* terms, we gain our subjective sense of well-being by looking at ourselves *relative* to some specific reference group (Merton, 1968; Mirowsky, 1987).

Ingroups and Outgroups

Because the members of various groups tend to think, look, and act differently, we value some over others. Students typically favor their own colleges, for example, looking critically at people who attend other schools.

This contrast illustrates an important process of group dynamics: the opposition of ingroups and outgroups. An **ingroup** is *an esteemed social group commanding a member's loyalty.* An **outgroup,** by contrast,

Many ingroups and outgroups are based on dimensions of inequality. In Joseph Decker's (1853–1924) painting *Our Gang* (1886), the artist suggests how readily race can lead some people to experience social marginality. The African-American boy has his back against a wall covered with weathered posters that seem to point to him like a finger of accusation (Decker originally named this painting *The Accused*). The reality of race in the United States is that people of color often find themselves existing as an outgroup in relation to the white majority ingroup.

is *a scorned social group toward which one feels competition or opposition.* Ingroups and outgroups work on the principle that "we" have valued traits that "they" lack. Tensions among groups sharpen their boundaries and give people a clearer social identity. However, members of ingroups generally hold overly positive views of themselves and unfairly negative views of various outgroups (Tajfel, 1982).

Powerful categories of people can sometimes define others as a disadvantaged outgroup. For example, whites have historically viewed African Americans as an outgroup and subjected them to social, political, and economic disadvantages. In the process, people targeted in this way often struggle to overcome negative self-images based on stereotypical group identity.

Group Size

If you are the first person to come to a party, you can observe some fascinating group dynamics. Until about six people enter the room, everyone generally shares a single conversation. But as more people arrive, the group soon divides into two or more smaller clusters. It is apparent that size plays a crucial role in how group members interact.

To understand why, consider the mathematical connection between the number of people in a social group and the number of relationships among them, as shown in Figure 5–2. Two people form a single relationship; adding a third person results in three relationships; adding a fourth person yields six. Adding people one at a time, in short, rapidly increases the number of relationships so that, by the time six people join one conversation, fifteen different relationships connect them. This explains why the group usually divides at this point.

German sociologist Georg Simmel (1858–1918) focused his research on social dynamics in the smallest social groups. Simmel (1950; orig. 1902) used the term **dyad** (from the Greek word for "pair") to designate *a social group with two members.* In the United States, love affairs, marriages, and the closest friendships are dyadic. Simmel identified two special qualities of the dyad. First, they are typically less stable than larger groups. Both members of a dyad must actively sustain the relationship; if either withdraws, the group collapses. Because the stability of marriage is important, society provides legal and religious support to this dyad.

Second, social interaction in a dyad is typically more intense than in larger groups. In a one-to-one relationship, neither member shares the other's attention with anyone else. Because marriage in our society is dyadic, strong emotional ties generally unite husbands and wives. As Chapter 12 ("Family and Religion") explains, however, in other societies marriage can involve more than two people. In that case, the marriage itself is more stable, even though the many marital relationships, viewed individually, are typically weaker.

A **triad** is *a social group with three members.* A triad encompasses three relationships, each uniting two of the three people. Simmel noted that any two members can form a coalition transforming the triad into a dyad with a "third wheel." Two members of a triad who develop a romantic interest, for example, quickly see the wisdom in the old saying "Two's company, three's a crowd."

Generally, however, a triad is more stable than a dyad. If the relationship between any two group members becomes strained, the third can act as a mediator to restore stability. Similarly, members of a dyad (such as a married couple) often seek out a third person (a trusted friend or counselor) to air tensions between them.

Social groups with more members are typically more secure because, even if several members lose interest, the group's existence is not directly threatened. Larger social groups also develop formal rules and regulations that stabilize their operation. Yet, larger groups inevitably lack the intense personal interaction that is possible only in the smallest groups.

Social Diversity and Group Dynamics

Race, ethnicity, and gender also affect group dynamics, especially the likelihood that members will interact with outsiders. Peter Blau (1977; Blau et al., 1982; South & Messner, 1986) points to three ways in which social diversity influences intergroup contact.

First, Blau explains, the larger a group, the more likely its members will focus their attention on one another to the exclusion of people in other groups. To illustrate, increasing the number of international students on campus may promote social diversity, but it also enables these students to maintain their own distinctive social group. For the same reason, members of large ethnic communities are more likely to marry within their group than members of small communities are (Gurak & Fitzpatrick, 1982).

Second, Blau argues that the more internally heterogeneous a group is, the more likely it is to interact with outsiders. Members of campus groups that recruit people of various social backgrounds typically have more intergroup contact than those who draw members from only one social category.

Third, Blau notes that physical boundaries promote social boundaries. To the extent that a social group is physically segregated from others (by having its own dorm or dining area, for example), its members are less likely to engage others in social interaction.

Networks

A **network** is *a web of weak social ties*. Unlike members of a social group, people linked by networks usually feel little sense of membership and interact only occasionally. The boundaries of networks are also less clear than those of groups.

Some networks approximate groups, such as those comprising college chums who maintain their friendship by mail and telephone. More commonly, however, networks involve weak ties, often including people we know of—or who know of us—but with whom we have rare contact (Granovetter, 1973). As one woman with a widespread reputation as a community organizer explains, "I get calls at home, someone says, 'Are you Roseann Navarro? Somebody told me to call you. I have this problem . . .'" (Kaminer, 1984:94).

Network ties may be weak, but they may serve as a valuable resource. Nan Lin (1981) discovered that subjects he surveyed relied primarily on networks to find their jobs. He also found that men whose fathers

FIGURE 5–2 Group Size and Relationships

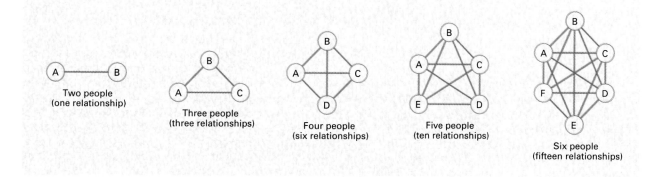

Today's college campuses value social diversity. One of the challenges of multiculturalism is ensuring that all categories of students are integrated into campus life. This is not always easy. Following Blau's theory of group dynamics, as the number of minority students increases, these individuals are able to form a group unto themselves, perhaps interacting less with others.

held important occupational positions gained the greatest advantages from networks. This finding underscores the fact that networks link people of similar social background, thereby perpetuating their social position from generation to generation.

Peter Marsden (1987) determined that the most extensive social networks are maintained by young, well-educated urbanites. The networks of men and women tend to be the same size, but women include more relatives in their networks while men count more co-workers among theirs. Women's networks, therefore, may not carry the clout that the "old-boy" networks do, although research suggests that this difference is diminishing over time (Moore, 1991, 1992).

Formal Organizations

A century ago, social life was centered in small groups of family, friends, and neighbors. Today, our lives are framed by **formal organizations,** *large, secondary groups organized to achieve specific goals.* Formal organizations such as corporations or government agencies differ from small primary groups in their impersonality and decidedly planned or formal atmosphere.

Keeping a society of more than 250 million people running smoothly is truly a remarkable feat. Countless tasks must be accomplished, ranging from educating expectant parents to delivering the mail. Most of these responsibilities are carried out by formal organizations, which develop a life and culture of their own beyond the individual members who may come and go.

Types of Formal Organizations

Amitai Etzioni (1975) has identified three organizational types based on how members are linked to an organization. *Normative organizations* pursue goals that their members consider morally worthwhile, offering personal satisfaction, perhaps social prestige, but no monetary reward. Sometimes called *voluntary associations*, these include community service groups (such as the PTA, the Lions Club, the League of Women Voters, and the Red Cross), political parties, and religious organizations. Because our society has historically excluded women from much of the paid labor force, they have traditionally played a greater part than men in civic and charitable organizations.

Coercive organizations enroll members involuntarily and subject them to punishment (a prison) or treatment (a mental hospital). Their extraordinary character is reflected in structural features such as locked doors and barred windows, as well as the presence of security personnel (Goffman, 1961). Designed to segregate inmates for a period of time, they sometimes seek to radically alter the attitudes and behavior of people confined within their walls (recall the section on resocialization in Chapter 3, "Socialization: From Infancy to Old Age").

According to Etzioni, people join *utilitarian organizations* in pursuit of income. Large business enterprises, for example, generate profits for their owners and salaries and wages for their employees. While utilitarian organizations offer greater individual freedom than coercive organizations, they provide less autonomy than normative organizations. Most people have little choice but to spend half of their waking hours at work, where they have limited control over their jobs.

From differing vantage points, a particular formal organization can fall into *all* of these categories. A mental hospital, for example, is a coercive organization to a patient, a utilitarian organization to a psychiatrist, and a normative organization to a hospital volunteer.

Although formal organization is vital to modern, industrial societies, it is far from new. Twenty-five centuries ago, the Chinese philosopher and teacher K'ung Fu-Tzu (known to Westerners as Confucius) endorsed the idea that government offices should be filled by the most talented young men. This led to what was probably the world's first system of civil service examinations. Here, would-be bureaucrats compose essays to demonstrate their knowledge of Confucian texts.

Origins of Bureaucracy

Formal organizations date back thousands of years to the religious and political administrations employed by elites to collect taxes, administer military campaigns, and construct monumental structures like the Great Wall of China and the Great Pyramids of Egypt.

The effectiveness of these early organizations was limited, however, by the traditional character of preindustrial societies. The influential German sociologist Max Weber defined **tradition** as *sentiments and beliefs about the world passed from generation to generation.*

Tradition fuels conservatism, Weber maintained, restraining the growth of formal organizations.

Weber characterized the contemporary world view as one of **rationality,** *deliberate, matter-of-fact calculation of the most efficient means to accomplish a particular task.* A rational world view is indifferent to the past and open to change in whatever way promises efficient realization of goals. Modern society, therefore, embraces formal organization.

The key to the rise of the "organizational society" is the process Weber termed **rationalization,** *the change from tradition to rationality as the dominant* *mode of human thought.* Modern society, he claimed, became "disenchanted" as sentimental ties to the past gave way to greater reliance on scientific thinking, complex technology, and the organizational structure called *bureaucracy.*

Characteristics of Bureaucracy

Bureaucracy is *an organizational model designed to perform tasks efficiently.* Bureaucratic officials formulate and modify policy to make an organization as effective as possible. To appreciate the efficiency of bureaucratic organization, consider our country's telephone system. Each of more than 160 million telephones can be used to reach any other telephone in homes, businesses, and automobiles within seconds. Of course, the telephone system depends on technological developments such as electricity and computers. But it could not operate without the organizational capacity to keep track of every telephone call—noting which phone called which other phone, when, and for how long—and presenting all this information to tens of millions of telephone users in the form of a monthly bill.

In global context, the availability of facsimile (fax) machines and other forms of electronic communication is one indicator of the extent of bureaucratic organization. As shown in Global Map 5–1, these devices are most common in the United States and Canada, Western Europe, Japan, and Australia and New Zealand. In poor nations of the world, by contrast, this equipment is limited to government officials, large businesses, and urban elites. Thus the proliferation of bureaucracy is closely tied to economic development.

What traits promote organizational efficiency? Max Weber (1978; orig. 1921) identified six elements of the ideal bureaucratic organization.

1. **Specialization.** Most of our ancestors were preoccupied with securing food and shelter. Bureaucratic societies, by contrast, assign people to highly specialized roles that correspond to organizational offices.
2. **Hierarchy of offices.** Bureaucratic offices form a hierarchy, according to their responsibilities. Each person is supervised by "higher-ups" in the organization while, in turn, supervising those in lower positions.
3. **Rules and regulations.** Bureaucratic operations are guided by rationally enacted rules and regulations. Ideally, a bureaucracy seeks to operate in a completely predictable fashion.

4. **Technical competence.** Bureaucratic officials must have the technical competence to carry out their duties. Bureaucracies typically recruit new members based on set criteria and, later, monitor their performance. Such impersonal evaluation contrasts sharply with the custom, through most of human history, of favoring relatives—whatever their talents—over strangers.
5. **Impersonality.** Bureaucracy places rules ahead of personal feelings. Ideally, offices provide uniform treatment for each client and worker. From this detached approach stems the notion of the "faceless bureaucrat."
6. **Formal, written communications.** An old adage states that the heart of bureaucracy is not people but paperwork. Rather than face-to-face talk, bureaucracy relies on formal written memos and reports, which accumulate into vast *files.* Such documents guide an organization in roughly the same way that personality guides an individual.

Bureaucracy Versus Small Groups

Members of small groups, especially primary groups like the family, value one another in a personal sense. By contrast, bureaucrats value their organization as a way to get a job done.

Bureaucratic organization promotes efficiency by carefully recruiting personnel and demanding conformity to set rules and regulations. In small, informal groups, by contrast, members have considerable discretion to respond to each other personally, without regard for rules or rank. Table 5–2 on page 116 summarizes differences between small social groups and large formal organizations.

The Informal Side of Bureaucracy

In Weber's ideal bureaucracy, officials deliberately regulate every activity. Realistically, however, organizational behavior often diverges from the rules. In some cases, innovation and informality help meet legitimate needs overlooked by regulations. In other situations, such as cutting corners in one's job, informal behavior undermines efficiency (Scott, 1981). In any case, actual operations do not always reflect bureaucratic blueprints.

Although power formally resides in offices, studies of U.S. corporations reveal that the leadership styles and skills of individuals have a tremendous impact on organizational outcomes (Halberstam, 1986). Then,

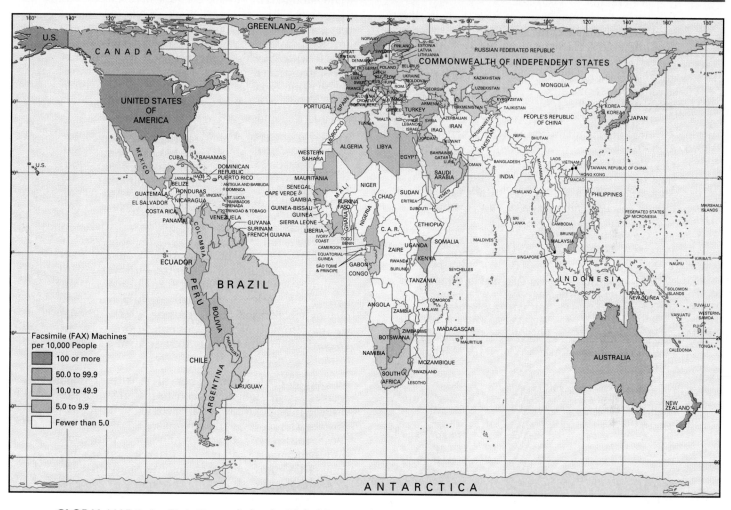

GLOBAL MAP 5–1   Data Transmission in Global Perspective

The expansion of formal organization depends partly on available technology. Facsimile (fax) machines and other devices for transmitting data are widespread in economically developed regions of the world, including the United States, Canada, Western Europe, Japan, and Australia. In poor societies, such devices are all but unknown to most people. Note, too, that the wealthy elite in small nations like Kuwait make extensive use of advanced technology to support their global business operations.

Source: *Peters Atlas of the World* (1990).

too, decision making does not always conform to a defined hierarchy and official regulations. In many organizations, people in leadership positions rely on subordinates to handle much of their own work. Many secretaries, for example, have more day-to-day responsibility than their job title and salary suggest.

Communication offers another example of organizational informality. Formally, memos and other written documents disseminate information through the chain of command. Typically, however, individuals cultivate informal networks or "grapevines" that spread information much faster, if not always accurately.

Grapevines are particularly important to subordinates because higher-ups often conceal important information from them.

Sometimes employees of formal organizations simply ignore bureaucratic structures to advance their own interests. A classic study of the Western Electric factory in Chicago revealed that few workers reported employees who violated rules, as company policy demanded (Roethlisberger & Dickson, 1939). On the contrary, those who *did* were socially isolated, labeled by other workers as untrustworthy "squealers." Although the company formally set productivity standards, workers informally created their own definition of a fair day's work, criticizing those who exceeded it as "rate-busters" and others who fell short as "chiselers." Such informal social patterns illustrate people's reluctance to accept bureaucratic rigidity.

TABLE 5–2 Small Groups and Formal Organizations: A Comparison

	Small Groups	Formal Organizations
Activities	Members typically engage in many of the same activities	Members typically engage in distinct, highly specialized activities
Hierarchy	Often informal or nonexistent	Clearly defined, corresponding to offices
Norms	Informal application of general norms	Clearly defined rules and regulations
Criteria for membership	Variable, often based on personal affection or kinship	Technical competence to carry out assigned tasks
Relationships	Variable; typically primary	Typically secondary, with selective primary ties
Communications	Typically casual and face to face	Typically formal and in writing
Focus	Person oriented	Task oriented

Limitations of Bureaucracy

Many members of our society view bureaucracy with more than a hint of ambivalence. While recognizing that formal organizations may be necessary to carry out many tasks in a vast and complex society, we are uneasy with "faceless" bureaucracy that seems indifferent to human concerns. Moreover, bureaucracy not only has the capacity to dehumanize and alienate individuals but it also poses dangers to personal privacy and political democracy.

Alienation. Max Weber touted bureaucracy as a model of productivity. Nonetheless, Weber was keenly aware of bureaucracy's potential to *dehumanize* those it purports to benefit. The impersonality that fosters efficiency, in other words, simultaneously denies officials and clients the ability to recognize each other's unique, personal needs. On the contrary, officials must treat each client impersonally as a standard "case."

The impersonal bureaucratic environment is also a source of *alienation* for organizational workers. All too often, Weber contended, formal organizations reduce the worker to "a small cog in a ceaselessly moving mechanism" (1978:988; orig. 1921). Although we may think that formal organizations serve us, Weber feared that humanity may well end up serving formal organizations.

Bureaucratic ritualism. Then there is the familiar problem of inefficiency, when formal organizations struggle to respond to special needs or circumstances. Anyone who has ever tried to replace a lost driver's license, return defective merchandise to a discount store, or change an address on a magazine subscription knows that bureaucracies sometimes can be maddeningly unresponsive.

The tedious preoccupation with organizational routines and procedures is captured in the concept of *red tape*, a term derived from the practice by eighteenth-century English administrators of using red tape to wrap official parcels and records (Shipley, 1985). Robert Merton (1968) points out that red tape constitutes a new twist in the already familiar concept of group conformity. He coined the term **bureaucratic ritualism** to designate *a preoccupation with rules and regulations to the point of thwarting an organization's goals.*

Ritualism impedes organizational performance by stifling creativity and imagination (Whyte, 1957; Merton, 1968). In doing so, it stands as another expression of the alienation that Weber feared would arise from bureaucratic rigidity.

Bureaucratic inertia. If bureaucrats are preoccupied with following the rules, they may also jealously seek to preserve their organization even when its goal has been accomplished. Weber noted that "once fully established, bureaucracy is among the social structures which are hardest to destroy" (1978:987; orig. 1921).

Bureaucratic inertia refers to *the tendency of bureaucratic organizations to perpetuate themselves.* Formal organizations, in other words, tend to take on a life of their own beyond their formal objectives. Occasionally, a formal organization that meets its goals will simply disband. More commonly, however, an organization stays in business by redefining its goals so it can continue to provide a livelihood for its members.

The National Association for Infantile Paralysis, sponsor of the well-known March of Dimes, came into being as part of the drive to find a cure for polio. Researchers accomplished this goal with the development of the Salk vaccine in the early 1950s. But, subsequently, the organization stayed in business redirecting its efforts toward other medical problems such as birth defects (Sills, 1969). It still exists today.

Bureaucracy and privacy. In the United States, more people now have more information about each and every citizen than ever before in our history. Bureaucracy may be essential to a vast and complex society, but the cost is ever-larger banks of personal information. As they issue driver's licenses, for example, government agencies gather information that they can dispatch to police or other officials at the touch of a button. Similarly, the Internal Revenue Service, the Social Security Administration, and programs that benefit veterans, students, the poor, and unemployed government agencies' people each collect extensive personal information (Long, 1967; Smith, 1979).

The U.S. Privacy Act of 1974 places limitations on government agencies' exchange of information about individuals. Additionally, the law gives people the right to examine and correct information contained in most government files. But, even as the United States seeks ways to limit bureaucratic invasion of privacy, many countries are developing new and complex systems for gathering, storing, and disseminating information about their people. The box on page 118 takes a closer look.

Bureaucratic waste and incompetence. "Work expands to fill the time available for its completion." Enough truth underlies C. Northcote Parkinson's (1957) tongue-in-cheek assertion that it is known today as Parkinson's Law.

To illustrate, assume that a bureaucrat processes fifty passport applications in an average day. If one

According to Max Weber, bureaucracy is an organizational strategy that promotes efficiency. Impersonality, however, also fosters alienation among employees, who may become indifferent to the formal goals of the organization. The behavior of this municipal employee in Bombay, India, is understandable to members of formal organizations almost anywhere in the world.

day this worker had only twenty-five applications to examine, how long would the task take? The logical answer is half a day; but Parkinson's Law suggests that if a full day is available to complete the work, a full day is how long it will take. After all, few members of formal organizations are going to seek out extra work to fill their spare time. What they do is try to appear busy, which only prompts organizations to take on more employees. The time and expense required to hire, train, supervise, and evaluate a larger staff makes everyone busier still, setting in motion the vicious cycle we call *bureaucratic bloat.* Ironically, the larger organization may accomplish no more real work than it did before.

Laurence J. Peter (Peter & Hull, 1969) devised the Peter Principle, which states that *bureaucrats are promoted to their level of incompetence.* The logic here is simple: Employees competent at one level of the organizational hierarchy are likely to advance to higher positions. Eventually, however, they reach a position

When Organizations Intrude: A Threat to Personal Privacy?

Thailand

Thailand's government will soon require all adults to carry an official identification card, which bears a photograph and a string of computer language. This card, inserted in a computer terminal, will provide a complete social profile of the individual, including physical description, fingerprints, home address, names of parents and children, marital status, education, job, income, religion, and police record.

Is this simply using advanced technology to assist officials in doing their jobs, as the Thai government claims? Or, as critics warn, is it a giant step toward giving "Big Brother" unprecedented information about citizens?

Expanding government bureaucracies coupled with sophisticated computer technology (much of which is supplied by U.S.

corporations) represents a growing threat to personal freedom in many nations of the world. Several countries—including Indonesia and the Philippines—are closely watching the Thai program unfold as they consider similar systems of their own.

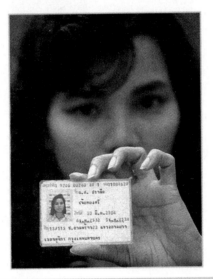

In other parts of the world, government agencies utilizing computer technology are also subjecting people to unprecedented scrutiny. Israel, for example, has long used such a system to monitor Palestinians living in occupied lands. And South Africa has also maintained technological surveillance over its black majority.

The danger of losing personal privacy is especially great in societies where certain categories of people suffer from social disadvantages and have few political rights to begin with. But the problem of declining privacy is growing everywhere as bureaucracy expands and new technology is developed that allows governments to more efficiently monitor people's lives.

Sources: Smith (1979), Dunn (1991), and Miller (1991).

---

where they are in over their heads, and they become ineligible for further promotion. This dooms them to a future of inefficiency, although they probably will avoid demotion or dismissal by hiding behind rules and regulations, taking credit for work actually performed by their more competent subordinates, or by building up a network of well-connected allies.

Oligarchy

Robert Michels (1876–1936) observed that bureaucracy fosters **oligarchy,** *the rule of the many by the few* (1949; orig. 1911). According to what Michels called "the iron law of oligarchy," the pyramid-like structure of bureaucracy places a few leaders in charge of entire government organizations.

Bureaucracy's strict hierarchy may promote efficiency, then, but it also discourages democracy. Moreover, organizational officials can—and often do—use their access to information and the media to promote their personal interests. Oligarchy, then, thrives in the hierarchical structure of bureaucracy and undermines people's confidence in their elected leaders.

Political competition and checks and balances in our country's government prevent the flagrant oligarchy found in some societies. Even here, incumbents generally enjoy enormous advantages of power and funding over challengers. But in the 1994 elections—a year the public was determined to "throw the bums out"—most incumbents who were Democrats (the party that had previously controlled Congress) were defeated by their challengers.

George Tooker's (1920–) painting *Government Bureau* is a powerful statement about the human costs of bureaucracy. The artist depicts members of the public in monotonous similitude—reduced from human beings to mere "cases" to be disposed of as quickly as possible. Set apart from others by their positions, officials are "faceless bureaucrats" concerned more with numbers (notice their hands on calculators) than with providing genuine assistance.

George Tooker, *Government Bureau*, 1956, Egg tempera on gesso panel. 19⅝ x 29⅝ inches. The Metropolitan Museum of Art, George A. Hearn Fund, 1956 (56, 78).

Gender and Race in Organizations

Rosabeth Moss Kanter (1977; Kanter & Stein, 1979) has shown that gender and race play an important part in organizational structure. In most organizations, a dominant category of people (usually white men) operates as an ingroup enjoying greater acceptance, credibility, and access to social networks. By contrast, women and minorities often feel like members of socially isolated outgroups. They may feel uncomfortably visible and think that they must work twice as hard as those in dominant categories in order to maintain their present standing, let alone advance to a higher position.

As Figure 5–3 on page 120 shows, white men in the United States represent about 42 percent of the U.S. population between the ages of twenty and sixty-five but hold two-thirds of management jobs. White women, a category of comparable size, trail with about 25 percent of managerial positions. The members of various minorities lag still further behind, even taking into account their smaller proportions in the overall population.

According to Kanter, organizations must offer everyone a fair chance for promotion in order to turn employees into "fast-trackers" committed to the organization. "Dead-end" jobs, she adds, produce only "zombies" with little aspiration or loyalty.

Kanter notes, too, that managers who enjoy both responsibility and opportunity become flexible leaders who build the morale of subordinates. People who

have little power, by contrast, often jealously guard what privileges they do have and rigidly supervise subordinates. Thus Kanter concludes that organizations must "humanize" their structure to bring out the best in their workers and improve the "bottom line."

Humanizing Organizations

"Humanizing" an organization refers to efforts to develop its human resources. Research by Rosabeth Kanter (1977, 1983, 1989; Kanter & Stein, 1980; cf. Peters & Waterman, Jr., 1982) shows that humanizing organizations produces both happier employees and healthier profits. Based on the discussion so far, we can identify three paths to more humane organizations:

1. **Social inclusiveness.** The performance of all employees will improve to the extent that no one is subject to social exclusion because of gender, race, or ethnicity.

2. **Sharing of responsibilities.** Humanizing organizations means relaxing rigid hierarchy. Spreading power and responsibility more widely encourages all employees to think creatively, increasing organizational effectiveness.

3. **Expanding opportunities for advancement.** Reducing the number of employees stuck in dead-end jobs encourages workers to perform better, to share ideas, and to try new approaches.

No position should be ruled out as the start of an upward career path.

Critical evaluation. Perhaps rigid formality made sense in the past, when organizations utilized uneducated workers simply as a source of physical labor. But today, Kanter suggests, employees will contribute a wealth of ideas to bolster efficiency if the organization rewards innovation.

Any plan to redistribute power is likely to be controversial. But, compared to rigidly bureaucratic companies, Kanter found that more flexible organizations are more profitable. She argues, therefore, that any organization's success depends on treating employees not as a group to be controlled but as a resource to be developed.

Organizational Environment

How organizations operate depends not just on their internal structure but on the organization's external environment, including available technology, economic and political systems, the available work force, and the presence of other organizations.

For example, modern organizations depend on the technology of telephone systems, fax machines, copiers, and computers. Today's organizations are also changing as the proliferation of personal computers gives employees access to more information than ever before and also allows executives to monitor the activities of workers (Markoff, 1991).

Similarly, economic and political trends may have dramatic consequences for the operation of an organization. All organizations are buoyed or burdened by periodic economic growth and recession, and many industries now face a host of new environmental standards (Pennings, 1982). The average age, typical education, and social diversity of a surrounding community shape both the available work force and the market for an organization's products or services. Finally, other organizations also contribute to the organizational environment. People who operate a hospital, for example, must contend not only with new government policies, but also with the insurance industry and organizations representing doctors, nurses, and other workers. And to remain competitive a hospital must keep abreast of the equipment, procedures, and prices at other, nearby medical facilities.

In sum, no organization operates in a social vacuum. But, just as formal organizations are shaped by their environment, they also influence society, as we shall now explain.

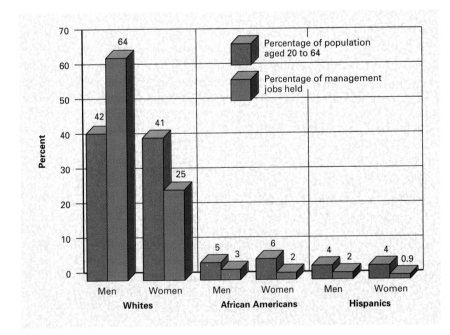

FIGURE 5–3
U.S. Managers by Race, Sex, and Ethnicity, 1993

Sources: U.S. Equal Employment Opportunity Commission (1993) and U.S. Bureau of the Census (1994).

The McDonaldization of Society[1]

This chapter began by noting the extraordinary success of the McDonald corporation. From its takeoff in the mid-1950s, there are now almost fifteen thousand McDonald's restaurants in the United States and around the world.

But the effect of McDonald's extends far beyond the sale of billions of hamburgers; our entire way of life is becoming "McDonaldized." This is an awkward way of saying that many other aspects of life are organized in ways that resemble the famous restaurant chain. Parents buy toys at worldwide chain stores like Toys-R-Us; we drive in to Jiffy Lube for a ten-minute oil change; communication is sliding more and more toward voice mail over the telephone, e-mail via computer, and junk mail in the box; more vacations take the form of packaged resorts and tours; television presents news in the form of ten-second sound bites; college admission officers size up students they have never met by glancing over their SAT and GPA scores; and professors assign ghost-written textbooks[2] and evaluate students with tests mass-produced for them by publishing companies. The list goes on and on.

Basic principles. What do all these developments have in common? According to George Ritzer, the "McDonaldization of society" involves four basic organizational principles.

1. **Efficiency.** Ray Kroc, the marketing genius behind the expansion of McDonald's, set out with the goal of serving a hamburger, french fries, and milkshake to a customer in fifty seconds. Today, one of the company's most popular items is the Egg McMuffin, an entire breakfast in a single sandwich. In the restaurant, customers bus their own trays or, better still, drive away from the pick-up window taking their trash and whatever mess they make with them. Almost everyone praises such efficiency. We tend to think that anything done quickly and cleanly is, for that reason alone, good.

2. **Calculability.** The first McDonald's operating manual declared the weight of a regular raw hamburger to be 1.6 ounces, its size to be 3.875

The "McDonaldization" of the United States has not only changed the way companies do business, it is also sparking new collaborative efforts among diverse business sectors. In Westchester, Illinois, Burger King and Amoco opened the nation's first fast-food gas station, where customers can gas up as they fill their own tank.

inches across, and its fat content to be 19 percent. A slice of cheese weighs exactly half an ounce, and french fries are cut precisely 9/32 inch thick. Think about how many objects around the home, the workplace, or the campus are mass produced uniformly in this way. Not just our environment but our life experiences—from traveling the nation's interstates to sitting at home viewing television—are now more deliberately planned than ever before.

3. **Predictability.** An individual can walk into a McDonald's restaurant anywhere in the world and receive the same sandwiches, drinks, and desserts prepared in precisely the same way. Such predictability results from a highly rational system that specifies every action and leaves nothing to chance.

4. **Control through automation.** The most unreliable element in the McDonald's system is human beings. To eliminate, as much as possible, the unpredictable human element, McDonald's has automated its equipment to cook food at fixed temperatures for set lengths of time. Even the cash register at a McDonald's restaurant is little more than pictures of the items to minimize the responsibility of the human being taking the customer's order.

---

[1]The material in this entire section is drawn from George Ritzer's (1993) book of the same name.

[2]More than half a dozen popular sociology texts were not authored by the person or persons whose names appear on the cover. This book is not one of them.

The scope of McDonaldization has expanded greatly in the United States. Highly automated bakeries now produce bread with scarcely any human intervention, just as chickens emerge from automated hatcheries. In supermarkets, scanners now are replacing human checkers. Most of this country's shopping now occurs in malls, in which everything from temperature and humidity to the kinds of stores and products is subject to continuous control and supervision.

Irrational rationality? There can be no argument about the popularity of McDonald's. Yet, as the rational McDonald's system spreads into other areas of social life, we need to recognize that there is a darker side to the story.

Max Weber observed the increasing rationalization of the world with alarm, fearing that formal organizations would overwhelm human creativity and crush the human spirit. As he saw it, rational systems exact a terrible price for their efficiency—*dehumanization*. Each of the four principles noted above depends on lessening the role of human creativity, discretion, and autonomy. Moreover, there is considerable evidence that McDonald's food is not particularly good for people or the natural environment. George Ritzer echoes Weber by asserting that "the ultimate irrationality of McDonaldization is that people could lose control over the system and it would come to control us" (1993:145).

Japanese Organizations

Not all types of formal organization are as impersonal as those found in the United States. Formal organizations in Japan, a small nation with a remarkable record of economic accomplishment, thrive in a distinctive organizational environment: a culture rooted in strong collective identity and solidarity.

While most members of our society prize rugged individualism, the Japanese cherish traditions of cooperation. This cohesiveness yields relatively low levels of social problems—such as alcoholism, violence, and drug abuse—compared to more rootless and competitive societies like the United States (Ouchi, 1981).

Japan's social solidarity makes formal organizations there remarkably personal, rather like extremely large primary groups. In the United States, by comparison, most companies cultivate secondary relationships. Indeed, as the box suggests, U.S. workers often oppose the highly personal way Japanese companies operate.

William Ouchi (1981) highlights five distinctions between formal organizations in Japan and their U.S. counterparts.

1. **Hiring and advancement.** U.S. organizations hold out promotions and higher salaries as prizes won through individual competition. In Japan, however, organizations hire new school graduates as a group and assign them comparable salaries and responsibilities. Only after several years is anyone likely to be singled out for special advancement. This policy generates a common identity, or team spirit, among employees of the same age.

2. **Lifetime security.** U.S. employees rarely remain with one company for their entire careers; U.S. companies are also quick to lay off employees in the face of economic setbacks. By contrast, Japanese corporations typically hire workers for life, so companies and their employees have strong, mutual loyalties.

3. **Holistic involvement.** While we tend to keep business and personal life distinct, the Japanese expect organizations to play a broad role in their lives. Companies may provide dormitory housing or offer mortgages for the purchase of homes, and sponsor a wide range of social events in which workers participate. Employee interaction beyond the workplace strengthens collective identity and offers respectful Japanese workers a chance to voice suggestions and criticisms in more casual settings.

4. **Nonspecialized training.** U.S. workers are highly specialized. But a Japanese employee learns all phases of organizational operation. Ideally, such general training helps workers understand how each job relates to the organization's overall operation.

5. **Collective decision making.** Typically, a handful of U.S. executives makes key decisions. Japanese executives, by contrast, give workers a say in decisions that affect them. This sense of cooperation is reinforced by the relatively small salary differential between Japanese executives and lower-level workers. Also, Japanese "quality circles" afford all Japanese employees a chance to participate in the company's day-to-day operations.

The Japanese Model: Will It Work Over Here?

What the company wants is for us to work like the Japanese. Everybody go out and do jumping jacks in the morning and kiss each other when they go home at night. You work as a team, rat on each other, and lose control of your destiny. That's not going to work in this country.

John Brodie
President, United Paperworkers
Local 448
Chester, Pennsylvania

Competition from Japan is forcing companies in the United States to reconsider long-held notions about corporate operations, from the assembly line right up to the board room. Moreover, Japanese "transplant organizations"—manufacturing plants built in this country by Honda, Nissan, and Toyota—achieve the same degree of efficiency and quality that have won these companies praise in Japan. Yet some workers, union leaders, and managers are speaking as bitterly about transplanting Japanese organizational techniques as they are about importing Japanese cars.

Many U.S. workers dislike the notion of worker participation, which they see as increasing their workload. While still responsible for building cars, for instance, workers are now asked to worry about quality control, unit costs, and overall company efficiency— tasks traditionally shouldered by management. Moreover, some employees do not want to move from job to job, since learning new skills is demanding and sometimes threatening. Many union leaders

To a large extent, organizational life reflects the surrounding culture. But, stirred by the economic power of Japanese corporations, more and more workers in the United States are employing some of Japan's organizational techniques, such as quality control groups. However, few experts think that organizational patterns can be easily transplanted from one society to another.

are also suspicious of any plans formulated by management, even those purporting to share power. Some managers, too, oppose worker participation programs since sharing power does not come easily to executives who are accustomed to top-down decision-making practices. Finally, U.S. corporations have a short-term outlook on profits, which discourages investing time and money in organizational restructuring.

Nonetheless, a recent government survey found that 70 percent of large U.S. businesses had initiated at least some reorganization along these lines. The advantages go right to the bottom line, since profits are usually higher when workers have a say in decision making. And most employees in worker-participation programs—even those who may not want to sign up for morning jumping jacks— seem significantly happier about their jobs. Workers who have long used only their bodies are now enjoying the opportunity to use their brains as well.

Sources: Hoerr (1989) and Florida & Kenney (1991).

Taken together, these traits generate a strong measure of organizational loyalty. The cultural emphasis on *individual* achievement in the United States thus finds its parallel in the value the Japanese place on success by the *group*. Workers tie their personal futures to those of the organization, and the company, in turn, places a high value on meeting employee needs.

Groups and Organizations in Global Perspective

In recent years, the emphasis in the study of formal organizations has shifted from the organizations themselves to the environment in which they operate. In part, this change stems from the recognition that, although Max Weber depicted bureaucracy as a singular form, actual organizations developed quite differently in various world regions.

In Europe and the United States, most businesses began as small family enterprises. But as Western societies became "rationalized" by the Industrial Revolution, people came to define nepotism (favoritism shown to a family member) or other primary relationships as barriers to organizational efficiency.

The development of formal organizations in Japan, meanwhile, followed a different route. Historically, that very cohesive society was built on family-based loyalties. As Japan industrialized, people there found no threat to efficiency in primary relationships, as Westerners did. On the contrary, the Japanese modeled their large businesses on the family and, as that nation modernized, they transferred some of their traditional family loyalty to corporations. Even though Japanese workers are now becoming more individualistic, the Japanese model still demonstrates that organizational life need not be impersonal.

Beyond Japan, organizations throughout the world are taking on particular forms based on distinctive environments. Businesses in Poland are gaining vitality as that country opens to global trade. European nations are engaged in forming a new multinational economic system. In the former Soviet Union and nations of Eastern Europe, associations of all kinds are coming out from under rigid political control for the first time in three-quarters of a century. In many respects, each of these developments will affect the shape of organizations in these regions.

As some analysts point out, organizations in our society are still the envy of the world for their efficiency; after all, where on earth does the mail arrive as quickly and dependably as in the United States (Wilson, 1991)? But global diversity and change call for us to be wary of any "absolute truths" about formal organizations and, just as important, to explore new possibilities for reorganizing our future.

SUMMARY

1. Social groups are important building blocks of society, fostering common identity among members.

2. Primary groups are small and person-oriented; secondary groups are typically large and goal-oriented.

3. Instrumental leaders are concerned with a group's goals; expressive leaders focus on the collective well-being of members.

4. Because group members often seek consensus, groups may pressure members toward conformity.

5. Individuals use reference groups—both in-groups and outgroups—to guide decisions and evaluations.

6. Georg Simmel argued that dyads have a distinctive intensity, but lack stability because of the effort necessary to maintain them. A triad can easily dissolve into a dyad by excluding one member.

7. Peter Blau explains that group size, homogeneity, and physical segregation each affect group behavior.

8. Social networks are group-like relational webs linking people with little common identity and limited interaction.

9. Formal organizations are large, secondary groups that try to perform complex tasks efficiently. Depending on their members' reasons for joining, formal organizations are considered normative, coercive, or utilitarian.

10. Bureaucratic organization, which expands in modern societies, is based on specialization, hierarchy, rules and regulations, technical competence, impersonal interaction, and formal, written communications.

11. Ideal bureaucracy may promote efficiency, but bureaucracy also generates alienation, tends to perpetuate itself, and contributes to the contemporary erosion of privacy.

12. Formal organization promotes oligarchy. Moreover, the concentration of power and opportunity in organizations can compromise organizational effectiveness.

13. Humanizing bureaucracy means recognizing people as an organization's greatest resource. To develop human resources, responsibility and opportunity should be made available to everyone.

14. Organizations operate not only according to their internal structures but also based on their external environments, responding to technological, economic, and political factors.

15. Formal organizations in Japan differ from the Western, bureaucratic model because of the collective spirit of Japanese culture.

KEY CONCEPTS

bureaucracy an organizational model designed to perform tasks efficiently

bureaucratic inertia the tendency of bureaucratic organizations to perpetuate themselves

bureaucratic ritualism a preoccupation with rules and regulations to the point of obstructing organizational goals

dyad a social group with two members

expressive leaders group leaders who emphasize collective well-being

formal organization a large secondary group that is organized to achieve specific goals

groupthink group conformity that limits understanding of an issue

ingroup an esteemed social group commanding a member's loyalty

instrumental leaders group leaders who emphasize the completion of tasks

network a web of weak social ties

oligarchy the rule of the many by the few

outgroup a scorned social group toward which one feels competition or opposition

primary group a small social group in which relationships are personal and enduring

rationality deliberate, matter-of-fact calculation of the most efficient means to accomplish any particular task

rationalization Max Weber's term for the change from tradition to rationality as the dominant mode of human thought

reference group a social group that serves as a point of reference for making evaluations and decisions

secondary group a large and impersonal social group based on some special interest or activity

social group two or more people who identify and interact with one another

tradition sentiments and beliefs about the world that are passed from generation to generation

triad a social group with three members

CRITICAL-THINKING QUESTIONS

1. What are the key differences between primary and secondary groups? Identify examples of each in daily life.

2. What are some of the positive functions of group conformity? Note several dysfunctions.

3. What does the "McDonaldization of society" mean? Cite familiar examples of this trend beyond those discussed in this chapter.

4. How do Japanese organizations differ from those common to the United States? What are several strengths and weaknesses of U.S. organizations in relation to their Japanese counterparts?

Deviance

Sirens sliced through the night as police cruisers joined in angry pursuit of the 1988 Hyundai speeding through a suburban Los Angeles neighborhood. As the black-and-white cars closed in, a helicopter chattered overhead, its powerful floodlight bathing the scene in a shimmering brilliance.

Twenty-five-year-old Rodney Glen King, the lone occupant of the Hyundai, brought his car to a halt, opened his door, and stumbled into the street. In an instant, police surrounded him, and a sergeant lunged forward, staggering King with the discharge of a 50,000-volt Taser stun gun. As eleven police officers looked on, three others took turns kicking King and striking him with their clubs as he tried to protect himself. By the time the beating ended, King had sustained a crushed cheekbone, a broken ankle, damage to his skull, a burn on his chest, and internal injuries.

The capture and beating of an unemployed construction worker by the police might have attracted little notice except for the extraordinary coincidence that a resident of a nearby apartment building had observed the event—through the eyepiece of his video camera. In a matter of hours, the violent confrontation was being replayed on television screens across the United States.

The King incident touched off a firestorm of public debate over the operation of police departments in Los Angeles and elsewhere. To some critics, the scene was all too familiar: an African-American man being brutalized by white police. The acquittal of the four officers—on charges of assault with a deadly weapon and use of excessive force—sparked several days of rioting in Los Angeles in which fifty-three people died. Subsequently, a federal prosecution charging that the officers had violated King's civil rights brought convictions for two of them.

Even as the furor over the incident subsided—and King won a multi-million dollar settlement from the city—many people maintain that poor people, and especially minorities, find little justice in our legal system. Others wonder if we ask the impossible of police who try to hold back a rising tide of crime and drug abuse in cities wracked by poverty. Routinely risking personal harm for relatively low pay, police officers often see themselves embroiled in a literal war on crime, in which atrocities are committed by people on both sides.

Every society struggles to establish and enforce standards of justice, to reward people who play by the rules, and to punish those who do not conform. But, as the Rodney King incident demonstrates, the line that separates good from evil is no simple matter of black and white. This chapter investigates many of the questions that underlie this case: How do societies both create and try to control crime? Why are some people more likely than others to be charged with offenses? And what are the legitimate purposes of the criminal justice system? We shall begin by defining several basic concepts.

What is Deviance?

Deviance is *the recognized violation of cultural norms.* Norms guide virtually all human activities, so the concept of deviance is also quite broad. One distinctive category of deviance is **crime,** *the violation of norms formally enacted into criminal law.* Even criminal deviance spans a wide range, from minor traffic violations to serious offenses such as rape and murder.

Not all deviance has to do with action or even choice. In some settings, minorities can feel deviant simply for *existing.* Similarly, being unusually tall or short, or grossly fat or exceedingly thin, or having a physical disability may brand a person as deviant. In addition, many people consider the poor to be disreputable to the extent that they do not measure up to middle-class standards.

Most examples of nonconformity that come readily to mind—such as stealing—involve *negative* definitions. However, since we all have shortcomings, we often define especially righteous people—those who never raise their voices or who enthusiastically pay their taxes—as deviant, even if we accord them a measure of respect (Huls, 1987). Whether negative or positive, then, deviance is matter of *difference,* leading us to react to people as "outsiders" (Becker, 1966).

All of us are subject to **social control,** *attempts by society to regulate the thought and behavior of individuals.* Like deviance itself, social control takes many forms. Socialization, the focus of Chapter 3, amounts to a lifelong process of social control in which family, peer groups, and the mass media influence people's attitudes and actions. A more complex and formal type of social control is the **criminal justice system,** *the lawful response to alleged crimes using police, courts, and state-sanctioned punishment.*

A society exerts social control by responding positively to conformity—including praise from parents, high grades in school, and positive recognition from people in the community—and reacting negatively to deviance—ranging from personal criticism to legal prosecution. Both positive reinforcement for socially accepted actions and fear of incurring society's wrath promote conformity to conventional patterns of thought and behavior.

The Biological Context

How do people come to be conformists or deviants in the first place? As noted in Chapter 3 ("Socialization: From Infancy to Old Age"), most people a century ago understood behavior as the product of biological instincts. Not surprisingly, then, early investigations of criminality focused on biological causes.

Born criminals? In 1876 Caesare Lombroso (1835–1909), an Italian physician who worked in prisons, asserted that criminals were physically distinctive, rather ape-like people, with low foreheads, prominent jaws and cheekbones, protruding ears, and lots of body hair. In essence, Lombroso depicted criminals as evolutionary throwbacks to lower forms of life.

But Lombroso failed to recognize that his "criminal" traits also existed in the population as a whole. British psychiatrist Charles Buckman Goring (1870–1919) and others probed the matter more carefully, comparing thousands of convicts and noncriminals, but produced no evidence of any physical differences distinguishing criminals from noncriminals of the kind noted by Lombroso (Goring, 1972; orig. 1913).

Research on body structure. William Sheldon (1949) contended that a person's physical build plays a role in criminality. He described three general body types: *ectomorphs,* who are tall, thin, and fragile; *endomorphs,* who are short and fat; and *mesomorphs,* people both muscular and athletic. Analyzing the body structure and criminal history of hundreds of young men, Sheldon reported a correlation between criminality and the mesomorphic body type. Criminality, according to Sheldon, was linked to a muscular, athletic build.

The kind of deviance people create reflects the moral values they embrace. The Berkeley campus of the University of California has long celebrated its open-minded tolerance of sexual diversity. Thus, in 1992, when Andrew Martinez decided to attend classes wearing virtually nothing, people were reluctant to accuse "The Naked Guy" of immoral conduct. However, in Berkeley's politically correct atmosphere, it was not long before school officials banned Martinez from campus—charging that his nudity constituted a form of sexual harassment.

Eleanor and Sheldon Glueck (1950) agreed. The Gluecks cautioned, however, that mesomorphic body structure is not necessarily a *cause* of criminality. Parents, they suggested, treat powerfully built males with greater emotional distance so that they, in turn, grow up to display less sensitivity toward others. Moreover, if people expect muscular, athletic boys to act like bullies, they may treat them accordingly, thereby prompting aggressive behavior in a self-fulfilling prophecy.

Genetic research. To date, there exists no conclusive evidence that criminality results from any simple genetic flaw (Hook, 1973; Vold & Bernard, 1986; Suzuki

& Knudtson, 1989). More likely, overall genetic composition, in combination with social influences, accounts for significant variation in criminality (Rowe, 1983; Rowe & Osgood, 1984; Wilson & Herrnstein, 1985; Jencks, 1987).

Sociobiologists (see Chapter 2, "Culture") suspect that certain deviant behavior can be traced to biology. For example, males engage in far more violence than females do, and parents are more likely to abuse disabled or foster children than healthy or natural children (Daly & Wilson, 1988).

Critical evaluation. Biological theories that explain crime in terms of specific physical traits of individuals, even if they are true, can explain only a small proportion of all crimes. Recent sociobiological research is intriguing but, at this point, we know too little about the links between genes and human behavior to draw any firm conclusions.

Besides, an individualistic biological approach cannot address the issue of how some kinds of behaviors come to be defined as deviant in the first place. Therefore, although there remains much to be learned about how human biology may affect behavior, research in the field of deviance currently places far greater emphasis on social influences (Gibbons & Krohn, 1986; Liska, 1991).

Personality Factors

Like biological theories, psychological explanations of deviance spotlight cases of *individual* abnormalities, this time involving personality. Some personality traits are hereditary, but psychologists view temperament as mostly the result of socialization. Psychologists treat deviance as the result of "unsuccessful" socialization.

Walter Reckless and Simon Dinitz (1967) hypothesized that boys who develop a negative self-image and who lack strong moral standards would be unable to contain delinquent urges. Reckless and Dinitz tested their "containment theory" by interviewing boys about twelve years of age, and asking teachers to assess the likelihood that each one would engage in delinquent behavior. The researchers discovered that the "good boys" shared a strong conscience (or superego, in Sigmund Freud's terminology), generally coped well with frustration, and identified positively with cultural norms and values. The "bad boys" had a weaker conscience, displayed a lower tolerance for frustration, and thought less of themselves. Tracking the boys over a four-year period, Reckless and Dinitz confirmed that the "good boys" experienced fewer run-ins with the police than the "bad boys." Since all the boys lived in neighborhoods known for delinquency, the researchers concluded that boys who stayed out of trouble had personalities that acted as an "internal buffer" against the forces leading to norm violation (Reckless, 1970:401).

Critical evaluation. Psychological research has demonstrated that personality patterns bear some connection to deviance. However, the value of this approach is limited by the fact that the vast majority of people who commit serious crimes are psychologically *normal.*

Both biological and psychological approaches fall short by considering deviance as an individual attribute without exploring how conceptions of right and wrong arise, why people define only some rule-breaking as deviant, and the role of power in shaping a society's system of social control. We now turn to these issues by presenting sociological explanations of deviance.

The Social Foundations of Deviance

Although we tend to view deviance in terms of the free choice or personal failings of individuals, all behavior—deviance as well as conformity—is guided by society. Three *social* foundations of deviance, identified below, are explored in detail later in this chapter.

1. **Deviance exists only in relation to cultural norms.** No thought or action is inherently deviant; it becomes so only when judged against particular norms. Texans, for example, can legally consume alcohol in a car, a practice outlawed in most other states. Gambling is a focal activity in Atlantic City, New Jersey, Las Vegas, Nevada, on Mississippi riverboats, and on a few Indian reservations elsewhere. Such activity is illegal everywhere else in the United States. Further, most cities and towns have at least one unique statute: Only in Seattle, for example, is a person suffering from the flu subject to arrest simply for appearing in public.

    In global context, deviance is even more diverse. Albania outlaws any public display of religious faith, such as "crossing" oneself; Cuba can prosecute its citizens for "consorting with foreigners"; police can arrest people in Singapore for selling chewing gum; U.S. citizens risk arrest by their own government for traveling to Libya or Iraq.

2. **People become deviant as others define them that way.** Each of us violates cultural norms, perhaps even to the extent of breaking the law.

For example, most of us have at some time walked around talking to ourselves or "borrowed" supplies, such as pens or paper, from the workplace. Whether such actions are sufficient to define us as mentally ill or criminal depends on how others perceive, define, and respond to any given situation.

3. **Both norms and the way people define situations involve social power.** Karl Marx viewed norms, and especially law, as a strategy by which powerful people protect their interests. A homeless person who stands on a street corner denouncing the government risks arrest for disturbing the peace; a presidential candidate doing the same thing during an election campaign receives extensive police protection. In short, norms and their application are linked to social inequality.

The Functions of Deviance: Structural-Functional Analysis

The key insight of the structural-functional paradigm is that deviance is a necessary element of society. This point was made a century ago by Emile Durkheim.

Durkheim's Basic Insight

In a pioneering study of deviance, Emile Durkheim (1964a, orig. 1895; 1964b, orig. 1893) recognized that there is nothing abnormal about deviance, since it performs four essential functions.

1. **Deviance affirms cultural values and norms.** Culture involves moral choices: People must prefer some attitudes and behaviors to others. Conceptions of "right" can exist only in relation to corresponding conceptions of "wrong." Just as there can be no righteousness without evil, there can be no justice without crime. Deviance, in short, is indispensable to the process of generating and sustaining morality.

2. **Responding to deviance clarifies moral boundaries.** By defining people as deviant, a society draws the boundary between right and wrong. For example, a college marks the line between academic honesty and cheating by taking disciplinary action against those who commit plagiarism.

Artists have an important function in any society: to explore alternatives to conventional notions about how to live. For this reason, while we celebrate artists' creativity, we also accord them a mildly deviant identity. Governments display this same ambivalence toward the artistic community, encouraging work that promotes patriotism but suppressing work that challenges conventional morality. When city officials in Cincinnati moved to block the display of photographs by the controversial photographer Robert Mapplethorpe, artists marched in outspoken defense of their freedom of expression.

3. **Responding to deviance promotes social unity.** People typically react to serious deviance with collective outrage. In doing so, Durkheim explained, they reaffirm the moral ties that bind them. For example, most members of our society joined together in condemning Susan Smith's apparent murder of her two young children in 1994.

4. **Deviance encourages social change.** Deviant people, claimed Durkheim, suggest alternatives to the status quo and help bring about change. Today's deviance, he noted, may well become tomorrow's morality (1964a:71).

For these four reasons, Durkheim concluded, deviance is a vital dimension of social organization. From the structural-functional perspective, then, there is nothing abnormal about deviance.

Merton's Strain Theory

While some deviance is inevitable in society, Robert Merton (1938, 1968) argues that certain social arrangements generate excessive norm violation. Merton's theory focuses on our society's *goals* (such as financial success) and the *means* (including education and hard work) available to achieve them. The essence of conformity lies in pursuing conventional goals by approved means.

But not everyone seeking conventional success has the opportunity to achieve it. Young people raised in poor inner-city neighborhoods, for example, may see little hope of becoming successful if they "play by the rules." As a result, they may pursue wealth through crime—say, by dealing cocaine. Such deviance, then, results from "strain" between our society's pronounced emphasis on material success and the limited opportunity it provides to become successful. Merton called this type of deviance *innovation*—the attempt to achieve a culturally approved goal (wealth) by unconventional means (drug sales). Figure 6–1 shows that innovators accept the goal of success but reject conventional means of becoming rich.

The inability to become successful by normative means may also prompt another type of deviance that Merton calls *ritualism* (see Figure 6–1). Ritualists resolve the strain of falling short of cultural goals by abandoning them in favor of almost compulsive efforts to live "respectably." In essence, they embrace the rules to the point that they lose sight of goals entirely. Lower-level bureaucrats, Merton notes, often succumb to ritualism as a way of gaining respectability.

A third type of deviance in our society is *retreatism*—a failure to succeed that results from rejecting both socially approved goals and normative means of success. Retreatists are society's dropouts. They include some alcoholics and drug addicts, and some of the street people found in U.S. cities. The deviance of retreatists lies in unconventional living and, perhaps more seriously, accepting this situation.

The fourth response to failure is *rebellion*. Like retreatists, rebels reject both the cultural definition of success and the normative means of achieving it. Rebels, however, go further by advocating radical alternatives to the existing social order. Whether they express their unconventional vision in political or religious language, rebels withdraw from society entirely, immersing themselves in a deviant counterculture.

Deviant Subcultures

Richard Cloward and Lloyd Ohlin (1966) extended Merton's theory in their investigation of delinquent youth. They maintain that criminal deviance results not simply from limited legitimate opportunity but also from readily accessible illegitimate opportunity. In other words, they explain deviance and conformity in terms of the *relative opportunity structure* young people face in their lives.

The life of Al Capone, a notorious gangster of the Prohibition era (which ran from 1920 to 1933), illustrates this concept. As a poor immigrant, Capone found few legitimate paths to success, such as a college education. Yet his world did provide illegitimate opportunity for success as a bootlegger. Where relative opportunity favors what Merton might call "organized innovation," Cloward and Ohlin predict the development of *criminal subcultures*. These subcultures confer knowledge, skills, and other resources people need to succeed in unconventional ways.

But, especially in poor neighborhoods, even illegal opportunity may be scarce. Here, delinquency is likely to surface in the form of *conflict subcultures* where violence explodes as an expression of frustration and a desire for respect. Alternatively, those who fail to achieve success, even by criminal means, may embrace

FIGURE 6–1   Merton's Strain Theory of Deviance
Source: Merton (1968).

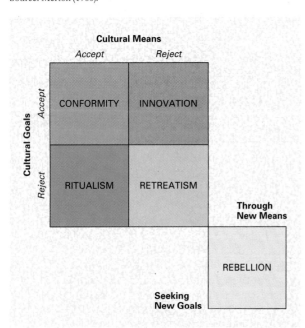

retreatist subcultures that advocate dropping out through abuse of alcohol or other drugs.

Albert Cohen (1971) asserts that criminality is most pronounced among lower-class youths because society offers them little opportunity to achieve success in conventional ways. With little access to wealth and all its trappings, these young people stake their self-respect on forging a deviant subculture that "defines as meritorious the characteristics [these youths] *do* possess, the kinds of conduct of which they *are* capable" (1971:66). In contrast to the dominant cultural value of being rich and well educated, for example, a deviant subculture may extol recklessness and even violence.

Walter Miller (1970) adds that deviant subcultures are likely to have six focal concerns: (1) *toughness,* the value placed on physical size, strength, and athletic skills, especially among males; (2) *trouble,* arising from frequent conflict with teachers and police; (3) *smartness,* the ability to succeed on the streets, to outthink or "con" others; (4) *excitement,* the search for thrills, risk, or danger; (5) *fate,* a sense that people lack control over their own lives; and (6) *autonomy,* a desire for freedom expressed as resentment toward all authority figures.

Hirschi's Control Theory

A final argument that builds on Durkheim's analysis of deviance is Travis Hirschi's (1969) *control theory.* Hirschi assumes that everyone finds deviance tempting. What requires explanation, then, is not deviance but *conformity.* He suggests that conformity arises from four types of social controls.

1. **Attachment.** Strong attachments to family, peer group, and school encourage conformity; weak relationships to others put people at greater risk of deviance.

2. **Commitment.** The higher one's commitment to legitimate opportunity, the greater the advantages of conformity. A young person bound for college, with good career prospects, has a high stake in conformity. By contrast, someone with little confidence in future success has a low investment in conformity and is more likely to drift toward deviance.

3. **Involvement.** Extensive involvement in legitimate activities such as holding a job or going to school inhibits deviance. By contrast, people who simply "hang out" waiting for something to happen have time and energy for deviant activity.

No social class stands apart from others as being either criminal or free from criminality. According to various sociologists, however, people with less stake in society and their own future typically exhibit less resistance to some kinds of deviance. Photographer Stephen Shames captured this scene on a Bronx, New York, rooftop in 1983.

4. **Belief.** Strong beliefs in conventional morality and respect for authority figures also limit deviance; people with weak beliefs are more vulnerable to temptation.

Hirschi's analysis explains many kinds of deviant behavior, and it has gained support from subsequent research (Wiatrowski, Griswold, & Roberts, 1981; Sampson & Laub, 1990). Here, again, a person's location in society is crucial in generating a stake in conformity or prompting people to cross the line into deviance.

Critical evaluation. Durkheim's pioneering work on the functions of deviance remains central to sociological thinking. Even so, recent critics point out that, in reality, a community does not always come together in reaction to crime; on the contrary, sometimes fear of

We create special settings that permit behavior that would otherwise be viewed as deviant. In this Los Angeles disco for young people, boisterous dancing, screaming, and body painting are the norm.

The Label of Deviance: The Symbolic-Interaction Approach

The symbolic-interaction paradigm casts light on how people construct reality in everyday situations. Applied to deviance, this theoretical paradigm reveals that definitions of deviance and conformity are surprisingly flexible.

The central contribution of symbolic-interaction analysis is **labeling theory,** *the assertion that deviance and conformity result, not so much from what people do, as from how others respond to those actions.* Labeling theory stresses the relativity of deviance, meaning that people may define the same behavior in any number of ways. Howard S. Becker claims that deviance is, therefore, nothing more than "behavior that people so label" (1966:9).

Consider these situations: A woman takes an article of clothing from a roommate; a married man at a convention in a distant city has sex with a prostitute; a member of Congress drives home gleefully intoxicated after a party. We might define the first situation as carelessness, borrowing, or theft. The consequences of the second situation depend largely on whether the news of his behavior follows the man back home. In the third situation, is the official an active socialite or a dangerous drunk? The social construction of reality, then, is a highly variable process of detection, definition, and response.

People sometimes contend with deviant labels because of events beyond their control. For example, victims of violent rape may be labeled deviant because of the misguided assumption that they encouraged the offender. Similarly, people with a terminal illness are sometimes shunned by employers, friends, and even family members who cannot face up to the reality of death.

Edwin Lemert (1951, 1972) notes that many episodes of norm violation are insignificant and transitory, provoking little reaction from others and with little effect on a person's self-concept. Lemert calls such passing episodes *primary deviance.*

But what happens if other people take notice of someone's deviance and make something of it? If, for example, people begin to think of a boisterous friend as an unsuitable social companion, that person, feeling left out, might become angry, escalating the level of criticism from others. Such a response constitutes *secondary deviance,* which may take the form of defending deviant actions, lying about them, or embracing them as part of personal identity. In other words, in response

crime drives people to withdraw from public life (Liska & Warner, 1991).

Derived from Durkheim's analysis, Merton's strain theory has also come under criticism for explaining some kinds of deviance (theft, for example) better than others (crimes of passion or mental illness). In addition, not everyone seeks success in conventional terms of wealth. As explained in Chapter 2 ("Culture"), members of our society embrace many different cultural values and are motivated by various notions of personal success.

The overarching argument of Cloward and Ohlin, Cohen, Miller, and Hirschi—that deviance reflects the opportunity structure of society—has been confirmed by subsequent research (cf. Allan & Steffensmeier, 1989). However, these theories, too, fall short in assuming that everyone shares the same cultural standards for judging right and wrong. Moreover, we must be careful not to define deviance in terms that unfairly focus attention on poor people. If crime is defined to include stock fraud as well as street theft, the typical criminal becomes much more affluent. Finally, all structural-functional theories imply that everyone who breaks the rules will be defined as deviant. Becoming deviant, however, is actually a highly complex process, as the next section explains.

to people's reaction to some earlier violation, secondary deviance may emerge with far greater consequences for social identity and self-definition. Initial labeling, then, may prompt individuals to develop deviant identities, thereby fulfilling the expectations of others.

Stigma

The emergence of secondary deviance marks the start of what Erving Goffman (1963) called a *deviant career.* Typically, this involves acquiring a **stigma,** *a powerfully negative label that radically changes a person's self-concept and social identity.* Stigma operates as a master status (see Chapter 4, "Social Interaction in Everyday Life"), overpowering other dimensions of identity so that a person is diminished and discredited in the minds of others.

Sometimes an entire community formally stigmatizes an individual through what Harold Garfinkel (1956) calls a *degradation ceremony.* Consider a criminal prosecution, for example, which operates much like a high school graduation except that a person stands before the community to be labeled in a negative rather than a positive way.

Once people have stigmatized a person, they may engage in **retrospective labeling,** *the interpretation of someone's past consistent with present deviance* (Scheff, 1984). For example, after discovering that a man who has taught at a boys' school for years has sexually molested a child, others rethink his past, perhaps musing, "He always did want to be around young boys." Retrospective labeling takes a highly selective and prejudicial view of a person's biography, and can reinforce a deviant identity.

Labeling and Mental Illness

Labeling theory is especially applicable to mental illness since a person's mental condition is often difficult to define. Psychiatrists generally assume that mental disorders, like diseases of the body, can be traced to verifiable causes. Certainly, we recognize that some mental disturbances arise from inherited predispositions, poor diet, and chemical imbalances. However, what we call "mental illness" is also a matter of social definitions sometimes designed to force others to conform to conventional standards (Thoits, 1985).

Is a woman who believes that Jesus rides the bus to work with her every day seriously deluded or merely

The world is full of people who are unusual in one way or another. This Indian man grew the fingernails on one hand for more than thirty years just to do something that no one else had ever done. Should we define such behavior as harmless eccentricity or as evidence of mental illness?

expressing her religious faith in a highly graphic way? If a man refuses to bathe, much to the dismay of his family, is he insane or just acting in an unconventional manner? Is a homeless woman who refuses to allow police to take her to a city shelter on a freezing night mentally ill or simply trying to live independently?

Psychiatrist Thomas Szasz charges that the label of insanity is widely applied to what is actually only "difference"; therefore, he claims, we should abandon the notion of mental illness entirely (1961, 1970; Vatz & Weinberg, 1983). Illness, Szasz argues, afflicts only the body, making mental illness a myth. Being "different" in thought or action may irritate others, but it is no grounds on which to define someone as sick. To do so, Szasz claims, simply enforces conformity to the standards of people powerful enough to get their way.

Szasz's views have provoked controversy; most of his colleagues reject the notion that all mental illness is a fiction. Some have hailed his work, however, for pointing out the danger of abusing medical practice in the interest of promoting conformity. Most of us, after all, have experienced periods of extreme stress or other mental disability. Such episodes, although upsetting, are usually of passing importance. If, however, they form the basis of a social stigma, they may lead to further deviance as a self-fulfilling prophecy (Scheff, 1984).

The Medicalization of Deviance

Labeling theory, particularly the ideas of Goffman and Szasz, underlies a recent shift in the way we understand deviance. Over the last fifty years, the growing influence of medicine—especially psychiatry—in the United States has propelled the **medicalization of deviance,** *the transformation of moral and legal issues into medical matters.* In essence, this amounts to a change in labels. In moral terms, we define people and their actions as "bad" or "good." However, the scientific objectivity of medicine replaces moral judgments with a clinical diagnosis of being "sick" or "well."

To illustrate, until the middle of this century, most people viewed alcoholics as morally deficient people easily tempted by the pleasure of drink. Gradually, however, medical specialists redefined alcoholism so that most people now regard it as a disease, rendering individuals "sick" rather than "bad." Similarly, obesity, drug addiction, child abuse, adultery, and even stealing—each of which used to be viewed as a moral issue—are defined in today's "culture of victimization" (see Chapter 2, "Culture") as illnesses for which "victims" need help rather than punishment.

Whether deviance is defined as a moral or medical issue has three important consequences. First, it affects *who responds* to deviance. An offense against common morality typically provokes a reaction from members of the community or the police. Applying medical labels, however, transfers the situation to the control of clinical specialists, including counselors, psychiatrists, and physicians.

A second issue is *how people respond* to a deviant. A moral approach defines the deviant as an "offender" subject to punishment. Medically, however, "patients" need treatment. Therefore, while punishment is designed to fit the crime, treatment programs are tailored to the patient and may involve virtually any therapy that might prevent future deviance (von Hirsh, 1986.)

Third, and most important, the two labels differ on the issue of *the personal competence of the deviant person.* Morally, people may do wrong but we understand our actions and must face the consequences.

Medically speaking, however, sickness implies that we are personally incompetent and unaware of our own best interest. Thus, we become vulnerable to involuntary treatment. For this reason alone, attempts to define deviance in medical terms should be made with extreme caution.

Differential Association Theory

Related to the issue of how we define others' behavior is the question of how we come to define our own. Edwin Sutherland (1940) observed that we learn social patterns, including deviance, through association with others, especially in primary groups.

We all regularly encounter situations promoting deviance as well as those supporting conformity. The likelihood that a person will engage in deviance, then, depends on the frequency of association with those who support norm violation compared with those who endorse conformity. This is Sutherland's theory of *differential association.*

Critical evaluation. All symbolic-interaction theories treat deviance, not as a fixed concept, but as one possible outcome in a process of reality construction. Thus an audience labels some people as deviant while choosing to ignore the same behavior in others. Yet, flexible as reality may be, the concepts of stigma, secondary deviance, and deviant career imply that the label of deviance can be incorporated into a lasting self-concept.

The labeling approach has several limitations. First, because it takes a highly relative view of deviance, labeling glosses over the fact that people everywhere condemn some kinds of behavior, such as murder (Wellford, 1980). Labeling theory is thus most usefully applied to less serious deviance, such as certain kinds of sexual behavior and mental illness. Second, the consequences of deviant labeling are unclear: Research is inconclusive as to whether deviant labeling encourages subsequent deviance or discourages further violations (Smith & Gartin, 1989). Third, not everyone resists the label of deviance; some people actually may want to be defined as deviant (Vold & Bernard, 1986). For example, individuals may engage in civil disobedience and court arrest to call attention to social injustice.

While Sutherland's differential association theory has had considerable influence in sociology, it provides little insight into why society's norms and laws define certain kinds of activities as deviant in the first

Artist Frank Romero painted *The Closing of Whittier Boulevard* based on a recollection of his youth in East Los Angeles. To many young Latinos, identified here by their distinctive "low-rider" cars, police represent a hostile Anglo culture likely to use heavy-handed tactics to discourage them from venturing out of their neighborhood.

place. This important question is addressed by social-conflict analysis, described next.

Deviance and Inequality: Social-Conflict Analysis

The social-conflict paradigm links deviance to social inequality. This approach suggests that *who* or *what* is labeled as deviant is based largely on the relative power of categories of people.

Deviance and Power

Alexander Liazos (1972) points out that deviance brings to mind "nuts, sluts, and 'preverts'" who share the trait of powerlessness. Bag ladies (not tax evaders) and unemployed men on street corners (not those who profit from wars) carry the stigma of difference.

Social-conflict theory explains how this works. First, the norms—including laws—of any society generally reflect the interests of the rich and powerful. People who threaten the wealthy, either by taking their property or by advocating a more egalitarian society, may find themselves defined as "thieves" or "political radicals." Karl Marx, one major architect of this approach, argued that all social institutions tend to support the capitalist economic system and protect the interests of the rich, capitalist class. Richard Quinney makes the point succinctly: "Capitalist justice is by the capitalist class, for the capitalist class, and against the working class" (1977:3).

Second, even if their behavior is called into question, the powerful have the resources to resist deviant labels. Corporate executives who might order or condone the dumping of hazardous wastes are rarely held personally accountable for these acts. While such actions pose dangers for all of society, courts rarely pronounce them as criminal.

Third, the widespread belief that norms and laws are natural and good masks their political character. For this reason, we may condemn the *unequal application* of the law but give little thought to whether the *laws themselves* are inherently unfair (Quinney, 1977).

Deviance and Capitalism

Steven Spitzer (1980) argues that deviant labels are applied to people who impede the operation of capitalism. First, because capitalism is based on private control of property, people who threaten the property of others—especially the poor who steal from the rich—are prime candidates for labeling as deviants. Conversely, the rich who exploit the poor are unlikely to be defined as deviant. Landlords, for example, who charge poor tenants high rents and evict those who cannot pay are not considered a threat to society; they are simply "doing business."

Second, because capitalism depends on productive labor, those who cannot or will not work risk deviant labeling. Many members of our society think of

Why was the trial of former football star and actor O. J. Simpson such a national obsession? Probably because, though we live in a society built on the principle of "equal justice under law," we are keenly aware that both race and class can affect legal outcomes. Surveys show that many people—and perhaps even most African Americans—think that people of color typically are not treated fairly by our criminal justice system And almost no one doubts that being very rich can tip the scales of justice; Simpson's wealth afforded him the services of dozens of the country's best attorneys, investigators, and scientific experts.

people who are out of work—even if through no fault of their own—as deviant.

Third, capitalism depends on respect for figures of authority, so people who resist authority are generally labeled as deviant. Examples are children who skip school or talk back to parents and teachers, adults who do not cooperate with employers or police, and anyone who stands up to "the system."

Fourth, capitalism rests on the widespread acceptance of the status quo; those who undermine or challenge the capitalist system risk deviant labeling. Into this category fall antiwar activists, environmentalists, labor organizers, and people who endorse an alternative economic system.

To turn the argument around, people label positively whatever enhances the operation of capitalism. Winning athletes, for example, have celebrity status because they express the values of individual achievement and competition vital to capitalism. Additionally, Spitzer notes, we define using drugs of escape (marijuana, psychedelics, heroin, and crack) as deviant, while sanctioning drugs that promote adjustment to the status quo (such as alcohol and caffeine).

Within a capitalist context, deviants fall into two general categories. People who do little work but are no threat to society (Robert Merton's retreatists who abuse drugs, the elderly, or people with physical or mental disabilities) are managed by social welfare agencies. People who directly threaten the capitalist system (including the inner-city "underclass" and Merton's rebels) come under the purview of the criminal justice system and, in times of crisis, military forces such as the National Guard.

Note that both systems apply labels that place responsibility for social problems on the people themselves. Welfare recipients are deemed unworthy freeloaders; poor people who vent rage at their plight are labeled as rioters; anyone who actively challenges the government is branded a radical or a communist; and those who attempt to gain illegally what they will never acquire legally are called common thieves.

White-Collar Crime

Until 1989, few people other than Wall Street stockbrokers had ever heard of Michael Milken. Yet Milken had accomplished a stunning feat, becoming the highest-paid U.S. worker in half a century. In a single year, his salary and bonuses totaled $550 million—*about $1.5 million a day*—placing Milken behind only Al Capone, whose 1927 earnings topped $600 million in current dollars (Swartz, 1989). Milken had something else in common with Capone: The government seized much of his fortune and sent him to jail, in this case for violations of securities and exchange laws.

Milken's activities exemplify **white-collar crime**, defined by Edwin Sutherland in 1940 as *crimes committed by people of high social position in the course of their occupations* (Sutherland & Cressey, 1978). As the Milken case suggests, white-collar crime rarely involves uniformed police converging on a scene with drawn guns and does not include crimes such as murder, assault, or rape that are committed by people of high social position. Instead, this concept refers only to acts by powerful people who make use of their occupational positions to enrich themselves or others illegally. For this reason, sociologists sometimes call white-collar offenses that occur in government offices and corporate board rooms *crime in the suites* as opposed to *crime in the streets*.

The most common white-collar crimes are bank embezzlement, tax fraud, credit fraud, bribery, and antitrust violations. Most cases of white-collar crime, like most street crimes, involve relatively little money and cause limited harm to individuals. But the occasional major crime—like the savings and loan scandal a few years ago—attracts a great deal of attention and results in substantial losses to many people (Weisburd et al., 1991). The government's program to bail out the savings and loan industry will end up costing U.S. taxpayers $600 billion—$2,500 for every adult and child in the country.

Sutherland (1940) argued that most white-collar offenses provoke little reaction from others. When they do, however, they are more likely to end up in a civil hearing rather than in a criminal courtroom. *Civil law* regulates economic affairs between private parties, while *criminal law* defines every individual's moral responsibilities to society. In civil settlements, a loser pays for damage or injury, but no party is labeled a criminal. Further, individuals who commit white-collar offenses are rarely prosecuted; instead, corporations, which have the legal standing of persons, are usually named as defendants in legal action.

And when white-collar criminals *are* charged and convicted, the odds are they will not go to jail. One accounting shows that fewer than three in ten embezzlers convicted in the U.S. District Court system spent a single day in prison; most were placed on probation (U.S. Bureau of Justice Statistics, 1992). Similarly, just ninety people were jailed for all federal environmental crimes between 1986 and 1991 (Gold, 1991).

The main reason for such leniency, as Sutherland noted years ago, is that the public sees white-collar crime as, in effect, victimizing everyone and no one.

TABLE 6–1 Theoretical Approaches to Deviance: A Summary

Theoretical Paradigm	Major Contributions
Structural-functional analysis	While what is deviant may vary, deviance itself is found in all societies; deviance and the social response it provokes bolster the moral foundation of society; deviance can also direct the course of social change.
Symbolic-interaction analysis	Nothing is inherently deviant but may become defined as such through the response of others; the reactions of others are highly variable; labeling a person as deviant can lead to secondary deviance and deviant careers.
Social-conflict analysis	Laws and other norms reflect the interests of powerful members of society; those who threaten the status quo are likely to be defined as deviant; social injury caused by powerful people is less likely to be defined as criminal than social injury caused by people who have little social power.

White-collar criminals do not stick a gun in anyone's ribs, and the economic costs are usually spread throughout the population.

Critical evaluation.   According to social-conflict theory, the inequality of wealth and power that pervades capitalist societies guides the creation and application of laws and other norms. This theory holds that the criminal justice system and social welfare organizations act as political agents controlling categories of people who threaten the capitalist system.

Yet while laws and other cultural norms do benefit the rich and powerful, as social-conflict theorists assert, laws also protect workers, consumers, and the environment, sometimes in opposition to the interests of the rich. In addition, this analytical approach implies that criminality springs up only to the extent that a society treats its members unequally. However, according to Durkheim, all societies generate deviance, and socialist countries fill their prisons just as capitalist societies do.

We have now presented various sociological explanations for crime and other types of deviance. Table 6–1 summarizes the contributions of each approach.

Date Rape: Exposing Dangerous Myths

Completing a day of work during a business trip to the courthouse in Tampa, Florida, thirty-two-year-old Sandra Abbott[1] pondered how she would return to her hotel. An attorney with whom she had been working—a pleasant enough man—made a kind offer of a lift. As his car threaded its way through the late afternoon traffic, their conversation was animated. "He was saying all the right things," Abbott recalled, "so I started to trust him."

He wondered if she would join him for dinner; she happily accepted. After lingering over an enjoyable meal, they walked together to the door of her hotel room. The new acquaintance angled for an invitation to come in, but Abbott hesitated. Sensing that he might have something more than conversation on his mind, she explained that she was old-fashioned about relationships. He could come in, she finally agreed, but only for a little while, and with the understanding that talk was *all* they would do.

---

[1]A pseudonym; the facts of this case are from Gibbs (1991a).

Sitting on the couch in the room, soon Abbott was overcome with drowsiness. Feeling comfortable in the presence of her new friend, she let her head fall gently onto his shoulder and, before she knew it, she fell asleep. That's when

The 1992 rape conviction of heavyweight boxing champion Mike Tyson suggests that our society is taking the problem of sexual violence against women more seriously.

the attack began. Abbott was startled back to consciousness as the man thrust himself upon her sexually. She shouted "No!" but he paid no heed. Abbott describes what happened next:

> I didn't scream or run. All I could think of was my business contacts and what if they saw me run out of my room screaming rape. I thought it was my fault. I felt so filthy, I washed myself over and over in hot water. Did he rape me?, I kept asking myself. I didn't consent. But who's gonna believe me? I had a man in my hotel room after midnight. (Gibbs, 1991a:50)

Abbott knew that she had said "No!" and thus had been raped. She notified the police, who conducted an investigation and turned their findings over to the state attorney's office. But the authorities backed away from Abbott. In the absence of evidence like bruises, a medical examination, and torn clothes, they responded, there was little point in prosecuting.

The upshot of Sandra Abbott's case was all too typical. In most

Deviance and Social Diversity

The shape deviance assumes in a society has much to do with the relative power and privilege of different categories of people. The following sections offer two examples: how gender is linked to deviance, and how racial and ethnic hostility motivates hate crimes.

Deviance and Gender

Virtually every society in the world applies more stringent normative controls to women than to men.

Historically, our society has limited the roles of women largely to the home. Even today, the United States and most other societies limit women's opportunities in the workplace, in politics, and in the military. Elsewhere in the world, the normative constraints placed on women are even greater. Saudi Arabian law prohibits women from operating motor vehicles; in Iran, women who dare to expose their hair or wear makeup in public can be whipped.

Gender also colors the theories about deviance noted earlier. Merton's strain theory, for example, defines cultural goals in terms of financial success. Traditionally, however, this preoccupation with material incidences of sexual attack, a victim makes no report to police, and no offender is arrested. Like Abbott, other rape victims face the bitter reality of simply trying as best they can to put a traumatic experience behind them. The reason for this official inaction is that many people have a misguided understanding of rape. Three inaccurate notions about rape are so common in the United States that they might be called "rape myths."

One myth holds that rape is predominantly a stranger-to-stranger crime. A sexual attack brings to mind young men who lurk in the shadows and suddenly spring on their unsuspecting victims. In truth, however, only one in five rapes involves strangers. For this reason, people have begun to speak more realistically about *acquaintance rape* or, more simply, *date rape*. A rape—legally speaking, the carnal knowledge of a female forcibly and against her will—is typically committed by a man who is known to, and even trusted by, his victim. But common sense dictates that being a "friend" (or even a husband) does not prevent a man from committing murder, assault, or rape.

A second myth about rape—that women provoke their attackers—recalls the familiar "blame the victim" scenario. Surely, many people think, a woman claiming to have been raped must have done *something* to encourage the man, to lead him on, to make him think that she really wanted to have sex.

In the case described above, didn't Sandra Abbott agree to have dinner with the man? Didn't she willingly admit him to her room? Such thinking often paralyzes victims. But having dinner with a man—or even inviting him into her hotel room—is hardly a woman's statement of consent to have sex with him any more than she has agreed to have him beat her with a club.

A third myth is the notion that rape is simply sex. If there is no knife held to a woman's throat, or if she is not bound and gagged, then how can sex become a crime? The answer is simply that *forcing a woman to have sex against her will is rape*. To accept the idea that rape is sex, one would also have to see no difference between brutal combat and playful wrestling. "Having sex" implies intimacy, caring, communication, and, most important of all, consent—none of which is present in cases of rape. In the absence of consent, as Susan Brownmiller (1975) explains, rape is not sex but violence.

The more people believe rape myths, the more women will become victims of sexual violence. The ancient Babylonians stoned married women who fell victim to rape, claiming that the women had committed adultery. To a startling extent, ideas about rape have not changed over thousands of years. As a result, even today, most rapes go unreported to police and, even when authorities are notified, prosecutions and convictions are rare. At present, perhaps one in twenty rapes results in an offender being sent to jail.

Sources: Gibbs (1991a, 1991b).

things has dominated the thinking of men, while women have been socialized to define success in terms of relationships, particularly marriage and motherhood (Leonard, 1982). Only recently have women and men come to recognize the "strain" caused by the cultural *ideals* of gender equity clashing with the *reality* of gender-based inequality.

Labeling theory, too, reflects ways in which gender influences how we define deviance. By bringing different standards to our judgments of men's and women's behavior, we bias the very process of labeling. Further, because of their greater social power, men often escape direct responsibility for actions that victimize women. In the past, at least, men engaging in sexual harassment or other assaults against women have been tagged with only mildly deviant labels and, sometimes, they even have won societal approval.

By contrast, women victims may have had to convince an unsympathetic audience that they are not to blame for their plight. A general rule holds that whether people define a situation as deviance—and, if so, whose deviance it is—depends on the sex of both the audience and the actors (King & Clayson, 1988). The box takes a closer look at the subject of date rape, an issue long fraught with double standards.

Hate Crimes: Punishing Actions or Attitudes?

On an October evening in 1989, Todd Mitchell, an African-American teenager, and a group of friends were milling about in front of their apartment complex in Kenosha, Wisconsin. They had just watched the film *Mississippi Burning*, and were fuming over a scene in which a white man beats a young black boy kneeling in prayer.

"Do you feel hyped up to move on some white people?" asked Mitchell. Minutes later, a young white boy walked toward the group on the other side of the street. Mitchell commanded: "There goes a white boy; go get him!" The group surrounded the white boy, brutally beating him and leaving him in a coma. They took his tennis shoes as a trophy of their conquest.

The boys were identified and charged with the assault. At the trial of Todd Mitchell, who acted as the ringleader, the jury took the unusual step of finding the young man guilty of aggravated battery *motivated by racial hatred*. Instead of the typical two-year prison sentence, the jury committed Mitchell to jail for four years.

Supporters of hate-crime legislation claim, first, that an offender's intentions have always been part of criminal deliberations, so this policy represents nothing new. Second, crimes motivated by racial or other bias inflame the public mood more than those carried out for more

Hostility has fueled attacks on Turks and other immigrants in Germany in recent years. In 1993, an angry mob burned this house causing loss of life and revealing the viciousness of racial and ethnic hatred.

common reasons like monetary gain. Third, supporters continue, because hate crimes are commonly carried out by groups rather than individuals and typically involve anger, they generally cause greater injury to the victims than other kinds of crime.

Critics, however, see in hate-crime laws a threat to free speech. Such a policy punishes offenders, not for their actions, but for their underlying attitudes. As Harvard law professor Alan Dershowitz laments, "As much as I hate bigotry, I fear much more the Court attempting to control the minds of its citizens." In short, critics condemn hate-crime statutes for punishing beliefs rather than behavior.

In 1993, the Supreme Court upheld the sentence handed down to Todd Mitchell. In a unanimous decision, the justices rejected the idea of punishing an individual's beliefs. At the same time, they reasoned, an abstract belief is no longer protected when it becomes the motive for a crime.

Sources: Greenhouse (1993) and Terry (1993).

Finally, a notable irony is that social-conflict analysis—despite its focus on social inequality—has long neglected the importance of gender. If, as conflict theory suggests, economic disadvantage is a primary cause of crime, why do women (whose economic position is much worse than that of men) commit far *fewer* crimes than men do? The crime discussion, beginning on page 143, which examines crime rates in the United States, answers this question.

Hate Crimes

More than a decade ago the concept of **hate crime** came into our language to designate *a criminal act*

motivated by racial or other bias. A hate crime may express hostility toward a person based not just on race but also on religion, ancestry, sexual orientation, or physical disability.

The federal government has tracked hate crimes since 1990. While still a small share of all crimes, their numbers are rising. An eight-city survey conducted by the National Gay and Lesbian Task Force (cited in Berrill, 1992:19–20) found that one in five lesbians and gay men had been physically assaulted because of their sexual orientation; more than 90 percent had experienced verbal abuse. Hate-motivated violence is especially likely to target people who contend with multiple stigmas, such as gay men of color.

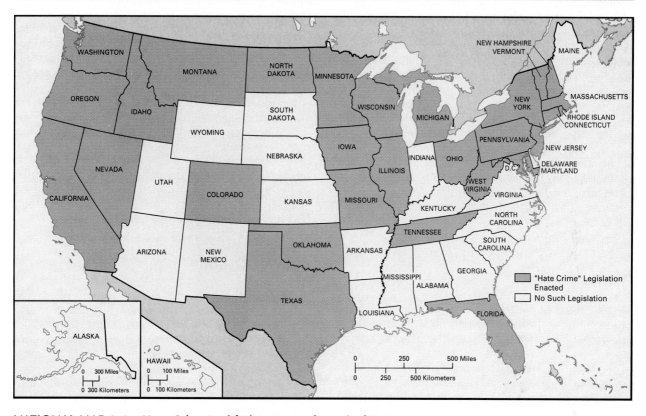

NATIONAL MAP 6–1   Hate-Crime Legislation Across the United States

The states shown in purple have legally mandated harsher penalties for crimes motivated by racial, ethnic, or other bias. Generally, laws of this kind are favored by political liberals. Can you see a pattern in the map? *Hint:* Most of the states that have enacted hate-crime laws supported Democrat Bill Clinton in the 1992 presidential election.

Source: Greenberg (1994).

What qualifies an offense as a hate crime is not the race or ancestry of the victim but the fact that such considerations *motivate* the offender. Such a crime, then, expresses hatred toward some category of people. The box describes a recent case—the basis for a Supreme Court ruling upholding stiffer sentences for crimes motivated by hate.

Extending the length of sentences for crimes motivated by bias is quickly becoming the law of the land. National Map 6–1 shows that, as of mid-1993, twenty-nine states had enacted hate-crime legislation.

Crime

Speak of crime and people immediately conjure up images of unsavory characters in alleyways, waiting to prey on unsuspecting victims. But crime covers a surprisingly wide range of behaviors. In centuries past, a Chinese commoner who simply looked at the emperor in public faced serious charges. Today a citizen of the People's Republic of China who expressed support for the nation's historic royalty would likely face arrest. The judicial system in the United States has also undergone considerable change, supporting slavery for two centuries, for example, then condemning racial discrimination.

Crime is the violation of the criminal law enacted by local, state, or federal government. Technically, all crimes are composed of two distinct elements: an *act* (or, in some cases, the failure to do what the law requires) and *criminal intent* (in legal terminology, *mens rea*, or "guilty mind"). Intent is a matter of degree, ranging from a deliberate action to negligence in which an individual behaves (or fails to act) in a manner that the person may reasonably expect to produce harm. Juries weigh the degree of intent in determining whether, for example, someone who kills another is guilty of first-degree murder, second-degree murder, or negligent manslaughter. Alternatively, a jury may also rule a killing justifiable, as in the case of self-defense.

Types of Crime

In the United States, the Federal Bureau of Investigation gathers information on criminal offenses. Two major types of crimes make up the official "crime index."

Crimes against the person are *crimes against people that involve violence or the threat of violence.* Such "violent crimes" include murder and nonnegligent manslaughter (legally defined as "the willful killing of one human being by another"), aggravated assault ("an unlawful attack by one person on another for the purpose of inflicting severe or aggravated bodily injury"), forcible rape ("the carnal knowledge of a female forcibly and against her will"), and robbery ("taking or attempting to take anything of value from the care, custody, or control of a person or persons by force or threat of force or violence and/or putting the victim in fear").

Crimes against property are *crimes that involve theft of property belonging to others.* "Property crimes" include burglary ("the unlawful entry of a structure to commit a [serious crime] or a theft"), larceny-theft ("the unlawful taking, carrying, leading, or riding away of property from the possession of another"), auto theft ("the theft or attempted theft of a motor vehicle"), and arson ("any willful or malicious burning or attempt to burn the personal property of another").

A third category of offenses, excluded from the crime index, is **victimless crimes,** *violations of law in which there are no readily apparent victims.* Examples of "crimes without complaint" are illegal drug use, prostitution, and gambling. However, "victimless crime" is often a misnomer. How victimless is a crime when young people purchasing drugs may be embarking on a life of crime to support a drug habit? Or if a young pregnant woman smoking crack causes the death or permanent injury of her baby? Or when a gambler falls so deeply into debt that he cannot make the mortgage payments on his house? In truth, the people who commit such crimes can themselves be both offenders and victims.

Laws regulating victimless crimes differ from place to place. In the United States, gambling is legal only in Nevada; Atlantic City, New Jersey; and a few other places. Prostitution is legal in part of Nevada; while homosexual (and some heterosexual) behavior is legally restricted in about half the states. Where such laws do exist, enforcement is typically uneven.

Criminal Statistics

Statistics gathered by the Federal Bureau of Investigation show that violent crime—but not property crime—increased dramatically in recent decades, despite greater government spending on various programs. Figure 6–2 tracks this trend.

Always read crime statistics with caution, however, since they cover only certain offenses. The official record is also limited to cases known to the police. Police become aware of almost all homicides, but rapes and other assaults—especially among acquaintances—are far less likely to be reported. Police records include an even smaller proportion of property crime, especially when thefts involve items of little value.

One way to evaluate official crime statistics is a *victimization survey,* in which researchers ask a representative sample of people about being victimized. According to these surveys, overall criminality occurs at a rate about three times higher than what official reports indicate.

The "Street" Criminal: A Profile

Using government crime reports, we can draw a general profile of people arrested for violent and property crimes.

Age. Official crime rates rise sharply during adolescence and the early twenties, declining thereafter. People between the ages of fifteen and twenty-four

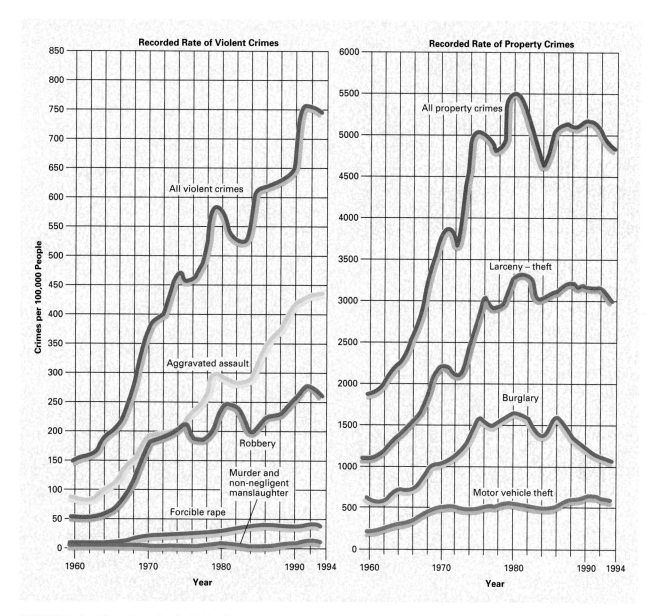

FIGURE 6–2 Crime Rates in the United States, 1960–1993

Source: U.S. Federal Bureau of Investigation (1993).

represent only 15 percent of our population, but they accounted for 42 percent of all arrests for violent crimes and 44 percent of arrests for property crimes in 1993.

Gender.   Official statistics suggest that males commit the vast majority of crimes. Although each sex constitutes roughly half the population, police collared males in 74 percent of all property crime arrests in 1993. In

the case of violent crimes, the disparity was even greater: 87 percent of arrests involved males (a seven-to-one ratio).

Some of this gender difference stems from the reluctance of law enforcement officials to define women as criminals. Even so, the arrest rate for women has been moving closer to that of men—one indication of increasing sexual equality in our society.

The creators of this photograph, part of the United Colors of Benetton advertising campaign, intended to make the statement that people are linked together regardless of color. But so strong are our notions about crime and race that many individuals mistakenly interpreted the photograph as a white police officer escorting a black suspect. What can sociology contribute toward a more accurate understanding of the connection between crime and color?

Between 1984 and 1993, the *increase* in arrests of women (37 percent) was more than double that for men (15 percent) (U.S. Federal Bureau of Investigation, 1994). In global perspective, we see the same pattern, with the greatest gender difference in crime rates marking societies that most limit the social opportunities of women.

Social class.   Criminality is more widespread among people of lower social position. But it is a mistake to assume that being socially disadvantaged means being criminal. While crime—especially violence—is a serious problem in the poorest inner-city neighborhoods, most people who live in these communities have no criminal records, and most crimes there are committed by relatively few hard-core offenders (Wolfgang, Figlio, & Sellin, 1972; Elliott & Ageton, 1980; Thornberry & Farnsworth, 1982; Wolfgang, Thornberry, & Figlio, 1987; Harries, 1990).

Moreover, as John Braithwaite (1981) reminds us, the connection between social standing and criminality depends on what kind of crime one is talking about. If we expand our definition of crime beyond street offenses to include white-collar crime, the "common criminal" has a much higher social position.

Race.   Both race and ethnicity show a strong correlation with crime rates, although the reasons are many and complex. Official statistics indicate that 67 percent of arrests for index crimes in 1993 involved white people. However, in proportion to their numbers in the overall population, African Americans are more likely than whites to be arrested—black people represent about 12 percent of the population and account for 33 percent of arrests for property crimes (versus 64 percent for whites) and 46 percent of arrests for violent crimes (53 percent for whites) (U.S. Federal Bureau of Investigation, 1994).

To explain this racial disparity, first, keep in mind that some degree of prejudice skews arrest data; white police tend to arrest blacks (and especially poor blacks) more readily. Similarly, racial and class bias may make citizens more likely to report black people to police as potential offenders (Liska & Tausig, 1979; Unnever, Frazier, & Henretta, 1980; Smith & Visher, 1981).

Second, race in the United States closely relates to social standing, which, as we have already explained, affects the likelihood of engaging in street crimes. Judith Blau and Peter Blau (1982) assert that the sting of being poor in the midst of affluence promotes criminality among people who come to perceive society as unjust. Note, too, that unemployment among African-American adults is double the rate among whites, and almost half of black children grow up in poverty in contrast to about one in six white children (Sampson, 1987).

Third, remember that the official crime index includes only so-called "street crimes." If we broaden our definition of crime to encompass driving while intoxicated, insider stock trading, embezzlement, and cheating on income tax returns, the proportion of white criminals rises dramatically.

Finally, some categories of the population have unusually low rates of arrest. People of Asian descent, who account for about 3 percent of the population, figure in only 1 percent of all arrests. As Chapter 9 ("Race and Ethnicity") documents, Asian Americans enjoy higher than average incomes, and have a particularly successful record of educational achievement which enhances job opportunities. Moreover, Asian-American communities place a strong cultural emphasis on family solidarity and discipline, both of which inhibit criminality.

Crime in Global Perspective

By world standards, the United States has a lot of crime. The New York metropolitan area recorded 2,401

There are almost enough guns in the United States to arm every woman, man, and child; about half of all households contain one or more such weapons. The "death clock" in New York City's Times Square tallies both the number of guns and the annual death toll from firearms. Guns are not the only key to our country's high crime rate, since unarmed criminality in the United States is also high by world standards. But the ready availability of guns does contribute to accidental shootings—especially by children—and it also raises the odds that interpersonal violence will become deadly.

murders in 1992. Rarely does a day pass with no murder in New York; typically, more New Yorkers are hit by stray bullets than are gunned down deliberately in cities elsewhere in the world.

The U.S. homicide rate stands at five times that of Europe, the rape rate is seven times higher, and our country endures twice the rate of property crime. The contrast is even greater between our society and the nations of Asia, including India and Japan, where rates of violent and property crime are among the lowest in the world.

Elliott Currie (1985) contends that crime stems from the overriding importance our culture assigns to individual economic success, frequently at the expense of family and community cohesion. The United States also has extraordinary cultural diversity, the legacy of centuries of immigration. Moreover, economic inequality is higher in this country than in most other industrial nations. Overall, these factors stitch together a relatively weak social fabric that, combined with considerable frustration among this country's have-nots, generates widespread criminal behavior.

Another contributing factor to the severity of violence in the United States is extensive private ownership of guns. There are now about as many guns as there are people in the United States. Moreover, of 22,540 murder victims in the United States in 1992, 68 percent died from shootings. By the early 1990s, Texas and several other southern states reported that deaths from gunshots exceeded automobile-related fatalities.

Of course, guns themselves do not cause crime. But a crime in which the offender is armed with a gun is more likely to result in serious injury or death. Even so, rising public demand for gun control led Congress in 1993 to pass the Brady Bill (named for former president Ronald Reagan's press secretary who was shot along with the president a decade before). This law requires a seven-day waiting period for the purchase of handguns in order to discourage impulse buying and allow police time to perform background checks on the purchasers of firearms.

However our society decides to deal with guns, they represent only one piece in the crime puzzle. As Elliott Currie notes, the number of Californians killed each year by knives alone exceeds the number of Canadians killed by weapons of all kinds. Most experts do think, however, that gun control will help curb the level of deadly violence.

It is true that crime rates are soaring in the largest cities of the world like São Paulo, Brazil, which have rapid population growth and millions of desperately poor people. However, the traditional character of most poor societies and their strong family structure make informal means of crime control the norm in local communities (Clinard & Abbott, 1973; *Der Spiegel*, 1989). By the same token, traditional social patterns promote crimes like prostitution by curbing the opportunities available to women. Global Map 6–1 shows the extent of prostitution in various world regions.

Finally, as noted in earlier chapters, a process of "globalization" is linking the world's societies more

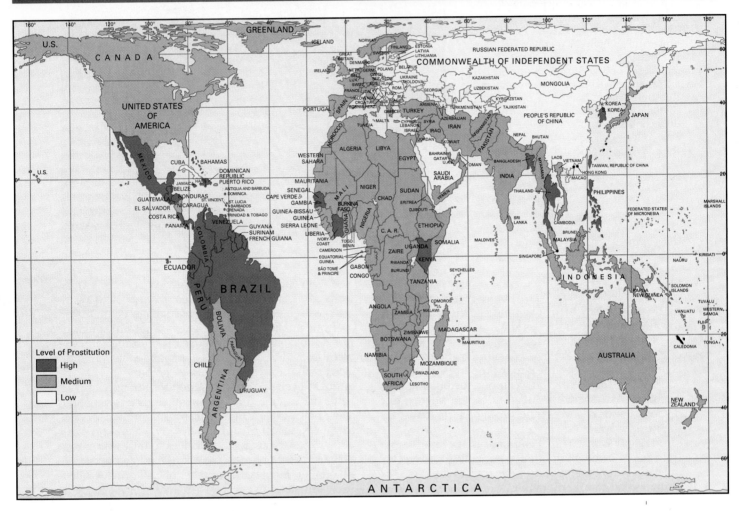

GLOBAL MAP 6–1   Prostitution in Global Perspective

Generally speaking, prostitution is widespread in societies of the world where women have low standing in relation to men. Officially, at least, the now-defunct socialist regimes in Eastern Europe and the former Soviet Union, as well as the People's Republic of China, boasted of gender equality, including the virtual elimination of prostitution. By contrast, in much of Latin America, a region of pronounced patriarchy, prostitution is commonplace. In many Islamic societies patriarchy also holds sway but religious forces restrain this practice. Western, industrial societies display a moderate amount of prostitution.

Source: *Peters Atlas of the World* (1990); updated by the author.

closely than ever before. Crime, too, crosses borders today. Some types of crimes have always been multinational, including terrorism, espionage, and arms dealing (Martin & Romano, 1992).

Of increasing importance on the international crime scene is the illegal drug trade. In part, the surge in illegal drug trafficking in the United States is a "demand" issue: There is a very profitable market for cocaine and other drugs in this country, and legions of young people are willing to risk arrest or even violent death by engaging in the lucrative drug trade. But the "supply" side of the issue is just as important. In the

South American nation of Colombia, 20 percent of the people depend on cocaine production for their livelihood. Furthermore, cocaine outsells coffee and all other Colombian exports combined. Clearly, then, understanding crimes such as drug dealing requires analyzing social conditions both in this country and elsewhere.

The Criminal Justice System

The criminal justice system is a society's formal response to crime. We shall briefly introduce the key elements of this system: police, the courts, and the punishment of convicted offenders.

The Police

The police generally serve as the point of contact between the population and the criminal justice system. In principle, the police maintain public order by enforcing the law. In reality, 554,000 full-time police officers in the United States (in 1993) cannot effectively monitor the activities of 250 million people. So the police exercise considerable discretion about which situations warrant their attention and how to handle them. Discretion is a two-edged sword, of course, enabling the police to work efficiently on the one hand, but opening the way to prejudicial treatment of some categories of people on the other hand. The Rodney King incident in Los Angeles, described at the beginning of this chapter, is a case in point.

How, then, do police carry out their duties? In a study of police behavior in five cities, Douglas Smith and Christy Visher (1981; Smith, 1987) concluded that, because they must act quickly, police rely on external cues to guide their actions. First, the more serious they perceive the situation to be, the more likely they are to make an arrest. Second, police also respond to the victim's preferences as to whether or not to make an arrest. Third, police more often arrest uncooperative suspects. Fourth, they are more likely to arrest suspects whom they have arrested before, presumably because this suggests guilt. Fifth, the presence of bystanders increases the probability of arrest. According to Smith and Visher, the presence of observers prompts police to take firm control of the situation, and also to use an arrest to move the interaction from the street (the suspect's turf) to the police department (where law officers have the edge). Sixth, all else being equal, police

are more likely to arrest minorities than whites. Smith and Visher concluded that police generally consider people of African or Latino descent as either more dangerous or more likely to be guilty.

Finally, the concentration of police is far from even in the United States. Washington, D.C., has the highest police-to-population ratio: 75 officers for every 10,000 people. Rural South Dakota has one fifth as many, proportionately, with 13 officers per 10,000 people (U.S. Federal Bureau of Investigation, 1994).

The Courts

After arrest, a court determines a suspect's guilt or innocence. In principle, our courts rely on an adversarial process involving attorneys—one representing the defendant and another the state—in the presence of a judge who monitors adherence to legal procedures.

In practice, however, about 90 percent of criminal cases are resolved prior to court appearance through **plea bargaining,** *a legal negotiation in which the prosecution reduces a charge in exchange for a defendant's plea of guilty.* For example, a defendant charged with burglary may agree to plead guilty to the lesser charge of carrying burglary tools; another charged with selling cocaine may go along with pleading guilty to mere possession.

Plea bargaining is widely used because it spares the system the time and expense of a court trial. A trial is usually unnecessary if there is little disagreement as to the facts of the case. By selectively trying only a small proportion of the cases, the courts can also channel their resources into those deemed most important (Reid, 1991).

But in the process, defendants (who are presumed innocent) are pressured to plead guilty. A person can exercise the right to a trial, but only at the risk of receiving a sentence more severe than the plea bargain if found guilty. In essence, then, plea bargaining is efficient, but it may undercut the rights of defendants as it circumvents the adversarial process.

Punishment

On January 5, 1993, a bound and hooded Westley Allan Dodd dropped through the trap door on a scaffold in Walla Walla, Washington, to his death. Few could feel compassion at the hanging of a man who admitted raping, torturing, and then killing three young boys. But any such event causes people to reconsider

Dutch painter Vincent Van Gogh (1853–1890) strongly identified with suffering people that he found around him. Perhaps this is why he included his own likeness in this portrait of the dungeon-like prisons of the nineteenth century. Since then, the stark isolation and numbing depersonalization of prison life have changed little. Prisons are still custodial institutions in which officials make few efforts at rehabilitation.

Vincent Van Gogh, *Prisoner's Round*. Dutch. Pushkin State Museum, Moscow.

crime as sin—an offense against God as well as society—that warranted a harsh response. While contemporary critics of retribution charge that this policy does little to reform the offender, it still carries weight as a means of reinforcing societal morality.

Deterrence.   A second justification for punishment is **deterrence,** *the attempt to discourage criminality through punishment.* Deterrence is based on the Enlightenment notion that humans are calculating and rational creatures. From this point of view, people will forgo deviance if they see that the pains of punishment outweigh the pleasures of mischief.

Initially, reformers promoted deterrence as a needed reform of the system of excessive punishments based on retribution. Why put someone to death for stealing, critics reasoned, if the crime can be discouraged by a lesser penalty? As the concept of deterrence gained broader acceptance, execution and physical mutilation of criminals were gradually replaced by milder forms of punishment such as imprisonment.

Punishment may deter in two ways. *Specific deterrence* demonstrates to an individual offender that crime does not pay. Through *general deterrence*, the punishment of one person serves as an example to others.

Rehabilitation.   The third justification for punishment, **rehabilitation,** involves *reforming the offender to preclude subsequent offenses.* This third justification for punishment arose along with the social sciences in the nineteenth century. Crime, the thinking goes, springs from an unfavorable social environment, perhaps blighted by poverty or a lack of parental supervision. Thus, the reasoning goes, just as offenders learn to be deviant, they will learn to obey the rules if placed in the right setting. *Reformatories* or *houses of correction* were established as controlled environments to help offenders learn proper behavior (recall the description of total institutions in Chapter 3, "Socialization: From Infancy to Old Age").

Rehabilitation resembles deterrence by motivating the offender to conform. But rehabilitation emphasizes constructive improvement while deterrence and retribution simply make the offender suffer. In addition, while retribution demands that the punishment fit the crime, rehabilitation focuses on the distinctive problems of each offender. Thus identical offenses might prompt similar acts of retribution but different programs of rehabilitation.

Societal protection.   A final justification for punishment is **societal protection,** or *rendering an offender incapable of further offenses either temporarily through*

the wisdom of legal execution and, more broadly, to ponder the purpose of punishment.

Scholars, too, reflect on the purposes of punishment. They commonly advance four justifications.

Retribution.   The most important justification for punishing is **retribution,** *inflicting on an offender suffering comparable to that caused by the offense.* As an act of social vengeance, retribution is based on viewing society as a moral system in balance. Criminality upsets this equilibrium; punishment, justly administered, restores it as suggested by the ancient dictum "An eye for an eye."

Retribution is the oldest justification for punishment. During the Middle Ages, most people viewed *incarceration or permanently by execution.* Like deterrence, societal protection is a rational approach to punishment and seeks to protect society from crime.

Table 6–2 summarizes these four justifications for punishment.

Critical evaluation. No society operates without some system to punish deviance. Assessing the actual consequences of punishment, however, is no simple task.

The value of retribution relates to Durkheim's ideas about the functions of deviance, presented earlier in this chapter. Recall that Durkheim believed that punishing the deviant person increases society's collective moral awareness. For this reason, punishment was traditionally a public event. Although the last public execution in the United States took place in Kentucky in 1936, today's mass media ensure public awareness of executions carried out inside prison walls (Kittrie, 1971).

Certainly, punishment deters some crime. Yet our society has a high rate of **criminal recidivism,** *subsequent offenses by people previously convicted of crimes.* One 1991 study found that 62 percent of state prison inmates had been incarcerated before, and 45 percent were repeat offenders with three or more convictions (U.S. Bureau of Justice Statistics, 1993). That means more than half of all inmates leave prison only to return within several years. Such a high rate of recidivism raises questions about the extent to which punishment actually deters crime. Then, too, police only find out about roughly one-third of all crimes, and of these, only about one in five results in an arrest. The old adage that "crime doesn't pay" rings rather hollow when we consider that such a small proportion of offenses ever result in punishment.

General deterrence is even more difficult to investigate scientifically, since we have no way of knowing how people might act if they were unaware of punishments meted out to others. In the debate over capital punishment, permitted in thirty-six states, critics of the practice point to research suggesting that the death penalty has limited value as a general deterrent in the United States, the only Western, industrialized society that routinely executes serious offenders (Sellin, 1980; van den Haag & Conrad, 1983; Archer & Gartner, 1987; Lester, 1987; Bailey & Peterson, 1989; Bailey, 1990; Bohm, 1991).

Efforts at rehabilitation have sparked controversy as well. Prisons accomplish short-term societal protection simply by keeping offenders off the streets, but they do very little to reshape attitudes and behavior in the long term. For this reason, penologists now concede that prisons rarely rehabilitate inmates (Carlson,

TABLE 6–2 Four Justifications for Punishment: A Summary

Retribution	The oldest justification for punishment that remains important today. Punishment is atonement for a moral wrong by an individual; in principle, punishment should be comparable in severity to the deviance itself.
Deterrence	An early modern approach. Deviance is viewed as social disruption, which society acts to control. People are viewed as rational and self-interested. Deterrence works, in theory, by making the pains of punishment outweigh the pleasures of deviance.
Rehabilitation	A modern approach linked to the development of social sciences. Deviance is considered the product of social problems (such as poverty) or personal problems (such as mental illness). Rehabilitation manipulates the inmates' environment in the hope of improving the inmates' behavior.
Societal protection	A modern approach easier to implement than rehabilitation. If society is unable or unwilling to improve offenders or reform social conditions, society gains protection from further deviance by incarceration or execution of offenders.

1976). Perhaps this is to be expected, since according to Sutherland's theory of differential association, placing a person among criminals for a long period of time should simply strengthen criminal attitudes and skills. And because incarceration severs whatever social ties inmates may have in the outside world, individuals may be prone to further crime upon their release, consistent with Hirschi's control theory.

Finally, inmates returning to the surrounding world contend with the stigma of being ex-convicts, often an obstacle to successful integration. One study of young offenders in Philadelphia found that boys who were sentenced to long prison terms—those likely to acquire a criminal stigma—later committed both more crimes and more serious ones (Wolfgang, Figlio, & Sellin, 1972).

Ultimately, we should never assume that the criminal justice system—the police, courts, and prisons—can eliminate crime. The reason, echoed throughout this chapter, is simple: Crime—in fact, all deviance—is more than simply the acts of "bad people"; it is inextricably bound up in the operation of society itself.

SUMMARY

1. Deviance refers to norm violations that span a wide range, from mild breaches of etiquette to serious violence.

2. Biological analysis, from Lombroso's research in the nineteenth century to ongoing research in human genetics, has yet to produce much insight into the causes of deviance.

3. Psychological explanations of deviance focus on abnormalities in the individual personality, which arise from either biological roots or the social environment. Psychological theories help to explain some kinds of deviance.

4. Social forces produce nonconformity because deviance (1) is defined in opposition to cultural norms, (2) is identified through a process of social labeling, and (3) is shaped by the distribution of social power.

5. Sociology links deviance to the operation of society rather than the deficiencies of individuals. Using the structural-functional paradigm, Durkheim claimed that responding to deviance affirms a society's norms and values, clarifies moral boundaries, promotes social unity, and stimulates social change.

6. According to the symbolic-interaction paradigm, the basis of labeling theory, deviance arises from the reaction of others to a person's behavior. Labeling theory explains that acquiring a stigma can generate secondary deviance and launch a deviant career.

7. Social-conflict theory draws a connection between deviance and inequality. Following the approach of Karl Marx, this paradigm holds that laws and other norms reflect the interests of the most powerful members of a society. White-collar crimes, for example, cause extensive social harm, but perpetrators rarely face criminal charges.

8. Official statistics indicate that arrest rates peak in adolescence, then drop steadily with advancing age. Males are arrested in three-fourths of property crimes; males also account for almost nine of ten arrests for violent crimes.

9. People of lower social position tend to commit more street crime than those with greater social privilege. When white-collar crimes are included among criminal offenses, however, this disparity in overall criminality diminishes.

10. More whites than African Americans are arrested for street crimes. However, African Americans are arrested more often than whites in proportion to their respective numbers in the population. Asian Americans have lower-than-average rates of arrest.

11. The police exercise considerable discretion in their work. Research suggests that factors such as the seriousness of the offense, the presence of bystanders, and the accused being African American make arrest more likely.

12. Although ideally an adversarial system, U.S. courts predominantly resolve cases through plea bargaining.

13. Punishment has been justified in terms of retribution, deterrence, rehabilitation, and social protection. Because its consequences are difficult to evaluate scientifically, punishment—like deviance itself—sparks considerable controversy among sociologists and the public as a whole.

KEY CONCEPTS

crime the violation of norms formally enacted into criminal law

crimes against the person (violent crimes) crimes against people that involve violence or the threat of violence

crimes against property (property crimes) crimes that involve theft of property belonging to others

criminal justice system the lawful response to alleged crimes using police, courts, and state-sanctioned punishment

criminal recidivism subsequent offenses committed by people previously convicted of crimes

deterrence the attempt to discourage criminality through punishment

deviance the recognized violation of cultural norms

hate crime a crime motivated by racial or other bias

labeling theory the assertion that deviance and conformity result, not so much from what people do, as from the response of others to those actions

medicalization of deviance the transformation of moral and legal issues into medical matters

plea bargaining a legal negotiation in which the prosecution reduces a charge in exchange for a defendant's guilty plea

rehabilitation reforming the offender to preclude further offenses

retribution inflicting on an offender suffering comparable to that caused by the offense

retrospective labeling the interpretation of someone's past consistent with present deviance

social control attempts by society to regulate the thought and behavior of individuals

societal protection rendering an offender incapable of further offenses either temporarily through incarceration or permanently by execution

stigma a powerfully negative label that radically changes a person's self-concept and social identity

victimless crime violation of law in which there is no readily apparent victim

white-collar crime crimes committed by people of high social position in the course of their occupations

CRITICAL-THINKING QUESTIONS

1. How does a sociological view of deviance differ from the common-sense notion that bad people do bad things?

2. Identify Durkheim's functions of deviance. From his point of view, would a society free from deviance be possible?

3. Suggest ways in which gender, race, and class affect the labeling of people's behavior.

4. What categories of people have high rates of arrest? Do these patterns square with predictions you would make using sociological theories of deviance?

Social Stratification

On April 10, 1912, the ocean liner Titanic *left the docks of Southampton, England, on its maiden voyage across the North Atlantic to New York. A proud symbol of the new industrial age, the towering ship carried twenty-three hundred passengers, some enjoying luxury that most travelers today could barely imagine. On the lower decks, however, poor immigrants crowded together in cramped quarters, journeying to what they hoped would be a better life in the United States.*

Two days out, the crew received reports of icebergs in the area but paid little notice. Then, near midnight, as the ship steamed swiftly and silently westward, a stunned lookout reported a massive shape rising directly ahead out of the dark ocean. Moments later, the ship collided with a huge iceberg, almost as tall as the ship itself, which ripped open its starboard side as if the grand vessel were a giant tin can.

Sea water burst into the ship's lower levels, and within twenty-five minutes people were rushing for the lifeboats. By 2 A.M. the bow of the Titanic was submerged with the stern high above the water. Clinging to the deck, quietly observed by those in lifeboats, hundreds of helpless passengers solemnly passed their final minutes before the ship disappeared into the frigid Atlantic (Lord, 1976).

The tragic loss of more than sixteen hundred lives made news around the world. Looking back dispassionately at this terrible event with a sociological eye, however, we see that some categories of passengers had much better odds of survival than others. Of those holding first-class tickets, more than 60 percent survived, primarily because they were on the upper decks, where warnings were sounded first and lifeboats were accessible. Only 36 percent of the second-class passengers were saved, and of the third-class passengers on the lower decks, only 24 percent escaped drowning. On board the Titanic, *class turned out to mean more than the degree of luxury of accommodations: It was truly a matter of life or death.*

The fate of those aboard the *Titanic* dramatically illustrates the enormous differences that social inequality can make in the way people live, or sometimes whether they live at all. This chapter introduces a number of concepts and sociological ideas concerning social stratification and surveys social inequality in the United States. Chapter 8 ("Global Stratification") enlarges our perspective by exploring how our society fits into a worldwide system of wealth and poverty.

What is Social Stratification?

Every society is marked by inequality, with some people having more money, schooling, health, and power than others. **Social stratification** refers to *a system by which a society ranks categories of people in a hierarchy.* Social stratification involves four fundamental principles.

1. **Social stratification is a characteristic of society, not simply a function of individual differences.** People in the United States tend to think of social standing in terms of individual achievement. But did a higher percentage of the first-class passengers on the *Titanic* survive because they were better swimmers than second- and third-class passengers? Hardly. They fared better because of their privileged position on the ship. Similarly, children born into wealthy families are more likely than those born into poverty to enjoy health, to become academic achievers, to succeed in their life's work, and to live well into old age. Neither rich nor poor children are responsible for creating social stratification, yet this system shapes the lives of them all.

2. **Social stratification persists over generations.** All societies recognize some degree of **social mobility,** *a change of position in a stratification system.* But in industrial societies like the United States, and even more so in agrarian societies, most people spend their lives at about the same social position, passing their social standing on to their children.

3. **Although universal, social stratification also varies in form.** Social stratification is found everywhere. Yet its character and intensity vary markedly from place to place. Some societies display more striking inequality than others. Similarly, as we shall see presently, some base their system of inequality primarily on prestige; others use wealth to establish people's place in the social hierarchy; still others focus on power as the key measure of social importance.

4. **Social stratification rests on widely held beliefs.** Systems of inequality not only give some people more resources than others, but also define these arrangements as fair. Just as *what* is unequal differs from society to society, then, so does the justification for inequality—the explanation of *why* people should be unequal.

Caste and Class Systems

Sociologists compare the world's systems of social inequality based on two opposing standards: "Closed" systems allow for little change in social position while "open" systems permit considerable social mobility (Tumin, 1985).

The Caste System

A **caste system** amounts to *social stratification based on ascription.* A pure caste system, in other words, is "closed," meaning that birth alone determines one's destiny. Rigid rankings characterize caste systems so that knowing your social category (rather than your particular talents and abilities) is sufficient to indicate your social ranking.

An illustration: India. Agrarian societies—including India—approximate caste systems. Caste holds sway in traditional Hindu villages where 80 percent of India's population live. In rural India, people are born into one of several thousand caste groups, which define their standing in the local community.

From birth, caste position determines the fundamental shape of people's lives. First, families in each caste perform one type of work from generation to generation. Although some vocations (like farming) are open to everyone, castes are identified with the work their members do (priests, barbers, fishers, and so on).

Second, to keep the hierarchy intact, Indian culture demands that people marry others of the same social ranking. Sociologists call this pattern *endogamous* marriage (*endo* stems from the Greek, meaning "within"). Tradition also directs parents to select marriage partners for their very young children (Srinivas, 1971).

Third, cultural beliefs also shore up caste systems. In India, tradition dictates that people accept their fate and carry out their life's work, whatever it may be, as a moral duty.

The personal experience of poverty is captured in Sebastiao Salgado's haunting photograph, which stands as a universal portrait of human suffering. The essential sociological insight is that, however strongly individuals feel its effects, our social standing is largely a consequence of the way in which a society (or a world of societies) structures opportunity and reward. To the core of our being, then, we are all the products of social stratification.

Fourth, caste systems organize everyday social contact. According to Indian traditions, relatively "pure" higher-caste people are "polluted" through contact with "unclean" members of lower castes. Such beliefs keep members of different categories apart and preserve the entire hierarchy.

Caste systems are typical of agrarian societies, because such beliefs foster the habits of diligence and discipline that agriculture demands. But the Hindu caste system has lost its hold in large cities, where most people now exercise greater choice in their marriage partners and their work (Bahl, 1991).

Another society that has been dominated by caste is South Africa, although the racially based system of *apartheid* is also now in decline. The box takes a closer look.

The Class System

A caste system bolsters stable, agrarian life; industrial societies, by contrast, depend on personal initiative and specialized talents. Industrialization thus propels social hierarchy toward a **class system,** *social stratification based on individual achievement.*

Race as Caste: A Report From South Africa

South Africa

At the southern tip of the African continent lies South Africa, a territory about the size of Alaska, with a population of more than 40 million. Long inhabited by people of African descent, the region attracted Dutch traders in the mid-seventeenth century. Early in the nineteenth century, a second wave of colonization, this time by British immigrants, pushed the Dutch inland. By the early 1900s, the British had gained control of the country, proclaiming it the Union of South Africa. In 1961, the United Kingdom recognized the independence of the Republic of South Africa.

But freedom was a reality only for white people. To ensure their political control over the black majority, whites relied on a policy of *apartheid,* or racial separation. A practice that developed over many years, apartheid was enshrined in law in 1948, denying blacks national citizenship, ownership of land, and any formal voice in the government. In effect, black South Africans became a subordinate caste, receiving little schooling and condemned to low-paying jobs. Under this system, even "middle-class" white housewives became accustomed to having a black household servant.

The prosperous white minority long defended apartheid as a way to preserve their cultural traditions and standard of living. But, as resistance to apartheid grew, the white minority government increasingly turned to military repression to maintain the status quo. At its peak, apartheid gave police the right to detain any black person who dared to oppose white rule in any way.

But criticism from most other industrial nations—including economic sanctions by the United States—helped to force South Africa to abandon apartheid. A decade ago, the South African government granted limited political rights to people of mixed race and Asian ancestry. Then came the right for all people to form labor unions, to enter occupations once restricted to whites, and to own property. Additionally, officials began to dismantle the system of "petty apartheid" regulations that segregated the races in all public places.

The process of change accelerated in 1990, with the release from prison of Nelson Mandela. In 1992, a majority of white voters endorsed the principle of bringing apartheid to an end and, in 1994, the first

Nelson Mandela, leader of the African National Congress (ANC), who was imprisoned by the white apartheid government for twenty-seven years, celebrates his election victory as South Africa's first black president.

national election open to all races elevated Mandela to the presidency, ending centuries of white minority rule.

But, despite this dramatic change, social stratification based on race still casts a long shadow over South Africa. Even with the right to own property, about one-third of black South Africans have no work and the majority remain dirt poor. The worst off are those termed *ukuhleleleka,* which means "marginal people" in the Xhosa language. Some 7 million blacks fall into this disadvantaged category. In Soweto-by-the-Sea, an idyllic-sounding community, thousands of people live crammed into shacks built of packing cases, corrugated metal, cardboard, and other discarded materials. There is no electricity for lights or refrigeration. Without plumbing, people use buckets to haul sewage; women line up awaiting their turn at a single water tap that serves more than one thousand people. Jobs are hard to come by, partly because Ford and General Motors have closed their factories in nearby Port Elizabeth, and partly because people keep migrating to the town from regions where life is even worse. Those who can find work are lucky to earn $200 a month.

Clearly, South Africa has taken dramatic strides toward ending its historic racial caste system. Yet this still-divided society faces the long-term challenge of providing real opportunity for the majority of people who still form a national underclass.

Sources: Based on Fredrickson (1981), Wren (1991), and Contreras (1992).

Social "classes" are not as rigidly defined as castes. As people gain skills and schooling and pursue new opportunities, they may experience social mobility in relation to their parents, blurring class distinctions. Under such a system, talent and effort—rather than birth—take on primary importance in social placement. Careers become matters of individual choice and achievement, not an ascribed status passed from generation to generation. Greater individuality also translates into more freedom in selecting a marital partner; parents and cultural traditions play a lesser role.

Status consistency. Status consistency refers to *the degree of consistency in a person's social standing across various dimensions of inequality.* By linking social ranking to birth, caste systems generate high status consistency; that is, people have similar relative standing with regard to wealth, prestige, power, and so on. Because of their characteristic mobility, class systems offer lower status consistency. In the United States, some people with prestigious occupations (such as priests or professors) accumulate little wealth and have limited social power. As a result of such inconsistencies, social classes (compared to castes) are poorly defined.

An illustration: the United Kingdom. There are no pure caste or class systems; social stratification in every society combines these two forms. Such a mix is evident in the United Kingdom (England, Wales, Scotland, and Northern Ireland), a society in which an agrarian history has given way to industrialization.

During the Middle Ages, England had a caste-like system of three *estates.* A hereditary nobility, or *first estate,* accounting for only 5 percent of the population, controlled most of the land—the chief form of wealth (Laslett, 1984). Typically, nobles had no occupation at all; to be "engaged in trade" or any other work for income was deemed "beneath" them. Well tended by servants, nobles used their extensive leisure time to cultivate refined tastes in art, music, and literature.

The estate system rested on the law of *primogeniture* (from Latin meaning "first born"), requiring one generation of nobles to pass their land intact to their eldest male descendant. This system forced younger noble sons to support themselves. Some entered the clergy—the *second estate*—where they exercised spiritual power and oversaw the church's extensive landholdings. Others became military officers or lawyers, or took up occupations that have come down to us today as "honorable" callings for "gentlemen." In an age when few women could expect to earn a living on their own, a daughter of nobility depended for her security on marrying well.

Below the nobility and the clergy, the vast majority of men and women formed the *third estate,* or "commoners." With little property, most commoners were serfs who worked plots of land owned by nobles. Unlike the nobility and the clergy, commoners had little access to schooling, so most remained illiterate.

As the Industrial Revolution steadily enlarged England's economy, some commoners gained wealth that rivaled—and sometimes surpassed—that of the nobility. Rapid economic growth, along with the extension of schooling and political rights to more people, undermined rigid social rankings as a class system emerged.

Yet the legacy of England's feudal past remains evident in today's social hierarchy. A small share of families enjoy considerable inherited wealth, which ensures the highest prestige, admission to expensive, elite universities, and political influence. A traditional monarch stands as the United Kingdom's head of state, and Parliament's House of Lords is composed of "peers" of noble birth. Yet, in a sign of the times, actual control of government resides in the House of Commons, where the prime minister and other legislators gain their position through election, not inheritance.

Below today's upper class, roughly one-fourth of the British people fall into the "middle class." Some earn high incomes from professions and business and are among the 10 percent of Britons who own stocks and bonds (Sherrid, 1986). Below the middle class, across a boundary that cannot be precisely defined, perhaps half of all Britons fall into the "working class," earning modest incomes, generally from manual labor. The remaining one-fourth of the British people form the lower class, the poor who lack steady work. They are concentrated in the nation's northern and western regions, which are plagued by the decline of mining and industrial factories.

Today, the United Kingdom is essentially a class system with unequally distributed wealth, power, and prestige, that affords people some opportunity to move upward or downward. One legacy of a long-established estate system, however, is that social mobility occurs less frequently in the United Kingdom than in the United States (Kerckhoff, Campbell, & Winfield-Laird, 1985). The relative rigidity of British stratification is exemplified in the importance attached to accent as a mark of social position. Distinctive patterns of speech develop in any society as stratification segregates categories of people from one another over many generations. In Great Britain, families of longstanding affluence and commoners speak so differently that

Eva Nagy, standing in front of her fashionable clothing store, represents the "new rich" class emerging in Hungary in the wake of that country's economic reforms. There seems to be little doubt that, in time, Eastern Europe's move toward a market economy will raise productivity and boost living standards. And it also seems likely that, in the process, economic inequality will increase as well.

they seem to be, as the old saying goes, a single people divided by a common language.

Classless Societies?

The former Soviet Union was born out of a revolution in 1917 that swept away a feudal estate system ruled by a hereditary nobility. The Russian Revolution transferred most farms, factories, and other productive property from private ownership to state control. Following the ideas of Karl Marx—who asserted that private ownership of such property is the basis of social classes—Soviet leaders boasted of forging a new, classless society.

But the former Soviet Union created a new social hierarchy, with high government officials dominating, in descending order, intellectuals and professionals, manual workers, and rural peasants. The fact that these categories enjoyed very different living standards indicates that the former Soviet Union never achieved the goals of social parity for everyone.

In 1985, Mikhail Gorbachev came to power with a new economic program, popularly known as *perestroika*, meaning "restructuring." Gorbachev recognized that,

while the Soviet system had reduced economic inequality, everyone was relatively poor, with living standards lagging far behind those of other industrial nations. Gorbachev hoped to stimulate economic expansion in the vast Soviet Union by reducing inefficient centralized control of the economy.

Gorbachev's reforms soon escalated into one of the most dramatic social movements in history, as popular uprisings toppled one after another socialist governments throughout Eastern Europe and, in 1991, in the Soviet Union itself. Those under the sway of Soviet socialism blamed their economic plight and their lack of basic freedoms on repression by small ruling classes of Communist Party officials.

Few are willing to predict the future of what is now called the Commonwealth of Independent States. But a look at the former Soviet Union reveals that social inequality has to do with much more than economic resources. While Soviet society lacked the extremes of wealth and poverty found in Great Britain and the United States, elite standing in that nation was based on *power* rather than wealth. Despite never earning as much as U.S. president Bill Clinton, both Mikhail Gorbachev and his successor Boris Yeltsin wielded awesome power.

And what about social mobility in so-called classless societies? Evidence suggests that, during this century, there has been more upward social mobility in the Soviet Union than in Great Britain or even the United States. But most of this difference is due to the rapid expansion of both industry and government that drew many rural peasants into factories and bureaucratic offices. This movement exemplifies what sociologists call **structural social mobility,** *a shift in the social position of large numbers of people due less to individual efforts than to changes in society itself.*

Now, with the recent introduction of private property into the economy and new laws sanctioning individual ownership of business enterprises, further structural social mobility should occur. Moreover, economic inequality probably will increase as well. Still, if the new direction translates into a higher standard of living, most would agree that the tradeoff of less equality for greater material plenty is definitely one worth making.

Ideology: Stratification's "Staying Power"

Looking around the world, we might wonder why people agree to live with so much inequality. The caste system of Great Britain lasted for centuries; even more striking, for two thousand years people in India accepted the idea that they should be privileged or poor due to the accident of birth.

A key reason for the remarkable persistence of social hierarchies is that they are built on **ideology,** *cultural beliefs that justify particular social arrangements.* The ancient Greek philosopher Plato (427–347 B.C.E.) treated justice as mostly a matter of agreement about who should have what. Societies, he explained, teach people to view their particular system of social stratification as "fair." Karl Marx, too, understood this fact, although he was more skeptical about claims of "fair inequality" than Plato was. Examining capitalist societies, Marx noted that, as the economy channels wealth and power into the hands of a few, culture defines the practice as simply "the laws of the marketplace." The legal system, furthermore, defines a basic right to own property and, tied to kinship, funnels money from one generation to the next. In short, Marx concluded, law, custom, and common sense work together to benefit a society's elite, which helps to explain why established hierarchies are so resistant to change.

Ideas that sustain social stratification change along with a society's economy and technology. Agrarian societies, dependent on the routine labor of most people, develop caste systems that define each person's work as a moral responsibility, all but ruling out the chance to change one's ranking. With the rise of industrial capitalism, a new idea came to the fore: Wealth and power became prizes won by those who display the greatest individual merit. This means that the poor, who were the objects of charity under feudalism, are denigrated by industrial capitalism as personally undeserving.

Human history reveals how difficult it is to change systems of social stratification. However, challenges to the status quo continue to arise as traditions weaken. Historic notions of a woman's place, for example, are losing their power to deprive women of economic opportunities. The continuing struggle for full-fledged racial equality in South Africa also exemplifies a widespread rejection of the ideology of apartheid.

The Functions of Social Stratification

Why are societies stratified at all? One answer, consistent with the structural-functional paradigm, is that social stratification has vital consequences for the operation of society. This argument was presented some fifty years ago by Kingsley Davis and Wilbert Moore (1945).

The Davis-Moore Thesis

Briefly stated, the *Davis-Moore thesis* asserts that social stratification is universal because it has beneficial consequences for the operation of a society. Why else,

---

In medieval Europe, people accepted rigid social differences, which divided them from birth until death, as part of a divine order for the world. This fifteenth-century painting by the Limbourg brothers—used to illustrate a book for the brother of the king—portrays life as orderly and cyclical. In this example, showing indoor life during January, the Duke of Berry is seated near the fireplace surrounded by a host of attendants that cater to his every whim. The firescreen behind him appears to give him a halo, surely intended by the artists to suggest the common notion of the time that nobles enjoyed their privileges by grace of God.

Limbourg Brothers, *Le Duc de Berry à table, Tres Riches Heures du Duc de Berry,* January, folio iv, Chantilly, Musée Conde.

Davis and Moore ask, would every known society have created some kind of social stratification? To explain the functions of inequality, Davis and Moore note that the many occupational positions found in a society are not all equal in importance. Some jobs—say, changing sparkplugs in a car—are relatively easy and can be done by virtually anyone. Other jobs—such as performing a human organ transplant—are only within the reach of people with scarce talents and expensive training.

In general, Davis and Moore explain, the greater the functional importance of an occupation, the more a society rewards those who perform it. Doing so makes sense, since rewarding important work with income, prestige, power, and leisure time encourages people to do these things. In effect, then, by distributing resources unequally, a society motivates people to develop their talents and to aspire toward the most significant work possible. Put otherwise, by directing rewards to those who work better, harder, or at least longer, social stratification makes a society more productive.

The Davis-Moore thesis does not deny that society can be egalitarian, but a system of equal rewards presumes that people are content to allow *any* person to perform *any* job. Equality also demands that good workers receive no more than those who perform poorly. Logic dictates that such a system does not motivate people toward their best efforts and thereby reduces a society's productive efficiency.

While the Davis-Moore thesis explains why stratification is universal, it does not endorse any *particular* system of inequality. Nor do Davis and Moore specify precisely what rewards a society should link to any occupational position. They merely point out that the positions a society deems crucial must yield sufficient reward to draw talent away from less important ones.

Meritocracy

The Davis-Moore thesis implies that societies become more productive as they approach **meritocracy,** *social stratification based on personal merit.* To the extent that a society is meritocratic ("merit" has Latin roots meaning "worthy of praise"), it uses unequal rewards to develop people's abilities and talents. Individuals, in turn, maximize their rewards by striving to be "all that they can be," as the army recruiters say. Meritocracy demands that a society promote *equality of opportunity* for everyone, but not *equality of condition.* Besides being unequal, a meritocracy also has extensive social mobility since individuals move upward or downward depending on their performance.

Relatively speaking, class systems are more meritocratic than caste systems. Through the eyes of caste societies, "merit" means a commitment to the low-skill labor necessary to the operation of an agrarian society. Caste systems, in short, confer honor on those who remain dutifully "in their place."

Caste systems inevitably waste human potential. Why, then, do modern industrial societies (including our own) limit meritocracy by allowing certain caste-like distinctions to persist? For one thing, more powerful categories of people (men or white people) benefit from a system that views other categories (women and minorities) as less meritorious by definition. In addition, left unchecked, meritocracy's focus on individuality erodes the social fabric of kinship and community; thus industrial class systems retain caste-like elements (including inheritance laws) to promote social cohesion and stability.

Critical evaluation. Although the Davis-Moore thesis has made a lasting contribution to sociological analysis, Melvin Tumin (1953) points to several flaws. First, Tumin notes the difficulty of assessing the functional importance of any occupation. As he sees it, the widespread respect for the work of physicians is partly engineered by medical schools that restrict admissions so the supply of physicians is kept low and the demand for their services remains high.

Second, actual rewards do not always seem to square with the contribution one makes to society. With an income of more than $50 million a year, television personality Oprah Winfrey earns more in one day than President Bill Clinton earns all year. Yet would anyone argue that hosting a talk show is of greater significance than the U.S. presidency?

A third charge made by Tumin is that Davis and Moore overlook how social stratification *prevents* the development of individual talent. While we expect rich people to develop their abilities, many gifted poor people never have the chance to realize their potential.

Fourth, by suggesting that social stratification benefits all of society, the Davis-Moore thesis ignores how social inequality promotes conflict and even outright revolution. This assertion leads us to the social-conflict paradigm, which offers a very different explanation for the persistence of social hierarchy.

Stratification and Conflict

Social-conflict analysis holds that, rather than promoting the operation of society as a whole, social stratification ensures that some people gain advantages at the expense of others. This analysis draws heavily on the ideas of Karl Marx, with additional insights from Max Weber.

Karl Marx: Class Conflict

The striking inequality of the early Industrial Revolution both saddened and angered Karl Marx. The technological miracle of industrialization meant that humanity could finally envision a society free from want. Yet, industrial capitalism had done little to improve the lives of most people. Marx devoted his life to explaining a glaring contradiction: how, in a society so rich, so many could be so poor.

In Marx's view, social stratification is rooted in people's relationships to the means of production. Either they are *owners* of productive property or they *provide labor* for enterprises controlled by others. In feudal Europe, the nobility and clergy owned the productive land, and the peasantry supplied labor. The rise of industrial capitalism changed only the identity of the contending classes, with the nobility replaced by **capitalists**, *people who own factories and other productive businesses.* Capitalists (sometimes termed the *bourgeoisie*, a French word meaning "of the town") use their property to gain profits. To do this, they employ the **proletariat**, *people who sell their productive labor.* Members of the industrial proletariat work for the wages needed to live. Marx predicted that the two great classes—separated by irreconcilable interests and great disparities in wealth and power—would inevitably clash in a thunderous confrontation.

Marx's analysis drew heavily on his observations of capitalism in the nineteenth century, when powerful new productive forces had elevated some to great wealth while subjecting most to monotonous toil for low wages. During this period, wealthy U.S. capitalists like Andrew Carnegie, J. P. Morgan, and John Jacob Astor (one of the few rich passengers to perish on the *Titanic*) lived in fabulous mansions filled with priceless art and staffed by dozens of servants. Even by today's standards, their incomes were staggering. Carnegie, for example, made more than $20 million in 1900 ($100 million in today's dollars)—at a time when the average worker earned about $500 a year in wages (Baltzell, 1964; Pessen, 1990).

In time, Marx believed, the working majority would overthrow the capitalists once and for all. Capitalism sowed the seeds of its own demise, Marx reasoned, by steadily reducing the living standards of workers and according them little control over their work or the product of their labor. Thus, Marx asserted, work under capitalism produced **alienation**, *the experience of powerlessness in social life*, rather than personal satisfaction.

In place of capitalism, Marx envisioned a *socialist* system he thought would respond to the needs of all—rather than merely boosting the profits of the few. Thus Marx, a relentless critic of the present, looked to the future with hope, claiming (1972:362; orig. 1848): "The proletarians have nothing to lose but their chains. They have a world to win."

This cartoon, titled "Capital and Labour," appeared in the English press in 1843, when the ideas of Karl Marx were first gaining attention. It links the plight of that country's coal miners to the privileges enjoyed by those who owned coal-fired factories.

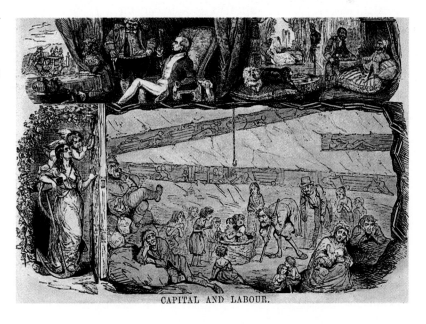

CAPITAL AND LABOUR.

John George Brown made a fortune a century ago as a painter who portrayed the world as most people wanted to see it (left). Photographer Jacob Riis, among others, found far less fame during his own lifetime by capturing something closer to the truth. This is Riis's well-known image of New York's "street arabs" (right), who survived as best they could on the mean streets of this growing industrial city.

Critical evaluation. By exploring how the capitalist economic system generates conflict between classes, Marx's analysis has had enormous influence on sociological thinking in recent decades. Its revolutionary implications also make it highly controversial.

Critics charge that the Marxist approach denies a crucial element of the Davis-Moore thesis: Motivating people to perform various social roles well requires a system of unequal rewards. Marx separated reward from performance, endorsing an egalitarian system based on the principle "from each according to his ability, to each according to his needs" (1972:388). Critics suggest that severing rewards from performance is what doomed the former Soviet Union and other socialist economies to low productivity.

A second flaw in Marx's analysis is that the revolutionary change he saw as inevitable failed to materialize. The next section considers why.

Why No Marxist Revolution?

Despite Marx's prediction, capitalism is still thriving. Why have workers in the United States not overthrown capitalism? Ralf Dahrendorf (1959) suggested four reasons.

1. **The fragmentation of the capitalist class.** Today, stockholders rather than single families typically own large companies. Moreover, the day-to-day operation of big corporations is now handled by many managers, who may or may not be major stockholders. With stock widely sold, an increasing number of people have a direct stake in preserving the capitalist system.

2. **A higher standard of living.** As Chapter 11 ("Economics and Politics") explains, a century ago most U.S. workers earned their livings in factories or on farms performing **blue-collar occupations**, *lower-prestige work that involves mostly manual labor.* Today, most workers hold **white-collar occupations**, *higher-prestige work that involves mostly mental activity.* These jobs include positions in sales, management, and other service work. Thus, most of today's white-collar workers do not think of themselves as an "industrial proletariat." Just as important, the

average income in the United States has risen almost tenfold over the course of this century in dollars controlled for inflation, even as the workweek has decreased. Is it any wonder, then, that workers typically perceive themselves as better off than their parents and grandparents? This structural mobility has certainly cooled revolutionary aspirations among working people (Edwards, 1979; Gagliani, 1981; Wright & Martin, 1987).

3. **More extensive worker organization.** Workers have organizational strengths they lacked a century ago. Employees have the right to organize into labor unions that can make demands of management, backed by threats of work slowdowns and strikes. If not always peaceful, then, worker-management disputes are now part of the fabric of corporate life.

4. **More extensive legal protections.** During this century, the government enacted laws to make the workplace safer and devised programs, such as unemployment insurance, disability protection, and Social Security, to provide workers with greater financial security.

Taken together, these developments suggest that, despite persistent inequality, our society has smoothed many of capitalism's rough edges. Advocates of social-conflict analysis, however, defend Marx's analysis of capitalism as still largely valid (Miliband, 1969; Edwards, 1979; Giddens, 1982; Domhoff, 1983; Stephens, 1986). First, they point out, wealth remains highly concentrated, with about half of all privately controlled corporate stock owned by 1 percent of our population. Second, many of today's white-collar jobs

offer no more income, security, or satisfaction than factory work did a century ago. Third, many of the benefits enjoyed by today's workers came about precisely through the class conflict Marx described, and workers still struggle to hold on to what they have. Fourth, workers may have gained some legal protections, but the law has changed little the overall distribution of wealth in this country. Therefore, social-conflict theorists conclude, the absence of a socialist revolution in the United States does not invalidate Marx's analysis of capitalism.

Table 7–1 summarizes the two contrasting explanations of social stratification.

Max Weber: Class, Status, and Power

Max Weber agreed with Karl Marx that social stratification sparks social conflict, but he thought Marx's two-class model was simplistic. Instead, he viewed social stratification as the interplay of three distinct dimensions.

First, Weber took note of economic inequality—the issue so vital to Marx—which he termed *class* position. Weber did not think of "classes" as crude categories but as a continuum ranging from high to low. Second, Weber highlighted *status*, or social prestige. Third, Weber emphasized the importance of *power* in a social hierarchy.

The socioeconomic status hierarchy. Marx regarded prestige and power as simple derivatives of economic position, and saw no reason to treat them as distinct dimensions of inequality. But Weber noted that status consistency in modern societies is often quite low: A local official, say, might wield considerable power yet

TABLE 7–1 Two Explanations of Social Stratification: A Summary

Structural-Functional Paradigm	Social-Conflict Paradigm
Social stratification keeps society operating. The linkage of greater rewards to more important social positions benefits society as a whole.	Social stratification is the result of social conflict. Differences in social resources serve the interests of some and harm the interests of others.
Social stratification encourages a matching of talents and abilities to appropriate positions.	Social stratification ensures that much talent and ability within society will not be tapped at all.
Social stratification is both useful and inevitable.	Social stratification is useful to only some people; it is not inevitable.
The values and beliefs that legitimize social inequality are widely shared throughout society.	Values and beliefs tend to be ideological; they reflect the interests of the more powerful members of society.
Because systems of social stratification are useful to society and are supported by cultural values and beliefs, they are usually stable over time.	Because systems of social stratification reflect the interests of only part of society, they are unlikely to remain stable over time.

Source: Adapted in part from Arthur L. Stinchcombe, "Some Empirical Consequences of the Davis-Moore Theory of Stratification," *American Sociological Review*, Vol. 28, No. 5 (October 1963):808.

have little wealth or social prestige. Weber's contribution, then, lies in showing that stratification in industrial societies comprises a multidimensional ranking. Following Weber's thinking, sociologists often use the term **socioeconomic status (SES)** to refer to *a composite social ranking based on various dimensions of inequality.*

A population that varies widely in class, status, and power—Weber's three dimensions of difference—displays a virtually infinite array of self-interested social groupings. Thus, unlike Marx, who concentrated on the conflict between two contending classes, Weber considered social conflict as a more complex, subtle, and variable process.

Inequality in history. Weber asserted that each of his three dimensions of social inequality stands out at a different point in history. Agrarian societies, he maintained, emphasize *prestige* in the form of honor or symbolic purity. Members of these societies gain prestige by conforming to cultural norms corresponding to their rank.

Industrialization and the development of capitalism level traditional rankings based on birth but generate striking financial differences. Thus, Weber argued, the crucial difference among people in capitalist societies lies in the economic dimension of *class.*

In time, industrial societies witness a surging growth in the bureaucratic state. This expansion of government, coupled with the proliferation of other types of formal organizations, means that official *power* gains primacy in the stratification system. Power is especially important to the organization of socialist societies, largely due to their extensive government regulation of many aspects of life. The elite members of such societies are likely to be high-ranking officials rather than rich people.

Based on this historical analysis, we can pinpoint a final difference between Weber and Marx. Marx believed that societies could virtually eliminate social stratification by abolishing private ownership of productive property. Weber doubted that overthrowing capitalism would significantly diminish social stratification. It might lessen economic disparity, he reasoned, but socialism would simultaneously increase inequality by expanding government and concentrating power in the hands of a political elite. Recent popular uprisings against entrenched bureaucracies in Eastern Europe and the former Soviet Union lend support to Weber's position.

Critical evaluation. Weber's multidimensional analysis of social stratification retains enormous influence among sociologists, especially in the United States.

Some analysts (particularly those influenced by Marx's ideas) argue that while social class boundaries have blurred, striking patterns of social inequality persist in the United States and elsewhere in the industrial world. Moreover, as we shall see presently, economic inequality has increased in recent years.

Stratification and Technology: A Global Survey

We can weave together a number of observations made in this chapter by considering the relationship between a society's technology and its form of social stratification. This analysis draws on Gerhard and Jean Lenski's model of sociocultural evolution, detailed in Chapter 2 ("Culture"), as well as both the structural-functional and social-conflict approaches (Lenski, 1966; Lenski, Lenski, & Nolan, 1991).

Simple technology limits the production of hunters and gatherers to what is necessary for day-to-day living. Although some individuals produce more than others, the group's survival depends on everyone sharing what they have. Thus, no categories of people emerge as better off.

As technological advances generate material surplus, social inequality intensifies. In horticultural and pastoral societies, a small elite gains control of most resources. Larger-scale agriculture produces still greater abundance as well as the most pronounced inequality of all. Various categories of people lead strikingly different lives, with nobles wielding god-like power over the masses.

Industrialization turns the tide, nudging inequality downward. Prompted by the need to develop individual talents, egalitarian thinking takes hold in these societies, lessening the power of elites. The increasing productivity of industrial technology steadily raises the living standards of the historically poor majority. Specialized work also demands the expansion of schooling, which sharply reduces illiteracy. A literate population, in turn, tends to press for a greater voice in political decision making. Industrialization also undermines the domination of women by men, since modern societies try to cultivate individual talent. In time, wealth becomes less concentrated (countering the trend predicted by Marx). Estimates suggest that the share of wealth controlled by the richest 1 percent of U.S. families peaked at about 36 percent just before the stock market crash in 1929, falling to about 30 percent by 1990

(Williamson & Lindert, 1980; Beeghley, 1989; *1991 Green Book*).

Considering the leveling effects of industrialization, we can understand why Marxist revolutions occurred in *agrarian* societies—such as Russia (1917), Cuba (1959), and Nicaragua (1979)—where social inequality is historically most striking, rather than in *industrial* societies, as Marx predicted more than a century ago.

In sum, reducing the intensity of social stratification is actually functional for industrial societies. This historical pattern, recognized by Nobel Prize-winning economist Simon Kuznets (1955, 1966; see also Berger, 1986), is illustrated by the "Kuznets Curve," shown in Figure 7–1.

Current patterns of social inequality around the world generally square with the Kuznets Curve. Global Map 7–1 on page 168 shows that industrial nations (including the United States) have less income inequality than predominantly agrarian countries (mostly found in Latin America, Africa, and Asia). Note, however, that income disparity reflects a host of factors beyond technology, especially political and economic realities. Consider countries that have had socialist economies (including the People's Republic of China, the Soviet Union, and the nations of Eastern Europe). While these countries exhibit relatively less income inequality than their capitalist counterparts, the people's average incomes in socialist nations are low by world standards. A closer look also reveals pronounced inequality on non-economic dimensions such as political power.

Inequality in the United States

The United States stands apart from most of the world's nations in never having had a titled aristocracy. With the significant exception of our racial history, we have never known a caste system that rigidly ranks categories of people.

Even so, U.S. society is highly stratified. The rich not only control most of the money, but they also benefit from the most schooling, they enjoy the best health, and they consume the greatest share of almost all goods and services. Such privilege contrasts sharply with the poverty of millions of women and men who struggle from day to day simply to survive. The widespread notion that the United States is a "middle-class society" does not square with several important facts.

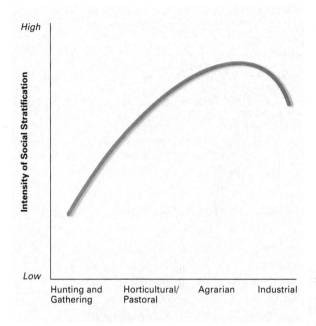

FIGURE 7–1   Social Stratification and Technological Development: The Kuznets Curve

The Kuznets curve posits that greater technological sophistication is generally accompanied by more pronounced social stratification. The trend reverses itself, however, as industrial societies gradually become more egalitarian. Rigid caste-like distinctions are relaxed in favor of greater opportunity and equality under the law. Political rights are extended more widely, and there is even some leveling of economic differences. The Kuznets curve may also be usefully applied to the relative social standing of the two sexes.

Income, Wealth, and Power

One important dimension of economic inequality involves **income,** *wages or salary from work and earnings from investments.* The government reports that the median U.S. family income[1] in 1992 was $36,812. The pie chart on the left of Figure 7–2 shows the distribution of income among U.S. families. Note that the 20 percent of families with the highest earnings (at least

---

[1]Reported for households rather than families, median income is somewhat lower: $30,786 in 1992. The Census Bureau defines a household as one or more persons in a living unit; a family, by contrast, is two or more persons related by blood, marriage, or adoption. Most of the difference between families and households is due to size: 1992 families contained, on average, 3.16 persons compared with 2.63 people for households.

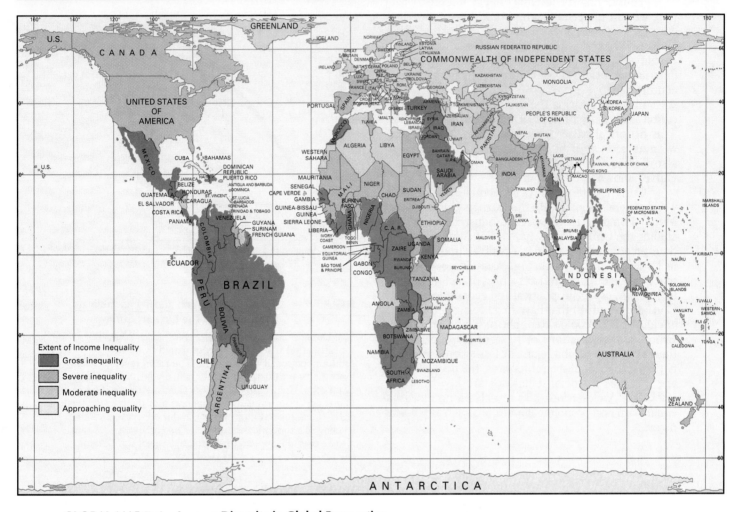

GLOBAL MAP 7–1   Income Disparity in Global Perspective

Societies throughout the world differ in the rigidity and intensity of social stratification as well as in overall standard of living. This map highlights income inequality. Generally speaking, countries that have had centralized, socialist economies (including the People's Republic of China, the former Soviet Union, and Cuba) display the least income inequality, although their standard of living has been relatively low. Industrial societies with predominantly capitalist economies, such as the United States and most of Western Europe, have higher overall living standards, accompanied by severe income disparity. The less-industrialized societies in Latin America and Africa (including Mexico, Brazil, and Zaire) exhibit the most pronounced inequality of income.

Source: *Peters Atlas of the World* (1990).

$64,000, with median income of about $100,000) received 44.6 percent of all income, while the bottom 20 percent (earning less than $17,000, with a median of $9,700) took in only about 4.4 percent. At the very top, the highest-paid 5 percent of families (who earn at least $110,000 annually, with a median of $156,000) secured

18 percent of all income, more than the lowest-paid 40 percent.

Income is but one component of the broader economic factor of **wealth,** *an individual's or family's total financial assets.* Wealth—including stocks, bonds, and real estate—is distributed less equally than income is. The pie chart on the right of Figure 7–2 breaks down the distribution of wealth in the United States in 1990. The richest 20 percent of U.S. families own an estimated four-fifths of the country's entire wealth. High up in this privileged category, the wealthiest 5 percent of families control over half of all property. Richer still—with wealth into the tens of millions of dollars—1 percent of our families possess about one-third of this country's resources. And at the very top of the wealth pyramid, the *three* richest families have a combined wealth in excess of $40 billion, which equals the total property of a million "average" individuals, representing enough people to fill the cities of Boston, Milwaukee, and New Orleans (Joint Economic Committee, 1986; Millman et al., 1993; Rogers, 1993).

The median wealth of U.S. families is about $40,000, roughly the same as the median annual family income (*1991 Green Book*). Lesser wealth is also different in *kind:* The richest people hold most of their property in the form of stocks and other income-producing investments. The wealth of average people resides primarily in property that generates no income, such as a home.

When financial assets are balanced against debts, the lowest-ranking 40 percent of families have little or no wealth. As the negative percentage shown on the right side of Figure 7–2 indicates, the bottom 20 percent actually live in debt.

In the United States, wealth confers power. Therefore, the small proportion of families that controls most of the wealth also has the ability to shape the agenda of the entire society through concerted political action. As explained in Chapter 11 ("Economics and Politics"), some sociologists argue that such concentrated wealth undermines democracy because the political system ends up serving the interests of "super-rich" families.

FIGURE 7–2   Distribution of Income and Wealth in the United States

Sources: Income data from U. S. Bureau of the Census (1993); wealth data are author estimates based on the Joint Economic Committee (1986) and Kennickell & Shack-Marquez (1992).

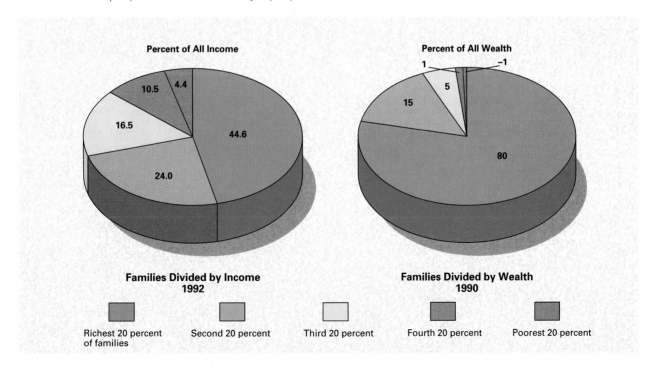

Occupational Prestige

Beyond generating income, occupation also serves as an important source of social prestige. We commonly evaluate each other according to the kind of work we do, envying some and looking down on others.

Sociologists have long monitored the relative social prestige of various occupations (Counts, 1925; Hodge, Treiman, & Rossi, 1966; NORC, 1993). Table 7–2 shows that people generally accord high prestige to occupations—such as physicians, lawyers, and engineers—that also produce high income. Favored occupations also require considerable ability and training.

By contrast, less prestigious work—as a waitress or janitor, for example—not only pays less, but usually requires less competence and schooling. Occupational prestige rankings are much the same in all industrial societies (Ma, 1987; Lin & Xie, 1988).

In any society, the most privileged categories of people tend to pursue occupations that yield the greatest prestige. Starting at the top of Table 7–2, one passes a dozen occupations before finding one ("registered nurse") in which most workers are women. Similarly, working your way up from the bottom, notice how many of these low-prestige jobs are commonly filled by minorities.

TABLE 7–2 The Relative Social Prestige of Selected Occupations in the United States

White-Collar Occupations	Prestige Score	Blue-Collar Occupations	White-Collar Occupations	Prestige Score	Blue-Collar Occupations
Physician	86		Bookkeeper	47	
Lawyer	75			47	Machinist
College/university professor	74			47	Mail carrier
Architect	73		Musician/composer	47	
Chemist	73			46	Secretary
Physicist/astronomer	73		Photographer	45	
Aerospace engineer	72		Bank teller	43	
Dentist	72			42	Tailor
Clergy person	69			42	Welder
Psychologist	69			41	Apprentice electrician
Pharmacist	68			40	Farmer
Optometrist	67			40	Telephone operator
Registered nurse	66			39	Carpenter
Secondary-school teacher	66			38	TV repairperson
Accountant	65			37	Security guard
Professional athlete	65			36	Brick/stone mason
Electrical engineer	64			36	Child care worker
Elementary-school teacher	64		File clerk	36	
Economist	63			36	Hairdresser
Veterinarian	62			35	Baker
Airplane pilot	61			34	Bulldozer operator
Computer programmer	61			34	Meter reader
Sociologist	61			32	Bus driver
Editor/reporter	60			31	Auto body repairperson
	60	Police officer	Retail apparel salesperson	30	
Actor	58			30	Truck driver
Radiologic technician	58		Cashier	29	
Dietician	56			28	Elevator operator
Radio/TV announcer	55			28	Garbage collector
Librarian	54			28	Taxi driver
	53	Aircraft mechanic		28	Waiter/waitress
	53	Firefighter		27	Bellhop
Dental hygienist	52			25	Bartender
Painter/sculptor	52			23	Farm laborer
Social worker	52			23	Household laborer
	51	Electrician		23	Midwife
Computer operator	50			22	Door-to-door salesperson
Funeral director	49			22	Janitor
Realtor	49			09	Shoe shiner

Source: Adapted from *General Social Surveys 1972–1993: Cumulative Codebook* (Chicago: National Opinion Research Center, 1993), pp. 937–45.

Schooling

In industrial societies, some schooling is mandatory for everyone, but all young people in the United States do not have an equal opportunity for formal education. Table 7–3 indicates the schooling of our population aged twenty-five and over in 1993. While more than three-fourths had completed high school, only about 22 percent were college graduates.

Dimensions of inequality are interconnected. Schooling affects both occupation and income, since most (but not all) of the better-paying, white-collar occupations shown in Table 7–2 require a college degree or other advanced study. Similarly, most blue-collar jobs that offer less income demand less schooling.

Ancestry, Race, and Gender

Although our class system does reward individual talent and initiative, the family into which we are born not only determines our initial social standing but also has a strong bearing on our future schooling, occupation, and income. Studies of our country's richest individuals—those with hundreds of millions of dollars in wealth—note that about half derived their fortunes primarily from inheritance (Thurow, 1987; Queenan, 1989). The "inheritance" of poverty and the lack of opportunity that goes with it just as surely shape the future of those in need.

Race, too, is closely linked to social position in the United States. White people have a higher overall occupational standing than African Americans, and also receive more schooling. These differences are reflected in median income: African-American families earned $21,161 in 1992, about 54 percent of the $38,909 earned by white families (U.S. Bureau of the Census, 1993). Differences in family patterns account for much of this income disparity. Comparing only families that include a married couple, African-American families earned 80 percent as much as white families.

Over time, this income differential builds into a considerable "wealth gap," with median wealth for African-American adults (about $4,100) equaling just 10 percent of that ($43,300) among white adults (O'Hare, 1989; *1991 Green Book*). Finally, race even shapes the lives of affluent families, as the box on page 172 explains.

Ethnicity, too, relates to social stratification. Traditionally, people of English ancestry have enjoyed the most wealth and exercised the greatest power. The rapidly growing Latino population of the United States, by contrast, has long been disadvantaged. In

**TABLE 7–3 Schooling of U.S. Adults, 1993
(aged 25 and over)**

	Women	Men
Not a high school graduate	20.1%	19.5%
8 years or less	9.2	9.4
9–11 years	10.9	10.1
High school graduate	80.0	80.6
High school only	37.4	33.2
1–3 years college	23.4	22.6
College graduate or more	19.2	24.8

Source: U.S. Bureau of the Census (1994).

1990, median income among Hispanic families was $23,901, about 61 percent of the comparable figure for all white families. Chapter 9 ("Race and Ethnicity") offers a detailed examination of how race and ethnicity affect social standing.

Societies also place men and women in different social positions. Of course, people of both sexes are born to families at every social level. Yet, on average, women claim less income, wealth, and occupational prestige than men. Even more important, as we shall explain later, households headed by women are nine times more likely to be poor than those headed by men. Chapter 10 ("Sex and Gender") fully examines the link between gender and social stratification.

Social Classes in the United States

As we have explained, rankings in a rigid caste system are obvious to all. Defining the social categories in a more fluid class system, however, poses a number of challenges. Taking Karl Marx's lead, we might identify two major social classes; other sociologists, however, have listed as many as six classes (Warner & Lunt, 1941) or even seven (Coleman & Rainwater, 1978). Still others endorse Max Weber's contention that industrial societies have not so much clear classes as a multidimensional continuum of difference.

The difficulty in defining classes in the United States arises from the relatively low status consistency in our society. Especially toward the middle of the hierarchy, people's social position on one dimension may contradict their standing on another (Gilbert & Kahl, 1993). Into what class would we place a member of the clergy who enjoys high prestige, but has moderate power and little wealth? And what of a lucky gambler who accumulates lots of money yet has little power and never completed high school? To make matters more

Two Colors of Affluence: Do Black People and White People Differ?

The typical African-American family earns only about 54 percent of the income of the average white family, establishing a strong link between race and poverty. But there is another side—an *affluent* side—to black America that has expanded in recent years.

In 1990, more than 1 million African-American families were affluent—with annual incomes exceeding $50,000. Adjusted for inflation, this represents a five-fold increase over two decades before. Today, almost 15 percent of African-American families—more than 2 million adults and their children—are affluent. About 15 percent of Latino families are affluent, too, as are 30 percent of white families and 35 percent of Asian families.

Black and white affluence differs in several key respects. First, well-off people of African descent are not *as rich* as their white counterparts. Almost 40 percent of rich white families (14 percent of all white families) earn more than $75,000 a year; only 26 percent of affluent African-American families (3 percent of all black families) reach this level of income. Second, African Americans are more likely than white people to achieve affluence through *multiple incomes*—from two employed spouses, or employed

parents and children. Third, affluent African Americans generally *earn* their income rather than deriving it from investments. Three-fourths of affluent white families have investment income, compared to only one-half of rich African-American families.

Beyond differences in income, affluent blacks still contend with social barriers based on color. Even African Americans with the money to purchase a home, for example, may find they are unwelcome as neighbors. For this reason, a smaller share of affluent African-American families (40 percent) live in the suburbs (the richest areas of the country) than do affluent white families (61 percent).

Affluent people come in all colors. Yet, race exerts a powerful influence on the lives of rich people, just as it influences the rest of us.

Sources: O'Hare (1989) and U.S. Bureau of the Census (1991).

---

complex, the social mobility characteristic of class systems—again, most pronounced near the middle—means that social position can change during one's lifetime, further blurring class boundaries. Keeping these problems in mind, we can break down U.S. society into four general rankings: the upper class, the middle class, the working class, and the lower class.

The Upper Class

Families in the upper class—3 or 4 percent of the U.S. population—have annual earnings of at least $100,000 and perhaps ten times that much. As a general rule, the stronger a family's claim to being upper class, the more they derive their income from inherited wealth.

In 1993, *Forbes* magazine profiled the richest four hundred people in the United States, estimating their combined wealth at $328 billion. These richest people had a *minimum* net worth of $300 million and included seventy-nine billionaires. The upper class thus comprises Karl Marx's "capitalists," those who own most of the nation's productive property.

Adding to their wealth and power, many members of the upper class work as top executives in large corporations and as senior government officials. Upper-class people also gain the most education, typically in expensive and highly regarded schools and colleges. Historically, although less so today, the upper class has been composed of white Anglo-Saxon Protestants (WASPs) (Baltzell, 1964, 1976, 1988).

People in the *upper-upper class*, sometimes termed "society" or "bluebloods," include about 1 percent of the nation's population (Warner & Lunt, 1941; Coleman & Neugarten, 1971; Rossides, 1990). Membership is almost always the result of birth, as suggested by the old quip that the easiest way to become an "upper-upper" is to be born one. These families possess enormous wealth, primarily inherited rather than earned. For this reason, we sometimes say that members of the upper-upper class have *old money*.

Most members of the upper-upper class live in exclusive neighborhoods such as Beacon Hill in Boston, the Rittenhouse Square section of Philadelphia, the Gold Coast of Chicago, and Nob Hill in San Francisco. Their children typically attend private secondary schools with others of similar background, completing their formal education at high-prestige colleges and universities. In the historical pattern of European aristocrats, they study liberal arts rather than vocational subjects. Women of the upper-upper class often engage in volunteer work for charitable organizations. While helping the larger community, these activities also forge networks that broaden this elite's power (Ostrander, 1980, 1984).

The remaining 2 or 3 percent of this elite category fall into the *lower-upper class*. For these families, the primary source of wealth is earnings rather than inheritance. While so-called "new rich" families generally live in expensive houses or condominiums, they are still excluded from the highest-prestige clubs and associations frequented by the "old-money" families of the upper-upper class.

The Middle Class

The middle class includes 40 to 45 percent of the U.S. population. Because it is so large and embodies the aspirations of many more people, the middle class exerts tremendous influence on our culture. Television and other mass media usually show middle-class men and women, and most commercial advertising is directed at these "average" consumers. The middle class encompasses far more ethnic and racial diversity than the upper class.

Families in the top third of this category are sometimes designated the *upper-middle class*, based on their above-average income in the range of $50,000 to $100,000 a year. This allows members of the upper-middle class gradually to accumulate considerable property—a comfortable house in a fairly expensive area, several automobiles, and some investments. Nearly all upper-middle-class people receive college educations, and postgraduate degrees are common. Many work in white-collar fields such as medicine, engineering, and law, or as business executives. Lacking

the power of the richest people to influence national or international events, the upper-middle class often plays an important role in local political affairs.

The rest of the middle class typically works in less prestigious white-collar occupations (as bank tellers, lower-level managers, and sales clerks) or in highly skilled blue-collar jobs (including electrical work and carpentry). Commonly, household income falls between $35,000 and $50,000 a year, which is at or slightly above the national average. Most middle-class people accumulate a small amount of wealth over the course of their working lives and eventually own a house. Middle-class men and women are likely to be high-school graduates, but only about four in ten young people at this class level attend college, usually at less expensive state-supported schools.

The Working Class

Including about one-third of the population, working-class people have lower incomes than those in the middle class and virtually no accumulated wealth. In Marxist terms, the working class forms the core of the industrial proletariat. Their blue-collar occupations generally yield a family income of between $15,000 and $35,000 a year, somewhat below the national average. Working-class families thus find themselves vulnerable to financial crises brought on by unemployment or illness.

Working-class jobs typically provide less personal satisfaction, and workers are usually subject to continual supervision. These jobs also offer fewer benefits such as medical insurance and pension plans. About half of working-class families own their homes, usually in lower-cost neighborhoods. Only about one-third of working-class children will attend college.

The Lower Class

The remaining 20 percent of our population make up the lower class. With little income, their lives are unstable and insecure. In 1992, the federal government classified some 37 million people (14.5 percent of the population) as poor. Millions more—the so-called "working poor"—are only marginally better off, typically holding low-prestige jobs with few intrinsic rewards and minimal satisfaction. Barely half manage to complete high school, and only one in four enrolls in college.

Society segregates the lower class, especially when the poor are racial or ethnic minorities. Although 40 percent of lower-class families manage to own their own home, most reside in the least-desirable neighborhoods. Poor districts generally are found in the inner cities, but lower-class families also live in rural communities, especially across the South.

The Difference Class Makes

Social stratification affects nearly every dimension of social life. Health is one of the most important correlates of social standing. Children born into poor families are at least twice as likely to die—from disease, neglect, accidents, or violence—during their first year of life than children born into privileged families. Among adults, people with above-average incomes are twice as likely to describe their health as excellent as are low-income people. Affluence supports longer life expectancy by providing more nutritious foods, a safer and less stressful environment, and more comprehensive medical care (Gortmaker, 1979; Children's Defense Fund, 1991).

Life expectancy is closely related to social-class position. Poor people—especially young males—who struggle to get by in cities around the world, have a strikingly high rate of death and injury from illness, accident, and violence. Some individuals caught up in poverty engage in perilous behavior because they have little reason to think the future will be brighter than the present. The boy shown here, from a poor neighborhood in Rio de Janeiro, died in a "train surfing" accident shortly after this photograph was taken.

Cultural values, too, vary somewhat from class to class. Women and men with the highest social standing have an unusually strong sense of family history since they enjoy wealth and social prestige passed down from generation to generation (Baltzell, 1979). Because their social standing is guaranteed as a birthright, the "old rich" also tend to be understated in their manners and tastes, while "new rich" people buy pricey homes, cars, and clothes as *status symbols* that "make a statement" about their owners.

People with substantial personal and financial security—and, therefore, greater latitude in their range of life choices—display more tolerance than their less-privileged counterparts toward controversial behavior on "family values" issues like premarital sexual activity and homosexuality. By the same token, working-class people grow up in an atmosphere of greater supervision and discipline at home that gives way later to a similar experience on the job as adults. In raising their children, then, they stress conformity to conventional beliefs and practices (Kohn, 1977; Humphries, 1984).

Political attitudes tend to follow class lines as well. Generally, more privileged people support the Republican Party while those with fewer advantages lean toward the Democrats. Looking to protect their wealth, people who are well off take a more conservative approach to economic issues, favoring a free-market economy unregulated by government. On social issues, such as support for the Equal Rights Amendment, abortion, and other feminist concerns, however, affluent people tend to be more liberal. People of lower social standing show the opposite pattern, backing liberal economic policies and conservative social goals (Nunn, Crockett, & Williams, 1978; Erikson, Luttbeg, & Tedin, 1980; Syzmanski, 1983; Humphries, 1984).

Finally, family life is also shaped by social class. Generally, lower-class families are larger than middle-class families, due to earlier marriage and less use of birth control. Upper-class families, too, have more children, partly because they can afford added child-rearing expenses. And it stands to reason that the greater a family's social resources, the more parents can develop their children's talents and abilities. According to a recent calculation, affluent families earning over $50,000 annually will spend more than $300,000 raising a child born in 1993 to the age of eighteen. Middle-class people, with income of about $40,000 a year, will spend about $200,000, while families earning less than $30,000 will spend about $170,000 (Lino, 1994). To be sure, children are a substantial financial expenditure for everyone, but privilege tends to beget privilege. In this way, family life reproduces a society's class structure from generation to generation.

Social Mobility

Ours is a dynamic society marked by a significant measure of mobility. Earning a college degree, securing a higher-paying job, or succeeding in a business endeavor contributes to *upward social mobility*, while dropping out of school, losing a job, or failing to sustain a business may signal *downward social mobility*.

But changes in society as a whole underlie most social mobility. As the United States industrialized, for example, the economy expanded, raising living standards for millions. Even without being good swimmers, so to speak, people were able to "ride a rising tide of prosperity." As explained presently, *structural social mobility* in a downward direction has more recently dealt many people economic setbacks.

Sociologists distinguish between one-generation and multigenerational transitions. **Intragenerational social mobility** refers to *a change in social position occurring during a person's lifetime.* **Intergenerational social mobility**, *the social standing of children in relation to their parents*, has special significance because it reveals long-term societal changes that affect everyone.

The "fear of falling" economically attends not only working-class people. In recent years, white-collar workers as well have been losing job security. Here, in Washington, D.C., professional men and women who are out of work line up in front of a federal employment office in hopes of landing a new job with the government.

Myth Versus Reality

In few societies do people dwell on social mobility as much as in the United States. Historically, moving ahead has been central to "the American Dream." But is there as much social mobility as we like to think?

Studies of intergenerational mobility (that, unfortunately, have focused almost exclusively on men), show that almost 40 percent of the sons of blue-collar workers attain white-collar jobs and almost 30 percent of sons born into white-collar families end up doing blue-collar work. *Horizontal social mobility*—changes of occupation at one class level—is even more common so that altogether about 80 percent of sons show at least some social mobility in relation to their fathers (Blau & Duncan, 1967; Featherman & Hauser, 1978).

Available research points to four general conclusions about social mobility in the United States.

1. **Social mobility, at least among men, has been fairly high.** The widespread notion that the United States does have considerable social mobility is basically true. This is what we would expect in an industrial class system.

2. **The long-term trend in social mobility has been upward.** Again, this is what most people think, and it squares with the facts. Industrialization, the expansion of the U.S. economy, and the growth of white-collar work over the course of this century have greatly boosted average incomes and living standards.

3. **Within a single generation, social mobility is usually incremental, not dramatic.** Only a very few move "from rags to riches." While sharp rises or falls in individual fortunes may command public attention, most instances of social mobility involve subtle shadings *within* one class level rather than striking changes *between* classes.

4. **The short-term trend has been stagnation, with some income polarization.** As we shall explain presently, the rising real income (that is, adjusted for inflation) that carried through most of this century hit a plateau in the early 1970s. Real income for the U.S. population as a whole also changed little during the 1980s, rising slowly in the early 1990s (Veum, 1992).

Mobility by Income Level

General trends often mask the different experiences of specific categories of people. Figure 7–3 shows how U.S. families fared during the 1980s, by income level.

Well-to-do people (the highest 20 percent) saw their incomes jump 27 percent, from $64,600 in 1980 to $82,350 in 1990. People in the second 20 percent also made gains, albeit more modest, during the 1980s. The middle fifth of the population, however, saw a slight decrease in income, a trend that carried through the fourth and fifth quintiles. These changes underlie the fact, noted earlier, that income disparity has grown in recent years.

Mobility by Race, Ethnicity, and Gender

African Americans traditionally have experienced less upward social mobility than white people, largely due to declining wage levels and rising unemployment. People of African descent lost some ground during the 1980s, with median family earnings sliding from 61 percent in 1980 to 54 percent of what white families earned in 1992. The picture is much the same for Latinos, who earned 73 percent as much as non-Latino whites in 1980, a figure that slipped to 61 percent by 1990 (Featherman & Hauser, 1978; Jacob, 1986; Pomer, 1986; DeParle, 1991b).

Women also have less opportunity for upward mobility than men do since the majority of working women hold clerical positions (such as secretaries) or low-paying service jobs (such as waitresses). But the long-term trend is a narrowing of the "gender gap" in earnings: Women working full-time earned 60 percent as much as comparable men in 1980, a figure that rose to 71 percent in 1991. Note, however, that this narrowing is due as much to a decline in men's pay as it is to a rise in women's earnings.

FIGURE 7–3 Median After-Tax Income, U.S. Families, 1980–1990 (in estimated 1992 dollars, adjusted for inflation)

Source: U.S. Bureau of the Census (1995).

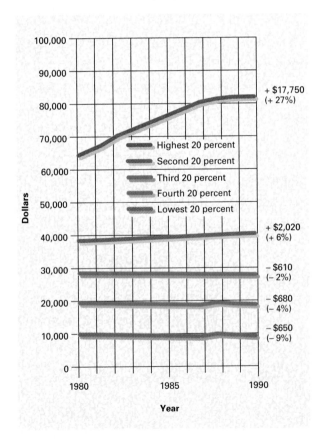

Waking Up From the "American Dream"

Through much of our history, economic expansion has fulfilled the promise of prosperity by raising living standards. Beginning about 1970, however, this upward trend ended, and we entered a period of "income stagnation" that has shaken our national confidence (Pampel, Land, & Felson, 1977; Blumberg, 1981; Levy, 1987). Note these disturbing trends:

1. **For many workers, earnings have stalled.** The annual income of a fifty-year-old man working full time climbed by 50 percent between 1958 and 1973 (from $21,000 to $32,000 in 1990 dollars adjusted for inflation). Between 1973 and 1990, however, this worker's income stayed the same, even as the cost of necessities like housing, education, and medical care rose rapidly (DeParle, 1991a).

2. **Multiple job holding is up.** According to the Census Bureau, in 1975 4.7 percent of the U.S. labor force worked at a second job beyond a full-time position; by 1991, the proportion had climbed to 6.2 percent.

3. **More jobs offer low pay.** In 1979, the Census Bureau classified 12 percent of full-time workers as "low-income earners" because they earned less than $6,905; by 1992, this segment of the labor force had swelled to 18 percent who earned less than the comparable figure that year of $13,091.

4. **Young people are remaining at home.** Fully 60 percent of young people aged 20–24 are now living with their parents. And the average age at

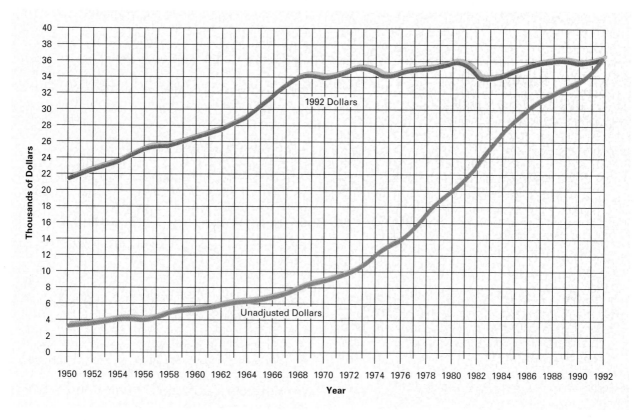

FIGURE 7–4   Median Income, U.S. Families, 1950–1992
Source: U.S. Bureau of the Census (1993).

marriage has moved upward three years (to 24.5 years for women and 26.5 years for men) from where it stood in 1975.

The brisk pace of economic expansion, long taken for granted, has now slowed for a generation. Figure 7–4 shows median U.S. family income from 1950 to 1992 in constant 1992 dollars. Between 1950 and 1973, median family income grew by almost 65 percent; however, it has remained roughly stable since then (U.S. Bureau of the Census, 1993).

The Global Economy and the U.S. Class Structure

Underlying the economic stagnation we have described is a global economic transformation. Much of the industrial production that offered U.S. workers high-paying jobs a generation ago has been transferred overseas. The United States now serves as a vast market for industrial goods—such as cars, and popular items like stereos and cameras—produced in Japan, South Korea, and other countries.

High-paying jobs in manufacturing, held by 26 percent of U.S. workers in 1960, employed just 17 percent of workers by 1993. As industrial jobs have dwindled, in their place appear various types of "service work," typically paying far less. Thus, traditionally high-paying corporations like USX (formerly United States Steel) have fallen on hard times and now employ fewer people than McDonald's, which is enjoying a rapid expansion. Not surprisingly, then, one study predicts the fastest-growing jobs in the 1990s will be cashiers, nurses, janitors, waiters, and truck drivers (Howe & Strauss, 1991).

The global reorganization of work is not bad news for everyone. On the contrary, the global economy has pushed the stock market upward, reaping profits for investors. But this trend has hurt many "average" workers whose factory jobs are now being done overseas. Moreover, many companies seeking to be more competitive in world markets are also cutting the ranks of their white-collar workers.

Just as industrialization spawned prosperity a century ago, today's deindustrialization has challenged the American Dream. The standard of living in the United States has stopped rising even though half of all households contain two or more workers, double the proportion in 1950. Compared to life at mid-century, far fewer now expect to improve their social position, and a growing number worry about being able to maintain the way of life they knew as children in their parents' home.

Poverty in the United States

Social stratification simultaneously creates "haves" and "have-nots," meaning that poverty is an inevitable product of any system of social inequality. Sociologists, however, recognize two different kinds of poverty. **Relative poverty**—which, by definition, is universal—refers to *the deprivation of some people in relation to those who have more.* Much more serious is **absolute poverty,** *a deprivation of resources that is life-threatening.* Defined in this way, poverty is a critical, but also solvable, human problem.

As the next chapter ("Global Stratification") explains, the global dimensions of absolute poverty place the lives of perhaps 800 million human beings—one in five of the earth's people—at risk. Even in the affluent United States, the wrenching reality of poverty results in hunger, inadequate housing, and poor health for millions.

The Extent of U.S. Poverty

In 1992, the government listed 37 million people—14.5 percent of the population—as poor. Under this relative definition of poverty, a poor urban family of four had an annual income not exceeding $14,335. This standard approximates three times the estimated minimum expense for food. But not all poor families are even this "well off": The income of the typical poor family was about $5,000 *below* that poverty threshold.

For at least half of poor families (and many near-poor families as well), hunger is a daily reality (Schwartz-Nobel, 1981; Physicians' Task Force on Hunger in America, 1987). Nor is absolute poverty unknown in this country. The Children's Defense Fund, a poverty-advocacy organization, estimates that ten thousand children die each year for various reasons stemming from poverty, making low income the leading cause of death among the youngest members of our society.

Who Are the Poor?

Although no single description covers all poor people, poverty is pronounced among certain segments of our population. Where these categories overlap, the ramifications of poverty are especially serious.

Age. A generation ago, the elderly were at greatest risk for poverty. But this is no longer the case. From 30 percent in 1967, the poverty rate for seniors over the age of sixty-five fell to 12.9 percent in 1992, yielding just over 4 million elderly poor. This figure is below the overall poverty rate of 14.5 percent. This dramatic decline is due to expanding financial support from private employers (in the form of pension plans) and the government (through Social Security and Medicare). Even so, because of the steadily increasing number of older people, 11 percent of the poor are still elderly people.

Today, the burden of poverty falls most heavily on children. In 1992, 22 percent of people under age eighteen (almost 13 million children) were officially counted as poor. Tallied another way, four in ten poor people in the United States are children under the age of eighteen. The box offers a closer look at the current problem of child poverty in this country.

Race and ethnicity. Two-thirds of all poor people are white; about 30 percent are African American. But in relation to their overall numbers, African Americans are about three times as likely as whites to be poor. In 1992, 33 percent of African Americans (about 11 million people) lived in poverty, compared to about 29 percent of Latinos (almost 7 million people), 13 percent of Asians and Pacific Islanders (1 million), and 12 percent of non-Hispanic whites (19 million). Since 1980, the "poverty gap" between the races has increased (U.S. Bureau of the Census, 1993).

Both young people and people of color are disproportionately poor, so minority children are at special risk of poverty. In 1992, 22 percent of all boys and girls under the age of eighteen were poor; this includes 17 percent of white children, 40 percent of young Latinos, and 47 percent of African-American youths.

U.S. Children: Bearing the Burden of Poverty

We cringe at the sight of hungry children in countries such as Somalia, the war-torn African nation in which the average person struggles to survive on less than $200 per year. But the persistence of child poverty in the United States is also a tragedy, since ours is a rich nation with per capita income one hundred times higher than Somalia.

One in five U.S. children under the age of eighteen (some 13 million boys and girls) are poor. Since the "war on poverty" began in 1964, our society has managed to cut poverty among senior citizens by more than half. But despite (some say because of) government efforts, the child poverty rate has actually been inching upward.

A good measure of the well-being of children is the infant mortality rate, the number of children who die during the first year of life for every 1,000 live births. The United States, which ranks twentieth in the world, is well ahead of poor countries but falls behind most other industrial societies, as the figure shows. The overall U.S. infant mortality rate in 1992 was 9. Among African Americans—three times as likely as white people to be poor—the rate is 19.

Poor children are a diverse category: 60 percent are white,

35 percent African American, and 5 percent are Asian. Of these, 20 percent are also culturally Hispanic. What they all have in common is living in households with low income.

But why the rise in the number of poor children? Liberals point to the trend toward lower-paying jobs noted earlier, and advocate greater government assistance to poor families with children. Conservatives point out that eight of ten poor children live in single-parent households, and in 80 percent of these households there is no full-time worker. They suggest, therefore, that government welfare programs actually make the problem worse by promoting family breakdown.

Children did not cause the problem of poverty in the United States, yet they are disproportionately its victims. Whether we address the suffering of poor children through additional government subsidies or by restructuring assistance programs to encourage self-sufficiency, a social policy that eliminates the deforming experience of poverty on children is certainly far less costly than dealing with the problems of unemployment, drug use, crime, and the violence that poverty breeds later on.

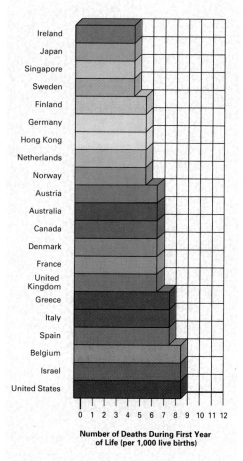

Infant Mortality Rates in Global Perspective, 1992

Source: The World Bank (1994).

Sources: Eggebeen & Lichter (1991), Children's Defense Fund (1992), and Marriott (1992).

Gender and family patterns. Of all poor people over eighteen, 63 percent are women, and 37 percent are men. This disparity reflects the fact that women who head households bear the brunt of poverty. Looking at all poor families, 53 percent are headed by women with no husband present. This represents a sharp rise from 25 percent in 1960, corresponding to the rising number of single women having children. Sociologists use the term **feminization of poverty** to designate *the trend by which women represent an increasing*

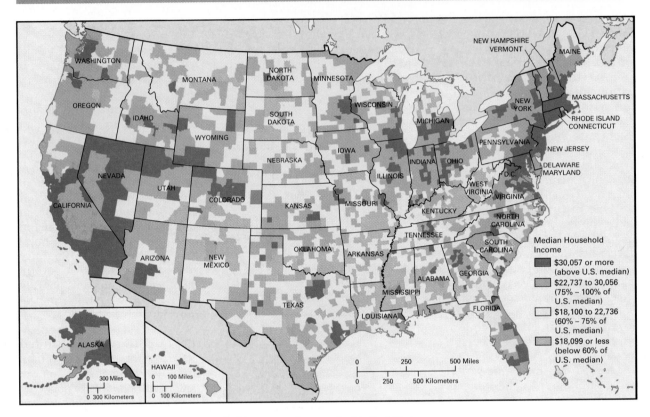

NATIONAL MAP 7–1   Median Household Income Across the United States

This map shows median household income for all 3,014 counties in the United States. Surprisingly, just 15 percent of all counties can boast of a median household income greater than the median for the entire country. What do these counties (shown in dark green) have in common? Low-income counties (shown in red) with high rates of poverty are also found in particular regions of the nation. What characteristics do low-income counties share? Do the patterns found here square with our assertion linking affluence to urban areas and poverty to rural places?

Sources: Map from *American Demographics* magazine, Oct. 1992, p. 9. Reprinted with permission. © 1992 *American Demographics* magazine, Ithaca, New York. Data from the 1990 decennial census.

proportion of the poor. In marked contrast, only 6 percent of poor families are headed by single men.

Area of residence.   The highest concentration of poverty is found among inner-city residents, 21 percent of whom were poor in 1992. For urban areas as a whole, however, the poverty rate was 14 percent, slightly below the 16 percent of rural residents who are poor. Suburbs, too, have destitute people, but their poverty rate stands at just 10 percent. National Map 7–1 sketches a visual picture of income levels across the

United States, indicating where poverty is most pronounced.

Explaining Poverty

In one of the richest countries on earth, how do we reconcile tens of millions of poor people in our midst? It is true, as some analysts remind us, that most poor people in the United States are far better off than the poor in other countries—40 percent of U.S. poor

African-American artist Henry O. Tanner (1859–1937) captured the humility and humanity of impoverished people in his painting *Thankful Poor*. This insight is important in a society that tends to dismiss poor people as morally unworthy and deserving of their bitter plight.

Henry O. Tanner, *Thankful Poor*, 1894. Oil on canvas. 35 x 44". William H. and Camille O. Cosby Collection. Philadelphia Museum of Art.

families own their home, for example, and 60 percent own a car (Jenkins, 1992). But it is also true, as noted earlier, that persistent malnutrition and outright hunger are a blight on this country.

What, then, are the causes of poverty? One approach holds that *the poor are primarily responsible for their own poverty.* Throughout our history, people in the United States have been a self-reliant lot, embracing the notion that social standing is mostly a matter of individual talent and effort. This view maintains that our society offers considerable opportunity for anyone able and willing to take advantage of it. Following this line of reasoning, we conclude that the poor are those who cannot or will not work, women and men with fewer skills, less schooling, or simply lower motivation.

Anthropologist Oscar Lewis (1961), in a study of Latin America, stated that the poor become entrapped in a *culture of poverty* that fosters resignation to one's plight. Socialized in poor families, children come to see little point in aspiring to a better life. The result is a self-perpetuating cycle of poverty. Taking this same approach, Edward Banfield (1974) characterized the U.S. poor as people who embrace a lower-class subculture that inhibits personal achievement. One element of this subculture, he claimed, is a present-time orientation, which places a premium on living for the moment rather than engaging in hard work, saving, and other behavior likely to promote upward social mobility. In

sum, Banfield portrays the poor as irresponsible, reaping more or less what they deserve. Government programs, as he sees it, at best accomplish little and, at worst, subsidize people who choose not to work.

An alternative position, argued by William Ryan (1976), holds that *society is primarily responsible for poverty.* In global perspective, societies that distribute resources more equally than our country does (including Sweden and Japan) also have less poverty. Ryan interprets any lack of ambition on the part of the poor as a *consequence* rather than a *cause* of inadequate opportunity. He dismisses Lewis's and Banfield's analysis as little more than "blaming the victims" for their own suffering. To combat poverty, he supports policies that would increase access to jobs, such as widely accessible child care for women, as well as tax policies that promote economic equality.

Critical evaluation. There is evidence to support both sides of the poverty debate. One fact that lends credence to the position of Lewis and Banfield is that most poor adults do not hold full-time jobs. Government statistics show that 41 percent of the heads of poor households did not work at all during 1992, and 85 percent of such households had, at best, a part-time adult worker (U.S. Bureau of the Census, 1993). Taken together, such facts suggest that one major cause of poverty is *not holding a job.*

An increase in homelessness since 1980 has intensified the controversy over poverty in the United States. Some homeless people—including individuals released from mental hospitals as part of the "deinstitutionalization movement"—have personal problems that render them unable to cope with a demanding world. But an increasing share of homeless people in the United States are families such as this one, who are victims of their economic situation. The predicament of homelessness caused by poverty, captured here by photographer Mary Ellen Mark, remains a hotly contested issue. What is clear is that major causes of rising homelessness include economic stagnation, a declining stock of low-income housing, and cutbacks in social service programs.

But the *reasons* that people do not work seem more consistent with Ryan's position. Middle-class women combine working and child rearing, but doing so is much harder for poor women whose earnings would be substantially eroded by child-care costs. Few U.S. employers provide child-care programs for their employees, and most low-paid workers cannot afford child care on their own. For their part, low-income men claim that there are no jobs to be found, that illness or disability has sidelined them, or, in the case of the elderly, that they have retired. Rightly or wrongly, most poor adults in the United States feel they have few options and alternatives (Popkin, 1990).

But not all poor people are jobless, and the *working poor* command the sympathy and support of people on both sides of the poverty debate. In 1992, 15 percent of poor heads of families (1.2 million people) labored for at least fifty weeks of the year and yet could not escape poverty; another 25 percent (2 million people) remained

poor despite working between 26 and 29 weeks. A key cause of "working poverty" is that, at the 1995 minimum wage level of $4.25 per hour, a full-time worker could not support a family above the poverty line.

Summing up, individual ability and personal initiative do play a part in shaping everyone's social position. On balance, though, evidence points toward society—not individual character traits—as the primary source of poverty. Some poor people do lack ambition. Overall, however, the poor are *categories* of people—women heads of families, people of color, people isolated from the larger society in inner-city areas—without the same opportunities as others.

Homelessness

Many low-income people in the United States cannot afford even basic housing. There is no precise count of homeless people. A special count by the Census Bureau (on March 20, 1991) tallied 178,828 people at shelters and 49,793 people on streets where the poor are known to congregate. But experts agree that a full count of this country's homeless would likely reach 500,000 *on any given night* with three times this number—1.5 million people—homeless *at some time during the course of a year* (Kozol, 1988; Wright, 1989).

The familiar stereotypes of homeless people—men sleeping in doorways and women carrying everything they own in shopping bags—have recently been undermined by the reality of the "new homeless," those thrown out of work because of plant closings, people forced out of apartments by rising rents, and others who cannot meet mortgage or rent payments due to their low wages. Today, no single stereotype paints a complete picture of the homeless.

But virtually all homeless people have one thing in common: *poverty.* For that reason, the approaches already used in explaining poverty also apply to homelessness. One side of the debate places responsibility on *personal traits* of the homeless themselves. One-third of homeless people are substance abusers, and one-fourth are mentally ill. The ranks of the homeless also include some who, for one reason or another, are unable to cope with our complex and highly competitive society (Bassuk, 1984; Whitman, 1989).

On the other side of the debate, advocates assert that homelessness results from *societal factors,* ranging from a lack of low-income housing to unemployment and the increasing number of low-income jobs (Kozol, 1988; Schutt, 1989). Adherents of this position point out that one-third of all homeless people are entire families, and children are the fastest-growing category of the homeless.

No one disputes that a large proportion of homeless people are personally impaired to some degree, although cause and effect issues are difficult to untangle. But structural changes in the U.S. economy, coupled with limited government support for lower-income people, have all contributed to homelessness.

Class and Welfare, Politics and Values

This chapter has focused on social stratification and presented many facts about social inequality. In the end, however, conclusions about what it means to be wealthy and privileged or poor and perhaps homeless turn on politics and values. Understandably, the notion that social standing reflects personal merit is most popular among well-off people. The opposing idea—that society should distribute wealth and resources more equally—finds greatest favor among the most disadvantaged (Rytina, Form, & Pease, 1970; NORC, 1993).

But most members of our society find some truth in the assertion that people have a good deal of control over their life circumstances. In response to the question, "How important is hard work for getting ahead in life?" almost 90 percent of respondents replied "essential" or "very important" (NORC, 1993:549). Such cultural values underlie our view of successful people as personally meritorious and the poor as personally deficient. These attitudes go a long way toward explaining why our society spends much more than other industrial nations on education (to promote opportunity) but much less on public assistance programs (which directly support the poor).

In addition, our cultural emphasis on individualism, rather than collective responsibility, has given rise to a higher level of poverty than that seen in most other industrial societies. Figure 7–5 shows that, while commanding majorities in Germany and the United Kingdom endorse government programs aimed at bringing about greater economic equality, such a view finds much less support in the United States.

The relatively high level of income disparity tolerated in our society translates into a harsh view of the poor, which Richard Sennett and Jonathan Cobb (1973) term the *hidden injury of class*. And, to the extent that we define poor people as undeserving, we perceive public assistance programs as, at best, a waste of money and, at worst, a threat to personal initiative. Ironically, the poor themselves share this thinking,

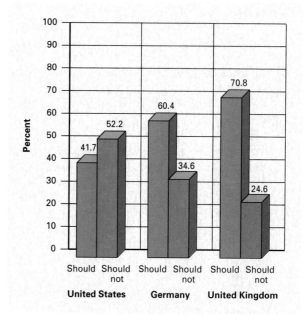

FIGURE 7–5   Attitudes Toward Government Action to Reduce Income Differences, 1990

Question: "On the whole, do you think it should or should not be the government's responsibility to reduce income differences between the rich and poor?"

Note: Adding undecided and non-responding individuals yields 100 percent.
Source: NORC (1994), International Social Survey Program.

which discourages half the people eligible for support from ever seeking it (Waxman, 1983; Handler & Hasenfeld, 1991; U.S. Bureau of the Census, 1993).

Curiously, this same value system paints a more positive picture of government benefits provided to "deserving" wealthy people. Current tax law, for example, allows homeowners to deduct from their income interest paid on home mortgages as well as real estate tax payments. The tax savings realized from this policy—which goes into the pockets of people affluent enough to own their own homes—amounts to more than $40 billion annually, more than *five times* the amount of government funds used to help house the poor. Our cultural tendency to equate privilege with personal merit leads us to nod approvingly at "wealthfare" while angrily denouncing welfare for the poor.

Finally, the drama of social stratification extends far beyond the borders of the United States. The most striking social disparities are found not by looking inside one country but by comparing living standards in various parts of the world. In Chapter 8, we broaden our investigation by focusing on global stratification.

SUMMARY

1. Social stratification refers to ranking categories of people in a hierarchy. Caste systems, which predominate in agrarian societies, are based on ascription and permit little or no social mobility. Class systems, characteristic of industrial societies, allow more social mobility based on individual achievement.

2. The Davis-Moore thesis states that social stratification is universal because it is useful to a society. In class systems, unequal rewards motivate all workers and draw the most able people toward the most important occupational positions.

3. For Karl Marx, conflict in industrial societies places the capitalists, who own the means of production and seek profits, in opposition to the proletariat, who provide labor in exchange for wages.

4. Max Weber envisioned social stratification in terms of three dimensions of inequality: economic class, social status or prestige, and power. Together, these three dimensions form a complex hierarchy of socioeconomic standing.

5. Gerhard and Jean Lenski observe that, historically, advancing technology tends to intensify social stratification. A limited reversal of this trend occurs in advanced industrial societies, as represented by the "Kuznets Curve."

6. In the United States, the upper class (3 to 4 percent of the population) includes this nation's richest and most powerful individuals. Members of the upper-upper class, or the old rich, typically inherit great wealth; those in the lower-upper class, or "new rich," derive most of their wealth from earned income.

7. The middle class (40 to 45 percent of the population) enjoys reasonable financial security, but only some of these people (the upper-middle class) accumulate significant wealth. With below-average incomes, members of the working class (33 percent) typically perform blue-collar work, and only one-third of their children reach college.

8. The lower class (20 percent of the U.S. population) includes individuals near or below the official poverty line. People of African and Latino descent, and all women, are disproportionately represented in the lower class.

9. Like other industrial societies, ours promotes social mobility; typically, however, only small changes in social position occur from one generation to the next.

10. The growing global economy has increased the wealth of rich families in the United States, but has stalled or even reduced the standard of living of other people.

11. Some 37 million people in this country are officially classified as poor. About 40 percent of the poor are children under the age of eighteen.

12. The "culture of poverty" thesis asserts that poverty is perpetuated by the personal flaws of the poor themselves. Opposing this view, others argue that poverty is caused by a society's unequal distribution of wealth.

KEY CONCEPTS

absolute poverty a deprivation of resources that is life-threatening

alienation the experience of powerlessness in social life

blue-collar occupation lower-prestige work that involves mostly manual labor

capitalist one who owns a factory or other productive enterprise

caste system social stratification based on ascription

class system social stratification based on individual achievement

feminization of poverty the trend by which women represent an increasing proportion of the poor

ideology cultural beliefs that justify particular social arrangements

income wages or salary from work and earnings from investments

intergenerational social mobility the social standing of children in relation to their parents

intragenerational social mobility a change in social position occurring during a person's lifetime

meritocracy social stratification based on personal merit

proletariat people who sell their productive labor

relative poverty the deprivation of some people in relation to others who have more

social mobility a change of position in a stratification system

social stratification a system by which a society ranks categories of people in a hierarchy

socioeconomic status (SES) a composite social ranking based on various dimensions of inequality

status consistency the degree of consistency in a person's social standing across various dimensions of inequality

structural social mobility a shift in the social position of large numbers of people due less to individual efforts than to changes in society itself

wealth an individual's or family's total financial assets

white-collar occupation higher-prestige work that involves mostly mental activity

CRITICAL-THINKING QUESTIONS

1. How is social stratification a product of society rather than simply an expression of individual differences?

2. How do caste and class systems differ? What do they have in common?

3. Distinguish between income and wealth. How is each distributed in the United States? Describe inequality with regard to occupational prestige and schooling.

4. What categories of people are at high risk of poverty in the United States? What evidence supports the assertion that the poor are responsible for their low social position? That society is responsible for poverty?

Global
Stratification

Half an hour from the center of Cairo, Egypt's capital city, the bus bumped along a dirt road and jerked to a stop. It was not quite dawn, and the Mo'edhdhins would soon climb the minarets of Cairo's many mosques to call the Islamic faithful to morning prayer. The driver turned, genuinely bewildered, to the busload of students from the United States and their instructor. "Why," he asked, mixing English with some Arabic, "do you want to be here? And in the middle of the night?"

Why, indeed? No sooner had we stepped down from the bus than smoke and stench, the likes of which we had never before encountered, swirled around us. Eyes squinting, handkerchiefs pressed against noses and mouths, we moved slowly uphill along a mile-long path ascending mountains of trash and garbage. We had reached the Cairo Dump, where one of the world's largest cities—with some 15 million people—deposits its trash and garbage.[1] We walked hunched over and with great care, since only a scattering of light came from small fires smoldering around us. Suddenly, from the shadows, spectral shapes appeared. After a moment, we identified them as dogs peering curiously through the curtain of haze. As startled as we were, they quickly bolted, vanishing into the thick air. Ahead of us, we could see blazing piles of trash circled by people huddling together against the cold and enjoying companionship.

Human beings actually inhabit this inhuman place, creating a surreal scene, like the aftermath of the next world war. As we approached, the fires cast an eerie light on their faces. We stopped some distance from them, separated by a vast chasm of culture and circumstances. But smiles eased the tension, and soon we were sharing the comfort of their fires. At that moment, the melodious call to prayer sounded across the city.

The people of the Cairo Dump, called the Zebaleen, belong to a religious minority—Coptic Christians—in a predominantly Muslim society. Barred by religious discrimination from many jobs, the Zebaleen use donkey carts and small trucks to pick up refuse throughout the city and bring it here. The night-long routine reaches a climax at dawn when hundreds of Zebaleen gather at the dump, swarming over the new piles seeking out anything of value.

That morning, we watched men, women, and children fill their baskets with bits of ribbon, scraps of discarded food—anything of value that would help them make it through another day. Watching in silence, we became keenly aware of our sturdy shoes and warm clothing, and self-conscious that our watches and cameras represented more money than most of the Zebaleen earn in a year.

Although they are unfamiliar to most members of our society, the Zebaleen of the Cairo Dump are hardly unique. Their counterparts live in the Philippines, India, Mexico, in fact, in almost every poor country of the world. In poor societies, as we shall see, poverty is not only more widespread than in the United States, but also far more severe.

Global Economic Development

Chapter 7 ("Social Stratification") explained that inequality is found everywhere, including the United States. In global perspective, however, social stratification is even more pronounced. The value of all the goods and services produced on earth each year (roughly $20 to $25 trillion) serves as the entire world's "income." In Figure 8–1 we see how total world income is split among fifths of the population, providing a distribution comparable to the one found in Figure 7–2 (page 169) that graphically illustrates inequality in the United States.

Recall that the richest 20 percent of the U.S. population earns about 45 percent of the national income; the richest 20 percent of humanity, however, garners 83 percent of global income. At the other end of the social pyramid, the poorest 20 percent of the U.S. population takes in about 5 percent of our national income; the poorest fifth of the world's people, by contrast, struggles to survive on just 1 percent of the global income.

---

[1]This portrayal is based on the author's visit to the Cairo Dump with more than one hundred students in 1988. It also draws on the discussion found in Spates & Macionis (1987).

In short, income is distributed far less equally in the world as a whole than it is in the United States. For this reason, the average member of our society lives very well by world standards. In fact, most of the people existing below our government's poverty line live much better than the majority of the earth's people.

The Problem of Terminology

To understand the unequal distribution of global income, social scientists have long divided the societies of the world into several broad classifications. A familiar scheme, which emerged after World War II, dubbed the rich, industrialized countries the "First World," the somewhat less industrialized, socialist countries the "Second World," and the largely nonindustrialized, poor countries the "Third World." In recent years, however, this "three worlds" model has lost some of its validity. For one thing, it was a product of cold war geopolitics by which the capitalist West (the First World) faced off against the socialist East (the Second World), while the rest of the world (the Third World) remained more or less on the sidelines. The sweeping transformations in Eastern Europe and the former Soviet Union mean that there no longer exists a distinctive "Second World"; just as importantly, the superpower tensions that defined the cold war have substantially abated.

Analysts also faulted the "Three Worlds" model because it lumped together as the "Third World" more than one hundred countries at significantly different levels of development. Some relatively better off nations of the Third World (such as Chile in South America) have ten times the per-person productivity seen in the poorest countries of the world (including Ethiopia in eastern Africa).

These concerns call for a modestly revised system of classification. As the following sections explain, the *most-developed countries* of the world have the most productive economies and the highest overall standard of living for their people. In the world's *less-developed countries*, economic development, while far below that of rich societies like the United States, is more or less typical for world nations taken as a whole. Finally, our planet's *least-developed countries* are marked by the lowest productivity and the most severe and extensive poverty.

Compared to the older "Three Worlds" system, this new form of classification has two prime advantages. First, it focuses on economic development while ignoring the earlier issue of whether societies are capitalist or socialist. Second, this revision sketches a more

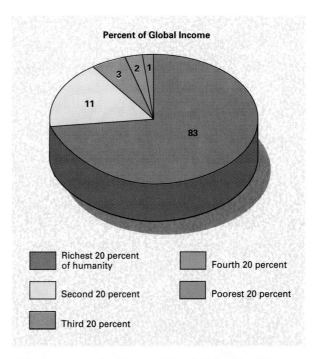

FIGURE 8–1   Distribution of World Income, 1990
Sources: Based on Sivard (1993) and The World Bank (1993).

precise picture of the relative economic development of the world's countries because it recognizes that not all less-industrialized countries fall into a single "Third World."

Still, to sort the 191 nations on earth into any three categories ignores striking differences in their ways of life. The societies we place at each of the three levels of economic development have rich and varied histories, speak dozens of languages, and encompass diverse peoples who take pride in their cultural distinctiveness.

Keep in mind, too, that just as the world's nations form a social hierarchy that ranges from very rich to very poor, so every country on earth is also internally stratified. This means that the extent of global inequality is actually greater than national comparisons suggest, because the most well-off people in rich societies live worlds apart from the poorest people in countries with the least-developed economies.

The Most-Developed Countries

Chapter 1 ("Sociology: Perspective, Theory, and Method") defined the world's *most-developed countries* as relatively rich, industrialized nations. These

Japan represents the world's high-income countries, in which industrial technology and economic expansion have produced material prosperity. The presence of market forces is evident in this view of downtown Tokyo (top left). The Commonwealth of Independent States represents the middle-income countries of the world. Industrial development has been slower in the former Soviet Union, as socialist economies have performed sluggishly. Residents of Moscow, for example, chafe at having to wait in long lines for their daily needs (above). The hope is that the introduction of a market system will raise living standards, although it probably will also increase economic disparity. Bangladesh (left) represents the low-income countries of the world. As the photograph suggests, these nations have limited economic development and rapidly increasing populations. The result is widespread poverty.

nations are rich because the Industrial Revolution first took hold there more than two centuries ago, increasing their productive capacity one hundred-fold. To grasp how this development enriched our own region of the world, the U.S. population now spends more money just in caring for household pets than Europeans did attending to all their needs during the Middle Ages.

A look back at Global Map 1–1 on page 6 identifies the roughly thirty-five high-income countries of the world. They include the United States and Canada, most of the nations of Western Europe, the Asian nations of Japan, Hong Kong, and Singapore, and, in the global region known as Oceania, Australia and New Zealand.

Taken together, countries with the most-developed economies cover roughly 25 percent of the earth's land area, including parts of five continents.

They lie mostly in the Northern Hemisphere, which is why people sometimes contrast the "rich North" with the "poor South." In 1995, the population of these nations was about 850 million, about 15 percent of the earth's people. By global standards, rich nations are not densely populated; even so, some countries (such as Japan) are crowded while others (like Canada) are sparsely settled. Inside their borders, however, about three-fourths of the people in high-income countries crowd together in cities.

Most-developed countries reveal significant cultural differences—the nations of Europe, for example, have more than thirty official languages. But these societies share an industrial capacity that generates, on average, a rich material life for their people. Per capita income in these societies ranges from about $8,000 annually (in Portugal) to more than $20,000 annually (in the United States and

Switzerland).[2] This income is so abundant that members of most-developed countries enjoy more than half the world's total income.

Generally speaking, high-income countries dominate global scientific efforts and employ the most complex technology. Production in rich societies is capital-intensive, depending on heavy investment in expensive factories and related machinery. The most-developed countries also stand at the forefront of new information technology; the majority of the largest corporations that design and market computers, for instance, are centered in rich societies. With the lion's share of wealth, high-income nations also control the world's financial markets; daily events in the financial exchanges of New York, London, and Tokyo affect people throughout the world.

The Less-Developed Countries

The *less-developed countries* of the world are those with per capita income of about $5,000, which is about the median for the world's nations (but above that for the world's *people* since most people live in the poorest countries). These societies have experienced only limited industrialization, primarily in cities. But about half of their people still live in rural areas and engage in agricultural production. Especially in the countryside, housing, schooling, and medical care are hard to come by and far below what members of high-income countries take for granted.

Typical incomes in these nations are substantially lower than those in rich societies. At the high end, residents of Greece (Europe) and Barbados (Latin America) earn about $8,000 in individual annual income. Panama (Central America), Albania (Europe), Algeria (Africa), and the Philippines (Asia) cluster at the lower end of this category with roughly $3,000 annually in per capita income. Looking back at Global Map 1–1 (page 6), we see that about one hundred of the world's nations fall into this classification, and they comprise a very diverse lot.

One group of middle-income countries includes the former Soviet Union and the nations of Eastern Europe (in the past, also known as the Second World). The former Soviet Union's military strength rivaled

that of the United States, giving it "superpower" status. Its satellites in Eastern Europe, including Poland, the German Democratic Republic (East Germany), Czechoslovakia, Hungary, Romania, and Bulgaria, had predominantly socialist economies until popular revolts between 1989 and 1991 toppled governments there. Since then, these nations have begun to introduce market systems and, so far, have compiled a mixed record of economic performance.

In a second category of less-developed countries are most of the oil-producing nations of the Middle East (or, less ethnocentrically, western Asia). These nations, including Saudi Arabia, Oman, and Iran, are very rich, but their wealth is concentrated so that most people receive little benefit and remain poor.

Countries considered to be in the third, and largest, category of less-developed nations are found in Latin America and northern and western Africa. These countries (which might be termed the better-off nations of the Third World) include Argentina and Brazil in South America, and Algeria and Botswana in Africa. Although South Africa's white minority lives as well as people in the United States, this country, too, must be considered less-developed because its majority black population subsists on far less income.

All told, less-developed countries span nearly 40 percent of the earth's land area. Roughly 2 billion people, or more than one-third of humanity, live in these nations. Compared to high-income countries, therefore, these societies are more densely populated as a rule, even though some of these nations (such as El Salvador) are far more crowded than others (like Russia).

The Least-Developed Countries

The *least-developed countries* of the world are primarily agrarian societies with little industry and in which most people are very poor. These fifty nations, identified in Global Map 1–1 on page 6, are found primarily in central and eastern Africa as well as Asia. Because they represent about 35 percent of the planet's land area but are home to half its people, population density is generally high in these nations, although it is much greater in Asian countries (such as India and the People's Republic of China) than in more sparsely settled central African nations (like Chad or Zaire).

In poor countries, barely 25 percent of the population live in cities; most inhabit villages and engage in farming as members of their families have done for centuries. In fact, about half of the entire world's population are peasants, and most of them live in the

[2]These data reflect the United Nations's (1993) recently introduced concept of "purchasing power parities," which avoids distortion caused by exchange rates when converting all currencies to U.S. dollars. Instead, the data reflect the local purchasing power of each nation's currency.

By and large, rich nations such as the United States wrestle with the problem of *relative* poverty, meaning that poor people get by with less than we think they should have. In poor countries such as Somalia, *absolute* poverty means that people lack what they need to survive. Here people gather near the Juba River to bury in a common grave family members who died from starvation.

least-developed countries. By and large, peasants are staunchly traditional, following the folkways of their ancestors. While cultural traditions may be rich, constant hunger, unsafe housing, and high rates of disease all plague members of the world's poorest societies.

This broad overview of global economic development frames our understanding of global stratification. For people living in affluent nations such as the United States, the scope of human want in much of the world is difficult to grasp. From time to time, televised scenes of famine in the poorest countries of the world, including Ethiopia and Bangladesh, give us a shocking glimpse of a daily struggle to survive. Behind these images lie cultural, historical, and economic forces that we shall explore in the remainder of this chapter.

Global Poverty

Poverty always means suffering. People in the world's poorest countries, however, contend with hardship that is both more severe and more widespread than that faced by the poor in the United States.

The Severity of Poverty

The data shown in Table 8–1 point up why poverty is more severe in poor countries. The first column of figures shows, for countries at each level of economic

development, the gross domestic product ("GDP").[3] Industrial societies typically have a high economic output, primarily due to their industrial technology. A large, industrial country like the United States had a 1992 GDP of about $5.9 trillion; Japan's GDP stood at about $3.6 trillion. Comparing the figures, we discover that the world's richest nations are a thousand times more productive than the poorest countries on earth.

The second column of figures in Table 8–1 indicates per capita GDP in terms of what the United Nations (1993) calls "purchasing power parities," giving some idea of what incomes can buy in a local economy. The resulting figures for rich countries like the United States, Switzerland, and Canada are very high—in the range of $20,000. Per capita GDP for less-developed countries, including Lithuania and Brazil, is much lower—in the $5,000 range. And in the world's least-developed countries, per capita annual income is down to just a few hundred dollars. In Zaire or Ethiopia, for example, a typical person labors all year to make what the average worker in the United States earns in several days.

The third column of Table 8–1 provides a measure of the quality of life in various nations. The index

---

[3]Gross domestic product refers to all the goods and services produced by a society's economy in a given year. Income earned outside the country by individuals or corporations is excluded from this measure, differentiating GDP from gross national product (GNP), which includes foreign earnings.

used here, calculated by the United Nations, incorporates income, education (adult literacy and average years of schooling), and longevity (how long people typically live). Index values are decimals that fall between hypothetical extremes of 1 (highest) and zero (lowest). By this calculation, Canada enjoys the highest quality of life (.932), and the African nation of Guinea has the lowest (.191). With a quality of life index of .925, the United States ranks eighth in the world.

Why does quality of life differ so dramatically among the societies of the world? One key reason: Economic productivity is lowest in precisely the regions of the globe where population is greatest. Figure 8–2 on page 194 shows the division of population and global income for countries at each level of economic development. The most-developed countries, home to 15 percent of the world's people, take in 55 percent of the planet's income. Less-developed countries, with 33 percent of total population, garner 37 percent of global income. This leaves fully half of the planet's population with a scant 8 percent of global income. Factoring together population and income shares, for every dollar earned by people in the least-developed countries, individuals in the most-developed nations receive 28 dollars.

Relative versus absolute poverty. A distinction made in the last chapter has an important application to global stratification. Members of rich societies generally focus on the *relative poverty* of some of their members, highlighting how some people lack resources that others take for granted. Relative poverty, by definition, exists in every society, whether rich or poor.

But especially important in global perspective is the concept of *absolute poverty*, a lack of resources that is life-threatening. Most human beings living in absolute poverty lack the nutrition for health and long-term survival.

In a rich nation like the United States, most people we consider poor are deprived in the relative sense. But some absolute poverty does exist in the United States. Inadequate nutrition that leaves children or elderly people vulnerable to illness or even outright starvation is a reality in this nation. But such immediate life-threatening poverty strikes a very small share of the U.S. population; in the least-developed countries of the world, one-third or more of the people are in desperate need.

Since absolute poverty threatens people with death, one revealing indicator of the extent of this global problem is a country's median age at death. Global Map 8–1 on page 195 identifies the age by

TABLE 8–1 Wealth and Well-Being in Global Perspective, 1992

Country	Gross Domestic Product ($ billion)	GDP Per Capita (PPP$)*	Quality of Life Index
Most-Developed Countries			
Canada	494	19,320	.932
Switzerland	241	21,780	.931
Japan	3,671	19,390	.929
Sweden	221	17,490	.928
Australia	295	16,680	.926
United States	5,920	22,130	.925
United Kingdom	903	16,340	.919
Germany	1,789	19,770	.918
Less-Developed Countries			
Eastern Europe			
Lithuania	5	5,410	.868
Hungary	35	6,080	.863
Russian Federation	387	6,930	.858
Poland	84	4,500	.815
Latin America			
Argentina	229	5,120	.853
Mexico	329	7,170	.804
Brazil	360	5,240	.756
Asia			
Korea, Republic of	296	8,320	.859
Thailand	110	5,270	.798
Middle East			
Saudi Arabia	111	10,850	.742
Iran, Islamic Republic of	110	4,670	.672
Africa			
Botswana	4	4,690	.670
Algeria	36	2,870	.553
Least-Developed Countries			
Latin America			
Honduras	3	1,820	.524
Haiti	3	925	.354
Asia			
China, People's Republic of	506	2,946	.644
India	215	1,150	.382
Africa			
Ethiopia	6.3	469	.341
Zaire	1	370	.249
Guinea	3	500	.191

* These data are the United Nations's new "purchasing power parity" calculations that avoid currency rate distortion by showing the local purchasing power of each domestic currency.

Sources: United Nations Development Programme, *Human Development Report 1994* (New York: Oxford University Press, 1994); The World Bank, *World Development Report 1994: Infrastructure for Development* (New York: Oxford University Press, 1994).

which half of all people born in a society die. In rich nations, most people die after the age of seventy-five; in poor countries, by contrast, half of all deaths occur among children under the age of ten.

The Extent of Poverty

Chapter 7 ("Social Stratification") explained that about 14 percent of the U.S. population is officially classified as poor. In less-developed countries, however, most people live no better than the poor in the United States; in the least-developed nations, the majority cling to the edge of survival. As the high death rates among children suggest, absolute poverty is greatest in Africa, where half the population is ill nourished. In the world as a whole, some 800 million people do not eat enough to allow them to work regularly, putting them at risk of their lives (Helmuth, 1989; Sivard, 1993; United Nations Development Programme, 1993).

Put more bluntly, people die—every minute of every day—from lack of basic nutrition. In the ten minutes it takes to read through this section of the chapter, about three hundred people in the world will die of

FIGURE 8–2 **The Relative Share of Income and Population by Level of Economic Development**
Source: Author calculations.

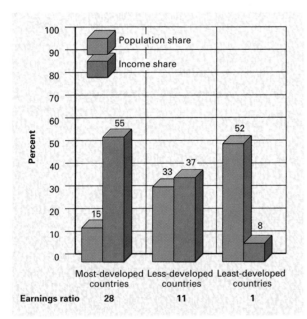

starvation. This amounts to more than 40,000 people a day, or 15 million people each year. Even more than in the United States, the burden of poverty in the least-developed countries falls on children: In the world's poorest nations, about one child in four dies before reaching the age of five.

Two further comparisons illustrate the human toll of global poverty. First, at the end of World War II, the United States obliterated the Japanese city of Hiroshima with an atomic bomb. The global loss of life from starvation today equals the Hiroshima death toll *every three days*. Second, the death toll from hunger in just the last five years equals the number of deaths from war, revolution, and murder over the last 150 years (Burch, 1983). Given the magnitude of this problem, easing world hunger is one of the most serious responsibilities facing humanity today.

Poverty and Gender

As Chapter 10 ("Sex and Gender") explains, the work women do is typically unrecognized, undervalued, and underpaid. And in poor societies, even though women do most of the work, they are disproportionately the poorest of the poor.

For one thing, women in poor countries receive grossly less pay for their efforts than men do. Moreover, families are much more likely to send sons than daughters to school. Without access to reliable birth control, many women in poor countries also have large families—five or six children is common in rural areas. Finally, the United Nations estimates, men own 90 percent of land in poor societies of the world, a far greater hold on wealth than men enjoy in industrial nations.

As the box on page 196 explains, gender bias frames virtually every dimension of life in poor countries, even a mother's decision whether or not to bear a child in the first place.

Poverty and Children

Child poverty, too, is greatest in the poorest societies of the world. We have already explained that death comes early in poor societies, where families lack adequate food, safe water, secure housing, and access to medical care. Organizations combating child poverty estimate that poverty forces some 75 million children in poor countries to work on the streets in order to assist their families. In many cases, this "work" translates into

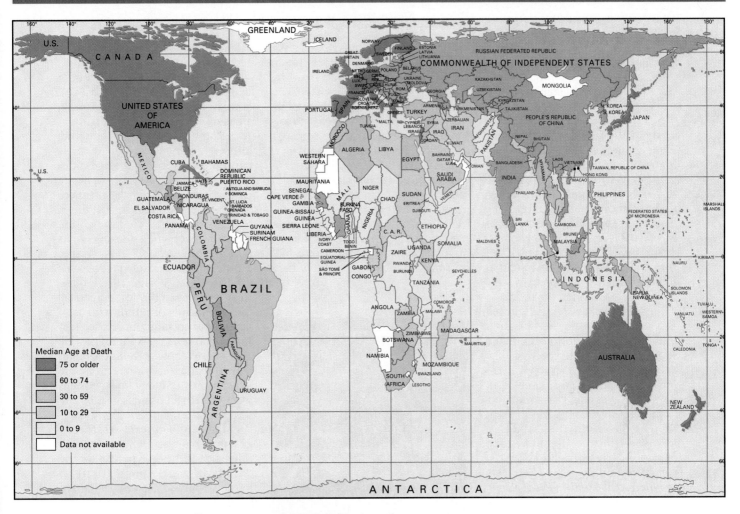

GLOBAL MAP 8–1   Median Age at Death in Global Perspective

This map identifies the age below which half of all deaths occur in any year. In the high-income countries of the world, including the United States, it is the elderly who face death—that is, people age seventy-five or older. In middle-income countries, including most of Latin America, most people die years or even decades sooner. In low-income countries, especially in Africa and parts of Asia, it is children who die, with half of all lives ending before individuals reach ten years of age.

Source: Adapted from *World Development Report* (The World Bank, 1993). Map projection from *Peters Atlas of the World* (1990).

begging, stealing, selling sex, or acting as a courier for drug gangs. Such a life almost always means dropping out of school and places children at high risk of illness and violence.

Another 25 million of the world's children have deserted their families altogether, getting by as best they can on their own. Perhaps half of such children are found in Latin America. Brazil, where much of the

Infanticide and Sexual Slavery: Reports From India and Thailand

Rani, a young woman living in a remote Indian village, returned home from the clinic after delivering a baby girl. There was no joy in the family. On the contrary, upon learning of the birth, the men somberly filed out of the mud house. Rani and her mother-in-law then set about the task of mashing oleander seeds into several drops of oil to make a poisonous paste, which they forced down the baby's throat. The day came to an end as Rani returned from a nearby field where she had buried the child.

As she walked home, Rani felt not sadness at losing her daughter but bitterness at not having had a son. Members of her village, like people living in poor societies across Asia and other world regions, favor boys while viewing girls as an economic liability. Why? Because in these male-dominated societies, men wield most of the power and control nearly all wealth. Parents recognize that boys are a better investment of their meager resources, since males have a better chance of surviving to earn income for their family. Then, too, custom dictates that parents of a girl offer a dowry to the family of her prospective husband. In short, given the existing social structure, families are better off with boys and without girls.

One consequence of this double standard is high rates of sex-selective

abortion throughout rural India, China, and other Asian nations. In India, villages that lack running water typically have a doctor who employs either amniocentesis or ultrasound—high-technology means to determine the sex of a woman's fetus. The pregnant woman's typical response, upon hearing the results of the test, is either elation at carrying a boy or resolve to terminate the pregnancy so that she can "try again." Although there exist no precise counts of such abortions and female infanticide, analysts point out that, in some rural regions of Asia, men

A global pattern is that poverty forces women into sexual slavery as prostitutes. These four Vietnamese women working in a brothel in Cambodia will never escape their poverty and may well fall victim to AIDS, which is spreading rapidly across Southeast Asia.

outnumber women by as many as ten to one.

Another dimension of gender bias is the exploding growth of sexual slavery involving young women. Bangkok, Thailand, is emerging as the sex-tourism capital of the world, although similar red-light districts can be found in other large cities throughout the region. In some cases, parents sell female infants to agents who pay others to raise them, then "harvest their crop" when the girls approach their teenage years and are old enough to work in a brothel. In other cases, girls who see little future in a rural village make their own way to the city, only to fall into the hands of pimps who soon have them soliciting in bars or performing in sex shows. Pimps provide girls with clothes and housing, but at a price that exceeds what they earn. This system of debt-bondage keeps women virtual prisoners of their unscrupulous employers.

The numbers involved are staggering: Thailand alone now has 2 million prostitutes (8 percent of the country's female population); as many as half of these are children. The future for these girls and women is bleak. Most suffer from a host of diseases brought on by abuse and neglect, and 40 percent are now infected with the virus that causes AIDS.

Sources: Anderson & Moore (1993) and Reaves (1993).

population has flocked to cities in a desperate search for a better life, faces the greatest problem of street children. Brazil has millions of street children living in

alleyways, under bridges, or in makeshift huts of their own construction. Surprisingly, perhaps, public response to the plight of street children is often anger—

directed at the children themselves. Police strive to rid shopping districts of "nuisance children" and, in some cases, death squads sweep through a neighborhood, engaging in a bloody act of "urban cleansing." In Rio de Janeiro, several hundred street children are murdered each year (U.S. House of Representatives, 1992; Larmer, 1992).

Correlates of Global Poverty

What accounts for the severe and extensive poverty throughout much of the world? The rest of this chapter weaves together explanations from various facts about poor societies.

1. **Technology.** Poor societies are largely agrarian, lacking the productive power of industrial technology. Energy from human muscles or beasts of burden falls far short of the force unleashed by steam, oil, or nuclear fuels, thus limiting the use of heavy machinery.

2. **Population growth.** As Chapter 14 ("Population and Urbanization") spells out, countries with the least-developed economies have the highest rates of population growth. High birth rates more than offset high death rates so that the populations of many countries in Africa, for example, double every twenty-five years. In these countries, half the people are teenagers or younger, so that they are just entering their childbearing years, making future population growth all but inevitable. Even a fast-developing economy would not be able to support future surges in population.

3. **Cultural patterns.** Poor societies usually embrace tradition. Families and neighbors pass down folkways and mores from generation to generation. Adhering to long-established ways of life, traditional people resist innovations—even those that promise a richer material life. The box on page 198 explains why traditional people in India regard their poverty differently than poor people in the United States commonly do.

4. **Social stratification.** The modest wealth of the least-developed nations is distributed very unequally among their populations. Chapter 7 ("Social Stratification") explained that social inequality is generally more pronounced in agrarian societies than in industrial societies. In many Asian and Latin American countries, for example, 10 percent of landowners control half the

All around the world, poverty weighs most heavily on children. Faced with little opportunity to improve their lives, many young people fall into despair and cushion their suffering with drugs. These boys in Guatemala sniff glue almost every day.

land, while half of all farming families have little or no land of their own (Hartmann & Boyce, 1982; Barry, 1983).

5. **Gender inequality.** As we have explained, poor societies exhibit striking gender inequality. Women who lack opportunity—and have many children—cannot be economically productive. Many analysts conclude that economic development in much of the world depends on improving the social standing of women.

6. **Global power relationships.** A final cause of global poverty lies in the relationships among the nations of the world. **Colonialism** is *the process by which some nations enrich themselves through political and economic control of other nations.* The nations of Western Europe colonized much of Latin America, Africa, and Asia beginning about five hundred years ago. Some analysts claim that this global exploitation allowed some nations to *develop* economically while others were deliberately *underdeveloped.*

   Although 130 former colonies gained their independence during this century, a continuing pattern of **neocolonialism** (*neo* comes from Greek, meaning "new") amounts to *a new form of economic exploitation involving not direct political control but the operation of multinational corporations.* **Multinational corporations,** in

A Different Kind of Poverty: A Report From India

Most North Americans know that India is one of the poorest societies of the world: Per capita income in this Asian nation stands at only $1,100 a year (see Table 8–1). Deprivation pervades this vast society, where one-third of the world's hungry people reside.

But few members of our society can fully comprehend the reality of poverty in India. Most of the country's 900 million people live in conditions far worse than those our nation labels as "poor." A traveler's first experience of Indian life is sobering and sometimes shocking; yet, in time, the outsider learns that, in India, people think about poverty differently than we do.

Arriving in Madras, one of India's largest cities with 6.5 million people, a visitor immediately recoils from the smell of human sewage, which hangs over much of the city like a malodorous cloud. Untreated sewage also makes much of the region's water unsafe to drink. The sights and sounds, too, are strange and intense—streets are choked by motorbikes, trucks, ox carts, and waves of people. Along the roads, vendors sit on burlap cloth hawking fruits, vegetables, and prepared foods. Seemingly oblivious to the surrounding urban chaos, people work, talk, bathe, and sleep in the streets. Tens of thousands of

homeless people fill this and other large cities of India.

Madras is also dotted by more than a thousand shanty settlements, encompassing half a million people, many of whom have converged on the city from rural villages where life is even harder. Shantytowns are clusters of huts constructed of branches, leaves, and discarded materials that offer little privacy and lack refrigeration, running water, and bathrooms. The visitor from the United States understandably feels uneasy entering such a community,

Less-developed societies may be poor, but strong traditions and vital families place most people in a network of social support. Thus people endure poverty with the help of their kin, which contrasts to the often isolating poverty in the United States.

since the poorest sections of inner cities in the United States seethe with frustration and, oftentimes, explode with violence.

But here, too, India presents a sharp contrast. No angry young people hang out at the corner, no drugs pervade the area, and there is surprisingly little danger. Instead, shantytowns comprise children, parents, and often grandparents who extend smiles and offer a welcome. To most rural Indians, life revolves around strong families and is shaped by *dharma*—the Hindu concept of duty and destiny. Mother Teresa, who has won praise for her devotion to the poorest of India's people, goes to the heart of the cultural differences: "Americans have angry poverty; in India, there is worse poverty, but it is a happy poverty."

No one who clings to the edge of survival can be called truly "happy." But the deadly horror of Indian poverty is eased by the warm embrace of families and traditional communities, a sense of purpose in life, and a world view that presses each person to accept whatever society offers. As a result, the U.S. visitor comes away from the first encounter with Indian poverty in confusion: "How can people be so poor, and yet apparently content, vibrant, and so *alive*?"

Source: Based on the author's research in Madras, India (1988).

turn, are *huge businesses that operate in many countries*. These corporations now wield such tremendous economic power that corporate

decision makers can—and often do—influence the political systems in countries where they do business.

Global Inequality: Theoretical Analysis

There are two major explanations for the unequal distribution of the world's wealth and power—*modernization theory* and *dependency theory*. Each presents a distinctive analysis of why so many of the world's people are poor and why we in the United States enjoy such comparative advantages.

Modernization Theory

Modernization theory is *a model of economic development that explains global inequality in terms of technological and cultural differences among societies.* Modernization theory emerged in the 1950s, a decade of fascination with technology in the United States and a time of hostility to U.S. interests in many poor countries. To counter the growing influence of the Soviet Union, U.S. policy makers framed principles of support for a free-market economy that has shaped this nation's foreign policy toward poor nations ever since.[4]

Historical perspective. Modernization theorists point out that the *entire world* was poor as recently as several centuries ago. Because poverty is the norm throughout human history, *affluence*—not deprivation—demands an explanation.

Affluence came within reach of a small segment of humanity during the twilight of the Middle Ages as economic activity expanded in Western Europe. Burgeoning urban trade, exploration of other parts of the world, and the onset of the Industrial Revolution transformed Western Europe and, soon after, North America. Industrial technology and the innovations of countless entrepreneurs created new wealth on a grand scale. At the outset, modernization theorists concede, this wealth benefited only a few. Yet industrial technology was so productive that gradually the standard of living of even the poorest people began to improve. The specter of absolute poverty, which had cast a menacing shadow over humanity for its entire history, was finally being routed.

Since then, the standard of living in the region where the Industrial Revolution first took hold has continued to rise. Many middle-income countries in

Asia and Latin America are now industrializing as well, spreading the fruits of technology ever more widely.

The importance of culture. Why haven't people everywhere shared in the bounty wrought by the Industrial Revolution? Modernization theory holds that people are likely to exploit new technology only in a *cultural environment* that emphasizes the benefits of materialism and innovation.

In a word, then, the greatest barrier to economic development is *tradition*. In societies that look to ancient ways to guide understanding of the present and the future, tradition operates as a form of "cultural inertia" that discourages people from adopting new technologies that would improve their living standards. Iran, for example, has fiercely resisted Western technological advances, seeing them as a threat to traditional Islamic ways of life.

Max Weber (1958; orig. 1904–5) argued that, at the end of the Middle Ages, Western Europe forged a distinctive cultural environment that favored change. As is noted in Chapter 12 ("Family and Religion"), this progress-oriented culture characterized societies where the Protestant Reformation had supplanted traditional Catholicism. Material affluence—regarded with suspicion by the Catholic Church—became a badge of personal virtue, and the growing importance of individualism steadily eroded the traditional emphasis on kinship and community. Taken together, these changing cultural patterns nurtured the Industrial Revolution, which allowed one region of the world to prosper.

Rostow's stages of modernization. Modernization theory maintains that low-income countries need not have a future as wretched as their past. As technological advances diffuse around the world, all societies are gradually converging on the industrial model. According to W. W. Rostow (1978), this process of modernization follows four general stages.

1. **Traditional stage.** Initially, cultural traditions are strong, so poor societies resist technological innovation. Socialized to venerate the past, people in poor societies cannot easily imagine how life could be different. They build their lives around their families and local communities, granting little individual freedom to one another, which, of course, inhibits change. Life is often spiritually rich, but lacking in material abundance.

   A century ago, much of the world was at this initial stage of economic development. Because Bangladesh, Somalia, and much of

---

[4]The following discussion of modernization theory draws primarily on Rostow (1978), Bauer (1981), and Berger (1986).

Early in the nineteenth century, exhausting and dangerous work was a fact of childhood in England. An unknown artist portrayed the perilous coal mines of Britain in this 1844 painting. Today, boys and girls in low-income societies around the world contend with grueling labor. Poor societies rely on the muscle power of everyone, so that childhood as we know it does not exist.

India, among other nations, are still at the traditional stage, they remain impoverished to this day.

2. **Take-off stage.** As a society's traditions begin to weaken, a market economy emerges, with people producing not just for their own consumption but to profitably trade with others. Paralleling these developments, greater individualism and a stronger achievement orientation take hold, often at the expense of family ties and time-honored norms and values.

   Great Britain reached this point by about 1800; the United States entered "take-off" by 1820. Thailand, a middle-income country in eastern Asia, has now entered this stage.

   Rostow argues that economic "take-off" depends on progressive influences—including foreign aid, the introduction of advanced technology and investment capital, and schooling abroad—that only rich nations can provide.

3. **Drive to technological maturity.** By this time, a society is in full pursuit of material prosperity. An active, diversified economy drives a population eager to enjoy the benefits of industrial technology. At the same time, however, people begin to realize (and sometimes lament) that industrialization is eroding traditional family and community life. Great Britain entered this stage by about 1840, the United States by about 1860. Today, Mexico and the People's Republic of China are among the nations driving to technological maturity.

   By this stage, absolute poverty is greatly reduced. Cities swell with people drawn from the rural hinterland in search of economic opportunity, occupational specialization renders relationships less personal, and heightened individualism often sparks movements for greater equality and expanded political rights. Societies approaching technological maturity also recognize the need to provide basic schooling to all their people, and advanced training for some. As people discredit tradition as "backward," they open the door to further change. The social position of women steadily becomes more equal to that of men. But, at least in the short term, the process of development may subject women to new and unanticipated problems, as the box explains.

4. **High mass consumption.** Economic development through industrial technology steadily raises living standards. This rise occurs, Rostow argues, as mass production stimulates mass consumption. More simply put, people soon learn to "need" the expanding array of goods that their society produces.

   The United States reached this stage of development by 1900; other rich countries were not far behind. For example, Japan was sufficiently industrialized to become a military power early

Modernization and Women: A Report From Rural Bangladesh

Bangladesh

In global perspective, gender inequality is greatest where people are poorest. Economic development, then, weakens traditional male domination and gives women opportunities to work outside the home. Birth control emancipates women from a continual routine of childbearing, allowing them to benefit from schooling and to earn more in the paid work force.

Even as living standards rise, however, economic development has drawbacks for women. Investigating a poor, rural district of Bangladesh, Sultana Alam (1985) reports that women confront several new problems as a result of modernization.

First, economic opportunity draws men from rural areas to cities in search of work, leaving women and children to fend for themselves. Men sometimes sell their land and simply abandon their wives, who are left with nothing but their children.

Second, the eroding strength of the family and neighborhood leaves women who are deserted in this way with few sources of assistance. The same holds true for women who become single through divorce or the death of a spouse. In the past, Alam reports, kin or neighbors readily took in a Bangladeshi woman

who found herself alone. Today, as Bangladesh struggles to advance economically, the number of poor households headed by women is

One consequence of modernization in developing societies might be termed "the sexualization of women." Rather than being defined in terms of traditional kinship roles, women are increasingly valued for their sexual attractiveness. It is noteworthy that many of the growing number of prostitutes in the cities of low-income countries have discarded traditional dress for Western styles of clothing.

increasing. Rather than enhancing women's autonomy, Alam argues, this spirit of individualism has actually reduced the social standing of women.

Third, economic development—as well the growing influence of Western movies and mass media—undermines women's traditional roles as wives, sisters, and mothers while redefining women as objects of men's sexual attention. The cultural emphasis on sexuality that is familiar to us now encourages men in poor societies to desert aging spouses for women who are younger and more physically attractive. The same emphasis contributes to the world's rising tide of prostitution noted earlier in this chapter.

Modernization, then, does not affect men and women in the same ways. In the long run, the evidence suggests, modernization does give the sexes more equal standing. In the short run, however, the economic position of many women actually declines, and women are also forced to contend with new problems that were virtually unknown in traditional societies.

Sources: Based on Alam (1985) and Mink (1989).

---

in this century. After recovering from the destruction of World War II, the Japanese entered an era of high mass consumption, and Japan now has the world's second largest economy. Closing in on this level of economic development are two of the most prosperous small societies of East Asia, Hong Kong and Singapore.

The role of rich nations. Modernization theory claims that high-income countries make four contributions to global economic development:

1. **Assisting in population control.** As we have already noted, population growth is greatest in the poorest countries of the world. Rich nations can

help curb global population by exporting birth control technology and promoting its use. Once economic development is under way, birth rates should decline as they have in industrial societies.

2. **Increasing food production.** Modernization theory asserts that "high-tech" farming methods, exported from rich societies to poor nations, will raise agricultural yields. Such techniques—collectively known as the *Green Revolution*—include the use of new hybrid seeds, modern irrigation methods, chemical fertilizers, and pesticides for insect control.

3. **Introducing industrial technology.** Rich nations can accelerate economic growth in poor societies by introducing machinery and information technology, which improve productivity and also transform the labor force from agricultural work to skilled industrial and service work.

4. **Providing foreign aid.** Investment capital from rich countries can boost the prospects of poor nations striving to reach the "take-off" stage. Foreign aid may be used to purchase fertilizers and construct irrigation projects that raise agricultural productivity, and to build power plants and factories to increase industrial output.

Critical evaluation. Modernization theory, which explains how and why industrialization transforms societies, has influential supporters among social scientists (Parsons, 1966; W. Moore, 1977, 1979; Bauer, 1981; Berger, 1986). It has also shaped U.S. foreign policy toward poor countries for decades. Proponents maintain that the economic development of Western societies serves as a useful blueprint for economic growth: Asian countries (especially South Korea, Taiwan, Singapore, and Hong Kong) have made impressive strides toward economic development by following the lead of Western countries.

From the outset, however, modernization theory came under fire from socialist nations (and sympathetic analysts in the West) as a thinly veiled defense of capitalism. Ideology aside, critics fault modernization theory, first and foremost, because it simply has not worked in many poor countries. Between 1980 and 1990, in fact, fifty low- and middle-income nations actually saw their living standards fall.

A second criticism is that modernization theory fails to recognize how the self-interest of rich nations is blocking paths to development for poor societies. In essence, critics charge, rich countries industrialized two centuries ago from a position of global *strength*:

Can we expect poor countries to make the same leap today from a position of *weakness*?

Third, critics continue, modernization theory treats rich and poor societies as worlds unto themselves, offering little insight into ways that international relations historically have affected all nations. It was colonization, they maintain, that boosted the fortunes of Europe to begin with; further, this economic windfall left in its wake the economic decimation of poor nations that are still reeling from the consequences.

Fourth, critics contend that modernization theory holds up the world's most economically developed countries as the standard by which the rest of humanity should be judged, thus betraying an ethnocentric bias. Keep in mind that the Western notion of "progress" has contributed to the degradation of the physical environment (see Chapter 15, "The Natural Environment"). In addition, not everyone buys into our ideas about competitive, materialistic living.

Fifth, and finally, modernization theory draws criticism for suggesting that the causes of global poverty lie almost entirely in the poor nations themselves. This amounts to "blaming the victims" for their own plight. Instead, critics argue, an analysis of global inequality should focus as much attention on the behavior of *rich* nations as that of poor nations (Wiarda, 1987).

From these concerns has emerged a second approach to understanding global inequality: dependency theory.

Dependency Theory

Dependency theory is *a model of economic development that explains global inequality in terms of the historical exploitation of poor societies by rich societies.* This analysis places primary responsibility for global poverty on rich nations. Dependency theory holds that rich societies have impoverished low-income countries, making poor societies *dependent* on rich ones. The roots of this destructive process, which dependency theorists claim continues today, extend back over centuries.

Historical perspective. Everyone agrees that, before the Industrial Revolution, there was little of the affluence present in some of the world today. Dependency theory asserts, however, that many people living in poor countries were actually better off economically in the past than their descendants are now. André Gunder Frank (1975), a noted proponent of this approach, argues that the development of rich

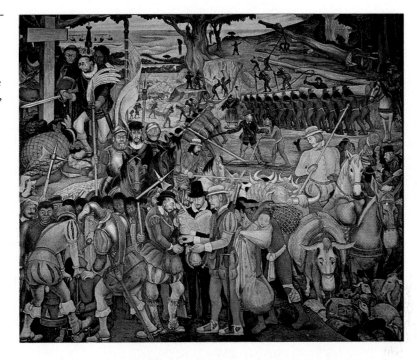

One side of the "Christopher Columbus controversy" is illustrated by artist Diego Rivera in his mural *Colonial Domination*. As this painting expresses in graphic detail, the arrival of Europeans to this hemisphere initiated considerable conflict and violence, placing the Americas under the political control of European nations for more than three hundred years.

societies resulted from the same colonial ties that *underdeveloped* poor societies.

Dependency theory hinges on the assertion that the economic positions of the rich and poor nations of the world are interconnected and cannot be understood in isolation from one another. This analysis argues that poor societies are not lagging behind rich ones on the "path of progress." Rather, the increasing prosperity of the most-developed countries came largely at the expense of less-developed nations. In short, some nations have become rich *only because others have become poor*. Both are the products of global commerce that intensified half a millennium ago.

The importance of colonialism. Late in the fifteenth century, Europeans began to explore North America to the west, the massive continent of Africa to the south, and the vast expanse of Asia to the east. The United States, itself originally a British colony, later colonized the Virgin Islands, Haiti, Puerto Rico, and part of Cuba in the Western Hemisphere, and Guam and the Philippines in Asia.

What Europeans have long celebrated as "the discovery of the New World" was—from the point of view of the people being "discovered"—the onset of centuries of exploitation. European nations set up colonies throughout much of Latin America, Africa, and Asia; a century ago, the English boasted that "The sun never

sets on the British Empire." Figure 8–3 shows the colonial territories that Britain and other European countries held in Africa until the early 1960s.

Formal colonialism broke down in Latin America by 1850, and most African and Asian colonies won their freedom during this century. However, according to dependency theory, political liberation has not meant economic autonomy. Far from it: The economic relationship between poor and rich societies continues to perpetuate the colonial pattern. This neo-colonialism is fueled by a capitalist world economy.

Wallerstein's capitalist world economy. According to Immanuel Wallerstein (1974, 1979, 1983, 1984), global stratification stems from the "capitalist world economy."[5] Wallerstein's term *world economy* suggests that the prosperity or poverty of all countries depends on the operation of a global economic system. He traces the roots of the global economy to the onset of colonization five hundred years ago as the emergent capitalist nations of Europe cast their eyes on the wealth of the rest of the world.

Wallerstein places rich nations at the *core* of the capitalist world economy. Colonialism enriched the

---

[5]While based largely on Wallerstein's ideas, this section also is informed by the work of Frank (1980, 1981), Delacroix & Ragin (1981), and Bergesen (1983).

core by funneling raw materials and other resources from around the globe to Western Europe, where they fueled the Industrial Revolution. Today, multinational corporations operate profitably around the globe by channeling the same resources and wealth to North America, Western Europe, Australia, and Japan.

Low-income countries, by contrast, represent the *periphery* of the world economy. Drawn into the world economy by colonial exploitation, poor countries continue to prop up rich ones by providing inexpensive labor and a vast market for industrial products.

In Wallerstein's view, the world economy benefits rich nations (by generating profits) and harms the rest of the world (by perpetuating poverty). The world economy thus imposes a chronic state of dependency on poor nations, which remain under the control of rich ones. This dependency turns on the following three factors:

1. **Narrow, export-oriented economies.** Unlike the diversified economies of rich countries, production in poor nations centers on a few crops for export, a pattern dating back to colonial times. Coffee and fruits from Latin American countries, oil from Nigeria, hardwoods from the Philippines, and palm oil from Malaysia are some of the products central to the economies of these poor nations. Multinational corporations maintain this reliance on single crops today as they purchase raw materials cheaply in poor societies and process them for profitable resale.

2. **Lack of industrial capacity.** Without an industrial base, poor countries face a double bind: They count on selling inexpensive raw materials to rich nations, from whom they buy whatever expensive manufactured goods they can afford. In a classic example of this dependency, British colonialists pressured the people of India to raise cotton, but prohibited them from manufacturing their own cloth. Instead, the British shipped Indian cotton to textile mills in Birmingham and Manchester back in England, wove it into cloth, and shipped finished goods back for profitable sale in India.

   Underdevelopment theorists also blast the Green Revolution, widely praised by modernization theory, for fostering dependency. To promote agricultural productivity, poor countries must purchase expensive fertilizers, pesticides, and mechanical equipment from core nations. Typically, rich countries profit from this exchange more than poor societies do.

3. **Foreign debt.** Such unequal trade patterns have plunged poor countries into debt to industrialized nations. Collectively, the poor countries of the world owe rich nations more than $1.7 trillion, including hundreds of billions of dollars owed to the United States (The World Bank, 1993). This staggering debt can paralyze a country with high unemployment and rampant inflation.

   Caught in the "debt trap," some poor countries (including Cuba) have simply stopped making payments. Because this threatens the economic well-being of the United States and other rich countries, these wealthy nations strongly

FIGURE 8–3 Africa's Colonial History

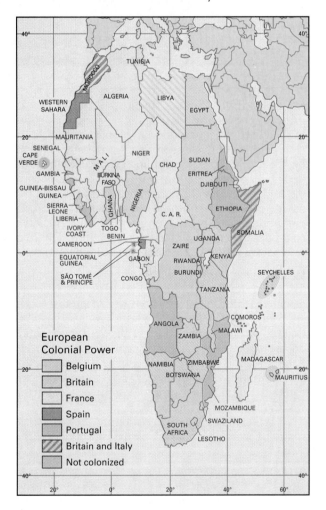

European Colonial Power

- Belgium
- Britain
- France
- Spain
- Portugal
- Britain and Italy
- Not colonized

oppose such actions by poor debtor nations and have proposed various refinancing programs.

The role of rich nations. Nowhere is the difference between modernization theory and dependency theory drawn more sharply than in the role they assign to rich nations. Modernization theory maintains that rich societies *produce wealth* through technological innovation. According to this view, as poor nations adopt pro-growth attitudes and more productive technology, they, too, will prosper. By contrast, dependency theory casts global stratification in terms of how countries *distribute wealth,* arguing that rich societies have *over*developed themselves as they have *under*developed the rest of the world.

Dependency theorists dismiss the idea that any program of population control, agricultural and industrial technology, or foreign aid is likely to help poor countries. Instead, they contend, rich nations act simply in pursuit of profit. Selling technology makes money, and foreign aid typically goes to ruling elites (rather than the poor majority) in exchange for ensuring a favorable "business climate" for multinational corporations (Lappé, Collins, & Kinley, 1981).

Additionally, dependency theorists Frances Moore Lappé and Joseph Collins (1986) assert that the capitalist culture of the United States underlies a widespread view of poverty as natural or inevitable. Following this line of reasoning, poverty stems from "natural" processes including having (too many) children, and natural disasters such as droughts. But global poverty is far from inevitable, they argue; rather, it results from deliberate policies. Lappé and Collins point out that the world already produces enough food to allow every person on the planet to grow quite fat. Moreover, India and most of Africa *export* food even though many of their people go hungry.

According to Lappé and Collins, the contradiction of poverty amid plenty is grounded in a rich-nation policy of producing food for profits, not people. That is, rich nations cooperate with elites in poor countries to grow and export profitable crops such as coffee while simultaneously curbing the production of staples consumed by local families. Governments of poor nations support this policy of "growing for export" because they need food profits to repay massive foreign debt. At the center of this vicious cycle, according to Lappé and Collins, is the capitalist corporate structure of the global economy.

After decades of war and communist rule, Vietnam is now attracting foreign investment, evident in this commercial display outside a Hanoi government building. Whether this inflow of capital will raise living standards, as modernization theory contends, or block development, as dependency theory maintains, remains to be seen.

Critical evaluation. The pivotal insight of dependency theory—that no society develops (or fails to develop) in isolation—points up how the global economy shapes the destiny of all nations. Citing Latin America and other poor regions of the world, dependency theorists claim that development simply cannot proceed under the constraints presently imposed by rich nations. Reducing global poverty, they conclude, demands more than change within poor societies. Rather, these theorists call for radical reform of the entire world economy so that it operates in the interests of the majority of people.

Critics, however, charge that dependency theory treats wealth as a zero-sum commodity, as if no one gets richer without someone else getting poorer. Not so, critics contend, since farmers, small-business owners, and industrialists can and do create new wealth through their drive and imaginative use of new technology. After all, they observe, the entire world's wealth has grown five-fold since 1950 because of technological innovations.

Second, critics reason, dependency theory is wrong in blaming rich nations for global poverty because many of the world's poorest countries (Ethiopia, for example) have had little contact with rich societies. Similarly, they continue, rapidly developing countries such as Singapore, South Korea, Japan, and Hong Kong (which became a British colony in 1841 and will remain so until 1997) have a long history of trade with rich countries. In addition, an increasing body of evidence bolsters the conclusion that foreign investment by rich nations fosters economic growth, as modernization theorists claim, not economic decline, as dependency theorists maintain (Vogel, 1991; Firebaugh, 1992).

Third, critics contend that dependency theory takes a simplistic approach by pointing the finger at a single factor—world capitalism—as the cause of global poverty. In doing so, dependency theory casts poor societies as passive victims, ignoring factors inside these countries that contribute to their economic plight. Sociologists have long recognized the vital role of culture in shaping human behavior, and some societies clearly embrace change readily while others staunchly resist economic development. Iran's fundamentalist brand of Islam has deliberately discouraged economic ties with other countries, especially nations of the West. Capitalist societies, then, can hardly be faulted for Iran's economic stagnation.

Nor can rich societies be saddled with responsibility for the reckless behavior of foreign leaders who engage in far-reaching corruption or militaristic campaigns to boost their own power (examples include the regimes of Marcos in the Philippines, Duvalier in Haiti, Noriega in Panama, Mobutu Sese Seko in Zaire, and Saddam Hussein in Iraq). Governments may even use food supplies as a weapon in internal political struggles: Leaders in Ethiopia, Sudan, and Somalia in Africa have all staged power plays with food intended for starving people. Other regimes (including many in Latin America and Africa) have done little to improve the status of women or control population growth.

Fourth, critics chide dependency theorists for downplaying the economic dependency fostered by the former Soviet Union. The Soviet army seized control of most of Eastern Europe during World War II and subsequently dominated these nations politically and economically for more than forty years. Critics of dependency theory see the popular uprisings against Soviet-installed governments, beginning in 1989, as rebellions against Soviet political domination and the ensuing economic dependency.

A fifth criticism holds that dependency theory advances only vague solutions to global poverty. Most dependency theorists urge poor societies to end all contact with rich countries, and some call for nationalizing foreign-owned industries. Dependency theory implies that global poverty could be eliminated by the overthrow of international capitalism. The bottom line, critics conclude, is that dependency theory is a thinly disguised call for some sort of world socialism. In light of the difficulties socialist societies have had in meeting the needs of their own people, critics ask, should we really expect such a system to lift the entire world toward prosperity?

Global Inequality: Looking Ahead

People in the United States, sociologists included, are discovering that our lives are caught up in global trends. We read, for instance, that U.S. corporations play a crucial role in the world while business interests from abroad gain control of properties here at home. As Chapter 7 ("Social Stratification") explained, the increasingly global economy is polarizing our society as it boosts the fortunes of the rich while cutting factory jobs and putting downward pressure on wages.

However, as we noted in this chapter, social inequality is far more striking in global context. The concentration of wealth among the most-developed countries, coupled with the grinding poverty in the least-developed nations, may well be the most pressing dilemma facing humanity in the twenty-first century. To some analysts, rich nations hold the key to ending world poverty; to others, they are the cause of this tragic problem.

But which of these two divergent approaches to understanding global inequality has more merit? As with many controversies, each view has some measure of truth as well as inherent limitations. Table 8–2 summarizes important arguments made by each approach.

Let us consider the empirical evidence. In some regions of the world, especially the "Pacific Rim" of eastern Asia, the market forces endorsed by modernization theory are raising living standards rapidly and substantially. Many Latin American nations, too, have recorded strong economic growth in recent years. At the same time, other poor societies, especially in Africa, are experiencing economic turmoil that frustrates hopes for market-based development.

The poor countries that have surged ahead economically have two factors in common. First, they are relatively small. Combined, the Asian nations of South Korea, Taiwan, Hong Kong, Singapore, and Japan equal only about one-fifth of the land area and population of India. The economic problems smaller countries face are more manageable; consequently, small nations more effectively administer programs of development. Second, these "best case" nations have cultural traits in common, especially an emphasis on individual achievement and economic success. In other areas of the world, where traditions inhibit individual achievement, even smaller nations have failed to turn development opportunities to their advantage.

The picture now emerging calls into question arguments put forward by both modernization and dependency theorists. On the one hand, few societies seeking economic growth now favor a market economy completely free of government regulation. This view challenges modernization theory, which endorses a free-market approach over government-directed initiatives. On the other hand, recent upheavals in the former Soviet Union and Eastern Europe demonstrate that a global reevaluation of socialism is currently under way. Decades of dismal economic performance and political repression make many poor countries wary of a socialist path to development. Because dependency theory has historically endorsed socialist economic systems, changes in world socialism will surely generate new thinking here as well.

In the short term, no plan for development is likely to effectively reduce the pressing problems of world hunger and rapid population growth. Moreover, as Chapter 15 ("The Natural Environment") points out, poverty is forcing people all over the world to exploit the earth's resources in ways that do permanent, global ecological damage.

Looking to the next century, however, there are reasons for hope. The approaches described in this chapter identify the two keys to combating global poverty. One insight, revealed by modernization theory, is that world hunger is partly a *problem of technology*. A higher standard of living for a surging world population depends on greater agricultural and industrial productivity. The second pivotal point, derived from dependency theory, is that global inequality is also a *political problem*. Even with higher productivity, the human community must address crucial questions about how resources are distributed—both within societies and around the globe.

People everywhere are coming to recognize that the security of the entire world depends on reducing the destabilizing extremes of global stratification. We can only hope that, as the cold war between the superpowers winds down, nations will redirect energy and resources to the needs of the vast majority of humanity trapped in a desperate struggle for survival.

TABLE 8–2 Modernization Theory and Dependency Theory: A Summary

	Modernization Theory	Dependency Theory
Historical pattern	The entire world was poor just two centuries ago; the Industrial Revolution brought affluence to high-income countries; as industrialization gradually transforms poor societies, people in all nations are likely to enjoy higher living standards.	Global parity was disrupted by colonialism, which made some countries rich while simultaneously making other countries poor; barring change in the world capitalist system, rich nations will grow richer and poor nations will become poorer.
Primary causes of global poverty	Characteristics of poor societies cause their poverty, including lack of industrial technology, traditional cultural patterns that discourage innovation, and rapid population growth.	Global economic relations—historical colonialism and the operation of multinational corporations—have enriched high-income countries while placing low-income countries in a state of economic dependency.
Role of rich nations	Rich countries can and do assist poor nations through programs of population control, technology transfers that increase food production and stimulate industrial development, and investment capital in the form of foreign aid.	Rich countries have concentrated global resources, conferring advantages on themselves while producing massive foreign debt in low-income countries; rich nations represent a barrier to the economic development of poor nations.

SUMMARY

1. Adopting a global perspective, we see the full extent of social stratification. About 15 percent of the world's people live in the most-developed countries, which are industrialized, rich nations such as the United States. Together, these advantaged countries take in 55 percent of the earth's total income. Another one-third of humanity live in less-developed countries with limited industrialization; they receive about 37 percent of all income. Half the world's population occupy the least-developed countries that have yet to industrialize, and earn only 8 percent of global income.

2. In addition to relative poverty, poor nations grapple with widespread absolute poverty. The typical member of a low-income society struggles to survive on a fraction of the income enjoyed by the average person in the United States.

3. Poverty places about 800 million of the world's people at risk. Some 15 million people, many of them children, die annually due to lack of nutrition.

4. Women are more likely than men to be poor nearly everywhere in the world. Gender bias against women is greatest in poor, agrarian societies. Children, too, bear a heavy burden of poverty, with perhaps 75 million children living on the streets.

5. The abject poverty found in much of the world is a complex problem rooted in a lack of industrial technology, rapid population growth, traditional cultural patterns, internal social stratification including male domination, and global power relationships that inhibit development.

6. Modernization theory maintains that poor societies seeking economic development must overcome the inertia of traditional cultural patterns and embrace more productive technology.

7. Modernization theorist W. W. Rostow identifies four stages of development: traditional, take-off, drive to technological maturity, and high mass consumption.

8. Arguing that rich countries hold the keys to creating wealth, modernization theory cites four ways rich nations can assist poor nations: through population control programs, by supplying food-producing technologies, by stimulating industrial development, and by providing investment capital and other foreign aid.

9. Critics of modernization theory argue that this approach has produced only limited economic development in the world, while ethnocentrically assuming that poor societies can—and want to—follow the path to development taken by rich nations centuries ago.

10. Dependency theory links global wealth and poverty to historical patterns of colonial exploitation. Today's world capitalist economy is fueled by neocolonialism, a form of exploitation by multinational corporations that parallels earlier exploitation by colonial powers.

11. Immanuel Wallerstein, the dependency theory pioneer, views high-income countries as the advantaged "core" of the capitalist world economy and the least economically developed societies as the global "periphery."

12. Three key factors—export-oriented economies, a lack of industrial capacity, and foreign debt—perpetuate poor countries' dependency on rich nations.

13. Critics of dependency theory argue that this approach overlooks how well many nations have done in creating new wealth. Contrary to the implications of this approach, these critics maintain, the poorest countries are not those with the strongest ties to rich nations.

14. Both modernization and dependency approaches offer useful insights into the origins of global inequality. Some evidence exists to support each view. Regardless of its origins, however, pervasive worldwide poverty undermines global stability.

KEY CONCEPTS

colonialism the process by which some nations enrich themselves through political and economic control of other nations

dependency theory a model of economic development that explains global inequality in terms of the historical exploitation of poor societies by rich societies

modernization theory a model of economic development that explains global inequality in terms of technological and cultural differences among societies

multinational corporation a large business that operates in many countries

neocolonialism a new form of economic exploitation involving not formal political control but the operation of multinational corporations

CRITICAL-THINKING QUESTIONS

1. In what ways is poverty in poor nations of the world a far more serious problem than poverty here in the United States?

2. What accounts for women's lower social standing in the poorest countries compared to their status in the United States?

3. State the basic tenets of modernization theory. How does this approach fall short?

4. What are the key arguments that support dependency theory? Identify several weaknesses of this model.

Race and Ethnicity

Chapter Outline

With his village in flames, twenty-four-year-old Hasan Mahmudagic fled for his life. The day had begun with the approach of Serbian soldiers; soon after, villagers were alarmed to discover the telephone lines were dead. That was enough for most people in the Bosnian village to pack up what they could carry and leave. When the soldiers arrived, they marched quickly from door to door, warning people to leave, and then splashed oil on the houses, igniting the town and the worst fears of its people.

Mahmudagic, a Muslim, hoped that a nearby Muslim city would offer safe haven. But, within days, Serbian soldiers captured him and took him to a detention camp. There, he discovered almost eight thousand men of his own kind. Discipline was harsh, and his captors demanded that each man sign away the right to his land. The choice was simple: Promise to leave Bosnia forever or die. After the camp's inmates complied, they boarded trucks carrying them across the Croatian border where they became refugees in a new country (Smolowe, 1992).

Since the latest outbreak of violent strife in the former Yugoslavia in 1991, the world has witnessed bitter "ethnic cleansing" by which one category of people tries to rid the region of others whose backgrounds differ from their own. Although the term is new, such conflict merely marks the latest outbreak in a long history of violent blood feuds that have wracked the Balkans time and again over the centuries.

Nor is ethnic or racial conflict limited to this one shuddering nation as it disintegrates. Across Eastern Europe, Ukrainians, Moldavians, Azerbaijanis, and a host of other ethnic peoples in the former Soviet Union are seeking to recover their cultural identity after decades of subjugation. In the Middle East, efforts continue to end decades of conflict between Arabs and Jews. In South Africa, democratic government is being born after centuries of racial separation. In India, Tibet, Malaysia, and other Asian nations as well, differences of color and culture frequently propel people into violent confrontation. Even in North America, where the magnitude of strife is less intense, social diversity continues to fuel conflict in countless communities.

In short, everywhere in the world race and ethnicity divide human beings. In one of life's greatest ironies, however, the same traits that infuse our lives with tremendous pride also underlie our propensity toward hatred and violence.

This chapter examines the meaning of race and ethnicity, explains how these social constructs have shaped our history, and explores why they continue to play a central part—for better or worse—in the world today.

The Social Significance of Race and Ethnicity

People frequently confuse the terms "race" and "ethnicity." For this reason, we begin with important definitions.

Race

A **race** is *a category composed of men and women who share biologically transmitted traits that members of a society deem socially significant*. People classify each other by race based on physical characteristics such as skin color, hair texture, facial features, and body shape. Racial features have nothing to do with being human; all people on earth are members of a single biological species. The biological variations that we describe as racial emerged over thousands of generations as a result of living in different areas of the world (Molnar, 1983). In hot regions, for example, humans developed darker skin (from the natural pigment melanin) that offers protection from the sun; in temperate regions, humans have lighter skin.

Over the course of history, migration spread genetic characteristics around much of the globe. In the world's "crossroads" of migration—like the Middle East—people display remarkable racial variation. In more isolated locales, such as Japan, people exhibit greater racial uniformity. No society, however, lacks genetic mixture, and increasing contact among the world's people ensures that racial blending will accelerate in the future.

Nineteenth-century biologists responded to racial diversity with a three-part classification scheme. They labeled people with relatively light skin and fine hair *Caucasian*; they applied the term *Negroid* to those

The range of biological variation in human beings is far greater than any system of racial classification allows. This fact is made obvious by trying to place all of the people pictured here into simple racial categories.

with darker skin and coarser, curlier hair; and they described people with yellow or brown skin and distinctive folds on the eyelids as *Mongoloid.* Such terms are misleading, however, because there are no biologically pure races. In fact, the traveler notices gradual and subtle variations all around the globe. The people we commonly call "Caucasians" or "white people" actually display skin color that ranges from very light (typical in Scandinavia) to dark (in southern India), and the same variation occurs among "Negroids" (that is, "black people") and "Mongoloids" (commonly called "Asians"). In fact, many "white people" born in southern India have darker skin than many "black" aborigines of Australia.

The population of the United States, too, is genetically mixed. Over many generations, the genetic traits of Negroid Africans, Caucasian Europeans, and Mongoloid Native Americans (whose ancestors were Asian) spread throughout the Americas. Many "black people," therefore, have a share of Caucasian genes, and many "white people" have some Negroid genes. In short, race is no black-and-white issue.

The reason people make so much of race is that societies rank people by genetic traits in systems of social inequality. In some cases, they defend this practice by asserting that physical traits are linked to innate intelligence and other mental abilities, although no sound scientific evidence supports such beliefs. With so much at stake, however, no wonder societies commonly strive to make social rankings more clear than facts permit. Earlier in this century, for example, many southern states labeled as "colored" anyone whose ancestry included even one African-American great-great-great grandparent. Today, with less of a racial caste system, state laws permit parents to declare the race of their child (if they wish to do so at all).

Ethnicity

Ethnicity is *a shared cultural heritage.* Members of an *ethnic category* may have common ancestors, language, and religion that confer a distinctive social identity. The United States is a multi-ethnic society in which

TABLE 9–1 Racial and Ethnic Categories in the United States, 1990

Racial or Ethnic Classification	Approximate U.S. Population	Percent of Total Population
African descent	29,986,060	12.1%
Hispanic descent*	22,354,059	9.0
Mexican	13,495,938	5.4
Puerto Rican	2,727,754	1.1
Cuban	1,043,932	0.4
Other Hispanic	5,086,435	2.1
Native-American descent	1,959,234	0.8
American Indian	1,878,285	0.8
Eskimo	57,152	<
Aleut	23,797	<
Asian or Pacific Islander descent	7,273,662	2.9
Chinese	1,645,472	0.7
Filipino	1,406,770	0.6
Japanese	847,562	0.3
Asian Indian	815,447	0.3
Korean	798,849	0.3
Vietnamese	614,547	0.2
Hawaiian	211,014	<
Samoan	62,964	<
Guamanian	49,345	<
Other Asian or Pacific Islander	821,692	0.3
European descent	200,000,000	80.0
German	57,947,000	23.3
Irish	38,736,000	15.6
English	32,652,000	13.1
Italian	14,665,000	5.9
French	10,321,000	4.1
Polish	9,366,000	3.8
Dutch	6,227,000	2.5
Scotch-Irish	5,618,000	2.3
Scottish	5,314,000	2.1
Swedish	4,681,000	1.9
Norwegian	3,869,000	1.6
Russian	2,953,000	1.2
Welsh	2,034,000	0.8
Danish	1,635,000	0.6
Hungarian	1,582,000	0.6

*People of Hispanic descent can be of any race. Many people also identify with more than one ethnic category. Thus figures total more than 100 percent. White people represent 80 percent of the U.S. population.

< Indicates less than 1/10 of one percent.

Source: U.S. Bureau of the Census (1993).

English is the favored language, but millions of people speak Spanish, Italian, German, French, or other tongues in their homes. Similarly, the United States is a predominantly Protestant society, but most people of Spanish, Italian, and Polish ancestry are Roman Catholic, while many others of Greek, Ukrainian, and Russian ancestry identify with the Eastern Orthodox Church. More than 6 million Jewish Americans (with ancestral ties to various nations) share a religious tradition. Similarly, several million men and women claim a Muslim religious heritage.

Race and ethnicity, then, are quite different, since one is biological and the other is cultural. But the two may go hand in hand. Japanese Americans, for example, have distinctive physical traits and—for those who maintain a traditional way of life—cultural attributes as well. People can fairly easily modify their ethnicity as, for instance, Polish immigrants discard their cultural background over time. Assuming people mate with others like themselves, however, racial distinctiveness persists over generations.

Minorities

A racial or ethnic **minority**[1] is *a category of people, distinguished by physical or cultural traits, that is socially disadvantaged.* Distinct from the dominant majority, in other words, minorities are set apart and subordinated. The scope of the term "minority" has expanded in recent years beyond race and ethnicity to include people with physical disabilities. As we shall see in Chapter 10 ("Sex and Gender"), some analysts also view gay people and women as minorities.

Table 9–1 tallies U.S. racial and ethnic minorities as recorded by the 1990 census. White people of non-Hispanic background (80 percent of the total) continue to predominate in the United States. But the absolute numbers and share of population for virtually every minority is growing rapidly so that, as the box explains, within a century minorities, taken together, may form a majority of the U.S population.

Minorities have two major characteristics. First, they share a *distinct identity.* Because race is highly visible (and virtually impossible for a person to change), minority men and women are set apart by their physical appearance. The significance of ethnicity (which people can change) is more variable. Throughout U.S. history, some people (such as Reform Jews) have downplayed their ethnicity, while others (including many Orthodox Jews) have maintained distinctive cultural traditions and neighborhoods.

A second characteristic of minorities is *subordination.* As we shall see presently, U.S. minorities have lower social standing. But not all minority members

---

[1]We use the term "minority" rather than "minority group" because, as explained in Chapter 5 ("Groups and Organizations"), a minority is a category, not a group.

The Coming Minority-Majority

A decade ago, Manhattan, the central borough of New York City, gained a "minority-majority." This means that people of African, Asian, and Latino descent became a majority of the population. As shown by National Map 9–1, on the next page, the same thing has occurred in 186 U.S. counties (6 percent of the total). In the final decades of the next century, according to some projections, minorities will be a majority in the United States as a whole.

The Census Bureau reports that, between 1980 and 1990, the white, non-Hispanic population increased by a modest 6 percent. The number of Asians or Pacific Islanders, however, soared 108 percent. The Hispanic population increased by more than half (53 percent), and the number of Native Americans, Eskimos, or Aleuts jumped by 37 percent. African Americans boosted their number by 13 percent.

But population projections are crude estimates. Stephan Thernstrom (1990) cautions that the "minority-majority" prediction is based on two questionable assumptions. First, he explains, the U.S. immigration rate would have to remain at its current high level—despite indications that immigration is subsiding. Second, the high birth rates that characterize new immigrants would have to continue. But, Thernstrom points out, past immigrants started behaving more like everyone else (reproductive patterns included) as years passed. To the extent that these two assumptions do not hold true, Thernstrom concludes, a minority-majority will be forestalled.

But, whatever the specific projections, few people doubt that a great change in the country's racial and ethnic profile is under way. As the twentieth century began, most people in the United States thought of "minorities" as people of German, Irish, or Italian background. It seems only a matter of time before people of European ancestry (other than Hispanics) once again become minorities in the United States.

---

are equally disadvantaged. Some Latinos, for example, are quite wealthy, certain Chinese Americans are celebrated business leaders, and a number of African Americans have joined the ranks of our nation's leading scholars. But even among the most successful individuals, race or ethnicity often serves as a master status (see Chapter 4, "Social Interaction in Everyday Life") that overshadows personal accomplishments (Benjamin, 1991).

While minorities usually constitute a small share of a society's population, there are exceptions to this rule. For example, even though black South Africans are a numerical majority in their own country, whites have deprived them of economic and political power. In the United States, too, women represent a slight majority of the population but still lack many opportunities and privileges enjoyed by men.

Prejudice and Stereotypes

Prejudice amounts to *a rigid and irrational generalization about a category of people.* Prejudice is irrational to the extent that people hold inflexible attitudes supported by little or no direct evidence. Prejudice can target people of a particular social class, sex, sexual orientation, age, political affiliation, race, or ethnicity.

Prejudices are *prejudgments* that can be positive or negative, and most people hold some of each type. With positive prejudices, we exaggerate the virtues of people like ourselves, while our negative prejudices condemn those who differ from us. A common form of prejudice is the **stereotype** (*stereo* is derived from Greek meaning "hard" or "solid"), *a prejudiced description of a category of people.* Because stereotypes often involve emotions like love and affection (generally toward members of ingroups) or hate or fear (toward outgroups), they are hard to change even in the face of contradictory evidence. For example, some people have a stereotypical understanding of the poor as freeloaders who would rather rely on welfare than work to support themselves (NORC, 1993). As Chapter 7 ("Social Stratification") explained, this stereotype distorts reality, since more than half of poor people in our nation are children, working adults, and elderly people.

People have devised stereotypes for virtually every racial and ethnic minority, and such attitudes often become deeply rooted in a society's culture. The

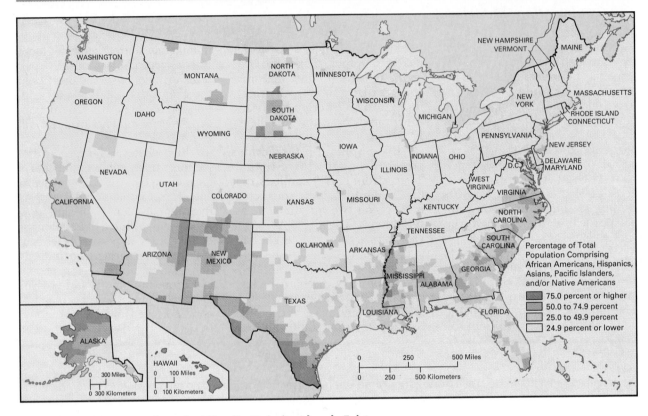

NATIONAL MAP 9–1 Where the Minority-Majority Already Exists

As recorded by the 1990 census, in 186 counties (out of about 3,000) minorities are already
a majority. That is, the total number of African Americans, Asian Americans, Hispanics,
and other minorities exceeds 50 percent of the population. The map also identifies some
40 counties in which minorities together exceed 75 percent of the population and more than
200 counties in which minority population surpasses the 25 percent mark. Why do you think
most of these counties are in the South and Southwest?

Sources: Map from *Time*, July 12, 1993, p. 15. Copyright ©1993 Time, Inc. Reprinted by permission. Data from the 1990
decennial census.

conflict in the war-torn Balkans, described in the opening to this chapter, is fueled by stereotypes that have
persisted for centuries.

Racism

A powerful and destructive form of prejudice, **racism**
refers to *the belief that one racial category is innately superior or inferior to another.* Racism has pervaded world

history: The ancient Greeks, as well as other people
from Africa to Asia, were quick to view anyone unlike
themselves as in some way inferior.

Racism has also been widespread in the United
States where, for centuries, notions about racial inferiority supported the enslavement of people of African
descent. Great Britain and other European powers
likewise defended their colonial empires by asserting
the innate inferiority of subjugated peoples. In this
century, racism animated the Nazi regime in Germany.

Nazi doctrine proclaimed a so-called "Aryan super-race" of blond-haired, blue-eyed Caucasians that was allegedly destined to rule the world. Such racism was used to justify the murder of anyone deemed inferior, including some 6 million European Jews and millions of Poles, Gypsies, and homosexuals.

More recently, growing public intolerance of immigrants has fueled a resurgence of Nazi rhetoric and tactics in Europe. In the United States racial tensions have arisen in cities and on college campuses as well.

Individual versus institutional racism. Stokely Carmichael and Charles Hamilton (1967) point out that we typically think of racism in terms of the ideas or actions of hateful individuals. But even more serious than *individual racism* is *institutional racism,* which refers to racism that guides the operation of schools, the police force, or the workplace. For example, some saw in the beating of Rodney King by police in Los Angeles (described at the beginning of Chapter 6, "Deviance") not just a case of wrongdoing by specific officers, but evidence of wide-ranging police violence targeting the city's black community. According to Carmichael and King, the public is slow to condemn institutional racism, since it involves established authority figures, even though powerful people sometimes seriously damage public welfare.

In a legal effort to improve the social standing of the lowest castes, India reserves half of all government jobs for members of particular castes deemed disadvantaged. Because the government is the largest employer, higher-caste students fear that this policy will keep them out of the labor force when they graduate from college. So intense are these concerns that recently eleven students killed themselves—five by fire—in public protest over this controversial policy.

Theories of Prejudice

If prejudice does not represent a rational assessment of facts, what are its origins? Social scientists have come up with various answers to this vexing question, citing the importance of frustration, personality, culture, and social conflict.

Scapegoat theory. *Scapegoat theory* holds that prejudice springs from frustration among people who are themselves disadvantaged (Dollard, 1939). A white woman unhappy with her low pay in a textile factory, for example, may direct hostility not at the powerful people who employ her but at powerless minority co-workers. Prejudice of this kind will not go far toward improving her situation in the factory, but it serves as a relatively safe way to vent anger and it may give the woman the comforting sense that at least she is superior to someone.

A **scapegoat** is thus *a person or category of people, typically with little power, whom people unfairly blame for their own troubles.* Because they are in no position to fight back, minorities make convenient scapegoats.

Authoritarian personality theory. T. W. Adorno (1950) and others claim that extreme prejudice forms a personality trait in some individuals. This conclusion is supported by research showing that people who display prejudice toward one minority are usually intolerant of all minorities. Such people have *authoritarian personalities,* rigidly conforming to conventional cultural values, envisioning issues as clear-cut matters of right and wrong, and voicing strong ethnocentrism. People with authoritarian personalities also look on society as naturally competitive and hierarchical, with "better" people (like themselves) inevitably dominating those who are weaker.

By contrast, Adorno found, people who are tolerant toward one minority are likely to be accepting of all. They express greater flexibility in their moral judgments and feel uncomfortable in any situation in which some people exercise excessive power over others.

The researchers contend that authoritarian personalities tend to develop in people with little education and those raised by cold and demanding parents. Socialized in this way, angry and anxious children may grow into hostile and aggressive adults who look down on scapegoats as inferior beings.

Cultural theory. A third approach contends that, while extreme prejudice may figure prominently in certain people's personalities, some prejudice is found in everyone. Emory Bogardus (1968) studied the effects of culturally rooted prejudices for more than forty years. He devised the concept of *social distance* to assess how closely we are willing to interact with members of various racial and ethnic categories. His research, which documented widespread agreement throughout our population, found that we feel closest to people of English, Canadian, and Scottish background, even welcoming marriage with them. Attitudes are somewhat less favorable toward the French, Germans, Swedes, and Dutch. According to Bogardus, the most negative prejudices target people of African and Asian descent.

If prejudice is so widespread, can we dismiss intolerance as merely a trait of a handful of abnormal people, as Adorno suggests? Rather, it seems that some bigotry is routinely expressed by people well adjusted to a "culture of prejudice."

Conflict theory. A fourth approach views prejudice as the product of social conflict. According to this theory, powerful people foster prejudice to justify their oppression of those with fewer advantages. To the extent that people devalue illegal Chicano immigrants in the Southwest, for example, rich landowners are able to pay these people low wages for their work.

Conflict theories of prejudice take various forms. According to one argument, based on Marxist theory, elites promote prejudice to divide workers along racial and ethnic lines. This strategy serves the interests of capitalists by discouraging workers from joining together to press for their common interests (Geschwender, 1978; Olzak, 1989).

A different argument, advanced by Shelby Steele (1990), holds that minorities themselves touch off conflict by playing up race as a political tactic to gain

The efforts of these four women advanced the United States toward the goal of equal opportunity regardless of a person's color. Sojourner Truth (1797–1883) (left), born a slave, became an influential preacher and later employed her charisma in the abolitionist cause. Near the end of the Civil War, President Abraham Lincoln honored her at the White House. Harriet Tubman (1820–1913) (bottom left), after escaping from slavery herself, masterminded the flight from bondage of hundreds of African-American men and women. She was one of the most successful participants in what came to be known as the "Underground Railroad." Ida Wells-Barnett (1862–1931) (bottom middle), born to slave parents, was outspoken in pursuit of social equality in the antebellum era. After becoming a partner in a Memphis newspaper, she was a tireless crusader against the terror of lynching. Marian Anderson (1897–1993) (bottom right) had an exceptional voice, which stood out in her church choir when she was six years old. For years, Anderson's career was restrained by racial prejudice. Thus, when she sang in the White House (1936), and on the steps of the Lincoln Memorial to a crowd of almost one hundred thousand people (1939), she symbolically broke an important "color line."

power. Such *race consciousness,* Steele explains, leads minorities—the historic victims of white oppression—to claim that they are now entitled to privileges based simply on their race. While such policies may yield short-term gains for minorities, he cautions, they are likely to spark a backlash from whites or others who condemn "special treatment" for anyone solely on the grounds of race or ethnicity.

Discrimination

Closely related to prejudice is **discrimination,** *treating various categories of people unequally.* While prejudice refers to attitudes, discrimination is a matter of action. Like prejudice, discrimination can be either positive (providing special advantages) or negative (subjecting people to special obstacles). Discrimination also varies in intensity, ranging from subtle avoidance to blatant barriers to opportunity.

Prejudice and discrimination often occur together, but not always. A prejudiced personnel manager, for example, may refuse to hire minorities. Robert Merton (1976) describes such a person as an *active bigot* (see Figure 9–1). Fearing legal action, however, the prejudiced personnel manager may not discriminate, thereby becoming a *timid bigot.* What Merton calls *fair-weather liberals* may be generally tolerant of minorities yet discriminate when it is expedient to do so, say when a superior demands it. Finally, Merton's *all-weather liberal* is free of both prejudice and discrimination.

Institutional discrimination. Like prejudice, discrimination involves not just the actions of individuals but the operation of society. **Institutional discrimination** refers to *discrimination that is a normative and routine part of the economy, educational system, or some other social institution.* As minorities in the United States have learned through painful experience, traditional ideas of people's "place" can be deeply embedded in the operation of the workplace or the legal system.

Until 1954, for example, the principle of "separate but equal" justified the practice of educating black and white children separately in different schools. Because the education received by African-American children lagged behind that of white children, the Supreme Court formally banned this institutional discrimination in the 1954 landmark decision *Brown* v. *The Board of Education of Topeka.* But because black and white people generally live in different neighborhoods, more

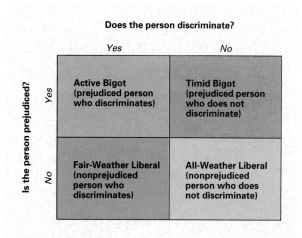

Does the person discriminate?

	Yes	No
Yes	**Active Bigot** (prejudiced person who discriminates)	**Timid Bigot** (prejudiced person who does not discriminate)
No	**Fair-Weather Liberal** (nonprejudiced person who discriminates)	**All-Weather Liberal** (nonprejudiced person who does not discriminate)

Is the person prejudiced?

FIGURE 9–1 Patterns of Prejudice and Discrimination
Source: Merton (1976).

than forty years after the *Brown* ruling, most young people of both races still attend racially imbalanced schools.

Prejudice and Discrimination: The Vicious Cycle

Prejudice and discrimination reinforce each other. W. I. Thomas offered a simple explanation of this fact, noted in Chapter 4 ("Social Interaction in Everyday Life"). The Thomas theorem states: *Situations that are defined as real become real in their consequences* (1966:301; orig. 1931).

Thomas recognized that people socially construct reality. Thus stereotypes become real to those who believe them, sometimes even to those who are victimized by them. Power also plays a role here, since some categories of people have the ability to enforce their prejudices to the detriment of others.

Prejudice on the part of whites toward people of color, for example, does not produce *innate* inferiority but it can produce *social* inferiority, consigning minorities to poverty, low-prestige occupations, and poor housing in racially segregated neighborhoods. If white people interpret social disadvantage as evidence that minorities do not measure up to their standards, they unleash a new round of prejudice and discrimination, giving rise to a *vicious cycle* whereby each perpetuates the other, even from generation to generation.

Majority and Minority: Patterns of Interaction

Social scientists describe patterns of interaction between minorities and more privileged members of a society in terms of four models: pluralism, assimilation, segregation, and genocide.

Pluralism

Pluralism is *a state in which people of all races and ethnicities are distinct but have social parity.* This means that, while people differ in appearance or social heritage, they all share resources more or less equally.

The United States is pluralistic in some respects. Large cities contain countless "ethnic villages" where people proudly display the traditions of their immigrant ancestors. In New York these include Spanish Harlem, Little Italy, and Chinatown; in Philadelphia, Italian "South Philly"; in Chicago, "Little Saigon"; and Latino East Los Angeles.

Nevertheless, the United States is not really pluralistic for three reasons. First, while many people appreciate their cultural heritage, only a small proportion want to live apart from others exclusively with their "own kind" (NORC, 1993). Second, our tolerance for

---

The ritual of Kwanzaa, devised in 1968, has gained popularity in recent decades as a celebration of African-American heritage. Observed soon after Chanukah and Christmas, Kwanzaa combines Christian and Jewish elements in a distinctly African ritual that builds the strength of families and communities.

social diversity is limited. One reaction to the growing proportion of minorities in the United States, for example, has been a social movement seeking to make English this country's official language, a drive some view as devaluing foreign-born people and their heritage. Third, as we shall see later in this chapter, people of various colors and cultures do not have equal social standing.

Assimilation

Assimilation is *the process by which minorities gradually adopt patterns of the dominant culture.* Assimilation involves changing modes of dress, values, religion, language, or friends.

Traditionally, the United States has styled itself as a "melting pot" in which various nationalities blended together. Rather than everyone "melting" into a new hybrid culture, however, minorities typically have adopted the traits of the dominant culture established by the earliest settlers. They have done so to position themselves for upward social mobility and to escape the prejudice and discrimination directed against more visible foreigners (Newman, 1973). But some critics of the assimilation model point out that it tends to paint minorities as "the problem" and define them (rather than elites) as the ones who need to do all the changing.

As a cultural process, assimilation focuses on changes in ethnicity but not in race. For example, many descendants of Japanese immigrants have discarded their ancestral traditions but retain their racial identity. However, distinctive racial traits do diminish over generations as a result of **miscegenation,** *the biological process of interbreeding among racial categories.* While resistance to such biological mixing remains strong—for example, only 1 percent of U.S. marriages joins black and white partners—miscegenation (often outside of marriage) has occurred throughout U.S. history.

Segregation

Segregation refers to *the physical and social separation of categories of people.* Sometimes minorities, especially religious orders like the Amish, voluntarily segregate themselves. Usually, however, majorities segregate minorities by excluding them from the mainstream of social and cultural life. Segregation characterizes neighborhoods, schools, occupations, hospitals, and even cemeteries. While pluralism fosters distinctiveness without disadvantage, segregation enforces separation to the detriment of a minority.

Racial segregation has a long history in the United States, marked first by centuries of slavery, and then followed by racially separated lodging, schooling, and transportation. Decisions such as the 1954 *Brown* case have reduced *de jure* (Latin meaning "by law") discrimination in the United States. However, *de facto* ("in fact") segregation continues.

Recent research by Douglas Massey and Nancy Denton (1989) documented the *hypersegregation* of African-American neighborhoods in some inner cities. Residents of such areas, they conclude, have little contact of any kind with people in the larger society.

Segregated minorities understandably oppose their second-class citizenship. Sometimes the action of even a single individual can have lasting consequences. On December 1, 1955, Rosa Parks was riding a bus in Montgomery, Alabama, sitting in a section designated by law for African Americans. When a crowd of white passengers boarded the bus, the driver asked four black people to give up their seats to white people. Three did so, but Rosa Parks refused. The driver left the bus and returned with police, who arrested her for violating the racial segregation laws. She was later convicted in court and fined $14. Her stand (or sitting) for justice sparked the African-American community of Montgomery to boycott city buses, ultimately bringing to an end this form of segregation (King, 1969).

Genocide

Genocide is *the systematic killing of one category of people by another.* This brutal form of racism and ethnocentrism violates nearly every recognized moral standard; nonetheless, it has recurred time and again in human history.

Genocide figured prominently in centuries of contact between Europeans and the original inhabitants of the Americas. From the sixteenth century on, the Spanish, Portuguese, English, French, and Dutch forcefully colonized vast empires in the Western Hemisphere. These conquests decimated the native populations of North and South America. Some native people fell victim to calculated killing sprees; most succumbed to diseases brought by Europeans and to which native peoples had no natural defenses (Matthiessen, 1984; Sale, 1990).

Genocide has also occurred in the twentieth century. Unimaginable horror befell European Jews in the

Only a full century after the abolition of slavery in the United States did the federal government take action to dismantle the "Jim Crow" laws that continued to enforce the separation of people of European and African ancestry in all aspects of public life. During the 1950s and 1960s, these laws, which formally segregated hotels, restaurants, parks, buses, and even drinking fountains, were finally abolished. Even so, *de facto* racial segregation in housing and schooling remains a reality for millions of people of color in the United States.

1930s and 1940s during Adolf Hitler's reign of terror, known as the Holocaust. Ultimately, the Nazis exterminated more than 6 million Jewish men, women, and children. Between 1975 and 1980 the Communist regime of Pol Pot in Cambodia slaughtered anyone thought to represent capitalist cultural influences. Condemned to death were people able to speak any Western language and even those who wore eyeglasses, construed as a symbol of capitalist culture. In all, some 2 million people (one-fourth of the population) perished in the "killing fields" of Cambodia (Shawcross, 1979).

These four patterns of minority-majority contact have all been played out in the United States. We proudly point to patterns of pluralism and assimilation; only reluctantly do we acknowledge the degree to which our society has been built on segregation (of African Americans) and genocide (of Native Americans). The remainder of this chapter examines how these four patterns have shaped the social standing of major racial and ethnic categories in the United States.

Race and Ethnicity in the United States

Give me your tired, your poor,
Your huddled masses yearning to breathe free,
The wretched refuse of your teeming shore,
Send these, the homeless, tempest-tossed to me:
I lift my lamp beside the golden door.

These words by Emma Lazarus, inscribed on the Statue of Liberty, express cultural ideals of human dignity, personal freedom, and opportunity. But, as the following history of our country's racial and ethnic minorities reveals, our nation's golden door has opened more widely for some than for others.

Native Americans

The term *Native Americans* refers to the hundreds of distinct societies—including Aleuts, Cherokee, Zuni,

---

In recent years, American Indians have taken advantage of the legal system to operate public gambling on reservation land in twenty-seven states. Some large casinos, such as this one in Ledyard, Connecticut, are extremely profitable. Gambling income reached $4 billion in 1993, making some American Indians quite rich.

Sioux, Mohawk, Aztec, and Inca—who first settled the Western Hemisphere. Some thirty thousand years before Columbus "discovered" the Americas, migrating peoples crossed a land bridge from Asia to North America where the Bering Strait (off the coast of Alaska) lies today. Gradually, they spread throughout North and South America.

When the first Europeans arrived late in the fifteenth century, Native Americans numbered in the millions. But by the beginning of this century, after relentless subjugation and even acts of genocide, the "vanishing Americans" numbered a mere 250,000 (Dobyns, 1966; Tyler, 1973).

It was Christopher Columbus (1446–1506) who first referred to Native Americans as *Indians*; when he landed in the Bahama Islands in the Caribbean, he thought he had reached India. Columbus found the indigenous people to be passive and peaceful, a stark contrast to the more materialistic and competitive Europeans (Matthiessen, 1984; Sale, 1990). Even as Europeans seized the land of Native Americans, they demeaned their victims as thieves and murderers to justify their actions (Unruh, 1979; Josephy, 1982).

After the Revolutionary War, the new United States government adopted a pluralist approach to Native-American societies and sought to gain more land through treaties. Payment for land was far from fair, however, and when Native Americans resisted surrender of their homelands, the U.S. government simply used superior military power to evict them. In perhaps the most regrettable incident of its kind, thousands of Cherokees died on a forced march—the Trail of Tears—from their homes in the southeastern United States to reservations in Indian Territory, later Oklahoma. By the early 1800s, few Native Americans remained east of the Mississippi River.

In 1871, the United States made Native Americans wards of the government and set out to resolve "the Indian problem" through forced assimilation. Native Americans continued to lose their land, and were well on their way to losing their culture as well. Reservation life fostered dependency, replacing ancestral languages with English and eroding traditional religion in favor of Christianity. Officials took many children from their parents and placed them in boarding schools, where they were to be resocialized as "Americans." Authorities gave local control of reservations to the few Native Americans who supported government policies, and distributed reservation land—traditionally held collectively—as the private property of individual families (Tyler, 1973). In the process, some whites grabbed still more land for themselves.

Not until 1924 were Native Americans entitled to U.S. citizenship. Since then, the government has encouraged their migration from reservations. Some have adopted mainstream cultural patterns and married non–Native Americans. Many large cities now have sizable Native-American populations. As shown in Table 9–2, however, median family income for Native Americans was far below the U.S. average in 1990, and relatively few Native Americans earn a college degree.[2]

From in-depth interviews with Native Americans in a Western city, Joan Albon (1971) concluded that this low social standing reflects cultural factors including a noncompetitive view of life and reluctance to pursue higher education. In addition, she noted, many Native Americans have dark skin that provokes prejudice and discrimination from others.

Like other racial and ethnic minorities in the United States, Native Americans have recently reasserted pride in their cultural heritage. Native-American organizations report a surge in new membership applications, and many children are learning to speak native tongues better than their parents (Fost, 1991; Johnson, 1991). In lawsuits against the federal government, some Native Americans have pressed for return of lands forcibly seized in the past, and they have sought self-rule over reservation lands. In a few cases, confrontations with federal officials have erupted into violence. Few Native Americans support this means of addressing grievances, but the vast majority share a profound sense of injustice suffered at the hands of white people (Josephy, 1982; Matthiessen, 1983).

White Anglo-Saxon Protestants

White Anglo-Saxon Protestants (WASPs) were not the first people to inhabit the United States, but they came to dominate this nation once European settlement began. Most WASPs are of English ancestry, but this category also includes people of Scottish and Welsh descent. With more than 50 million people of English ancestry, one in five members of our society claims some WASP background.

---

[2]In making comparisons of income and education, keep in mind that categories of the U.S. population vary in average age. The 1994 median age for all U.S. people was 34.1 years. White people have a median age of 35.1 years; for Native Americans, the figure is 26.7 years. Because people's income and schooling rise through adulthood, this age difference accounts for some of the disparities shown here.

TABLE 9–2 The Social Standing of Native Americans, 1990

	Native Americans	Entire United States
Median family income	$21,750	$35,225
Percent in poverty	30.9%	13.1%
Completion of four or more years of college (age 25 and over)	9.3%	20.3%

Source: U.S. Bureau of the Census (1993).

Historically, WASP immigrants were highly skilled and motivated toward achievement by what we now call the Protestant work ethic. Because of their numbers and power, WASPs were not subject to the prejudice and discrimination experienced by other categories of immigrants. The historical dominance of WASPs has been so great that, as noted earlier, members of all other groups have sought to become more like them.

During the nineteenth century, many WASPs bemoaned the growing presence of new arrivals whom they deemed "undesirable foreigners." Nativist political movements managed to legally limit the flow of immigrants. Those who could afford to pursued a personal solution to the "problem" by sheltering themselves in exclusive suburbs and restrictive clubs. Thus the 1880s—the decade in which the Statue of Liberty first welcomed immigrants to the United States—also saw the founding of the first country club (with all WASP members). Soon afterward, WASPs began publishing the *Social Register* (1887), a listing of members of "society," and established various genealogical societies such as the Daughters of the American Revolution (1890) and the Society of Mayflower Descendants (1894). These efforts served to further insulate wealthy WASPs from newly arrived immigrants (Baltzell, 1964).

By mid-century, the commanding wealth and privileges of the WASPs had peaked. Signaling a more egalitarian trend, John Fitzgerald Kennedy was elected as the first Irish-Catholic president of the United States in 1960. But the majority of people in the upper-upper class are still WASPs (Baltzell, 1964, 1976, 1979, 1988; Neidert & Farley, 1985). And the WASP cultural legacy still stands: English remains this country's dominant language and Protestantism is the majority religion. Our legal system, too, reflects its English origins. But the historical dominance of WASPs comes through most clearly in the widespread use of the terms "race" and "ethnicity" to describe everyone but them.

At its foundation, agrarian slavery was an institution built on coercion and violence. As African-American painter Jacob Lawrence shows here, planters utilized the most brutal treatment in an effort to obtain compliance. The wide stance and clenched jaw convey the planter's determination to control the bound man at his feet. But despite the fear that such tactics generated, they also provoked periodic rebellion on the part of slaves.

African Americans

Although African Americans accompanied Spanish explorers to the New World in the fifteenth century, most accounts mark the beginning of black history in the United States as 1619, when a Dutch trading ship brought twenty Africans to Jamestown, Virginia. Whether these people arrived as slaves or as indentured servants who paid for their passage by performing labor for a specified period, being of African descent on these shores soon became virtually synonymous with being a slave. In 1661, Virginia enacted the first law recognizing slavery (Sowell, 1981).

Slavery was the foundation of the southern colonies' plantation system. Some whites prospered as plantation owners and, until it was outlawed in 1808, as slave traders. Traders forcibly transported some 10 million Africans to various countries in the Americas; about four hundred thousand entered the United States. Hundreds of slaves were chained on board small sailing ships as human cargo during a voyage of several weeks across the Atlantic Ocean. Filth and disease killed many; the inhuman conditions drove others to suicide. Overall, perhaps half died en route (Tannenbaum, 1946; Franklin, 1967; Sowell, 1981).

Surviving the journey was a mixed blessing, bringing a life of servitude as the property of white owners. Although some worked in cities at a variety of trades, most slaves labored in the fields, often from daybreak until sunset and even longer during the harvest. The law allowed owners to impose whatever disciplinary measures they deemed necessary to ensure that slaves labored continuously. Even the killing of a slave by an owner rarely prompted legal action. Owners also divided slave families at public auctions where human beings were bought and sold as pieces of property. Unschooled and dependent on their owners for all their basic needs, slaves had little control over their destinies (Franklin, 1967; Sowell, 1981).

There were, however, free persons of color in both the North and the South, small-scale farmers, skilled workers, and small-business owners (Murray, 1978). But the lives of most African Americans stood in glaring contradiction to the principles of freedom on which the United States was founded. The Declaration of Independence states:

> We hold these Truths to be self-evident, that all Men are created equal, that they are endowed by their Creator with certain unalienable Rights, that among these are Life, Liberty, and the Pursuit of Happiness. . . .

Most white people, however, did not apply these ideals to black people. In the Dred Scott case in 1857, the U.S. Supreme Court addressed the question, "Are blacks citizens?" by writing, "We think they are not, and that they are not included, and were not intended to be included, under the word 'citizens' in the Constitution, and can therefore claim none of the rights and privileges which that instrument provides for and secures for citizens of the United States" (quoted in Blaustein & Zangrando, 1968:160). Thus arose what Swedish sociologist Gunnar Myrdal (1944)

The message of the Civil Rights movement was never stated more simply or clearly than it is here. The claim "I Am a Man"—regardless of color or class—is a bold challenge to the racism that continues to compromise the basic humanity of millions of women and men in the United States.

termed the *American dilemma:* the denial of basic rights and freedoms to an entire category of people. To resolve this dilemma, many white people simply defined African Americans as innately inferior.

In 1865 the Thirteenth Amendment to the Constitution outlawed slavery. Three years later the Fourteenth Amendment reversed the Dred Scott ruling, granting citizenship to all people born in the United States. The Fifteenth Amendment, ratified in 1870, stated that neither race nor previous condition of servitude should deprive anyone of the right to vote. However, especially in the South, so-called Jim Crow laws still segregated U.S. society into two racial castes (Woodward, 1974). White people beat and lynched black people (and some whites) who challenged this racial hierarchy.

The twentieth century has brought dramatic changes to African Americans. In the decades after World War I, tens of thousands of women and men deserted the rural South for jobs in northern factories. While some did find more economic opportunity, few escaped racial prejudice and discrimination, which placed them lower in the social hierarchy than white immigrants arriving from Europe at the same time (Lieberson, 1980).

In the 1950s and 1960s, a national civil rights movement of black people and sympathetic white people celebrated landmark judicial decisions that outlawed segregated schools and overt discrimination in employment and public accommodations. In addition, the "black power movement" gave African Americans a renewed sense of pride and purpose.

Gains notwithstanding, people of African descent continue to occupy a subordinate position in the United States. As shown in Table 9–3 on page 226, the median income of African-American families in 1992 ($21,161) was 54 percent of that earned by white families ($38,909).[3] Black families are also three times as likely as white families to be poor.

In 1992, about one in four African-American families was securely in the middle class with an annual income of at least $35,000—a 50 percent jump during the 1980s. Moreover, 15 percent of African-American families were affluent, with income exceeding $50,000. But, overall, African Americans have been hurt economically as factory jobs—vital to residents of inner cities—have been lost to other countries where labor costs are lower. Thus black unemployment stands

[3]Here, again, a median age difference (white people, 35.1; black people, 29.0) accounts for some of the income and educational disparities shown here. A higher proportion of one-parent families among blacks than whites also plays a role in these differences. If we were to compare only families headed by married couples, black families (earning $34,196 in 1992) received 80 percent as much as white families ($42,738).

TABLE 9–3 The Social Standing of African Americans, 1992*

	African Americans	Entire United States
Median family income	$21,161	$36,812
Percent in poverty	33.3%	14.5%
Median education (years; age 25 and over)	12.3	12.7
Completion of four or more years of college (age 25 and over)	11.5%	21.4%

*For purposes of comparison with other tables in this chapter, 1990 data are as follows: median family income, $21,423; percent in poverty, 31.9%; median education, 12.4 years; completion of four or more years of college, 11.3%.

Source: U.S. Bureau of the Census (1993).

at more than twice the level of whites; among African-American teenagers in many cities, the figure exceeds 40 percent (Wilson, 1984; Jacob, 1986; Lichter, 1989; U.S. Department of Labor, 1994).

By 1992, the historical gap in schooling between the races had almost closed: The median figures were 12.3 years for African Americans and 12.7 years for whites. But a striking racial disparity remains at the college level. Table 9–3 shows that African Americans are just half as likely as white people to complete four years of college. In fact, the share of black high school graduates who enter college (currently 31.5 percent) is now lower than a generation ago (U.S. Bureau of the Census, 1994).

The political clout of African Americans has increased, paralleling the number of registered voters and elected officials drawn from their ranks. Partly as a result of black migration to cities coupled with white movement to the suburbs, half of this country's ten largest cities have elected African-American mayors. At the national level, however, only 1 percent of elected leaders are African Americans. After the 1994 elections, thirty-nine men and women (out of 435) in the House of Representatives were African Americans, and only one U.S. Senator (out of 100) was black.

In sum, for more than 350 years people of African ancestry in the United States have struggled for social equality. As a nation, we can certainly take pride in how far we have come in this pursuit. A century ago slavery was outlawed and, during the twentieth century, this nation has banned most forms of overt discrimination.

Assessing the state of African Americans in 1913—fifty years after the abolition of slavery—W. E. B.

Du Bois proudly recounted the extent of black achievement, but cautioned that racial bigotry remained strong. Clearly this is still the case. One response to this problem is the government policy of affirmative action, or preferential treatment for categories of people historically subjected to prejudice and discrimination. The box examines this controversial policy.

Asian Americans

Although Asian Americans share some racial traits, enormous cultural diversity marks this category of people. The 1990 census placed their number at more than 7 million—approaching 3 percent of the population. In the largest category of Asian Americans are people of Chinese ancestry (1.6 million), followed by those of Filipino (1.4 million), Japanese (850,000), Asian-Indian (815,000), and Korean (800,000) background. Forty percent of Asian Americans reside in California.

Young Asian Americans have commanded attention and respect as high achievers who are disproportionately represented at our country's best colleges and universities. Many of their elders have also made significant economic and social gains in recent years. Yet some people take a negative view of Asian Americans, expressing attitudes toward them ranging from aloofness to outright hostility despite (and sometimes because of) this record of achievement.

But, as we shall see, the "model minority" image of Asian Americans obscures the poverty found within their ranks. We now focus on the history and current standing of Chinese Americans and Japanese Americans—the longest-established Asian-American minorities—and conclude with a brief look at the most recent arrivals.

Chinese Americans. Chinese immigration to the United States began with the economic boom of the California Gold Rush in 1849. With new towns and businesses springing up overnight, entrepreneurs met their pressing need for cheap labor by employing some one hundred thousand Chinese immigrants. Most Chinese workers were young, hard-working men willing to take lower-status jobs shunned by whites. But the economy soured in the 1870s, and desperate whites were thrown into keen competition with the Chinese for jobs. Suddenly the industriousness of the Chinese posed a threat. Following a well-known pattern, economic hard times led to prejudice and discrimination ((Ling, 1971; Boswell, 1986).

Affirmative Action: Problem or Solution?

After World War II, the U.S. government funded higher education for veterans of all races. The G.I. Bill held special promise for African Americans, sending some 350,000 black men and women to college by 1960. But these men and women were not finding the kinds of jobs for which they were qualified.

The government responded with a program that came to be known as "affirmative action." In the early 1960s, the Kennedy Administration defined affirmative action as efforts by employers to find the qualified minorities they knew were out there. This program won widespread support for helping thousands of African Americans gain jobs in line with their skills and training.

But, by the 1970s, critics complained, affirmative action was coming to mean "group preferences" for minorities. Some advocates of affirmative action wanted to go further toward a quota system, claiming that minorities should be represented in jobs (or on campus) in proportion to their numbers in the overall population. The "quota" concept is highly controversial, because it guarantees some minority members favorable treatment regardless of how they stack up against other applicants.

U.S. courts have rejected rigid quota systems. Even so, the law allows for preferences based on race and ethnicity as a means of increasing the proportion of minorities in settings that have historically excluded them.

Advocates applaud affirmative action as a fair and necessary corrective for historical discrimination. Everybody alive today, they argue, has been affected by privileges accorded or denied to their parents and grandparents. "Special treatment," from this point of view, is nothing new and is necessary for those denied opportunity through no fault of their own. Only in this way, supporters claim, can we break the vicious cycle of prejudice and discrimination.

Opponents of affirmative action concede that minorities have historically suffered from discrimination, but they view affirmative action as *reverse discrimination.* Why should today's whites—most of whom are not especially privileged—be penalized for past discrimination for which they were in no way responsible? Critics of affirmative-action programs also point out that many minorities have overcome historical barriers to opportunity through hard work, not requests for special treatment. In effect, they say, affirmative

action requires employers to find the best *minority person,* rather than the best *individual,* for a job. Such categorical preferences, opponents continue, inevitably compromise standards, foster race consciousness, provoke a hostile backlash from whites, and, perhaps worst of all, undermine the real accomplishments of minorities. Finally, the critics conclude, affirmative action generally benefits minorities with more schooling (who, presumably, need help the least) while doing little for the persistently poor who really need a hand.

When applied to African Americans, the U.S. population tends to oppose affirmative-action policies, as the following survey responses suggest. Those polled responded to the following statement:

> Some people think that blacks have been discriminated against for so long that the government has a special obligation to help improve their living standards. Others believe that the government should not be giving special treatment to blacks.

The numbers 1 through 5 show the range of opinion in relation to the three responses.

Source: NORC (1994).

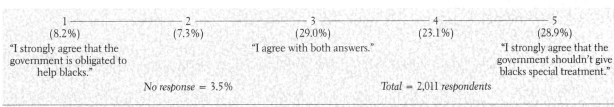

Source: Survey data from *General Social Surveys, 1972–1994: Cumulative Codebook* (Chicago: National Opinion Research Center, 1994), p. 272.

Given the extent of global inequality, it is not surprising that tens of millions of people each year leave their homes in search of more opportunity. This ship, which recently sailed into San Francisco, contained some of the one hundred thousand Chinese immigrants who annually try to enter this country any way they can.

Soon, whites acted to bar the Chinese from many occupations. Courts also withdrew legal protections, unleashing vicious campaigns by some whites against the so-called "Yellow Peril" (Sowell, 1981). Everyone seemed to line up against the Chinese, a sentiment captured in a popular phrase of the time that a person "didn't have a Chinaman's chance" (Sung, 1967).

In 1882, the U.S. government passed the first of several laws curtailing Chinese immigration. This action created domestic hardship because, in the United States, Chinese men outnumbered women by twenty to one (Hsu, 1971; Lai, 1980). This sex imbalance sent the Chinese population plummeting to only sixty thousand by 1920. Chinese women already in the United States, however, were in high demand and they soon became far less submissive to men (Sowell, 1981).

Responding to their plight, some Chinese moved eastward; many more sought the relative safety of urban Chinatowns (Wong, 1971). There, Chinese traditions flourished, and kinship networks, called *clans*, offered financial assistance to individuals and represented the interests of all. At the same time, however, Chinatowns discouraged their residents from learning English and taking jobs outside the local community.

A renewed need for labor during World War II prompted President Franklin Roosevelt to end the ban on Chinese immigration in 1943 and extend the rights of citizenship to Chinese Americans born abroad. Many responded by moving out of Chinatowns and pursuing cultural assimilation. In turn-of-the-century Honolulu, for example, 70 percent of the Chinese people lived in Chinatown; today, the figure is down to 20 percent.

By 1950, many Chinese Americans had experienced upward social mobility. Today, people of Chinese ancestry are no longer restricted to self-employment in laundries and restaurants; many now work in a host of high-prestige occupations. Other Chinese Americans—including several Nobel Prize winners—have excelled in science and technology (Sowell, 1981).

As shown in Table 9–4, the median family income of Chinese Americans in 1990 ($41,316) stood above the national average ($35,225). Note, however, that the higher income of all Asian Americans reflects a larger number of family members in the labor force.[4] Chinese Americans also have an enviable record of educational achievement, with twice the national average of college graduates.

Despite this record of success, many Chinese Americans still grapple with subtle (and sometimes overt) prejudice and discrimination. Such hostility is one reason that poverty among Chinese Americans ranks above the national average. Poverty is higher still among those who remain in the protective circle of Chinatowns working in restaurants or other low-paying jobs. This fact has sparked a debate over whether racial and ethnic enclaves assist their residents economically or exploit them (Portes & Jensen, 1989; Zhou & Logan, 1989; Kinkead, 1992).

Japanese Americans.   Japanese immigration to the United States began slowly in the 1860s, reaching only three thousand by 1890. Most of these immigrants settled in the Hawaiian Islands (annexed by the United States in 1898 and made a state in 1959), where they served as a source of cheap labor. Early in this century, however, as the number of newcomers to California rose along with demands for higher pay, white people responded by setting limits on immigration (Daniels, 1971). In 1907 the United States signed an agreement with Japan curbing the entry of men—the chief economic threat—while allowing Japanese women to immigrate to ease the sex-ratio imbalance. In the 1920s,

---

[4]Median age for all Asian Americans is 30.4, somewhat below the median of 34.1 for the entire U.S. population and below the 35.1 years for whites.

state laws in California and elsewhere mandated segregation and prohibited interracial marriage, virtually ending further Japanese immigration. Not until 1952 did the United States extend citizenship to foreign-born Japanese.

Japanese and Chinese immigrants differed in three ways. First, the number of Japanese immigrants was lower, so they escaped some of the hostility directed at the more numerous Chinese. Second, the Japanese knew much more about the United States before migrating than the Chinese did, which eased their assimilation (Sowell, 1981). Third, Japanese immigrants favored rural farming to clustering together in cities.

But many white people objected to Japanese ownership of farmland. California acted in 1913 to bar further purchases. Foreign-born Japanese (called the *Issei*) responded by placing farmland in the names of their U.S.-born children (*Nisei*), who were Constitutionally entitled to citizenship. Others leased farmland with great success.

Japanese Americans faced their greatest crisis after December 7, 1941, when the nation of Japan destroyed much of the U.S. naval fleet at Hawaii's Pearl Harbor. Rage toward Japan was directed at the Japanese living in the United States. Some feared that Japanese here would commit acts of espionage and sabotage on behalf of Japan. Within a year, President Franklin Roosevelt signed Executive Order 9066, an unprecedented policy to protect national security by rounding up people of Japanese descent and placing them in military camps. Shortly thereafter, authorities relocated 110,000 people of Japanese ancestry (90 percent of the total) to remote, inland reservations.

While concern about national security always rises in times of war, this policy was criticized, first, because it targeted an entire category of people, not one of whom was ever known to have committed a disloyal act. Second, roughly two-thirds of those imprisoned were *Nisei*—U.S. citizens by birth. Third, although the United States was also at war with Germany and Italy, no such action was taken against people of German or Italian ancestry.

Relocation meant selling homes, furnishings, and businesses on short notice for pennies on the dollar. As a result, the Japanese-American population was economically devastated. In military prisons—surrounded by barbed wire and guarded by armed soldiers—families crowded into single rooms, often in buildings that had previously sheltered livestock (Fujimoto, 1971; Bloom, 1980). The internment ended in 1944, when the Supreme Court declared the policy unconstitutional. In 1988 Congress awarded $20,000 as token compensation to each victim of this program.

After World War II, Japanese Americans staged a dramatic recovery. Having lost their traditional businesses, many entered a wide range of new occupations. Because their culture places a high value on education and hard work, Japanese Americans have enjoyed remarkable success. In 1990, the median income of Japanese-American households was almost 50 percent above the national average. And the rate of poverty among Japanese Americans was only half that for the United States as a whole.

Upward social mobility has propelled cultural assimilation. The third and fourth generations of Japanese Americans (the *Sansei* and *Yonsei*) rarely live in residential enclaves, as many Chinese Americans still do, and a majority marry non–Japanese Americans. In the process, many have abandoned their traditions, including the ability to speak Japanese. A high proportion of Japanese Americans participate in ethnic associations, however, as a way of maintaining their ethnic identity (Fugita & O'Brien, 1985). Still, some appear to be caught between two worlds, belonging to neither. As one Japanese-American man put it, "I never considered myself 100 percent American because of obvious

TABLE 9–4 The Social Standing of Asian Americans, 1990

	All Asian Americans	Chinese Americans	Japanese Americans	Korean Americans	Filipino Americans	Entire United States
Median family income	$42,240	$41,316	$51,550	$33,909	$46,698	$35,225
Percent in poverty	14.0%	14.0%	7.0%	13.7%	6.4%	13.1%
Median education (years; age 25 and over)	13.7	NA	NA	NA	NA	12.7
Completion of four or more years of college (age 25 and over)	37.7%	40.7%	34.5%	34.5%	39.3%	20.3%

Source: U.S. Bureau of the Census (1993).

Asian Americans are more likely than any other category of people in the United States to be small-scale entrepreneurs. Although families may earn above-average incomes operating businesses such as this New York grocery store, they typically rely on the labor of many people for long hours.

physical differences. Nor did I think of myself as Japanese" (Okimoto, 1971:14).

Recent Asian immigrants. More recent immigrants from Asia include Koreans, Filipinos, Indians, Vietnamese, Samoans, and Guamanians. When added to the existing population of Chinese and Japanese descent, Asian Americans are this country's fastest growing minority, accounting for almost half of all immigration to the United States (Winnick, 1990).

Generally speaking, the entrepreneurial spirit remains strong among Asian immigrants. When it comes to owning and operating small businesses, Asians are slightly more likely than white people, three times more likely than Latinos, and four times more likely than African Americans and Native Americans to be entrepreneurs (U.S. Bureau of the Census, 1992).

Koreans are the most likely to earn a living by operating small businesses. They own a majority of grocery stores in New York City, for example, and a large share of neighborhood liquor stores in Los Angeles. Many Koreans work long hours; nonetheless, Korean-American families have slightly lower than average incomes, as shown in Table 9-4. Moreover, Korean Americans have experienced limited social acceptance, even among other categories of Asian Americans.

The data in Table 9–4 show that Filipinos generally have fared well. A closer look at this category of Asian Americans, however, reveals a mixed pattern by which some Filipinos stand out among successful professionals (especially in medicine), while others struggle to survive in low-skill jobs (Parillo, 1994).

The key to the relatively high income of Filipino-American families is gender. Almost three-fourths of Filipino-American women are in the labor force, compared to about half of Korean-American women. Moreover, 42 percent of Filipino-American women have a four-year college degree, an achievement equaled by just 25 percent of Korean-American women. Thus, the typical Filipino-American family has relatively high income because both wives and husbands work, in many cases at high-paying, professional occupations.

In sum, the social history of Asians in this country is a mix of discrimination, opportunity, and success. The Japanese come closest to having achieved widespread social acceptance; for the Koreans and other Asian Americans, even economic success has not eradicated historical prejudice and discrimination. And, along with prosperity for many, some Asian Americans remain poor. Their exceptionally high immigration rate guarantees that people of Asian ancestry will play a central role in U.S. society in the century to come.

Hispanic Americans

In 1994, Hispanics numbered some 26 million, about 10 percent of the U.S. population. Few people who fall in this category actually describe themselves as "Hispanic" or "Latino." Like Asian Americans, Hispanics comprise a cluster of smaller populations, each of which identifies with a particular country.

More than half (at least 14 million) of Latinos are Mexican Americans, commonly called *Chicanos*. Puerto Ricans are next in population size (3 million), followed by Cuban Americans (1 million). Many other societies of Latin America are represented in smaller numbers. Because of a high birth rate and significant immigration, analysts predict that Hispanics will surpass African Americans to become this nation's largest racial or ethnic minority by 2010 (U.S. Bureau of the Census, 1993).

The U.S. Hispanic population resides primarily in the Southwest. One of four Californians is Latino (in greater Los Angeles, the share is closer to one-half). National Map 9–2 pinpoints counties across the

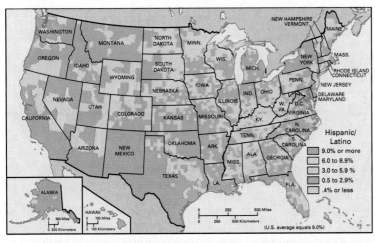

(U.S. average equals 9.0%)

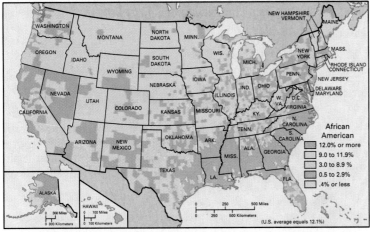

(U.S. average equals 12.1%)

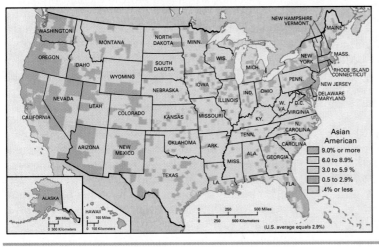

(U.S. average equals 2.9%)

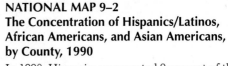

NATIONAL MAP 9–2
The Concentration of Hispanics/Latinos, African Americans, and Asian Americans, by County, 1990

In 1990, Hispanics represented 9 percent of the U.S. population, compared with 12 percent for African Americans and 3 percent for people of Asian descent. These three maps show the geographic distribution of these categories of people. Comparing them, we see that the southern half of the United States is home to far more minorities than the northern half. But are the three concentrated in the same specific areas? What patterns do the maps reveal?

Sources: Maps from *American Demographics Desk Reference Series*, No. 1, June 1991, pp. 8, 14, 16. Reprinted with permission. © 1991, *American Demographics* magazine, Ithaca, New York. Data from the 1990 decennial census.

Chapter 9 Race and Ethnicity 231

TABLE 9–5 The Social Standing of Hispanic Americans, 1990

	All Hispanics	Mexican Americans	Puerto Ricans	Cuban Americans	Entire United States
Median family income	$23,431	$23,240	$18,008	$31,439	$35,225
Percent in poverty	25.0%	25.0%	37.5%	13.8%	13.1%
Median education (years; age 25 and over)	12.0	10.8	12.0	12.4	12.7
Completion of four or more years of college (age 25 and over)	9.2%	6.2%	10.1%	18.5%	20.3%

Source: U.S. Bureau of the Census (1993).

United States where Hispanics predominate and contrasts them with counties containing large African-American and Asian-American populations.

Median family income for all Hispanics—about $23,431 in 1990—stands well below the national average.[5] As the following sections reveal, however, some categories of Hispanics have fared better than others.

Mexican Americans. Some Chicanos are descendants of people who lived in a part of Mexico annexed by the United States after the Mexican-American War (1846–1848). Most Mexican Americans, however, are recent immigrants. Between 1970 and 1990, more immigrants came to the United States from Mexico than from any other country.

Like many other immigrants, many Mexican Americans have worked as low-wage laborers, on farms or elsewhere. Table 9–5 shows that the 1990 median family income for Mexican Americans was $23,240, about two-thirds the national standard. One-fourth of Chicano families are poor—almost twice the national average. Finally, despite gains since 1980, Mexican Americans still acquire significantly less education than U.S. adults as a whole and have a high drop-out rate.

Puerto Ricans. Puerto Rico (like the Philippines) became a possession of the United States when the Spanish-American War ended in 1898. In 1917, islanders (but not Filipinos) became U.S. citizens, and Puerto Ricans now move freely to and from the mainland (Fitzpatrick, 1980).

New York City is the center of Puerto Rican life in the continental United States. Once the airlines began running regular flights between New York City and San Juan, Puerto Rico's capital, migration took

off. Today, New York is home to about 1 million Puerto Ricans.

However, life in New York has not met the expectations of many Puerto Ricans, and one-third of that city's Puerto Rican community is severely disadvantaged. Adjusting to unfamiliar cultural elements on the mainland—including, for many, learning English—is one major challenge; Puerto Ricans with darker skin also encounter prejudice and discrimination. As a result, about as many families return to Puerto Rico annually as arrive from the island.

This "revolving door" pattern hampers assimilation. About three-fourths of Puerto Rican families in the United States speak Spanish at home, compared with about half of Mexican-American families (Sowell, 1981; Stevens & Swicegood, 1987). Speaking only Spanish maintains a strong ethnic identity but it also limits economic opportunity. In addition, Puerto Ricans also have the highest incidence of women-headed households among Hispanics, a pattern that places these families at greater risk of poverty (Reimers, 1984). Table 9–5 shows that in 1990 the median household income for Puerto Ricans was $18,008, about half the national average. This low income marks Puerto Ricans as the most socially disadvantaged Hispanic minority.

Cuban Americans. Within little more than a decade after the 1959 Marxist revolution led by Fidel Castro, four hundred thousand Cubans had emigrated to the United States. Most settled in Miami. Many Cuban Americans were highly educated business and professional people who wasted little time building much the same success in the United States that they had enjoyed in their homeland (Fallows, 1983; Krafft, 1993). Table 9–5 shows that the median household income for Cuban Americans in 1990 was $31,439—well above that of other Hispanics yet still below the national standard.

[5]The 1990 median age of the U.S. Hispanic population was 26.2 years, well below the national median of 34.1 years. This difference accounts for some of the disparity in income and education.

The 1 million Cuban Americans living in the United States today have managed a delicate balancing act—achieving success in the larger society while retaining much of their traditional culture. Of all Hispanics, Cubans are the most likely to speak Spanish in their homes; eight out of ten families do (Sowell, 1981). However, cultural distinctiveness and living in highly visible communities like Miami's Little Havana do provoke some hostility.

White Ethnic Americans

The term *white ethnics* recognizes the ethnic heritage—and social disadvantages—of many working-class white people. White ethnics are non-WASP people whose ancestors lived in Germany, Ireland, Italy, or other European countries. More than half of the U.S. population falls into one or another white ethnic category.

Unprecedented immigration from Europe during the nineteenth century first brought Germans and Irish and then Italians and Jews to our shores. Despite cultural differences, all shared the hope that the United States would offer greater political freedom and economic opportunity than they had known in their homelands. Most lived better in this country, but the belief that "the streets of America are paved with gold" turned out to be a far cry from reality. Many immigrants found here only hard labor for low wages.

White ethnics also endured their share of prejudice and discrimination. Nativist organizations opposed the entry of non-WASP Europeans to the United States, and many newspaper ads seeking workers in the mid-nineteenth century carried a warning to new arrivals: "None need apply but Americans" (Handlin, 1941:67).

Some of this prejudice and discrimination actually was based on class rather than ethnicity, since most immigrants with little command of English were poor. But even distinguished achievers faced hostility. Fiorello La Guardia, the half-Italian, half-Jewish son of immigrants, served as mayor of New York between 1933 and 1945 despite being rebuked by President Herbert Hoover in words that reveal unambiguous ethnic hatred:

> You should go back where you belong and advise Mussolini how to make good honest citizens in Italy. The Italians are preponderantly our murderers and bootleggers. . . . Like a lot of other foreign spawn, you do not appreciate the country that supports and tolerates you. (Mann, 1959, cited in Baltzell, 1964:30)

This country's immigration policies have changed over time; today, as in the past, we have also seen fit to apply different standards to different categories of people. A recent case in point is Haitians who have fled their Caribbean nation because of poverty and political turbulence. The U.S. government has refused to allow most Haitians to enter this country, claiming that they are not true political refugees. Critics ask whether this policy would stand if the people in question were not both poor and dark skinned.

Nativists were finally victorious. In 1921, the government applied immigration quotas to each foreign country; these quotas remained in effect until 1968. The most severe restrictions targeted southern and eastern Europeans—people likely to have darker skin and to differ culturally from the dominant WASPs (Fallows, 1983).

In response to widespread bigotry, white ethnics, like other immigrants before them, formed tightly knit residential enclaves. Some also gained footholds in specialized occupations: Italian Americans entered the construction industry; Irish Americans worked in the building trades and took civil service jobs; Jews predominated in the garment industry; many Greeks (like the Chinese) worked in the retail food business (Newman, 1973).

White ethnics who prospered were likely to assimilate into the larger society; some working-class people, however, still live in the traditional neighborhoods. For virtually all white ethnics, however, cultural heritage serves as a source of immense pride.

U.S. Minorities: Looking Ahead

The United States has been, and will probably remain, a land of immigrants. Immigration has generated striking cultural diversity, as well as tales of success, hope, and struggle, told in hundreds of tongues.

Most who came to this country during the first wave of immigration that peaked about 1910 saw the next generations achieve gradual economic gains and at least some cultural assimilation. The government also granted basic freedoms where they earlier had been denied, extending citizenship to African Americans (1868), Native Americans (1924), Chinese Americans (1943), and Japanese Americans (1952).

A second wave of immigration began after World War II, and swelled as immigration laws were relaxed in the 1960s. Since 1990, more than 1 million people have made their way to the United States each year, more than twice the number that arrived during the "Great Immigration" a century ago (although newcomers now enter a country with five times as many people). But today most immigrants come not from Europe but from Latin America and Asia, with Mexicans, Filipinos, and South Koreans arriving in the largest numbers.

Many new arrivals face much the same prejudice and discrimination as those who came before them. Indeed, in 1994, California voters passed Proposition 187, which threatens to cut off social services (including schooling) to illegal immigrants—a clear indication of rising hostility toward minorities. Even so, like European immigrants of the past, many coming today now struggle to enter the United States without giving up their traditional culture. Some have also built racial and ethnic enclaves: The Little Havana and Koreatown of today stand alongside the Little Italy and Germantown of the past. Today's immigrants also share the traditional hope of their predecessors that racial and ethnic diversity, while a dimension of difference, will not be a badge of inferiority.

SUMMARY

1. Race involves a cluster of biological traits. Although a century ago scientists identified three broad categories—Caucasians, Negroids, and Mongoloids—there are no pure races. Ethnicity is based not on biology but shared cultural heritage. Minorities—including people of certain races and ethnicities—are both socially distinct and socially disadvantaged.

2. Prejudice is an inflexible and distorted generalization about a category of people. Racism, a destructive form of prejudice, asserts that one race is innately superior or inferior to another.

3. Discrimination is a pattern of action by which a person treats various categories of people unequally.

4. Pluralism refers to a state in which distinct racial and ethnic categories have equal social standing. Assimilation is a process by which minorities gradually adopt the patterns of the dominant

culture. Segregation is the physical and social separation of categories of people. Genocide is the extermination of a category of people.

5. Native Americans—the original inhabitants of the Americas—have endured genocide, segregation, and forced assimilation. Today their social standing is well below the national average.

6. WASPs predominated among the original European settlers of the United States, and they continue to enjoy high social standing today.

7. African Americans experienced two centuries of slavery. Emancipation in 1865 led to rigid segregation by law. Despite equality under the law, African Americans are still relatively disadvantaged today.

8. Chinese and Japanese Americans historically have suffered both racial and ethnic discrimination. Today, however, both categories have

above-average income and schooling. Recent Asian immigration—especially of Koreans and Filipinos—has made this the fastest-growing racial category of the U.S. population.

9. Hispanics represent many ethnicities sharing a Spanish heritage. Mexican Americans, the largest Hispanic minority, are concentrated in the Southwest. Puerto Ricans, most of whom live in New York, are poorer. Cubans, centered in Miami, are the most affluent category of Hispanics.

10. White ethnics include non-WASPs of European ancestry. While making gains during the last century, many white ethnics still struggle for economic security.

11. Immigration has increased in recent years. No longer primarily from Europe, most immigrants now arrive from Latin America and Asia.

KEY CONCEPTS

assimilation the process by which minorities gradually adopt patterns of the dominant culture

discrimination treating various categories of people unequally

ethnicity a shared cultural heritage

genocide the systematic killing of one category of people by another

institutional discrimination discrimination that is a normative and routine part of the economy, educational system, or some other social institution

minority a category of people, distinguished by physical or cultural traits, that is socially disadvantaged

miscegenation the biological process of interbreeding among racial categories

pluralism a state in which people of all races and ethnicities are distinct but have social parity

prejudice a rigid and irrational generalization about a category of people

race a category composed of men and women who share biologically transmitted traits that members of a society deem socially significant

racism the belief that one racial category is innately superior or inferior to another

scapegoat a person or category of people, typically with little power, whom others unfairly blame for their own troubles

segregation the physical and social separation of categories of people

stereotype a prejudiced description of a category of people

CRITICAL-THINKING QUESTIONS

1. Clearly differentiate between race and ethnicity. What is a minority?

2. In what ways are prejudice and discrimination mutually reinforcing?

3. Are all generalizations about minorities wrong? What makes a stereotype unfair?

4. Specify the relative social standing of the various minorities considered in this chapter. Assess how factors such as prejudice, discrimination, average age, family patterns, and cultural traits affect this hierarchy.

Sex
and
Gender

Chapter Outline

The Duchess of Windsor once quipped, "A woman cannot be too rich or too thin." The first half of this observation may apply to men as well, but certainly not the second. After all, don't the cosmetics and diet industries—together generating $60 billion annually—aim their product advertising almost exclusively at women?

Naomi Wolf (1990) claims that our culture embraces a "beauty myth." This means, first, that society teaches women to measure their importance in terms of their physical appearance. At the same time, however, society sets unrealistic standards of beauty (embodied by the voluptuous Playboy centerfold or the one-hundred-pound New York fashion model).

Second, the beauty myth teaches women to let men assess their beauty and, thus, their personal significance. The relentless pursuit of beauty, argues Wolf, drives women toward living to please men.

Third, the beauty myth primes men to seek and possess physically beautiful women. In this way, Wolf maintains, our society's concept of beauty both reduces women to objects and motivates men toward seeing women as dolls rather than human beings.

In reality, Wolf concludes, our cultural notions about beauty are more about behavior *than about* appearance. *Perhaps, she points out, this is why our society became particularly attuned to female beauty during the 1890s, the 1920s, and the 1980s—all decades in which women were challenging male power.*

This chapter explores how conceptions of beauty—and countless other elements of social life—operate to define the relative social positions of women and men. In most cases, as we shall see, the social system gives men the upper hand.

Sex and Gender

Is there something innate that prompts men to pursue wealth while women spend countless hours—and dollars—on improving their looks? Hardly. As we shall see, the different social experiences of women and men are the creation of society far more than biology. To begin, we shall distinguish between the key concepts of sex and gender.

Sex: A Biological Distinction

Sex refers to *the biological distinction between females and males.* Sex is determined at the moment of conception as a female ovum and a male sperm join to form a fertilized embryo. An ovum and sperm each contains twenty-three pairs of chromosomes—biological codes that guide physical development—and one such pair determines the child's sex. The mother always contributes an X chromosome. If the father contributes an X chromosome, a female embryo (XX) develops; a father's Y chromosome results in a male embryo (XY).

Within weeks of conception, the sex of an embryo begins to emerge. If the embryo is male, testicular tissue produces testosterone, a hormone that stimulates the growth of the male genitals. Without testosterone, the embryo develops female genitals. Upon reaching puberty, most often in the early teens, humans experience further biological differentiation. To accommodate pregnancy, childbearing, and nurturing infants, adolescent females develop wider hips, breasts, and soft fatty tissue that provide a reserve supply of nutrition for pregnancy and breast feeding (Brownmiller, 1984). Usually slightly taller and heavier than females from birth, adolescent males typically develop more muscles in the upper body, more extensive body hair, and voices deeper in tone. These are only general differences, however, since some males are smaller, have less body hair, and speak in a higher tone than some females.

Hermaphrodites. In rare cases, a hormone imbalance before birth produces a **hermaphrodite** (a word derived from the mythological character Hermaphroditus, the offspring of the Greek gods Hermes and Aphrodite, who embodied both sexes), *a human being possessing some combination of female and male internal and external genitalia.* Members of our society generally regard hermaphrodites with confusion and even disgust. By contrast, the Pokot of eastern Africa are indifferent to what they define as a simple biological error, and the Navajo look on hermaphrodites with awe, viewing them as the embodiment of the full potential of both the female and the male (Geertz, 1975).

Transsexuals. Further complicating the story of human sexuality, some people deliberately decide to change their sex. Hermaphrodites may undergo genital surgery to gain the appearance (and occasionally the function) of a sexually normal female or male. Surgery may also be considered by **transsexuals,** *people who feel they are one sex though biologically they are the other.* Tens of thousands of transsexuals in the United States have surgically altered their genitals to escape the sense of being "trapped in the wrong body" (Restak, 1979, cited in Offir, 1982:146).

Sexual Orientation

Sexual orientation is *the manner in which people experience sexual arousal and achieve sexual pleasure.* For most living things, sexuality is biologically programmed. In humans, however, sexual orientation is bound up in the complex web of cultural attitudes and rules. The norm in all industrial societies is *heterosexuality (hetero* is a Greek word meaning "the other of two"), by which a person is attracted to someone of the opposite sex. However, *homosexuality (homo* is the Greek word for "the same"), by which a person is sexually attracted to others of the same sex, is not uncommon.

Although all cultures endorse heterosexuality, many tolerate—and a few have even encouraged—homosexuality. Among the ancient Greeks, for instance, elite intellectual men celebrated homosexuality as the highest form of relationship, shunning women, whom they considered incapable of philosophical discussion. In this light, heterosexuality amounted to little more than a reproductive necessity, and men who spurned homosexuality were looked upon as deviant. But because homosexual relations do not permit reproduction, no record exists of an entire society that favored homosexuality over heterosexuality (Kluckhohn, 1948; Ford & Beach, 1951; Greenberg, 1988).

Gay rights. Tolerance of *gay* people (a label homosexuals adopted in the 1960s) has increased during this century. In 1974 the American Psychiatric Association removed homosexuality from its roster of mental disorders. Yet gays experienced increasing prejudice and discrimination during the 1980s as the deadly disease AIDS became publicly identified with homosexual men. Today, about 60 percent of U.S. adults condemn homosexuality as morally wrong; even so, the same share thinks our society should allow gay people and straight people equal opportunities in the workplace (Salholz, 1990; NORC, 1993).

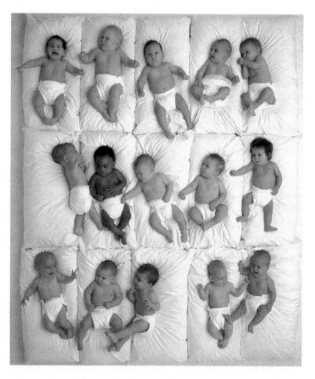

Sex is a biological distinction that develops prior to birth. Gender is the meaning that a society attaches to being female or male. That is, culture divides the range of human feelings, thoughts, and behavior into what people define as feminine or masculine. Moreover, gender differences are also a matter of power, as what is masculine typically has social priority over what is feminine. Gender differences are not evident among infants, of course, but the ways in which we think of boys and girls set in motion patterns that will continue for a lifetime.

For their part, many organizations of gay people are struggling to overcome the stereotypes of gay men and gay women (commonly called *lesbians*). Supporters of gay rights now use the term *homophobia* (with Greek roots meaning "fear of sameness") to designate an irrational fear of gay people (Weinberg, 1973). This label implies that the problem lies not with gay people, but with those intolerant of their sexual orientation.

How many gay people? Determining the number of people with a homosexual orientation is a vexing problem. For one thing, people may be reluctant to describe their sexuality to researchers; for another, sexual orientation is not a matter of neat, mutually exclusive categories. Pioneering investigator Alfred

Kinsey (1948, 1953) described sexual orientation as a continuum, from exclusively homosexual at one extreme, to equally homosexual and heterosexual in the middle, to exclusively heterosexual at the other extreme. Kinsey estimated that about 4 percent of males and 2 percent of females have an exclusively same-sex orientation, although he suggested that one-third of men and one-eighth of women had at least one homosexual experience leading to orgasm.

In the wake of the Kinsey studies, many social scientists—and the gay rights movement—settled on the idea that 10 percent of the U.S. population is gay. In the last several years, however, studies conducted by the Centers for Disease Control, National Opinion Research Center (NORC), and social scientists in various nations have refined this estimate. The evidence indicates that, while the share of men having *some* homosexual experience is at least 10 percent, those having an exclusively homosexual orientation is no more than 3 or 4 percent. In the case of women, the percentages are about half as large (Crispell, 1992; Cole & Gorman, 1993; Horowitz et al., 1993; Laumann et al., 1994).

Bisexuality.   Kinsey and his colleagues treated sexual orientation as a single continuum, claiming that people who are more homosexual are, by definition, less heterosexual. But other researchers take issue with this "either-or" view of sexuality (Storms, 1980). They contend that some individuals experience little sexual attraction to anyone else—an orientation termed *asexuality*—while others are *bisexual*, feeling strong attraction to people of both sexes.

This means that bisexuals may not think of themselves as either gay or straight. Bisexuality, therefore, is a distinct sexual orientation in its own right.

The roots of sexual orientation.   Mounting evidence suggests that sexual orientation is rooted in biological factors present at birth and further reinforced by the hormone balance in the body as we grow (Gladue, Green, & Hellman, 1984; Weinrich, 1987; Isay, 1989; Puterbaugh, 1990; Angier, 1992; Gelman, 1992). Still other research points to the importance of the social environment in promoting particular sexual attitudes and behaviors (Troiden, 1988). Considering that most adults who describe themselves as homosexuals have had some heterosexual experience, we conclude that society steers our actions, thoughts, and feelings to some degree, regardless of what biological forces are at work.

In short, both nature and nurture figure in anyone's sexual orientation. To complicate matters further,

there is no reason to think that sexual orientation is set in precisely the same way for everyone. At this point, although we have discovered a great deal about sexual orientation, we still have much to learn.

Gender: A Cultural Distinction

Gender refers to *the significance a society attaches to biological categories of female and male.* Gender guides how we think about ourselves, how we interact with others, and what opportunities and constraints we face throughout our lives.

Gender deals not only with difference but also with hierarchy. This inequality, which has historically favored males, is no simple matter of biological differences. Females and males do differ biologically, of course, but these variations are complex and inconsistent. Men around the world average about 150 pounds compared to about 120 pounds for women; men also have more muscle in the arms and shoulders, so the average man can lift more weight than the average woman can. Yet, women outperform men in some tests of long-term endurance because they can draw on the energy contained in greater body fat. Females also outperform males in life itself. According to the Bureau of the Census (1994), the average life expectancy for men is now 72.3 years, while women can expect to live 79.0 years.

Adolescent males exhibit greater mathematical ability, while adolescent females excel in verbal skills, differences that reflect both biology and patterns of socialization (Maccoby & Jacklin, 1974; Baker et al., 1980; Lengermann & Wallace, 1985). But research supports the conclusion that there exist no overall differences in intelligence between males and females.

Biologically, then, the sexes are distinguished in limited ways, with neither one naturally superior. Nevertheless, the deeply rooted *cultural* notion of male superiority may seem so natural that we assume it is the inevitable consequence of sex itself. But society is at work here, much more than biology, as the global variability of gender attests.

Cultural variability in gender.   Researchers investigating the roots of gender have focused on collective settlements in Israel called *kibbutzim*. The kibbutzim are important for gender research because people there historically have embraced social equality, with men and women sharing in both work and decision making.

In the kibbutz (the singular form), both sexes typically perform child care, building repair, cooking, and cleaning. Boys and girls are raised in the same way and, from the first weeks of life, live in dormitories under the care of specially trained personnel. Members of kibbutzim, then, regard sex as barely relevant to much of everyday life.

Some observers suggest that biological dispositions underlie a movement by the two sexes in the kibbutzim toward more traditional social roles (Tiger & Shepher, 1975). Even if this were so—and this research has its critics—the kibbutzim stand as evidence of wide cultural latitude in defining what is feminine and masculine. They also exemplify how, through conscious efforts, a society can promote sexual equality just as it can reinforce domination of one sex by the other.

Well-known anthropologist Margaret Mead also carried out comparative research on gender. To the extent that gender reflects the biological facts of sex, she reasoned, people everywhere should define the same traits as feminine and masculine; if gender is cultural, these conceptions should vary.

Mead's best-known gender research involved three societies in New Guinea (1963; orig. 1935). In the mountainous home of the Arapesh, Mead observed men and women with remarkably similar attitudes and behavior. Both sexes, she reported, were cooperative and sensitive to others: in short, what our culture would label "feminine." Among the Mundugumor, who lived to the south, Mead also found females and males to be alike; however, the Mundugumor culture of head-hunting and cannibalism stood in striking contrast to the gentle ways of the Arapesh. Both sexes were typically selfish and aggressive, traits we define as more "masculine." Finally, traveling west to observe the Tchambuli, Mead discovered a culture that, like our own, defined females and males differently. Yet the Tchambuli *reversed* many of our notions of gender, raising females to be dominant and rational, while males were submissive, emotional, and nurturing toward children. From these comparisons, Mead concluded that culture is the key to how the sexes differ.

A broader study of more than two hundred preindustrial societies by George Murdock (1937) revealed some global agreement about which tasks are feminine or masculine. Hunting and warfare, Murdock found, generally fall to men, while home-centered tasks such as cooking and child care tend to be defined as women's work. With their simple technology, preindustrial societies benefit from men's greater size and

In every society, people assume certain jobs, patterns of behavior, and ways of dressing are "naturally" feminine while others are just as obviously masculine. But, in global perspective, we see remarkable variety in such social definitions. These men, Wodaabe pastoral nomads who live in the African nation of Niger, are proud to engage in a display of beauty most people in our society would consider feminine.

short-term strength when it comes to hunting and defense; because women bear children, their activities focus on domestic duties.

But beyond these general patterns, Murdock discovered striking variation. About the same number of societies considered agriculture to be feminine as masculine; most, in fact, divided this responsibility between the sexes. Many other tasks—from building shelters to tattooing the body—were as likely to be assigned to one sex as the other, Murdock observed.

In global perspective, then, societies consistently define only a few specific activities as feminine or masculine. And as societies industrialize, with a resulting decrease in the significance of muscle power, even those distinctions are minimized (Lenski, Lenski, & Nolan, 1991). Gender, in sum, is simply too variable across cultures to be considered a simple expression of biology. Instead, as with many other elements of culture, what it means to be female and male is mostly a creation of society.

The cultural variability of gender also means that the lives of women and men may change over

Patriarchy Under Fire: A Report From Botswana

When the judge announced the court's decision, Unity Dow beamed and people around her joined in hugs and handshakes. Dow, a thirty-two-year-old lawyer and citizen of the African nation of Botswana, had won the first round in her efforts to overturn the laws by which, she maintains, her country defines women as second-class citizens.

The law in question specifies the citizenship rights of Botswanan children. This nation is traditionally patrilineal, meaning that people trace kinship through men, so children are part of their father's—but not their mother's—family line. Citizenship law reflects this tradition and has special importance for anyone who marries a citizen of another country, as Unity Dow did. Under the law, a child of a Botswanan man and a woman with other citizenship would be a citizen of Botswana, since legal standing passes through the father. But the child of a Botswanan woman and a man from another nation has no rights of citizenship. Because she married a man from the United States, Unity Dow's children had no citizen's rights in the country where they were born.

The significance of the Dow case extends beyond citizenship to the general legal standing of women and men. In rendering the decision in Dow's favor, High Court Judge Martin Horwitz declared, "The time that women were treated as chattels or were there to obey the whims and wishes of males is long past." In support of his decision, Horwitz pointed to the constitution of Botswana, which guarantees fundamental rights and freedoms to both women and men. Arguing for the

Patrilineal descent often characterizes less economically developed societies in which men dominate women.

government against Dow, Ian Kirby, a deputy attorney general, conceded that the constitution confers equal rights on the two sexes, but he claimed that the law can and should take account of sex where such patterns are deeply rooted in Botswanan culture. To challenge national traditions in the name of Western feminism, he continued, amounts to cultural imperialism by foreign influences.

Women from many African nations attended the Dow court case, suggesting that a push for sexual equality is not as foreign to African cultures as some might think. Analysts on both sides of the issue agreed that the victory signals the beginning of historic change.

To many people in the United States, the Dow case may seem strange, since the notion that men and women are entitled to equal rights and privileges is widely endorsed here. But, worth noting is the fact that the United States—not Botswana—lacks a constitutional guarantee of equal standing under the law for women and men.

Sources: Author's personal communication with Unity Dow and Shapiro (1991).

time. Looking to the African nation of Botswana, the box points up how and why such change is often controversial.

Patriarchy and Sexism

Although conceptions of gender certainly vary, a universal pattern among world societies is some degree of **patriarchy** (literally, "the rule of fathers"), *a form of social organization in which males dominate females.* Despite mythical tales of societies dominated by female "Amazons," the contrasting pattern of **matriarchy,** *a form of social organization in which females dominate males,* is not at present part of the human record (Gough, 1971; Harris, 1977; Kipp, 1980; Lengermann & Wallace, 1985).

While some degree of patriarchy may be universal, however, world societies reveal significant variation in the relative power and privilege of females and males. In Saudi Arabia, for example, the power of men over women is as great as anywhere in the world; in the Nordic nation of Norway, by contrast, the two sexes approach equality in many respects.

An important ideological underpinning of patriarchy is **sexism,** *the belief that one sex is innately superior to the other.* Historically, patriarchy has rested on a belief in the innate superiority of men. In effect, sexism justifies men dominating women in much the same way that racism (discussed in Chapter 9, "Race and Ethnicity") legitimizes the practice of white people dominating people of color. Also like racism, sexism is more than a matter of individual attitudes. The notion that one sex is superior to the other is built into various institutions of our society. As we shall see presently, *institutionalized sexism* pervades the operation of the economy, with women concentrated in low-paying jobs. Similarly, the legal system historically has winked at violence against women, especially abuse committed by boyfriends, husbands, and fathers (Landers, 1990).

The costs of sexism. Sexism burdens all of society by stunting the talents and abilities of women—half the population. Men, too, suffer from sexism because, as Marilyn French (1985) argues, patriarchy compels men to relentlessly seek control—not only of women, but of themselves and the entire world. Such impossible goals extract a high price among males in terms of accidents, stress, and heart attacks. The so-called Type A personality—characterized by chronic impatience, driving ambition, competitiveness, and free-floating hostility—is known to be linked to heart disease. This personality profile is also precisely the behavior that our culture defines as masculine (Ehrenreich, 1983). Furthermore, insofar as men try to control others, they lose the ability to experience intimacy and trust. As one researcher put it, becoming masculine is supposed to separate "the men from the boys," but in practice it separates men from men (Raphael, 1988:184).

Is patriarchy inevitable? In preindustrial societies, women have little control over pregnancy and childbirth, limiting the scope of their lives. Similarly, men's greater height and short-term strength are vital resources. Patriarchy thrives in such societies. But with the advent of industrialization and birth control technologies, people gain greater choice over how to live. Today, in societies like ours, biological differences provide little justification for patriarchy.

Yet male dominance still holds sway in the United States and elsewhere in the world. Does this mean that patriarchy is inevitable? Some sociologists claim that biological factors "wire" the sexes with different motivations and behaviors—particularly more aggressiveness on the part of males—that make the eradication of patriarchy difficult, and perhaps even impossible (Goldberg, 1974, 1987; Rossi, 1985; Popenoe, 1993). Most sociologists, however, contend that gender is primarily a social construction that can be changed. Thus, simply because no society has eliminated patriarchy up to this point does not mean we must remain prisoners of the past.

To understand the persistence of patriarchy, we now examine how gender is rooted and reproduced in society, a process that spans the way we learn to think of ourselves as children through the work we perform as adults.

Gender and Socialization

From birth until death, human feelings, thoughts, and actions reflect social definitions of the sexes. Children quickly learn that their society defines females and males as different kinds of human beings; by about the age of three, they begin to apply gender standards to themselves (Kohlberg, 1966, cited in Lengermann & Wallace, 1985:37; Bem, 1981).

Table 10–1 sketches the traits that people in the United States traditionally have used to distinguish "feminine" from "masculine" in largely opposing terms. Such thinking remains part of our culture, even though research reveals that most young people do not develop consistently feminine or masculine personalities (L. Bernard, 1980).

TABLE 10–1 Traditional Notions of Gender Identity

Feminine Traits	Masculine Traits
Submissive	Dominant
Dependent	Independent
Unintelligent and incapable	Intelligent and competent
Emotional	Rational
Receptive	Assertive
Intuitive	Analytical
Weak	Strong
Timid	Brave
Content	Ambitious
Passive	Active
Cooperative	Competitive
Sensitive	Insensitive
Sex object	Sexually aggressive
Attractive because of physical appearance	Attractive because of achievement

Masculinity as Contest

By the time I was ten, the central fact in my life was the demand that I become a man. By then, the most important relationships by which I was taught to define myself were those I had with other boys. I already knew that I must see every encounter with another boy as a contest in which I must win or at least hold my own. . . . The same lesson continued [in school], after school, even in Sunday School. My parents, relatives, teachers, the books I read, movies I saw, all taught me that my self-worth depended on my manliness, my willingness to stand up to the other boys. This usually didn't mean a physical fight, though the willingness to stand up and "fight like a man" always remained a final test. But the relationships between us usually had the character of an armed truce. Girls weren't part of this social world at all yet, just because they weren't part of this contest. They didn't have to be bluffed, no credit was gained by cowing them, so they were more or less ignored. Sometimes when there were no grownups around we would let each other know that we liked each other, but most of the time we did as we were taught.

Source: Silverstein (1977).

Just as gender affects how we think of ourselves, so it teaches us to act in normative ways. **Gender roles** (or sex roles) are *attitudes and activities that a society links to each sex*. Insofar as our culture defines males as ambitious and competitive, we expect them to engage in team sports and aspire to positions of leadership. To the extent that we define females as deferential and emotional, we look to them to be good listeners and supportive observers.

Gender and the Family

The first question people usually ask about a newborn—"Is it a boy or a girl?"—looms large because the answer involves not just sex but the likely direction of the child's entire life.

In fact, gender is at work even before the birth of a child, since parents the world over generally hope to have a boy rather than a girl. In China, India, and other strongly patriarchal societies, female embryos are at risk of abortion, with parents hoping later to produce a boy, whose social value is greater (United Nations Development Programme, 1991).

Sociologist Jessie Bernard (1981) asserts that, soon after birth, family members usher infants into the "pink world" of girls or the "blue world" of boys. Parents convey gender messages to children by how they, themselves, act and even unconsciously in the way they handle daughters and sons. One researcher at an English university presented an infant dressed as either a boy or a girl to a number of women; her subjects handled the "female" child tenderly, with frequent hugs and caresses, while treating the "male" child more aggressively, often lifting him up high in the air or bouncing him on the knee (Bonner, 1984). The lesson is clear: The female world revolves around passivity and emotion, while the male world places a premium on independence and action.

Gender and the Peer Group

As they reach school age, children's lives spill outside the family as they forge ties with others their own age. Peer groups further socialize their members according to normative conceptions of gender. The box explains how play groups shaped one young boy's sense of himself as masculine.

Janet Lever (1978) spent a year observing fifth graders at play. She concluded that boys engage more in team sports—such as baseball and football—that involve many roles, complex rules, and clear objectives such as scoring a run or a touchdown. These games are nearly always competitive, separating winners from losers. Male peer activities reinforce masculine traits of aggression and control.

By contrast, girls play hopscotch or jump rope, or simply talk, sing, or dance together. Such spontaneous activities have few rules and rarely is "victory" the ultimate goal. Instead of teaching girls to be competitive, Lever explains, female peer groups promote interpersonal skills of communication and cooperation—resumably the basis for family life.

Carol Gilligan (1982), whose work is highlighted in Chapter 3 ("Socialization: From Infancy to Old

Age"), explains Lever's observations from the perspective of a gender-based theory of moral reasoning. Boys, Gilligan contends, reason according to abstract principles. For them, "rightness" amounts to "playing by the rules." Girls, by contrast, consider morality more a matter of their responsibilities to others. Thus, the games we play as children have serious implications for our larger lives.

Gender and Schooling

Once in school, the classroom curriculum encourages children to fall in step with culturally approved gender patterns. For example, schools have long offered to young women instruction in typing and home-centered skills such as nutrition and sewing. Classes in woodworking and auto mechanics, conversely, generally attract young men.

In college, the pattern continues, with men and women tending toward different majors. Men are disproportionately represented in the natural sciences—including physics, chemistry, biology, and mathematics. Women cluster in the humanities (such as English), the fine arts (painting, music, dance, and drama), or the social sciences (including anthropology and sociology). New areas of study also perpetuate gender distinctions. Computer science, for example, with its grounding in engineering, logic, and abstract mathematics, predominantly appeals to men (Klein, 1984); courses in gender studies, by contrast, tend to enroll women.

Gender and the Mass Media

Since it first captured the public imagination in the 1950s, television has placed the dominant segment of our population—white males—at center stage. Racial and ethnic minorities were all but absent from television until the early 1970s, and only in the last decade have programs featured women in prominent roles.

Even when both sexes appear on camera, men generally play the brilliant detectives, fearless explorers, and skilled surgeons. Women, by contrast, come through as less capable, often valued in TV scripts primarily for their sexual attractiveness.

Change has come most slowly to advertising, which sells products by conforming to widely established cultural norms. Advertising thus presents the two sexes, more often than not, in stereotypical ways. Historically, ads have shown women at home, happily using cleaning products, serving food, modeling cloth-

Some recent advertising reverses traditional gender definitions by portraying men as the submissive sex objects of successful women. Although the reversal is new, the use of gender stereotypes to sell consumer products is very old indeed.

ing, and trying out appliances. Men, on the other hand, predominate in commercials for cars, travel, banking services, industrial companies, and alcoholic beverages. The authoritative "voiceover" in television and radio advertising is almost always male (Busby, 1975; Courtney & Whipple, 1983).

Advertising also actively perpetuates Naomi Wolf's "beauty myth," described in the opening of this chapter. The argument runs something like this: By embracing traditional notions of femininity and masculinity, we raise our prospects for personal and professional success. With that groundwork in place, advertising then dictates that masculine men drive the "right" car while feminine women lavish themselves with beauty aids designed to make them look younger and more attractive to men.

Gender and Social Stratification

Gender implies more than the differences in how people think and act. The concept of **gender stratification** refers to *the unequal distribution of wealth,* *power, and privilege between the two sexes.* The lower social standing of women can be seen, first, in the world of work.

Working Women and Men

In 1993, 66.2 percent of people in the United States over the age of sixteen were working for income: As shown in Figure 10–1, this represents 75.2 percent of men and 57.9 percent of women (U.S. Department of Labor, 1994). This is an increase from 1900, when only about one-fifth of women were in the labor force. Furthermore, three-fourths of the women in the labor force now work full time. The traditional view that being the breadwinner is "man's work" no longer holds true.

Among the factors at work in the changing U.S. labor force are the decline of farming, the growth of cities, shrinking family size, a rising divorce rate, and households that rely on more than one income. Today, 60 percent of married couples count on two incomes.

In the United States and other industrial societies, then, a majority of women work for income. Therefore, in rich societies, women now make up something approaching half of the labor force. As Global Map 10–1 shows, however, this is not the case in many of the poorer societies of the world.

A common misconception (especially among middle-class people) holds that women in the labor force are childless. But, today, 60 percent of married women with children under the age of six earn a living; among married women with children between six and seventeen years of age, 75 percent are employed. For divorced women with children, the comparable figures are 60 percent of women with younger children and 80 percent of women with older children (U.S. Bureau of the Census, 1993). A gradual increase in employer-sponsored child-care programs is giving more women and men the opportunity to combine working and parenting, a trend that is especially important for divorced mothers.

Gender and occupations. While the proportions of women and men in the labor force have been converging, the work done by the two sexes remains different.

FIGURE 10–1 **Men and Women in the U.S. Labor Force**
Source: U.S. Department of Labor (1994).

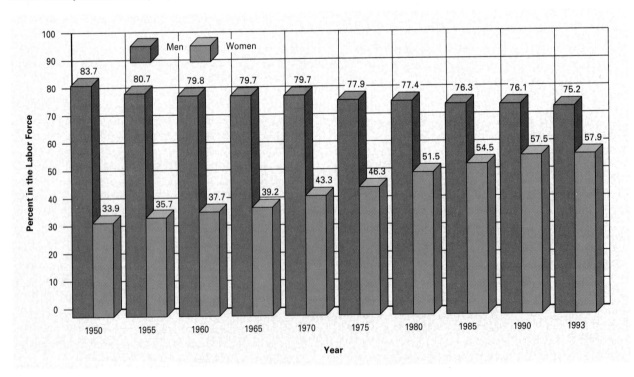

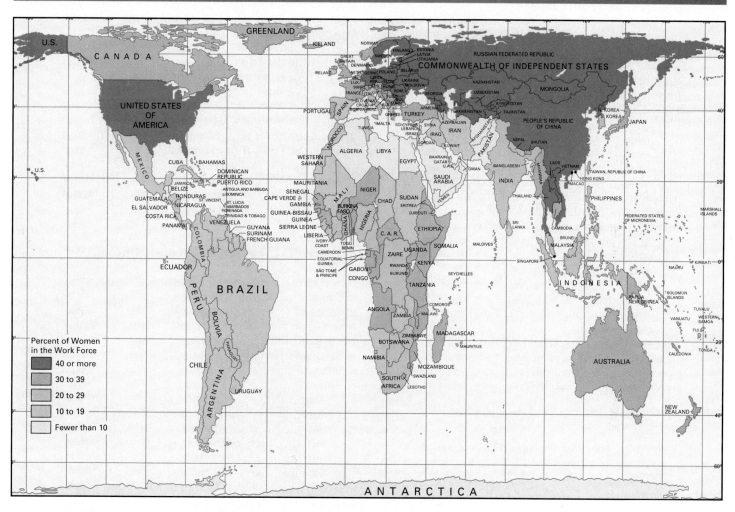

GLOBAL MAP 10–1   Women's Paid Employment in Global Perspective

In 1991, women comprised 45.4 percent of the labor force in the United States—up almost 10 percent over the last generation. Throughout the industrialized world, at least one-third of the labor force is made up of women. In poor societies, however, women work even harder than they do in this country, but they are less likely to be paid for their efforts. In Latin America, for example, women represent only about 15 percent of the paid labor force; in Islamic societies of northern Africa and the Middle East, the figure is even lower.

Source: *Peters Atlas of the World* (1990).

The U.S. Department of Labor (1994) reports that women engage in a narrow range of occupations, with half of working women holding just two types of jobs. Administrative support work, first, draws 27 percent of working women, most of whom serve as secretaries, typists, or stenographers. Viewed from another perspective, about 80 percent of these "pink-collar" jobholders are women.

The second broad category is service work, performed by 18 percent of employed women. These jobs include waitressing and related food-service employment as well as health-care positions. Both categories

Chapter 10   Sex and Gender   247

of jobs lie at the low end of the pay scale, offer limited opportunities for advancement, and are subject to supervision—most often by men.

Table 10–2 lists the ten occupations with the highest concentrations of women. The bottom line is that, even though increasing numbers of women are working for pay, women remain highly segregated in the labor force, suggesting that our society continues to perceive work through the lens of gender (Roos, 1983; Kemp & Coverman, 1989; U.S. Department of Labor, 1994).

Men predominate in most other job categories. Men overwhelmingly control the building trades; 98 percent of brick and stone masons, structural metal workers, and heavy-equipment mechanics are men. Men also hold the lion's share of positions that provide high income, prestige, and power. For example, more than 92 percent of engineers, 78 percent of physicians, judges, and lawyers, and 69 percent of corporate managers are men. Only 3 percent of the top executives of large U.S. corporations are women.

Interestingly, however, 30 percent of small businesses are now owned and operated by women, a share that is rising. Although 90 percent of these businesses are sole proprietorships with a single employee, the success of tens of thousands of these entrepreneurs demonstrates that women have the power to create opportunities for themselves. Many female business owners find the rewards of working this way far greater than those offered by larger, male-dominated companies (Ando, 1990; O'Hare & Larson, 1991; U.S. Bureau of the Census, 1993).

Overall, then, gender stratification permeates the workplace. This hierarchy is easy to spot in the job setting: Male physicians are assisted by female nurses, male executives have female secretaries, and male airline pilots work with female flight attendants.

And, in any field, the greater the income and prestige that is associated with any job, the more likely it is that the position will be held by a man. For example, women represent 98 percent of kindergarten teachers; 86 percent of elementary teachers; 58 percent of secondary-school educators; 43 percent of professors in colleges and universities; and 12 percent of college and university presidents (U.S. Department of Labor, 1994).

Housework: Women's "Second Shift"

As we have already noted, housework—maintaining the home and caring for children—is primarily the province of women throughout the world (see Global Map 4–1 on page 86). In the United States, housework has always embodied a cultural contradiction: Touted as essential to family life and therefore valuable on the one hand, it carries little reward or social prestige on the other (J. Bernard, 1981).

Surprisingly, despite their rapid entry into the labor force, women still perform about forty hours of housework each week (down only slightly in recent decades) while men, on average, put in about thirteen hours (up slightly in recent decades) (Demo, 1994). The typical couple shares only the disciplining of children and managing finances. Men routinely perform home repairs and yardwork; women see to most daily tasks of shopping, cooking, and cleaning, which, on average, consume thirty to forty hours a week. Little wonder, then, that women commonly return from the workplace to face a "second shift" of unpaid work on the home front (Schooler et al., 1984; Benokraitis & Feagin, 1986; Fuchs, 1986; Hochschild, 1989; Presser, 1993).

In sum, men endorse the idea of women entering the labor force and many depend on the money women earn. Nevertheless, most men have done little to modify their own behavior to help their partners establish careers and manageable home lives. Further, men make a point of calling special attention to housework they perform, while taking the contributions of women for granted (Komarovsky, 1973; Cowan, 1992; Robinson & Spitze, 1992).

TABLE 10–2 Jobs with the Highest Concentrations of Women, 1993

Occupation	Number of Women Employed	Percent in Occupation Who Are Women
1. Dental hygienist	75,468	99.3%
2. Child-care provider	298,980	99.0%
3. Secretary	3,546,554	98.9%
4. Dental assistant	117,018	97.8%
5. Prekindergarten and kindergarten teachers	489,477	97.7%
6. Receptionist	873,828	97.2%
7. Child-care/private household worker	335,340	97.2%
8. Early childhood teacher's assistant	403,788	96.6%
9. Licensed practical nurse	402,050	94.6%
10. Typist	465,842	94.3%

Source: U.S. Department of Labor, Bureau of Labor Statistics, *Employment and Earnings*, vol. 41, no. 1, January 1994, pp. 205–10.

African-American artist Jacob Lawrence painted *Ironers* (1943) to depict the daily lives of women in his working-class neighborhood in New York's Harlem. The painting suggests that the work women perform in the labor force often parallels the tasks women perform in the home.

Gender, Income, and Wealth

In 1992, the median earnings for women working full time were $22,167, while men working full time earned $31,128. This means that, for every dollar earned by men, women earned about 71 cents.

Among full-time workers, 58 percent of women earned less than $25,000 in 1992, compared to 36 percent of comparable men. At the upper end of the income scale, men were five times more likely than women (7.5 percent versus 1.5 percent) to earn more than $75,000 (U.S. Bureau of the Census, 1993).

The most important reason for the lower earnings of working women is the *kind* of work they do: largely clerical and service jobs. In effect, jobs and gender interact: Members of our society tend to perceive jobs with less clout as "women's work" just as people devalue work simply because it is performed by women (Parcel, Mueller, & Cuvelier, 1986; Blum, 1991; England, 1992).

During the 1980s, proponents of gender equality responded to this mind-set by proposing a policy of "comparable worth," which means that people should be paid not according to a historical double standard but based on the worth of what they actually do. Several nations, including Great Britain and Australia, have adopted such policies, which have found limited acceptance in the United States. Still, critics argue,

women in this country are losing as much as $1 billion annually based on their sex.

A second cause of this gender-based income disparity has to do with the family. Both men and women have children, of course, but our culture defines parenting as more of a woman's responsibility than a man's. Pregnancy and raising small children keep many younger women out of the labor force altogether at a time when their male peers stand to make significant occupational gains. As a result, women workers build up less job seniority than their male counterparts (Fuchs, 1986).

Moreover, women who choose to have children may be reluctant or unable to maintain fast-paced jobs that tie up their evenings and weekends. Career women with children may resolve this classic case of role strain by favoring jobs that offer a shorter commuting distance, more flexible hours, and employer-sponsored child-care services. We can see the seriousness of the dilemma faced by women opting for both a career and a family in one salient fact: Among executive men at the age of forty, 90 percent have had a child; among executive women at age forty, only 35 percent have had a child. And in general, women who do have children fall behind childless women in terms of earnings.

The two factors noted so far—type of work and family responsibilities—account for about two-thirds of the earnings disparity between women and men.

Researchers conclude that a third factor—discrimination against women—is responsible for most of the remainder (Pear, 1987; Fuller & Schoenberger, 1991).

Because discrimination is illegal, it is often practiced in subtle ways (Benokraitis & Feagin, 1994). Corporate women may encounter a so-called *glass ceiling*, a barrier, formally denied by high company officials, which effectively prevents women from rising above middle management.

For all these reasons, then, women earn less than men in all major occupational categories. As shown in Table 10–3, this disparity varies from job to job, but in only four of these major job classifications do women earn more than 70 percent as much as men do.

Finally, perhaps because women typically outlive men, many people think that women own most of the country's wealth. Government statistics tell a different story: 57 percent of individuals with $1 million or more in assets are men, although widows are highly repre-sented in this elite category (U.S. Bureau of the Census, 1993). And just 20 percent of the individuals identified by researchers at *Forbes* and *Fortune* magazines as the richest people in the United States are women.

Gender and Education

In the past, our society deemed higher education irrelevant for women, whose lives revolved around the home. In 1990, however, women earned 54 percent of associate's and bachelor's degrees, with the remaining 46 percent earned by men (National Center for Education Statistics, 1991).

And while colleges enroll as many women as men today, the two sexes still tend to pursue different courses of study, although to a decreasing degree. In 1970, for example, women earned just 17 percent of bachelor's degrees in the natural sciences, computer science, and engineering; by 1990 the proportion had doubled to one-third.

Today's women also enjoy more opportunities for post-graduate education, often a springboard to high-prestige jobs. Counting all areas of study, women earn a larger share of master's degrees (53.6 percent) than men do (46.4 percent). And a growing number of women are pursuing programs that until recently were virtually all-male provinces. For example, in 1970 only a few hundred women received master's of business administration (M.B.A.) degrees; in 1991, the number exceeded twenty-seven thousand (35 percent of all such degrees) (Kaufman, 1982; U.S. Bureau of the Census, 1994).

Most professional fields, however, remain predominantly male. In 1991, men received 63 percent of doctorates (however, women earned 52 percent of all Ph.D.s in sociology). Men also were awarded 57 percent of law degrees (LL.B. and J.D.), 64 percent of medical degrees (M.D.), and 68 percent of dental degrees (D.D.S. and D.M.D.) (U.S. Bureau of the Census, 1994). Nonetheless, the proportion of women in all these professions is steadily rising.

Gender and Politics

A century ago, virtually no women held elected office in the United States. In fact, women were legally barred from casting a vote in national elections until the adoption of the Nineteenth Amendment to the Constitution in 1920. A few women, however, were candidates for political office even before they could

TABLE 10–3 Earnings of Full-Time U.S. Workers, by Sex, 1992*

Selected Occupational Categories	Median Income (dollars) Men	Women	Women's Income as a Percentage of Men's
Executives, administrators, and managers	$42,509	$27,494	65%
Professional specialties	$44,015	$31,261	71%
Technical workers	$32,720	$24,767	76%
Sales	$31,346	$17,924	57%
Precision production, craft, and repair workers	$28,923	$19,045	66%
Clerical and other administrative support workers	$27,186	$20,321	75%
Transportation workers	$25,787	$20,131	78%
Machine operators and tenders	$23,884	$15,714	66%
Service workers	$20,606	$12,931	63%
Farming, forestry, and fishing workers	$14,897	$10,079	68%
All occupations listed above	$30,358	$21,440	71%

*Workers aged 15 and over.

Source: U.S. Bureau of the Census, *Current Population Reports*, ser. P-60, no. 184 (Washington, D.C.: U.S. Government Printing Office, 1993).

vote. The Equal Rights Party supported Victoria Woodhull for the U.S. presidency in 1872; perhaps it was a sign of the times that she spent election day in a New York City jail. Table 10–4 cites subsequent milestones in women's gradual movement into political life.

Today, thousands of women serve as mayors of cities and towns across the United States, and tens of thousands more hold responsible administrative posts in the federal government. Less change has occurred at the highest levels of politics, although a majority of citizens claim that they would support a woman for any office, including the presidency. After the 1994 national elections, 1 of the 50 state governors was a woman (2 percent); in Congress, women held 49 of 435 seats in the House of Representatives (11 percent), and 8 of 100 seats (8 percent) in the Senate.

Minority Women

If minorities are socially disadvantaged, as Chapter 9 explained, are minority women doubly handicapped? Generally speaking, the answer is yes.

First, there is the disadvantage associated with race and ethnicity. For example, in 1992, median annual income for African-American women working full time was $20,229—90 percent as much as the $22,423 earned by white women. Hispanic women earned $17,743—79 percent as much as their white (non-Hispanic) counterparts.

Second, there is the obstacle associated with sex. Thus, African-American women earned 89 percent as much as African-American men, while Hispanic women earned 87 percent as much as Hispanic men.

Combining these disadvantages, African-American women earned 64 percent as much as white men, and Hispanic women earned 56 percent as much (U.S. Bureau of the Census, 1993). These disparities reflect minority women's lower position on the occupational and educational ladders in comparison to white women (Bonilla-Santiago, 1990). Further, whenever the economy sags, as it has in recent years, minority women are especially likely to experience declining income and unemployment.

Chapter 7 ("Social Stratification") explained that women are becoming a larger proportion of the U.S. poor. Overall, 53 percent of poor families are headed by single women, compared to 6 percent headed by men alone. But the connection between women and poverty is especially strong among African Americans because of a higher incidence of single parenthood. Thus, three-fourths of poor African-American families

TABLE 10–4 Significant "Firsts" for Women in U.S. Politics

1869	Law allows women to vote in Wyoming territory; Utah follows suit in 1870.
1872	First woman to run for the presidency (Victoria Woodhull) represents the Equal Rights Party.
1917	First woman elected to the House of Representatives (Jeannette Rankin of Montana).
1924	First women elected state governors (Nellie Taylor Ross of Wyoming and Miriam ["Ma"] Ferguson of Texas); both followed their husbands into office. First woman to have her name placed in nomination for vice-presidency at the convention of a major political party (Lena Jones Springs).
1931	First woman to serve in the Senate (Hattie Caraway of Arkansas); completed the term of her husband upon his death and won reelection in 1932.
1932	First woman appointed to the presidential cabinet (Frances Perkins, secretary of labor in F. D. Roosevelt's administration).
1964	First woman to have her name placed in nomination for the presidency at the convention of a major political party (Margaret Chase Smith, a Republican).
1972	First African-American woman to have her name placed in nomination for the presidency at the convention of a major political party (Shirley Chisholm, a Democrat).
1981	First woman appointed to the U.S. Supreme Court (Sandra Day O'Connor).
1984	First woman to be successfully nominated for the vice-presidency by a major party (Democrat Geraldine Ferraro).
1988	First woman chief executive to be elected to a consecutive third term (Madeleine Kunin, governor of Vermont).
1992	Political "Year of the Woman" yields record number of women in the Senate (six) and the House (forty-eight), as well as (1) first African-American woman to win election to U.S. Senate (Carol Moseley-Braun of Illinois); (2) first state (California) to be served by two women senators (Barbara Boxer and Dianne Feinstein); (3) first Puerto Rican woman elected to the House (Nydia Valasquez of New York).

Source: Adapted from Sandra Salmans, "Women Ran for Office Before They Could Vote," *New York Times*, July 13, 1984, p. A11, and news reports.

are headed by single women, compared to about 40 percent of poor white families.

Are Women a Minority?

Given the clear economic disadvantage of being a woman in our society, it seems reasonable to count all U.S. women as a minority. But, in fact, most white women do *not* think of themselves as members of a minority (Hacker, 1951; Lengermann & Wallace, 1985). This is partly because, unlike racial and ethnic

In general, women earn less income than men do. But the economic disparity linked to gender is especially pronounced among single parents. Single mothers are ten times more likely to be poor than fathers who are raising children alone. And when single mothers are from racial or ethnic minorities, the odds are greater still that they will live in poverty. Then, too, the daughters of single mothers often become single mothers themselves, creating a multigenerational pattern of poverty.

minorities, white women are well represented at all levels of the class structure, including the very top. But, at every class level, women typically have less income, wealth, education, and power than men do. In fact, patriarchy makes women dependent for much of their social standing on men—first their fathers and later their husbands (Bernard, 1981).

Violence Against Women

Perhaps the most wrenching kind of suffering endured by women is violence. As Chapter 6 ("Deviance") explained, official statistics paint criminal violence as overwhelmingly the actions of men—hardly surprising, since aggressiveness is a trait our culture defines as masculine. Most victims of violence are also men, but much male violence is directed at women (Straus & Gelles, 1986; Shupe, Stacey, & Hazelwood, 1987; Gelles & Cornell, 1990).

The majority of gender-linked violence happens at home. Richard Gelles (cited in Roesch, 1984) argues that, with the exception of the police and the military, the family is the most violent organization in the United States.

Violence toward women also occurs in casual relationships. As Chapter 6 ("Deviance") noted, most rapes involve not strangers but men known (and often trusted) by women. Citing the extent of sexual abuse in our society, Dianne Herman (1995) argues that some

tendency toward sexual violence is built into our way of life. All forms of violence against women—from the wolf whistles that intimidate women on city streets to a pinch in a crowded subway to physical assaults that take place at home—are facets of what she calls a "rape culture" by which men try to impose their will on women. Sexual violence, then, is fundamentally about *power* rather than sex, making it a dimension of gender stratification.

Sexual harassment. The 1991 Senate confirmation hearings of Supreme Court Justice Clarence Thomas drew national attention to the concept of **sexual harassment,** widely defined as *comments, gestures, or physical contact of a sexual nature that are deliberate, repeated, and unwelcome.* Anita Hill, a law professor and former colleague, alleged that Thomas had harassed her during the time they worked together for the federal government. The Senate never clearly resolved the specific allegations made by Hill and vigorously denied by Thomas, but people across the United States lined up on one side or the other as the episode touched off a national debate that has already redefined the rules for workplace interaction between the sexes.

Most victims of sexual harassment are women. This is because, first, our culture encourages men to be sexually assertive and to perceive women in sexual terms; social interaction in the workplace, on the campus, and elsewhere, then, can readily take on sexual overtones. Second, most individuals in positions of power—including business executives, physicians, bureau chiefs, assembly line supervisors, professors, and military officers—are men who oversee the work of women. Surveys carried out in widely different work settings reveal that half of women respondents experience some unwanted sexual attention (Loy & Stewart, 1984; Paul, 1991).

Sexual harassment is sometimes blatant and direct: A supervisor may solicit sexual favors from an employee coupled with the threat of reprisals if the advances are refused. Courts have declared such *quid pro quo* sexual harassment (the Latin phrase means "one thing in return for another") to be an illegal violation of civil rights.

However, the issue is often a matter of subtle behavior—sexual teasing, off-color jokes, pin-ups displayed in the workplace—which a man may not intend to be harassing to a subordinate or co-worker. But, using the *effect* standard favored by many feminists, such actions add up to a *hostile environment* (Cohen, 1991; Paul, 1991). Incidents of this kind are far more complex because they involve very different perceptions of the same behavior. For example, a man may think that showing romantic interest in a co-worker is paying the woman a compliment; she, on the other hand, may deem his behavior offensive and a hindrance to her job performance.

Women's entry into the workplace does not, in itself, ensure that everyone is treated equally and with respect. Untangling precisely what constitutes a hostile working environment, however, demands clearer standards of conduct than exist at present. Creating such guidelines—and educating the public to embrace them—is likely to take some time (Cohen, 1991; Majka, 1991). In the end, courts (and, ultimately, the court of public opinion) will draw the line between what amounts to "reasonable friendliness" and behavior that constitutes "unwarranted harassment."

Pornography. *Pornography,* too, underlies sexual violence. Defining pornography has long challenged scholars and law makers alike. The Supreme Court allows local cities and counties to decide for themselves what violates "community standards" of decency and lacks any redeeming social value. There is little doubt, however, that pornography (loosely defined) is popular in the United States: X-rated videos, 900 telephone numbers providing sexual conversation, and a host of sexually explicit magazines together make up a 7-billion-dollar-a-year industry.

Traditionally, we have viewed pornography as a *moral* issue. National survey data show that 60 percent of the U.S. population still think that "sexual materials lead to a breakdown of morals" (NORC, 1993:266).

A more recent view holds that pornography demeans women. That is, pornography is really a *power* issue because it fosters the notion that men should control both sexuality and women. Catharine MacKinnon (1987) has branded pornography as one foundation of male dominance because it portrays women in dehumanizing fashion as the subservient playthings of men. Worth noting, in this context, is that the term pornography is derived from the Greek word *porne,* meaning a harlot who acts as a man's sexual slave.

A related charge is that pornography promotes violence against women. Certainly, anyone who has viewed "hard-core" videos finds this assertion plausible. Yet, researchers have not demonstrated a scientific cause-and-effect relationship between what people. view and how they act. Research does support the contention, however, that pornography tends to make men think of women as objects rather than people. The public at large shares this concern about the effects of pornography, with 55 percent of adults voicing the opinion that pornography prompts people to commit rape (NORC, 1993:266).

Like sexual harassment, pornography raises complex and sometimes conflicting concerns. While

A debate over the concept of sexual harassment is now underway in the United States. No one doubts that supervisors who demand sexual favors from subordinates as a condition of employment or advancement are wrong to do so. But people do disagree as to precisely where to draw the line between friendly conversation and contact and unwarranted imposition of sexuality on another.

Many public organizations and private companies now have elaborate policies to ensure that the workplace is free of any behavior, conversation, object, or image that might contribute to a "hostile or intimidating environment." In essence, such policies attempt to remove sexuality from the work setting so that employees can do their jobs while steering clear of traditional notions about female and male relationships.

everyone objects to material he or she finds offensive, many also endorse the rights of free speech and artistic expression. But pressure to restrict this kind of material is building as a result of an unlikely coalition of conservatives (who oppose pornography on moral grounds) and progressives (who condemn it for political reasons).

Theoretical Analysis of Gender

Each of sociology's major theoretical paradigms addresses the significance of gender and the role that it plays in social organization.

Structural-Functional Analysis

The structural-functional paradigm views society as a complex system of many separate but integrated parts. From this point of view, gender enables us to organize key facets of social life.

As Chapter 2 ("Culture") explained, the earliest hunting and gathering societies had little power over the forces of biology. Lacking effective birth control, women experienced frequent pregnancies, and the responsibilities of child care kept them close to home. Likewise, to take advantage of men's greater short-term strength, norms guided them toward the pursuit of game and other tasks away from the home. Over many generations, this sex-based division of labor became entrenched and was largely taken for granted (Lengermann & Wallace, 1985).

Industrial technology opens up a vastly greater range of cultural possibilities. Human muscle power no longer serves as a vital source of energy, so the physical strength of men loses much of its earlier significance. At the same time, the ability to control reproduction gives women greater choice in shaping their lives. Members of modern societies come to see that traditional gender roles waste an enormous amount of human talent; yet change comes slowly, because gender is deeply embedded in social mores.

In addition, as Talcott Parsons (1951, 1954) has explained, gender differences help to integrate society—at least in its traditional form. Gender, Parsons claimed, forms a *complementary* set of roles that links women and men into family units that carry out various tasks vital to the operation of society. Women assume primary responsibility for the household and raising children; men, by contrast, connect the family to the larger world, primarily by participating in the labor force.

Parsons further argued that distinctive socialization teaches the two sexes their appropriate gender identity and skills needed for adult life. Thus society teaches boys—presumably destined for the labor force—to be rational, self-assured, and competitive. This complex of traits Parsons termed *instrumental*. To prepare girls for child rearing, their socialization stresses *expressive* qualities, such as emotional responsiveness and sensitivity to others.

Finally, according to Parsons, society promotes gender-linked behavior as people incorporate cultural definitions about gender into their own identities, so that deviance produces guilt. Society further bolsters gender conformity by conveying subtle and not-so-subtle messages that straying too far from accepted standards courts rejection by members of the opposite sex. In simple terms, women learn to view nonmasculine men as sexually unattractive, while men learn to shun unfeminine women.

Critical evaluation. Structural-functionalism advances a theory of complementarity by which gender integrates society both structurally (in terms of what people do) and morally (in terms of what they believe).

Given our notions about power being a masculine trait, it is little wonder that our popular culture typically portrays powerful women as decidedly unfeminine. This recent cartoon about Hillary Rodham Clinton depicts her in decidedly masculine terms.

The Gore/Perot debate on "Larry King Live" set the precedent. NOW, see HILLARY CLINTON and BOB DOLE face off over HEALTH CARE on....

AMERICAN GLADIATORS

But one limitation of this approach is that it assumes a singular vision of society that is simply not shared by everyone. For example, many women have traditionally worked outside the home out of economic necessity. Second, critics charge, Parsons's analysis ignores personal strains and social costs produced by rigid gender roles (Giele, 1988). Third, and finally, to those whose goals include sexual equality, this analysis seems to legitimize the status quo. What Parsons describes as gender "complementarity," say some critics, amounts to little more than male domination.

Social-Conflict Analysis

From a social-conflict point of view, gender involves not just differences in behavior but disparities in power. Conventional gender patterns historically have benefited men while subjecting women to prejudice and discrimination, in a striking parallel to the treatment of racial and ethnic minorities (Hacker, 1951, 1974; Collins, 1971; Lengermann & Wallace, 1985). Thus, conflict theorists claim, conventional ideas about gender thinly disguise sexism that promotes not cohesion but tension and strife, with men seeking to protect their privileges while women challenge the status quo.

As earlier chapters noted, the social-conflict paradigm draws heavily on the ideas of Karl Marx. Yet Marx was a product of his time insofar as his writings focused almost exclusively on men. His friend and collaborator Friedrich Engels, however, did explore the link between gender and social stratification (1902; orig. 1884).

Looking back through history, Engels noted that in hunting and gathering societies the activities of women and men were different, yet the two sexes had comparable importance. As technological advances led to a productive surplus, however, social equality and communal sharing gave way to private property and, ultimately, a class hierarchy. At this point, men gained pronounced power over women. With surplus wealth to pass on to heirs, upper-class men took a keen interest in their children. The desire to control property, then, prompted the creation of monogamous marriage and the family. Ideally, men could be certain of paternity—especially who their sons were—and the law ensured that wealth passed to them. For their part, women were taught to remain virgins until marriage, to remain faithful to their husbands thereafter, and to build their lives around bearing and rearing children.

According to Engels, capitalism intensified male domination. First, capitalism created more wealth, which conferred greater power on men as the owners of property, the heirs of property, and the primary wage earners. Second, an expanding capitalist economy depended on defining people—especially women—as consumers and convincing them that personal fulfillment derived from buying and owning products. Third, while men worked in factories, women were

"Hire him. He's got great legs."

SEX DISCRIMINATION ISN'T FUNNY
SUPPORT THE NATIONAL ORGANIZATION FOR WOMEN
28 EAST 56 STREET N.Y.C. 10022

For generations, our society's evaluation of women in terms of physical appearance instead of job performance contributed to unequal occupational opportunities. By turning the tables, this educational poster helps people to see how grossly unfair this practice really is.

assigned the task of maintaining the home. The double exploitation of capitalism, as Engels saw it, lies in paying low wages for male labor and *no* wages for female work (Eisenstein, 1979; Barry, 1983; Jagger, 1983; Vogel, 1983).

Critical evaluation. The social-conflict analysis of gender highlights how society places the two sexes in unequal positions of privilege, prestige, and power.

Social-conflict analysis, too, has its critics. One problem, they suggest, is that this approach casts conventional families—historically viewed by traditionalists as morally good—as a social evil. Second, from a more practical standpoint, social-conflict analysis

minimizes the extent to which women and men live together cooperatively, and often quite happily, in families. A third problem with this approach, at least for some critics, is the idea that capitalism stands at the root of gender stratification. In fact, industrial-capitalist societies are typically less patriarchal than agrarian societies are. Moreover, societies with socialist economic systems—including the People's Republic of China and the former Soviet Union—have also been strongly patriarchal.

Feminism

Feminism is *the advocacy of social equality for the sexes, in opposition to patriarchy and sexism.* The "first wave" of the feminist movement in the United States swelled in the 1840s, as women opposed to slavery, including Elizabeth Cady Stanton and Lucretia Mott, drew parallels between the exploitation of African Americans and the oppression of women (Randall, 1982). The primary objective of the early women's movement was securing the right to vote, which was achieved in 1920. But other disadvantages persisted and a "second wave" of feminism arose in the 1960s and continues today.

Basic Feminist Ideas

Feminism views the personal experiences of women and men through the lens of gender. How we think of ourselves (gender identity), how we act (gender roles), and our sex's social standing (gender stratification) are all rooted in the operation of our society.

Although people who consider themselves feminists disagree about many things, most support the following five ideas.

1. **The importance of change.** Feminist thinking is decidedly political, linking ideas to action. Feminism is critical of the status quo, advocating instead social equality for women and men.
2. **Expanding human choice.** Feminists argue that cultural conceptions of gender divide the full range of human qualities into two opposing and limiting spheres: the female world of emotions and cooperation, and the male world of rationality and competition. As an alternative, feminists propose a "reintegration of humanity" by which each human being develops *all* human traits (French, 1985).

3. **Eliminating gender stratification.** Feminism opposes laws and cultural norms that limit the education, income, and job opportunities of women. For this reason, feminists have long pressed for passage of the Equal Rights Amendment (ERA) to the U.S. Constitution, which states simply:

> Equality of rights under the law shall not be denied or abridged by the United States or any State on account of sex.

The ERA, first proposed in Congress in 1923, and never enacted into law, has the support of two-thirds of U.S. adults (NORC, 1993:287).

4. **Ending sexual violence.** The contemporary women's movement focuses on eliminating sexual violence. Feminists argue that patriarchy distorts the relationships between women and men, encouraging violence against women in the form of rape, domestic abuse, sexual harassment, and pornography (Millet, 1970; J. Bernard, 1973; Dworkin, 1987).

5. **Sexual autonomy.** Finally, feminism promotes women's control over their sexuality and reproduction. Feminists advocate the free availability of birth control information. In addition, most feminists support a woman's right to choose whether to bear a child or to terminate a pregnancy, rather than allowing men—as husbands, physicians, and legislators—to make that decision. Many feminists also join forces with gay people in their efforts to overcome prejudice and discrimination in a predominantly heterosexual culture (Deckard, 1979; Barry, 1983; Jagger, 1983).

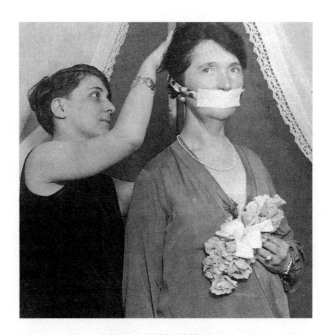

Margaret Higgins Sanger (1883–1966) was a pioneer activist in the crusade for women's reproductive rights, a cause that led her into frequent conflict with the laws of the time. Threatened with arrest if she spoke to a gathering in Boston in 1929, she made a powerful statement by appearing in public with tape over her mouth. Decades later, at the time of her death, some birth control devices (including condoms) still were not freely available in stores everywhere in the United States.

Variations Within Feminism

People pursue the goal of sexual equality in various ways, yielding three general types of feminism (Barry, 1983; Jagger, 1983; Stacey, 1983; Vogel, 1983).

Liberal feminism is grounded in classic liberal thinking that individuals should be free to develop their own talents and pursue their own interests. Adherents of liberal feminism accept the basic organization of our society but seek to expand rights and opportunities for women. Liberal feminism endorses the Equal Rights Amendment and opposes all prejudice and discrimination that block the aspirations of women.

Liberal feminists also support reproductive freedom for all women. They respect the family as a social institution, but call for widely available maternity leave and child care for women who wish to work. Liberal feminists applauded Congressional passage of the Family Leave Act in 1992, by which the United States joined more than one hundred nations that guarantee maternity leave for all working women.

Socialist feminism evolved from the ideas of Karl Marx and Friedrich Engels, in part as a critical response to how little attention Marx paid to gender. From this point of view, capitalism intensifies patriarchy by concentrating wealth and power in the hands of a small number of men. Socialist feminists view the reforms sought by liberal feminism as shortsighted. The bourgeois family fostered by capitalism must be restructured, they argue, in favor of some collective means of carrying out housework and child care. The key to this goal, in turn, is a socialist revolution. (Further discussion of socialism is found in Chapter 11, "Economics and Politics.")

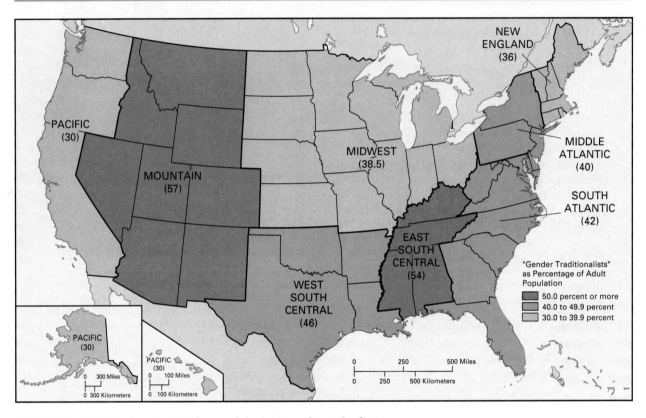

NATIONAL MAP 10–1   Support for Feminism Across the United States

Nationally, only about 35 percent of all adults support a gender-based division of labor, claiming that men should work outside the home while women take care of home and family. But, as the map shows, whether people support or oppose feminism varies significantly by region. In the Mountain states and the East South Central states, more than half of adults are "gender traditionalists." Across the remainder of the South and right up through the Middle Atlantic region, traditionalists make up more than 40 percent of the population. In New England and the Midwest, between 35 and 40 percent of all adults embrace traditional beliefs. The Pacific Coast states are the least traditional with regard to gender: Just 30 percent of adults out West endorse traditional gender-linked roles for men and women. How would you explain these regional differences? One key clue: Generally speaking, feminism takes root in regions where the level of education is highest and people's average age is lowest.

Sources: Map prepared by the author. Data from NORC (1991).

Radical feminism, too, finds the reforms proposed by liberal feminism inadequate. Moreover, radical feminists claim that even a socialist revolution would not end patriarchy. Instead, this variant of feminism holds that gender equality can be realized only by eliminating the cultural notion of gender itself. Radical feminists look toward the new reproductive technology (see Chapter 12, "Family and Religion") as one means of achieving this goal. They posit that by separating women's bodies from the process of childbearing, people could reproduce in the absence of conventional families. Thus, radical feminism envisions a revolution much more sweeping than that sought by Marx—an egalitarian and gender-free society.

Opposition to Feminism

Feminism has provoked criticism and resistance from men and women who embrace conventional ideas about gender. Some men oppose sexual equality for the same reasons that many white people have historically opposed social equality for minorities: They do not want to give up their privileges. Other men and women criticize feminism for undermining the family and rejecting what traditionalists see as time-honored male-female relationships that have guided social life for centuries.

Further, for some men, feminism threatens an important basis of their status and self-respect: their masculinity. Men who have been socialized to value strength and dominance understandably feel uneasy about feminist contentions that they can also be gentle and warm (Doyle, 1983). Similarly, for women who have centered their lives around their husbands and children, feminism may pose a challenge to cherished social roles that have imbued their lives with meaning and a sense of identity (Marshall, 1985).

Resistance also comes from some academics who charge that feminism chooses to ignore a growing body of evidence that men and women do think and act in somewhat different ways (which, presumably, makes the goal of gender equality illusory). Moreover, say these critics, by focusing on enhancing women's presence in the workplace, feminism has all but ignored women's crucial and unique contributions to the development of children—especially in the first years of life (Popenoe, 1993).

Finally, there is the question of *how* women should seek to improve their social standing. A large majority of U.S. adults believe that women should have equal rights, but most also think that women should advance individually, according to their abilities. Only 10 percent support collective action through women's-rights groups as the best approach (NORC, 1993:395).

In sum, opposition to feminism is primarily directed against its socialist and radical variants; there is widespread support for the principles that underlie liberal feminism. Furthermore, over time, we see a clear trend toward gender equality. In 1977, 65 percent of all adults endorsed the statement "It is much better for everyone involved if the man is the achiever outside the home and the woman takes care of the home and family." By 1993, however, the share supporting this statement had dropped sharply to 35 percent (NORC, 1993:286). Even so, some regions of the country offer more support for feminism than others do. National

Many of today's young women are keenly aware of continuing gender inequality. Yet, in historical perspective, the two sexes have never had more comparable social standing. Women today enjoy many rights and privileges won by the persistent efforts of feminists in past generations.

Map 10–1 on page 258 illustrates the extent of support for feminism across the United States.

Gender: Looking Ahead

Predictions about the future are, at best, informed speculation. Just as economists disagree about the projected inflation rate a year from now, sociologists differ in their views of the future state of society. Based on past trends, however, we can venture some likely directions of future change.

To begin, change has been remarkable. The position of women a century ago was one of clear and striking subordination. Husbands controlled property in marriage, women were barred from most areas of the labor force, and no woman could vote. Although women remain socially disadvantaged, the movement toward equality has surged ahead. Note, further, that two-thirds of people entering the work force during the 1990s will be women.

Many factors have contributed to this change. Perhaps most important, industrialization has both broadened the range of human activity and shifted the nature of work from physically demanding tasks that favored male strength to jobs that require human thought and imagination, placing the talents of women and men on an even footing. Additionally, medical technology now gives us control over reproduction, so women's lives are less constrained by unwanted pregnancies.

Many women and men have also made deliberate efforts to lessen the impact of patriarchy at home and on the job. Sexual harassment complaints, for example, are now taken much more seriously in the workplace. As more women enter positions of commanding power on the national stage, social changes in the twenty-first century may turn out to be as great as those we have already witnessed.

Yet strong opposition to feminism persists. Gender still forms an important foundation of personal identity and family life, and it is deeply woven into the moral fabric of our society. Therefore, attempts to rethink cultural ideas about the two sexes will continue to provoke resistance. On balance, however, while change is likely to proceed incrementally, the movement toward a society in which women and men enjoy equal rights and opportunities seems certain to gain strength.

SUMMARY

1. Sex is a biological concept; a human fetus is female or male from the moment of conception. Hermaphrodites combine the biological traits of both sexes; transsexuals have chosen to alter their sex surgically.

2. Heterosexuality is the dominant sexual orientation in every society, although people with an exclusively homosexual orientation make up a small percentage of the human population.

3. Gender refers to how societies assign human traits and power to each sex. Gender varies historically and across cultures; some degree of patriarchy, however, exists in every society.

4. Through the socialization process, people fuse gender with personal identity (gender identity) and distinctive activities (gender roles). The major agents of socialization—the family, peer groups, schools, and the mass media—reinforce cultural definitions of what is feminine and masculine.

5. Gender stratification entails numerous social disadvantages for women. Although most women are now in the paid labor force, a majority of working women hold clerical or service jobs. Unpaid housework remains predominantly a task performed by women.

6. On average, women earn about 71 percent as much as men do. This disparity stems from differences in jobs and family responsibilities, as well as discrimination.

7. Women now earn a slight majority of all associate's, bachelor's, and master's degrees. Men still receive a majority of doctorates and professional degrees.

8. The number of women in politics has increased sharply in recent decades. Still, the vast majority of elected officials nationwide are men.

9. Minority women experience greater social disadvantages than white women. Overall, minority women earn only half as much as white men, and half the households headed by African-American women are poor.

10. Because of their distinct identity and social disadvantages, women represent a social minority, although many do not think of themselves in such terms.

11. Violence against women is a widespread problem in the United States. Our society is also grappling with the issues of sexual harassment and pornography.

12. Structural-functional analysis suggests that distinct roles for females and males constitute a survival strategy in preindustrial societies. In industrial societies, pronounced gender inequality becomes dysfunctional, yet long-established gender norms change slowly. According to Talcott Parsons, complementary gender roles help integrate the family.

13. Social-conflict analysis views gender as a dimension of social inequality and conflict. Friedrich Engels linked gender stratification to the emergence of private property. He claimed that capitalism devalues women and housework.

14. Feminism endorses the social equality of the sexes and actively opposes patriarchy and sexism. Feminism also seeks to eliminate sexual violence against women, and to give women control over their sexuality.

15. There are three variants of feminist thinking. Liberal feminism strives to ensure equal opportunity for the two sexes within current social arrangements; socialist feminism advocates abolishing private property as the means to social equality; radical feminism seeks to create a gender-free society.

16. Because gender distinctions stand at the core of our way of life, feminism has encountered strong resistance. Although two-thirds of U.S. adults support the Equal Rights Amendment, this legislation—first proposed in Congress in 1923—has yet to become part of the U.S. Constitution.

KEY CONCEPTS

feminism the advocacy of social equality for the sexes, in opposition to patriarchy and sexism

gender the significance a society attaches to the biological categories of female and male

gender roles (sex roles) attitudes and activities that a society links to each sex

gender stratification the unequal distribution of wealth, power, and privilege between the two sexes

hermaphrodite a human being possessing some combination of female and male internal and external genitalia

matriarchy a form of social organization in which females dominate males

patriarchy a form of social organization in which males dominate females

sex the biological distinction between females and males

sexism the belief that one sex is innately superior to the other

sexual harassment comments, gestures, or physical contact of a sexual nature that are deliberate, repeated, and unwelcome

sexual orientation the manner in which people experience sexual arousal and achieve sexual pleasure

transsexuals people who feel they are one sex though biologically they are the other

CRITICAL-THINKING QUESTIONS

1. Distinguish between sex and gender. What impact do the biological forces of sex have in shaping cultural patterns of gender?

2. How do the family, peer groups, schools, and the mass media affect our thinking about gender?

3. What makes gender a dimension of social stratification? How does gender interact with other dimensions of inequality such as race and class?

4. What principles underlie feminism? Distinguish among liberal, socialist, and radical feminism.

Economics
and Politics

"America First!" proclaimed the mayor of Greece, New York, an upstate community outside of Rochester. Amid bad economic news—a continuing recession, rising unemployment, and a deepening federal deficit—the town leaders had symbolically voted to cancel the purchase of a $40,000 piece of excavating equipment from Japan's Komatsu Corporation in order to give the business to U.S. manufacturer John Deere, even at a higher price.

The action prompted much applause, but its impact was muted indeed: It turns out that the Komatsu model is actually built in the United States, while the John Deere is powered by an engine—you guessed it—manufactured in Japan. Appearances aside, the emerging global economy is making conventional political boundaries almost irrelevant.

This chapter delves into the economy and politics, two vital dimensions of social life. First, we explore the economy, with special attention to the Industrial Revolution that ushered in the modern world, and the burgeoning global economy that is already reshaping the workplace both here and around the globe. Second, our attention turns to politics, highlighting the growth and changing character of government in the United States, and surveying political systems of various stripes found elsewhere in the world.

The economy and polity each constitute a major **social institution,** *an organized sphere of social life.* The two chapters that follow consider the other key social institutions: Chapter 12 examines the family and religion, and Chapter 13 investigates education and medicine. In focusing on social institutions, we probe how they function as strategies by which society meets its basic needs while, at the same time, serving to maintain social inequality. We shall discover, too, that these institutions have been quite variable over human history.

The Economy: Historical Overview

The **economy** is *the social institution that organizes a society's production, distribution, and consumption of goods and services.* To say that the economy is *institutionalized* means that it operates in a well established manner. *Goods* are commodities ranging from necessities (such as food, clothing, and shelter) to luxury items (such as automobiles and swimming pools), while *services* refer to activities that benefit others (including the work of religious leaders, physicians, teachers, and telephone operators).

The Agricultural Revolution

As Chapter 2 ("Culture") noted, the earliest societies relied on hunting and gathering to live off the land. There was no distinct economic life: Production, distribution, and consumption of goods were all dimensions of family life.

The development of agriculture some five thousand years ago brought revolutionary change to these societies. Agriculture emerged as people harnessed animals to plows, magnifying the productivity of hunting and gathering more than tenfold. The resulting surplus meant that not everyone had to produce food, and many people adopted specialized economic roles, forging tools, raising animals, and constructing dwellings. This economic expansion, in turn, gave rise to towns, which were soon linked by networks of traders (Jacobs, 1970). These four factors—agricultural technology, productive specialization, permanent settlements, and trade—were the keys to the growth of the economy as a distinct social institution and propelled the first revolutionary change in human society.

The Industrial Revolution

Beginning in mid-eighteenth-century England, industrialization introduced five revolutionary changes to the economies of Western societies.

1. **New forms of energy.** Throughout history, people had generated energy with their own muscles or those of animals. At the dawn of industrialization in 1765, however, the English inventor James Watt pioneered the application of steam power to machinery. Surpassing muscle power a hundred times over, steam engines soon made production far more efficient than ever before.
2. **The spread of factories.** Steam-powered machinery rendered cottage industries obsolete. Factories—centralized workplaces apart from the home—proliferated. A more productive system, factory work nonetheless lacked the personal ties that had characterized earlier, family-based production.

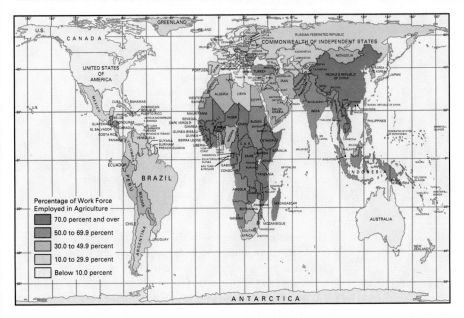

GLOBAL MAP 11–1
Agricultural Employment in Global Perspective

The primary sector of the economy predominates in societies that are least developed. Thus, in the poor countries of Africa and Asia, half, or even three-fourths, of all workers are farmers. This picture is altogether different among the world's most economically developed countries—including the United States, Canada, Great Britain, and Australia—which have less than 10 percent of their work force in agriculture.

Source: *Peters Atlas of the World* (1990).

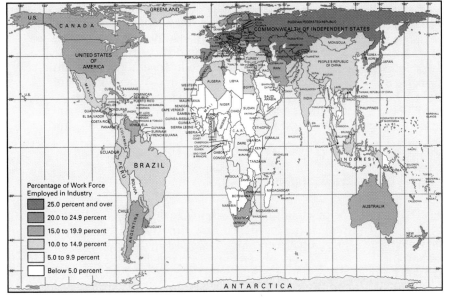

GLOBAL MAP 11–2
Industrial Employment in Global Perspective

The world's poor societies, by and large, have yet to industrialize. For this reason, in the countries of Latin America, Africa, and Asia, a small proportion of the labor force engages in industrial work. The nations of Eastern Europe, along with the Commonwealth of Independent States, have far more of their workers in industry. In the world's richest societies, we see a reversal of this trend, with more and more workers moving from industrial jobs to service work. Thus, the postindustrial economy of the United States now has about the same share of workers in industrial jobs as the much poorer nation of Argentina.

Source: *Peters Atlas of the World* (1990).

3. **Manufacturing and mass production.** Before the Industrial Revolution, most work involved cultivating and gathering raw materials, such as crops, wool, and wood. The industrial economy shifted that focus to manufacturing raw materials into a wide range of salable products. For example, factories mass produced lumber into furniture and transformed wool into clothing.

4. **Specialization.** A skilled laborer working at home fashioned a product from beginning to end. Factory work, by contrast, was highly specialized

so that laborers repeated a single task, making only a small contribution to the finished product.

5. **Wage labor.** Instead of laboring for themselves or joining together as households, factory workers became wage laborers. This meant that they sold their labor to strangers who often cared less for them than for the machines they operated.

After the Industrial Revolution took hold, greater productivity steadily raised living standards as countless new products filled an expanding economy. Especially at the outset, however, the benefits of industrial technology were shared very unequally. Some factory owners made vast fortunes, while the majority of workers hovered perilously close to poverty. Children, too, worked in factories or coal mines for pennies a day.

The Information Revolution

Industrialization is an ongoing process. In Europe and North America, workers gradually formed labor unions to collectively represent their interests in dealings with factory owners. During this century, governments outlawed child labor, forced wages upward, improved workplace safety, and extended schooling and political rights to a larger segment of the population.

By about 1950, the United States had developed a **postindustrial economy,** *a productive system based on service work and high technology.* Automated machinery reduced the role of human labor in production, while bureaucracy simultaneously expanded the ranks of clerical workers and managers. Service industries—such as public relations, advertising, banking, and sales—now employ most of our country's labor force. The postindustrial era, then, is marked by a shift from industrial production to service jobs.

The crucial technology of a postindustrial age revolves around information. Computer technology forms the core of an *Information Revolution,* which is generating a host of new, specialized occupations. Just as gaining technical skills held the key to success in the past, now workers must enhance their literacy skills.

The Information Revolution is changing not just what people do but where they do it. Just as factories centralized the work force (because of the enormity of the machinery), a service economy allows salespeople, architects, writers, and others to work virtually anywhere equipped with computers, facsimile (fax) machines, electronic notebooks, and other lightweight and portable information-processing devices. Today's

more educated and skilled workers also no longer require—and some do not tolerate—the close supervision that marked yesterday's factories.

Sectors of the Economy

The broad historical changes just described reflect a shifting balance among three sectors of a society's economy. The **primary sector** is *the part of the economy that generates raw materials directly from the natural environment.* The primary sector, which includes agriculture, raising livestock, fishing, forestry, and mining, holds sway in preindustrial societies. Global Map 11–1 on page 265 shows that the economies of poor nations of the world, such as India and the People's Republic of China, are still dominated by the primary sector.

The **secondary sector** is *the part of the economy that transforms raw materials into manufactured goods.* This sector grows as societies industrialize. Secondary sector production includes the refining of petroleum and the use of metals to manufacture tools and automobiles. Global Map 11–2 on page 265 illustrates the scope of industrial production in global perspective.

The **tertiary sector** is *the part of the economy involving services rather than goods.* Accounting for only a tiny share of work in preindustrial economies, the tertiary sector grows with industrialization and gains primacy in postindustrial societies. Almost 70 percent of the U.S. labor force is now employed in service occupations, including secretarial and clerical work, and positions in food service, sales, law, advertising, and teaching.

The Global Economy

As new information technology draws nations of the world closer together, we are witnessing the emergence of a **global economy,** *economic activity across national borders.* The development of a global economy has three main consequences.

1. **Products pass through many national economies.** Workers in Taiwan may make shoes, for example, which a Hong Kong distributor sends to Italy, where an Italian company stamps a designer label on them. Then another distributor in Rome might forward the shoes to New York where they sell in a department store owned by a firm with its headquarters in Tokyo.

The productivity of capitalist Hong Kong is evident in the fact that streets are choked with advertising and shoppers. Socialist Beijing, by contrast, is dominated by government buildings rather than a central business district. Here bicyclists glide past the Great Hall of the People.

2. **National governments no longer control their economies.** Today, governments cannot even control the value of their national currencies, since dollars, pounds sterling, yen, and other currencies are now traded around the clock in the financial centers of New York, London, and Tokyo. Global markets are one consequence of satellite communications that forge information links among the various cities of the world.

3. **Large companies control more economic activity.** In the global economy, as we shall explain presently, a small number of multinational businesses now dominate economic activity the world over. One estimate concludes that the six hundred largest international companies account for half of the earth's entire total economic output (Kidron & Segal, 1991).

The world is still divided into 191 politically distinct nations. But, in light of the proliferation of international economic activity, "nationhood" has lost much of its former significance.

Global Economic Systems

We can describe the economies of world societies in terms of two general models: capitalism and socialism. These models represent two ends of a continuum on which all actual economies are located.

Capitalism

Capitalism refers to *an economic system in which natural resources and the means of producing goods and services are privately owned.* Ideally, a capitalist economy has three distinctive features.

1. **Private ownership of property.** A capitalist economy supports the right of individuals to own almost anything. The more capitalist an economy is, the more private ownership there is of wealth-producing property like factories, real estate, and natural resources.

2. **Pursuit of personal profit.** A capitalist society promotes the accumulation of private property and defines a profit-minded orientation as the natural order of "doing business." Further, claimed the Scottish economist Adam Smith (1723–1790), the drive of individuals pursuing their own self-interest helps an entire society prosper (1937; orig. 1776).

3. **Free competition and consumer sovereignty.** A purely capitalist economy would operate with no government interference, sometimes called a *laissez-faire* (a French expression meaning "to leave alone") system. Adam Smith contended that a freely competitive economy regulates itself through the "invisible hand" of the laws of supply and demand.

Consumers control a market economy, Smith continued, as they select goods and services offering the greatest value. Producers must compete with one another for business; thus, everyone benefits from more efficient production and ever-increasing value. In Smith's time-honored phrase, from narrow self-interest comes "the greatest good for the greatest number of people." Government control of an economy would distort market forces, reducing producer motivation, diminishing the quality of goods, and shortchanging consumers.

Most of the world's nations have economies that are largely capitalist. But nowhere does pure laissez-faire capitalism exist. In the United States, for example, government policies influence what companies produce, affect the quality and cost of merchandise, oversee imports and exports, and regulate our use of natural resources. The federal government also owns and operates many productive organizations, including the U.S. Postal Service, the Amtrak railroad system, and the entire U.S. military. Further, government policies set minimum wage levels and enforce workplace safety standards, regulate corporate mergers, provide farm price supports, and funnel income in the form of Social Security, public assistance, student loans, and veterans' benefits to a majority of people in the United States. Not surprisingly, local, state, and federal governments together make up this nation's biggest employer, with 15 percent of the labor force (some 19 million people) on their payrolls (U.S. Bureau of the Census, 1994).

Socialism

Socialism is *an economic system in which natural resources and the means of producing goods and services are collectively owned.* In its ideal form, a socialist economy opposes each of the three tenets of capitalism just described.

1. **Collective ownership of property.** An economy is socialist to the extent that it limits the right to private property, especially property used to generate income. Such laws are designed to make housing and other goods available to all, not just those with the most money.
2. **Pursuit of collective goals.** The individualistic pursuit of profit also stands at odds with the collective orientation of socialism. Socialist values and norms define as illegal what capitalists celebrate as the entrepreneurial spirit.
3. **Government control of the economy.** Socialism rejects the notion that a free-market economy

regulates itself. Instead of a laissez-faire approach, socialist governments oversee a *centrally controlled* or *command* economy.

Socialism also rejects the idea that consumers guide capitalist production. From this point of view, consumers lack the information necessary to evaluate products and are manipulated by advertising to buy what is profitable rather than what they genuinely need. Commercial advertising thus plays little role in socialist economies.

The People's Republic of China and a number of societies in Asia, Africa, and Latin America—some two dozen in all—model their economies on socialism, placing almost all wealth-generating property under state control (McColm et al., 1991). The extent of world socialism has declined in recent years as societies in Eastern Europe and the former Soviet Union have been dramatically transformed. As change continues, these countries will eventually forge new economic systems from some combination of market forces and government regulation.

Democratic Socialism and State Capitalism

A look at the world's nations reveals various ways of fusing capitalist and socialist principles. A number of countries in Western Europe—including Sweden and Italy—have blended socialist economic policies with democratic political systems. This hybrid is called **democratic socialism,** *an economic and political system that combines significant government control of the economy with free elections.*

Under democratic socialism, the government owns and operates some of the largest industries and services, such as transportation, education, and health care. In Sweden and Italy, about 12 percent of total production is state-controlled. That leaves most industry in private hands but subject to extensive government regulation. High taxation (aimed especially at the rich) funds a wide array of social welfare programs that transfer wealth to less advantaged members of society.

Yet another variant of this economic form is *state capitalism,* in which privately owned companies cooperate closely with the government. Systems of state capitalism thrive in many rapidly developing Asian countries including Japan, South Korea, and Singapore. There, governments and large companies work hand in hand, with government supplying financial assistance or controlling imports of foreign products to help locally

Not all linkages between government and the private sector of the economy are constructive; some are even illegal. In recent years, Italy has been rocked by charges that high government officials have corrupt deals with business leaders. In this protest march, supporters of Umberto Bossi, a political leader in northern Italy who is contemptuous of the government in Rome, carry aloft a huge figure of their leader holding a saw symbolizing his desire to gain political independence for his region of the country.

based corporations remain competitive in world markets. In sum, besides the traditional capitalist and socialist models, we see throughout the world a range of private-public partnerships between companies and governments.

Relative Advantages of Capitalism and Socialism

In practice, how do economic systems differ? Assessing economic models is difficult because nowhere do they exist in their pure states. Societies mix capitalism and socialism to varying degrees, and each country has distinctive cultural attitudes toward work, different natural resources, unequal levels of technological development, and disparate patterns of trade (Gregory & Stuart, 1985). Despite such complicating factors, we can draw some crude comparisons.

Productivity.   Perhaps the most important dimension of economic performance is productivity. A commonly used measure of economic output is Gross Domestic Product (GDP), the total value of all goods and services produced annually by an economy. "Per capita" (or per person) GDP allows us to compare societies of different population size.

The economic output of predominantly capitalist countries at the end of the last decade varied from country to country; yet averaging the figures for the United States, Canada, and the nations of Western Europe yields a per capita GDP of about $13,500. The comparable average based on the output of the former Soviet Union and the nations of Eastern Europe was about $5,000. This means that the capitalist countries outproduced the socialist nations by a ratio of 2.7 to 1 (United Nations Development Programme, 1990).

Economic inequality.   We also need to consider how resources are distributed within a population. In a comparative study completed in the mid-1970s, researchers calculated the degree of economic inequality in societies by comparing the incomes of the richest 5 percent of the population and the poorest 5 percent (Wiles, 1977). The result: Societies with predominantly capitalist economies had an income ratio of about 10 to 1; the corresponding figure for socialist countries was 5 to 1.

This comparison of economic performance supports the conclusion that *capitalist economies produce a higher overall standard of living but with greater income disparity.* Or, put otherwise, *socialist economies create less income disparity but generate a lower overall standard of living.*

Civil liberties.   Economics and politics are closely linked. Capitalism depends on the freedom of producers and consumers to interact without extensive interference from the state. Thus economic capitalism fosters broad political freedoms. Socialist governments, by contrast, strive to maximize economic equality. This requires considerable state intervention in the economy, limiting the personal liberty of citizens. It appears, therefore, that efforts to achieve the goals of political liberty and economic equality work at cross purposes. The implications of this tension are nowhere more evident than in Eastern Europe, where previously socialist countries are undergoing significant economic transition.

Changes in Socialist Countries

The countries of Eastern Europe, all of which had fallen under the political control of the former Soviet Union at the end of World War II, shook off socialist regimes in 1989 and 1990. These nations—including the German Democratic Republic (East Germany), the Czech Republic, Slovakia, Hungary, Romania, and Bulgaria—have now introduced capitalist elements into what had for decades been state-controlled economies. In 1992, the Soviet Union itself formally dissolved, following a similar path.

The reasons for these sweeping transformations are many and complex. In light of earlier discussion, however, two factors stand out. First, these predominantly socialist economies grossly underproduced their capitalist counterparts. They were, as we have noted, somewhat successful in achieving economic equality; living standards for everyone, however, were low compared to those in Western Europe. Second, the brand of socialism that was imprinted on Eastern Europe by the former Soviet Union burdened citizens with heavy-handed and unresponsive government that rigidly controlled the media as well as the ability of individuals to move about, even in their own countries.

In short, the socialist systems in these societies did do away with *economic* elites, as Karl Marx predicted. But, as Max Weber might have foreseen, they expanded the clout of *political* elites, and party bureaucracies grew to gargantuan proportions.

At this stage, the market reforms in the former Soviet Union and Eastern Europe have been proceeding unevenly, with some nations faring better than others. For the short term at least, Eastern Europe has been buffeted by price increases, which have further eroded living standards. In the long term, however, officials in these countries hope that an expanding market will raise living standards through greater productivity. If that happens, based on the experience of Western societies, a rising standard of living will almost certainly be accompanied by increasing economic inequality.

Work in the Postindustrial United States

Change is not restricted to the socialist world; the last century has also dramatically transformed the economy of the United States. In 1993, 128 million people were in the labor force, representing two-thirds of those aged sixteen and over. As explained in Chapter 10 ("Sex and Gender"), a larger proportion of men (75.2 percent) than women (57.9 percent) held income-producing jobs, but this gap has diminished in recent decades. Among men, the share of people of African descent in the labor force (68.6 percent) is somewhat lower than the proportion of whites (76.1 percent); among women, about the same percentage of African Americans (57.4 percent) and whites (58.0 percent) are employed.

National Map 11–1 shows labor-force participation by county for the United States. Since work and income go hand in hand, regions of the country with above average labor-force participation are typically more affluent.

The Changing Workplace

In 1900, 40 percent of the U.S. labor force engaged in farming. By 1993, this proportion had dropped to less than 3 percent. Figure 11–1 on page 272 illustrates this rapid decline, which reflects the diminished role of the primary sector in the U.S. economy.

Industrialization swelled the ranks of blue-collar workers a century ago. By 1950, however, a white-collar revolution had carried a majority of workers into service occupations. By 1993, more than two-thirds of employed men and women held white-collar jobs. As Chapter 7 ("Social Stratification") explained, many so-called "white-collar" positions are "service" jobs, including sales and clerical occupations, and work in fast-food restaurants. Such jobs yield little of the income and prestige of professional white-collar occupations, and often provide fewer rewards than factory work. More and more jobs in this postindustrial era, then, afford workers only a modest standard of living.

Labor Unions

The changing economy has been accompanied by a decline in the strength of labor unions, worker organizations that seek to improve wages and working conditions. Membership in labor unions increased rapidly after 1935 to more than one-third of nonfarm workers by 1950. Union membership peaked during the 1970s at almost 25 million people. Since then, it has dropped to about 16 percent of the nonfarm labor force, or about 17 million men and women.

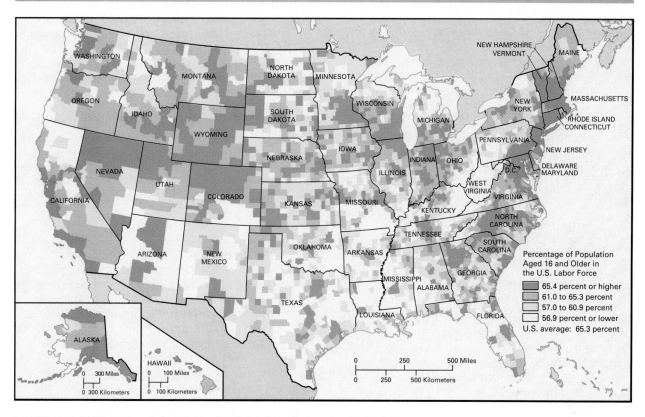

NATIONAL MAP 11–1   Labor Force Participation Across the United States

Counties with high levels of labor-force participation have within their borders steady sources of employment, including military bases, recreation areas, and large cities. By contrast, counties with low employment rates typically have a high share of elderly people (as well as students). Gender also plays an important role: In regions of the country (stretching from the South up to coal-mining districts of Kentucky and West Virginia) where traditional cultural norms encourage women to stay home, how do employment levels compare to other areas?

Source: *American Demographics Desk Reference Series # 4.* Reprinted with permission. ©1992 *American Demographics* magazine, Ithaca, New York. Data from the 1990 decennial census.

Unions are weaker in the United States than in other industrial societies. More than 90 percent of workers in Denmark and Sweden belong to unions, as do half in Great Britain, and about one-third in Canada, Switzerland, and Japan. Our country's low union membership can be traced, in part, to a decrease in the highly unionized industrial sector of the economy coupled with growth in service jobs, which are far less likely to be unionized. But unions still exert power in the workplace and, since 1990, economic uncertainty appears to have given some new life to unions.

According to some analysts, falling job security may well make union affiliation a higher priority for workers in the years to come. But to expand their membership, unions will also have to adapt to the new global economy. Instead of seeing foreign workers as a threat to their interests, in short, union leadership will have to forge new international alliances (Goldfield, 1987; Mabry, 1992; Western, 1993).

Professions

All kinds of work today are called *professional*—we hear of professional tennis players and even professional exterminators. As distinct from an *amateur* (from Latin for "lover," meaning one who acts out of love for the activity itself), a professional pursues some task for a living.

More precisely, a **profession** is *a prestigious, white-collar occupation that requires extensive formal education.* The term suggests a profession—or public declaration—of willingness to abide by certain principles. Traditional professions include the ministry, medicine, law, and academia (W. Goode, 1960). Today, more workers describe their occupations as professional to the extent that they demonstrate the following four characteristics (Ritzer & Walczak, 1990).

1. **Theoretical knowledge.** Professionals have a theoretical knowledge of their field rather than mere technical training. Anyone can learn first aid, for example, but physicians draw on a theoretical understanding of human health.

2. **Self-regulating practice.** The typical professional is self-employed, "in practice" rather than working for a company. Professionals oversee their own work and embrace a code of ethics.

3. **Authority over clients.** Based on extensive training, professionals claim authority over clients, and expect "lay people" to follow their direction.

4. **A profession of altruism.** Professionals assert that they serve the community rather than merely seeking income. Some professional associations (such as the American Medical Association) forbid their members from advertising.

Not every category of highly skilled workers claims full professional status. Some *paraprofessionals*, including paralegals and medical technicians, possess specialized training but lack the extensive theoretical education required of full professionals.

Self-Employment

Self-employment—in effect, earning a living without working for a large organization—was once commonplace in the United States. From about 80 percent of the labor force in 1800, self-employment now accounts for only 8 percent of workers (11 percent of men and 6 percent of women).

Lawyers, physicians, and some other professionals are represented strongly among the ranks of the self-employed. But most self-employed workers are farmers, small-business owners, plumbers, carpenters, freelance writers, editors, artists, and long-distance truck drivers. Overall, the self-employed are more likely to have blue-collar jobs than white-collar work.

Unemployment

Every society has some unemployment. Few young people entering the labor force find a job right away; some older workers temporarily leave their jobs to seek new work, to have children, or because of a labor strike; others suffer from long-term illnesses; and still others are illiterate or without the skills to perform useful work.

But unemployment is also caused by the economy itself. Jobs disappear as occupations become obsolete, as businesses close in the face of foreign competition, or as recession forces layoffs. Since 1987, the "downsizing" of U.S. companies has eliminated 6 million jobs including both blue-collar and white-collar positions.

In 1993, 8.7 million people over the age of sixteen were unemployed—about 7 percent of the civilian

FIGURE 11–1   The Changing Pattern of Work in the United States, 1900–1992

Source: U.S. Department of Labor (1994).

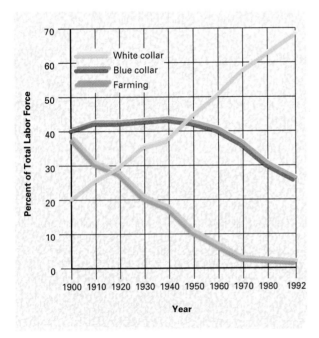

During the Great Depression, a time of catastrophic unemployment in the United States, Isaac Soyer painted *Employment Agency,* a powerful statement of the personal collapse and private despair that afflict men and women who are out of work.

labor force. As a glance back at National Map 11–1 suggests, some regions of the country, including parts of West Virginia and New Mexico, contend with unemployment at twice the national rate.

Figure 11–2 on page 274 shows the official unemployment rate for various categories of U.S. workers in 1993. Unemployment among African Americans stood more than twice as high (12.9 percent) as that found among white people (6.0 percent). For both races, men now have higher unemployment than women—a reversal of a historical pattern. The economic recession in male-dominated blue-collar industries accounts for this change.

Social Diversity in the Workplace

Another major change involves the composition of the workplace. Traditionally, white men have been the mainstay of the U.S. labor force. As explained in Chapter 9 ("Race and Ethnicity"), however, our country's proportion of minorities is rising rapidly, substantially boosting social diversity on the job. During the 1980s, the increase in African Americans (13 percent) was twice as great as for white people (6 percent); even higher was the jump in the Hispanic population (more than 50 percent), and in the numbers of Asian Americans (topping 100 percent). Should these trends continue, there will be a "minority-majority" in the

United States by the end of the next century. The box takes a closer look at how growing social diversity is affecting the workplace in the 1990s.

Technology and Work

The central feature of the emerging postindustrial economy is the computer and related information-processing technology. The Information Revolution is changing both the workplace and the nature of work itself.

Shoshana Zuboff (1982) points out four ways in which computers have already transformed the character of work.

1. **Computers are deskilling labor.** Just as industrial machines deskilled the master craftsworker of an earlier era, so computers now threaten the skills of managers. More and more business decisions are based not on the judgment of executives but rather on computer modeling, in which a machine determines whether to make a new product or to approve a loan application.

2. **Computers are making work more abstract.** Industrial workers generally have a "hands-on" relationship with their product. Postindustrial workers manipulate symbols in pursuit of some sales goal or other abstract business objective.

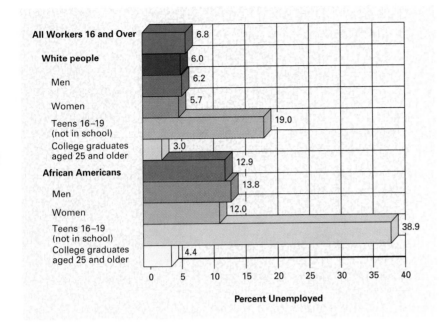

FIGURE 11–2
Official U.S. Unemployment Rate
Among Various Categories
of Adults, 1993
Source: U.S. Department of Labor (1994).

3. **Computers limit workplace interaction.** The Information Revolution is placing employees at computer terminals, isolating them from one another.

4. **Computers enhance employers' control of workers.** Computers allow supervisors to monitor each worker's output precisely and continuously, whether workers are at computer terminals or on an assembly line.

Making a broader point, Zuboff contends that technology is not socially neutral; rather, it reconfigures how we work in ways not always to workers' liking.

Corporations

At the core of today's capitalist economy lies the **corporation,** *an organization with a legal existence, including rights and liabilities, apart from those of its members.* By incorporating, an organization becomes a legal entity unto itself, able to enter into contracts and own property. Of some 20 million businesses in the United States, 4 million are incorporated (*Statistics of Income Bulletin,* 1991). The advantages of incorporating span a wide range from protecting the personal wealth of owners from lawsuits arising out of business operations to lowering taxes on profits.

Economic Concentration

About half of U.S. corporations are quite small, with assets of less than $100,000. The largest corporations, however, dominate our nation's economy. Corporations of record in 1990 included 367 with assets exceeding $1 billion, representing 71 percent of all corporate assets and 73 percent of total corporate profits (U.S. Bureau of the Census, 1992).

The largest U.S. corporation in terms of sales is General Motors, which has $190 billion in total assets. GM's sales ($132 billion) equal the combined tax revenues of half the states. GM also employs more people than the governments of all states on the West Coast including Alaska and Hawaii.

Conglomerates and Corporate Linkages

Economic concentration has spawned *conglomerates,* giant corporations composed of many smaller corporations. Conglomerates emerge as corporations enter new markets, spinning off new companies or carrying

The Work Force of the Twenty-First Century

The significant rise in the U.S. minority population in recent years means a marked transformation of the labor force. The figure shows that the number of white men in the labor force is projected to rise by a modest 10 percent from 1992 to 2005. The anticipated increase among African-American working men will be far greater, at 21 percent. Among Hispanic men, the rise will be 58 percent, and, among Asian-American/Native-American men, a whopping 77 percent.

Among women, projected increases across the board are even larger. And, here again, the gains among minorities will be greatest of all: A 21 percent rise among white women will be surpassed by a 29 percent jump among African-American women, a 72 percent increase in Hispanic women, and an 86 percent surge in Asian-American/Native-American women.

Thus, non-Hispanic white men will represent only 10 percent of new workers by 2005, for a total of just 40 percent of all workers. Because this figure will continue to drop, companies that begin now to plan for growing social diversity in the labor force will tap the largest talent pool and enjoy a competitive advantage in the next century.

Responding effectively to workplace diversity means more than maintaining affirmative action programs, which are primarily aimed at recruiting. The broader challenge—and greater opportunity—is to transform the workplace environment to develop the potential of all workers. Employees, after all, are any company's most important resource, and utilizing them to the best advantage will require change in several key areas.

First, companies must realize that the needs and concerns of women and minorities may not be the same as those of white men. For example, corporations will be pressed to provide workplace child care in the future.

Second, businesses will have to devise effective strategies for defusing tensions that arise from social differences. They will have to work harder at treating all workers equally and respectfully; also, the emerging corporate culture must not tolerate harassment related to gender and race.

Third, companies will have to rethink current promotion practices. At present, only 2 percent of Fortune 500 top executives are women, and just 1 percent are other minorities. In a broad survey of U.S. companies, the U.S. Equal Opportunity Commission confirmed that white men (40 percent of adults aged twenty to sixty-four) hold 68 percent of management jobs; the comparable figures for white women are 41 and 23 percent; for African Americans, 12 and 5 percent; and, for Hispanics, 8 and 2 percent.

Any informal "glass ceiling" that prevents advancement by skilled workers clearly discourages achievement. In the emerging labor force of the next century, such barriers will deprive companies of their largest source of talent—women and minorities.

Projected Increase in the Numbers of People in the U.S. Labor Force, 1992–2005

*Hispanics can be of any race.

Source: Data from Fullerton, Jr. (1993).

Sources: Bureau of National Affairs (1990) and Crispell (1990).

out "takeovers" of existing companies. Forging a conglomerate is also a strategy to diversify a company, so that new products can provide a hedge against declining profits in the original market. Faced with declining sales of tobacco products, for example, R. J. Reynolds merged with Nabisco foods, forming a conglomerate called RJR-Nabisco that sells dozens of familiar household products.

Another type of corporate linkage is the *interlocking directorate*, a social network of people who serve simultaneously on the boards of directors of many corporations (Marlios, 1975; Herman, 1981; Scott & Griff, 1985). These connections give corporations access to valuable information about each other's products and marketing strategies. Beth Mintz and Michael Schwartz (1981) found that General Motors was directly linked through board members to twenty-nine other major corporations, and indirectly to another seven hundred companies. Although corporate linkages do not necessarily run counter to the public interest, they can facilitate illegal activity such as price fixing, and they certainly concentrate corporate power.

Corporations and Competition

The capitalist model assumes that businesses operate independently in a competitive market. However, large corporations do not truly compete because, first, extensive linkages mean that they are not independent. Second, a small number of corporations hold sway over many large markets.

No large corporation can legally engage in **monopoly**, *domination of a market by a single producer*, because such a company could simply dictate prices. But a common practice is **oligopoly**, *domination of a market by a few producers*. Because of the vast investment needed to enter a new market like the auto industry, oligopoly has become the norm in big business. Moreover, true competition means risk, which corporate leaders try to avoid.

Corporations and the Global Economy

Corporations have grown in size so fast that they now account for most of the world's economic output. The largest corporations—centered in the United States, Japan, and Western Europe—have spilled across national borders and view the world as one vast marketplace.

Corporations become multinational in order to make more money. Because three-fourths of the world's people and most of the planet's resources are found in poor nations, global corporations enter these countries to gain access to raw materials, inexpensive labor, and vast markets. Developing an international profile also permits corporations to lower their tax liabilities and to move money from country to country, profiting from fluctuating currency rates.

Yet the impact of multinationals on poor societies is controversial, as we saw in Chapter 8 ("Global Stratification"). On one side of the argument, modernization theorists claim that multinationals unleash the great productivity of the capitalist economic system to the benefit of poor nations (Rostow, 1978; Madsen, 1980; Berger, 1986). Advocates of modernization theory assert that corporations offer poor societies tax revenues, capital investment, new jobs, and advanced technology that combine to accelerate economic growth. On the other side, dependency theorists respond that multinationals have intensified global inequality (Vaughan, 1978; Wallerstein, 1979; Delacroix & Ragin, 1981; Bergesen, 1983). Multinational investment, they contend, actually creates few jobs, inhibits the growth of local industries, and pushes developing countries to produce goods for export rather than food and other products for local consumption. From this standpoint, multinationals make poor societies poorer and increasingly dependent on rich societies.

Looking Ahead: The Economy of the Twenty-First Century

Through social institutions, societies strive to meet basic human needs. But as societies themselves change over time, various social institutions may be hard-pressed to keep pace.

One important transformation highlighted in this chapter revolves around the Information Revolution. New information technology is propelling the emerging postindustrial economy in the United States. The share of the U.S. labor force engaged in manufacturing is now half of what it was in 1960, while service work has increased at a comparable rate. As a society, we must recognize that millions of men and women lack the language and computer skills needed to participate in the postindustrial economy. Therefore, in the next century, families and schools must face up to the challenge of preparing young people to perform the kind of work their society makes available to them.

A second key transformation is the growth of a global economy. In the earliest phase of our country's history, the ups and downs of a local economy depended on events or trends that took place within a single town. In time, local communities across the country became linked economically so that one town's prosperity typically depended on producing goods demanded by people elsewhere. The global economy now taking hold will gradually erode national economies so that what people, say, in a Kansas farm

The expansion of Western multinational corporations has altered patterns of consumption throughout the world, creating a homogeneous "corporate culture" that is—for better or worse—undermining countless traditional ways of life.

town buy and sell may be affected more by what transpires in the wheat-growing region of Russia than by events in their own state capital. In short, U.S. workers are not only generating new products and services, but we are doing so in response to factors and forces distant and unseen.

Finally, change is causing analysts around the world to rethink conventional economic models. The emerging global economy laid bare the inefficiency of socialist economies; the socialist economic system—which, at its peak, organized the productive lives of about one-fourth of humanity—is in decline around the world. But the new global economic realities are forcing changes in capitalism, too: Capitalist economies now operate with a significant degree of government regulation. As an offshoot of capitalist dominance in the world economy, we can expect multinational corporations to extend their reach into more parts of the world, just as foreign-based corporations will increase their investment in the United States. At this point, foreign corporations own more property in the United States than U.S. corporations own abroad.

How will these changes shake out in the long term? Two conclusions seem inescapable. First, the economic future of the United States and other nations will be played out around the world. The postindustrial economy in the United States now dovetails with the increasing industrial production of other nations, especially in Asia's rapidly developing Pacific Rim. Second, we all confront the ever-pressing issue of global inequality. Whether the world economy ultimately reduces or deepens the disparity between rich and poor societies will determine whether our planet moves toward peace or belligerence.

Politics: Historical Overview

Closely related to economics is **politics**, *the social institution that distributes power and makes decisions.* Early in this century, Max Weber (1978; orig. 1921) defined **power** as *the ability to achieve desired ends despite opposition.*

Brute force is certainly the most basic form of power. But a society cannot long exist if power derives *only* from force, at least not without more efficient means of government control than exist at present. More realistically, social organization depends on consensus about proper goals (cultural values) and the suitable means of attaining them (cultural norms). This brings us to the concept of **authority**, *power people perceive as legitimate rather than coercive.*

The way a society generates authority depends, in turn, on its economy. According to Max Weber, preindustrial societies rely on *traditional authority*, power legitimized by respect for long-established cultural patterns. Once woven into a society's collective memory, *traditional authority* may seem almost sacred. The might of Chinese emperors in antiquity rested on tradition, as did the rule of nobles in medieval Europe.

Traditional authority declines as societies industrialize. Royal families still preside ceremonially in several European societies, but a more democratic culture has shifted power to commoners elected to office. Yet, Weber observed that the expansion of rational bureaucracy enhances another, distinctly modern path to legitimizing power. *Rational-legal authority* (sometimes called *bureaucratic authority*), said Weber, is power legitimated by legally enacted rules and regulations.

Rationally enacted rules underlie most authority in the United States today. Political leaders draw their authority from offices in vast governmental organizations. Compared to traditional authority, rational-legal authority flows not from family background but from organizational position. Thus while a traditional monarch rules for life, a modern president accepts and relinquishes power according to law, with presidential authority residing in the office rather than the individual.

Weber described one additional type of authority that has surfaced throughout history. Chapter 12 ("Family and Religion") explores *charisma*, exceptional personal qualities that play a key role in many religious movements. *Charismatic authority*, then, is power legitimated by the extraordinary personal qualities of an individual leader. Unlike its traditional and rational-legal counterparts, charismatic authority depends less on a person's ancestry or office and more on the force of individual personality. Followers are drawn to a charismatic leader with special magnetism, believing that person to be imbued with divine power. Charisma characterized leaders as different as Jesus of Nazareth, Adolf Hitler, and Mahatma Gandhi. But all charismatics share a desire to transform the existing social order, which, of course, makes them highly controversial.

Because charismatic authority emanates from a single individual, any charismatic regime faces a crisis of survival upon the death of its leader. The persistence of a charismatic movement, Max Weber explained, depends on the **routinization of charisma,** *the transformation of charismatic authority into some combination of traditional and bureaucratic authority.* Initially, the personal charisma of Jesus of Nazareth, for example, gave momentum to Christianity. After the death of Jesus, followers institutionalized his teachings, and the Christian church, eventually centered in Rome, was built into a massive institution based on tradition and bureaucracy. The Roman Catholic church still flourishes today, two thousand years later.

Global Political Systems

Government refers to *a formal organization that directs the political life of a nation.* The governments of the world's 191 nations differ in countless ways. Yet

A majority of the world's poor societies do not accord extensive rights and liberties to their citizens, and many undergo continuous political turmoil. The people of Haiti, which is among the poorest countries in the Western Hemisphere, elected Jean-Bertrand Aristide, a popular activist priest, as their president in 1990. Aristide soon found himself at odds with Haiti's business and military elites and, amid escalating tensions, was deposed less than one year after taking office. Haiti remains a long way from political stability.

virtually all bear a close resemblance to one of four political systems.

Monarchy

Monarchy (with Latin and Greek roots mean "ruling alone") is *a type of political system that transfers power from generation to generation within a single family.* Monarchy dates back to earliest human history: The Bible, for example, tells of great kings such as David and his son Solomon; similarly, British monarchs trace their ancestry through centuries of nobility. In terms of Weber's analysis, monarchy is legitimated by tradition.

During the medieval era, *absolute monarchy,* in which hereditary rulers claimed a virtual monopoly of power based on divine right, flourished from England to China and in parts of the Americas. Monarchs in some nations—including Saudi Arabia—still exercise virtually absolute control over their people.

During this century, however, elected officials have gradually replaced hereditary nobility. In those European societies where royal families remain—including Great Britain, Spain, Norway, Sweden, Belgium, Denmark, and the Netherlands—they now preside over *constitutional monarchies,* in which monarchs are little more than symbolic heads of state. Actual governing is the responsibility of elected officials, led by a prime minister, and guided by a constitution. In these countries, the nobility may reign, but elected officials actually rule (Roskin, 1982).

Democracy

The historical trend in the modern world has favored **democracy,** *a political system giving power to the people as a whole.* Members of democratic societies rarely participate directly in decision making; numbers alone make this an impossibility. Instead, a system of *representative democracy* places authority in the hands of elected leaders who are accountable to the people.

Industrialization and democratic government go together because both depend on a literate populace who turn away from traditions. Additionally, in every industrial society, corporations and other formal organizations have a say in political outcomes. Thus, in modern democratic societies, power is not as concentrated as it was in feudal monarchies.

The traditional legitimization of power in a monarchy gives way in democratic political systems to rational-legal authority. Elections place leaders in offices regulated by law. Even so, the vast majority of the 19 million people who operate federal, state, and local governments in the United States are not elected leaders but bureaucrats. Thus, much decision making in nominally democratic societies is actually performed in an undemocratic way (Scaff, 1981; Edwards, 1985; Etzioni-Halevy, 1985).

Economic systems and "freedom." Despite their differences, virtually all industrialized nations in the world claim to be democratic and politically free. Capitalist countries, including the United States, Canada, and the nations of Western Europe, grant individuals a high level of personal freedom to pursue their self-interest. The capitalist approach to political freedom, in short, means personal *liberty.* On the down side, capitalist liberty translates into some people being far more "free" than others because of a striking inequality of wealth.

In socialist nations, by contrast, political officials closely regulate social life in order to provide every citizen with a job, housing, schooling, and medical care. The socialist approach thus emphasizes not *freedom to act* but *freedom from want.* The problem here, as recent uprisings in Eastern Europe and the former Soviet Union revealed, is that such governments typically tolerate low standards of living and generally prohibit any form of political opposition.

Change in much of the socialist world has led to an expansion of Western-style freedoms. Global Map 11–3 shows that by 1991, an unprecedented share of the world's people had sufficient political rights and civil liberties to be called "free," at least in the capitalist sense.

Authoritarianism

Despite the trend toward democracy in most parts of the world, not all nations give their people a say in politics. **Authoritarianism** refers to *a political system that denies popular participation in government.* Authoritarian systems are indifferent to people's lives and offer neither free elections nor the legal means to remove leaders from office. The absolute monarchies that rule Saudi Arabia and Kuwait are highly authoritarian, as are the military juntas in Congo, Ethiopia, and Haiti. A recent and interesting development, detailed in the box, is a form of "soft authoritarianism" that now thrives in the small Asian nation of Singapore.

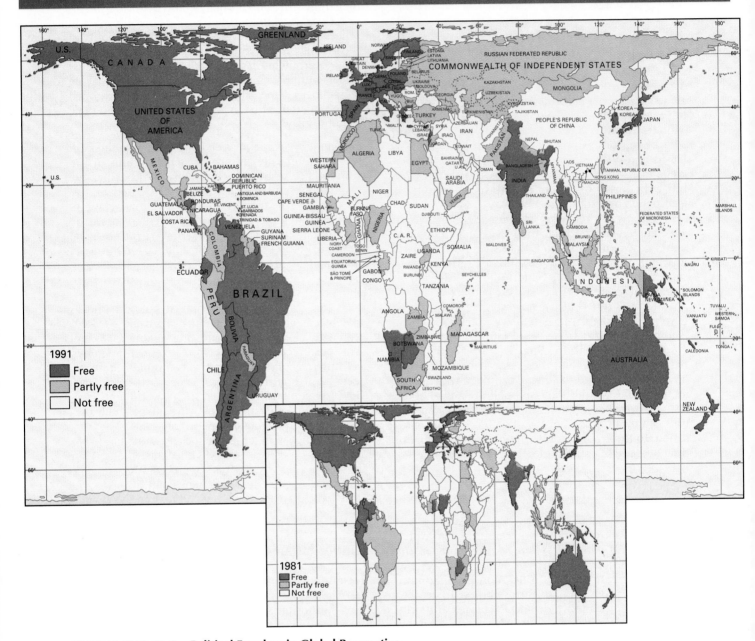

GLOBAL MAP 11–3 **Political Freedom in Global Perspective**

In 1991, seventy-five of the world's nations, containing almost 40 percent of all people, were politically "free"—that is, they offered their citizens extensive political rights and civil liberties. Another seventy-three nations that included almost 30 percent of the world's people were "partly free," with more limited rights and liberties. The remaining forty-two nations, with about one-third of humanity, fall into the category of "not free." In these countries government sharply restricts individual initiative. Comparing the two maps shows that, during the 1980s, democratic gains were made in Eastern Europe, the former Soviet Union, and South America. Political liberties are most extensive in the rich nations of the world and most restricted in the poorer countries of Africa and Asia.

Source: McColm et al. (1991).

"Soft Authoritarianism" or Planned Prosperity? A Report From Singapore

Singapore

Singapore, a tiny nation on the tip of Asia's Malay Peninsula with a population of about 3 million people, looks at first glance like a slice of paradise. Surrounded by poor societies that grapple with squalid, sprawling cities and rising crime rates, the cleanliness and tranquility of Singapore make the North American visitor think more of a theme park than a country.

In fact, since its independence from Malaysia in 1965, Singapore[1] has startled the world with its breakneck economic development; today, its per capita income rivals that of the United States. But, unlike the United States, Singapore has never struggled with social problems such as crime, slums, unemployment, or children living in poverty. In fact, people in Singapore don't have to fume about traffic jams, scowl at graffiti on subway cars, or dodge litter in the streets.

The key to Singapore's orderly environment is the omnipresence of government, which regulates just about everything. The state owns and manages most of the country's housing and has a hand in many businesses. It provides tax incentives for family planning and completing

[1]Singapore is one of the four rapidly developing "Little Dragons" of Asia, along with South Korea, Hong Kong, and Taiwan.

additional years of schooling. To keep traffic under control, the government slaps hefty surcharges on cars, pushing the price of a basic sedan up around $40,000.

Singapore made headlines in the United States in 1994 after the government punished U.S. citizen Michael Fay for vandalism by caning—a penalty illegal in the United States. Singapore's laws permit police to detain a person suspected of a crime without charge or trial. The government bans pornography outright. Even smoking in public brings a heavy fine, and drug offenders face death by hanging. To keep the city streets clean, the state forbids eating on a subway, imposes stiff fines for littering, and has even outlawed the sale of chewing gum.

In economic terms, Singapore defies familiar categories. As in

socialist societies, the government retains control of scores of businesses, from television stations to the telephone service, from airlines to taxis. Yet, unlike socialist enterprises, these businesses are highly efficient and extremely profitable. Moreover, Singapore's capitalist culture celebrates the relentless pursuit of wealth, and this nation is home to hundreds of multinational corporations.

Singapore's political climate is as unusual as its economy. A single political organization—the People's Action Party—has ruled Singapore without opposition since the nation's independence thirty years ago.

Clearly, Singapore is not a democratic country. But most people in this prospering nation seem content—even enthusiastic—about their lives. What Singapore's political system offers is a simple bargain: Government operates diligently to maintain public order and prosperity; in return, it demands unflinching loyalty. Critics charge that this amounts to a "soft authoritarianism" that stifles dissent and gives government unwarranted control over people's lives. Most of the citizens of Singapore, however, know the struggles of living elsewhere and, for now at least, consider the tradeoff a good one.

Source: Adapted from Branegan (1993).

Totalitarianism

The most intensely controlled political form is **totalitarianism,** *a highly centralized political system that extensively regulates people's lives.* Totalitarian government depends on communications technology that permits officials to rigidly regulate people's lives; thus, it is a creation of this century. The Nazi regime in

Germany, finally crushed at the end of World War II, was able to maintain extensive surveillance and terror. More recently, information technology—especially computers—has increased the potential for government manipulation of a large population.

Although some totalitarian governments claim to represent the will of the people, most seek to bend people to the will of the government. Such governments

The concept of political liberty burned brightly in the minds of many European thinkers during the eighteenth and nineteenth centuries; authoritarian regimes were often just as intent on stamping out dissent. In *The Third of May, 1808*, the Spanish painter Francisco Goya (1746–1828) commemorated the death of Madrid citizens at the hands of the faceless soldiers. The martyrs shown here are dying not for religious salvation, as is depicted in so much medieval art, but for the modern principle of political freedom.

constitute *total* concentrations of power, allowing no organized political opposition. Denying the populace the right to assemble for political purposes, these governments also limit the access of citizens to information: The former Soviet government, for example, restricted public access to telephone directories, copying machines, fax machines, even city maps.

Socialization in totalitarian societies puts political ideology at center stage, pressing not just for outward compliance but for inward commitment to the system. In North Korea, one of the most totalitarian states in the world, pictures of leaders and political messages blaring over loudspeakers are virtually everywhere reminding citizens at every turn that they owe total support to the state. Government also controls all the mass media, presenting only official versions of events (Arendt, 1958; Kornhauser, 1959; Friedrich & Brzezinski, 1965; Nisbet, 1966; Goldfarb, 1989).

Totalitarian governments span the political spectrum from the far right (including Nazi Germany) to the far left (such as North Korea). Many people in the United States view socialist societies as totalitarian by definition, because of their extensive government regulation of the economy. Democratic socialist systems, like Sweden's, however, do not generate a totalitarian political climate. Then, too, some societies with capitalist economies (Chile and South Africa, for example) have exercised totalitarian control over the lives of at least most of their citizens in recent years.

A Global Political System?

We have already noted the emergence of a global economy; are we forging a parallel global political system as well? At one level, the answer is no. Although most of the world's economic activity now crosses national borders, the planet remains divided into nation-states just as it has been for centuries. The United Nations, founded in 1945, may seem like a step toward global government, but it has played only a limited role in global politics up to this point.

At another level, however, politics has gone global. Some analysts contend that multinational corporations represent a new political order, since they have enormous power to shape social life throughout the world. From this standpoint, politics is dissolving into business as corporations grow larger than governments. As one multinational leader asserted, "We are not without cunning. We shall not make Britain's mistake. Too wise to govern the world, we shall simply own it" (cited in Vaughan, 1978:20).

Then, too, the Information Revolution has created a global audience for political events. Satellite transmission systems and even home fax machines mean that few countries can conduct their political affairs "in private." In short, just as nations are losing control of their own economies to multinational corporate conglomerates, so they can no longer fully manage the political events that occur within their boundaries.

In 1994, a Republican sweep of Congressional elections signalled a national desire to reduce the scope—and expense—of the federal government.

Politics in the United States

After fighting a revolutionary war against Great Britain to gain political independence, the United States replaced the British monarchy with a democratic political system. Our nation's commitment to democratic principles has persisted through two centuries, shaped by a distinctive history, geography, economy, and cultural heritage.

The Growth of Government

Our cultural emphasis on individualism is written into the Bill of Rights (the first ten amendments to the U.S. Constitution), which guarantees freedom from undue government interference. Many people in the United States, no doubt, share the sentiment of nineteenth-century philosopher and poet Ralph Waldo Emerson: "The government that governs best is the government that governs least."

Yet few of us would do away with government entirely because almost everyone thinks it is necessary for some purposes, including maintaining national defense, a system of schools, and public law and order. In fact, as the United States has become larger, government has expanded even faster, from an annual federal budget of $4.5 million in 1789 ($1.50 per person) to well over $1.5 trillion ($6,000 per person) in 1994. In terms of numbers, from one government employee serving every eighteen hundred citizens at the nation's

founding, today we have one official for every thirteen citizens, counting government at all levels (U.S. Bureau of the Census, 1994). This amounts to 19 million people, a number that now exceeds the U.S. labor force in manufacturing. These bureaucrats manage schools, monitor civil rights, set safety standards that protect consumers and workers, run programs that benefit students, veterans, and the elderly, and oversee our vast system of national defense. Just as important, a majority of U.S. adults depend on government for at least part of their income (Caplow et al., 1982; Devine, 1985).

The Political Spectrum

Political labels—including "conservative," "liberal," and "middle-of-the-roader"—are shorthand for an individual's attitudes on the *political spectrum*, ranging from extreme liberalism on the left to extreme conservatism on the right.

One cluster of attitudes concerns *economic issues*. Economic liberals support extensive government regulation of the economy with the goal of reducing disparities in income and wealth. Economic conservatives press for limits on government control of the economy and freer reign for market forces.

Social issues are moral questions ranging from abortion and the death penalty to gay rights and treatment of minorities. Social liberals endorse equal rights and opportunities for all categories of people, view abortion as a matter of individual choice, and oppose the death penalty because it has been unfairly applied to minorities. The "family values" agenda of social conservatives promotes traditional gender roles, while opposing gay rights, affirmative action, and other "special programs" for minorities. Social conservatives condemn abortion as morally wrong and call for the death penalty as a response to heinous crimes.

Of the two major political parties in the United States, the Republican Party is more conservative on both economic and social issues while the Democratic Party is more liberal. But most individuals do not voice consistently conservative or liberal views. With wealth

One good indication of the steadily increasing size of government in the United States is the rising tide of paperwork completed by businesses. These workers in one company stand alongside copies of government forms they have completed in just one year.

to protect, well-to-do people generally hold conservative views on economic issues. Yet their extensive schooling and secure social standing encourage them to be social liberals. Individuals of low social position exhibit the opposite pattern, tending toward liberal views on economic policy and embracing a socially conservative agenda (Nunn, Crockett, & Williams, 1978; Erikson, Luttbeg, & Tedin, 1980; Syzmanski, 1983; Humphries, 1984). African Americans, regardless of social standing, take more liberal positions (especially on economic issues) and, for half a century, have voted Democratic. Historically, Latinos and Jews have also formed bastions of support for the Democratic Party. Asian Americans, by contrast, stand out as the only minority to vote Republican in the 1992 presidential election.

Because many people hold mixed political attitudes—espousing liberal views on some issues and conservative stands on others—party identification is weak in the United States. Table 11–1 shows the results of a national survey of party identification among U.S. adults. About 46 percent identified themselves—to some degree—as Democrats and about 40 percent favored the Republicans. Thirteen percent claimed to be independents, voicing no preference for either major party. Although more than eight in ten have a preference, however, most are not strongly committed to their party. In 1994, for example, the Republicans gained control of Congress buoyed by the support of millions of people who had voted Democratic just two years earlier.

Special-Interest Groups

In 1993, President Bill Clinton repealed the luxury tax on expensive boats. The boating industry, which had complained that this regulation was choking their business, applauded loudly.

The boating industry, as well as associations of elderly people, women's organizations, and environmentalists, each exemplify a *special-interest group* with an interest in some economic or social issue. Special-interest groups flourish in societies where political parties are weak, and the United States encompasses a vast array of them. Many special-interest groups employ *lobbyists* as their professional advocates in political circles.

Political action committees (PACs), formed by special-interest groups, raise and spend money to advance political aims. Political action committees channel most of their funds directly to candidates likely to bolster their interests. Since the 1970s, the number of

PACs has grown rapidly to more than four thousand (U.S. Bureau of the Census, 1994).

Because of the rising costs of campaigns, most candidates eagerly accept financial contributions from political action committees. In the 1992 congressional elections, 27 percent of all funding came from PACs and two-thirds of all senators seeking reelection received at least $1 million each in PAC contributions. Supporters maintain that PACs represent the interests of a vast array of businesses, unions, and church groups, thereby increasing political participation. Critics claim that organizations supplying cash to politicians expect to be treated favorably in return so that, in effect, PACs are buying political influence (Sabato, 1984; Allen & Broyles, 1991; Cook, 1993).

Voter Apathy

In light of the courageous drive of people around the world to gain a greater voice in government—sometimes at the cost of their very lives—why do so many people here in the United States seem indifferent to voting at all? In fact, U.S. citizens are less likely to cast ballots today than they were a century ago. Even with a slight uptick in turnout, only 60 percent of U.S. adults claim to have voted in the 1992 presidential election.

Who is and is not likely to vote? Women and men are equally likely to cast a ballot. People over sixty-five are twice as likely to vote as young adults. Voting is also higher among white people (64 percent voted in the 1992 presidential election) than African Americans (59 percent), with Hispanics (32 percent) the least likely of all to vote (U.S. Bureau of the Census, 1993).

What accounts for voter apathy? First, at any given time, millions of people are sick or disabled; millions more are away from home having made no arrangement to submit an absentee ballot. Second, many people forget to re-register after moving from one election district to another. Third, registration and voting require the ability to read and write, which discourages the tens of millions of people with limited literacy skills.

But the main cause of voter apathy, as conservatives see it, is *indifference* to politics, suggesting that people are by and large content with life in the United States. Liberals, and especially political radicals, counter that many people are so deeply dissatisfied with society that they doubt elections will make any real difference; thus, from this perspective, voter apathy signifies political *alienation*. There is, no doubt,

TABLE 11-1 Political Party Identification in the United States, 1993

Party Identification	Proportion of Respondents
Democrat	45.9%
Strong Democrat	14.1
Not very strong Democrat	20.0
Independent, close to Democrat	11.8
Republican	39.6
Strong Republican	11.2
Not very strong Republican	18.6
Independent, close to Republican	9.8
Independent	12.8
Other party, no response	1.6

Source: *General Social Surveys, 1972–1993: Cumulative Codebook* (Chicago: National Opinion Research Center, 1993), p. 104.

some truth to each view. A final possibility is that apathy stems from how little the two major parties differ from one another. If the parties represented a wider spectrum of political opinion—as in European countries—our population might have more reason to vote (Zipp & Smith, 1982; Zipp, 1985; Piven & Cloward, 1988).

Theoretical Analysis of Politics

Sociologists have long debated how power is distributed in the United States. Power is one of the most difficult topics of scientific research because decision making is complex and often occurs behind closed doors. Moreover, theories about power are hard to separate from the political beliefs of social thinkers themselves. From this mix of facts and values, two competing models of power in the United States have emerged.

The Pluralist Model: Structural-Functional Analysis

Formally, the **pluralist model** is *an analysis of politics that views power as dispersed among many competing interest groups.* Pluralists claim, first, that politics is an arena of negotiation. With limited resources, no organization can expect to achieve all its goals. Organizations, therefore, operate as *veto groups* realizing some objectives but mostly keeping opponents from achieving all of their ends. The political process, then, relies heavily on forging alliances and compromises that bridge differences among various interest groups so that policies reflect consensus (Dahl, 1961, 1982).

African-American artist Thomas Waterman Wood painted *American Citizens (To the Polls)* in 1876 to acclaim the new right of black men to vote. We see an affluent Yankee, a working-class Irishman, a Dutch transportation worker, and an African American, whose clothing provides little clue as to his occupation or his social standing. Despite differences of class, ethnicity, and race, in other words, Wood was optimistic that our political system would forge a representative, democratic government.

Supporting the pluralists' vision of society, Nelson Polsby (1959) found in a study of New Haven, Connecticut, that key decisions involving urban renewal, selecting political candidates, and running the city's schools were made by different groups. Polsby concluded that no one group—not even members of the New Haven upper class—were always able to get their way.

The pluralist model implies that the United States is reasonably democratic, granting at least some power to everyone. From this point of view, even disadvantaged people are able to band together to ensure that government addresses some of their political interests.

The Power-Elite Model: Social-Conflict Analysis

The **power-elite model** is *an analysis of politics that views power as concentrated among the rich.* The term *power elite* was coined by C. Wright Mills (1956), who argued that the upper class holds the bulk of society's wealth, prestige, and power.

Through business and marital alliances, Mills contended, the "super-rich" are able to dominate the three major sectors of U.S. society—the economy, the government, and the military. Elites circulate from one sector to another, Mills continued, consolidating power as they go. Alexander Haig, for example, has held top positions in private business, was secretary of state under Ronald Reagan as well as a 1988 presidential candidate, and is a retired army general. Most political leaders, in fact, enter public life from highly paid positions in private business, and most return to the corporate world later on (Brownstein & Easton, 1983).

Power-elite theorists challenge claims that the United States is a democracy; the concentration of

wealth and power, they maintain, is simply too great for the average person's voice to be heard. Rejecting pluralist assertions that competing centers of power serve as checks and balances on one another, the power-elite model holds that those at the top encounter no real opposition.

Making the case for the power-elite position, Robert and Helen Lynd (1937) studied Muncie, Indiana, and documented the fortune amassed by one family—the Balls—from their business producing glass canning jars. The Lynds showed how the Ball family dominated many dimensions of the city's life. If anyone doubted the Balls' prominence, the Lynds explained, there was no need to look further than a local bank, a university, a hospital, and a department store, which all bear the family's name. In Muncie, according to the Lynds, the power elite more or less boiled down to a single family.

Critical evaluation. While these two models of power, summarized in Table 11–2, paint quite different pictures of U.S. politics, some evidence does bolster each interpretation. Reviewing all the research on this issue, however, we find greater support for the power-elite model. Even Robert Dahl (1982)—one of the stalwart advocates of the concept of pluralism—concedes that the marked concentration of wealth, as well as the barriers to equal opportunity faced by minorities, constitute basic flaws in our nation's drive toward a truly pluralist democracy.

Do these flaws mean that the pluralist model is entirely wrong? No, but they do suggest that our political system is not as democratic as most people think it is. The right to vote and to form political organizations are pluralist achievements; yet major candidates usually come out in favor of positions acceptable to the most powerful segments of society (Bachrach & Baratz, 1970).

TABLE 11–2 The Pluralist and Power-Elite Models: A Comparison

	Pluralist Model	Power-Elite Model
How is power distributed in the United States?	Dispersed.	Concentrated.
How many centers of power are there?	Many, each with a limited scope.	Few, interconnected, with broad control over society.
How do centers of power relate to one another?	They represent different political interests and thus provide checks on one another.	They represent the same political interests and face little opposition.
What is the relationship between power and the system of social stratification?	Some people have more power than others, but even minority groups can organize to gain power. Wealth, social prestige, and political office rarely overlap.	Most people have little power, and the upper class dominates society. Wealth, social prestige, and political office regularly overlap.
What is the importance of voting?	Voting provides the public as a whole with a political voice.	Voting involves choosing between alternatives acceptable to elites.
What, then, is the most accurate description of the U.S. political system?	A pluralist democracy.	An oligarchy—rule by the wealthy few.

Power Beyond the Rules

Politics is always a matter of disagreement about a society's goals and the means to achieve them. Yet a political system tries to resolve controversy within a system of rules. But political activity sometimes exceeds—or tries to do away with—established practices.

Political Revolution

Political revolution is *the overthrow of one political system in order to establish another.* In contrast to reform, which involves change *within* a system, revolution implies change *of the system itself.* In the extreme case of reform, one leader overthrows another—a *coup d'état* (in French, literally "blow concerning the state")—making for change only at the top. And while reform rarely escalates into violence, revolution often does. The revolutions in Eastern Europe beginning in 1989 were, on the whole, surprisingly peaceful, although violent upheaval in Romania resulted in thousands of deaths.

No type of political system is immune to revolution; nor does revolution invariably produce any one kind of government. The U.S. Revolution transformed colonial rule by the British monarchy into democratic government. French revolutionaries in 1789 also overthrew a monarch, only to set the stage for the return of monarchy in the person of Napoleon Bonaparte. In 1917, the Russian Revolution replaced monarchy with a socialist government built on the ideas of Karl Marx. In 1992, the Soviet Union formally came to an end, as revolutionary change propelled the new Commonwealth toward a market system and greater political democracy.

Despite their striking variety, claim analysts, revolutions share a number of traits (Tocqueville, 1955, orig. 1856; Davies, 1962; Brinton, 1965; Skocpol, 1979; Lewis, 1984).

1. **Rising expectations.** Although common sense tells us that revolution should be more likely when people are grossly deprived, history shows that revolutions generally occur when people's lives are improving. Rising expectations, rather than bitter resignation, fuel revolutionary fervor.

2. **Unresponsive government.** Revolutionary zeal gains strength to the extent that a government is unable or unwilling to reform, especially when such demands are made by powerful segments of society (Tilly, 1986).

3. **Radical leadership by intellectuals.** The English philosopher Thomas Hobbes (1588–1679) observed that intellectuals often make the case for revolution; ever since, universities have been at

leaders are installed. Revolutionaries must also guard against counter-revolutionary drives led by past leaders. This explains the speed and ruthlessness with which victorious revolutionaries typically dispose of their predecessors.

Scientific research cannot pronounce the effects of revolution as good or bad. The consequences of such upheaval depend on one's values and, in any case, cannot be fully assessed until many years have passed. In the wake of its recent revolution, for example, who can predict with certainty the future of the former Soviet Union?

Terrorism

Terrorism is *violence or the threat of violence employed by an individual or group as a political strategy.* Like revolution, terrorism is a political act beyond the rules of established political systems. Paul Johnson (1981) offers three insights about terrorism.

First, terrorism tries to paint violence as a legitimate political tactic, ignoring the fact that such acts are condemned by virtually every society. Terrorists also bypass (or are excluded from) established channels of political negotiation. Terrorism, therefore, serves as a weak organization's strategy to harm a stronger foe. The people who held U.S. hostages in the Middle East until 1991 may have been morally wrong to do so, but they succeeded in focusing the world's attention on that region of the globe.

Second, terrorism is employed not just by groups but also by governments against their own people. *State terrorism* is the use of violence, usually without support of law, by government officials. While contrary to democratic political principles, state terrorism is lawful in some authoritarian and totalitarian states, which rule through a combination of fear and intimidation. Saddam Hussein, for example, has built his government in Iraq on the use of terror to suppress those who oppose him.

Third, although democratic principles oppose state terrorism, democracies are especially vulnerable to terrorism because these governments afford extensive civil liberties to their people and have limited police networks. In striking contrast, totalitarian regimes make widespread use of state terrorism, yet their immense police power minimizes opportunities for individual acts of terror.

Hostage-taking and outright killing provoke widespread anger, but devising an effective response to

Because of highly publicized acts of violence against U.S. citizens by Middle Eastern people in recent years, some members of our society tend to link Islam with terrorism. More correctly, however, this religion (like Christianity) seeks harmony and justice. Officials in Egypt have countered a recent wave of terrorism by a few religious extremists by reminding citizens (and outsiders) of their religious responsibility to promote peace.

the center of such change. Students played a key role in China's recent pro-democracy movement, as they did in Eastern Europe.

4. **Establishing a new legitimacy.** The overthrow of a political system rarely comes easily, but more difficult still is ensuring a revolution's long-term success. Some revolutionary movements are unified merely by hatred of the past regime, and may fall victim to internal division once new

such acts challenges democratic societies. The immediate concern is identifying those responsible. Because terrorist groups are often shadowy organizations with no formal connection to any established state, targeting reprisals may be impossible. Yet, terrorism expert Brian Jenkins warns, the failure to respond "encourages other terrorist groups, who begin to realize that this can be a pretty cheap way to wage war on the United States" (cited in Whitaker, 1985:29). Then, too, a forcible military reaction to terrorism may broaden the scope of violence, increasing the risk of confrontation with other governments.

Finally, terrorism is always a matter of definitions. Governments claim the right to maintain order, even by force, and may brand opponents who use violence as "terrorists." In the process, however, one person's "terrorist" may be another's "freedom fighter."

War and Peace

Perhaps the most critical political issue is **war,** *armed conflict among the people of various countries, directed by their governments.* While war is as old as humanity, understanding it now takes on greater urgency. Because we possess the technological capacity to destroy ourselves, war poses unprecedented danger to the entire planet. Most scholarly investigation of war looks toward promoting peace, meaning the absence of war (but not necessarily all conflict).

Many people think of war as extraordinary, yet for almost all of this century wars were ongoing in at least some part of the globe. In our nation's short history, we have participated in ten significant wars, which, as shown in Figure 11–3, resulted in the deaths of more than 1.3 million men and women and caused injury to many times that number. Thousands more died in "undeclared wars" and limited military actions, in countries from the Dominican Republic to Lebanon, Grenada, and Panama.

The Causes of War

Considering the frequency of war in human affairs, we might suspect that there is something "natural" about armed confrontations. But while many animals are naturally aggressive (Lorenz, 1966), research provides no evidence that human beings inevitably go to war under any particular circumstances. As Ashley Montagu (1976) observes, governments around the

world must resort to considerable coercion in order to mobilize their people for wars.

Like other forms of social behavior, warfare is a product of *society* that varies in purpose and intensity from place to place. The Semai of Malaysia, among the most peace-loving of the world's peoples, rarely resort to violence. In contrast, the Yąnomamö, described at the beginning of Chapter 2 ("Culture"), are quick to wage war with others.

If society holds the key to war or peace, under what circumstances *do* humans engage in warfare? Quincy Wright (1987) cites five factors that promote war.

1. **Perceived threats.** Societies mobilize in response to a perceived threat to their people, territory, or culture. The likelihood of armed conflict with the former Soviet Union, for example, has subsided to the extent that our nation now defines that country as more friendly toward us.

2. **Social problems.** Internal problems that cause widespread frustration prompt a society's leaders to become aggressive toward others as a form of scapegoating. The lack of economic development in the People's Republic of China, for example, sparked that nation's hostility toward Vietnam, Tibet, and the former Soviet Union.

3. **Political objectives.** Leaders sometimes settle on war as a desirable political strategy. Poor nations,

FIGURE 11–3   Deaths of Americans in Ten U.S. Wars

Sources: Compiled from various sources by Maris A. Vinovskis (1989) and the author.

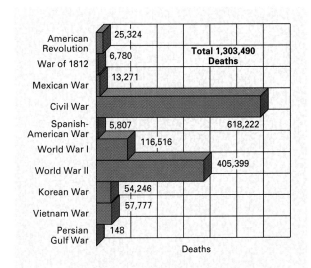

Violence Beyond the Rules: A Report From the Former Yugoslavia

Former
Yugoslavia

War is violent, but it also has rules. Many of the current rules of warfare emerged from the ashes of World War II, when the victorious Allies, including the United States, brought to trial German and Japanese military officials for war crimes. Subsequently, the United Nations added to the broad principles of fair play in war that have become known as the "Geneva Conventions" (which date back to 1864).

One of the most important principles of the rules of war is that, whatever violence soldiers inflict upon each other, they cannot imprison, torture, rape, or murder civilians; nor can they deliberately destroy civilian property or wantonly bomb or shell cities to foster widespread terror.

A growing body of evidence suggests that all these crimes have occurred as part of the protracted and bloody civil war in the former Yugoslavia. Serbs, Croats, and Muslims, according to the United States, have committed war crimes, which have involved tens of thousands of deaths, rapes, and serious

Civil wars, such as the conflict in the former Yugoslavia, are among the most tragic forms of bloodshed because a large proportion of casualties are not soldiers but civilians who find themselves in harm's way. Dozens of people died on this street in Sarajevo as mortar rounds fired from the mountains surrounding the city rained down on men, women, and children who were going about their daily lives.

injuries and an incalculable loss of property. Late in 1993, therefore, a United Nations tribunal convened in the Netherlands to assess the evidence and consider possible responses.

After World War II, the Allies were able to successfully prosecute (and, in several cases, execute) German officers for their crimes against humanity based on evidence obtained from extensive Nazi records. This time around, however, the task of punishing offenders will be far more difficult. For one thing, there appear to be no written records of the Yugoslav conflict, so that many allegations stand with little or no proof and not one alleged war criminal is in United Nations custody.

The United Nations has decided not to try war criminals *in absentia.* Thus, the investigation will continue, but most observers suspect that no one will ever be convicted of war crimes in this tragic situation.

Sources: Adapted from Nelan (1993) and various news reports.

such as Vietnam, have fought wars to end foreign domination. Powerful countries like the United States may periodically make a "show of force" (such as sending troops to the eastern African country of Somalia in 1993) to enhance their global political stature.

4. **Moral objectives.** Nations rarely claim to fight simply to increase their wealth and power. They infuse military campaigns with moral urgency, rallying around visions of "freedom" or the "fatherland." Although few doubted that the Persian Gulf War was largely about *oil*, the United States

portrayed the mission as a drive to halt a Hitler-like Saddam Hussein.

5. **The absence of alternatives.** A fifth factor promoting war is the lack of alternatives. As previously noted, the ability of the United Nations to resolve tensions among self-interested countries has been limited.

In short, war is rooted in the operation of society. Moreover, war is also a form of social organization subject to its own system of rules. The box takes a look at situations in which combatants act violently, contravening the norms of war—behavior termed *war crimes.*

Militarism and the Arms Race

The costs of warfare extend far beyond battlefield casualties. Together, the world's nations spend some $5 billion annually on militarism. While such expenditures, at least in part, may be justifiable, they divert resources from the desperate struggle for survival by millions of poor people throughout the world. Assuming the will and the political wisdom of doing so, there is little doubt that the resources currently spent on militarism could be used to greatly reduce global poverty.

In recent years, defense has long been the largest single expenditure by the U.S. government, accounting for 19 percent of spending, or $280 billion, in 1994. The reason for such sums—$1,085 for every man, woman, and child in the country—is the *arms race*, a mutually reinforcing escalation of military power, between the United States and the former Soviet Union.

Some analysts claim that the United States is dominated by a **military-industrial complex,** *a close association among government, the military, and defense industries.* From this point of view, the U.S. economy has become dependent on military spending as a source of jobs and corporate profits (Marullo, 1987). Even so, in response to the dissolution of the Soviet Union, the U.S. government has made significant reductions in military spending. How deep these cuts will continue to be—given the ongoing need for national security and the economic pressure by some special-interest groups to keep military spending high—will remain a pressing issue for some time to come.

Nuclear Weapons and War

Almost twenty-five thousand nuclear warheads are deployed around the world, representing a destructive power equivalent to five tons of TNT for every person on the planet. Should even a small fraction of this arsenal be consumed in war, life as we know it might cease on much of the earth. Albert Einstein, whose genius contributed to the development of nuclear weapons, reflected: "The unleashed power of the atom has changed everything *save our modes of thinking,* and we thus drift toward unparalleled catastrophe." In short, nuclear weapons have rendered unrestrained war unthinkable in a world not yet capable of peace.

At present, although Great Britain, France, and the People's Republic of China also have a substantial nuclear capability, the vast majority of nuclear weapons are held by the United States and Russia. These two nations have agreed to further cuts in their stockpiles over the next decade. But even as the superpower rivalry has diminished, the danger of catastrophic war has escalated as a result of *nuclear proliferation*, the acquisition of nuclear weapons by more and more nations. Most experts agree that Israel, India, Pakistan, and South Africa already possess some nuclear weapons, and other nations (including Argentina, Brazil, Iraq, Libya, and North Korea) are in the process of developing them. By early in the next century, as many as fifty nations could have the capacity to fight a nuclear war. Because many of these countries have longstanding conflicts with their neighbors, nuclear proliferation places the entire world at risk (Spector, 1988).

Social Diversity and the Military

Debate about our country's military does not focus solely on halting nuclear proliferation or curbing the arms race. Policy makers are also addressing barriers that limit opportunity in the military for women and gay people.

Military women. Although women have served in the armed forces even before this country's Revolutionary War, their representation began rising only recently. Today, 12 percent of all military personnel are women. In the 1991 war in the Persian Gulf, 35,000 women represented 6.5 percent of a total deployment of 540,000 U.S. troops. Five of the 148 Gulf War casualties were women.

In the past several years, the armed services have made great strides toward opening their ranks to women. Figure 11–4 shows that the Coast Guard, Air Force, and Navy now open all or almost all jobs to both sexes; the Army and the Marine Corps, however, still limit women's roles.

This gender-based prohibition is most pronounced when it comes to women serving in combat roles. Defenders of this policy argue that, on average, women lack the physical strength of men. Critics respond by pointing out that military women are better educated and score higher on intelligence tests than their male counterparts. The heart of the issue, however, turns on our society's deeply held view of women as *nurturers*—people who give life and help others—which clashes intolerably with the image of women as professional killers.

Still, women are taking on more and more military assignments. Recent policy changes opening more military jobs to women rest on the fact that the technology of war has undermined traditional distinctions between combat and noncombat personnel. For example, a combat pilot may fire missiles at a radar-screen

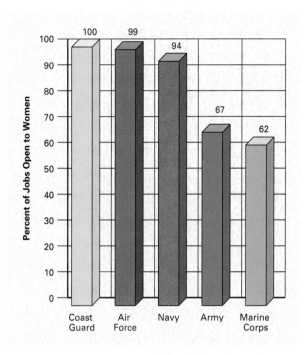

FIGURE 11–4 Proportion of Assignments Open to Women by Branch of Armed Forces

Source: U.S. Department of Defense (1994).

target miles away while nonfighting medical evacuation teams are called on to enter the immediate heat of battle (Stiehm, 1989; McNeil, Jr., 1991; May, 1991; Segal & Hansen, 1992; Wilcox, 1992).

Gays and the military. Until 1993, all military services formally barred homosexual men and women. Nonetheless, tens of thousands of gay people have served their country. In the past, any individual even suspected of having a homosexual orientation was automatically discharged from the military. Roughly one thousand men and women were being expelled annually from the armed forces on such grounds.

Several official reasons underlie this historical policy. First, soldiers live in close quarters with minimal privacy; the presence of homosexuals, the argument goes, puts discipline at risk and may undercut the military's morale and effectiveness. Second, officials worry that soldiers exposed as gay could be blackmailed into compromising military security. More recently, critics of gays in the military cite the danger of spreading the virus that causes AIDS as an additional reason to bar homosexuals from the armed forces.

As in the case of military women, policies relating to gays have more to do with traditional stereotypes than facts. Studies conducted by the military document that gay people have commendable performance records. Furthermore, gay people are not disqualified from civilian jobs that are far more sensitive than those of rank-and-file soldiers.

President Bill Clinton moved to lift the ban on homosexuals in the military in 1992. Military leaders launched a major campaign against this change, resulting in a "Don't ask; don't tell" compromise. According to the new policy, similar to those in place in many European nations, the military does not ask recruits about their sexual orientation, thus allowing gay people to join up. At the same time, however, homosexual behavior—that is, acting on that orientation—remains grounds for dismissal.

In light of this new policy—as well as the "tailhook" scandal involving charges of sexual harassment of women by naval aviators—the military is looking to generate new standards of sexual conduct during the next few years (Davis, 1993; Segal, Gade, & Johnson, 1993).

The Pursuit of Peace

How can the world reduce the dangers of war? Here are brief sketches of several approaches to promoting peace.

1. **Deterrence.** The logic of the arms race has long held that security derives from a balance of terror between the superpowers. During the so-called "cold war," the principle of *mutually assured destruction* (MAD) ensured that either side launching a first strike against the other would sustain massive retaliation. This deterrence policy did keep the peace for forty years; yet it encouraged the arms race and it cannot control nuclear proliferation, which now poses a growing threat to peace.

2. **High-technology defense.** If technology created the weapons, perhaps it can also deliver us from the threat of war. This is the idea behind the *strategic defense initiative* (SDI), proposed by the Reagan administration in 1981. SDI is a complex plan for satellites and ground installations to provide a protective shield or umbrella against enemy attack. Missiles would be detected soon after launch and destroyed by lasers and particle beams before reentering the atmosphere.

But, many analysts claim, "star wars" would produce at best a leaky umbrella. The collapse of the Soviet Union also calls into question the need for such an extensive—and expensive—defense scheme.

3. **Diplomacy and disarmament.** Some analysts conclude that diplomacy rather than technology holds the best chance for peace (Dedrick & Yinger, 1990). Diplomacy has the appeal of achieving security through reducing rather than increasing weapons stockpiles.

   But disarmament has its own dangers. No nation wishes to become vulnerable by reducing its defenses. Successful diplomacy, then, depends not on "soft" concession-making, or "hard" demands, but on all sides sharing responsibility for a common problem (Fisher & Ury, 1988).

4. **Resolving underlying conflict.** In the end, reducing the dangers of war may depend on resolving the conflicts that provoke nations to make war in the first place. Regional conflicts are festering in Latin America, Africa, Asia, the Balkans, and the Middle East. Moreover, with hundreds of millions of people teetering on the brink of absolute poverty, we might wonder why the world spends *three thousand times* as much money on militarism as we allocate for peacekeeping efforts (Sivard, 1988).

Looking Ahead: Politics in the Twenty-First Century

Just as economic systems are changing, so are political systems. As we look ahead to the next century, several important dilemmas and trends are certain to command widespread attention.

One key transformation noted in this chapter is the growth of global politics. Through the Information Revolution, news and political analysis are now broadcast instantly from one point in the world to another. This global flow of information promises to empower individuals, since governments can no longer seal their borders to new ideas. Today anyone with a television or short-wave radio (not to mention fax machines and

Attitudes in the United States toward gay people in the military are mixed. Public opinion polls show that a majority of people support the military's historic ban on gay recruits. At the same time, paradoxically, a majority of people also assert that gay people should have no special exemption from serving their country.

other computer-based devices) has access to an unprecedented amount of political information.

Second, now that the cold war is over, we are moving away from a rigid model of two antithetical political alternatives—the West's market-based capitalism and the East's state-centered socialism. Today, we are seeing a broader range of political systems that integrate economics and politics in novel ways. The "state capitalism" characteristic of Japan and South Korea is but one case in point.

Third, and finally, the danger of war looms large. We must grapple with vast stockpiles of nuclear weapons, and this technology is spreading around the world. New superpowers are likely to arise in the century ahead (the People's Republic of China, for example, seems poised to reach for superpower status), just as surely as regional conflicts will continue to smolder. Even so, humanity can still enlist forces working for peace—including the United Nations, expanding international trade, widespread and rapid communication, and an evolving sense of political justice—in hopes of devising a nonviolent solution to the age-old problems that provoke war.

SUMMARY

Economics

1. The economy is the institutional means by which a society produces, distributes, and consumes goods and services.

2. The primary sector of the economy, which generates raw materials, dominates in preindustrial societies. The secondary, or manufacturing, sector prevails in industrial societies. The tertiary, or service, sector gains primacy in postindustrial societies.

3. Capitalism is based on private ownership of productive property and the pursuit of profit in a competitive marketplace. Socialism is grounded in collective ownership of productive property through government control of the economy.

4. Capitalism is highly productive, providing a high overall standard of living; socialism is typically less productive but generates less economic inequality.

5. Only a small percentage of U.S. workers make their living in agriculture; just one-fourth hold blue-collar occupations; two-thirds have white-collar service jobs.

6. A profession is a special category of white-collar work based on theoretical knowledge, occupational autonomy, and authority over clients, with an emphasis on community service.

7. About 7 percent of U.S. workers are unemployed; young people and minorities are most likely to be without jobs.

8. Women and other minorities are likely to represent 60 percent of all workers in the United States by the year 2005.

9. Corporations are the core of the U.S. economy. Most large corporations now operate in many countries.

Politics

1. Politics is the social institution that distributes power and organizes decision making. Legitimate, rather than coercive, power is based on tradition, rationally enacted rules or regulations, or a leader's personal charisma.

2. Monarchy is common to preindustrial societies; industrialization parallels the development of democracy.

3. Authoritarian political systems deny popular participation in government. Totalitarian political systems go even further, monitoring and controlling people's everyday lives.

4. People's political views fall along a spectrum from the left to the right. Opinions vary on economic issues (such as the degree of government regulation of the economy) and social issues (moral questions about the rights and opportunities of various segments of the population).

5. Interest groups tend to be strong in countries like the United States with weak political parties. Only 60 percent of eligible voters cast ballots in the 1992 U.S. presidential election.

6. The pluralist model views power as widely dispersed; the power-elite model claims that power is concentrated in a small, wealthy segment of our society.

7. Revolution radically transforms a political system. Terrorism employs violence in pursuit of political goals.

8. War is armed conflict between governments. The development of nuclear weapons, and their proliferation, has increased the threat of global catastrophe. Enhancing world peace ultimately depends on resolving the tensions that underlie militarism.

KEY CONCEPTS

Economics

capitalism an economic system in which natural resources and the means of producing goods and services are privately owned

corporation an organization with a legal existence, including rights and liabilities, apart from those of its members

democratic socialism an economic and political system that combines significant government control of the economy with free elections

economy the social institution that organizes a society's production, distribution, and consumption of goods and services

global economy economic activity across national borders

monopoly domination of a market by a single producer

oligopoly domination of a market by a few producers

postindustrial economy a productive system based on service work and high technology

primary sector the part of the economy that generates raw materials directly from the natural environment

profession a prestigious, white-collar occupation that requires extensive formal education

secondary sector the part of the economy that transforms raw materials into manufactured goods

social institution an organized sphere of social life such as the economy or the family

socialism an economic system in which natural resources and the means of producing goods and services are collectively owned

tertiary sector the part of the economy involving services rather than goods

Politics

authoritarianism a political system that denies popular participation in government

authority power that people perceive as legitimate rather than coercive

democracy a type of political system giving power to the people as a whole

government a formal organization that directs the political life of a nation

military-industrial complex a close association among the government, the military, and defense industries

monarchy a type of political system that transfers power from generation to generation within a single family

pluralist model an analysis of politics that views power as dispersed among many competing interest groups

political revolution the overthrow of one political system in order to establish another

politics the social institution that distributes power and makes decisions

power the ability to achieve desired ends despite opposition

power-elite model an analysis of politics that views power as concentrated among the rich

routinization of charisma the transformation of charismatic authority into some combination of traditional and bureaucratic authority

terrorism violence or the threat of violence by an individual or a group as a political strategy

totalitarianism a highly centralized political system that extensively regulates people's lives

war armed conflict among the people of various countries, directed by their governments

CRITICAL-THINKING QUESTIONS

1. What is a social institution? How do economic and political systems affect each other?

2. How did the Industrial Revolution reshape the economy of the United States? How is the Information Revolution transforming the U.S. economy once again?

3. How would you describe the attitudes of the U.S. population on the political spectrum? How do political opinions reflect class position?

4. What sociological factors (1) make war more likely and (2) enhance prospects for peaceful relations among nations?

Chapter

12

Family
and Religion

Verna Terry thought she had found the perfect apartment. But she soon found herself in a complicated legal tangle when John and Agnes Donahue, who own and reside on the Los Angeles property where the apartment was located, discovered that Terry intended to live there with a man to whom she was not married. The Donahues, a very religious couple, are opposed to sex before marriage. To them, renting the property to Verna Terry amounted to helping someone commit the sin of fornication, an immoral situation for all concerned. Terry, on the other hand, felt she was the victim of housing discrimination and filed suit in court against the Donahues.[1]

This case, which is currently wending its way through the court system, illustrates the controversy that surrounds the changing definition of families in the United States. We can see, too, how the current "family values" debate pits some people's rights against others' religious beliefs.

This chapter examines the family and religion, which are closely linked as society's prominent *symbolic institutions*. Through both family and religious life, we establish morality, observe traditions, and bond into durable social units. Not surprisingly, change in these institutions is sparking spirited disagreement. Not long ago, the cultural ideal in the United States was a family made up of a working father, a homemaker mother, and their young children; today, fewer people embrace such a singular vision of the family, and, at any given time, only about one in ten U.S. households fits that description. Similar changes have shaken the foundations of religion in the United States. Membership in most long-established churches is dwindling, while many new sects are flourishing.

With an eye on the United States, and making comparisons to other countries, we will examine why some people maintain that the family and religion are bedrock foundations of social life, while others predict—and some even campaign for—the demise of both institutions.

The Family: Basic Concepts

Kinship refers to *a social bond, based on blood, marriage, or adoption, that joins people into families.* Throughout this century, most members of our society have regarded a **family** as *a relatively permanent group of two or more people, who are related by blood, marriage, or adoption and who usually live together.* Over the life course, the members of a family unit change. Individuals are born into a family composed of parents and siblings (sometimes termed the *family of orientation* since this group is central to socialization); in adulthood, people form a *family of procreation* in order to have or adopt children of their own. In the United States, as elsewhere, families form around **marriage,** *a legally sanctioned relationship, involving economic cooperation as well as normative sexual activity and childbearing, that people expect to be enduring.*

Language offers an insight into our cultural belief that marriage alone is the appropriate setting for procreation: Traditionally, people have attached the label of "illegitimacy" to children born out of wedlock; moreover, "matrimony," in Latin, means "the condition of motherhood." The link between childbearing and marriage is growing weaker, however, as the share of children born to single women (currently about one in four) has increased.

The traditional family, comprising married parents and their children, has been giving way in recent years to all sorts of new family arrangements—from unmarried couples living together, as noted in the chapter opening, to gay couples, and single parents and their children. Some people, especially those calling for a return to "family values," view these new family patterns with concern. But others welcome the proliferation of *families of affinity,* that is, people with or without legal or blood ties who feel they belong together and want to define themselves as a family. These families of affinity reflect a national trend toward a broader, more inclusive definition of "family."

Interestingly, the Census Bureau plays a role in how the concept of "family" is defined. Because Census Bureau officials still use the traditional definition of a family unit, sociologists who rely on Census Bureau data describing "families" must accept this definition.[2]

---

[1]This account is based on Niebuhr (1992).

[2]According to the Census Bureau, there were 96.4 million U.S. households in 1993, of which 68.1 million (71 percent) were family households. The remaining living units contain single people or unrelated people living together. For comparison, in 1960, 85 percent of all households were families.

In modern industrial societies, the members of extended families pursue their careers independently and usually live apart from one another. However, various nuclear families may assemble periodically for rituals such as weddings, funerals, and family reunions.

The Family: Global Variations

Although people the world over recognize families, just who is included under the umbrella of kinship varies from one society to another. Preindustrial societies attach great importance to the **extended family,** *a social unit including parents and children, but also other kin.* This group is also called the *consanguine family,* meaning that it includes everyone with "shared blood."

The onset of industrialization, a process detailed in the previous chapter, shifts work away from the home and gives rise to the **nuclear family,** *a social unit containing one or, more commonly, two adults and any children.* The nuclear family is also called the *conjugal family,* meaning "based on marriage." Although many members of our society live in extended families, the nuclear family has long been the predominant form in the United States.

Marriage Patterns

Cultural norms, and often laws, determine who is (and is not) a suitable marriage partner. Some norms promote **endogamy,** *marriage between people of the same social category.* Endogamy norms constrain marriage prospects to others of the same age, village, race, religion, or social class. Other norms encourage **exogamy,** *marriage between people of different social categories.* In rural India, for example, people expect a person to marry someone from the same caste (endogamy) but from a different village (exogamy). Throughout the world, societies pressure people to marry someone of the same social background but of the other sex.

In every industrial society, laws prescribe a form of marriage called **monogamy** (from the Greek meaning "one union"), *marriage involving two partners.* Global Map 12–1 on page 300 shows that while monogamy is the rule throughout the Americas and in Europe, preindustrial societies—especially in Africa and southern Asia—permit **polygamy** (from Greek meaning "many unions"), *marriage that unites three or more people.*

Polygamy takes two forms. By far the more common is *polygyny* (Greek meaning "many women"), a form of marriage that joins one male with more than one female. Islamic societies in the Middle East and Africa, for example, permit men up to four wives. Even so, most Islamic families are monogamous because few men have the wealth required to support several wives and even more children. *Polyandry* (from the Greek, meaning "many men") unites one female with more than one male. This pattern appears only rarely. One example can be found among Tibetan Buddhists, perhaps because agriculture is difficult in this mountainous region: Polyandry discourages the division of land and divides the support of families among many men. Polyandry also appears in societies that engage in female infanticide—the abortion of female fetuses or the killing of female infants. There, the female population plunges, forcing men to share women.

Looking at the issue historically and globally, the majority of world societies have permitted more than one marital pattern; even so, most marriages have been monogamous (Murdock, 1965). This predominance of monogamy reflects, first, the financial burden of supporting multiple spouses, and, second, the rough numerical parity of the sexes, which limits the possibilities for polygamy.

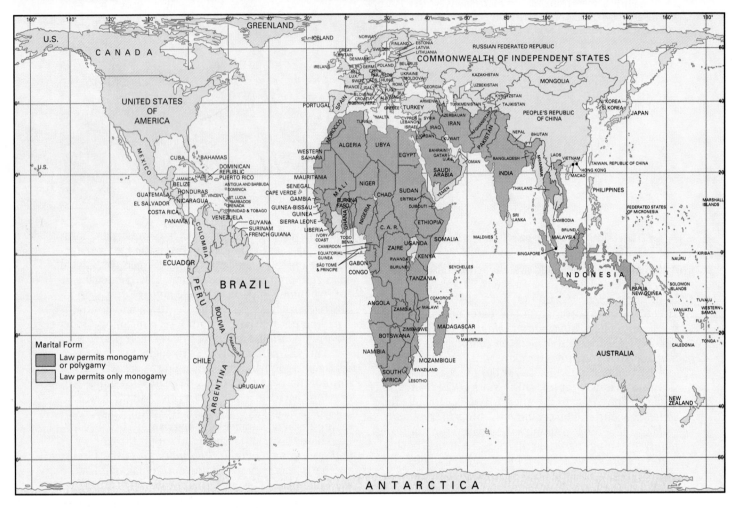

GLOBAL MAP 12–1   Marital Form in Global Perspective

Monogamy is the legally prescribed form of marriage in all industrial societies and throughout
the Western Hemisphere. In most African nations, as well as in southern Asia, however,
polygamy is permitted by law. In the majority of cases, this practice reflects the historic
influence of Islam, a religion that allows a man to have no more than four wives. Even so,
most marriages in these traditional societies are monogamous, primarily for financial reasons.

Source: *Peters Atlas of the World* (1990).

Residential Patterns

Just as societies regulate mate selection, so they designate where a couple resides. In preindustrial societies,
most newlyweds live with one set of parents, gaining
economic assistance and security in the process. Most

such societies have adopted *patrilocality* (Greek for
"place of the father"), which guides a married couple to
live with or near the husband's family. But some
societies (such as the North American Iroquois)
endorse *matrilocality* (meaning "place of the mother"),
so that couples live with or near the wife's family.

A society's inclination toward one variant or the other often corresponds to military and economic patterns. Societies that engage in frequent, local warfare tend toward patrilocality, since families want their sons close to home to offer protection. Societies that engage in distant warfare present a mixed picture, favoring patrilocality or matrilocality depending on whether sons or daughters have greater economic value (Ember & Ember, 1971, 1991).

Industrial societies show yet another pattern. When finances permit, at least, they favor *neolocality* (Greek meaning "new place"), by which a married couple lives apart from the parents of both spouses.

Patterns of Descent

Descent refers to *the system by which members of a society trace kinship over generations*. Most preindustrial societies trace kinship through only one side of the family—the father or the mother. The more prevalent pattern is *patrilineal descent,* meaning people trace their relations through males and pass property from fathers to sons. Patrilineal descent generally characterizes pastoral and agrarian societies, in which men produce the most valued resources. Less common is *matrilineal descent,* by which people define only the mother's side as kin, and daughters inherit property from mothers. Matrilineal descent is found more frequently in horticultural societies where women are the primary food producers (Haviland, 1985).

Industrial societies, with greater gender equality, recognize *bilateral descent* ("two-sided descent"), tracing kinship through both men and women. In this pattern, children count among their relatives the families of both parents.

Patterns of Authority

The predominance of polygyny, patrilocality, and patrilineal descent in the world reflects the universal presence of patriarchy. Without denying that wives and mothers exercise considerable power in every society, as Chapter 10 ("Sex and Gender") explains, no truly matriarchal society has ever existed. In industrial countries like the United States, more egalitarian family patterns are evolving, especially as increasing numbers of women enter the labor force. However, even here, men are typically viewed as heads of households. Parents in the United States also still prefer boys to girls, and most give children their father's last name.

Theoretical Analysis of the Family

As in earlier chapters, we draw on various theoretical approaches to provide useful insights into the family.

Functions of the Family: Structural-Functional Analysis

The structural-functional paradigm reveals that the family performs several of society's basic tasks. This view explains why we sometimes think of the family as "the backbone of society."

1. **Socialization.** As noted in Chapter 3 ("Socialization: From Infancy to Old Age"), the family is the first and most important setting for socialization. In ideal terms, parents help their children learn to be well-integrated and contributing members of society (Parsons & Bales, 1955). Of course, family socialization continues throughout the life cycle. Adults change within marriage and, as any parent knows, mothers and fathers learn as much from raising their children as their children learn from them.

2. **Regulation of sexual activity.** Every culture regulates sexual activity in the interest of maintaining kinship organization and property rights. One universal proscription is the **incest taboo,** *a norm forbidding sexual relations or marriage between certain kin*. Precisely which kin fall under the incest taboo varies from one culture to another. The matrilineal Navajo, for example, forbid marrying any relative of one's mother. Our bilateral society applies the incest taboo to both sides of the family but limits it to close relatives, including parents, grandparents, siblings, aunts, and uncles. But even brother-sister marriages found approval among the ancient Egyptian, Incan, and Hawaiian nobility (Murdock, 1965).

    Reproduction between close relatives can adversely affect the mental and physical health of offspring. But this fact fails to explain why, among all species of life, the incest taboo is observed only by human beings. The key reason to control incest, then, is social. Why? First, the incest taboo minimizes sexual competition within families by restricting legitimate sexual activity to spouses. Second, it forces people to marry outside of their immediate families, forging useful alliances. Third, since kinship defines people's rights and obligations toward each other, forbidding reproduction among close relatives protects kinship from collapsing into chaos.

3. **Social placement.** Families are hardly necessary for people to reproduce, but they do maintain social organization. Parents confer their own social identity—in terms of race, ethnicity, religion, and social class—on children at birth, which accounts for the longstanding preference for so-called "legitimate" childbearing.

4. **Material and emotional security.** People have long viewed the family as a "haven in a heartless world," looking to kin for physical protection, emotional support, and financial assistance. To a greater or lesser extent, most families do provide all these things, although not without periodic conflict. Not surprisingly, then, people living in families tend to be healthier than those living alone.

Critical evaluation. Structural-functional analysis explains why society, at least as we know it, could not exist without families. But this approach virtually ignores the great diversity of U.S. family life. Moreover, it pays little attention to how other social institutions (say, government) could meet at least some of the same human needs. Finally, structural-functionalism overlooks many controversial elements of family life, including the prevalence of patriarchy, and the alarming extent of family violence.

Inequality and the Family: Social-Conflict Analysis

Like the structural-functional approach, the social-conflict paradigm also sees the family as central to the operation of society. But rather than concentrating on ways that kinship benefits society, conflict theorists investigate how families reproduce patterns of inequality from one generation to the next.

1. **Property and inheritance.** Friedrich Engels (1902; orig. 1884) traced the origin of the family to the need to identify heirs so that men (especially in the higher classes) could transmit property to their sons. Families thus promote the concentration of wealth and reproduce the class structure in each succeeding generation (Mare, 1991).

2. **Patriarchy.** Engels explained that men determine their heirs only by controlling the sexuality of women. Thus, Engels continued, families transform women into the sexual and economic property of men. A century ago in the United States, most wives' earnings belonged to their husbands. Today, while women have moved rapidly into the paid work force, they still bear major responsibility for child rearing and housework (Haas, 1981; Schooler et al., 1984; Fuchs, 1986).

3. **Race and ethnicity.** Racial and ethnic categories persist over generations only to the degree that people marry others like themselves. Thus endogamous marriage shores up the racial and ethnic hierarchy in our society and elsewhere.

Later in this chapter, we will explore how the connection between the traditional family and social

The family is a basic building block of society because it performs important functions such as conferring social position and regulating sexual activity. To most family members, however, the family (at least in ideal terms) is a "haven in a heartless world" in which individuals find a sense of belonging and emotional support, an idea conveyed in Marc Chagall's *Scène Paysanne.*

inequality relates to other issues, such as violence against women, divorce, and the increasing number of women raising children outside of marriage.

Critical evaluation. Social-conflict analysis reveals another side of family life: its role in maintaining social inequality. During his era, Engels condemned the family as part and parcel of capitalism. Yet societies that have rejected the capitalist system have families (and family problems) all the same. The family and social inequality are deeply intertwined, as Engels argued, but the family appears to carry out various societal functions that are not easily accomplished by other means.

Micro-Level Analysis

Both structural-functional and social-conflict analyses take a broad view of the family as a structural system. Micro-level approaches, by contrast, explore how individuals shape and experience family life.

Socially constructing family life. From a symbolic-interaction perspective, individuals construct family life, and they do so variably. Women and men, parents and children—all tend to see family life differently, with no two individuals experiencing precisely the same reality.

Family life also changes over time. A newlywed couple's initial expectations about their relationship will almost certainly change as they face the daily realities of life together. A new role for a spouse, such as a wife entering law school, alters the lives of all family members. Thus, from this micro perspective, marriage and the family are less rigid patterns than they are ongoing processes.

Family life as exchange. Social-exchange analysis is another micro-level approach that depicts courtship and marriage as forms of negotiation (Blau, 1964). Dating allows each person to assess the other as a potential spouse, weighing a prospective partner's advantages and disadvantages against one's own. In essence, exchange analysts point out, individuals seek to make the best "deal" they can in selecting a marriage partner.

Physical attractiveness is one critical dimension of exchange. In patriarchal societies around the world, beauty has long been a commodity offered by women on the marriage market. The high value assigned to beauty explains women's traditional concern with physical appearance and their sensitivity about revealing their age. For their part, men traditionally

stack up according to their financial resources. As women have joined the labor force and gained more financial independence, however, the terms of exchange are converging for men and women.

Critical evaluation. Micro-level analysis offers a useful balance to structural-functional and social-conflict visions of the family as an institutional system. Adopting an interactional or exchange viewpoint, we derive a better sense of the individual's experience of family life, and appreciate how people creatively shape this reality for themselves.

Using this approach, however, we run the risk of missing the bigger picture that family life is similar for people affected by the same set of economic and cultural forces. That is, U.S. families vary in some predictable ways according to social class and ethnicity, and, as the next section explains, they typically evolve through stages linked to the life course.

Stages of Family Life

The family shows marked changes over the life course. Members of our society recognize several distinct stages of family life.

Courtship

Adults in preindustrial societies (who represent most of the world's people) generally consider courtship too important to be left to the young (Stone, 1977; Haviland, 1985). *Arranged marriages* represent an alliance of two extended families, a negotiation involving wealth, power, and prestige. Romantic love has little to do with it, and parents often make such arrangements when their children are quite young. A century ago in India, for example, half of all girls married before reaching the age of fifteen (Mayo, 1927; Mace & Mace, 1960).

Industrialization erodes the importance of extended families, weakens traditions, and enhances personal choice in courtship. Young people now expect to choose mates for themselves, and they delay doing so until gaining the experience they need to select a suitable marriage partner. Dating sharpens their skills, and may serve as a period of sexual experimentation as well.

Our culture elevates *romantic love*—the experience of affection and sexual passion toward another person—as the basis for marriage. For us, marriage

students in industrial societies say they would enter a loveless marriage.

Our society's emphasis on romance has some useful consequences. Passionate love motivates individuals to leave their original families to form new ones, and it may also carry a new couple through difficult adjustments to the realities of living together (Goode, 1959). On the other hand, because feelings wax and wane, romantic love makes for a less stable foundation for marriage than social and economic considerations—an assertion borne out by the fact that the U.S. divorce rate is much higher than that found in, say, India.

But even in this age of choice, sociologists have long recognized that Cupid's arrow is aimed by society more than we like to think. Most people fall in love with others of the same race, comparable age, and similar social class. All societies "arrange" marriages to the extent that they encourage **homogamy** (literally, "like marrying like"), *marriage between people with the same social characteristics.*

Settling In: Ideal and Real Marriage

Our society presents marriage to the young in idealized, "happily-ever-after" terms. One consequence of such optimistic thinking is the danger of disappointment, especially for women—who, more than men, are taught to look to marriage for the key to future happiness.

Then, too, fantasy infuses romantic love. We fall in love with others, not necessarily as they are, but as we want them to be (Berscheid & Hatfield, 1983). Only after marriage do many spouses regularly confront each other as they carry out the day-to-day routines of maintaining a household.

Sexuality is one source of disappointment. In the romantic haze of falling in love, people may envision marriage as an endless sexual honeymoon only to face the sobering realization that sex becomes less than an all-consuming passion. But while the frequency of sexual intercourse does decline over the years, a majority of married people claim to be satisfied with the sexual dimension of their relationship.

Many experts agree that couples with the most fulfilling sexual relationships experience the greatest satisfaction in their marriages. This connection does not mean that sex is the key to marital bliss, but it does suggest that good sex and good relationships go together (Hunt, 1974; Tavris & Sadd, 1977; Blumstein & Schwartz, 1983; Laumann et al., 1994).

Although people in every society recognize the reality of physical attraction and romantic love, members of traditional societies often arrange marriages between people of the same social position with little consideration given to the partners' feelings for each other. In Japan, a society that has long been more traditional than our own, marriages guided by the head instead of the heart have been common. As the country has industrialized during this century, however, attitudes have changed so that most individuals, rather than their parents, now take primary responsibility for selecting a spouse.

without love is difficult to imagine, and popular culture—from fairy tales like "Cinderella" to today's paperback romance novels—portrays love as the key to a successful marriage. Figure 12–1 provides a comparative look at the importance of romantic love in various countries. About half of today's college students in Pakistan and India claim they would marry partners they did not love; however, only a small percentage of

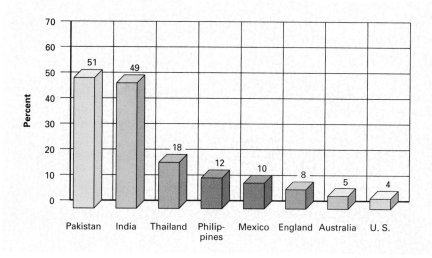

Child Rearing

Adults in the United States overwhelmingly identify raising children as one of life's great joys (NORC, 1993:616). This despite the undeniable fact that children make substantial demands on the time, energy, and income of parents. Given this fact, we can understand why few people want more than three children, as Table 12–1 on page 306 documents.[3] Two centuries ago, *eight* children was the U.S. average.

Families in preindustrial societies depend on children to provide labor, and generally regard having children as a wife's duty. This assumption, coupled with unreliable birth control technology, makes childbearing a regular event. Finally, a high death toll prevents many of these children from reaching adulthood; as late as 1900, about one-third of children in the United States died by age ten (Wall, 1980).

Industrialization transforms children, economically speaking, from a vital asset into a burdensome liability. The expense of raising even one child exceeds $100,000, a figure that doubles if the child goes to college (Lino, 1994). This helps to explain the steady drop in U.S. family size during this century. Such low rates of childbirth in industrial societies contrast sharply with high birth rates in poor societies in Latin America, Asia, and, especially, Africa, where women

have few alternatives to bearing children. In such societies, four to six children is still the norm.

Parenting is not only expensive but represents a lifetime commitment. In recent years, more U.S. adults have opted to delay childbirth or to remain childless. In 1960, almost 90 percent of women between twenty-five and twenty-nine who had ever married had at least one child; by 1990 this proportion had tumbled to 71 percent (U.S. Bureau of the Census, 1993). One recent survey indicated that about two-thirds of parents in the United States would like to devote far more of their time to child-rearing (Snell, 1990). But, unless we are willing to suffer a decline in our material standard of living, economic realities demand that most parents pursue careers outside the home. Thus the child-rearing patterns we have described reflect ways of coming to terms with economic change.

Now that two-thirds of women with children under eighteen work for income, both mothers and fathers have less time for parenting. Some 7 million young children—sometimes called *latchkey kids*—are left by working parents to fend for themselves for some part of the day, and half of all nine-year-olds are unsupervised after school (U.S. Women's Bureau, 1989).

Congress took a step toward easing the conflict between family and job responsibilities by passing a "family leave" bill in 1993. This law allows up to ninety days' leave from work in order to care for a new child or to assist with a family emergency. But most adults in this country still juggle parental and occupational responsibilities with only limited success. This dilemma points to the heightened importance of child-care facilities, as the box on page 307 explains.

---

[3]The median number of children (under age eighteen) per family was 0.96 in 1993. The median number of children among only married couples with children was about twice as great: 1.87 for whites, 1.92 for African Americans, and 2.08 for Hispanics (U.S. Bureau of the Census, 1994).

The Family in Later Life

Increasing life expectancy in the United States means that, barring divorce, couples are likely to remain married for a long time. By age fifty, most have completed the task of raising children. The remaining years of marriage—the "empty nest"—bring a return to living alone with one's spouse.

Like the birth of children, their departure requires adjustments, although the marital relationship often becomes closer and more satisfying once children are on their own (Kalish, 1982). A healthy marriage at this stage of life is generally characterized by companionship. Years of living together may have diminished a couple's sexual passion for each other, but mutual understanding and commitment have generally grown stronger.

Contact with children usually continues, and most older adults live within a short distance of at least one of their children. Moreover, one-third of all U.S. adults are grandparents (50 million in all), many of whom help daughters and sons with child care and a host of other responsibilities. Among African Americans (who have a high rate of single parenting), many grandmothers assume a central position in family life (Shanas, 1979; Cherlin & Furstenberg, 1986; Crispell, 1993).

An increasing number of adults also find that they must provide care for their own aging parents. The "empty nest" may not be filled by a parent coming to stay in the home, but many adults find that parents living eighty years and beyond require practical, emotional, and financial attention that can be more taxing than raising young children. Analysts tout people in their forties as the "sandwich generation" because they will spend as many years tending to the needs of their aging parents as they did caring for their own offspring.

Retirement further transforms family life. If the wife has been a homemaker, the husband's retirement means spouses will be spending much more time together. Although this change may be a source of pleasure to both, it can dramatically upset wives' established routines. As one woman bluntly put it: "I may have married him for better or worse, but not for lunch" (quoted in Kalish, 1982:96).

The final and surely the most difficult transition in married life comes with the death of a spouse. Wives typically outlive husbands because of women's greater life expectancy, and also because women usually marry men several years older to begin with. Wives can thus expect to spend a significant period of their lives as widows. The bereavement and loneliness accompanying the death of a spouse are always difficult. This experience may be even more difficult for widowers, who usually have fewer friends than widows do, and may be unskilled at cooking and housework (Berardo, 1970).

U.S. Families: Class, Race, and Gender

Dimensions of inequality—social class, race and ethnicity, and gender—are powerful forces that shape marriage and family life. Keep in mind that while we will address each factor separately, they overlap in our lives.

Social Class

Social class molds a family's financial security and shapes its range of opportunities. Interviewing working-class women, Lillian Rubin (1976) found that wives deemed a good husband to be one who held a steady job and refrained from violence and excessive drinking. Rubin's middle-class respondents, by contrast, never mentioned such concerns; these women simply *assumed* a husband would provide a safe and secure home. Their ideal husband was a man with whom they could communicate easily and share feelings and experiences. Clearly, what women (and men) feel they can hope for in marriage—and what they end up with—is substantially linked to the social level that circumscribes their entire lives (Komarovsky, 1967; Bott, 1971; Rubin, 1976; McLeod & Shanahan, 1993).

TABLE 12–1 The Ideal Number of Children for U.S. Adults, 1990

Number of Children	Proportion of Respondents
0	1.1%
1	2.7
2	52.4
3	21.6
4	10.1
5	1.4
6 or more	0.7
As many as you want	6.0
No response	3.9

Source: *General Social Surveys, 1972–1993: Cumulative Codebook* (Chicago: National Opinion Research Center, 1993), p. 260.

Who's Minding the Kids?

Traditionally, the task of providing daily care for young children fell to mothers. But with a majority of mothers and fathers now in the labor force, securing quality, affordable child care has become a high priority for parents.

The figure displays the source of care for U.S. children under five years of age whose mothers are working. The most common location of child care—utilized in 36 percent of all cases—is the child's own home where a father or other relative usually provides supervision. An additional 31 percent of children are attended to in another person's home, with either relatives or perhaps neighbors or friends looking after them. A small share of children accompany their mothers to work.

An organized day-care facility or preschool is the setting for the remaining 23 percent of young children with working mothers. The proportion in day-care centers has doubled over the last decade because many parents have difficulty finding in-home care for their children.

Some day-care centers handle dozens of children at one time, amounting to "tot lots" in which children, "parked" by their parents for the day, receive little love and minimal attention. The impersonality of such settings, coupled with rapid turnover in staff, can undermine the warm and consistent nurturing that young children (especially under the age of three) need to develop a sense of trust. Other child-care centers, however, offer a secure and healthful environment for children. The balance of research points to a simple conclusion: *Good* child-care centers are good for children; *bad* facilities are not.

Identifying high-quality child-care facilities is not always easy. Parents need to inspect centers carefully, determining the ratio of children to caregivers, inquiring about discipline policies, and noting the cleanliness and safety of the surroundings. Such personal investigation is especially important because few states have comprehensive guidelines for operating child-care centers—and some states have none at all.

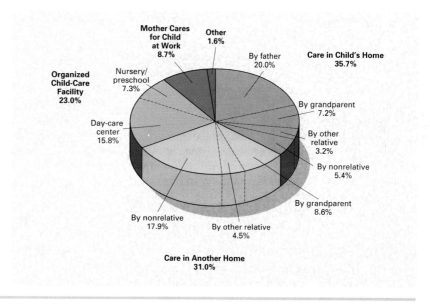

Ethnicity and Race

Ethnicity, too, shapes the family. Latinos generally enjoy the loyalty and support of extended families. Traditionally, too, Hispanic parents exercise greater control over their children's courtship, defining marriage as an alliance of families rather than a union born of romantic love. In addition, the Hispanic heritage places great stock in conventional gender roles. *Machismo*—masculine strength, daring, and sexual prowess—is pronounced in this culture, while women are both honored and closely supervised.

Assimilation into the larger society is gradually tempering these traditional patterns, however. Many Puerto Ricans who immigrated to New York, for example, do not maintain the strong extended families they knew in Puerto Rico. Especially among affluent Latino families—whose number has tripled in the last

Latinos traditionally have maintained strong kinship ties. Carmen Lomas Garza's 1988 painting, *Tamalada* ("*Making Tamales*"), portrays the extended family that historically has undergirded Hispanic culture.

twenty years—the traditional authority of men over women has diminished (Fitzpatrick, 1971; Moore & Pachon, 1985; O'Hare, 1990).

Analysis of African-American families must begin with the stark reality of economic disadvantage. As explained in earlier chapters, the typical African-American family earned $21,161 in 1992, not quite 55 percent of the national income standard. People of African ancestry are also three times as likely as white people to be poor so that family patterns reflect unemployment, underemployment, and, in some cases, a physical environment replete with crime and drug abuse.

Under these circumstances, maintaining stable family ties is difficult. For example, 25 percent of African-American women now in their forties have never married, compared with about 10 percent of white women of the same age (Bennett, Bloom, & Craig, 1989). This means that women of color—often with children—are more likely to be heads of households. Figure 12–2 shows that women headed 47 percent of African-American families in 1993, compared with 23 percent of Hispanic families, 14 percent of Asian and Pacific Islander families, and 14 percent of white families (U.S. Bureau of the Census, 1994).

Regardless of race, families of single women and children are always at high risk of poverty. About one-third of families headed by white women are poor, and the proportion is closer to half among people of African or Hispanic ancestry—strong evidence of how class, race, and gender overlap to create special disadvantages for many women. Note that African-American families with both wife and husband in the home—which represents half of the total—are less economically vulnerable, earning about 80 percent as much as comparable white families. But two-thirds of African-American children are born to single women, and half of all African-American boys and girls are growing up poor, meaning that such families carry much of the burden of child poverty in the United States (Hogan & Kitagawa, 1985; U.S. Bureau of the Census, 1994).

Gender

Among all races, Jessie Bernard (1982) asserts, every marriage is actually *two* different relationships: the woman's marriage and the man's marriage. Although the extent of patriarchy has diminished, few of today's marriages are composed of two equal partners. As an example, we still expect husbands to be older and taller than their wives, and to have more important careers (McRae, 1986).

Curiously, in light of these patterns, most people hold fast to the belief that marriage benefits women more than men (Bernard, 1982). The positive stereotype of the carefree bachelor contrasts sharply with the negative image of the lonely spinster. These ideas are rooted in women's historic exclusion from the labor force, which made a woman's financial security dependent on having a husband.

But, Bernard claims, married women have poorer mental health and more passive attitudes toward life than single women and report less personal happiness. Married men, by contrast, live longer than single men, are mentally better off, and report being happier. As a result, after divorce, men are more eager than women to secure a new partner.

Bernard concludes that there is no better guarantor of long life, health, and happiness for a man than a woman well socialized to the role of a traditional wife, devoted to taking care of him and providing the regularity and security of a well-ordered home. She is quick to add that marriage *could* boost the health and happiness of women if society would only end the practice of husbands dominating wives and expecting them to perform virtually all the housework.

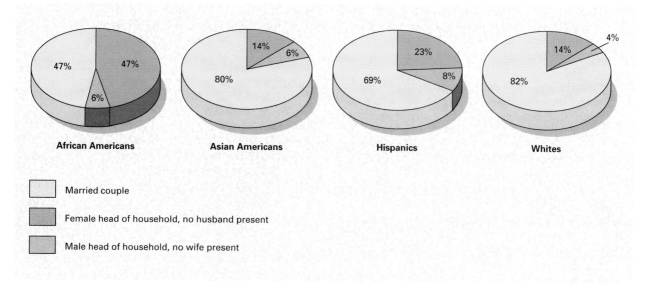

Married couple

Female head of household, no husband present

Male head of household, no wife present

FIGURE 12–2   Family Form in the United States, 1993
Source: U.S. Bureau of the Census (1994).

Transitions and Problems in Family Life

Ann Landers, a well-known observer of the U.S. scene, once characterized one marriage out of twenty as wonderful, five in twenty as good, ten of twenty as tolerable, and the remaining five as "pure hell." Families can be a source of joy, but the reality of family life often falls short of this ideal.

Divorce

Our society strongly supports marriage, and about nine out of ten people "tie the knot" at some point in their lives. But many of today's marriages eventually unravel. Figure 12–3 on page 310 depicts a tenfold increase in the U.S. divorce rate over the last century. By 1995, about four in ten marriages were ending in divorce (for African Americans, the comparable figure was about six in ten).

Causes of divorce.   The high U.S. divorce rate is linked to a number of factors (Huber & Spitze, 1980; Kitson & Raschke, 1981; Thorton, 1985; Waite, Haggstrom, & Kanouse, 1985; Weitzman, 1985; Gerstel, 1987; Furstenberg & Cherlin, 1991).

1. **Individualism is on the rise.** Members of families spend less time together than in the past. We have become more individualistic, seemingly more concerned with personal happiness than with family well-being.

2. **Romantic love often fades.** Our culture bases marriage on romantic love, and marriages may collapse as sexual passion subsides. Many people now see nothing wrong with ending a marriage in which the spark has fizzled in favor of a new relationship that renews excitement and romance.

3. **Women are less dependent on men.** Their increasing participation in the labor force has reduced wives' financial dependency on husbands. As a practical matter, then, women can more easily walk away from unhappy marriages.

4. **Many of today's marriages are stressful.** A majority of today's couples both work outside the home, consuming time and energy people used to direct toward family life. Under such circumstances (and given the difficulty of securing high-quality, affordable child care), raising children is harder than ever. Children do stabilize some marriages, but divorce is most common during the early years of marriage when many couples have young children.

5. **Divorce is more socially acceptable.** Divorce no longer carries the powerful, negative stigma it did a century ago. Family and friends are now less likely to discourage couples from considering divorce.

6. **Divorce is legally easier to accomplish.** In the past, courts required divorcing couples to demonstrate that one or both were guilty of behavior such as adultery or physical abuse. Now most states allow divorce simply because a couple thinks their marriage has failed.

Who divorces? At greatest risk of divorce are young spouses, especially those who marry after a brief courtship, have few financial resources, and have yet to mature emotionally. The chance of divorce rises if a couple marries in response to an unexpected pregnancy, and when one or both partners have alcohol or other substance-abuse problems. People who are not religious are more likely to divorce than those who are.

Divorce also is more common among women with successful careers, perhaps due to the strains of a two-career marriage but also because financially secure women do not feel compelled to stay in an unhappy marriage. Moving, which weakens ties with family and friends, also boosts the odds of divorce. Finally, people who divorce once tend to divorce again, presumably because problems follow them from one marriage to another (Booth & White, 1980; Yoder & Nichols, 1980; Glenn & Shelton, 1985). National Map 12–1 provides a look at where in the United States we find the highest percentages of divorced people.

Finally, after divorce, mothers usually secure custody of children but fathers typically earn more income. Thus, the well-being of children often depends on fathers making court-ordered child-support payments. Courts award child support in 58 percent of all divorces involving children. Yet, in any given year, half of those required by court order to pay child support make only partial payments or none at all. Faced with some 2.5 million "dead-beat dads," Congress mandated that employers withhold money from the earnings of parents who fail to pay up. Still, many fathers evade their responsibilities by moving or switching jobs (Weitzman, 1985; Waldman, 1992).

Remarriage

Despite our high divorce rate, four out of five people who divorce remarry, most within five years. Almost half of all marriages are now remarriages for at least one partner. Men, who derive greater benefits from marriage, are more likely to remarry than women are.

Remarriage often creates *blended families*, composed of children and some combination of biological parents and stepparents. Members of blended families thus have to specify precisely who is part of the child's nuclear family. Blended families also require children to reorient themselves; an only child, for example, may suddenly find that she now has two older brothers. But, despite the challenges of blended families, these groups sometimes free both young and old from rigid family roles (Furstenberg, 1984).

Family Violence

The ideal family showers love and support on its members. The disturbing reality in many homes, however, is *family violence*, emotional, physical, or sexual abuse of one family member by another. Richard J. Gelles

FIGURE 12–3   The Divorce Rate for the United States, 1890–1992

Source: U.S. Bureau of the Census (1994).

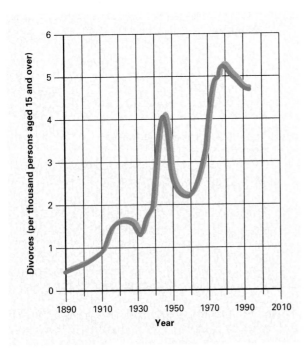

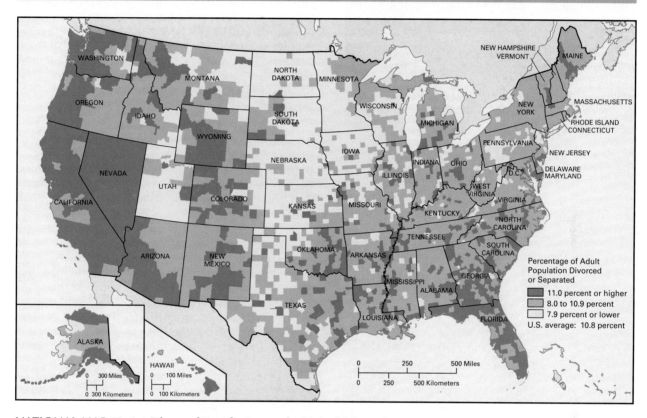

NATIONAL MAP 12–1   Divorced People Across the United States

Overall, about 11 percent of the U.S. population aged fifteen or over are divorced or separated. However, marriages are more vulnerable to breakup in the Pacific region of the country. Nevada has long been the U.S. divorce capital, due to its exceedingly liberal divorce laws. But divorce is also pronounced where religious values are weaker and where people are more likely to move often, thus distancing themselves from family and friends. How would you characterize the West Coast with regard to these factors?

Sources: Map from *American Demographics* magazine, October 1992, p. 5. Reprinted with permission. © 1992 *American Demographics* magazine, Ithaca, New York. Data from the 1990 decennial census.

characterizes the family as "the most violent group in society with the exception of the police and the military" (quoted in Roesch, 1984:75).

Violence against women.   Family brutality often goes unreported to police, but researchers estimate that about 9 million couples—or one in six—endure some domestic violence each year. About six hundred thousand women (and perhaps fifty thousand men) suffer serious injuries as a result (Straus & Gelles, 1986;

Schwartz, 1987; Shupe, Stacey, & Hazelwood, 1987; Bachman, 1994).

Government statistics show that almost 30 percent of murdered women (but just 4 percent of murdered men) are killed by partners or ex-partners. Nationwide, the death toll from family violence is four thousand women each year. This makes women more likely to be injured by a family member than to be mugged or raped by a stranger or injured in an automobile accident.

In the past, the law regarded domestic violence as a private family matter, giving victims few options. Now, even without separation or divorce, a woman can obtain court protection from an abusive spouse. Since 1990, forty-eight states have added "stalking laws" that prohibit an ex-partner from following or otherwise threatening a woman. Finally, communities across North America have established domestic abuse shelters that provide counseling as well as temporary housing for women and children driven from their homes by domestic violence.

Violence against children. Family violence also victimizes children. Child abuse entails more than physical injury because abusive adults also violate trust, which undermines a child's emotional well-being. Upwards of 2 million children each year—roughly 3 percent of all youngsters—suffer abuse, including several thousand who die as a result. Child abuse is most common among the youngest and most vulnerable children (Straus & Gelles, 1986; U.S. House of Representatives, 1987).

About 90 percent of child abusers are men, but they conform to no simple stereotype. As one man who entered a therapy group reported, "I kept waiting for all the guys with raincoats and greasy hair to show up. But everyone looked like regular middle class people" (quoted in Lubenow, 1984). Most abusers, however, share one common trait: having been abused themselves as children. Researchers have found that violent behavior in close personal relationships is learned; in families, then, violence begets violence (Gwartney-Gibbs, Stockard, & Bohmer, 1987).

Nations, as well as parents, can abuse children. Prior to the fall of the Ceauçescu regime in 1989, the Romanian government denied women any form of birth control and banned abortion. Tens of thousands of unwanted children were the result, many of whom remain warehoused in orphanages like this one.

Historically, the law defined wives as the property of husbands, so that no man could be charged with raping his wife. By 1994, however, all fifty states had passed *marital rape* laws although, in many cases, the law considers an act as marital rape only under specific circumstances such as after legal separation (Margolick, 1984; Goetting, 1989; National Center on Women and Family Law, 1991).

Alternative Family Forms

Most families in the United States are still composed of a married couple who raise children. But, in recent decades, our society has displayed increasing diversity in family life.

One-Parent Families

About three in ten families with children under eighteen years of age have only one parent in the household—a proportion that doubled during the last generation. At some point in their lives, half of our children now live with a single parent. *One-parent families*—four times more likely to include a mother than a father—may result from divorce, death, or from the choice of an unmarried woman to have a child.

Entering the labor force has bolstered women's financial capacity to be single mothers, but single parenthood still increases a woman's risk of poverty because it limits her ability to gain education or to work. At least one-third of the women in the United States now become pregnant as teenagers, and many decide to raise their children. As shown earlier in Figure 12–2, 53 percent of African-American families are headed by a single parent. Single parenthood is less common among Hispanics (31 percent), Asian Americans (20 percent), and non-Hispanic whites (18 percent) (U.S. Bureau of the Census, 1994). Many such families are multigenerational, with single parents (most of whom are mothers) turning to their own parents (again, typically, mothers) for help in raising the children. Thus, more than 3.4 million U.S. children today are living with grandparents (U.S. Bureau of the Census, 1994).

Much research points to the conclusion that growing up in a one-parent family disadvantages children. Some studies suggest that a father and a mother each make a distinctive contribution to a child's social development, so it is unrealistic to expect a single parent to do as good a job. But the most serious problem among families with one parent—especially if that parent is a woman—is poverty. On average, children growing up in a single-parent family start out poorer, gain less schooling, and end up with lower incomes as adults. Such children are also more likely to become single parents themselves (Mueller & Cooper, 1984; McLanahan, 1985; Weisner & Eiduson, 1986; Wallerstein & Blakeslee, 1989; Astone & McLanahan, 1991; Li & Wojtkiewicz, 1992; Biblarz & Raftery, 1993; Popenoe, 1993).

Cohabitation

Cohabitation is *the sharing of a household by an unmarried couple.* The number of cohabiting couples in the United States increased from about five hundred thousand in 1970 to more than 3.5 million by 1993. However, this number represents only 6 percent of all couples (U.S. Bureau of the Census, 1994).

In global perspective, cohabitation is common in Sweden and other Scandinavian societies as a long-term form of family life, with or without children. By contrast, this family form is rare in more traditional

More than 1 million gay and lesbian couples in the United States are currently raising children. This trend suggests that people of all sexual orientations support "traditional family values."

(and Roman Catholic) nations such as Italy. While cohabitation is gaining in popularity here—some 25 percent of U.S. adults cohabit at some point in their lives—such partnerships are still usually short term, with roughly 40 percent of couples marrying after several years, and the remainder splitting up (Blumstein & Schwartz, 1983; Macklin, 1983; Popenoe, 1988, 1991, 1992).

Gay and Lesbian Couples

In 1989, Denmark became the first country to legally recognize homosexual marriages. This change extended to gay and lesbian couples advantages in inheritance, taxation, and joint property ownership as well as social legitimacy. Danish law, however, stops short of permitting homosexual couples to adopt children. While our society legally prohibits homosexual marriage, some cities (including San Francisco and New York) confer limited marital benefits on gay and lesbian couples.

A decade ago, most gay couples in households with children were raising the offspring of previous, heterosexual unions. But a "gay-by boom" trend is under way as more gay partners are adopting children. A gay male couple can have a child by hiring a surrogate mother who agrees to allow doctors to impregnate her with the sperm of one of the men. By turning to sperm banks, one or both lesbian partners may become pregnant.

There are at least 1 million gay and lesbian couples in the United States who are now raising one or more children. While this trend challenges many traditional notions about families in the United States, it also indicates that many gay and lesbian couples derive the same rewards and fulfillment from child rearing as heterosexual couples do (Bell, Weinberg, & Kiefer-Hammersmith, 1981; Gross, 1991; Pressley & Andrews, 1992).

Singlehood

Because nine out of ten people in the United States marry, we tend to see singlehood as a transitory stage of life that ends with marriage. In recent decades, however, more people have deliberately chosen to live alone. In 1950 only one household in ten contained a single person. By 1994, this proportion had risen to one in four households: a total of 25 million single adults.

Most striking is the surging number of single young women. In 1960, 28 percent of women aged twenty to twenty-four were single; by 1993 the proportion had soared to two-thirds. Underlying this trend is women's greater participation in the labor force. Women who are economically secure view a husband as a matter of choice rather than a financial necessity.

By midlife, however, unmarried women sense a lack of available men. Because our culture frowns on women marrying men much younger than they are (while encouraging men to pursue "May-September" unions), middle-aged women who wish to marry find the odds rising against them. In 1993, there were four unmarried men aged forty to forty-four for every five unmarried women of the same age (U.S. Bureau of the Census, 1994).

New Reproductive Technology

Recent medical advances, generally called *new reproductive technology,* are changing families, too. In the twenty years since England's Louise Brown became the world's first "test-tube" baby, thousands of people have been conceived in this way. Early in the next century, 2 or 3 percent of the population of industrial societies may be the result of new birth technologies.

Technically, test-tube babies result from *in vitro fertilization* whereby doctors unite a woman's egg and a man's sperm "in glass," that is, in a laboratory dish. When successful, this complex medical procedure produces embryos, which doctors implant in the womb of the woman who is to bear the child; alternatively, these embryos may be frozen for use at a later time.

In vitro fertilization helps some couples who cannot conceive normally to become parents. Looking further ahead, new birth technologies may reduce the incidence of birth defects. But new reproductive technologies force us to consider whether what is scientifically possible is necessarily morally desirable. The Catholic church, for example, condemns turning human life into an object of research, and points to past efforts by Nazi scientists to generate a race of "superhumans." Endorsing this position, half the states in this country and many European nations currently regulate genetic experimentation.

Looking Ahead:
The Family in the Twenty-First Century

Family life in the United States is undergoing sweeping change and will continue to do so. These transformations generate controversy, with advocates of "traditional family values" opposing supporters of greater "personal choice." Sociologists cannot predict the outcome of this debate but our discussions do suggest five directions of future change.

First, a high divorce rate has dissolved the idea that marriage is a lifetime commitment. This change does not mean that today's relationships are less durable than they were a century ago, since, back then, many marriages were cut short by death (Kain, 1990). The point is that more couples now *choose* to end their marriages.

Second, family life in the twenty-first century will be highly variable. We have noted an increasing number of cohabiting couples, one-parent families, gay and lesbian families, and blended families. Most families, of course, are still based on marriage, and most married couples still have children. But, taken together, the variety of family forms represents a growing conception of family life as a matter of choice.

Third, in most families, men will continue to play only a limited role in child rearing. In the 1950s, a decade many people see as the "golden age" of families, "hands-off" parenting became the norm among men (Snell, 1990; Stacey, 1990). A countertrend is emerging now as some fathers—older, on average, and more established in their careers—eagerly jump into the parenting role. But, on balance, the high U.S. divorce rate and a surge in single motherhood translate into more children growing up with weaker ties to fathers. Is the absence of fathers directly and significantly detrimental to children? Research is inconclusive on this point, but there is little doubt that families without husbands and fathers contribute to rising levels of childhood poverty in the United States.

Fourth, as Arlie Hochschild (1989) points out, it is in the family that we often feel the effects of economic changes. As economic pressures mount, both household partners now work in most families, rendering marriage the interaction of weary men and women who try to squeeze in a little "quality time" for their children (Dizard & Gadlin, 1990). While two-career couples may advance the goal of gender equality, the long-term effects of this new parenting pattern on children and families are likely to yield mixed reviews.

Fifth and finally, new reproductive technology will make substantial inroads. Ethical concerns will slow these developments to some extent, but new forms of reproduction will continue to challenge traditional notions about parenthood.

Despite social changes that have buffeted the family in the United States, most people still report being happy as partners and parents (Cherlin & Furstenberg, 1983). Controversy may now swirl around marriage and family life, but both will likely remain the foundation of our society for some time to come.

Religion: Basic Concepts

Like the family, religion has played a central part in the drama of human history. Families gathered together have long surrounded birth, the passage into adulthood, and death with religious rituals.

French sociologist Emile Durkheim described the focus of religion as "things that surpass the limits of our knowledge" (1965:62; orig. 1915). As humans, he

For better or worse, the family is certainly changing. But the fact that young people still find marriage so attractive—even amid the most severe adversity—suggests that families will continue to play a central role in society for centuries to come.

continued, we set apart some ideas, objects, events, and experiences as **sacred,** *that which people define as extraordinary, inspiring a sense of awe and reverence.* Most, by contrast, we treat as **profane** (from the Latin for "outside the temple"), meaning *an ordinary element of everyday life.* **Religion,** then, is *a social institution, involving beliefs and practices, that distinguishes the sacred from the profane.*

In global perspective, matters of faith vary greatly, with nothing sacred to everyone on earth. Although people regard most books as profane, Jews view the Torah (the first five books of the Hebrew Bible or the Old Testament) as sacred, in the same way that Christians revere the entire Bible and Muslims exalt the Qur'an (Koran).

However a community of believers draws religious lines, Durkheim (1965:62) claimed, people

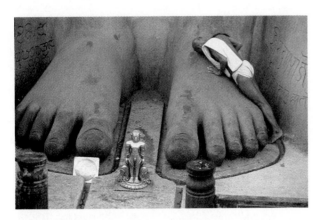

Religion is founded on the idea of the sacred, that which is set apart as extraordinary and which demands our submission. Bowing, kneeling, or prostrating oneself—each a common element of religious devotion—symbolizes this submissiveness.

understand profane things in terms of everyday usefulness: We sit down at a computer or turn the key of a car to accomplish various jobs. What is sacred, however, we reverently separate from daily life. For example, to make clear the boundary between the sacred and the profane, Muslims remove their shoes before entering a mosque to avoid defiling a sacred place with soles that have touched the profane ground outside.

The sacred is the focus of *ritual,* or formal, ceremonial behavior. Holy communion is the central ritual of Christianity; to the Christian faithful, the wafer and wine consumed during communion symbolize the body and blood of Jesus Christ, and are never treated as food.

Further, since religion deals with ideas that transcend everyday experience, neither common sense nor science can verify or disprove religious doctrine. Religion is a matter of **faith,** *belief anchored in conviction rather than scientific evidence.* For example, the New Testament of the Bible defines faith as "the conviction of things not seen" (Heb. 11:1) and exhorts Christians to "walk by faith, not by sight" (2 Cor. 5:7).

Some people with strong religious beliefs may be disturbed by the thought of sociologists studying what the faithful hold to be sacred. Yet sociological study carries no threat to anyone's faith. Just as sociologists study the family, they seek to understand the common and distinctive features of religious experiences around the world and how religion relates to other social institutions. In doing so, they make no claims about whether a particular religious belief is right or wrong. Sociological analysis, then, investigates the social *consequences* of religious activity, but can never assess the *validity* of any religious doctrine because religious truth rests on faith rather than empirical evidence.

Theoretical Analysis of Religion

Sociologists have examined religion through the lens of various theoretical paradigms. Each provides distinctive insights about religious life.

Functions of Religion: Structural-Functional Analysis

Emile Durkheim pointed out that society has an existence and power of its own beyond the life of any individual. Thus, society itself is "god-like": It survives the ultimate deaths of its members, whose lives it shapes. Durkheim concluded that, in religion, people celebrate the awesome power of their society (1965; orig. 1915).

This insight explains why, around the world, people transform everyday objects into sacred symbols of their collective life. Members of technologically simple societies do this by fashioning a **totem,** *an object collectively defined as sacred.* The totem—perhaps an animal or an elaborate work of art—becomes the centerpiece of ritual. In our society, the flag is a quasi-religious totem that should never be used in a profane way (say, as clothing) or allowed to touch the ground.

Durkheim pointed out three major functions of religion for the operation of society:

1. **Social cohesion.** Religion unites people through shared symbolism, values, and norms. Religious thought and ritual establish morality and rules of "fair play" that make organized social life possible.

2. **Social control.** Each society uses religious imagery and rhetoric to promote conformity. In medieval Europe, where monarchs claimed to rule by divine right, any challenge to the social order meant defiance of God's will. Today, our leaders publicly ask for God's blessing, implying to audiences that their efforts are just and even sanctioned by a higher authority.

3. **Providing meaning and purpose.** Religious beliefs offer the comforting sense that the vulnerable human condition serves a greater purpose. Strengthened by such beliefs, people are less likely to collapse in despair when confronted by life's calamities. For this reason, we mark major life transitions—including birth, marriage, and death—with religious observances.

Critical evaluation. Durkheim's structural-functional analysis of religion asserts that religious symbolism, in essence, makes society possible. This approach falls short, however, by downplaying the dysfunctional consequences of religion—especially the capacity of strong belief to generate destructive conflict. Nations have long marched to war under the banner of their god; few people would dispute that religious beliefs have provoked more killing than have differences of social class.

Constructing the Sacred: Symbolic-Interaction Analysis

From a symbolic-interactionist point of view, religion, like all of society, is socially constructed. To give our fallible, transitory lives "the semblance of ultimate security and permanence," we (perhaps with God's inspiration) fashion "sacred canopies" of meaning—beliefs and rituals that place our actions in a larger context (Berger, 1967:35–36).

Marriage is a good example. If we look on marriage as just a contract, it has no special hold on the two partners. Defined as holy matrimony, however, this bond makes moral claims on us and confers meaning on our lives. Especially when humans face uncertainty and life-threatening situations—such as illness, war, and natural disaster—we bring sacred symbols to the fore.

Critical evaluation. The symbolic-interaction approach views religion as a strategy by which people's lives gain meaning that transcends their day-to-day existence. Of course, as Peter Berger notes, elements viewed as sacred can only legitimize and stabilize society if people ignore their constructed character. After all, we could derive little strength from sacred beliefs we saw as mere devices for coping with tragedy. Then, too, this micro-level view pays little attention to how religion dovetails with social inequality, the issue to which we now turn.

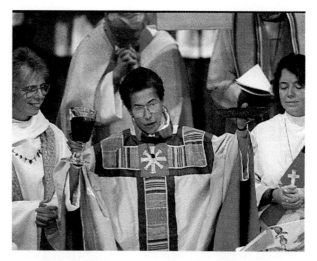

One way that religions support social inequality is by admitting to positions of leadership only certain categories of people. Historically, this has meant the dominance of white men, but this pattern has eroded in recent years. In 1989, for example, Barbara Harris became the first woman of color to be ordained as a bishop in the Episcopal Church.

Religion and Inequality: Social-Conflict Analysis

The social-conflict paradigm highlights religion's link to social hierarchy. According to Karl Marx, religion serves elites by legitimizing the status quo and diverting people's attention from social inequities.

The British monarch, for example, is even today crowned by the head of the Church of England, illustrating the close alliance between religious and political elites. In practical terms, working for political change may mean opposing the church—and, by implication, God. Religion also encourages people to look hopefully to a "better world to come," minimizing the social problems of *this* world. In one of his best-known statements, Marx offered a stinging criticism of religion as "the sigh of the oppressed creature, the sentiment of a heartless world, and the soul of soulless conditions. It is the opium of the people" (1964:27; orig 1848).

Religion reinforces social inequality in one other way: Virtually all the world's major religions are patriarchal. For example, the Qur'an (Koran)—the sacred text of Islam—asserts that men are to have social dominance over women:

Men are in charge of women. . . . Hence good women are obedient. . . . As for those whose rebelliousness you fear,

Religion has always held a special promise to the poor, reaffirming the dignity of people flogged by famine and holding out hope of a better life to come. Christian churches are currently thriving in the poorest regions of southern Africa. There, Christian ideals are expressed passionately in some of the world's most inspirational religious art.

admonish them, banish them from your bed, and scourge them. (cited in Kaufman, 1976:163)

Christianity—the dominant religion in the Western Hemisphere—has also supported patriarchy. Although Christians revere Mary, the mother of Jesus, the New Testament instructs us:

A man . . . is the image and glory of God; but woman is the glory of man. For man was not made from woman, but woman from man. Neither was man created for woman, but woman for man. (I Corinthians 11:7–9)

As in all the churches of the saints, the women should keep silence in the churches. For they are not permitted to speak, but should be subordinate, as even the law says. If there is anything they desire to know, let them ask their husbands at home. For it is shameful for a woman to speak in church. (I Corinthians 14:33–35)

Wives, be subject to your husbands, as to the Lord. For the husband is the head of the wife as Christ is the head of the church. . . . As the church is subject to Christ, so let wives also be subject in everything to their husbands. (Ephesians 5:22–24)

Judaism, too, has traditionally elevated men over women. Male Orthodox Jews include the following words in daily prayer:

Blessed art thou, O Lord our God, King of the Universe, that I was not born a gentile.
Blessed art thou, O Lord our God, King of the Universe, that I was not born a slave.
Blessed art thou, O Lord our God, King of the Universe, that I was not born a woman.

Despite their patriarchal heritage, many religions are gradually opening the way for women to assume leadership roles. Such developments, coupled with linguistic revisions in hymnals and prayer books, have delighted progressives while outraging traditionalists. These changes have far-reaching consequences: Beyond mere shifts in organizational patterns, they reflect new conceptions of God. Theologian Mary Daly puts the matter bluntly: "If God is male, then male is God" (cited in Woodward, 1989:58).

Critical evaluation. Social-conflict analysis reveals how religion perpetuates social inequality. Yet, in some instances, religion has also pressed for greater equality. Nineteenth-century religious groups in the United States, for example, played a key role in the abolition of slavery. During the 1950s and 1960s, religious organizations and their leaders stood at the core of the civil rights movement. Then, in the 1960s and 1970s, many members of the clergy protested the Vietnam War and, as we explain presently, some have championed revolutionary change in Latin America and elsewhere.

Religion and Social Change

Religion is not the monolithic conservative force portrayed by Karl Marx. As Max Weber (1958; orig. 1904–5) explained, religion can promote dramatic social change.

Max Weber: Protestantism and Capitalism

Weber contended that particular religious ideas set into motion a wave of change that brought about the industrialization of Western Europe. According to Weber, industrial capitalism developed in the wake of Calvinism, a Christian movement within the Protestant Reformation.

Central to the religious thought of John Calvin (1509–1564) is the doctrine of *predestination*. This means that the all-knowing, all-powerful God has selected some people for salvation while condemning most to eternal damnation. With each individual's fate sealed before birth and known only to God, the only certainty is what hangs in the balance: eternal glory or hellfire.

Driven by anxiety over their fate, Calvinists understandably sought signs of God's favor in *this* world and gradually settled on prosperity as a mark of divine favor. This conviction, together with a rigid devotion to duty, prompted Calvinists to concentrate on the pursuit of wealth, which was used neither to fuel self-indulgent spending nor to aid the poor, whose plight Calvinists saw as a mark of God's scorn. As agents for God's work on earth, Calvinists believed that their life-long "calling" was best fulfilled by reinvesting profits and reaping ever-greater success in the process. All the while, they practiced personal thrift and eagerly embraced technological advances, thereby laying the groundwork for the rise of industrial capitalism.

In time, the religious fervor that motivated early Calvinists weakened, so that their habits of success-seeking and personal discipline evolved into a profane "Protestant work ethic." Thus Max Weber described industrial capitalism as a "disenchanted" religion. But his analysis leaves little doubt as to the power of religion to alter the basic shape of society.

Liberation Theology

Christianity has a longstanding concern for the suffering of poor and oppressed people. Historically, the Christian response has been to strengthen the believer's faith in a better life to come. In recent decades, however, some church leaders and theologians have fashioned **liberation theology,** *a fusion of Christian principles with political activism, often Marxist in character.*

This social movement started in the late 1960s in Latin America's Roman Catholic church. In addition to the church's efforts to free humanity from sin, Christian activists are helping people in the least-developed countries to liberate themselves from abysmal poverty. Their message is simple: Human suffering runs counter to Christian morality and is also preventable. Therefore, as a matter of faith and social justice, Christians must promote greater social equality.

This mix of religion and politics has attracted a large following among church leaders and lay people alike. Yet Pope John Paul II condemns this movement for tainting traditional church doctrine with left-wing politics. Despite the pontiff's objections, however, the liberation theology movement is gaining strength in Latin America, fueled by the belief that Christian faith should propel the drive to improve the condition of the world's poor (Boff, 1984; Neuhouser, 1989).

Church, Sect, and Cult

Sociologists describe religious organizations in terms of three general types: church, sect, and cult. Drawing on the ideas of his teacher Max Weber, Ernst Troeltsch (1931) defined a **church** as *a formal religious organization well integrated into the larger society.* Church-like organizations typically persist for centuries and count among their members generations of the same families. Churches favor formality, enacting many rules and regulations to guide ritual observances and requiring leaders to undergo approved training and formal ordination.

While concerned with the sacred, a church tends to accept the ways of the profane world. Church members conceive of God in highly intellectualized terms (say, as a force for good) and endorse general moral doctrine ("Do unto others as you would have them do unto you"). By teaching morality in safely abstract terms, church leaders need not engage in divisive social controversies. For example, clergy have long preached about the unity of all peoples to all-white congregations (Troeltsch, 1931; O'Dea & Aviad, 1983).

A church generally operates as an ecclesia or a denomination. An **ecclesia** is *a church that is formally allied with the state.* Ecclesias have been common in human history: For centuries, the Catholic church was allied with the "Holy" Roman Empire; Confucianism was the state religion in China until early in this century; the Anglican church remains the official church of England; and Islam is today the official religion of Morocco, Pakistan, and Iran. State churches typically define everyone in the society as a member, a policy that sharply limits tolerance of religious differences.

A **denomination,** by contrast, is *a church, not linked to the state, that accepts religious pluralism.* Denominations thrive in societies like ours that formally separate church and state. In the United States, religious pluralism flourishes, with dozens of Christian denominations—including Catholics, Baptists, Methodists, and Lutherans—as well as various denominations of Judaism and other traditions. While members of any denomination hold particular religious beliefs, they recognize the right of others to disagree.

A second religious form is the **sect,** *a type of religious organization that stands apart from the larger society.* Simply put, sect members place their own convictions ahead of what others around them believe to be true. In extreme cases, members of a sect may withdraw entirely from the larger society to practice their faith without interference from outsiders. The Amish are one example of a North American sect that has long isolated itself (Kraybill & Olshan, 1994). Since

In global perspective, the range of human religious activity is truly astonishing. Members of one Christian cult in the Latin American nation of Guatemala observe Good Friday by vaulting over fire, an expression of faith that God will protect them.

our culture holds up religious tolerance as a virtue, members of sects are sometimes accused of being dogmatic in their insistence that they alone follow the true religion.

In organizational terms, sects are less formal than churches. Thus sect members often engage in highly spontaneous and emotional practices as they worship, while members of churches are more passive and attentive to their leader. Sects also reject the intellectualized religion of churches, stressing instead the personal experience of divine power. Rodney Stark (1985:314) contrasts a church's vision of a distant God—"Our Father, who art in Heaven"—with a sect's more immediate God—"Lord, bless this poor sinner kneeling before you now."

A further distinction between church and sect turns on patterns of leadership. The more church-like an organization, the more likely that its leaders are formally trained and ordained. Because more sect-like organizations celebrate the personal presence of God, members expect their leaders to exude divine inspiration in the form of **charisma** (from Greek meaning "divine favor"), *extraordinary personal qualities that can turn an audience into followers*, infusing them with the emotional experience that sects so value.

Sects usually form as breakaway groups from established churches or other religious organizations (Stark & Bainbridge, 1979). Their psychic intensity and informal structure render them less stable than churches, and many sects blossom only to fade away soon after. The sects that do endure typically become more like churches, losing fervor as they become more bureaucratic and entrenched.

To sustain their membership, sects rely on active recruitment, or *proselytizing*, of new members. Successful proselytizing leads to *conversion*, or religious rebirth. Members of Jehovah's Witnesses, for example, share their faith with others in the hope of attracting new members.

Finally, churches and sects differ in their social composition. Because they are more closely tied to other social institutions, well-established churches tend to bring into their fold people of high social standing. Sects, by contrast, attract more disadvantaged people. A sect's openness to new members and promise of salvation and personal fulfillment may be especially appealing to people widely regarded as social outsiders. However, as we shall explain presently, many established churches in the United States have lost membership in recent decades. As a result, a number of sects now count more affluent members among their ranks.

A **cult** is *a religious organization that is substantially outside the cultural traditions of a society*. Whereas a sect emerges from within a conventional religious organization, a cult represents something else entirely. Cults typically form around a highly charismatic leader who offers a compelling message of a new way of life.

Because some cult principles or practices are unorthodox, many people view cults as deviant or even evil. Negative publicity given to a few cults in recent years has raised suspicion about any unfamiliar religious group. Members of the Branch Davidian cult in

Waco, Texas, for example, held federal officers at bay for more than fifty days in 1993 before almost one hundred cult members died in a shootout and subsequent fire. Based on public reaction to such cases, some scholars assert that to call a religious community a "cult" amounts to declaring it unworthy (Richardson, 1990).

This is unfortunate because there is nothing intrinsically wrong with this kind of religious organization. Many longstanding religions—Christianity, Islam, and Judaism included—began as cults. Of course, not all or even most cults last for very long. For one thing, cults are even more at odds with the larger society than sects. Many cults demand that members not only accept their doctrine but adopt a radically new lifestyle. This is why people sometimes accuse cults of brainwashing new members. Yet researchers have found that most people who join cults experience no psychological harm (Barker, 1981; Kilbourne, 1983).

Religion in History

Like the family, religion is a part of every known society. But, also like the family, religion shows marked historical and cross-cultural variation.

Religion in Preindustrial Societies

Religion predates written history. According to archaeological evidence, our human ancestors routinely engaged in religious rituals some forty thousand years ago.

Early hunters and gatherers embraced **animism** (from Latin meaning "the breath of life"), *the belief that natural objects are conscious forms of life that affect humanity.* Animistic people view forests, oceans, mountains, and even the wind as spiritual forces. Many Native-American societies were animistic, which accounts for their historical reverence for the natural environment.

Belief in a single divine power responsible for creating the world paralleled the rise of pastoral and horticultural societies. We can trace our society's conception of God as a "shepherd," directly involved in the world's well-being, to the origins of Christianity, Judaism, and Islam among pastoral peoples.

In agrarian societies, the institution of religion gains in prominence, as evidenced by the centrality of the church in medieval Europe. The physical design of the medieval city even casts this dominance in stone: The cathedral rises above all other structures.

Religion in Industrial Societies

With the Industrial Revolution, people came to rely on science as the primary source of truth. Even so, religious thought persists simply because science cannot address issues of ultimate meaning in human life. In other words, *how* this world works is the purview of scientists; but *why* we and the rest of the universe exist at all is a question that lies outside the scientific realm. So while science may help us grasp the workings of the physical world, religion has a unique capacity to address the *spiritual* dimension of human existence.

Still, because they both offer powerful but distinctive visions of the universe, science and religion have often fallen into an uneasy relationship. This tension peaked after the publication, in 1859, of Charles Darwin's *On the Origin of Species*, a biological treatise on human origins. Darwin's theory of evolution holds that, far from being present at the earth's creation (as stated in the Biblical account of creation in Genesis), humans evolved from lower forms of life over billions of years.

Some celebrated Darwin's work as a rational chronicle of creation, while others condemned his conclusions as an attack on sacred beliefs. For the next century, the two sides battled for dominance, with legislatures (especially in Southern states) banning the teaching of Darwin's theory of evolution in public schools. By 1968, however, the U.S. Supreme Court had ruled that such laws violated the Constitution's ban on government support for religion.

But decisions by the High Court have not resolved the matter because many people continue to see in religion and science two incompatible ways of understanding the world. Yet it is more accurate to say that the two approaches represent different ways of answering different questions. For example, John S. Spong, Episcopal bishop of Newark, New Jersey, argues that everyone should accept the "enormous amount of evidence" that humanity did evolve over a billion years as Darwin contended. But, he adds, science merely investigates *how* the natural world operates; only religion can address *why* we exist and God's role in this process.

Religion in the United States

Just as people debate the current health of families in the United States, so analysts disagree as to the strength of religion in our society. While research certainly shows that changes are underway in this area, it also confirms the ongoing role of religion in social life (Collins, 1982; Greeley, 1989).

Religious Commitment

National surveys reveal that 90 percent of adults identify with a particular religion (NORC, 1993:148). Looking at Table 12–2, we see that almost two-thirds of the population are affiliated with a Protestant denomination, 22 percent claim to be Catholics, and 2 percent say they are Jews. In addition, significant numbers of people adhere to dozens of other religions—from animism to Zen Buddhism—making our society more religiously diverse than virtually any on earth.

The religious diversity of the United States stems from two key factors: a Constitutional ban on any government-sponsored religion and a high rate of immigration. But, in any particular region of the country, one religious denomination stands out, as National Map 12–2 shows.

Religiosity is *the importance of religion in a person's life*. By global standards, North Americans are a relatively religious people, more so, for example, than Europeans or the Japanese. Quantitative measures of religiosity, however, depend on precisely how one operationalizes this concept (see Chapter 1, "Sociology: Perspective, Theory, and Method"). Almost everyone in the United States (95 percent) claims to believe in a divine power of some kind, although only about 60 percent assert that they "know that God exists and have no

doubts about it" (NORC, 1993:409). Responding to other survey items, just half of U.S. adults claim to pray at least once a day, and 40 percent report that they attend religious services on a weekly or almost-weekly basis (NORC, 1993:144, 152, 158).

Clearly, the question "How religious are we?" yields no easy answers. Keep in mind, too, that being religious is normative in our culture, so that people probably claim to be more religious than they really are. One team of researchers, who recently tallied the actual church attendance of the people living in Ashtabula County in northeast Ohio, concluded that twice as many people said they attended church on a given Sunday as really did so. Their estimate, in other words, is that no more than 20 percent of people attend church regularly (Hadaway, Marler, & Chaves, 1993). Our general conclusion, then, is that while most people in the United States claim to be at least somewhat religious, only about one-third are, in fact, strongly religious.

Finally, religiosity varies among denominations. In general, Catholics are more religious than Protestants, and members of sects are the most religious of all (Stark & Glock, 1968; Hadaway, Marler, & Chaves, 1993).

Religion and Social Stratification

Religious affiliation is related to a number of other factors. We now examine how religions are linked to dimensions of social stratification.

Social class. Wade Roof (1979) found that Jews, Episcopalians, and Presbyterians had the highest overall social standing in the United States. In a middle position were Congregationalists and Methodists; lower social standing was typical of Catholics, Lutherans, Baptists, and members of sects. All categories, of course, show internal variation.

Ethnicity. Throughout the world, religion is tied to ethnicity, largely because one religion may predominate in a single region or society. The Arab cultures of the Middle East, for example, are mostly Islamic; Hinduism closely reflects the culture of India. Christianity and Judaism diverge from this pattern; while these religions are primarily Western, followers live in numerous societies.

Religion and ethnicity also dovetail in the United States. Our society encompasses *Anglo-Saxon* Protestants, *Irish* Catholics, *Russian* Jews, and *Greek* Orthodox. This fusion of nationality and religion derives

**TABLE 12–2 Religious Identification
in the United States, 1993**

Religion	Proportion Indicating Preference
Protestant denominations	64.1%
Baptist	19.5
Methodist	10.6
Lutheran	7.3
Presbyterian	4.4
Episcopalian	2.1
All others or no denomination	20.2
Catholic	22.0
Jewish	2.1
Other or no answer	2.7
No religious preference	9.1

Source: *General Social Surveys, 1972–1993: Cumulative Codebook* (Chicago: National Opinion Research Center, 1993), pp. 148–49.

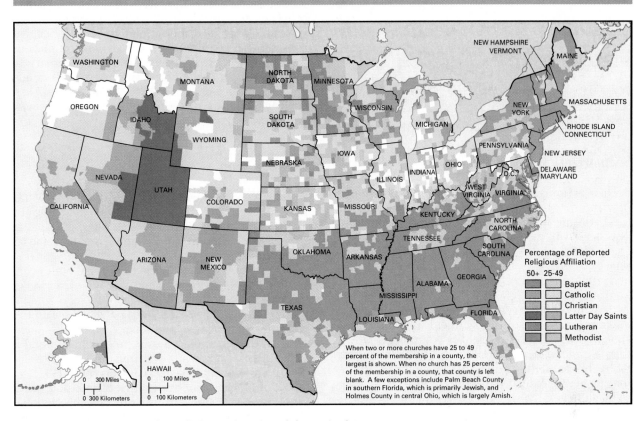

NATIONAL MAP 12–2   The Religious Diversity of the United States

In the vast majority of counties, at least 25 percent of people who report having a religious affiliation are members of the same religious organization. Thus, while the United States is religiously diverse at the national level, most people live in communities where one denomination predominates. What historical facts might account for this pattern?

Source: Glenmary Research Center (1990).

from an influx of immigrants from societies with a single major religion. Still, nearly every U.S. ethnic group incorporates at least some religious diversity. People of English ancestry, for instance, may be members of a Protestant denomination, Roman Catholics, Jews, or affiliated with some other religion.

Race.   Historically, the church has been central to the spiritual—and also political—lives of African Americans. Transported to the Western Hemisphere, most people of African descent became Christians— the dominant religion in the Americas—but they

blended Christian belief and practice with elements of African religions. Guided by this multicultural religious heritage, many people of color even today participate in rituals that are—by European standards— both spontaneous and emotional (Frazier, 1965; Roberts, 1980).

As African Americans migrated from the rural South to the industrial cities of the North, the church played a key role in addressing problems of dislocation, poverty, and prejudice. Further, black churches have provided an important avenue of achievement for talented men and women. Ralph Abernathy, Martin

Luther King, Jr., and Jesse Jackson each gained world recognition as a religious leader.

Religion in a Changing Society

As we have seen with family life, religion is changing in the United States. Analysis of religious change revolves around the concept of *secularization*.

Secularization

Secularization refers to *the historical decline in the influence of religion*. Secularization (derived from the Latin, meaning "the present age") is commonly associated with modern, technologically advanced societies (Cox, 1971; O'Dea & Aviad, 1983). Conventional wisdom holds that secularization parallels the increasing importance of science in understanding human affairs.

More adults today, for example, experience the transitions of birth, illness, and death in the presence of physicians (with scientific knowledge) rather than church leaders (whose knowledge is based on faith). To some, this means that religion's relevance for our everyday lives has diminished. Harvey Cox elaborates:

> The world looks less and less to religious rules and rituals for its morality or its meanings. For some, religion provides a hobby, for others a mark of national or ethnic identification, for still others an aesthetic delight. For fewer and fewer does it provide an inclusive and commanding system of personal and cosmic values and explanations. (1971:3)

If Cox is right, should we expect that religion will someday completely disappear? The consensus among sociologists is "no" (Hammond, 1985; McGuire, 1987). Recall that the vast majority of people in the United States continue to profess a belief in God and as many claim to pray each day as vote in national elections. Further, religious affiliation today is actually several times higher than it was in 1850.

Secularization does not, then, signal the impending death of religion. More correctly, a decline in some dimensions of religion (like belief in life after death) is being accompanied by an increase in others (such as religious affiliation). Furthermore, our society is of two minds about whether secularization is good or bad. Conservatives tend to equate any erosion of religion with moral decline. But many progressives hail secularization as liberation from the all-encompassing beliefs of the past, so that people can take greater responsibility for what they choose to believe. Secularization has also brought the practices of many religious organizations more in line with widespread social attitudes. The Catholic church, for example, abandoned Latin in religious services in favor of commonly spoken languages, and an increasing number of religions now permit the ordination of women.

Civil Religion

Secularization takes many forms, including what Robert Bellah (1975) calls **civil religion**, *quasi-religious loyalty based on citizenship*. Even in a basically secular society, in other words, our citizenship retains some religious qualities.

Certainly, most people in the United States consider our way of life to be moral and a force for good in the world. People differ as to what our society's moral purpose should be, but individuals at all points on the political spectrum also find religious qualities—such as a sense of belonging, a drive to make the world a better place, and a feeling of shared mission in life—in political movements (Williams & Demerath, 1991).

Civil religion, like its spiritual counterpart, takes in a range of rituals from rising to sing the National Anthem at sporting events to watching public parades several times a year. And like the Christian cross or the Jewish Star of David, the flag serves as a symbol of our national identity that we expect people to treat with reverence.

Religious Revival

From a distance, the evidence shows a stable pattern of religiosity in the United States in recent decades. But inside the world of organized religion, a great change is underway. Membership in established, "mainstream" churches like the Episcopalian and Presbyterian denominations has plummeted by almost 50 percent since 1960. During the same period, affiliation with other religious organizations (including the Mormons, Seventh-Day Adventists, and especially Christian sects) has risen just as dramatically. Secularization may turn out to be self-limiting; that is, as church-like organizations become more worldly, many people abandon them in favor of sect-like communities

The Changing Face of Religion: A Report From Great Britain

Although the Church of England is still that nation's official religious organization, Anglicans number only one-fifth of regular worshipers in Great Britain today. Like their counterparts in the United States, Britain's established, "mainstream" churches have lost members; as the figure shows, support for the Anglican, Roman Catholic, Presbyterian, and Baptist churches has plunged substantially in recent years.

Even so, religiosity in Great Britain is holding steady (although at a level below that of the United States). The reason is that, while the established churches are losing members, newer religious organizations are showing surprising strength.

Immigration lies behind some of this religious revival: As large numbers of Asians settle rapidly in Britain, the proportion of Muslims, Sikhs, and Hindus in the country steadily increases. Newly formed cults, too, contribute to religious resurgence; experts contend that as many as six hundred British cults exist at any one time.

But the most significant surge in British religious affiliation has occurred among fundamentalist Christian organizations that embrace highly energetic and musical forms of worship, often under the direction of charismatic leaders. Like fundamentalist denominations in the United States, these religious communities typically cherish and share the experience of God's presence in a way that the more staid, "mainstream" churches do not.

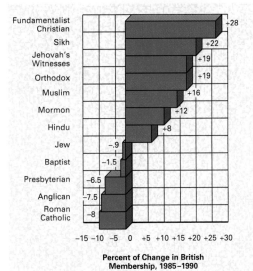

Percent of Change in British Membership, 1985–1990

Group	Percent of Change
Fundamentalist Christian	+28
Sikh	+22
Jehovah's Witnesses	+19
Orthodox	+19
Muslim	+16
Mormon	+12
Hindu	+8
Jew	−.9
Baptist	−1.5
Presbyterian	−6.5
Anglican	−7.5
Roman Catholic	−8

Sources: Barker (1989) and *The Economist* (1993).

---

that better address their spiritual concerns (Stark & Bainbridge, 1981; Roof & McKinney, 1987; Jacquet & Jones, 1993).

Much the same pattern of change can be seen in other industrial societies. The box takes a look at the state of religious affiliation in Great Britain.

A key dimension of religious revival everywhere is the growth of **religious fundamentalism,** *a conservative doctrine that opposes intellectualism and worldly accommodation in favor of restoring traditional, otherworldly religion.* In the United States, fundamentalism has made the greatest gains among Protestants. Southern Baptists, one such organization, form the largest religious community in the United States. But fundamentalist groups have also proliferated among Roman Catholics and Jews.

In response to what they see as the growing influence of science and the erosion of the conventional family, religious fundamentalists defend their version of traditional values. From this point of view, the liberal churches are simply too tolerant of religious diversity and too open to change. Religious fundamentalism is distinctive in five ways (Hunter, 1983, 1985, 1987, 1989; Willcox, 1989).

1. **Fundamentalists interpret the Scriptures literally.** Fundamentalists insist on a literal interpretation of Scripture to counter what they see as excessive intellectualism among more liberal Christian organizations. For example, many fundamentalists dismiss evolution, believing that God created the world, including human beings, precisely as described in Genesis.

2. **Fundamentalists do not accept religious diversity.** Fundamentalists maintain that tolerance and relativism water down personal faith. They

The painting *Arts of the South*, by Thomas Hart Benton (1889–1975), suggests that religious fundamentalism is strongly integrated into the community life of rural people in the southern United States.

maintain, therefore, that their religious beliefs are valid while those of others are not.

3. **Fundamentalists pursue the personal experience of God's presence.** In contrast to the worldliness and intellectualism of other religious organizations, fundamentalism seeks to propagate "good old-time religion" and spiritual revival. To fundamentalist Christians, the experience of being "born again" and establishing a personal relationship with Jesus Christ should be clearly evident in a person's everyday life.

4. **Fundamentalism opposes "secular humanism."** Fundamentalists reject accommodation with the changing world because, to them, contemporary life undermines religious conviction. Secular humanism is a general term that refers to our society's tendency to look to scientific experts (including sociologists) rather than God for guidance about how to live.

5. **Many fundamentalists endorse conservative political goals.** Although fundamentalism tends to shy away from worldly concerns, some fundamentalist leaders have weighed in to the political arena in recent years to oppose what they see as the "liberal agenda" of feminism and gay rights. Fundamentalists oppose abortion as a matter of choice, seek to preserve the traditional

two-parent family, press for the return of prayer in the public schools, and scold the mass media for coloring the stories they report with liberal sentiments (Viguerie, 1981; Hunter, 1983; Speer, 1984; Ostling, 1985; Ellison & Sherkat, 1993; Green, 1993).

Taken together, these traits suggest why some people view fundamentalists as somewhat rigid and self-righteous. At the same time, this brief sketch also helps us to understand why adherents find in fundamentalism—with its greater religious certainty and its emphasis on experiencing God's presence—an appealing alternative to the more intellectual, tolerant, and worldly "mainstream" denominations.

Which religious organizations are "fundamentalist"? This term is most correctly applied to conservative organizations in the larger evangelical tradition, including Southern Baptists, Pentecostals, Seventh-Day Adventists, and the Assembly of God. In national surveys, about 35 percent of U.S. adults describe their upbringing as "fundamentalist"; 38 percent claim a "moderate" religious upbringing; and 24 percent call their religious background "liberal" (NORC, 1993:169).

Finally, in contrast to small village congregations of years past, some fundamentalist organizations have become *electronic churches* dominated by "prime-time preachers" (Hadden & Swain, 1981). Electronic religion, a pattern known only in the United States, has propelled Oral Roberts, Pat Robertson, Robert Schuller, and others to greater prominence than all but a few clergy enjoyed in the past. Perhaps 5 percent of the national television audience (about 10 million people) are regular viewers of religious television, while 20 percent (about 40 million people) watch some religious programming every week (Martin, 1981; Gallup, 1982; NORC, 1993).

Looking Ahead:
Religion in the Twenty-First Century

Despite periodic soul searching over whether God is dead, the power of media ministries, the surging growth of sects, and the adherence of millions more people to "mainstream" churches suggest that religion will remain a central element of modern society (Stark & Bainbridge, 1981; Bateson & Ventis, 1982; Hunter, 1985; Greeley, 1994). The world is becoming more complex, with rapid change almost outstripping our ability to keep pace. But rather than undermining religion, these processes end up firing the religious imagination of people who seek a sense of religious community and ultimate meaning in life.

Science simply cannot address humanity's spiritual needs and questions. Moreover, technological advances are presenting us with moral dilemmas as never before—from new technologies for creating life to techniques for sustaining the lives of dying people. Against this backdrop of uncertainty, it is little wonder that many of us rely on our faith for assurance and hope (Cox, 1977; Barker, 1981).

SUMMARY

Family

1. The family is a major social institution found everywhere in the world; even so, the forms families take vary around the world and over time.

2. In industrial societies such as the United States, marriage is monogamous. Many preindustrial societies, however, permit polygamy, of which there are two types: polygyny and polyandry.

3. In global perspective, patrilocal residence is most common, while industrial societies favor neolocality, and a few cultures are matrilocal. Industrial societies utilize bilateral descent, while preindustrial societies tend to be either patrilineal or matrilineal.

4. Structural-functional analysis identifies major family functions: socializing the young, regulating sexual activity, and providing social placement and emotional support. Social-conflict theories explore how the family perpetuates inequality based on class, ethnicity, race, and gender. Symbolic-interaction analysis highlights the dynamic and changeable nature of family life.

5. In the United States and elsewhere, family life evolves over the life course beginning with courtship, extending through child rearing, and ending with the loss of a spouse, usually in old age.

6. Families also differ according to class position, race, ethnicity, and gender. Few family patterns apply to all household groups.

7. The divorce rate today is ten times higher than it was a century ago; about 40 percent of current marriages will end in divorce. Most people who divorce—especially men—remarry.

8. Family violence, victimizing both women and children, has captured public attention.

9. Our society's family life is becoming more varied. Singlehood, cohabitation, and one-parent families are on the rise. While homosexual men and women cannot legally marry, many form long-lasting relationships.

10. Although ethically controversial, new reproductive technology is altering traditional notions of parenthood.

Religion

1. Religion is a major social institution based on distinguishing the sacred from the profane. Religion is a matter of faith, not scientific evidence. Therefore, sociologists study religion's effects on society while making no claim as to the ultimate truth of any religious belief.

2. Emile Durkheim argued that, through religion, individuals celebrate the power of their society. His structural-functional analysis holds that religion promotes social cohesion and conformity, and confers meaning and purpose on life.

3. Using the symbolic-interaction paradigm, Peter Berger explains that people socially construct religious beliefs in response to life's uncertainties and disruptions.

4. Social-conflict analyst Karl Marx claimed that religion supports inequality. Yet religious ideals, as Max Weber countered, can trigger change and even promote social equality.

5. Churches, which are formal religious organizations well integrated into their societies, fall into two categories—ecclesias and denominations.

6. How religious we conclude our society is depends on how we operationalize the concept of religiosity. The vast majority of people say they believe in God, but only about one-fifth of the U.S. population attends religious services regularly.

7. The concept of secularization refers to the diminishing importance of the sacred in everyday life. Looking at the United States, we see that some measures of religiosity (including membership in "mainstream" churches) have declined, while others (such as membership in sects) are gaining ground. This complex mosaic of religious faith casts doubt on the assertion that secularization will eventually lead to the demise of religion.

8. Religious fundamentalism opposes accommodation to the world, advocates literal interpretation of sacred texts, and pursues the personal experience of God's presence. Some fundamentalist Christians have become galvanized into a conservative political force.

Sects, the result of religious division, are marked by suspicion of the larger society as well as charismatic leadership. Cults are religious organizations that embrace new and unconventional beliefs and practices.

KEY CONCEPTS

Family

cohabitation the sharing of a household by an unmarried couple

descent the system by which members of a society trace kinship over generations

endogamy marriage between people of the same social category

exogamy marriage between people of different social categories

extended family (consanguine family) a social unit including parents, children, and other kin

family a relatively permanent group of two or more people, who are related by blood, marriage, or adoption and who usually live together

homogamy marriage between people with the same social characteristics

incest taboo a norm forbidding sexual relations or marriage between certain kin

kinship a social bond, based on blood, marriage, or adoption, that joins people into families

marriage a legally sanctioned relationship, involving economic cooperation as well as normative sexual activity and childbearing, that people expect to be enduring

monogamy marriage involving two partners

nuclear family (conjugal family) a social unit containing one or, more commonly, two adults and any children

polygamy marriage that unites three or more people

Religion

animism the belief that natural objects are conscious forms of life that affect humanity

charisma extraordinary personal qualities that can turn an audience into followers

church a formal religious organization well integrated into the larger society

civil religion a quasi-religious loyalty based on citizenship

cult a religious organization that is substantially outside the cultural traditions of a society

denomination a church, not linked to the state, that recognizes religious pluralism

ecclesia a church that is formally allied with the state

faith belief anchored in conviction rather than scientific evidence

liberation theology a fusion of Christian principles with political (often Marxist) activism

profane that which people define as an ordinary element of everyday life

religion a social institution, involving beliefs and practices, that distinguishes the sacred from the profane

religiosity the importance of religion in a person's life

religious fundamentalism a conservative religious doctrine that opposes intellectualism and worldly accommodation in favor of restoring traditional, otherworldly religion

sacred that which people define as extraordinary, inspiring a sense of awe and reverence

sect a type of religious organization that stands apart from the larger society

secularization the historical decline in the influence of religion

totem an object collectively defined as sacred

CRITICAL-THINKING QUESTIONS

1. Identify several ways in which families have changed since 1960. What causes family transformation?

2. On balance, are families in the United States becoming weaker or not? Cite evidence to back up your contention.

3. Explain Karl Marx's assertion that religion tends to support the status quo. Develop a counterargument, based on Max Weber's analysis of Calvinism, that religion serves as a major force for social change.

4. What facts point to religion's waning importance in the United States? In what ways is religion getting stronger?

Education
and Medicine

Thirteen-year-old Naoko Matsuo has just returned from school to her home in suburban Yokohama, Japan. Instead of dropping off her books and beginning an afternoon of fun, she settles in to do her homework. Several hours later, her mother reminds her that it is time to leave for the juku *or "cram school" that she attends three evenings a week. After a short subway trip downtown, Naoko joins dozens of other girls and boys for intensive training in Japanese, English, math, and science.*

Tuition for the juku *costs the Matsuo family several hundred dollars a month. They hope, however, that the investment will pay off when Naoko begins a series of national examinations to determine her school placement, an ordeal that culminates in the achievement test that determines whether or not she will attend an exclusive national university—the gateway to a high-paying, prestigious career (Simons, 1989).*

This chapter begins by exploring *education,* a vital social institution in societies such as Japan and the United States. We shall explain *why* schooling is important in modern societies, as well as *who* reaps most educational benefits. The second half of the chapter examines *medicine,* another social institution with great importance in the modern world. Good health, like quality schooling, is distributed unequally throughout our society's population. And like education, medicine reveals striking variation from society to society.

Education: A Global Survey

Education refers to *the social institution through which society provides its members with important knowledge, including facts, skills, and values.* Education takes place in a host of ways, many of them as informal as a family discussion. A central component of education in industrial societies is **schooling**, *formal instruction under the direction of specially trained teachers.*

Education in Poor Societies

In preindustrial societies—in which most of the world's people live—families and local communities teach their members specialized productive skills. But formal schooling, and especially learning not directly linked to work, is generally available only to wealthy people. This fact is suggested by the Greek root of the word "school," which is "leisure." In ancient Greece, renowned teachers such as Plato, Socrates, and Aristotle taught only aristocratic men; similarly, in ancient China, the famous philosopher Confucius shared his wisdom with only a privileged few (Rohlen, 1983).

The influence of thousands of local cultural traditions produces marked diversity in schooling throughout poor countries today. In Iran (Middle East), for example, education and religion are closely linked, so Islam figures prominently in schooling there. In Bangladesh (Asia), Zimbabwe (Africa), and Nicaragua (Latin America), distinctive cultural systems have molded the process of schooling. Schooling in poor societies also reflects historic colonialism by which various rich nations imposed their culture on others.

But all poor societies have one trait in common: limited access to schooling. Only half of all children living in poor countries enroll in secondary school; in the least economically developed nations (including several in central Africa), only half of all children even enter primary school (Najafizadeh & Mennerick, 1992). As a result, illiteracy disadvantages one-third of Latin Americans, almost half of Asians, and about two-thirds of Africans. Global Map 13–1 displays the extent of illiteracy around the world.

Education in Industrial Societies

Industrial societies, by contrast, embrace the principle of schooling for everyone. Industrial production demands that workers gain at least basic skills in the so-called "three Rs"—reading, 'riting, and 'rithmetic. Our society also looks to schooling as a way to forge a literate citizenry capable of actively participating in political life.

The United States was among the first countries to pursue the goal of mass education. By 1850, half the U.S. population between the ages of five and nineteen were enrolled in school. By 1918, however, every state had enacted a *mandatory education law* requiring children to attend school until age sixteen or completion of the eighth grade. Such laws drew children from farms and factories to classrooms.

Table 13–1 on page 334 shows that a milestone was reached in the mid-1960s when a majority of U.S. adults had completed high school. In 1993, four in five adults had a high school education and more than one in five had completed four years of college.

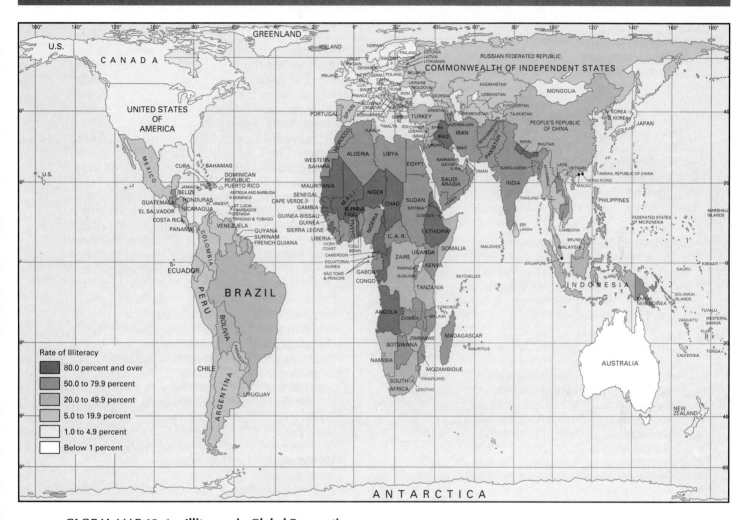

GLOBAL MAP 13–1   Illiteracy in Global Perspective

Reading and writing skills are widespread in every industrial society, with illiteracy rates generally below 5 percent. Throughout Latin America, however, illiteracy is more commonplace—one consequence of limited economic development. In about three dozen nations of the world—many of them in Africa—illiteracy is the rule rather than the exception. In such societies, people rely on what sociologists call the "oral tradition" of face-to-face communication rather than communicating by the written word.

Source: *Peters Atlas of the World* (1990).

Schooling in Japan

Before industrialization brought mandatory education to Japan in 1872, only a privileged few received schooling. Today's educational system in Japan is widely praised for generating some of the world's highest achievers.

The early grades concentrate on transmitting Japanese traditions, including obligation to family. By their early teens, students (including Naoko Matsuo,

TABLE 13–1 Educational Achievement in the United States, 1910–1993*

Year	High School Graduates	College Graduates	Median Years of Schooling
1910	13.5%	2.7%	8.1
1920	16.4	3.3	8.2
1930	19.1	3.9	8.4
1940	24.1	4.6	8.6
1950	33.4	6.0	9.3
1960	41.1	7.7	10.5
1970	55.2	11.0	12.2
1980	68.7	17.0	12.5
1993	80.2	21.9	12.7

*For persons twenty-five years of age and over. Percentage for high school graduates includes those who go on to college.

Source: U.S. Bureau of the Census (1994).

described at the beginning of this chapter) encounter Japan's system of rigorous and competitive examinations. These written tests, which resemble the Scholastic Aptitude Tests (SATs) used for college admissions in the United States, all but determine a young Japanese student's future.

More men and women graduate from high school in Japan (90 percent) than in the United States (80 percent). But competitive examinations sharply curb the number of college-bound youths, so that only 30 percent of high school graduates—compared to 60 percent in the United States—end up entering college. Understandably, then, Japanese students take these examinations with the utmost seriousness and about half attend "cram schools" to better prepare for them. Japanese women, most of whom are not in the labor force, often devote themselves to their children's success in school.

Despite—or perhaps because of—the pressure it places on students, Japanese schooling produces impressive results. In a number of fields, notably mathematics and science, young Japanese outperform students in every other industrial society, including the United States (Benedict, 1974; Hayneman & Loxley, 1983; Rohlen, 1983; Brinton, 1988; Simons, 1989).

Schooling in Great Britain

During the Middle Ages, schooling was a privilege of the British nobility, who studied classical subjects since they had little need for the practical skills related to earning a living. As the Industrial Revolution created a need for an educated labor force, and as working-class people demanded access to schools, a rising share of the British population entered the classroom. Law now requires every British child to attend school until age sixteen.

Traditional social distinctions, however, persist in British education. Many wealthy families send their children to what the British call *public schools,* the equivalent of private boarding schools in the United States. Such elite schools not only teach academic subjects, they also convey to children from wealthy (especially *newly rich*) families the distinctive patterns of speech, mannerisms, and social graces of the British upper class. These schools are far too expensive for most students, however; the majority attend state-supported day schools.

To lessen the influence of social background on schooling, the British expanded their university system during the 1960s and 1970s, and inaugurated a system of competitive examinations for admission. For those who score highest, the government pays most tuition and living expenses. Still, class differences figure more prominently in British education than they do in more meritocratic Japan. Thus, many students who do not perform well on the examinations—but are well-connected in terms of social class—still manage to attend Oxford and Cambridge, high-prestige British universities roughly on a par with Yale, Harvard, and Princeton in the United States. These "Oxbridge" graduates assume their place at the core of the British power elite (Sampson, 1982; Gamble, Ludlam, & Baker, 1993).

Schooling in the United States

The educational system in the United States, too, has been shaped by our cultural traditions. Thomas Jefferson thought that the new nation could become democratic only if schooling enabled people to "read and understand what is going on in the world" (quoted in Honeywell, 1931:13). The United States now has a larger proportion of its people attending colleges and universities than any other industrial society—twice the share in Australia or Sweden, for example, and three times the proportion in France or Ireland (U.S. Bureau of the Census, 1993).

Schooling in the United States also reflects the value of *equal opportunity.* National surveys show that most people think schooling is crucial to personal success, and a majority of respondents also believe that people have a chance to get an education consistent with their abilities and talents (NORC, 1993). But this view better expresses our aspirations than our achievement. Until this century, our society all but excluded women from higher education, and only among the wealthy do a majority of young people attend college even today.

Besides trying to make schooling more widely available, our educational system has also stressed the value of *practical* learning, that is, knowledge that has a direct bearing on people's work and interests. The educational philosopher John Dewey (1859–1952) maintained that children would readily learn those things that they found useful, rather than a fixed body of knowledge passed down from generation to generation. Thus Dewey (1968; orig. 1938) championed *progressive education* that addressed people's changing concerns and needs. Reflecting this practical emphasis, today's college students select areas of major study with an eye toward future employment. As a consequence of the Information Revolution, for example, the number of bachelor's degrees awarded in computer science during the 1980s more than doubled, while the number of degrees in agriculture tumbled by almost half (U.S. Bureau of the Census, 1993).

The Functions of Schooling

Structural-functional analysis focuses on ways in which schooling enhances the operation and stability of society.

1. **Socialization.** Technologically simple societies rely on the family to transmit knowledge about a way of life from one generation to another. As societies acquire complex technology, formal systems of education emerge, with highly trained teachers to convey specialized knowledge.

2. **Social integration.** Schools help to forge a diverse population into a unified culture sharing norms and values. It is no coincidence that states enacted mandatory education laws a century ago during a time of unparalleled immigration. Schooling operates the same way in many of today's cities, in which a majority of students come from the ranks of racial and ethnic minorities.

3. **Social placement.** Schools identify the talents of students and see that they receive instruction appropriate to their abilities. Schooling thus enhances meritocracy by rewarding talent and hard

Wealth and power in Great Britain have long been linked to attending "public" schools—actually privately funded boarding schools for young men and, to a lesser extent, women. The most elite of these schools transmit the way of life of the upper class not so much in the classroom as on the playing fields, in the dining halls, and in the dormitories where informal socialization goes on continuously. Elite boarding schools are especially important to new-rich families; parents with modest backgrounds and big bank accounts send their children to these schools to mix with and learn from the offspring of "old-money" families.

work regardless of students' social background. Historically, schooling has been the key to upward social mobility in the United States (Hurn, 1978).

4. **Cultural innovation.** Schools create as well as transmit culture. Especially at centers of higher education, scholars engage in critical inquiry and research that lead to innovation and discovery.

5. **Latent functions of schooling.** Besides these widely recognized functions of formal education, schools also serve as a source of child care for the rising number of one-parent and two-career families. Among teens, schooling consumes much time and considerable energy, inhibiting deviant behavior. Schooling also usefully occupies

Proponents of Afrocentric schooling argue that teaching African languages and cultures will foster children's self-esteem and interest in learning. Critics respond that Afrocentrism promotes racial separation and diverts resources from the teaching of basic skills that children need to succeed in the larger society.

thousands of young people in their twenties for whom few jobs may be available. High schools, colleges, and universities bring together people of marriageable age, many of whom meet their future spouse in the classroom. School networks provide not only friendship, but valuable career opportunities and resources later on in life.

Critical evaluation. Structural-functional analysis of formal education stresses the ways in which this social institution supports the operation of an industrial society. However, functionalism overlooks the extent of inequality inherent in our educational system and, indeed, how schooling actually operates to reproduce the class structure in each generation. In the next section, social-conflict analysis casts a critical eye on these issues.

Schooling and Social Inequality

Social-conflict analysis examines how formal education promotes social inequality. From this point of view, schooling perpetuates social inequality and acceptance of the status quo.

1. **Social control.** Samuel Bowles and Herbert Gintis (1976) claim that the clamor for public

education in the late nineteenth century arose just as capitalists were demanding a docile and disciplined work force. Mandatory education laws ensured that schools taught immigrants the English language as well as cultural values, such as punctuality and discipline, which enhance the operation of capitalism.

2. **Testing and social inequality.** Educators developed intelligence and aptitude tests early in this century to evaluate innate ability, not social background. But such tests have questionable validity insofar as scores also reflect a subject's cultural environment. Critics charge that any test reflects a society's dominant culture, thereby placing minority students at some disadvantage. Thus, in effect, standardized tests transform privilege into personal merit (Owen, 1985; Crouse & Trusheim, 1988; Putka, 1990).

3. **Tracking and social inequality.** Despite their alleged deficiencies, tests are the basis for educational **tracking,** *the division of a school's students into different educational programs.* Defenders contend that tracking helps teachers tailor lessons to students' individual aptitudes and interests. Thus some enroll in college preparatory classes, others receive a general education, and still others gain vocational and technical training. Critics charge that tracking undermines meritocracy because, in practice, schools place students from privileged backgrounds in higher tracks where they receive the best the school offers. Those from disadvantaged backgrounds, by contrast, end up in lower tracks in which rote memorization and classroom drill are commonplace (Bowles & Gintis, 1976; Persell, 1977; Davis & Haller, 1981; Oakes, 1982, 1985; Hallinan & Williams, 1989; Kilgore, 1991).

Public and Private Education

Just as students are treated differently within schools, so do schools vary among themselves. In 1993 almost 90 percent of the 65 million primary and secondary school children in the United States attended state-funded public schools. The remainder were enrolled in private schools.

A majority of private-school students attend one of more than eight thousand *parochial* schools (from the Latin meaning "of the parish"), operated by the Roman Catholic church. The Catholic school system grew rapidly a century ago, as cities swelled with

From a functionalist point of view, schooling provides children with the information and skills they will need as adults. A conflict analysis adds that schooling differs according to the resources available to the local community. To the extent that some schools offer children much more than others do, education falls short of its goal of enhancing equality of opportunity.

immigrants who were glad to find schools that would help maintain their cultural traditions. Today, after millions of white people have fled the inner cities, many parochial schools enroll non-Catholics, including a growing number of African Americans whose families eagerly embrace this alternative to the neighborhood public school.

Protestants, too, have private schools or Christian academies. Both kinds of schools offer religious instruction, a more rigorous academic environment, and—in some cases—a racially exclusive classroom (James, 1989).

Some fifteen hundred nonreligious private schools enroll young people mostly from well-to-do families. These prestigious and expensive preparatory schools—many modeled after boarding schools in Great Britain—not only provide a strong academic program, but teach the mannerisms, attitudes, and social graces of the socially prominent. Many "preppies" maintain lifelong social networks with other graduates of their school that confer numerous social advantages.

Two influential reports (Coleman, Hoffer, & Kilgore, 1981; Coleman & Hoffer, 1987) indicate that, holding social background constant, students in private schools perform better than public-school students. This advantage appears to be due to the typical private school's smaller classes, more rigorous curricula, and greater discipline.

But even the public schools are not all the same. For example, Winnetka, Illinois, one of the richest towns in the United States, spends more than $8,000

annually per student, compared to $3,000 spent in Socorro, Texas, one of the poorest. Although cost-of-living differences account for a portion of this disparity, some of our country's fifteen thousand school districts clearly enjoy far more resources than others (Carroll, 1990).

Most affluent, suburban school districts offer better schooling than less well-funded systems in central cities. This pattern—which benefits whites—has prompted a policy of *busing*—transporting students to achieve racial balance and equal opportunity in schools. Although busing currently affects only 5 percent of U.S. school children, it has generated enormous controversy. Advocates claim that, given the reality of racial segregation, governments will earmark adequate funding for schools in poor, minority neighborhoods only if white children from richer areas attend them. Critics respond that busing is expensive and undermines the concept of neighborhood schools. But both sides acknowledge that, because of the racial imbalance in contemporary urban areas, any effective busing scheme would have to join inner cities and suburbs—a plan that has never been politically feasible.

A report by a research team headed by James Coleman (1966) confirmed that predominantly minority schools suffered problems ranging from larger class size to insufficient libraries and fewer science labs. But the Coleman report cautioned that money alone would not magically improve academic quality. More important are the cooperative efforts and enthusiasm of teachers,

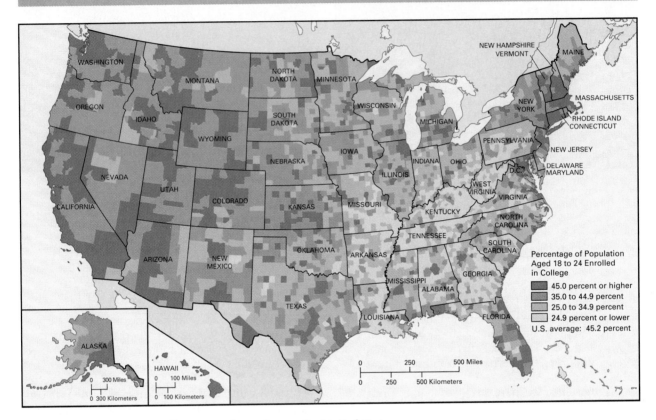

NATIONAL MAP 13–1   College Attendance Across the United States

Generally speaking, college attendance is most common among adults along the Northeast and West coasts. By contrast, adults living in the Midwest and the South (especially the Appalachian region) are the least likely members of our society to enroll in college. How would you explain this pattern? (Income is one obvious consideration. Would people's ideas about gender equality be another?)

Source: *American Demographics* magazine, April 1993, p. 60. Reprinted with permission. ©1993 *American Demographics* magazine, Ithaca, New York.

parents, and the students themselves. Supporting this conclusion, Christopher Jencks (1972) asserted that even if schools were exactly the same everywhere, the students whose families value and encourage learning would still perform better.

The point is that we should not expect schools alone to alleviate marked social inequality in the United States. Yet our society can hardly afford to ignore the educational needs of poor minority children, who will represent a growing proportion of tomorrow's work force (Cohen, 1989).

Access to Higher Education

Higher education is a path to occupational achievement; not surprisingly, then, the vast majority of parents would send their children to college if they could (Gallup, 1982). Yet only 60 percent of high school graduates enroll in college the following fall, and among the U.S. population aged twenty-five and older, only one-fifth are college graduates. National Map 13–1 shows where in the United States people are more or less likely to reach college.

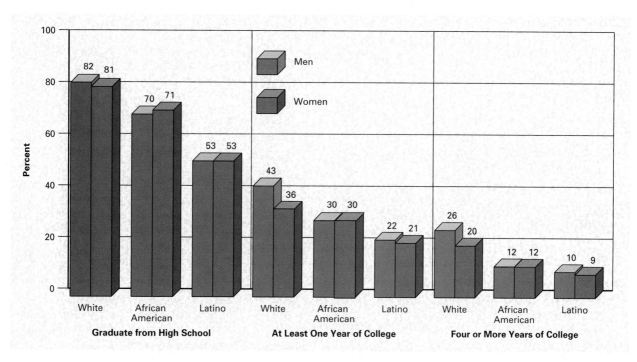

FIGURE 13–1   Educational Achievement for Various Categories of People, Aged 25 Years and Over

Source: U.S. Bureau of the Census (1994).

In the United States, the most crucial factor affecting access to higher education is money. College is expensive and the cost is rising rapidly. Even at state-supported colleges and universities, annual tuition averages about $2,600, and the most expensive private colleges and universities reach $25,000 a year. This is why, among affluent families earning $75,000 per year or more, two-thirds of young people attend college; the same is true of less than one-fifth of young people from families earning $10,000 or less each year.

The financial burden of higher education discourages many minorities, typically with below-average incomes, from enrolling in college. Figure 13–1 shows that white people are more likely than African Americans and Hispanics to complete high school to begin with, and this disparity widens with each step in the educational system. The long-term trend, however, may be toward greater equality. During the 1980s, the number of Latinos attending college rose by about 63 percent and African-American enrollments increased by 21 percent; the non-Hispanic white rise was a modest 16 percent (U.S. Bureau of the Census, 1993).

For those who do complete college, rewards include not just intellectual and personal growth but higher income. Table 13–2 presents the 1993 median income for full-time workers aged twenty-five and over according to their education. Women with five to eight years of schooling typically earned about $6,493; income rose to about $11,000 for high school graduates, and averaged $22,416 for college graduates and $39,614 for women with doctorates. The numbers in parentheses are ratios, showing that a woman with a doctorate or professional degree earns six or seven times as much as her counterpart with four or fewer years of schooling. Men earn considerably more across the board than women do; moreover, more schooling boosts men's income at an even greater rate. Finally, bear in mind that some of the earning differential based on education has to do with social background, since the people with the most schooling are likely to come from relatively well-to-do families to begin with.

Credentialism

Sociologist Randall Collins (1979) has dubbed the United States a *credential society*, because people view diplomas and degrees as evidence of ability to perform

TABLE 13–2 Median Income by Sex and Educational Attainment*

Education	Men	Women
Professional degree	$68,824 (9.2)	$36,645 (6.4)
Doctorate	51,790 (6.9)	39,614 (6.9)
Master's	44,271 (5.9)	30,190 (5.2)
Bachelor's	36,779 (4.9)	22,416 (3.9)
1–3 years of college	26,374 (3.5)	14,408 (2.5)
4 years of high school	21,673 (2.9)	10,909 (1.9)
9–11 years of school	14,220 (1.9)	7,294 (1.3)
5–8 years of school	11,089 (1.5)	6,493 (1.1)
0–4 years of school	7,464 (1.0)	5,759 (1.0)

*Persons aged twenty-five years and over, working full-time, 1993. The earnings ratio, in parentheses, indicates how many times the lowest income level an individual with additional schooling earns.

Source: U.S. Bureau of the Census (1994).

specialized occupational roles. In modern, technologically advanced societies, credentials now say "who you are" as much as family background does.

Credentialism, then, means *evaluating people on the basis of educational degrees.* On the one hand, credentialism is the way our society fills jobs with well-trained people. On the other hand, however, credentials often bear little relation to the responsibilities of a specific job. Collins (1979) suggests that advanced degrees serve as a shorthand way to sort out people with the manners, attitudes, and even color desired by many employers. In short, credentialism amounts to a gatekeeping strategy that restricts important occupations to a small segment of the population.

Privilege and Personal Merit

If, as social-conflict analysis suggests, attending college is a rite of passage for affluent men and women, then *schooling transforms social privilege into personal merit.* But our cultural emphasis on individualism pushes us to see credentials as "badges of ability," as Richard Sennett and Jonathan Cobb (1973) put it, rather than as symbols of family affluence. Thus, when we congratulate the new graduate, we usually overlook the social resources that made this achievement possible. In the same way, we are quick to condemn the high school dropout as personally deficient with little thought to the social circumstances that surround that person's life.

Critical evaluation. Social-conflict analysis links formal education to social inequality and shows how schooling transforms privilege into personal worthiness,

and disadvantage into personal deficiency. Critics claim that the social-conflict approach minimizes the extent to which schooling has provided upward mobility for talented women and men—especially those from modest backgrounds. Further, especially in recent years, "politically correct" educational curricula—inspired by conflict theory—are challenging the status quo on many fronts.

Problems in the Schools

An intense debate revolves around schooling in the United States. Because people expect schools to do so much—equalize opportunity, instill discipline, and fire the individual imagination—few people think public schools are doing an excellent job; about half of adults give our schools a grade of "C" or below (Roper Center for Public Opinion Research, 1994).

Discipline and Violence

While most people think schools should instill personal discipline (NORC, 1993:525), many suspect that the job is not being done. The government estimates that, each year, several hundred thousand students and at least one thousand teachers are physically assaulted on school grounds. And according to news reports, thousands of young people now routinely arrive at school armed with guns and other deadly weapons (U.S. Bureau of Justice Statistics, 1991).

Disorder spills into schools from the surrounding society. Nevertheless, schools do have the power to effect change for the better. The key to success appears to be firm disciplinary policies, backed up by parents and, if necessary, law enforcement officials. Schools are unlikely to solve problems of violence that have roots deep in society itself, but they can control violence by forging alliances with parents and community leaders (Reed, 1983; Burns, 1985; Gup, 1992).

Bureaucracy and Student Passivity

If some schools are plagued by violence, many more are afflicted by passive, bored students. Some of the responsibility for failing to take advantage of educational opportunity can be placed on television (which now consumes more of young people's time than school does), on parents (who fail to foster a desire to learn), and on students themselves. But schools, too, must share the blame, since our educational system has long generated student passivity (Coleman, Hoffer, & Kilgore, 1981).

The small, personal schools that served countless local communities a century ago have evolved into huge educational factories. A study of high schools across the United States led Theodore Sizer (1984) to identify five ways in which large, bureaucratic schools undermine education (1984:207–9).

1. **Rigid uniformity.** Bureaucratic schools are typically insensitive to the cultural character of local communities. Outside "specialists" (such as state education officials) operate schools with too little understanding of the needs of particular students.

2. **Numerical ratings.** School officials focus on attendance rates, dropout rates, and achievement test scores. In doing so, they overlook dimensions of schooling difficult to quantify, such as the creativity of students and the energy and enthusiasm of teachers.

3. **Rigid expectations.** Officials expect fifteen-year-olds to be in the tenth grade, and eleventh-graders to score at a certain level on a standardized verbal achievement test. Rarely are exceptionally bright and motivated students permitted to graduate early. Likewise, the system pushes along students who have learned little so they can graduate with their class.

4. **Specialization.** High school students learn Spanish from one teacher, receive guidance from another, and are coached in sports by still others. No school official comes to know the "complete" student. Students experience this division of labor as a continual shuffling among fifty-minute periods throughout the school day.

5. **Little individual responsibility.** Highly bureaucratic schools do not empower students to learn on their own. Similarly, teachers have little latitude in what and how they teach their classes; they dare not accelerate learning for fear of disrupting "the system."

Of course, some formal organization in schools is inevitable given the immense size of the task. The number of students in the New York City public schools alone now exceeds the population of the entire country a century ago. But, Sizer maintains, we can humanize schools to make them more responsive to

In some cities of the United States, the level of violence has escalated to the point that students are in danger of harm not only while traveling to and from school but also in school itself. Estimates indicate that thousands of young people come to school each day carrying guns and other deadly weapons, forcing administrators to adopt desperate security measures.

those they claim to serve. He recommends eliminating rigid class schedules, reducing class size, and training teachers more broadly to help them become fully involved in the lives of their students. Perhaps his most radical suggestion is that graduation from high school should depend on what students have learned rather than simply on the length of time they spend in school.

College: The Silent Classroom

Passivity is also common among college and university students (Gimenez, 1989). Sociologists have done little research on the college classroom—a curious fact considering how much time they spend there. An exception is a study in which David Karp and William Yoels

(1976) observed classes at a coeducational university. Even in small classes, they found, only a few students actively participate. Sometimes, they noticed, students even become irritated with one of their peers who is especially talkative.

Survey responses revealed that most students consider classroom passivity to be their own failing. But, Karp and Yoels reasoned, the educational system itself teaches students to view passively their instructors as "experts" who impart "truth." Students come to see their proper role as quietly listening and respectfully taking notes. As a result, the researchers estimate that only a scant 10 percent of college class time is devoted to discussion.

Professors, for their part, typically enter the classroom ready to deliver a lecture and dislike being sidetracked by student questions or comments (Boyer, 1987). Thus, early in a course, a handful of students assume the role of providing whatever occasional, limited comments the instructor may desire.

Dropping Out

If many students are passive in class, others are not there at all. The problem of *dropping out*—quitting before earning a high school diploma—leaves young people (many of whom are disadvantaged to begin with) ill-equipped for the world of work and at high risk for poverty.

The dropout rate has eased slightly in recent decades; currently about 9 percent of people between the ages of fourteen and twenty-four leave school before graduating, a total of 3.5 million young women and men. Dropping out is least pronounced among non-Hispanic white people (9 percent), higher among African Americans (11 percent), and far higher among Hispanics (24 percent) (U.S. Bureau of the Census, 1994).

The reasons for dropping out include difficulty with the English language, pregnancy among women, and the need to work among those whose families are poor. The dropout rate among children growing up in the poorest 20 percent of all households (27 percent) is ten times higher than that for youngsters living in the richest 20 percent of households (National Center for Education Statistics, 1992). These data point to the fact that many dropouts are young people whose parents also have little schooling and who provide minimal encouragement to continue. Thus low educational achievement often takes the form of a multigenerational cycle of disadvantage.

Academic Standards

Perhaps the most serious educational issue confronting our society involves the quality of schooling. A *Nation at Risk*, a 1983 study of the quality of U.S. schools prepared by the National Commission on Excellence in Education, began with an alarming statement:

> If an unfriendly foreign power had attempted to impose on America the mediocre educational performance that exists today, we might well have viewed it as an act of war. As it stands, we have allowed this to happen to ourselves. (1983:5)

Supporting this conclusion, the report points out that "nearly 40 percent of seventeen-year-olds cannot draw inferences from written material; only one-fifth can write a persuasive essay; and only one-third can solve mathematical problems requiring several steps" (1983:9). Furthermore, scores on the Scholastic Aptitude Test (SAT) have declined since the early 1960s. Then, median scores for students were 500 on the mathematical test and 480 on the verbal test; by 1993, the averages had slipped to 478 and 424. Some of this decline may stem from the broader range of students taking the test, but few doubt that schooling has suffered a setback.

A *Nation at Risk* also notes with alarm the extent of **functional illiteracy,** *reading and writing skills inadequate for everyday living.* Roughly one in eight children—one in three African Americans—completes secondary school without learning to read or write very well. The box takes a closer look at this national problem.

A *Nation at Risk* recommends drastic reform. First, it calls for schools to require all students to complete several years of coursework in English, mathematics, social studies, general science, and computer science. Second, schools should stop pushing along failing students and keep them in the classroom as long as necessary to teach basic skills. Third, teacher training and salaries must be improved in order to attract more talent into the profession. A *Nation at Risk* concludes that educators must ensure that schools meet public expectations, and we citizens must be prepared to bear the costs of good schools.

A final concern is the low performance of U.S. students in global context. Our students are generally less motivated than their counterparts in Japan, for example, and also do less homework. Moreover, Japanese young people spend sixty more days in school each year than U.S. students do. Perhaps we could remedy

Functional Illiteracy: Must We Rethink Education?

Imagine being unable to read labels on cans of food, instructions for assembling a child's toy, the dosage on a medicine bottle, or even the information on your own paycheck. These are some of the debilitating experiences of *functional illiteracy*, reading and writing skills that are inadequate for carrying out everyday responsibilities.

Some 25 million U.S. adults read and write at no more than a fourth-grade level, and another 25 million have just eighth-grade skills. Functional illiteracy, then, is a complex social problem afflicting one in four adults. It is caused partly by bureaucratic schools, communities indifferent to their own children, and homes in which parents (often functionally illiterate themselves) offer little encouragement to their children.

Functional illiteracy costs our society more than $100 billion a year in decreased productivity (by workers who perform their jobs improperly) and increased accidents (by people unable to understand written instructions). This disability also forces society to support people (on welfare or in prison) unable to

Paco learned to read last year. So did Dad.

Literacy Volunteers of America, Inc.

The problem of illiteracy in the United States is most serious among Latinos. In part this is due to a dropout rate among fourteen- to twenty-four-year-olds of 24 percent, which is almost three times the rate among whites and more than twice the rate of African Americans. The broader issue is that schools fail to teach many Spanish-speaking people to read and write any language very well.

read and write well enough to earn a living themselves.

Addressing this national problem requires one approach for young people and another for adults. To head off functional illiteracy before it happens, the public must demand that schools stop graduating students who have yet to learn basic language skills. For adults who lack the ability to read and write, and who often feel deep shame at their plight, we must begin by urging them to seek assistance while not making them feel more inadequate.

Ours is one of the richest and most powerful nations on earth, yet at least a dozen other countries have a more literate population than we do. For those struggling to get by with limited literacy skills, functional illiteracy is a personal disaster; for all of us, it is an urgent national problem.

Sources: Based on Kozol (1980, 1985a, 1985b).

---

our schools' poor performance, at least in part, simply by requiring that students spend more time there.

Contemporary Issues in U.S. Education

Our society's schools must respond to new challenges and technological innovation. The following sections explore several pressing educational issues.

School Choice

Some analysts claim that our schools do not teach very well because they have no competition. Thus, giving parents a range of options about where to educate their children may force all schools to do a better job. This is the essence of the *school choice* proposal.

Proponents of school choice advocate creating an education marketplace so that parents and students can shop for the best value. According to one proposal, the government would provide vouchers to all families with school-aged children, allowing them to spend the money at public, private, or parochial schools. Indianapolis, Minneapolis, and Milwaukee adopted such a plan in 1990 in the hope that public schools would be forced to perform better in order to win the confidence of families. But critics charge that school choice amounts to abandoning our nation's commitment to public schools and does little to improve schooling where the need is greatest—in central cities.

Another development in the school choice movement is *schooling for profit.* According to advocates of this proposal, private profit-making companies can operate school systems more effectively than local governments can. Of course, private schooling is nothing new; more than ten thousand schools are currently operated by private organizations and religious groups. What is new, however, is the assertion that private companies can carry out *mass* education in the United States.

Research confirms that many public school systems suffer from bureaucratic bloat, spending far too much and teaching far too little. Further, in a society that has long looked to competition as a strategy to improve quality, it is not surprising that various "choice" proposals are gaining favor. But many wonder whether education will respond positively to commercial incentives and whether such plans will improve schools for everyone or only for some of our population (Putka, 1991; Toch, 1991).

Schooling People With Disabilities

Bureaucratic school systems do not always meet the special needs of particular children. Schooling some 5 million U.S. children with disabilities is a case in point. Many children with physical impairments have difficulty getting to and from school, and those with crutches or wheelchairs cannot negotiate stairs and other obstacles inside school buildings. Children with developmental disabilities like mental retardation require extensive personal attention from specially trained teachers. As a result, many children with mental and physical disabilities have received a public education only because of persistent efforts by parents and other concerned citizens.

About one-fourth of children with disabilities are schooled in special facilities; the rest attend public schools, many participating in regular classes. This reflects the policy of *mainstreaming* of students with disabilities into the overall educational program. An alternative to segregated "special education" classes, mainstreaming (also termed *inclusive education*) works best for physically impaired students who have no difficulty keeping up with the rest of the class. As an added advantage, children with disabilities learn how to interact with others just as other children learn how to interact with them.

Mainstreaming is typically less effective for students who have serious mental or emotional impairments. These children may have difficulty matching the performance of other students, and they may simultaneously be deprived of appropriate special education. In any case, mainstreaming can be as expensive as special programs, requiring adaptive facilities and skilled and committed teachers.

Adult Education

Most schooling involves young people. However, the share of U.S. students aged twenty-five and older is rising steadily and now accounts for nearly one in five people in the classroom.

By 1993, more than 25 million U.S. adults were enrolled in school. They range in age from the mid-twenties to well past sixty-five. Adult students are generally a fairly privileged slice of the population with above-average incomes.

What propels adults to go back to school? The reasons are as varied as the students themselves, but most return to the classroom to enhance their careers, enrolling in business, health, and engineering courses. But others, who study everything from astronomy to zen, return to school simply for the pleasure of learning.

Looking Ahead: Schooling in the Twenty-First Century

Nowhere on earth does a larger proportion of people attend college than in the United States. Yet, our public school system continues to struggle with serious problems, many of which have their roots in the larger society. Thus, as we approach the next century, we should not expect schools—by themselves—to raise the quality of education. Schools will only improve to the extent that teachers, parents, and students themselves are committed to the pursuit of excellence. In short, educational dilemmas are *social problems* for which there is no "quick fix."

Another important trend already reshaping schools involves the technology of the Information Revolution. Today, more than 95 percent of schools report using computers for instruction. Interacting with computers prompts students to be more active learners, and has the added benefit of allowing them to progress at their own pace. Even so, the enthusiasm sparked by computers should not blind us to their limitations. For example, computers will never bring to the educational process the personal insight or imagination of a motivated human teacher. And technology simply cannot solve many of the problems—including violence and rigid bureaucracy—that plague our schools. What we need is a broad plan for social change that refires this country's early ambition to provide quality universal schooling—a goal that has so far eluded us.

Health

Another social institution that burgeons in modern societies is **medicine,** *the social institution that focuses on combating disease and improving health.* In ideal terms, according to the World Health Organization, **health** is *a state of complete physical, mental, and social well-being* (1946:3).

Health: A Social Issue

The remainder of this chapter demonstrates that health is as much a social as a biological issue. To begin, society affects health in three basic ways.

1. **Cultural patterns define health.** Standards of health vary from culture to culture. René Dubos (1980; orig. 1965) points out that, early in this century, the contagious skin disease yaws was so common in tropical Africa that people there considered it normal.
    What members of a society view as healthful also reflects what they think is morally good; conversely, illness has much to do with what people define as morally wrong. People who believe homosexuality is wrong, for example, may view this sexual orientation as "sick," although, medically speaking, it is quite natural. Ideas about health, therefore, act as a form of social control, encouraging conformity to cultural standards.
2. **Technology affects health.** Even a century ago, before the United States had fully industrialized,

Medieval medical practice was heavily influenced by astrology, so that physicians and lay people alike attributed disease to astral influence; this is the root of our word "influenza." In this woodcut by Swiss artist Jost Amman (1580), as midwives attend a childbirth astrologers cast a horoscope for the newborn.

our society was ravaged by malnutrition and infectious disease. Today, poor societies are in much the same situation; here, however, a high standard of living and advanced medical care have greatly improved health.

3. **Social inequality affects health.** All societies distribute health-promoting resources unequally. Therefore, the physical, mental, and emotional health of well-to-do people is far better than that of the poor.

Health: A Global Survey

Because health is so closely tied to other dimensions of social life, we find pronounced change in human well-being over the long course of history. Similarly, striking differences in health also distinguish nations of the world today.

Health in Preindustrial Societies

Simple technology limited the ability of hunting and gathering societies to generate a healthful environment. Food shortages sometimes even forced nursing mothers to abandon infants. Children fortunate enough to survive infancy were still vulnerable; perhaps half died before the age of twenty. Few lived to forty.

The agricultural revolution expanded the supply of food and other resources. Yet, due to increasing social inequality, elites enjoyed far better health while peasants and slaves faced hunger daily and lived in crowded, unsanitary shelters. Especially in the growing cities of medieval Europe, human waste and other refuse accelerated the spread of infectious diseases, including plagues that periodically wiped out entire towns (Mumford, 1961).

Severe poverty persists in poor societies today (see Chapter 8, "Global Stratification"), limiting life expectancy to between forty and sixty years. A look back at Global Map 8–1 on page 195 shows that, in the poorest countries of the world, most people die before reaching their teens.

According to the World Health Organization, 1 billion people around the world—one in five—suffer from serious illness because of poverty. Poor sanitation and malnutrition cause widespread infectious diseases that kill people of all ages, just as they did centuries ago in the United States. The box takes a closer look at the link between poverty and poor health in Africa.

Improving health in poor societies presents a monumental challenge. First, in a classic vicious cycle, poverty breeds disease, which, in turn, undermines people's ability to earn income. Second, when medical technology does control infectious disease, the populations of poor nations soar. Without resources to ensure the well-being of the people they have now, poor societies can ill afford population growth. Thus, efforts to reduce death rates will have little beneficial effect without programs to reduce birth rates as well.

Health in Industrial Societies

Industrialization dramatically changed patterns of human health in Europe, although, at first, not for the better. As the Industrial Revolution took hold in the nineteenth century, factories drew people from the countryside, swelling the cities. Such dense living conditions produced serious problems of sanitation. Factories made matters worse, fouling the air with smoke nonstop (although no one at the time recognized this as a health hazard).

But as the nineteenth century progressed, health in Western Europe and North America began to improve, mainly due to a rising standard of living that translated into better nutrition and safer housing for most people. After 1850, medical advances promoted even better health by controlling infectious diseases in cities. To illustrate, in 1854 researcher John Snow noted the street addresses of cholera victims in London and traced the source of this disease to contaminated drinking water (Mechanic, 1978). Soon after, scientists linked cholera to specific bacteria and developed a protective vaccine against the deadly disease. Armed with scientific knowledge, early environmentalists campaigned against age-old practices such as discharging raw sewage into rivers used for drinking water. By the early twentieth century, death rates from infectious diseases had fallen sharply.

Thus the leading killers in 1900—influenza and pneumonia—account for only a fraction of all deaths in the United States today. Table 13–3 on page 348 indicates that various infectious diseases—all once major killers—no longer pose much threat to health. Living longer, two-thirds of our population now typically die from chronic illnesses including heart disease, stroke, and cancer. Nothing alters the reality of death, of course; but, industrial societies manage to delay our demise until old age.

Health in the United States

Living in an affluent, industrial society, people in the United States have good health by world standards. Sociological researchers examine patterns of health among various categories of people; they also study health issues that affect everyone.

Social Epidemiology: Who Is Healthy?

Social epidemiology is *the study of how health and disease are distributed throughout a society's population.* Social epidemiologists investigate the origin and spread of epidemic diseases, and also contrast the health of various categories of people.

Poverty and Poor Health: A Report From Africa

Recent famine in Africa brought home to people in the affluent United States images of starving children. Some of the children portrayed by the mass media appear bloated, while others seem to have shriveled to little more than skin drawn tightly over bones. Both of these deadly conditions, Susan George explains, are direct consequences of poverty.

Children with bloated bodies are suffering from protein deficiency. In West Africa this condition is known as *kwashiorkor*, which means literally "one-two." The term derives from the common practice among mothers of abruptly weaning a first child upon the birth of a second. Deprived of mother's milk, an infant may receive virtually no protein.

Children with shriveled bodies lack both protein and calories. This deficiency is the result of eating little food of any kind.

In either case, children usually do not die of starvation, strictly speaking. Their weakened condition makes them vulnerable to stomach ailments such as gastroenteritis or diseases like measles. The death rate

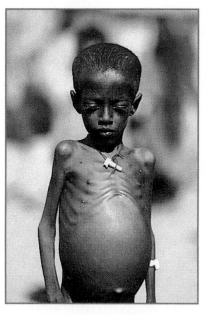

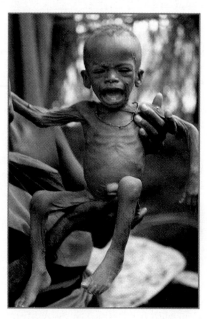

from measles, for example, is a thousand times greater in parts of Africa than in North America.

Depending on a single food also undermines nutrition, causing a deficiency of protein, vitamins, and minerals. Millions of people in the least-developed societies of the world suffer from goiter, a debilitating, diet-related disease of the thyroid gland. Pellagra, a disease common to people who consume only corn, is equally serious, frequently leading

to insanity. Those who consume mostly processed rice are prone to beriberi.

We grasp the idea that society shapes the health of its members by simply taking note of the fact that a host of diseases virtually unknown now in rich societies are a common experience of life—and death—in poor countries.

Source: Based, in part, on George (1977).

Age and gender. In general, death is now rare among young people, with two notable exceptions: a rise in mortality resulting from accidents and, more recently, from acquired immune deficiency syndrome (AIDS).

Across the life course, women fare better than men. Females have a slight biological advantage that renders them less likely to die before or immediately after birth. Then, as socialization takes over, more aggressive and individualistic males experience higher rates of accidents, violence, and suicide.

Doctors describe "coronary-prone behavior" (sometimes dubbed the "Type-A personality") as a combination of chronic impatience, uncontrolled ambition, and frequent outbursts of hostility toward one's surroundings. This syndrome also mirrors our culture's definition of masculinity.

Social class and race. Infant mortality—the death rate among newborns—is twice as high for disadvantaged children as for children born to privilege. While

**TABLE 13–3 The Leading Causes of Death
in the United States, 1900 and 1992**

1900	1992
1. Influenza and pneumonia	1. Heart disease
2. Tuberculosis	2. Cancer
3. Stomach/ intestinal diseases	3. Cerebrovascular diseases
4. Heart disease	4. Lung disease (noncancerous)
5. Cerebral hemorrhage	5. Accidents
6. Kidney disease	6. Pneumonia and influenza
7. Accidents	7. Diabetes
8. Cancer	8. Suicide
9. Diseases in early infancy	9. HIV virus
10. Diphtheria	10. Homicide

Sources: Information for 1900 is from William C. Cockerham, *Medical Sociology*, 2d ed. (Englewood Cliffs, N.J.: Prentice-Hall, 1986), p. 24; information for 1992 is from U.S. National Center for Health Statistics, *Monthly Vital Statistics Report* (Hyattsville, Md.: The Center, 1993), vol. 42, no. 2 (Aug. 31, 1993).

our richest children have the best health in the world, our poorest children are as vulnerable to health crises as those in poor countries such as Sudan and Lebanon.

As noted in Table 13–4, almost 80 percent of people in the United States with family incomes over $35,000 evaluate their health as excellent or very good, while not quite half of those in families earning less than $10,000 make this claim. Conversely, while only about 4 percent of higher-income people describe their own health as fair or poor, almost one-fourth of low-income people respond this way.

Bear in mind that just as income shapes health, so does health affect income. Members of low-income families miss eight days of school or work each year due to illness, while higher-income people lose only five days a year for this reason (U.S. National Center for Health Statistics, 1992).

Because people of color are three times as likely as whites to be poor, they are more prone to die in infancy and to suffer the effects of violence and illness as adults. Table 13–5 shows that the projected life expectancy for white people born in 1992 is more than seventy-six years, almost seven years longer than for African Americans.

But sex is a stronger predictor of health than race, since African-American women can expect to outlive males of either race. The table also indicates that 76 percent of white men—but only about 58 percent of African-American men—will live to sixty-five. The comparable chances for women are about 86 percent for whites and 78 percent for African Americans.

Eating Disorders

Eating disorders, which are a dangerous and intense striving to become very thin, are widespread in the United States. Anorexia nervosa is a disorder marked by radical, often compulsive dieting; bulimia couples binge eating with induced vomiting to inhibit weight gain.

Eating disorders have a significant cultural component. Consider this fact: Ninety-five percent of people who suffer from anorexia nervosa or bulimia are women, mostly from white, relatively affluent families. Michael Levine (1987) explains that our culture transmits powerful messages that, just as men cannot be too rich, women cannot be too thin. For women, in other words, being slender is almost synonymous with being successful.

Research reveals that most college-age women (1) widely accept the idea that "guys like thin girls," (2) think being thin is crucial to physical attractiveness, and (3) believe that they are not as thin as men would like them to be. In fact, most college women want to be even thinner than most college men say women should be. When it comes to men, most do not dwell on their physiques; unlike women, they tend to express satisfaction with their overall appearance (Fallon & Rozin, 1985).

The "beauty myth" embedded deep in our culture (see Chapter 10, "Sex and Gender") teaches women to relentlessly pursue being slender, sometimes at the cost of their health. Many young girls learn such attitudes from mothers and fathers—especially affluent parents—who pressure them to be "The Best Little Girl in the World." Reinforcing this message, television and other mass media set up as exemplars actresses and models who are unnaturally thin and unrealistically beautiful.

Cigarette Smoking

Many threats to health are matters of specific behavior, and cigarette smoking tops the list of preventable hazards. Smoking became popular in the United States after World War I. Fashionable just a generation ago, today smoking carries a mild stigma of deviance.

Consumption of cigarettes has fallen since 1960, when almost 45 percent of U.S. adults smoked. By 1992, only 26 percent were smokers (U.S. Bureau of the Census, 1994). Quitting is difficult because cigarette smoke contains nicotine, which is physically addictive. People also smoke to cope with stress. Because of this psychological dependence, divorced and separated

TABLE 13-4 Assessment of Personal Health by Income, 1992

Family Income	Excellent	Very Good	Good	Fair	Poor
$35,000 and over	48.7%	29.9%	17.1%	3.5%	0.8%
$20,000–$34,999	36.3	30.8	24.1	6.8	2.1
$10,000–$19,999	28.7	25.8	29.3	11.7	4.5
Under $10,000	25.2	24.5	28.4	14.6	7.3

Source: U.S. National Center for Health Statistics, *Current Estimates from the National Health Interview Survey United States, 1992*, series 10, no. 189 (Washington, D.C.: U.S. Government Printing Office, 1994).

people are more likely to smoke, as are the unemployed, and people in the military services.

Generally speaking, the less education people have, the greater their chances of smoking. A larger share of men (28 percent) than women (25 percent) smoke. But cigarettes—the only form of tobacco use to gain popularity among women—has become a major health threat, with lung cancer surpassing breast cancer a decade ago as a leading cause of death among U.S. women.

The number of men and women who die prematurely each year (most often from cancer or heart disease) as a result of cigarette smoking approaches 450,000—more than the combined death toll from alcohol, cocaine, heroin, homicide, suicide, accidents, and AIDS (Mosley & Cowley, 1991). Because smoking lowers a person's resistance, smokers are also susceptible to frequent bouts with infectious diseases such as the flu, and pregnant women who smoke increase the likelihood of spontaneous abortion, prenatal death, and low birth-weight babies. Even nonsmokers exposed to secondhand tobacco smoke have a higher risk of smoking-related diseases.

Tobacco remains a $30 billion industry in the United States. According to the tobacco industry the precise link between cigarettes and disease cannot be specified, so the health effects of smoking remain "an open question." But the tobacco industry is not breathing as easily today as it once did. Laws mandating a smoke-free environment are spreading rapidly. Furthermore, courts have increased the liability of cigarette manufacturers in lawsuits brought by victims of smoking-related illnesses, or their survivors.

In response to these antismoking drives in the United States, the tobacco industry has been selling more products abroad, especially in poor countries where tobacco is subject to little regulation. In the United States, however, more and more smokers are trying to break the habit, taking advantage of the fact that someone who has not smoked for ten years has about the same pattern of health as a lifelong non-smoker (Shephard, 1982; Rudolph, 1985).

Sexually Transmitted Diseases

Sexual activity, while both pleasurable and vital to our species, can transmit some fifty illnesses. Sometimes called *venereal diseases* (from Venus, the Roman goddess of love), these ailments date back to humanity's origins. Our culture has long linked sex to sin; therefore, some people regard venereal diseases not only as illness, but also as a mark of immorality.

Sexually transmitted diseases (STDs) became a national issue during the "sexual revolution" of the 1960s, which prompted people to begin sexual activity at an earlier age and to have sex with a greater number of partners. As a result, STDs stand out as an exception to the general decline in infectious ailments during this century.

Gonorrhea and syphilis. Gonorrhea and syphilis, among the oldest diseases, are caused by a microscopic organism almost always transmitted by sexual contact. Untreated, gonorrhea can cause sterility, while syphilis can damage major organs and result in blindness, mental disorders, and death.

Officials record about five hundred thousand cases of gonorrhea and one hundred thousand instances of syphilis annually in the United States, although the actual numbers may be several times higher. According to reports, 77 percent of cases involve African

TABLE 13-5 Life Expectancy for U.S. Children Born in 1992

	Females	Males	Both Sexes
Whites	79.7 (86%)	73.2 (76%)	76.5 (81%)
African Americans	73.9 (78%)	65.5 (58%)	69.8 (67%)
All races	79.0 (85%)	72.3 (74%)	75.7 (79%)

Figures in parentheses indicate the chances of living to age sixty-five.

Source: U.S. Bureau of the Census (1994).

Experts—and the public—disagree as to the best strategy for combating the spread of HIV. Liberals support the distribution of condoms to young people because condom use significantly reduces the chances for sexual transmission of the virus. Conservatives object to this policy, claiming it encourages casual sex, which, for them, is the heart of the problem: From this point of view, rethinking the notion that young people should be sexually active is a better approach.

Americans, 12 percent affect white people, 4 percent target Latinos, and less than 1 percent affect Asian Americans and Native Americans (Masters, Johnson, & Kolodny, 1988; Moran et al., 1989; U.S. Centers for Disease Control and Prevention, 1993).

Most cases of gonorrhea and syphilis are easily cured with antibiotics such as penicillin. Thus neither disease currently represents a major health problem in the United States.

Genital herpes.   An estimated 20 to 30 million adults in the United States (one in seven) are infected with the genital herpes virus. The infection rate among African Americans, however, is about twice as high as among white people (Moran et al., 1989).

Although far less serious than gonorrhea and syphilis, herpes is incurable. People with genital herpes may exhibit no symptoms or they may experience periodic, painful blisters on the genitals accompanied by fever and headache. While not fatal to adults, women with active genital herpes can transmit the disease during a vaginal delivery to infants, to whom it may be deadly. Such women, therefore, often give birth by Caesarean section.

AIDS.   The most serious of all sexually transmitted diseases is acquired immune deficiency syndrome, or AIDS. Identified in 1981, this disease is incurable and fatal. AIDS is caused by a human immunodeficiency virus (HIV). This virus attacks white blood cells, the core of the immune system, rendering a person vulnerable to a wide range of infectious diseases that eventually bring on death. During the twelve-month period ending June, 1994, 82,376 new cases were reported in the United States, raising the total to almost 400,000. About 240,000 of these people have already died (U.S. Centers for Disease Control and Prevention, 1994).

In global perspective, as many as 10 million people are infected with HIV, a figure that could increase three- or four-fold by the end of this decade. Global Map 13–2 shows that the African continent (more specifically, countries south of the Sahara Desert) has the highest HIV infection rate and currently accounts for almost two-thirds of all world cases. In the cities of central African nations such as Burundi, Rwanda, Uganda, and Kenya, roughly one-fifth of all young adults are infected with HIV (Tofani, 1991). About 10 percent of global HIV is found in North America. In the United States, officials place the number of infected people at 1 million.

People with HIV typically display no symptoms for at least a year and, therefore, most are unaware of their infection. Within five years, about one-third of infected persons develop AIDS; half exhibit symptoms within a decade, and medical experts state that all but a few will do so eventually. With four hundred thousand active cases in the United States as of mid-1994, the infection rate is still rising, although at a slowing rate of increase as people adopt safe-sex practices. With the death toll mounting, AIDS has turned out to be nothing less than catastrophic—potentially the most serious epidemic of modern times.

Transmission of HIV almost always occurs through blood, semen, or breast milk. This means that HIV is not spread through casual contact—that is, by shaking hands or hugging. There is no known case of the virus being transmitted through the sharing of towels or dishes, swimming together, or even through coughing and sneezing. The risk of transmitting HIV through saliva (as in kissing) is extremely low. Oral and especially genital sex are dangerous, but the risk is reduced by the use of latex condoms. In the age of AIDS, the only sure ways to avoid contracting HIV are abstinence or maintaining an exclusive relationship with an uninfected person.

Specific behaviors place people at high risk for HIV infection. The first is *anal sex*, which can cause

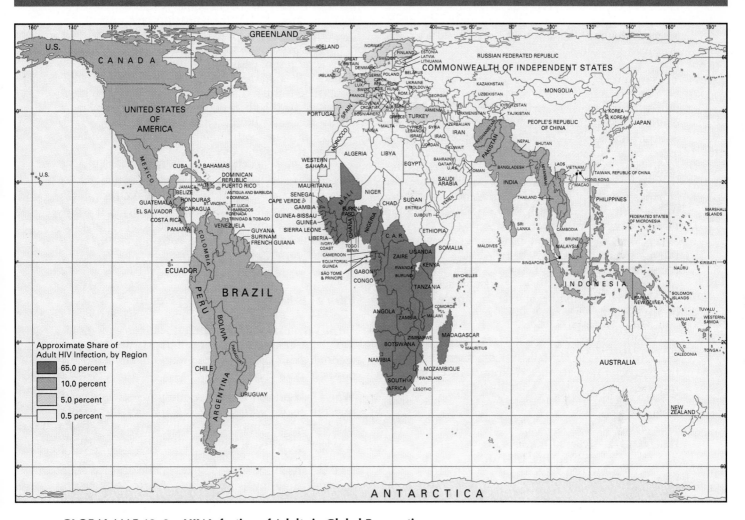

GLOBAL MAP 13–2   HIV Infection of Adults in Global Perspective

Approximately two-thirds of all global HIV cases are recorded in sub-Saharan Africa. This high infection rate reflects the prevalence of other venereal diseases and infrequent use of condoms, factors that promote heterosexual transmission of HIV. South and North America each represent another 10 percent of all cases. The incidence of infection is still low in Europe. Southeast Asia, where HIV is spreading most rapidly, accounts for another 10 percent of infections. Least affected by HIV are countries in North Africa and the Middle East, and the nations of Australia and New Zealand.

Sources: Data from The World Bank (1993); map projection from *Peters Atlas of the World* (1990).

rectal bleeding, allowing easy transmission of HIV from one person to another. This practice is extremely dangerous, and the greater the number of sexual partners, the greater the risk. Anal sex is commonly practiced by gay men, in some cases with multiple partners. As a result, homosexual and bisexual men represent about 60 percent of people with AIDS in the United States. In response to the devastating effect of AIDS on gay communities across this country, gays (as well as non-gays) have begun to shun sexual promiscuity (McKusick et al., 1985; Kain, 1987; Kain & Hart, 1987).

Sharing needles used to inject intravenous drugs is a second high-risk behavior. At present, intravenous drug users account for 31 percent of people with AIDS. Sex with an intravenous drug user is also very risky. Because intravenous drug use is more common among poor people in the United States, AIDS is becoming a disease of the socially disadvantaged. Overall, 49 percent of AIDS patients are white (non-Hispanic), with African Americans (12 percent of the population) accounting for 32 percent of people with AIDS (and half of all women with the disease). Latinos (7 percent of the population) represent 17 percent of AIDS cases. Asian Americans and Native Americans together account for 0.7 percent of people with AIDS (U.S. Centers for Disease Control and Prevention, 1994).

Using any drug, including alcohol, also increases the risk of being infected with HIV to the extent that it impairs judgment. In other words, even people who understand what places them at risk may act irresponsibly (say, by having unprotected sex) once they are under the influence of alcohol, marijuana, or some other drug.

As Figure 13–2 shows, only 7 percent of people with AIDS in the United States became infected through heterosexual contact (although heterosexuals, infected in various ways, account for almost 30 percent of AIDS cases). But heterosexual activity does

transmit HIV, and the danger rises with the number of sexual partners, especially if they fall into high-risk categories. Worldwide, heterosexual relations are the primary means of HIV transmission, accounting for two-thirds of all infections (Eckholm & Tierney, 1990).

AIDS is throwing our health-care system into crisis. The cost of treatment for one person has already soared to hundreds of thousands of dollars. In addition, there is the mounting cost of caring for children orphaned by this disease, whose numbers may reach eighty thousand by the end of this decade. Overall, AIDS represents both a medical and a social problem of staggering proportions.

Funding for AIDS research (now exceeding $4 billion annually) has increased rapidly, and researchers have found that some drugs, such as AZT, suppress the symptoms of the disease. But educational programs remain our most effective weapon against AIDS, since prevention is the only way to stop a disease that currently has no cure.

Ethical Issues: Confronting Death

Health issues always involve ethical considerations. Moral questions are more pressing than ever now that technological advances have given human beings the power to define life and death.

When is a person dead? Common sense suggests that life ceases when breathing and heartbeat stop. But with the technology to revive or replace a heart and to artificially sustain respiration, such notions about death have become obsolete. Thus, medical and legal experts in the United States define death as an *irreversible* state involving no response to stimulation, no movement or breathing, no reflexes, and no indication of brain activity (Ladd, 1979; Wall, 1980).

Do people have a right to die? Today, medical personnel, family members, and patients themselves face the agonizing burden of deciding when a terminally ill person should die. To illustrate this process, in 1990, twenty-six-year-old Nancy Cruzan fell into an irreversible coma after an automobile accident. Physicians exhausted their efforts and solemnly assured Cruzan's parents that their daughter would never recover. Certain that their daughter would not wish to live in a permanent vegetative state, the Cruzans sought a legal decision to let Nancy die, which required taking their case all the way to the U.S. Supreme Court. In 1990, the court issued a judgment supporting a patient's right to die, declaring that any person deemed competent

FIGURE 13–2 Types of Transmission for Reported U.S. AIDS Cases, 1994

Source: U.S. Centers for Disease Control and Prevention (1994).

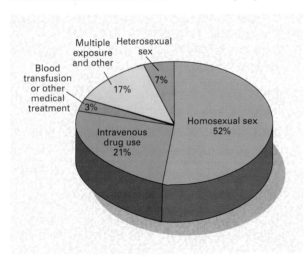

can refuse medical treatment or nutrition. Because the Cruzans were able to present "clear and convincing evidence" that this would be Nancy's wish, the court permitted removal of the feeding tube keeping her alive. Nancy Cruzan died twelve days later (Mauro, 1990).

Ten thousand people in the United States are in the same kind of permanent vegetative state as Nancy Cruzan (Howlett, 1990). Thousands more, facing a terminal illness that may cause terrible suffering, consider ending their own lives. Thus courts and government commissions continue to weigh patients' rights against practitioners' obligations to provide all appropriate care to those in need. Generally speaking, the first responsibility of physicians and hospitals is to keep patients alive. Even so, terminally ill patients can refuse heroic treatment (either at the time, or through a living will) that may extend their lives but offer no hope of recovery. But when family members speak for an incompetent person, they must act in the interest of that patient—no one else.

What about mercy killing? *Mercy killing* is the common term for **euthanasia,** *assisting in the death of a person suffering from an incurable disease.* Euthanasia (from the Greek, meaning "a good death") poses the ethical dilemma of being both an act of kindness and a form of killing.

Although a patient's right to die has widespread support in the United States, assisting in the death of another person still provokes controversy. Jack Kevorkian, a Michigan physician who helped more than a dozen people end their lives with his "suicide machine," has been in and out of court on murder charges. No one thinks that the people involved—all suffering from terminal illnesses—looked on Kevorkian as their murderer. But our society remains uneasy about empowering physicians to actively end a life in response to a patient's request.

The debate breaks down roughly as follows. Those who view life—even with suffering—as preferable to death categorically reject euthanasia. People who recognize circumstances under which death is preferable to life support euthanasia, but they face the practical problem of determining just when life is no longer worth living. Such a decision can be an enormous burden on family members who are already emotionally strained. Then, too, they must confront the reality of medical costs, which skyrocket when heroic care is undertaken. Opponents of euthanasia fear that such costs will enter into a family's decision regarding life-sustaining treatment, perhaps compromising the interests of the patient.

The Medical Establishment

Through most of human history, health care was the responsibility of individuals and their families. Members of preindustrial societies also turn to various health practitioners—including acupuncturists and herbalists—who tend to the sick in much of the world today.

As a society industrializes, health care becomes the responsibility of specially trained and legally licensed healers. The medical establishment in modern, industrial societies took form over the last 150 years as healers and researchers applied the logic of science to their work.

The Rise of Scientific Medicine

In colonial times, doctors, herbalists, druggists, midwives, and ministers each engaged in some form of healing arts but agreed on few principles or procedures (Stevens, 1971). Unsanitary instruments, lack of anesthesia, and simple ignorance made surgery a terrible ordeal in which doctors killed as many patients as they saved.

Medical specialists gradually learned about human anatomy, physiology, and biochemistry. By about 1850, doctors had established themselves as self-regulating professionals with medical degrees. The American Medical Association (AMA), founded in 1847, symbolized the growing acceptance of a scientific model of medicine. The AMA widely publicized the successes of its members in identifying the causes of life-threatening diseases—bacteria and viruses—and developing vaccines against them.

Still, other approaches to health care, such as encouraging proper nutrition, also had defenders. The AMA responded boldly—some thought arrogantly—to these alternate health-care methods, trumpeting the superiority of its practitioners. By the early 1900s, state licensing boards agreed to certify only physicians trained in the scientific programs approved by the AMA (Starr, 1982). With control of the certification process, the AMA effectively closed down schools teaching other healing skills, limiting the practice of medicine mainly to those with an M.D. degree. In the process, both the prestige and income of physicians rose dramatically; today, doctors in the United States earn, on average, $175,000 per year.

Practitioners of other approaches, such as osteopathic physicians, concluded that they had no choice but to fall in line and follow AMA standards. Thus

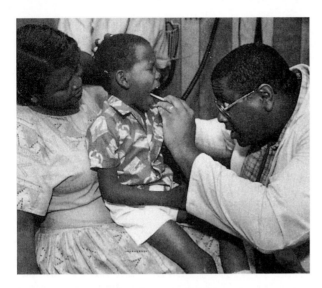

The rise of scientific medicine sparked stunning achievements in our ability to control disease. But it also effectively reduced the number of African Americans in the medical professions and opposed many kinds of healers who traditionally have served rural areas. Michael Cheers, M.D., has tried to turn the tide by transforming an abandoned restaurant into a medical clinic in Tchula, Mississippi. Cheers, who is also an ordained minister and jazz pianist, accepts donations and works overtime in hospital emergency rooms to enable him to treat people who cannot afford to pay for care.

osteopaths (with D.O. degrees), originally concerned with manipulating the skeleton and muscles, today treat illness much as medical doctors (with M.D. degrees) do. Other practitioners—such as chiropractors, herbal healers, and midwives—adhere more to their traditional practices but at the cost of being pushed from the mainstream of the medical profession (Gordon, 1980).

Scientific medicine, taught in expensive, urban medical schools, also changed the social profile of doctors. Most physicians soon came from privileged backgrounds and practiced in cities. Furthermore, women, who had played a key role in many forms of healing, were denigrated by the AMA. Some early medical schools did train women and African Americans but, with few financial resources, most of these schools soon closed. Only in recent decades have women and minorities increased their representation in medicine (Stevens, 1971; Starr, 1982; Huet-Cox, 1984).

Holistic Medicine

The scientific model of medicine has recently been tempered by the more traditional notion of **holistic medicine,** *an approach to health care that emphasizes prevention of illness and takes account of the person's entire physical and social environment.*

Holistic practitioners also embrace the use of drugs, surgery, artificial organs, and high technology, but they caution that these developments risk transforming medicine into narrow specialties concerned with symptoms rather than people, and with disease instead of health. The following are foundations of holistic health care (Gordon, 1980).

1. **A holistic approach.** Holistic practitioners are concerned with how environment and lifestyle affect an individual's health. Holistic healers extend the bounds of conventional medicine, taking an active role in combating environmental pollution and other dangers to public health.

2. **Responsibility, not dependency.** The complexity of contemporary medicine fosters patients' dependence on physicians. Holistic medicine tries to shift some responsibility for health from physicians to people themselves by enhancing their abilities to engage in health-promoting behavior (Ferguson, 1980). Holistic medicine favors a more *active* approach to *health*, rather than a *reactive* approach to *illness.*

3. **Personal treatment.** Conventional medicine locates medical care in impersonal offices and hospitals, which are disease-centered settings. Holistic practitioners favor, as much as possible, a personal, relaxed, home-like environment. In light of the current policy of the AMA of certifying more than fifty specialized areas of medical practice, the holistic approach reminds us of the need for practitioners concerned with the patient in the broadest sense.

Holistic care does not oppose scientific medicine. But it does shift the emphasis in health care away from narrowly treating disease toward the goal of achieving the highest possible level of well-being for everyone.

Paying the Costs: A Global Survey

Today's medicine relies on high technology; as a result, the costs of health care in industrial societies have skyrocketed. Countries employ various strategies to meet these costs.

The People's Republic of China.

The People's Republic of China, a poor, agrarian society only beginning to industrialize, faces the daunting task of attending to the health of more than a billion people. The Chinese embrace traditional healing arts, including acupuncture and the prescription of medicinal herbs, and hold fast to a holistic concern for the interplay of mind and body. China's famed barefoot doctors, roughly comparable to U.S. paramedics, have brought some modern methods of medical care to millions of peasants in remote rural villages (Sidel & Sidel, 1982b; Kaptchuk, 1985).

China recently experimented with private medical care. But by 1990 the government had re-established control over this dimension of life, closely monitoring the practices of healers and hospitals.

The former Soviet Union.

The former Soviet Union is currently struggling to transform its state-dominated economy into more of a market system. As part of this process, the scheme for providing medical care is also in transition. Like their counterparts in the People's Republic of China, people in the former Soviet Union do not choose a physician, but rather report to a local government health facility, funded through taxes.

Physicians in the former Soviet Union have lower prestige and income than their counterparts in the United States. They receive about the same salary as skilled industrial workers (compared to roughly a five-to-one ratio in this country). Worth noting, too, is that about 70 percent of physicians in the new Commonwealth of Independent States are women, compared with 16 percent in the United States, and, as in our society, occupations dominated by women yield fewer financial rewards.

The former Soviet Union has trained enough physicians to meet the basic needs of a large population. However, rigid bureaucracy still makes for highly standardized and impersonal care. As market reforms proceed, uniformity will likely diminish, and disparities in the quality of medical care available to richer and poorer people may well increase.

Sweden.

In 1891, Sweden instituted a compulsory, comprehensive system of government medical care. Citizens of this Scandinavian country pay for this program through taxes, which are among the highest in the world. Typically, physicians receive salaries from the government rather than fees from patients, and most hospitals are government managed. Because this medical system resembles that of socialist societies, it is often described as **socialized medicine,** *a medical-care system in which the government owns most facilities and employs most physicians.*

Great Britain.

In 1948, Great Britain, too, instituted socialized medicine. The British did not do away with private care, however, creating a "dual system" of medical services. All British citizens are entitled to medical care provided by the National Health Service, but those who can afford to may purchase more extensive care from doctors and hospitals that operate privately.

Canada.

Like a vast insurance company, the Canadian government is the "single payer" of regulated fees to doctors and hospitals. But because medical personnel operate privately, Canada's system does not exemplify true socialized medicine. Moreover, some physicians work entirely outside the government-funded system, charging whatever fees they wish (Grant, 1984; Vayda & Deber, 1984; Rosenthal, 1991).

Japan.

Physicians and hospitals in Japan operate privately. In general, employers provide comprehensive health coverage as an employee benefit. For those without such programs, government medical insurance covers most costs, and the elderly receive free care (Vogel, 1979).

Medicine in the United States

The United States is unique among industrialized nations in having no universal, government-subsidized medical program. On average, European governments pay about 75 percent of medical costs; the U.S. government pays 40 percent (Lohr, 1988). For the most part, then, medicine in this country is handled as a private, profit-making industry. Called a **direct-fee system,** ours is *a medical-care system in which patients pay directly for the services of physicians and hospitals.*

People with comfortable incomes can purchase outstanding medical care, yet lower-income people fare worse than their counterparts in Europe. This translates into relatively high death rates among both infants and adults in the United States compared to many European countries (Fuchs, 1974; United Nations Development Programme, 1991).

Why does the United States have no national health-care program? First, our society has historically favored limited government. Second, support for a national medical program has not been strong even among labor unions, which have concentrated on winning private health-care benefits from employers. Third, the AMA and the insurance industry have consistently opposed any such program (Starr, 1982).

As Figure 13-3 shows, medical expenditures in the United States increased dramatically from $12 billion (5 percent of the gross national product) in 1950 to $750 billion (14 percent of GNP) by 1991. Who pays the medical bills?

Private insurance programs. In 1992, 180 million people in the United States (71 percent) received medical-care benefits from a family member's employer or labor union or purchased coverage on their own. Three-fourths of our population thus have private insurance (such as Blue Cross and Blue Shield), although few such programs pay all medical costs (U.S. Bureau of the Census, 1994).

Public insurance programs. In 1965 Congress created Medicare and Medicaid. Medicare pays some of the medical costs for people over sixty-five; in 1992 it covered 34 million men and women, 14 percent of the population. Medicaid, a medical insurance program for the poor, provides benefits to some 29 million people, about 11 percent of the population. An additional 25 million veterans (10 percent) can obtain free care in government-operated hospitals. In all, 35 percent of this country's people take advantage of some government-subsidized benefits, but most also participate in private insurance programs.

Health maintenance organizations. An increasing number of people in the United States belong to a **health maintenance organization** (HMO), *an association that provides comprehensive medical care for a fixed fee*. In 1992, 550 HMOs enrolled some 37 million individuals, about 15 percent of the population. HMOs vary in costs and benefits, and none provides full coverage. But fixed costs give these organizations a financial interest in keeping their subscribers healthy; therefore, many have adopted a preventive approach to health (Ginsburg, 1983).

In all, 85 percent of the U.S. population has some medical-care coverage, either private or public. Yet most plans pay only part of the cost of treatment for a serious illness, threatening even middle-class people with financial ruin. And most programs also exclude many medical services, such as dental care and treatment for mental-health problems. Most seriously, 31 million people (about 13 percent of the population) have no medical insurance at all. Almost as many lose their coverage temporarily each year, generally because of layoffs or job changes. Caught in the medical-care bind are mostly low- and moderate-income people who can neither afford to become ill nor to purchase the medical care they need to remain healthy.

Recent debate. By 1994, there was growing public support for establishing some form of universal health care coverage in the United States. Congress has considered a number of plans ranging from a conservative Republican proposal to offer tax credits to people who purchase health insurance to a Canadian-type "single-payer" system sponsored by liberal Democrats.

President Clinton advocates a hybrid approach called "managed competition." Under this plan, Clinton claims, "competition" would lower costs because employees would join together to bargain with competing medical providers to receive the greatest value. To make the proposal "managed," the government would ensure that almost everyone—regardless of income or present state of health—would have substantial medical coverage.

The Clinton proposal intends to shift medical care away from the traditional private fee-for-service

FIGURE 13–3   The Rising Cost of Medical Care in the United States

Sources: U.S. Bureau of the Census (1970, 1993).

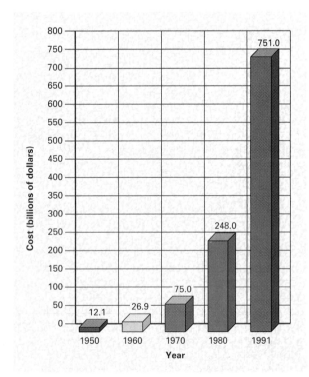

system toward various types of health maintenance organizations (HMOs) and government-funded programs. In the process, supporters claim, costs would fall even as coverage became virtually universal. Critics, however, counter with a "pro-choice" argument that patients should be able to choose their own doctor without government interference. Further, because Clinton favors creating a new government bureaucracy, critics fear his plan would raise—not lower—the costs of health care. In the end, critics maintain, the government would control costs through rationing care.

Even though Clinton's proposed reforms never emerged from Congress in 1994, the debate over health care will hold center stage for some time to come. Most analysts agree that people should have greater financial security in the face of illness than they do at present (Anders, 1993; Church, 1993; Goodgame, 1993).

Theoretical Analysis of Medicine

Each of the theoretical paradigms in sociology helps to organize and make sense of the various facts presented in this chapter.

Structural-Functional Analysis

Talcott Parsons (1951) viewed medicine as a social system's strategy for keeping its members healthy. In this scheme, illness amounts to a form of system dysfunction, undermining the performance of social roles.

The sick role. Society responds to illness, Parsons argued, by having the afflicted assume the **sick role,** *patterns of behavior defined as appropriate for those who are ill.* Insofar as people suffer from poor health, the sick role exempts them from everyday responsibilities. However, Parsons added, people cannot simply declare themselves ill; this assessment falls to a recognized medical expert. Parsons noted further that, upon taking on the sick role, the patient is obligated to do whatever is needed to regain good health, including cooperating with health professionals.

The physician's role. Physicians function to assess claims of sickness, and to restore sick people to normal routines. The physician's power and responsibility in relation to the patient derive from specialized knowledge, Parsons explained. Physicians expect patients to follow "doctor's orders," and to provide whatever personal information may reasonably assist their efforts.

Critical evaluation. Parsons's work links illness and medicine to the broader organization of society. Others have extended the useful concept of the sick role to some nonillness situations such as pregnancy (Myers & Grasmick, 1989).

However, the concept of the sick role applies to acute conditions (like the flu) better than chronic illness (like heart disease), which may not be reversible. Moreover, a sick person's ability to regain health depends on available resources. Many poor people can ill afford either medical care or time off from work.

Symbolic-Interaction Analysis

Viewed according to the symbolic-interaction paradigm, society is less a grand system than a complex and changing reality. Both health and medical care are thus human constructions that people perceive subjectively.

Socially constructing illness. Since we socially construct both health and illness, members of a society where most people go hungry may view malnutrition as quite normal. Similarly, members of our own society remain complacent about the unhealthful effects of a rich diet.

How we respond to illness, too, is based on social definitions that may or may not square with medical facts. For instance, people with AIDS contend with fear and sometimes outright bigotry that has no basis in medical fact.

Constructed or not, how people define a medical situation can sometimes affect how they actually feel. Medical experts have long noted the existence of *psychosomatic* disorders (a fusion of Greek words for "mind" and "body"), in which state of mind guides physical sensations (Hamrick, Anspaugh, & Ezell, 1986). If we think we are (or want to be) sick, in other words, we may soon feel that way.

Socially constructing treatment. In Chapter 4 ("Social Interaction in Everyday Life"), we used the dramaturgical approach of Erving Goffman to explain how physicians craft their physical surroundings ("the office") and present themselves to others to foster specific impressions of competence and power.

Sociologist Joan Emerson (1970) further illustrates this process of reality construction by analyzing a situation familiar to women, a gynecological examination conducted by a male doctor. After observing seventy-five such examinations, she explains that this situation is vulnerable to serious misinterpretation since we commonly consider a man's touching of a woman's genitals as a sexual act and possibly even an assault.

To ensure that the situation is defined as impersonal and professional, the medical staff carefully furnishes the examination room with nothing but medical equipment, and all personnel wear uniforms. The staff also acts as if such examinations are simply routine although, from the patient's point of view, they may be highly unusual. Further, the doctor's performance suggests to the patient that inspecting the genitals is no different from surveying any other part of the body. A nurse is often present during the examination not only to assist the physician, but to dispel any impression that a man and woman are "alone in a room."

The need to manage situational definitions has long been overlooked by medical schools. This omission is unfortunate because, as Emerson's analysis shows, understanding how reality is socially constructed in the examination room is just as crucial as mastering the medical skills required for effective treatment.

Critical evaluation. One strength of the symbolic-interaction paradigm lies in revealing that what people view as healthful or harmful depends on a host of factors, many of which are not, strictly speaking, medical. This approach also shows that all medical procedures involve subtle reality construction by patient and physician.

Yet this approach seems to deny that there are any objective standards of well-being. Certain physical conditions do indeed cause specific changes in human capacities, whether we think so or not. And people who lack sufficient nutrition and safe water, for example, suffer from their unhealthy environment however they define their surroundings.

Social-Conflict Analysis

Social-conflict analysis draws a connection between health and social inequality and, following Karl Marx, ties health to the operation of capitalism. Researchers have focused on three main issues: access to medical care, the effects of the profit motive, and the politics of medicine.

The access issue. Most of the 31 million people in the United States who lack any health-care coverage at present have low incomes. Conflict theorists claim that, while capitalism does offer excellent health care for the rich, it simply does not provide very well for the rest of the population. And, as already noted, the pattern by which health follows wealth is more pronounced in the United States than in most other industrial societies since we have no comprehensive, universal medical-care system.

The profit motive. Some social-conflict analysts go further, arguing that the real problem is not access to medical care but the character of capitalist medicine itself. The profit motive turns physicians, hospitals, and the pharmaceutical industry into multibillion-dollar corporate conglomerates. The quest for ever-increasing profits underlies unneccessary tests and surgery and an overreliance on drugs (Ehrenreich, 1978; Kaplan et al., 1985).

Of the 30 million surgical operations performed in the United States each year, three-fourths are "elective," meaning that they are intended to promote long-term health rather than being prompted by a medical emergency. Critics charge that the decision to perform surgery reflects the financial interests of surgeons and hospitals as well as the medical needs of patients (Illich, 1976). Perhaps 10 percent of this elective surgery could safely be refused or deferred, saving patients more than $1 billion each year. More important, since about one in two hundred patients dies from elective surgery (because surgery itself is dangerous), thousands of lives a year are needlessly lost (Sidel & Sidel, 1982a).

Finally, critics point out, our society is too tolerant of physicians having a direct, financial interest in the tests and procedures they order for their patients (Pear & Eckholm, 1991). In short, they conclude, health care should be motivated by a concern for people, not profits.

Medicine as politics. Although science declares itself to be politically neutral, scientific medicine frequently takes sides on significant social issues. For example, the medical establishment has long voiced strong opposition to government-sponsored health-care programs. The history of medicine, critics contend, is replete with racial and sexual discrimination justified by "scientific" facts. For example, a century ago, medical men declared women unfit for higher education, lest learning harm their reproductive systems (Zola, 1978; Brown, 1979; Leavitt, 1984).

Even today, critics continue, scientific medicine explains illness in terms of bacteria and viruses rather than citing the effects of social inequality on health. In this way, scientific medicine depoliticizes health in the United States by reducing social issues to simple biology.

Critical evaluation. Social-conflict analysis asserts that some people have far better health than others because of social inequality. Yet the most common objection to the conflict approach is that it minimizes the advances in U.S. health brought about by scientific medicine and higher living standards. Though there is plenty of room for improvement, health indicators for our population have risen steadily over the course of this century and compare fairly well with those of other industrial societies.

In sum, sociology's three major theoretical paradigms convincingly argue that social arrangements have a key impact on human health. The famous French scientist Louis Pasteur (1822–1895) spent much of his life studying how bacteria cause disease. Yet just before his death, he concluded that health depends less on bacteria than on the social environment in which bacteria thrive (Gordon, 1980:7). Explaining Pasteur's insight is sociology's contribution to human health.

Looking Ahead: Health in the Twenty-First Century

At the beginning of this century, deaths from infectious disease were widespread, and scientists had yet to develop basic antibiotics like penicillin. Today, members of our society take for granted far better health and longer lives. There is every reason to expect the upsurge in U.S. health to continue into the next century.

Another positive trend, drawing on the holistic health movement, is the public recognition that, to a significant extent, we can take responsibility for our own health (Caplow et al., 1991). All of us improve our health by avoiding tobacco, eating sensibly and in moderation, and exercising regularly.

Even so, health problems persist. For one thing, with no cure in sight, the AIDS epidemic will continue to plague our society. And the changing social profile of people with AIDS—which increasingly afflicts the poor—reminds us that the United States has a long way to go in order to improve the health of marginalized members of our society.

Finally, echoing a thought noted in earlier chapters, we see that problems of health are far greater in the poor nations of the world than they are in the United States. The good news is that life expectancy

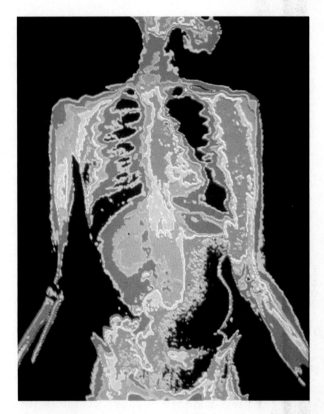

Advances in medicine utilizing computers and other new technology offer significant health benefits to many people. But they have also contributed to the soaring cost of medical care. This country is now developing a national health care package in response to charges that we have two standards of health: one for those who can afford the best care and another for everyone else.

for the world as a whole has been rising—from forty-eight years in 1950 to about sixty-five years today—and the biggest gains have been in poor countries (Mosley & Cowley, 1991). But in most poor societies, hundreds of millions of adults and children lack adequate food, safe water, and medical attention. As we enter the next century, global economic development depends on improving health in the world's poorest societies.

SUMMARY

Education

1. Education is a major social institution for transmitting knowledge and skills as well as passing on norms and values. In preindustrial societies, education occurs informally within the family; industrial societies develop more formal systems of schooling.

2. The United States was among the first societies to institute compulsory mass education, reflecting both democratic political ideals and the needs of the industrial-capitalist economy.

3. The primary functions of schooling include socialization, social placement, and fostering social integration and innovation. Additional latent functions range from child care to forging social networks.

4. Social-conflict analysis points out that schooling helps perpetuate social inequality based on class, race, and gender. Formal education also instills conformity as a way to produce compliant adult workers.

5. The great majority of young people in the United States attend state-funded public schools. Most privately funded schools are affiliated with religious organizations. A small proportion of young people—generally well-to-do—attend elite private schools.

6. One-fifth of U.S. adults over the age of twenty-five are now college graduates, signaling the emergence of a credential society.

7. Most adults in the United States are critical of public schools. Violence permeates many schools, and educational bureaucracy also fosters high dropout rates and widespread student passivity. Declining standardized test scores point to a slide in academic achievement.

8. The school choice movement seeks to make educational systems more responsive to the public they serve.

9. Children with mental or physical disabilities historically have been schooled in special classes or not at all. Mainstreaming affords broader opportunities to students with disabilities.

Medicine

1. Health is a social issue because well-being depends on a society's technology and distribution of resources. Culture shapes both definitions of health as well as patterns of health care.

2. Health improved dramatically in Western Europe and North America in the nineteenth century, first due to industrialization and later because of medical advances.

3. Infectious diseases were leading killers at the beginning of this century. Today most people in the United States die in old age of chronic illnesses like heart disease, cancer, or stroke.

4. Poor nations suffer from inadequate sanitation, hunger, and other problems stemming from poverty. Life expectancy in these impoverished countries is about twenty years less than in the United States; in the least economically developed societies, half of all children do not survive to adulthood.

5. Three-fourths of U.S. children born today can expect to reach age sixty-five. Throughout the life course, women have relatively better health than men, and people of high social position enjoy better health than others.

6. Cigarette smoking stands as the greatest preventable cause of death in the United States.

7. While the incidence of most types of infections has dropped, the frequency of sexually transmitted diseases has risen in recent decades.

8. Advancing medical technology prompts us to confront ethical dilemmas concerning how and when death should occur.

9. Historically a family concern, health care is now the responsibility of trained specialists. The model of scientific medicine underlies the U.S. medical establishment. The holistic approach stresses greater individual responsibility for one's own health.

10. Socialist societies define medical care as a right that governments offer equally to everyone. Capitalist societies view medical care as a commodity to be purchased, although most capitalist

governments support medical care through socialized medicine or national health insurance.

11. Central to the structural-functional analysis of health is the concept of the sick role, in which illness frees people from routine responsibilities.

The symbolic-interaction paradigm investigates the social construction of both health and medical treatment. Social-conflict analysis focuses on the unequal access to health care and criticizes our medical system for its profit orientation.

KEY CONCEPTS

Education

credentialism evaluating people on the basis of educational degrees

education the social institution through which society provides its members with important knowledge, including facts, skills, and values

functional illiteracy reading and writing skills inadequate for everyday living

schooling formal instruction under the direction of specially trained teachers

tracking the division of a school's students into different educational programs

Medicine

direct-fee system a medical-care system in which patients pay directly for the services of physicians and hospitals

euthanasia (mercy killing) assisting in the death of a person suffering from an incurable illness

health a state of complete physical, mental, and social well-being

health maintenance organization (HMO) an organization that provides comprehensive medical care for a fixed fee

holistic medicine an approach to health care that emphasizes prevention of illness and takes account of a person's entire physical and social environment

medicine the social institution that focuses on combating disease and improving health

sick role patterns of behavior defined as appropriate for those who are ill

social epidemiology the study of how health and disease are distributed throughout a society's population

socialized medicine a medical-care system in which the government owns most facilities and employs most physicians

CRITICAL-THINKING QUESTIONS

1. Why did the institutions of schooling and medicine expand after the onset of the Industrial Revolution?

2. Do you agree with research findings in this chapter that, by and large, college students are passive in class? If so, how do you think colleges could make students more active learners?

3. Explain the assertion that health is as much a social as a biological issue.

4. How do sexually transmitted diseases represent an exception to the historical decline in infectious diseases?

Chapter

14

Red Grooms, *Taxi to the Terminal*, 1993.

Population and Urbanization

In 1519 a band of Spanish conquistadors led by Hernando Cortés reached Tenochtitlán, the capital of the Aztec empire. They were stunned by the beautiful, lake-encircled city, teeming with some three hundred thousand people. Walking down broad streets, exploring magnificent stone temples, and gazing on the golden treasures of the royal palace, Cortés and his soldiers wondered if they were dreaming.

Cortés soon woke up and set his mind to looting the city. Unable at first to overcome the superior forces of Montezuma and the Aztecs, Cortés spent the next two years raising a vast army and finally returned to totally destroy Tenochtitlán. On the rubble of this ancient urban center, he constructed a new city in the European fashion—Ciudad Imperial de México—Mexico City.

Today Mexico City is once more fighting for its life. Its soaring population will reach 28 million by the end of the 1990s—one hundred times the number of people that astonished Cortés. This huge population is grappling with a host of problems common to poor societies, including poverty and a deteriorating environment.

A triple burden of rising population, urban sprawl, and desperate poverty weighs on much of today's world. This chapter examines both population growth and urbanization—two powerful forces that have shaped and reshaped our planet for thousands of years. The increasing population will be one of the most serious challenges facing the world in the coming century, and this compelling drama will be played out in cities of unprecedented size.

Demography: The Study of Population

From the point at which the human species emerged, roughly 200,000 B.C.E., until several centuries ago, the earth's population climbed slowly to about 250 million—about the same number as the population of the United States today. Life for our ancestors was uncertain at best; people were vulnerable to countless diseases and frequent natural disasters. For ten thousand generations, however, our species has managed to flourish. Ironically, global population is now so large (5.7 billion in 1995), and growing so rapidly (by about 100 million annually), that the future of humanity is in doubt once again.

The causes and consequences of this growth form the core of **demography**, *the study of human population.* Demography (from Greek meaning "description of people"), a close cousin of sociology, analyzes the size and composition of a population, as well as the migration of people from place to place. Although much demographic research is a numbers game, the discipline also poses crucial questions about the effects of population growth and its control.

The following sections explain basic demographic concepts.

Fertility

The study of human population begins with how many people are born. **Fertility** is *the incidence of childbearing in a society's population.* During a woman's childbearing years, from the onset of menstruation (typically in the early teens) to menopause (usually in the late forties), she is capable of bearing over twenty children. But *fecundity,* or potential childbearing, is sharply reduced by illness, finances, and personal choice.

Demographers measure fertility using the **crude birth rate,** *the number of live births in a given year for every thousand people in a population.* They calculate the crude birth rate by dividing the number of live births in a year by a society's total population, and multiplying the result by 1,000. In the United States in 1994, there were 4.0 million live births in a population of 261 million (U.S. Bureau of the Census, 1994). According to this formula, then, the crude birth rate was 15.3.

This birth rate is "crude" because it is based on the entire population, not just women in their childbearing years. National comparisons can be misleading, then, if one country has a larger share of women of childbearing age than another. A crude birth rate also tells us nothing about how fertility differs among a society's racial and ethnic categories. But this measure is easy to calculate and serves as a good indicator of a society's overall fertility. Table 14–1 shows that the crude birth rate of the United States is low by global standards.

Mortality

Population size is also affected by **mortality,** *the incidence of death in a society's population.* Corresponding to the crude birth rate, demographers use a **crude death rate,** *the number of deaths in a given year for every thousand people in a population.* This time, we take the number of deaths in a year, and again divide by the total population, multiplying the result by 1,000. In 1994 there were 2.3 million deaths in the U.S. population of 261 million, yielding a crude death rate of 8.8. As Table 14–1 shows, this rate is low in global context.

A third widely used demographic measure is the **infant mortality rate,** *the number of deaths among infants under one year of age for each thousand live births in a given year.* This rate is derived by dividing the number of deaths of children under one year of age by the number of live births during the same year and multiplying the result by 1,000. In 1994 there were 32,200 infant deaths and about 4.0 million live births in the United States. Dividing the first number by the second and multiplying the result by 1,000 produces an infant mortality rate of 8.1.

Here again, we need to bear in mind variation among different categories of people. For example, African Americans, with three times the burden of poverty as whites, have an infant mortality rate of about 19—the same as the people of Jamaica and more than twice the white rate of 8 (U.S. Bureau of the Census, 1994). But infant mortality offers a good general measure of overall quality of life. Table 14–1 shows that U.S. infant mortality, while low compared to poor countries, is slightly higher than in Canada, Denmark, and other nations that make medical care more widely available to their people.

Low infant mortality greatly raises **life expectancy,** *the average life span of a society's population.* Males born in the United States in 1992 can expect to live 72.3 years, while females can look toward living 79.0 years. In poor societies with high infant mortality, however, life expectancy is about twenty years less.

Migration

Population size is also affected by **migration,** *the movement of people into and out of a specified territory.* Migration is sometimes involuntary, such as the forced transport of 10 million Africans to the Western Hemisphere as slaves (Sowell, 1981). Voluntary migration is usually motivated by complex "push-pull" factors.

TABLE 14–1 Fertility and Mortality Rates in Global Perspective, 1994

	Crude Birth Rate	Crude Death Rate	Infant Mortality Rate
North America			
United States	15	9	8
Canada	14	7	7
Europe			
Belgium	12	10	7
Russia	13	11	27
Denmark	13	11	7
France	13	9	7
Spain	11	9	7
United Kingdom	13	11	7
Latin America			
Chile	21	6	15
Cuba	17	7	10
Haiti	40	19	109
Mexico	27	5	27
El Salvador	33	6	41
Puerto Rico	19	8	17
Africa			
Algeria	30	6	52
Cameroon	41	11	77
Egypt	29	9	76
Ethiopia	45	14	106
Nigeria	44	12	75
South Africa	34	8	47
Asia			
Afghanistan	44	19	156
Bangladesh	35	12	107
India	29	10	78
Saudi Arabia	38	6	52
Japan	11	7	4
Vietnam	28	8	46

Source: U.S. Bureau of the Census (1994).

Dissatisfaction with life may "push" people to move, while a common "pull" factor is the opportunity for a better life in a big city.

Movement into a territory—commonly termed *immigration*—is measured as an *in-migration rate,* calculated as the number of people entering an area for every thousand people in the population. Movement out of a territory—or *emigration*—is measured in terms of the *out-migration rate,* the number leaving for every thousand people. Both types of migration usually occur simultaneously, their difference being the *net-migration rate.*

African-American artist Jacob Lawrence completed a series of paintings that he titled *The Migration of the Negro* (1940–41) to document a major population movement among people of color from the rural South to the urban centers of the Northeast and Midwest.

Population Growth

Fertility, mortality, and migration all affect the size of a society's population. In general, rich nations (like the United States) grow as much from immigration as natural increase; less economically developed societies (like Mexico) grow almost entirely from natural increase.

To calculate a population's natural growth rate, subtract the crude death rate from the crude birth rate. The natural growth rate of the U.S. population in 1994 was 6.5 per thousand (the crude birth rate of 15.3 per thousand minus the crude death rate of 8.8 per thousand), or 0.65 percent annual growth.

Global Map 14–1 shows that annual population growth in the United States and other industrialized nations is well below the world average of 1.6 percent. In Europe, the current rate of growth is just 0.2 percent, and in Japan population is holding steady. By contrast, high annual growth rates are the norm in Asia (1.6 percent) and Latin America (1.8 percent). Africa is witnessing the greatest population surge, with annual growth of 3.1 percent.

As a handy rule-of-thumb, dividing a society's growth rate into the number seventy yields the *doubling time* in years. Thus, an annual growth rate of 2 percent (as in Latin America) doubles a population in thirty-five years, and a 3 percent growth rate (as in Africa) pares the doubling time to twenty-four years. The rapid population growth of the poorest countries is deeply troubling because they can barely support the populations they have now.

Population Composition

Demographers also study the composition of a society's population at a given point in time. One simple variable is the **sex ratio,** *the number of males for every hundred females in a given population.* In 1994 the sex ratio in the United States was 95.1, or roughly 95 males for every 100 females. Sex ratios are usually below 100 because women typically outlive men. In India, however, the sex ratio is 108, because parents value sons more than daughters and sometimes abort a female fetus or, after birth, provide less care to a female infant, leading to premature death.

A more complex measure is the **age-sex pyramid,** *a graphic representation of the age and sex of a population.* Figure 14–1 on page 368 presents two age-sex pyramids, which show the contrasting compositions of the populations of the United States and Mexico. The rough pyramid shape of these figures results from higher mortality as people age. Looking at the U.S. pyramid, the bulge corresponding to ages twenty through forty-nine reflects high birth rates during the *baby boom* from the mid-1940s to 1970. The contraction just below—that is, people under twenty—represents the subsequent *baby bust* as the crude birth rate dipped from 25.3 in 1957 to a low of 15.3 in 1994.

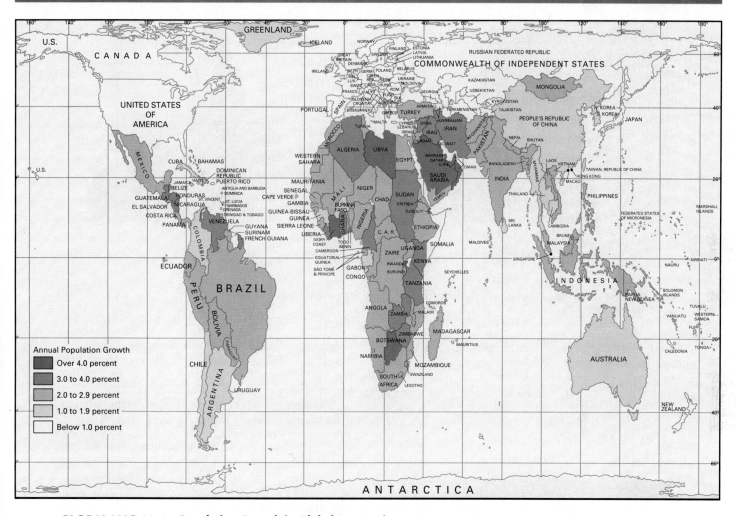

GLOBAL MAP 14–1   Population Growth in Global Perspective

The richest countries of the world—including the United States, Canada, and the nations of Europe—have growth rates below 1 percent. The nations of Latin America and Asia typically have growth rates of about 2 percent, which double a population in thirty-five years. The continent of Africa has an overall growth rate of 3.1 percent, which cuts the doubling time to less than twenty-four years. In global perspective, we see that a society's standard of living is closely related to its rate of population growth: Population is rising fastest in the world regions that can least afford to support more people.

Sources: *Peters Atlas of the World* (1990), with statistics updated by the author.

Comparing the U.S. and Mexican pyramids, we can predict different demographic trends. The age-sex pyramid for Mexico, like that of other less economically developed countries, is wider at the bottom (reflecting higher birth rates) and narrows quickly by what we would term middle age (due to higher mortality). Mexico, in short, is a much younger society with a median age of 20.4 compared to 34.1 in the United States. With a larger share of females still in their childbearing years, we can see why Mexico's

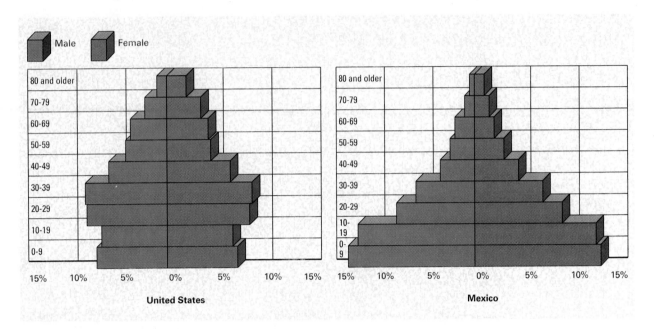

FIGURE 14–1   Age-Sex Population Pyramids for the United States and Mexico
Sources: U.S. Bureau of the Census and Mexican Census data.

crude birth rate (27) is considerably higher than our own (15.3), a fact that contributes to greater population growth.

History and Theory of Population Growth

Through most of human history, people favored large families because human labor was the key to productivity. Additionally, until rubber condoms appeared 150 years ago, controlling birth was uncertain at best. But high death rates, resulting from widespread infectious diseases, served as a constant brake on population growth. World population at the dawn of civilization, about 6000 B.C.E., was just 50 million.

A demographic shift began as the earth's population turned sharply upward, reaching the 1 billion mark about 1800. This milestone (requiring some forty thousand years) was repeated by 1930 (barely a century later) when a second billion was added to the planet. In other words, not only did population increase, but the *rate* of growth accelerated. Population reached a third billion by 1962 (after just thirty-two years) and a fourth billion by 1974 (a scant twelve years later). The rate of world

population increase has recently slowed, but our planet passed the 5 billion mark in 1987. In no previous century did the world's population even double. In the twentieth century, it has increased *fourfold*.

Currently, experts predict that global population will exceed 6 billion early in the next century, and it will probably reach 8 billion by 2025. Little wonder, then, that global population has become a matter of urgent concern.

Malthusian Theory

It was the sudden population growth two centuries ago that sparked the development of demography. Thomas Robert Malthus (1766–1834), an English clergyman and economist, warned that population increase would soon lead to social chaos. Malthus (1926; orig. 1798) began by claiming that population would rise according to what mathematicians call a geometric progression, illustrated by the series of numbers 2, 4, 8, 16, 32, and so on. At such a rate, Malthus concluded, world population would soon soar out of control.

Food production would also increase, Malthus reasoned, but only in arithmetic progression (as in the series 2, 3, 4, 5, 6) because, even with agricultural innovation, farmland is limited. Malthus's analysis yielded a troubling vision of the future: people reproducing beyond what the planet can feed, leading ultimately to widespread starvation.

Malthus recognized that artificial birth control or sexual abstinence might change the equation, but he found them either morally wrong or practically impossible. Thus, famine and war stalked the future of humanity, in Malthus's scheme, a vision that earned him the moniker of the "dismal parson."

Critical evaluation. Fortunately, Malthus's prediction was flawed. First, by 1850 the European birth rate began to drop, partly because children were becoming less of an economic asset, and partly because people did adopt artificial birth control. Second, Malthus underestimated human ingenuity: Irrigation, fertilizers, and pesticides have greatly boosted farm production just as factories have generated a bounty of other products.

Critics also chided Malthus for ignoring the role of social inequality in world abundance and famine. Karl Marx (1967; orig. 1867) objected to viewing suffering as a "law of nature" rather than the mischief of capitalism.

Still, we should not entirely dismiss Malthus's dire prediction. First, habitable land, clean water, and fresh air are certainly finite. And greater agricultural productivity has taken a toll on the natural environment. Finally, as medical advances have lowered death rates, world population has risen even faster.

In principle, some analysts conclude, no level of population growth is sustainable over the long run. Thus, people everywhere must fix their sights on the long-range dangers of population increase.

Demographic Transition Theory

Malthus's rather crude analysis has been superseded by **demographic transition theory,** *a thesis linking population patterns to a society's level of technological development.*

Figure 14–2 shows the demographic consequences of four stages of technological development. Preindustrial agrarian societies—at Stage 1—have high birth rates because of the economic value of children and the absence of birth control. Death rates are also high, the result of low living standards and limited medical technology. But deaths neutralize births, so population rises and falls with a modest, overall increase, as was the case for thousands of years before the Industrial Revolution in Europe.

Stage 2—the onset of industrialization—brings a demographic transition as population surges upward. Technology expands food supplies and combats disease. Death rates fall sharply although birth rates remain high, resulting in rapid population growth. It was in an era like this that Malthus formulated his ideas, which explains his pessimism. Most of the world's poorest countries today are still in this high-growth stage.

In Stage 3—a mature industrial economy—the birth rate drops, curbing population growth once again. Fertility falls, first, because most children now survive to adulthood and, second, because high living standards make raising children expensive. Affluence, in short, transforms children from economic assets into economic liabilities. Smaller families are also favored by women working outside the home, prompting widespread use of birth control. As birth rates follow death rates downward, population growth slows further.

FIGURE 14–2
Demographic Transition Theory

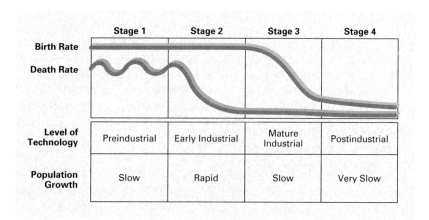

The birthrate in Europe has dropped so low that some analysts foresee an absolute drop in population in this world region. The French government, which sees children as a national resource, has turned to advertising to encourage people to have children. The ad implies children are becoming so rare that this baby can remark: "It appears that I am a sociocultural phenomenon." At the bottom right is added, "France needs children."

The most recent stage corresponds to a postindustrial economy. The birth rate in such societies continues to fall, in part because the costs of rearing children keep on rising and also because dual-income couples gradually become the norm, which diverts time from parenting. This trend, together with steady death rates, means that, at best, population grows only very slowly. In many European countries and Japan, for example, population is now virtually stable or falling slightly (van de Kaa, 1987).

Critical evaluation. Demographic transition theory suggests that technology holds the key to population control. Instead of the runaway population increase Malthus feared, this analysis foresees technology both controlling population growth and ensuring material plenty.

Demographic transition theory dovetails with modernization theory, one approach to global development examined in Chapter 8 ("Global Stratification"). Modernization theorists take the optimistic view that poor societies will solve their population problems as they industrialize. But critics—notably dependency

theorists—argue that global economic arrangements will only perpetuate poverty in much of the world. Unless there is a significant redistribution of the world's resources, they claim, our planet will become increasingly divided into industrialized "haves," enjoying low population growth, and nonindustrialized "have-nots," struggling in vain to feed soaring populations.

Global Population: A Survey

What demographic patterns characterize today's world? Drawing on the discussion so far, we can highlight several key trends.

The Low-Growth North

When the Industrial Revolution began, population growth in Western Europe and North America peaked at 3 percent annually. But in the centuries since, it steadily declined and, in 1970, dropped below 1 percent. As our postindustrial society reaches Stage 4, the U.S. birth rate is approaching the replacement level of 2.1 children per woman, a point demographers term *zero population growth*.

Factors holding down population growth in postindustrial societies include the high proportion of men and women in the labor force, the rising cost of raising children, trends toward later marriages and singlehood, and the use of contraceptives by about two-thirds of women of childbearing age (including U.S. Catholics). Finally, abortion has been legal in the United States since 1973, and each year women decide to terminate 1.5 million pregnancies in this way (Westoff & Jones, 1977; Moore & Pachon, 1985; U.S. Bureau of the Census, 1994).

Overall, population growth in industrial nations does not present the pressing problem that it does in poor countries. Even so, as Chapter 15 ("The Natural Environment") explains, the typical individual in our society uses many times the resources that the average person in a poor country does, placing that much more stress on the physical environment.

The High-Growth South

Population growth remains a serious problem in poor nations of the Southern Hemisphere. Only a few societies lack industrial technology altogether, placing them at demographic transition theory's Stage 1. Most countries in Latin America, Africa, and Asia have agrarian economies with some industry, locating them in Stage 2. Advanced medical technology supplied by rich societies has sharply reduced death rates, but birth rates remain high. Figure 14–3 shows the result. These societies now account for two-thirds of the earth's people and 90 percent of global population growth.

Cultural imperatives play a role here. In poor countries, birth rates remain high because children still work eight- or ten-hour days to generate income; later, as adults, they care for aging parents. Throughout the less-developed world, families average four or five children; in rural areas, the number may reach six or eight (The World Bank, 1991). But we must be careful about extending generalizations to more than one hundred societies. The box on page 372 contrasts the demographic profiles of the two Chinas—the People's Republic of China and Taiwan, Republic of China.

Any society's demographic profile has much to do with the options and opportunities available to women. Worldwide, societies that define women's primary responsibilities as bearing children experience high population growth. One study focusing on Sudan (Africa) and Colombia (South America) concluded that women with seven years of schooling had half as many children as women with no education (Ross, 1985; Salas, 1985).

In Latin America, a combination of poverty, traditional patriarchy, and Roman Catholic doctrine discourages women from using birth control devices, with predictable effects on fertility. In much of Africa, women in poor villages have no access at all to effective birth control (Salas, 1985). As we have seen, Asia is a study in contrasts with some countries pressing couples to have children while others wage aggressive campaigns to limit births.

Taken together, various strategies to control fertility in developing countries have met with some success. But, in most cases, birth rates are still too high to be sustainable. Just as important, death rates are falling too, which, although good news, pushes population upward.

In point of fact, population growth in poor countries is due *primarily* to declining death rates. After about 1920, when Europe and North America began to export scientific medicine, nutrition, and sanitation to poor societies, mortality there tumbled. Since then, inoculations against infectious diseases and the use of antibiotics and insecticides have continued to lower death rates with stunning effectiveness. For example, in Sri Lanka, malaria caused half of all deaths in the mid-1930s; a decade later, use of insecticide to kill malaria-carrying mosquitoes cut the death toll in half. Although we hail such an achievement, over the long run, it sent Sri Lanka's population soaring. Similarly, India's infant mortality rate fell from 130 in 1975 to 90 in 1990, a decline that helped boost that nation's population to more than 850 million.

In short, in much of the world life expectancy is up and infant mortality is down. But birth control policies are now vital in countries where "death control" programs worked well several generations ago (Ehrlich, 1978; Piotrow, 1980).

Looking Ahead: Population in the Twenty-First Century

Demographic analysis sheds light on how and why the earth is gaining unprecedented population. Only through such study can humankind address this pressing problem.

But even if we grasp the causes of the problem, controlling global population in the next century will

FIGURE 14–3   The Increase in World Population, 1700–2100

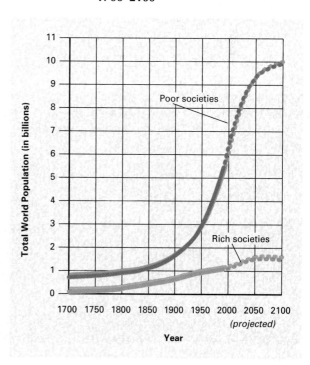

Demographic Contrasts: A Report From the Two Chinas

P.R. China
Taiwan, R.O.C.

The People's Republic of China and Taiwan, Republic of China, contend with different population problems. The former—the world's most populous country with 1.3 billion people—is aggressively trying to limit its population growth. The latter, by contrast, has initiated programs to raise its birth rate.

With fully one-fifth of humanity within its borders, it is no surprise that individuals in the People's Republic of China say they "count mouths" rather than "count heads" as we do. Ominously, more than half these people are under thirty, raising the specter of an unprecedented baby boom that could overwhelm the nation's food supply. As a result, since 1979, the government has pursued a tough "single-child" policy by which local officials give people strong incentives to delay childbirth and, once one child is born, to submit to sterilization or abort subsequent pregnancies. One-baby couples who comply enjoy income bonuses and special treatment for their children in school and, later, in employment and housing. This program has nudged annual population growth downward from 2.0 percent in 1960 to 1.8 percent today.

Some critics charge that such efforts amount to forcing sterilization on people. Moreover, this policy prompts some parents to abort female fetuses or even kill female infants since, by tradition, Chinese parents look to sons (not daughters) to care for them in old age. In response, the government has displayed some leniency in recent years. Yet the price of failure to curb fertility is high: At the present rate of increase, China's population will double by 2025, undermining the struggle of a vast society to raise its standard of living.

Taiwan faces a different problem, as its annual rate of population growth has fallen to 0.9 percent (almost as low as the 0.65 percent U.S. rate). The reason for the downward trend is that this nation (one of the four prospering "Little Dragons" along with South Korea, Hong Kong, and Singapore) is currently experiencing rapid economic development. Taiwanese women are leaving the home to enter the labor force, and the two-income family is becoming the norm as it already has in the United States. With affluence also comes independence, and an increasing share of Taiwan's adult population is choosing to remain single and childless.

If fertility continues its downward slide, Taiwan's government is concerned that there will soon be too many elderly people and not enough younger workers to support them. As a result, officials have launched public relations campaigns to convince couples that "Two children is just right." In addition, to counter the traditional prejudice against having girls, Taiwan has outlawed using medical procedures to discover the sex of a fetus.

Comparisons of this kind show that countries monitor demographic patterns for very different reasons. They also reveal how misleading any one stereotype of developing societies can be.

FAMILY PLANNING—A BASIC NATIONAL POLICY OF CHINA

Sources: The World Bank (1984), Brophy (1989a, 1989b), Tien (1989), and The Economist (1993b).

pose a monumental challenge. As we have seen, population growth is currently greatest in the poorest countries of the world, those that lack the productive capacity to support their present populations, much less their future ones. Most of the inhabitants of rich nations are spared the trauma of poverty. But adding almost 90 million people to our planet each year—80 million of these in poor societies—will require a global commitment to provide not only food, but housing, schools, and employment—all of which are in tragically short supply. The well-being of the entire world may ultimately depend on resolving many of the economic and social problems of poor, overly populated countries and bridging the widening gulf between the "have" and "have-not" societies. Describing recent population growth as "a great wave," one official of the United States government concluded:

> I see the world population movement as the effort to construct a breakwater—a structure that will stop the wave and prevent it from engulfing and sweeping away centuries of human development and civilization. (cited in Gupte, 1984:323)

Urbanization: The Growth of Cities

For most of human history, the small populations found around the world lived in nomadic groups, moving as they depleted vegetation or searched for migratory game. Small settlements marked the emergence of civilization in the Middle East some ten thousand years ago, but they held only a small fraction of the earth's people. Today each of the largest cities contains as many people as the entire planet did then.

Urbanization is *the concentration of humanity into cities.* Urbanization both redistributes population within a society and transforms many patterns of social life. We will trace these changes in terms of three urban revolutions—the emergence of cities beginning ten thousand years ago, the development of industrial cities after 1750, and the explosive growth of cities in poor countries today.

The Evolution of Cities

Cities are a relatively new development in human history. Only about ten thousand years ago did our ancestors begin creating permanent settlements, initiating the *first urban revolution.*

Sex selection, the use of amniocentesis to determine the sex of a fetus, coupled with a decision to abort females, has become a popular practice in traditional, patriarchal societies of the world. This poster, by an organization in Bombay, India, reads "Once the woman becomes pregnant, after determination of the sex, everywhere there is murder of girls. Let's stop sex determination."

From "Sex Selection in India as a Bad Investment," an article by Les Levidow, in the premiere issue of *Science as Culture,* a quarterly published by Free Association Books in London. This poster was created by the Forum Against Sex Discrimination and Sex Pre-Selection Techniques in Bombay.

Preconditions of cities. The first precondition of urban development was a *favorable ecology.* As glaciers melted at the end of the last ice age, people were drawn to warm regions with fertile soil. The second was *changing technology.* At about the same time, humans discovered how to cultivate animals and crops. Whereas hunting and gathering demanded continual movement, raising food required people to remain in one place (Lenski, Lenski, & Nolan, 1991). Domesticating animals and plants also produced *a material surplus,* which freed some people from concentrating on food production and allowed them to build shelters, make tools, weave clothing, and lead religious rituals. Thus, the founding of cities was truly revolutionary, raising living standards and magnifying specialization.

The first cities. Historians identify the first city as Jericho, a settlement to the north of the Dead Sea in disputed land currently occupied by Israel. Around 8000 B.C.E., Jericho had a permanent population of about six hundred (Kenyon, 1957; Hamblin, 1973). By 4000 B.C.E., numerous cities were flourishing in the Fertile Crescent between the Tigris and Euphrates rivers in present-day Iraq and, soon afterward, along the Nile River in Egypt. Some, with populations as high as fifty thousand, became centers of urban empires. Priest-kings wielded absolute power over lesser nobles, administrators, artisans, soldiers, and farmers. Slaves, captured in frequent military campaigns, labored to build monumental structures like the pyramids of Egypt (Wenke, 1980; Stavrianos, 1983; Lenski, Lenski, & Nolan, 1991).

Humans independently developed cities in at least three other areas of the world. Several large cities bordered the Indus River of present-day Pakistan starting about 2500 B.C.E. Scholars date Chinese cities from 2000 B.C.E. And in Central and South America, urban centers began about 1500 B.C.E. In North America, however, Native-American societies rarely formed settlements; significant urbanization did not begin until the arrival of European settlers in the sixteenth century (Lamberg-Karlovsky, 1973; Change, 1977; Coe & Diehl, 1980).

Preindustrial European cities. Urbanization in Europe first took hold around 1800 B.C.E. on the Mediterranean island of Crete. Cities soon spread throughout Greece, resulting in more than one hundred city-states, of which Athens is the most famous. During its Golden Age, lasting barely a century, from 500 to 400 B.C.E., some three hundred thousand people living within roughly one square mile made major contributions to

the Western way of life in philosophy, the arts, and politics. Despite such achievements, Athenian society rested on the labor of slaves, one-third of the population. Their democratic principles notwithstanding, Athenian men also denied the rights of citizenship to women, foreigners, and slaves (Mumford, 1961; Gouldner, 1965; Stavrianos, 1983).

As Greek civilization faded, the city of Rome grew to almost 1 million inhabitants and became the center of a vast empire. By the first century C.E., the Roman army had subdued much of northern Africa, Europe, and the Middle East. In the process, Rome spread its language, arts, and technology across its huge sphere of influence. Four centuries later, the Roman Empire fell into disarray, a victim of its gargantuan size, internal corruption, and militaristic appetite. Yet, between them, the Greeks and Romans founded cities across Europe, including London, Paris, and Vienna.

The fall of the Roman Empire ushered in an era of urban decline and stagnation lasting six hundred years. Cities became smaller as people drew back within defensive walls and competing warlords battled for territory. Around the eleventh century, the "Dark Ages" came to an end; with a semblance of peace, trade began to flourish and cities came back to life once again.

Medieval cities slowly tore down their walls as trade expanded. Beneath towering cathedrals, the narrow and winding streets of London, Brussels, and Florence soon teemed with merchants, artisans, priests, peddlers, jugglers, nobles, and servants. Typically, bakers, keymakers, carpenters, and other occupational groups clustered together in distinct sections or "quarters." Ethnic groups also inhabited their own neighborhoods, often because people kept them out of other districts. The term ghetto (from the Italian word *borghetto*, meaning "outside the city walls") first described the segregation of Jews in Venice.

Industrial European cities. Throughout the Middle Ages, steadily increasing commerce created an affluent urban middle class or *bourgeoisie* (French, meaning "of the town"). By the fifteenth century, the wealth-based power of the bourgeoisie rivaled the traditional authority of the hereditary nobility.

By about 1750 industrialization was proceeding apace, triggering a *second urban revolution*, first in Europe and then in North America. Factories unleashed productive power as never before, causing cities to grow to unprecedented size, as Table 14–2 shows. During the nineteenth century the population

The eruption of Mount Vesuvius in the year 79 C.E. buried the Italian city of Pompeii in lava, mud, and ash, killing the population before they knew what had happened. Now that archaeologists have excavated the region, visitors can see what life was like in this preindustrial city. Although modern conveniences such as electricity and indoor plumbing were absent, many of the residents of ancient Pompeii lived relatively comfortable lives.

of Paris soared from five hundred thousand to over 3 million, and London's population exploded from eight hundred thousand to 6.5 million (A. Weber, 1963, orig. 1899; Chandler & Fox, 1974). Most of this increase was due to migration from rural areas by people seeking a better standard of living.

So prominent was commerce in urban life that the industrial-capitalist city forged a new urban form. Broad, straight boulevards replaced older irregular streets to accommodate the flow of commercial traffic and, eventually, motor vehicles. Steam and electric trolleys crisscrossed the expanding cities. Lewis Mumford (1961) explains that developers divided cities into regular-sized lots, making land a commodity to be bought and sold. Finally, the cathedrals that had dominated the life of medieval cities were soon dwarfed by towering, brightly lit, and frantic central business districts made up of banks, office buildings, and retail stores.

Focused on business, cities became increasingly crowded and impersonal. Crime rates rose. Especially at the outset, a small number of industrialists lived in grand style, while for most men, women, and children, factory work proved exhausting and provided barely a subsistence wage.

Table 14–2 shows that European cities continued to grow during this century, although at a slower rate. Organized efforts by workers to improve their plight led to legal regulation of the workplace, better housing, and the right to vote. Public services such as water, sewage, and electricity further enhanced urban living. Today some urbanites still live in poverty, but a rising standard of living has partly fulfilled the city's historical promise of a better life.

The Growth of U.S. Cities

Inhabiting this continent for tens of thousands of years, Native Americans were migratory people, establishing few permanent settlements. Cities first sprang up, then, as an offshoot of European colonization. The Spanish made an initial settlement at St. Augustine, Florida, in 1565, and the English founded Jamestown, Virginia, in 1607. In 1624, the Dutch established New Amsterdam (later called New York), which soon overshadowed these smaller settlements. In 1990, the United States had 195 cities comprising more than one hundred thousand inhabitants. How ours became an urban society is explained in the brief history that follows.

TABLE 14–2 Population Growth in Selected Industrial Cities of Europe (in thousands)

| City | Year | | | |
	1700	1800	1900	1992*
Amsterdam	172	201	510	713
Berlin	100	172	2,424	3,020
Lisbon	188	237	363	2,505
London	550	861	6,480	9,168
Madrid	110	169	539	4,577
Paris	530	547	3,330	8,589
Rome	149	153	487	3,028
Vienna	105	231	1,662	2,392

* for entire urban area

Sources: Based on data from Tertius Chandler and Gerald Fox, *3000 Years of Urban History* (New York: Academic Press, 1974), pp. 17–19; and U.S. Bureau of the Census (1993).

Colonial settlement: 1624–1800. The metropolises of New York and Boston started out as tiny villages in a vast wilderness. Dutch New Amsterdam (1624) and English Boston (1630) each resembled medieval towns, with narrow, winding streets that still exist in lower Manhattan and downtown Boston. New Amsterdam was walled on the north, the site of today's Wall Street. In 1700, Boston was the largest U.S. city, with just seven thousand people.

The rational and expansive culture of capitalism soon transformed these quiet villages into thriving towns built with wide thoroughfares. Figure 14–4 contrasts the medieval winding street patterns of New Amsterdam with the modern grid system of Philadelphia, founded in 1680 after another half-century of economic development.

On the heels of independence from Great Britain, the United States was still an overwhelmingly rural society. In 1790 the government's first census tallied roughly 4 million people. As Table 14–3 shows, just 5 percent of them resided in cities.

Urban expansion: 1800–1860. Early in the nineteenth century, towns began springing up along transportation routes that opened the American West. In 1818 the National Road (now Route 40) funneled settlers from Baltimore to the Ohio Valley. A decade later the Baltimore and Ohio Railroad and the Erie Canal (1825) from New York sparked the development of cities along the Great Lakes, including Buffalo, Cleveland, and Detroit.

By 1860 about one-fifth of the U.S. population lived in cities. Underlying this urban expansion was the Industrial Revolution, which most transformed cities in

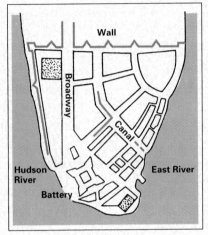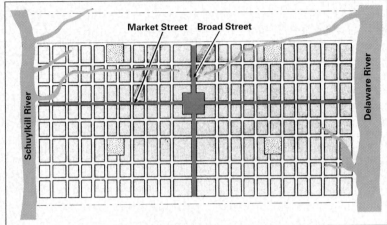

FIGURE 14–4   The Street Plans of Colonial New Amsterdam and Philadelphia

The plan of colonial New Amsterdam, shown at left, exemplifies the preindustrial urban pattern of walls enclosing a city of narrow, irregular streets. Colonial Philadelphia, founded fifty years later, reflects the industrial urban pattern of accessible cities with wide, regularly spaced, parallel and perpendicular streets to facilitate economic activity.

the northern states. In 1850, for example, New York City had ten times the population of Charleston, South Carolina. This division of the United States into the industrial-urban North and the agrarian-rural South aggravated tensions that touched off the Civil War (Schlesinger, 1969).

The metropolitan era: 1860–1950.   The Civil War gave an enormous boost to urbanization, as factories strained to produce the tools of combat. Waves of people fled the countryside for cities in hopes of obtaining better jobs. Soon after, tens of millions of immigrants—most from Europe—joined in to form a culturally diverse urban mix. Table 14–4 reveals the rapid growth of U.S. cities in the late nineteenth century.

In 1900 New York boasted 4 million residents, and Chicago—a city of scarcely one hundred thousand people in 1860—was closing in on 2 million. This growth marked the era of the *metropolis*, from Greek meaning a great "mother city." Dozens of metropolises became the manufacturing, commercial, and residential centers of the United States.

Industrial technology further changed the physical shape of cities, pushing buildings well above the three or four stories common up to that point. By the 1880s, steel girders and mechanical elevators raised structures over ten stories high. In 1930, New York's

Empire State Building became an urban wonder, a true "skyscraper" stretching 102 stories into the clouds. Railroads and highways drew cities outward so that, by 1920, the United States was a predominantly urban society.

Urban decentralization: 1950–present.   The industrial metropolis reached its peak about 1950. Since then, something of a turnaround has occurred as people have deserted the downtowns in a process known as *urban decentralization* (Edmonston & Guterbock, 1984). As Table 14–4 shows, large cities of the Northeast and Midwest stopped growing—and some even lost population—after 1950. The 1990 census count found New York, for example, to have half a million fewer people than at mid-century.

But decentralization has not ended urbanization; cities simply continue to change their form. Instead of densely populated central cities, the urban landscape now looks more and more like sprawling urban regions, with expanding suburbs.

Suburbs and Central Cities

Just as central cities flourished a century ago, we have recently witnessed the expansion of **suburbs**, *urban areas beyond the political boundaries of a city.* Suburbs began to grow late in the nineteenth century as railroad and trolley lines enabled people to live beyond the commotion of the city while still being able to commute "downtown" to work (Warner, 1962).

The first suburbanites were well-to-do people, imitating the European nobility who shuttled between their country estates and town houses (Baltzell, 1979). And mounting immigration prompted many urbanites to flee to homogeneous, high-prestige enclaves beyond the reach of the masses. In time, less wealthy people came to view a single-family house on its own piece of leafy suburban ground as part of the American Dream.

The postwar economic boom of the late 1940s, coupled with the mobility offered by affordable automobiles, placed suburbia within the grasp of the average household. After World War II, men and women eagerly returned to family life, igniting the baby boom described earlier. Since central cities had little space left for new housing, suburbs blossomed almost overnight. The government weighed in with guaranteed bank loans, and developers built and marketed new, prefabricated homes at unheard-of low prices.

Some people poked fun at the "cookie-cutter" houses of the new suburbs, but others snatched up tract homes as fast as they went up. By 1970, more of our population lived in the suburbs than in the central cities. Business followed the flow of people, and soon the suburban mall replaced downtown stores of the metropolitan era. Manufacturing companies, too, decentralized, favoring suburban industrial parks over the congested streets, high taxes, and soaring crime rates of inner cities. The interstate highway system, with its beltways encircling central cities, made moving out to

TABLE 14–3 The Urban Population of the United States, 1790–1990

Year	Population (in millions)	Percent Urban
1790	3.9	5.1
1800	5.3	6.1
1820	9.6	7.3
1840	17.1	10.5
1860	31.4	19.7
1880	50.2	28.1
1900	76.0	39.7
1920	105.7	51.3
1940	131.7	56.5
1960	179.3	69.9
1980	226.5	73.7
1990	253.0	75.2

Source: U.S. Bureau of the Census (1993).

the suburbs almost irresistible for residents and businesses alike (Rosenthal, 1974; Tobin, 1976; Geist, 1985).

Decentralization was not good news for everyone, however. Rapid suburban growth soon threw older cities of the Northeast and Midwest into financial chaos. Population decline meant reduced tax revenues. Further, cities that lost affluent people to the suburbs were left with the burden of providing expensive social programs for the poor who stayed behind. And so inner-city decay began after 1950 in major cities throughout the Northeast. Especially to white people, the deteriorating inner cities became synonymous with slum housing, crime, drugs, unemployment, the poor, and minorities. This perception fed on

TABLE 14–4 Population Growth in Selected U.S. Cities, 1870–1990

City	Population (in thousands)						
	1870	1890	1910	1930	1950	1970	1990
Baltimore	267	434	558	805	950	905	736
Boston	251	448	671	781	801	641	574
Chicago	299	1,100	2,185	3,376	3,621	3,369	2,784
Dallas	7	38	92	260	434	844	1,007
Detroit	80	206	466	1,569	1,850	1,514	1,028
Los Angeles	6	50	319	1,238	1,970	2,812	3,485
Milwaukee	71	204	374	578	637	717	628
New Orleans	191	242	339	459	570	593	497
New York*	942	2,507	4,764	6,930	7,892	7,896	7,323
Philadelphia	674	1,047	1,549	1,951	2,072	1,949	1,586
St. Louis	311	452	687	822	857	622	397
San Francisco	149	299	417	634	775	716	724

*Population figures for New York in 1870 and 1890 reflect that city as presently constituted.

Source: U.S. Bureau of the Census (1993).

itself, fueling wave after wave of "white flight" and pushing some cities (like New York) to the brink of bankruptcy (Clark, 1979; Gluck & Meister, 1979; Sternlieb & Hughes, 1983; Logan & Schneider, 1984; Stahura, 1986; Galster, 1991).

The official response to the plight of the central cities was *urban renewal*. Under this program, federal and local governments have paid to rebuild many inner cities. Yet critics of urban renewal charge that these programs have benefited downtown businesses while doing little to meet the housing needs of low-income residents (Jacobs, 1961; Greer, 1965; Gans, 1982).

Postindustrial Sunbelt Cities

In the new postindustrial economy (see Chapter 11, "Economics and Politics"), people are not only moving beyond the boundaries of central cities, they are also migrating from the Snowbelt to the Sunbelt. The Snowbelt—the traditional industrial heartland of the United States—runs from the Northeast to the Midwest and was home to 60 percent of the U.S. population in 1940. By 1975, however, the Sunbelt—the South and the West—had surpassed the Snowbelt in overall population and, by 1992, it was home to 56 percent of our people.

This demographic shift is shown in Table 14–5, which compares the ten largest cities in the United States in 1950 and in 1990. In 1950, eight of the top ten were industrial cities of the Snowbelt whereas, in 1990, six out of ten were postindustrial cities of the Sunbelt. The box takes a closer look at this shift.

Why are Sunbelt cities faring so well? Unlike their counterparts in the Snowbelt, the postindustrial cities of the Sunbelt grew *after* urban decentralization began. Since Snowbelt cities have long been closed in by a ring of politically independent suburbs, outward migration took place at the expense of the central city. Suburbs have played a smaller role in the history of Sunbelt cities, which have simply expanded outward, gaining population in the process. Chicago, for example, covers 228 square miles, whereas Houston sprawls over 565.

Through physical expansion, Sunbelt cities have retained population even as people have moved outward from the urban center. Yet traveling across town is time-consuming in Sunbelt cities, and owning an automobile is almost a necessity. Lacking a dense center, Sunbelt cities also generate far less of the excitement and intensity that draw people to New York or Chicago. Critics have long tagged Los Angeles, for example, as a vast cluster of suburbs in search of a center.

Megalopolis: Regional Cities

Urban decentralization has produced vast urban areas that encompass numerous cities. In 1993 the Bureau of the Census recognized 253 regional cities, which they call *metropolitan statistical areas* (MSAs). Each MSA includes at least one city with fifty thousand or more people plus densely populated surrounding counties. Almost all of the fifty fastest-growing MSAs are in the Sunbelt.

The biggest MSAs, containing more than 1 million people, are called *consolidated metropolitan statistical areas* (CMSAs). In 1993, there were twenty CMSAs. Heading the list was New York and adjacent urban areas in Long Island, western Connecticut, and northern New Jersey, with a total population approaching 20 million. Next in size was the CMSA in southern California that includes Los Angeles, Riverside, and Anaheim, with a population of 15 million.

Some regional cities have grown so large that they have collided with one another. The East Coast now

TABLE 14–5 The Ten Largest Cities in the United States, 1950 and 1990

1950		
Rank	City	Population
1	New York	7,892,000
2	Chicago	3,621,000
3	Philadelphia	2,072,000
4	Los Angeles	1,970,000
5	Detroit	1,850,000
6	Baltimore	950,000
7	Cleveland	915,000
8	St. Louis	857,000
9	Boston	801,000
10	San Francisco	775,000

1990		
Rank	City	Population
1	New York	7,323,000
2	Los Angeles	3,485,000
3	Chicago	2,784,000
4	Houston	1,631,000
5	Philadelphia	1,586,000
6	San Diego	1,111,000
7	Detroit	1,028,000
8	Dallas	1,007,000
9	Phoenix	983,000
10	San Antonio	936,000

Source: U.S. Bureau of the Census (1993).

Snowbelt and Sunbelt: Contrasts in Urbanization

Just as the twentieth century opened with tremendous urban growth in the North and Midwest, the twenty-first century will witness rapid urbanization in the South and West. The official tally from the 1990 census indicates that Snowbelt cities suffered a moderate drop in population while the Sunbelt population is soaring.

The figure shows how the largest Snowbelt and Sunbelt cities fared between 1980 and 1992. While two of the six most populous Snowbelt cities posted slight population increases, four recorded substantial losses. Each of these six cities is now well below its size in 1950, when Snowbelt cities reached their peak population.

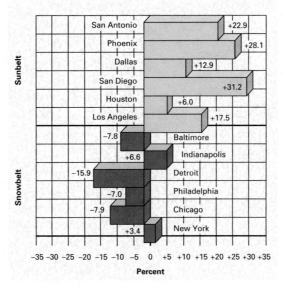

Percent Population Change, 1980–1992
Source: U.S. Bureau of the Census (1994).

The picture is very different if we turn to the cities of the Sunbelt, where population has grown rapidly since mid-century. All six of the largest Sunbelt cities registered population gains during the 1980s—even Houston and Dallas, which were hard hit by the economic downturn. The population growth in the other four Sunbelt cities is dramatic—similar to the explosive increases found in the Snowbelt a century ago.

Which cities—of any size—grew fastest of all during this period? Across the United States, Mesa, Arizona, led the way with an 89 percent gain (to 288,000). Nine other cities had population increases of over 60 percent during the 1980s—every one in the Sunbelt.

---

comprises a four-hundred-mile supercity extending from New England to Virginia. In the early 1960s, French geographer Jean Gottmann (1961) coined the term *megalopolis* to designate a sprawling urban region. Although composed of hundreds of politically independent cities and suburbs, from an airplane at night, a megalopolis appears to stretch to the horizon like a single continuous city. Other megalopolises cover the eastern coast of Florida and stretch from Cleveland to Chicago. Future supercities will undoubtedly emerge, especially in the fast-growing Sunbelt.

Urbanism as a Way of Life

Various sociologists in Europe and the United States were among the first to contrast urban and rural life. We will briefly present their views of urbanism as a way of life.

Ferdinand Toennies: *Gemeinschaft* and *Gesellschaft*

In the late nineteenth century, the German sociologist Ferdinand Toennies (1855–1937) set out to study the social traits defining the industrial metropolis. He contrasted rural and urban life using two concepts now etched into sociology's terminology.

In Toennies's (1963; orig. 1887) scheme, the German word **Gemeinschaft** (meaning roughly "community") referred to *a type of social organization by which people are bound closely together by kinship and tradition*. The *Gemeinschaft* of the rural village, Toennies explained, joins people into what amounts to a single primary group.

By and large, Toennies continued, *Gemeinschaft* is absent in the modern city. On the contrary, urbanization enhances **Gesellschaft** (a German word meaning roughly "association"), *a type of social organization by which people stand apart based on self-interest*. In the *Gesellschaft* model, individuals are motivated by their own needs rather than a desire to enhance the well-being of everyone. City dwellers, Toennies noted, display little sense of neighborhood and look to others mostly as a means of advancing their individual goals. Thus Toennies saw in urbanization the erosion of primary social relations in favor of the temporary, impersonal ties typical of business.

Emile Durkheim: Mechanical and Organic Solidarity

The French sociologist Emile Durkheim agreed with much of Toennies's thinking about cities. Yet, Durkheim countered, urbanites do not lack social bonds; they simply organize social life differently than rural people do.

Traditional, rural life expresses what Durkheim called **mechanical solidarity,** *social bonds based on collective conformity to tradition.* Durkheim's concept of mechanical solidarity bears a striking similarity to Toennies's *Gemeinschaft.* Urbanization erodes some mechanical solidarity, Durkheim explained, but it also generates a new type of bonding, which he termed **organic solidarity,** *social bonds based on specialization and interdependence.* This concept, which parallels Toennies's *Gesellschaft,* reveals a key difference between the two thinkers. While each thought the expansion of industry and cities would undermine traditional social patterns, Durkheim was more optimistic about this historical transformation. Where societies had been built on *likeness,* in short, Durkheim now saw social life based on *difference.* And Durkheim found in urban society more individual choice, increasing moral tolerance, and greater personal privacy than rural villages offer. In short, Durkheim concluded, something may be lost in urbanization, but much is gained.

Georg Simmel: The Blasé Urbanite

German sociologist Georg Simmel (1858–1918) offered a micro-analysis of cities by probing how urban life shaped people's behavior and attitudes. Individuals, Simmel (1964; orig. 1905) explained, experience the city as a crush of people, objects, and events. Easily overwhelmed by this hyperstimulation, he continued, urbanites develop a *blasé attitude,* selectively tuning out much of what goes on around them. This trait does not mean that city dwellers lack sensitivity and compassion, although they often seem aloof. Urban detachment, as Simmel saw it, is simply a strategy for social survival by which people devote their time and energy to those who really matter.

Robert Park: Walking the Streets

Sociologists in the United States soon focused their attention on rapidly growing cities on this side of the Atlantic. Robert Park (1864–1944), a leader of the first major U.S. sociology program at the University of Chicago, did study the European theorists. But Park urged his students and colleagues to walk the streets and study real cities. In one of his most memorable comments, Park said of himself:

> I suspect that I have actually covered more ground, tramping about in cities in different parts of the world, than any other living man. (1950:viii)

What did Park conclude from his lifetime of travel? He found the city to be a carefully organized mosaic of distinctive ethnic communities, commercial districts, and industrial sectors. Over time, he observed, these "natural areas" develop and change in relation to one another. To Park, then, the city was a living, pulsating organism, truly the human kaleidoscope.

Louis Wirth: Urbanism as a Way of Life

A second major figure in the Chicago School of urban sociology was Louis Wirth (1897–1952). Wirth's (1938) best-known contribution is a brief essay in which he blended the ideas of Toennies, Simmel, Durkheim, and Park into a comprehensive theory of urban life.

Wirth began by defining the city as a center of large population, dense settlement, and social diversity. These traits, he argued, combine to form an impersonal, superficial, and transitory way of life. Living among millions of others, urbanites come into contact with many more people than rural residents do. Thus, if city people notice others at all, they usually know them only in terms of *what they do:* as bus driver, florist, or grocery store clerk, for instance.

Specialized, urban relationships are sometimes pleasant for both parties. But, Wirth reminded us, self-interest rather than friendship is the main reason for the interaction. Finally, limited social involvement coupled with great social diversity also make city dwellers more tolerant than rural villagers. Rural

The painting *Peasant Dance*, by Pieter Breughel the Elder (c. 1525/30–1569), conveys the essential unity of rural life forged by generations of kinship and neighborhood. By contrast, Fernand Léger's painting *The City* (1919) communicates the disparate images and discontinuity of experience that are commonplace in urban areas. Taken together, these two paintings capture Toennies's distinction between *Gemeinschaft* and *Gesellschaft*.

communities often jealously defend their narrow traditions, but the heterogeneous population of a city rarely shares—or enforces—any single code of moral conduct (T. Wilson, 1985).

Critical evaluation. Both in Europe and the United States, early sociologists cast an inquisitive eye on urban life. On balance, this research offers a mixed view of urban living. On the one hand, rapid urbanization troubled the sociological pioneers. Toennies and Wirth, especially, recognized that the personal ties and traditional morality of rural life are lost in the anonymous rush of the city. On the other hand, Durkheim and Park emphasized urbanism's positive face, including greater personal autonomy and a wider range of life choices.

And what of Wirth's specific claims about urbanism? Decades of research have provided support for only some of his conclusions. Wirth correctly maintained that urban settings do sustain a weaker sense of community than do rural areas. But one can easily forget that conflict is found in the countryside as well as the city. Furthermore, while urbanites treat most people impersonally, they typically welcome such privacy and, of course, do maintain close personal relationships with a select few (Keller, 1968; Cox, 1971; Macionis, 1978; Wellman, 1979; Lee et al., 1984).

Where the analysis of Wirth and others falls short, too, is in painting urbanism in broad strokes that

overlooks the effects of class, race, and gender. There are many types of urbanites—rich and poor, black and white, Anglo and Latino, women and men—all leading distinctive lives (Gans, 1968). In fact, cities can intensify these social differences. That is, we see the extent of social diversity most clearly in cities where different categories of people reside in the largest numbers (Spates & Macionis, 1987).

Urban Ecology

Sociologists (especially members of the Chicago School) also developed **urban ecology,** *the study of the link between the physical and social dimensions of cities.* Consider, for example, why cities are located where they are. The first cities emerged in fertile regions where the ecology favored raising crops. Preindustrial societies, concerned with defense, built their cities on mountains (ancient Athens was situated on an outcropping of rock) or surrounded by water (Paris and Mexico City were founded on islands). After the Industrial Revolution, when economics gained increasing importance, all major U.S. cities developed next to rivers or natural harbors that facilitated trade and transport of materials.

Urban ecologists also study the physical design of cities. In 1925 Ernest W. Burgess, a student and

Perhaps the greatest U.S. urban sociologist was Robert Park, who taught generations of students to base their conclusions on the direct observation of city life.

colleague of Robert Park, described land use in Chicago in terms of *concentric zones.* City centers, Burgess observed, are business districts bordered by a ring of factories, followed by residential rings that become more expensive with greater distance from the noise and pollution of the city's core.

Homer Hoyt (1939) refined Burgess's observations by noting that distinctive districts often form *wedge-shaped sectors.* For example, one fashionable area may develop next to another, or neighborhoods may extend outward from a city's center along a train or trolley line.

Chauncy Harris and Edward Ullman (1945) added yet another insight: As cities decentralize, they take on a *multi-centered* form. As cities grow, residential areas, industrial parks, and shopping districts typically push away from one another. Few people wish to live close to industrial areas, for example, so the city becomes a mosaic of distinct districts.

Social area analysis adds another twist to urban ecology by investigating what people in specific neighborhoods have in common. Three factors explain most of the variation—family patterns, social class, and race and ethnicity (Shevky & Bell, 1955; Johnston,

1976). Families with children gravitate to areas offering large apartments or single-family homes and good schools. The rich generally seek high-prestige neighborhoods, often in the central city near many of the city's cultural attractions. People with a common social heritage tend to cluster together in distinctive communities.

Finally, Brian Berry and Philip Rees (1969) tied many of these insights together. They explain that distinct family types tend to settle in the concentric zones described by Ernest Burgess. Specifically, households with few children cluster toward the city's center, while those with more children live farther away. Social class differences generate the sector-shaped districts described by Homer Hoyt as, for instance, the rich occupy one "side of the tracks"; the poor, the other. And racial and ethnic neighborhoods are found at various points throughout the city, consistent with Harris and Ullman's multiple-center model.

Looking at the entire United States, cities have a special appeal to young adults. National Map 14–1 shows the attraction of urban places for today's baby boomers.

Critical evaluation. Urban ecologists link the physical and social dimensions of cities. But, as ecologists themselves concede, their conclusions paint an overly simplified picture of urban life. Critics chime in that urban ecology wrongly implies that cities take shape simply from the choices people make. Rather, they assert, urban development responds more to power elites than to ordinary citizens (Molotch, 1976; Feagin, 1983).

A final criticism holds that urban ecologists have studied only U.S. cities and only during a single historical period. What we have learned about industrial cities may not apply to preindustrial towns; similarly, even among industrial cities, socialist settlements differ from their capitalist counterparts. In sum, there is good reason to doubt that any single ecological model will account for the full range of urban diversity.

Urbanization in Poor Societies

Twice in history the world has experienced a revolutionary expansion of cities. The first urban revolution began about 8000 B.C.E. with Jericho and continued until permanent settlements were in place around the globe. The second urban revolution began about 1750 and lasted for two centuries as the Industrial

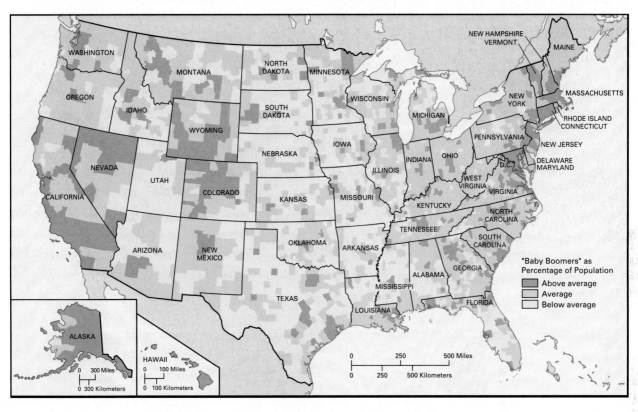

NATIONAL MAP 14–1   Baby Boomers: Residential Patterns Across the United States

About 30 percent of the U.S. population fall into the category of "baby boomers," the generation born between the end of World War II, in 1945, and 1970. The map identifies counties that have an above-average population of baby boomers. What can you say about the places that these men and women have chosen to live? Why do you think they have moved there?

Sources: Adapted from *American Demographics* magazine, Dec. 1992, p. 2. Reprinted with permission. ©1992 *American Demograhics* magazine, Ithaca, New York. Data from the 1990 decennial census.

Revolution touched off the rapid growth of cities in Europe and North America.

A third urban revolution began around 1950 and continues to this day, but this time the change is taking place not in industrial societies where, as Global Map 14–2 on page 384 shows, 75 percent of people are already city dwellers. Extraordinary urban growth is now occurring in poor societies. In 1950, about 25 percent of people living in poor countries inhabited cities; by 1990, the proportion surpassed 40 percent; by 2000, it will exceed 50 percent. Moreover, in 1950, only seven cities

in the world had populations over 5 million, and just two of these were in poor societies. By 1990, thirty-three cities had passed this mark, and twenty-four of them were in less-developed countries (U.S. Bureau of the Census, 1994).

Table 14–6 looks back to 1980 and ahead to 2000, comparing the size of the world's ten largest urban areas (cities and surrounding suburbs). In 1980, six of the top ten were in industrialized countries; three were in the United States. By the beginning of the next century, however, only four of the ten will be found in

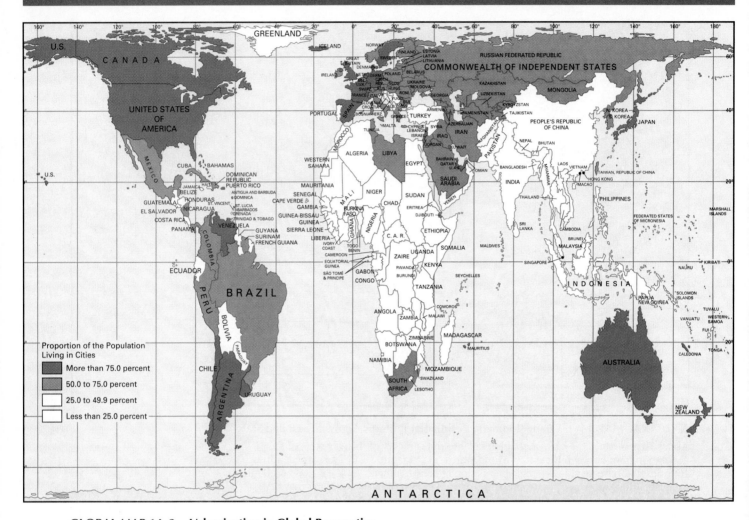

GLOBAL MAP 14–2   Urbanization in Global Perspective

Urbanization is closely linked to economic development. Thus rich nations—including the United States and Canada—have more than three-fourths of their populations in cities, while in the poorest countries of the world—found in Africa and Asia—fewer than one-fourth of the people live in urban centers. Urbanization is now proceeding rapidly in poor countries, however, with emerging "supercities" of unprecedented size.

Source: *Peters Atlas of the World* (1990).

industrialized nations: two in Japan, one in South Korea, with just one in the United States. The majority will be in less economically developed societies.

These urban areas not only will be the world's largest, they will encompass unprecedented populations.

Relatively rich countries such as Japan may have the resources to provide for cities with upwards of 30 million people, but for poor nations, such as Mexico and Brazil, such supercities will tax resources that are already severely strained.

Causes of Urbanization in Poor Societies

To understand the third urban revolution, recall that many nonindustrial societies are now entering the high-growth stage of demographic transition. Falling death rates have fueled a population explosion in Latin America, Asia, and, especially, Africa. For urban areas, the rate of growth is *twice* as high because, in addition to natural increase, millions of migrants leave the countryside each year in search of jobs, health care, education, and conveniences like running water and electricity. Political events, such as the recent military and economic crisis in Haiti, can also "push" migration.

Cities do offer more opportunities than rural areas, but they provide no quick fix for escalating population and grinding poverty. Many burgeoning cities in less-developed societies—including Mexico City, described at the beginning of this chapter—are simply unable to meet the basic needs of much of their population. Thousands of rural people stream into Mexico City every day, although more than 10 percent of the *current* 25 million residents have no running water in their homes, 15 percent lack sewerage facilities, and the city can process only half the trash and garbage produced now. To make matters worse, exhaust from factories and cars chokes everyone, rich and poor alike (Friedrich, 1984; Gorman, 1991).

Like other major cities throughout Latin America, Africa, and Asia, Mexico City is surrounded by wretched shantytowns—settlements of makeshift homes built from discarded materials. As explained in Chapter 8 ("Global Stratification"), even city dumps are home to thousands of poor people, who pick through the waste hoping to find enough to ensure their survival for another day.

Looking Ahead: Urbanization in the Twenty-First Century

The problems now facing cities in poor countries seem to defy solution, and the end of this remarkable urban growth is nowhere in sight. What hope is there of relieving the plight of people in emerging megacities like Mexico City, São Paulo (Brazil), Kinshasa (Zaire), Bombay (India), and Manila (the Philippines)?

Earlier chapters point up two different answers to this question. One view, linked with modernization

TABLE 14–6 The World's Ten Largest Urban Areas, 1980 and 2000

1980	
Urban Area	Population (in millions)
New York, U.S.A.	16.5
Tokyo–Yokohama, Japan	14.4
Mexico City, Mexico	14.0
Los Angeles–Long Beach, U.S.A.	10.6
Shanghai, China	10.0
Buenos Aires, Argentina	9.7
Paris, France	8.5
Moscow, U.S.S.R.	8.0
Beijing, China	8.0
Chicago, U.S.A.	7.7

2000 (projected)	
Urban Area	Population (in millions)
Tokyo–Yokohama, Japan	30.0
Mexico City, Mexico	27.9
São Paulo, Brazil	25.4
Seoul, South Korea	22.0
Bombay, India	15.4
New York, U.S.A.	14.7
Osaka–Kobe–Kyoto, Japan	14.3
Tehran, Iran	14.3
Rio de Janeiro, Brazil	14.2
Calcutta, India	14.1

Sources: United Nations Development Programme (1993) and U.S. Bureau of the Census (1993).

theory, holds that as poor countries undergo industrialization (as Western Europe and North America did a century ago), greater productivity will simultaneously raise living standards and this, in turn, will reduce population growth. A second view, associated with dependency theory, argues that such progress is unlikely as long as poor nations remain economically dependent on rich countries.

We know that, throughout history, the city has improved people's living standards more than any other settlement pattern. The question facing humanity now is whether cities in poor societies will be able to meet the needs of vastly larger populations in the coming century. The answer—which rests on issues of international relations, global economic ties, and simple justice—will affect us all.

SUMMARY

Population

1. Fertility and mortality are major factors affecting population size. In global terms, fertility, mortality, and population growth in North America are relatively low.

2. Migration, another key demographic concept, has special importance to the historical growth of cities.

3. Demographers construct age-sex pyramids to graphically represent the composition of a population and to project population trends.

4. Historically, world population grew slowly because high birth rates were offset by high death rates. About 1750, a demographic transition began as world population rose sharply, mostly due to declining death rates.

5. Two centuries ago, Thomas Robert Malthus warned that population growth would outpace food production, resulting in social calamity. Contradicting Malthus's ominous predictions, demographic transition theory holds that technological advances gradually prompt a drop in birth rates.

6. World population is expected to reach 8 billion by the year 2025. Such an increase will likely overwhelm many poor societies, where 90 percent of the increase is taking place.

Urbanization

1. The first urban revolution began with the appearance of cities after 8000 B.C.E.; by the start of the Common Era, cities had emerged in most regions of the world except for North America.

2. Preindustrial cities are characterized by small buildings; narrow, winding streets; and strong interpersonal social ties.

3. A second urban revolution began about 1750, with the Industrial Revolution propelling rapid urban growth in Europe. The structure of cities changed, as planners created wide, regular streets to facilitate trade.

4. Urbanism came to North America with European settlers. A string of colonial towns dotting the Atlantic coastline gave way by 1850 to hundreds of new settlements from coast to coast. By 1920, a majority of the U.S. population lived in urban settings, and several metropolises encompassed millions of people. About 1950, cities began to decentralize so that, by 1970, most urbanites lived in suburbs.

5. Rapid urbanization in Europe during the nineteenth century led early sociologists to contrast rural and urban life. Ferdinand Toennies built his analysis on the concepts of *Gemeinschaft* and *Gesellschaft*. Emile Durkheim's concepts of mechanical solidarity and organic solidarity closely parallel those of Toennies. Georg Simmel claimed that overstimulation produced a blasé attitude in urbanites.

6. At the University of Chicago, Robert Park hailed cities for enhancing social freedom. Louis Wirth offered a mixed review, suggesting that great size, density, and heterogeneity render cities impersonal, self-interested, and tolerant. Other researchers have explored urban ecology, the interplay of social and physical dimensions of cities.

7. A third urban revolution is now occurring in poor countries, where most of the world's largest cities will soon be found.

KEY CONCEPTS

Population

age-sex pyramid a graphic representation of the age and sex of a population

crude birth rate the number of live births in a given year for every thousand people in a population

crude death rate the number of deaths in a given year for every thousand people in a population

demographic transition theory a thesis linking population patterns to a society's level of technological development

demography the study of human population

fertility the incidence of childbearing in a society's population

infant mortality rate the number of deaths among infants under one year of age for each thousand live births in a given year

life expectancy the average life span of a society's population

migration the movement of people into and out of a specified territory

mortality the incidence of death in a society's population

sex ratio the number of males for every hundred females in a given population

Urbanization

Gemeinschaft a type of social organization by which people are bound together by kinship and tradition

Gesellschaft a type of social organization by which people stand apart due to self-interest

mechanical solidarity social bonds based on collective conformity to tradition

organic solidarity social bonds based on specialization and interdependence

suburbs urban areas beyond the political boundaries of a city

urban ecology study of the link between the physical and social dimensions of cities

urbanization the concentration of humanity into cities

CRITICAL-THINKING QUESTIONS

1. Explain the significance of fertility and mortality. Change in which variable has been of greater importance in increasing global population?

2. How does demographic transition theory link population patterns to technological development?

3. Identify the three urban revolutions in human history and explain the consequences of each.

4. According to Ferdinand Toennies, Emile Durkheim, Georg Simmel, and Louis Wirth, what characterizes urbanism as a way of life? Note several differences in the ideas of these thinkers.

The Natural Environment

Where would you go to enjoy truly "natural" surroundings? Surely not to the crowded and often litter-strewn beaches of New Jersey or the boat-choked waters of the midwestern Great Lakes. Farther west, mining, development, and tourism have transformed many of the scenic peaks and valleys of the Rocky Mountains; and the great forests of the Pacific Northwest are falling under the march of commercial logging, road construction, and new housing.

Nor would we have an easier time finding "natural" surroundings elsewhere in the world. Industry in Latin America is expanding rapidly, leaving its mark on the land, the water, and the air. With the population of African nations rising faster than anywhere on earth, villages and cities are pushing further into the countryside. To the east, even Nepal—a remote Asian kingdom high in the Himalaya Mountains—now swarms with visitors, and is awash with everything they leave behind.

Perhaps the single remaining "natural" region of the world is Antarctica, the frozen continent that covers the earth's South Pole. This expanse of ice and snow—spanning five million square miles, making it larger than Europe—is essentially the same today as it was when British sea captain James Cook skirted it in 1773. What accounts for this remarkable stability? Simply put, Antarctica is the only continent on earth that is virtually uninhabited by human beings.

A steady-state environment seems odd to members of our society. After all, over the last two hundred years, the United States and other industrial nations have been the architects of bewildering transformations. According to one analyst, humanity's remaking of the earth during the last two centuries actually exceeds changes to our planet from all causes over the course of the last billion years (Milbrath, 1989).

To be sure, many of these changes have been beneficial to humanity. As noted in past chapters, life expectancy has risen steadily to an unprecedented level. Moreover, as members of rich societies, we enjoy material comforts that our ancestors scarcely could have imagined. However, as this chapter explains, we now know that the way of life that has evolved in rich societies is seriously straining the earth's natural environment and threatening the future of the entire

planet. The alarming state of the natural environment can be traced directly to one key factor: *how human beings organize social life.* So while science and technology certainly figure in any plans to restore ecological balance to the planet, we must address environmental concerns from a sociological perspective as well.

Ecology: The Study of the Natural Environment

Ecology is *the study of the interaction of living organisms and the natural environment.* An interdisciplinary field, ecology draws on the work of both social and natural scientists. The present discussion, however, is limited to those aspects of ecology that have a direct connection to other, now-familiar sociological ideas and issues.

The concept of the **natural environment** refers to *the earth's surface and atmosphere, including living organisms as well as the air, water, soil, and other resources necessary to sustain life.* Like every other living species, humans depend on the natural environment in countless ways. Yet humans stand apart from other species of life in our capacity for culture; that is, we alone take deliberate action to remake the world according to our own interests and desires.

Slowly, we have come to recognize that the choices we have made in building a life for ourselves are threatening the natural environment. Ecologists describe this situation as an **environmental deficit,** *a situation in which the negative, long-term consequences of decisions about the natural environment outweigh whatever short-term benefits people derive* (Bormann, 1990).

Embedded within the concept of environmental deficit are three important ideas. First, we are reminded that the state of the environment is a *social issue,* because it reflects choices people make about how we live. Second, this concept suggests that much environmental damage—to the air, land, or water—is *unintended.* That is, by focusing on the short-term benefits of, say, cutting down old-growth forests or using easily disposable packaging, we avoid confronting the long-term environmental impact of these choices. Third, in some but not all respects, the environmental deficit is *reversible.* Inasmuch as societies have created environmental problems, in other words, societies can undo many of them.

The earth's rain forests—vital to the planet's ecology—are now half their original size and become smaller every year. Once the lush vegetation of such forests is lost, the soil is at risk of drying out and turning into a desert. Thus, environmental damage is often irreversible.

The Global Dimension

Any study of the natural environment calls for a global approach. Regardless of national divisions, the earth constitutes a single **ecosystem,** defined as *the system composed of the interaction of all living organisms and their natural environment.*

The Greek meaning of *eco* is "house," which reminds us that our planet is our home and, further, that all living things and their natural environment are *interrelated.* In practice, this connectedness means that changes in any part of the natural environment ripple throughout the entire global ecosystem.

To illustrate, consider the effects of using chlorofluorocarbons (CFCs, marketed under the brand name "Freon") as a propellent in aerosol spray cans containing hair spray, deodorant, or a host of other household items. Once released into the air, CFCs accumulate in the upper atmosphere where, in chemical reactions with sunlight, they form chlorine atoms. These, in turn, destroy ozone, the layer in the atmosphere that limits the amount of the sun's ultraviolet radiation reaching the earth. Observing a "hole" in the ozone layer (in the atmosphere over Antarctica), scientists predict a rise in human skin cancers and other deleterious effects to plants and animals (Clarke, 1984a).

The use of CFCs illustrates the three principles of environmental deficit we have already noted: (1) Its harmful consequences result from human decision making; (2) they are largely unintended, and (3) they are mostly reversible. In response to the dangers of ozone depletion, the United States and a number of other nations began to restrict the use of CFCs in the early 1980s.

But, in a world of countless environmental connections, we fail to see many threats to the global environment. The box explains that the popular, and seemingly innocent, act of eating hamburgers threatens the environment in other parts of the world.

Technology

Humanity's capacity to threaten the natural environment is rooted in culture, specifically *technology.* Chapter 2 ("Culture") defined technology as knowledge that a society applies to the task of living in its natural surroundings. The more complex a society's technology, the greater its ability to affect the natural environment.

Societies with simple technology, such as bands of hunters and gatherers, have little impact on the environment. On the contrary, natural forces, including the migration of game and the rhythm of the seasons, determine the shape of their lives. Moreover, people using simple technology are vulnerable to catastrophic natural events, such as fires, floods, droughts, and storms.

As societies gain greater technological sophistication, they also boost their capacity to influence the environment. But horticulture (small-scale farming),

Deforestation and Hamburgers: A Report From Costa Rica

Costa Rica

The earth constitutes a single ecosystem, but not every region of the globe has the same power to shape the natural environment. Members of rich societies like our own consume a disproportionate share of all the world's resources, so it stands to reason that even small decisions we make every day can add up to large consequences for the planet as a whole.

Consider how we relish the all-American hamburger. McDonald's and dozens of other fast-food chains serve billions of hamburgers each year to eager customers across North America, Europe, and Japan. This appetite for beef creates a large market for cattle, which, in turn, has greatly expanded cattle-farming in Latin America. As our consumption of hamburgers grows, ranchers in Costa Rica and other Latin American countries devote more and more land to cattle-grazing.

Cattle in Latin America graze on grass (rather than feeding on grain—as is the practice in this country). This diet produces the lean meat demanded by the fast-food corporations, but it also requires a great deal of grazing land. Where is the land to come from? Ranchers in Latin America solve this problem by clearing forests at the rate of thousands of square miles each year. Tropical forests, as we explain in this chapter, are vital

to maintaining the earth's atmosphere. Therefore, forest destruction threatens the well-being of everyone—even the people back in the United States who savor the hamburgers.

Despite the high stakes involved, most people have no idea about the long-term consequences of satisfying their taste for beef. Fast-food companies, meanwhile, are just trying to make money by meeting a demand. Ranchers, too, need to make a living, so they seek out grazing land wherever they can find it. But, taken together, these actions set in motion trends that may have serious repercussions for everyone on earth. Thus, in a world of countless connections, we must think critically about the effects of choices we make every day—like what's for lunch!

Source : Based on Myers (1984a).

---

pastoralism (the herding of animals), and even agriculture (the use of animal-drawn plows) have only limited environmental impact because these technologies rely on human and animal muscle power for production of food and other goods.

The picture changes dramatically, however, with the introduction of industrial technology. First, industry draws on far more powerful sources of energy to operate large machinery. Burning fossil fuels, including coal and oil, both consumes natural resources and releases pollutants into the atmosphere. Furthermore, armed with industrial technology, humans now bend nature to their will much more than ever before, tunneling through mountains, damming rivers, irrigating deserts, and drilling for oil on the ocean floor.

Industrialization and high energy consumption also go hand in hand. The typical adult in the United States uses up to one hundred times more energy each year than the average person living in one of the world's poorest nations. The members of industrial societies total 20 percent of humanity but utilize 80 percent of the world's energy: The United States alone consumes one-third of the total energy output worldwide (Connett, 1991; Miller, 1992).

Besides disproportionate energy consumption, industrial societies also *produce* one hundred times more goods than agrarian societies do. While this mass production enhances people's material standard of living, it also generates problems of solid waste (since people ultimately throw away much of what is produced) and pollution (in the form of smoke and other toxic substances, spewed into the air and water as by-products of industrial production).

From the outset, people eagerly acquired the material benefits of industrial technology. But only after a century did people begin to recognize the long-term consequences of the new technology for the natural environment. Indeed, one defining trait of postindustrial societies is a growing concern for environmental quality.

From today's perspective, we reach an ironic and sobering conclusion: At the height of our technological prowess, we have placed the natural environment—including ourselves and all other living things—at significant risk (Voight, cited in Bormann & Kellert, 1991:ix–x).

Population Growth

Paralleling the development of more powerful technology, population increase stands as a second major factor threatening the natural environment. Five thousand years ago, at the dawn of civilization, the entire world's population barely topped 50 million. That number today represents those residing just on the West Coast of the United States.

But with the advent of the Industrial Revolution, rising living standards and improving medical technology combined to send death rates in Western Europe plummeting. The predictable result: A sharp upward spike in population. By 1800, global population had soared to the unprecedented level of 1 billion.

But that was just the beginning. In the decades that followed, global population accelerated, reaching the 2 billion point by 1930, 3 billion in 1962, 4 billion in 1974, and 5 billion in 1987. In 1995, the world's population stands at roughly 5.7 billion, with 90 million people added to the world's total annually (250,000 each day).

Population growth can quickly overwhelm available resources. Consider this old illustration about how runaway growth can wreak havoc on the natural environment (Milbrath, 1989:10):

> A pond has a single water lily growing on it. The lily doubles in size each day. In thirty days, it covers the entire pond. On which day did the lily cover half the pond?

The answer that springs readily to mind—the fifteenth day—is wrong because the lily was not increasing in size at a steady rate. The correct answer is that the lily covered half the pond on the twenty-ninth day. The point of the riddle is that, at an increasing rate of growth, the small lily increases from one-eighth of the surface to covering the entire pond in just three days.

To apply the same logic to the earth, most experts now conclude that between 8 and 10 billion people will inhabit the earth by the end of the next century. As Chapter 8 ("Global Stratification") explained, the most rapid population growth is now occurring in the poorest regions of the world. A glance back at Global Map 14–1 on page 367 reveals the growth rates for nations around the world. The nations of Africa, taken together, are adding to their population at an annual rate exceeding 3 percent. If such a high growth rate continues, the continent will almost double its population over the course of the next generation.

Rapid population growth dovetails with poverty. For one thing, a surging population quickly neutralizes any increase in living standards. If a society's population doubles, doubling its productivity amounts to no gain at all.

Poverty itself strains the natural environment. Preoccupied with survival, members of poor societies must consume whatever resources are available, without the luxury of considering the long-term impact of their actions.

And if poor societies suddenly industrialized, what would be the environmental consequences for

We blithely assume that eradicating the persistent poverty that paralyzes societies around the world is a desirable goal. But the environmental impact of global economic development might be devastating. What would happen, for example, if 850 million people in India became "middle class" and began operating that many automobiles, the way we in the United States do?

the billions of people living there? Even at their current population levels, the economic development of poor nations would impose unprecedented stress on the natural environment. To offer just one example, imagine if a poor country like India were suddenly transformed into a land of prosperity. With its population of more than 850 million, a "middle class" India would put almost 1 billion additional cars on its streets. What would that mean for the world's oil reserves or for global air quality?

Cultural Patterns: Growth and Limits

What if, overnight, the poor nations of Latin America, Africa, and Asia were blessed with the material prosperity that we in the United States take for granted? Such global affluence would soon overwhelm the world's environment. This conclusion suggests that our planet suffers not just from the problem of economic *under*development in some regions, but also from economic *over*development in others.

Let us consider how we construct our cultural notion of "the good life." Our cultural outlook, in addition to technology and population growth, is a third factor contributing to the environmental deficit.

The logic of growth. Why does our society designate specific areas as "parks" or "game reserves"? Doing so implies that, except for these special areas, we may freely use the earth and its resources for our own purposes (Myers, 1991). Such an aggressive approach to the natural environment has long been a central element of our way of life.

Chapter 2 ("Culture") described many of the core values that underlie social life in the United States (Williams, 1970). These include an emphasis on *material comfort*, the belief that money and the things it buys enrich our lives. We also embrace the idea of *progress*, thinking that the future will be better than the present. Moreover, we rely on *science*, looking to experts to apply technology to make our lives better. Taken together, these cultural values form the foundation for the *logic of growth*.

The logic of growth is an optimistic view of the world holding, first, that society has improved people's lives by devising more productive technology and, second, that we shall continue to do so into the future. The logic of growth thus boils down to the arguments that "people are clever," "having things is good (having more is better)," and "life will improve." A powerful force throughout the history of the United States and other Western, industrial societies, the logic of growth has driven individuals to settle the wilderness, clear the land, build towns and roads, and pursue material affluence.

But even optimistic people realize that "progress" generates unanticipated problems, environmental or otherwise. The logic of growth responds by arguing that people (especially scientists and other technology experts) are inventive and will find a way out of any problems that growth places in our path. If, say, present resources should prove inadequate to our future needs, we will come up with some new alternative resources that will do the job just as well.

To illustrate, most people in the United States would probably agree that the development of automobiles has greatly improved our lives by providing a swift and comfortable means of travel. Automobiles have also made us dependent on oil, but, according to the logic of growth, by the time the growing number of cars in the world threatens to deplete the planet's oil reserves, scientists will have come up with electric, solar, or nuclear engines, or some as-yet-unknown technology to free us from oil dependence.

The logic of growth still infuses U.S. culture. But many environmentalists challenge this line of reasoning. Lester Milbrath (1989) argues that natural resources such as oil, clean air, fresh water, and the earth's topsoil—all finite—simply cannot be replaced by technologically engineered alternatives. He warns that we can and will exhaust these irreplaceable assets if we continue to pursue growth at any cost.

And what of our faith in human ingenuity to address problems of a scarcity of resources? While conceding that humans are clever at solving problems, Milbrath adds that human resourcefulness, too, has limits. Do we dare to assume that we have it in our power to defuse every crisis that confronts us, especially those wreaking serious damage on the life-giving environment? Moreover, the more powerful and complex the technology (nuclear reactors, say, compared to gasoline engines), the greater the dangers posed by miscalculation and the more significant the unintended consequences are likely to be. Thus, Milbrath concludes that as we are called on to support more and more people using finite resources, we will almost certainly cause irreparable injury to the environment and, ultimately, to ourselves.

The limits to growth. If we cannot "invent" our way out of the problems created by the "logic of growth," perhaps we need to come up with an alternative way of thinking about the world. Environmentalists, therefore, propose the counterargument that growth must have *limits* (Meadows et al., 1972). The *limits to growth* thesis, stated simply, is that humanity must implement policies to restrain the growth of population, cut back on production, and use fewer natural resources in order to head off environmental collapse.

The Limits to Growth, a book published in 1972 that helped launch the environmentalism movement, uses a computer model of the environment to calculate available resources, rates of population growth, amount of land free for cultivation, levels of industrial and food production, and amount of pollutants released into the atmosphere. The authors contend that the model reflects changes that had occurred since 1900, and then projects forward to the end of the next century. Long-range predictions using such a complex model are always speculative, and some critics have challenged their validity (Simon, 1981). But the general conclusions of the study, shown in Figure 15–1, have remained influential ever since.

Following the limits to growth logic, humanity is quickly consuming the earth's finite resources. Supplies of oil, natural gas, and other sources of energy will fall sharply, a little faster or slower depending on policies in rich nations and the speed at which other countries industrialize. While food production per person should continue to rise into the next century, the authors calculate, millions will go hungry because existing food supplies are not equally distributed throughout the world. By mid-century, however, the model predicts a hunger crisis severe enough that rising mortality rates will first stabilize population and then send it plunging downward. Depletion of resources will eventually cripple industrial output as well. Only then will pollution rates fall.

The lesson of this study is grim: Current patterns of life are not sustainable for even another century. This leaves us with a fundamental choice: Either we make deliberate changes in how we live, or calamity will overtake us and force changes upon us.

Environmental Issues

We have now reviewed how technological development, population growth, and cultural orientations have placed increasing demands on the natural environment. What, then, is the state of the natural environment today?

Public opinion surveys in the United States and elsewhere reveal serious concern about the natural environment. In general, as Figure 15–2 shows, people

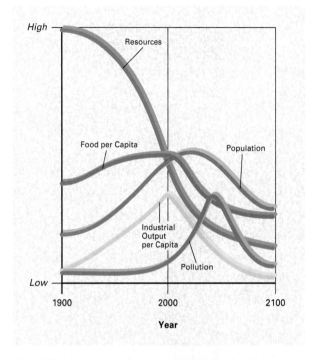

FIGURE 15–1   The Limits to Growth: Projections
Source: Meadows et al. (1972).

in poor societies who contend with the greatest problems of overpopulation and poverty are most unhappy with their surroundings (Dunlap, Gallup, & Gallup, 1992).

People in the United States have a more favorable view of their local environments than people in poor countries do. But we, too, are becoming more concerned about the natural environment. In one national poll, two-thirds of respondents said they believed the natural environment had "gotten worse" over the last twenty years, with 80 percent now claiming to consider themselves "environmentalists" (Gutfeld, 1991a).

In sum, we certainly *perceive* threats to the natural environment. But does our perception accurately mirror reality? In the following survey, we shall briefly examine several key environmental issues, paying particular attention to the United States.

Solid Waste: The "Disposable Society"

As an interesting exercise, carry a large trash bag over the course of a single day, collecting all the materials you throw away. Most people would be surprised to

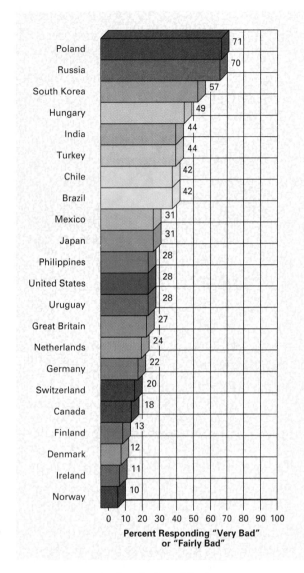

**FIGURE 15–2   Rating the Local Environment:
A Global Survey**

Question: "When we say environment, we mean your
surroundings—both the natural environment, namely, the
air, water, land, plants, and animals—as well as buildings,
streets, and the like. Overall, how would you rate the
quality of the environment in your local community: very
good, fairly good, fairly bad, or very bad?"

Source: Based on Dunlap, Gallup, & Gallup (1992).

find that the average person in the United States
would almost fill the bag with close to five pounds of
paper, metal, plastic, and other disposable material.

For the country as a whole, this amounts to about 1 billion pounds of solid waste produced *each and every day.*

It is easy to see why the United States has been
dubbed a *"disposable society."* Not only are we material-
ly rich, but ours is a culture that values convenience. As
a result, we consume more products than virtually any
nation on earth, and we purchase much of it with a
great deal of packaging. The most commonly cited case
is fast food, served with cardboard, plastic, and styro-
foam containers we throw away within minutes. But
countless other products—from film to fishhooks—are
sold with excessive packaging for the purpose of
making the product more attractive to the customer
(or harder to shoplift or tamper with).

Consider, too, that manufacturers market soft
drinks, beer, and fruit juices in aluminum cans, glass
jars, or plastic containers, which not only consume
finite resources but generate mountains of solid waste.
Then there are countless items specifically designed to
be disposable. Stroll through any local supermarket and
you can spot shelves filled with pens, razors, flashlights,
batteries, and even cameras that are intended to be
used only a few times and then dropped in the nearest
trash can. In a process called "planned obsolescence,"
other products—from light bulbs to automobiles—are
designed to have a limited useful life, and then become
unwanted junk. As Paul H. Connett (1991:101) points
out, even the words we use to describe what we throw
away—*waste, litter, trash, refuse, garbage, rubbish*—
reveal how little we value what we can no longer use
and how we quickly try to push these items out of sight
and out of mind.

Living in a "disposable society," the average person
in the United States consumes 50 times more steel,
170 times more newspaper, 250 times more gasoline,
and 300 times more plastic each year than the typical
resident of India (Miller, 1992). This high level of consumption means that we in the United States not only
use a disproportionate share of the planet's natural resources, but we also generate the lion's share of the
world's refuse.

We like to say that we "throw things away." But 80
percent of our solid waste that is not burned or recycled
never "goes away"; rather, it ends up in landfills. Landfills
pose several threats to the natural environment.

First, the sheer volume of discarded material is
literally filling up landfills all across the country.
Especially in large cities like New York, there is simply
no room left for disposing of trash. Second, material
placed in landfills contributes to water pollution.
Although, in most jurisdictions, law now regulates
what can be placed in a landfill, the Environmental

Protection Agency has identified thirty thousand dump sites across the United States that contain hazardous materials that are polluting water both above and below the ground. Third, what goes into landfills all too often stays there—sometimes for centuries. Tens of millions of tires, diapers, and other items that we bury annually in landfills do not readily decompose and will become an unwelcome legacy for future generations.

Fifty years ago, it was common practice for manufacturing plants to dispose of all types of hazardous wastes by dumping them in nearby woods or discharging them into streams. Today, laws in most states impose stiff penalties for such actions, but enforcement has been lax. The problem of solid waste encompasses both the waste products of manufacturing and the solid waste each of us throws away. To cope with its sheer volume, environmentalists argue that we must turn "waste" into a resource, one that will benefit, rather than burden, our descendants. One way to do this is through **recycling,** *programs to reuse resources we would otherwise discard as "waste."* But, as the box on page 398 explains, the United States lags behind Japan and many other industrial societies in implementing recycling programs.

Preserving Clean Water

The oceans and other bodies of water supply the lifeblood of the global ecosystem. Throughout the history of our species, humans have relied on water for drinking, bathing, cooling, and cooking, for recreation, and for a host of other activities.

Yet, the oceans have long served as a vast dumping ground for all kinds of waste. No one can calculate the precise amount of solid waste that has been poured into the world's oceans, but the total would certainly exceed millions of tons. The problems caused by disposing of solid waste in this way are crystal clear: Polluted water kills fish or makes them dangerous to eat, and also spoils a source of great beauty and recreational pleasure.

According to what scientists call the *hydrological cycle,* the earth naturally recycles water and refreshes the land. The process begins as heat from the sun causes sea water, 97 percent of the earth's total water reserve, to evaporate and form clouds. Next, water returns to earth as rain, which drains into streams and rivers and rushes toward the sea. The hydrological cycle not only renews the supply of water, but cleans it as well. Because water evaporates at lower temperatures

Recycling is one strategy for controlling the amount of solid waste a society generates. The Japanese recycle three times the share of solid waste that we in the United States do.

than most pollutants, the water vapor that rises from the seas is relatively pure and free of contaminants that are left behind. Although the hydrological cycle generates clean water in the form of rain, however, it does not destroy pollutants that steadily build up in the oceans.

Two key concerns, then, dominate discussions of water and the natural environment. The first is supply; the second is pollution.

Water supply. Concern over an ample supply of water is nothing new. For thousands of years, since the time of the ancient civilizations in China, Egypt, and Rome, water rights have figured prominently in codes of law. Throughout Europe, aqueducts of brick, built by the Romans, stand as testimony to the importance of readily available water.

Today, some regions of the world—the tropics, for example—enjoy a plentiful supply of water, although most of the annual rainfall occurs over a relatively brief season. Other regions of Asia, North America, and Africa, however, are more arid and draw their water from rivers. Egypt, for instance, has long depended on the Nile River for most of its water. There, as population increases, the problem of water supply is fast reaching the critical stage. Egyptians today must make do with one-sixth as much water per person from the Nile as they did in 1900, and the supply will shrink by half again over the next twenty years (Myers, 1984c; Postel, 1993).

The Second Time Around: Recycling in the United States

Walking around neighborhoods in Japanese cities, the observer notes large receptacles in which residents are required, by law, to place bottles, cans, and newspapers. Person for person, the Japanese consume only half as much of these things as individuals in the United States do. In addition, they recycle over three times more of their disposable waste than we do.

While recycling is the accepted practice in Japan and a number of other industrial nations, it is a relatively new idea in the United States. Here, just 10 percent of solid waste is recycled (compared to at least one-third in Japan), with another 10 percent being burned in incinerators. Most solid waste ends up in landfills.

A growing number of communities, however, realize that this trend cannot continue. As a result, these municipalities have initiated recycling programs. By 1990, thirty-eight states had enacted at least one law regarding recycling (Gutfeld, 1991b). Some programs are voluntary, while others are mandatory, sometimes complete with "trash cops" who inspect roadside cans and issue tickets to residents who fail to separate recyclable material from other refuse. All in all, the United States is leaning toward the Japanese approach, since a national program of recycling could prevent more than 100 billion pounds of solid waste from being consigned to landfills each year.

Most of what the typical household throws away could be recycled. As the figure shows, paper represents the largest share of household trash (about 50 percent by volume). Glass, metals, and plastic (totaling an additional 24 percent) are also candidates for recycling. In the same spirit of conserving resources and

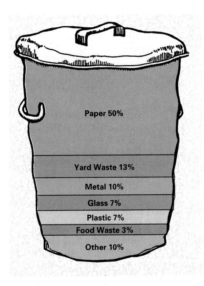

Paper 50%
Yard Waste 13%
Metal 10%
Glass 7%
Plastic 7%
Food Waste 3%
Other 10%

Sources: Based on Franklin Associates (1986) and Corley et al. (1993).

lessening the load on landfills, households could donate old appliances, furniture, carpeting, and other unwanted items to technical schools or thrift shops for repair. Yard and food waste could also be recycled through composting, which involves placing organic materials (that is, what is or was living) in piles or containers to allow them to decompose naturally (and produce soil-enriching humus in the process).

In assessing the prospects for widespread recycling in countries with market-based economies like the United States, profitability plays a key role. At present, the demand for some recycled materials (such as paper products) is not strong enough to make recycling profitable. As a result, most recycling programs are operated by volunteers or municipal governments. But as recycling processes become more efficient, industries will likely come to see "waste" as a useful resource.

Still, not all environmentalists think recycling should be left to market forces. Some propose earmarking public funds for this purpose since local governments already operate landfills (rarely at a profit). Moreover, most taxpayers would agree that any program to improve the natural environment would certainly be in the public interest.

Much of the remainder of northern Africa and the Middle East faces an even more critical situation. Within thirty years, according to current predictions, 1 billion people in this region will lack necessary water. The world has recently witnessed the tragedy of hunger in the African nations of Ethiopia and Somalia. While we recognize the impact of food shortages there, an even more serious problem for these nations is the lack of adequate water for irrigation and drinking.

Surging population and complex technology—especially in manufacturing and power-generation facilities—have greatly increased societies' appetite for water. The global consumption of water (estimated at about 5 billion cubic feet per year) has tripled since 1950, and is expanding faster than the world's population (Postel, 1993).

As a result, even in areas of the earth that receive significant rainfall, people are using groundwater faster than it can be naturally replenished. Take the Tamil Nadu region of southern India, for example. There, the fast-growing population is drawing so much groundwater that the local water table has fallen one hundred feet over the last several decades. And, in the United States, the pumping of water from the massive Ogallala aquifer, which lies below seven states from South Dakota to Texas, is now so rapid that some experts fear it could be depleted several decades into the next century.

In light of such developments, we must face the reality that water is a valuable, finite resource. Greater conservation of water by individuals in the home is part of the answer. However, households around the world account for no more than 10 percent of total water use. We need to curb water consumption by industry, which currently uses 25 percent of the global total. And, most crucial of all, agricultural irrigation absorbs two-thirds of humanity's consumption of water.

New irrigation technology may well reduce this demand in the future. Yet technological advances must still be balanced with plans for economic growth, taking into account available natural resources and, of course, the urgent need to establish effective controls on population growth (Myers, 1984a; Goldfarb, 1991; Falkenmark & Widstrand, 1992; Postel, 1993).

Water pollution. Still, in large cities—from Mexico City to Cairo to Shanghai—many people have little choice but to drink contaminated water. The poor people of the world suffer most as a result of unsafe water. As Chapter 13 ("Education and Medicine") explained, infectious diseases like typhoid, cholera, and dysentery, all caused by micro-organisms that contaminate water, run rampant in poor nations. Throughout less-developed regions of the world, then, we can trace the source of much illness and death to microbes thriving in polluted water (Clarke, 1984b; Falkenmark & Widstrand, 1992).

Thus, besides ensuring ample *supplies* of water, we must recognize that no society has done an exemplary job of protecting the *quality* of its water. In most areas of the world, tap water is not safe for drinking.

Most people living in the United States take for granted that tap water is free from contaminants, and water quality in our country is good by global standards. However, even here the problem of water pollution is growing steadily. According to the Sierra Club, an environmental activist organization, rivers and streams across the United States take in some 500 million pounds of toxic waste each year. This pollution results not just from intentional dumping, but also from the

The Aral Sea, which straddles Kazakhstan and Uzbekistan in the southwest region of the former Soviet Union, was once a plentiful source of water and fish. Today, due to policies that overly exploited this resource, the sea has all but vanished.

runoff of agricultural fertilizers and lawn chemicals. Groundwater supplies, as we have already noted, are also endangered as hazardous substances leech from thousands of landfills and dump sites across the country.

While even small amounts of pollutants can damage the aquatic ecosystem, only recently have water supplies had the protection of law. The federal government's Clean Water Act of 1972 was a major step toward cleaning up this country's water. Before its passage, many urban rivers were so polluted that the water was dangerous for drinking or even bathing, and deadly to fish and other aquatic life. In one of the most egregious examples, Cleveland's Cuyahoga River became so choked with oil and other toxic substances in the late 1960s that it actually caught fire.

Clearing the Air

Most people in the United States are more aware of air pollution than they are of contaminated water, in part because air serves as our constant and immediate environment. Then, too, large numbers of people in the United States deal daily with the mix of smoke and fog (the origin of the word "smog") that hangs over many of our urban centers.

One of the unanticipated consequences of industrial technology—especially the factory and the motor vehicle—has been a deterioration of air quality. The thick, black smoke belching from factory smokestacks,

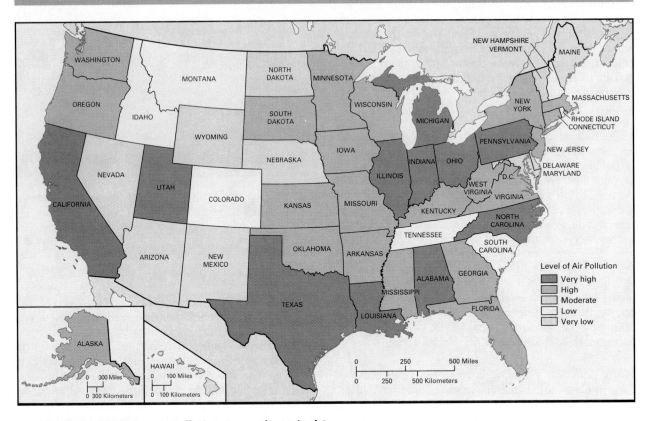

NATIONAL MAP 15–1   Air Pollution Across the United States

The Environmental Protection Agency (EPA) monitors the emission of 173 compounds into the atmosphere. In 1991, the five states that polluted the air the least were Hawaii, Nevada, Wyoming, North Dakota, and Vermont (although these states each emitted five hundred thousand pounds of toxics that year). High-pollution states—including California, Texas, Illinois, Ohio, and Pennsylvania—each sent one hundred times as much toxic material into the atmosphere. What traits distinguish high-pollution from low-pollution states?

Source: Prepared by the author using data from the Environmental Protection Agency.

often twenty-four hours a day, alarmed residents of early industrial cities a century ago. Writing about Pittsburgh in 1884, for instance, Williard Glazier was stunned by the nighttime view from the hills surrounding his city, the air ablaze with the fires of steel mills and swirling with factory smoke. It was as if someone had lifted the lid of hell itself, Glazier mused, and his fellow urbanites were "tortured spirits writhing in agony" as they fought simply to breathe (quoted in Glaab, 1963).

By the end of World War II, such scenes were commonplace in industrial cities of the Northeast and Midwest. By 1950, automobiles were adding to the problem of air pollution, their exhaust fumes shrouding cities like Los Angeles that had escaped the earlier rush of industrial development. On a clear day Angelenos could see across the city, but there were few clear days.

In mid-century London, factory discharge, automobile emissions, and smoke from coal fires used to heat households combined to create what was probably the worst urban air quality of the century. What some British jokingly called "pea soup" was, in reality, a deadly mix of pollution: In the course of just five days in 1952, an especially thick haze that hung over London killed four thousand people (Clarke, 1984a).

Fortunately, great strides have been made in combating air pollution brought on by our industrial way of life. Laws now mandate the use of low-pollution heating fuels in most cities, and the coal fires that choked London are now forbidden. In addition, scientists have devised new technology to reduce the noxious output of factory chimneys and, even more importantly, to lessen the pollution caused by the growing number of automobiles and trucks. The switch to unleaded gasoline, initiated in the early 1970s, coupled with changes in engine design and exhaust systems, have reduced the automobile's detrimental environmental impact. Still, with almost 200 million motor vehicles in the United States alone, the challenge of cleaning the air remains daunting. National Map 15–1 identifies the states with the worst air quality.

If the rich societies of the world can breathe a bit more easily than they once did, the problem of air pollution in poor nations is becoming more and more serious. For one thing, people in less economically developed countries still rely on wood, coal, peat, or other "dirty" fuels to generate heat. Moreover, many nations are so eager to promote short-term industrial development that they pay little heed to the longer-term dangers of air pollution. As a result, many cities in Latin America, Eastern Europe, and Asia are plagued by air pollution rivaling that found in London fifty years ago.

Acid Rain

Acid rain refers to *precipitation made acidic by air pollution that destroys plant and animal life.* The complex reaction that generates acid rain (or snow) begins when power plants burning fossil fuels (oil and coal) to produce electricity release sulphur and nitrogen oxides into the air. Once the winds sweep these gases into the atmosphere, a chemical reaction with the air yields sulphuric and nitric acids, which make atmospheric moisture acidic. Figure 15–3 illustrates the process that creates acid rain.

Taking a closer look at this figure, we also observe that one type of pollution often causes another. In this case, air pollution (from smokestacks) ends up contaminating water (in lakes and streams that collect acid rain). Notice, too, that acid rain is a global phenomenon because the regions that suffer its deleterious effects may be thousands of miles from the site of the original air pollution. For instance, tall chimneys of

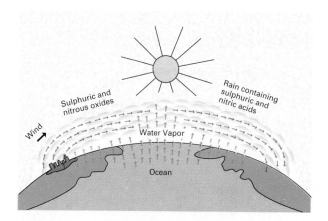

FIGURE 15–3   The Formation of Acid Rain

British power plants are the source of the acid rain that has devastated forest and marine life in Norway and Sweden a thousand miles to the northeast. In the United States, we see a similar pattern, with midwestern chimneys poisoning the natural environment of New England (Clarke, 1984a).

The Rain Forests

Rain forests are *regions of dense forestation, most of which circle the globe close to the equator.* Global Map 15–1 shows that the largest rain forests are in South America (notably Brazil), but west central Africa and southeast Asia also have sizable rain forests. In all, the world's rain forests cover an area of some 2 billion acres, which accounts for 7 percent of the earth's total land surface.

Like the rest of the world's resources, the rain forests are falling victim to the needs and appetites of the surging human population. As noted earlier in this chapter, the demand for beef has sparked more cattle-grazing in Latin America; ranchers typically burn forested areas to increase their supply of grazing land. Just as important is the lucrative hardwood trade. High prices are paid for mahogany and other timber by people in rich societies who have, as environmentalist Norman Myers (1984b:88) puts it, "a penchant for parquet floors, fine furniture, fancy paneling, weekend yachts, and high-grade coffins."

Under such pressure, the world's rain forests are now just half their original size, and they continue to shrink by about one percent (65,000 square miles) annually. If this rate of destruction proceeds unchecked,

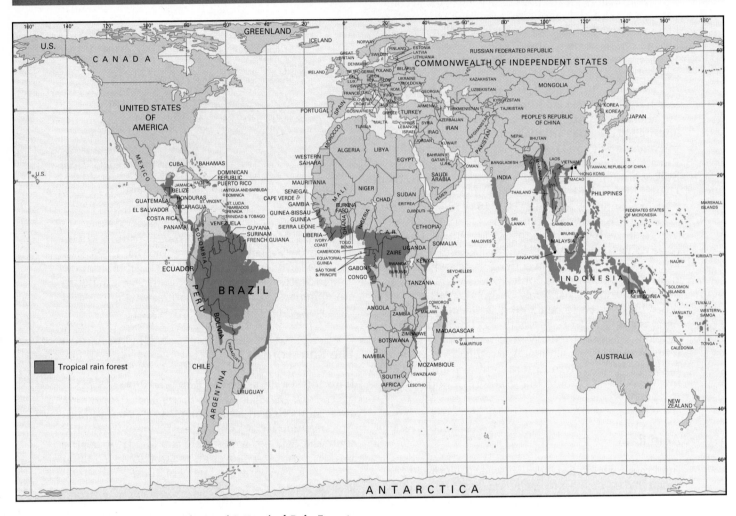

GLOBAL MAP 15–1   The Earth's Tropical Rain Forests

The earth's rain forests are situated along the equator in Latin America, Africa, and southeast
Asia. The most massive rain forest is in the Amazon River region of South America, largely
within the borders of Brazil. Although rain forests account for only 7 percent of the earth's
land area, they play a key role in the global ecosystem.
Source: Prepared by the author. Map projection from *Peters Atlas of the World* (1990).

these forests will vanish before the end of the next
century and, with them, protection for the earth's biodiversity and climate.

Global warming.   Natural scientists explain that rain
forests figure prominently in the process of removing
carbon dioxide (CO_2) from the earth's atmosphere.

From the time of the Industrial Revolution, the amount
of carbon dioxide humanity has produced (most generated by factories and automobiles) has risen tenfold.
Much of this CO_2 is absorbed by the oceans. But
plants, which take in carbon dioxide and expel oxygen,
also play a major part in maintaining the chemical balance of the atmosphere.

The problem, then, is that production of carbon dioxide is rising while the amount of plant life on the earth is shrinking. To make matters worse, rain forests are being destroyed mostly by burning, which releases even more carbon dioxide into the atmosphere. Experts estimate that the atmospheric concentration of carbon dioxide is now 10 to 20 percent higher than it was just 150 years ago.

In the atmosphere, carbon dioxide behaves much like the glass roof of a greenhouse, letting in heat from the sun to warm the earth while preventing much of it from radiating back away from the planet. Thus scientists speculate about a possible **greenhouse effect,** *a rise in the earth's average temperature due to an increasing concentration of carbon dioxide in the atmosphere.*

Some analysts warn that our planet is currently experiencing a rise in average temperature: From the current mean of 60 degrees Fahrenheit, they claim, the planet's average temperature could go up ten degrees by 2050. This warming trend would melt much of the polar icecaps, raise sea levels, and push the oceans up over low-lying land around the world, flooding Bangladesh, for example, and much of the coastal United States, including Washington, D.C., right up to the steps of the White House. On the other hand, the U.S. Midwest—currently one of the most productive agricultural regions in the world—would likely become arid.

Not all scientists share this vision of future global warming. Some point out that global temperature changes have been taking place throughout history, apparently with little or nothing to do with rain forests. Moreover, higher concentrations of carbon dioxide in the atmosphere might actually accelerate plant growth (since plants thrive on this gas). This trend would serve to correct the present imbalance and nudge the earth's temperature downward once again (Silverberg, 1991).

Declining biodiversity. Whatever the effects on this planet's climate, rain forest clearing has another undeniable impact. The disappearance of rain forests is eroding the earth's *biodiversity,* or, more simply, causing many thousands of species of plant and animal life to disappear forever. While rain forests account for just 7 percent of the earth's surface, they are home to almost half of this planet's living species.

Estimates of the number of living species of animals, bacteria, and plants range from 1.5 million to more than 30 million. Researchers, in fact, have identified more than one thousand species of ants alone (Wilson, 1991). Several dozen species cease to exist each day; but, given the vast number of species living on earth, why should we be concerned with this loss of biodiversity? Environmentalists cite three reasons. First, our planet's biodiversity provides a vast and varied source of human food. Agricultural technology currently "splices" familiar crops with more exotic species, yielding plants that are more productive or have greater resistance to insects and disease. In addition, plant geneticists looking into the properties of unfamiliar plant and animal life are working toward generating the quantity and quality of foods necessary to nourish our rapidly increasing population.

Second, the earth's biodiversity is a vital genetic resource. Medical and pharmaceutical industries depend on animal and plant biodiversity in their research to discover and formulate compounds that will cure disease and improve our lives. Children in the

The so-called mud men of the Asaro Valley of the Eastern Highlands province of Papua New Guinea are in increasing contact with outsiders (and, indeed, now perform their "mud men" ritual primarily for tourists). The way of life of these people, along with that of hundreds of other indigenous peoples around the world, is in danger of disappearing. Paralleling the loss of the planet's biodiversity, therefore, is the decline of humanity's cultural diversity.

United States, for example, now have a good chance of surviving leukemia, a disease that was almost a sure killer two generations ago, because of a compound derived from a tropical plant called the rosy periwinkle. The oral birth control pill, used by tens of millions of women in this country, also stemmed from plant research, this time using the Mexican forest yam. Scientists have examined tens of thousands of plants for medicinal properties, and hundreds of medicines are developed each year based on this research.

Third, with the loss of any species of life— whether it is one variety of ant, the spotted owl, the magnificent California condor, or the famed Chinese panda—the beauty and complexity of our natural environment is diminished. And there are clear warning signs: Three-fourths of the world's nine thousand species of birds are currently declining in number.

Finally, keep in mind that, unlike pollution and other environmental problems, the extinction of species is final and irreversible. As a matter of ethics, then, should those who live today make decisions that will impoverish the world for those who live tomorrow (Myers, 1984b; Myers, 1991; Wilson, 1991; Brown et al., 1993)?

Society and the Environment: Theoretical Analysis

We have now introduced a number of key concepts and outlined prominent issues facing the natural environment. Sociological theory can help tie this material together to see how environmental concerns reflect the operation of society.

Structural-Functional Analysis

The structural-functional paradigm offers three significant insights about the natural environment. First, as earlier chapters have made clear, this approach highlights the importance of *values* and *beliefs* to the operation of a social system. Thus, in simple terms, the state of the environment depends largely on how we think about the natural world, for values guide human actions.

Members of industrial societies generally see in nature resources to serve our needs; this point of view (discussed earlier as the "logic of growth") justifies imposing our human will on the planet. With this orientation as a springboard, our forebears cleared forests for farmland, dammed rivers for irrigation and water power, covered vast areas with asphalt and concrete, and erected buildings to make cities.

Moreover, Western cultures historically have embraced both materialism and acquisitiveness. That is, we have looked to *things* (more than, say, kinship or spirituality) as a source of comfort and happiness. At the same time, we tend to think that if owning *some* things is good, having *more* things is better. Our tendency toward "conspicuous consumption" leads us to use the purchase and display of material possessions as a way to indicate our social position to others. Such values, not surprisingly, set the stage for the kinds of environmental problems that this chapter has described.

A second contribution of structural-functionalist theory is pointing up the interconnectedness of the environment and various dimensions of social life. Our ideas about the value of efficient and private travel, for example, have much to do with the dizzying rate at which industrial societies have produced and consumed motor vehicles. Building and operating hundreds of millions of trucks and automobiles, in turn, has placed far greater stress on natural resources (like oil) and the environment (especially the air).

Third, structural-functional analysis suggests that, given the many ways in which the operation of society affects the natural environment, environmental problems demand far-reaching, imaginative, and multifaceted solutions. We cannot hope to curb the rate at which humanity is consuming the earth's resources, for example, as long as almost 2 million people are added to the global population each week. Controlling population growth, in turn, depends on expanding the range of occupational and educational opportunities open to women so they have alternatives to staying home and having more children.

However difficult the task may be, structural-functionalism offers grounds for optimism that societies can constructively respond to threats to the environment. Consider, once again, the case of air pollution. Air quality plunged with the onset of the Industrial Revolution. But gradually societies in Europe and North America recognized and responded to this problem, enacting new laws and employing new technology to improve air quality. Similarly, just as companies once fouled the natural environment in the process of making money, now a host of new companies profit from cleaning up our physical surroundings. In short, because we need a livable natural environment, determined efforts will undoubtedly cope with whatever environmental problems arise.

Critical evaluation. Structural-functional analysis shows that the condition of the natural environment cannot be analyzed apart from the operation of society itself. To its credit, this approach reveals the extent to which the environment is a sociological concern.

But, as we have seen before, this approach overlooks the issues of inequality and power arrangements in society. In other words, who benefits from environmental pollution, and who bears the consequences of a spoiled environment? As we shall see presently, the answer may turn out to be, respectively, the rich and the poor.

Furthermore, many environmentalists are skeptical about society's capacity to restore the natural world. On the one hand, many people have vested interests in continuing past ways, even if they threaten the well-being of the general public. Moreover, many of the environmental problems we face—especially rapid population growth—are simply too far out of control at present to justify the optimism voiced by functionalists.

Social-Conflict Analysis

Social-conflict theory casts a spotlight on the very issues that structural-functionalism glosses over: power and inequality. Far from being inevitable, conflict theorists believe that problems of the natural environment spring from social arrangements favoring elites. In other words, social-conflict theory indicts elites for directly or indirectly aggravating environmental problems as they pursue their self-interest. Extending this idea, social-conflict analysis also reminds us that the global disparity of wealth and power has important environmental consequences.

First, there is the issue of elites. As conflict theorists see it, in the hierarchical organization of contemporary U.S. society, a small proportion of the population—what Chapter 11 ("Economics and Politics") called the "power elite"—set the national and global agenda by controlling the world's economy, law, and view of the natural environment.

Early capitalists shepherded the United States into the industrial age, hungrily tapping the earth's resources and frantically turning out manufactured goods in pursuit of profits. They did so with little regard for environmental consequences. By and large, it was they who reaped the benefits of the new industrial wealth, while workers toiled in dangerous factories and lived in nearby neighborhoods clogged with smoke and shaken round the clock by the vibrations of the big machines.

The poor of the world suffer most from environmental degradation. Tragically, poverty pushes people toward short-term strategies to survive (including cutting forests or hunting game to extinction) that have detrimental long-term consequences.

Just as important, our society has long winked at the most blatant instances of environmental destruction, even when elite perpetrators run afoul of the law. Corporate pollution, as Chapter 6 ("Deviance") explains, falls under the category of white-collar crime. Such offenses typically escape prosecution; when action is taken, it is usually in the form of fines levied on a company rather than criminal penalties imposed on individuals. Thus, corporate executives who order the burial or dumping of toxic waste have been subject to penalties no greater (and sometimes less) than ordinary citizens who throw litter from car windows.

Conflict theorists who embrace a Marxist view of society argue that capitalism itself poses a threat to the environment. This is simply because the logic of capitalism is the pursuit of profit, which demands continuous economic growth. As Marxists see it, what is profitable does not necessarily advance the public welfare, nor is it likely to be good for the natural environment. As noted earlier in this chapter, for example, capitalist industries have long shored up their profits by designing products to have a limited useful life (the concept of "planned obsolescence"). Such policies may improve the "bottom line" in the short term, but raise the risk of depleting natural resources as well as generating solid waste.

A second issue raised by social-conflict theory is inequality. Generally, members of rich societies consume most of the earth's resources and, in the process, generate the most pollution. We have achieved our affluent way of life, in short, by exploiting the earth and the poor in the less-developed countries, poisoning the air and water in the process.

From this point of view, rich nations are actually *over*developed and consume too much. No one should expect that the majority of the earth's people, who live in poor societies, will be able to match the living standards in this country; nor, given the current environmental crisis, would that be desirable. Instead, they call for a more equitable distribution of resources among all people of the world both as a matter of social justice and as a strategy to preserve the natural environment.

Critical evaluation. The social-conflict paradigm complements other analyses by raising the important questions of who sets a society's agenda and who benefits (and suffers) most from decisions that are made. Environmental problems, from this point of view, are consequences of a society's class structure and the world's hierarchy of nations.

Yet critics point out that while elites may have always dominated U.S. society, they have not been able to prevent the passage of laws protecting the natural environment. These protections, in turn, have resulted in some significant improvements in air and water quality.

And what of the charge that capitalism is particularly hostile to the natural world? There is little doubt that capitalism's logic of economic growth does place stress on the environment. At the same time, however, capitalist societies in North America and, especially, in Europe have made notable strides toward environmental protection. By contrast, the environmental record of socialist societies is far from exemplary. A look back to Figure 15–2 shows that citizens of Poland and Russia—two societies ruled for a half-century by socialist governments—are highly critical of environmental quality in their local communities (Dunlap, Gallup, & Gallup, 1992). This record reflects decades of policies that pursued industrialization in utter neglect of environmental concerns, without challenge and with tragic consequences in terms of human health.

Finally, there is little doubt that rich nations currently place the greatest demands on the natural environment. However, this pattern is beginning to shift as global population swells in poor countries. And, environmental problems will grow worse to the extent that poor societies develop economically, using more resources and producing more waste and pollutants in the process.

In the long run, all nations of the world share a vital interest in protecting the natural environment. This concern leads us to the final topic of this chapter, the concept of a sustainable environment.

Looking Ahead: Envisioning a Sustainable Society and World

India's great leader Mahatma Gandhi once declared that societies must provide "for people's need, but not for their greed." From an environmental point of view, this means that the earth will be able to sustain future generations only if humanity refrains from rapidly and thoughtlessly consuming resources such as oil, hardwoods, and water. Nor can we persist in polluting the air, water, and soil at anything like the current levels. The loss of forests—through cutting of trees and the destructive effects of acid rain—threatens to undermine the global climate. And we risk the future of the planet by adding people to the world at the rate of 90 million each year.

As we noted, on every part of the earth inhabited by humanity, an environmental deficit is growing. This means that our present way of life is borrowing against the well-being of our children and their children. And, taking a global perspective, we see that members of rich societies, who currently consume so much of the earth's resources, are mortgaging the future security of the majority of people who live in the poor countries of the world.

In principle, we could solve the entire range of environmental problems described in this chapter by living in a way that is *sustainable*. A **sustainable ecosystem** refers to *the human use of the natural environment to meet the needs of the present generation without threatening the prospects of future generations.*

Sustainable living calls for three basic strategies. The first is the *conservation of finite resources*. We must balance the desire to satisfy our present wants with our responsibility to preserve the resources needed by future generations. Conservation means using resources more efficiently, seeking alternative resources, and, in some cases, learning to live with less.

Technology, no doubt, will furnish us with household devices (from light bulbs to furnaces) that are far more energy efficient than those available at present. Moreover, we should expand development of alternative energy sources, including harnessing the power of the sun, wind, and tides. But while relying on help from new technology, a sustainable way of life will require rethinking the pro-consumption attitudes formed during decades of "cheap electricity" and "cheap oil."

The second strategy toward achieving a sustainable society is *reducing waste*. Whenever possible, simply using less is the most effective way to do this. In addition, societies around the world need to expand recycling programs. Success will depend on the dual incentives of educational efforts to enlist widespread support for these initiatives and on legislation requiring the recycling of certain materials. Looking down the road, as recycling programs become commercially profitable, they will be adopted more readily by market-based economies around the world.

The third key element in any plan for a sustainable ecosystem is to *bring world population growth under control*. As we have explained, the current (1995) population of 5.7 billion is already straining the natural environment. Clearly, the higher world population climbs, the more serious environmental problems will become. Global population is now increasing at a rate of about 1.6 percent each year, which, if unchecked, will double the world's people in about forty years. Few analysts think that the earth can support a population of 10 billion or more; most argue that we must hold the line at about 7 billion. Reaching this goal will require urgent steps in poor regions of the world where growth rates are highest.

But even sweeping environmental strategies—put in place with the best intentions—will fail without some basic changes in the ways we think about ourselves and our world. By setting up our own immediate interests as the standards for how to live, we have overlooked several important connections.

First of all, we need to recognize that, environmentally speaking, *the present is tied to the future*. Simply put, today's actions shape tomorrow's world. Thus, we must learn to evaluate our present choices in terms of their long-range consequences for the natural environment.

Second, rather than viewing humans as "different" from all other life forms and assuming that we have every right to dominate the planet, we must

Although the problem of topsoil erosion in the United States is serious primarily in California, desertification is also widespread in many countries of the world, including Nepal (Asia), Peru (Latin America), Turkey (bridging Europe and Asia), and Sudan and Lesotho (Africa). The causes of desertification are less climatic than human: The cutting of trees, burning of vegetation, and allowing cattle to overgraze land are the major causes of this problem. The overall effect is that, as the world's forests shrink in size, the planet's deserts are expanding.

acknowledge that *all forms of life are interdependent*. Ignoring this truth not only harms other life forms, it will eventually undermine our own well-being. From the realization that all of life figures in the ecological balance must follow specific programs to protect the earth's biodiversity.

Third, and finally, achieving a sustainable ecosystem will require *global cooperation*. The planet's rich and poor nations are currently separated by a vast chasm of divergent interests, cultures, and living standards. On the one hand, most countries in the northern half of the world are overdeveloped, using more resources than is sustainable over the long term. On the other hand, most nations in the southern half of the world are underdeveloped, unable to meet the basic needs of many of their people. A sustainable ecosystem depends on bold and unprecedented programs of cooperation. And while the cost of change will certainly be high, it pales before the eventual cost of not responding to the growing environmental deficit (Humphrey & Buttel, 1982; Burke, 1984; Kellert & Bormann, 1991; Brown et al, 1993).

In tandem with the shifts in focus just outlined, we will only reach the goal of a sustainable society by critically re-evaluating the logic of growth that has dominated our way of life for several centuries. There is already evidence that the tide is turning on this issue: A recent Gallup poll found that majorities of people in twenty of twenty-two nations surveyed endorsed stronger action to protect the environment, even if doing so slowed economic growth (Dunlap, Gallup, & Gallup, 1992).

In closing, we might think back on the great dinosaurs that dominated this planet for some 160 million years before they perished forever. Humanity is far younger, having existed for a mere quarter of a million years. Compared to the rather dim-witted dinosaurs, our species has the gift of great intelligence. But how will we use these abilities? What are the chances that our species will continue to flourish on the earth 160 million years—or even one thousand years—from now? As Tom Burke (1984) points out, it would be foolish to assume that our present civilization is about to collapse. But it would be equally foolish to ignore the warning signs. One certainty is that the state of tomorrow's world will depend on choices we make today.

SUMMARY

1. Because the most crucial factor affecting the state of the natural environment is how human beings organize social life, ecology, the study of how living organisms interact with their environment, is one important focus of sociology.

2. Societies increase the environmental deficit by focusing on short-term benefits and ignoring long-term environmental damage brought on by their ways of life.

3. Studying the natural environment demands a global perspective. All parts of the ecosystem—including the air, soil, and water—are interconnected. Similarly, actions in one part of the world have an impact on the natural environment elsewhere.

4. Humanity's enormous influence on the natural environment springs from our capacity for culture. Our manipulation of the environment has expanded over time with the development of complex technology.

5. Through population growth, too, humanity affects the natural environment. The world population has soared upward over the course of the last two centuries and now threatens to overwhelm available resources.

6. The "logic of growth" argument defends economic development and asserts that people can solve environmental problems as they arise. In opposition to this position, the "limits to growth" thesis states that societies have little choice but to curb development to head off eventual environmental collapse.

7. As a "disposable society," the United States generates 1 billion pounds of solid waste each day. Currently, our society incinerates 10 percent of solid waste, recycles another 10 percent, and disposes of the remaining 80 percent in landfills.

8. Water consumption is rapidly increasing throughout the world. Much of the world—notably Africa and the Middle East—is currently approaching a water-supply crisis.

9. The hydrological cycle purifies rainwater, but pollution from dumping and chemical contamination still poses a serious threat to water quality in the United States. This problem is even more serious in the world's poor societies.

10. Air quality became steadily worse in Europe and North America after the Industrial Revolution. About 1950, however, a turnaround took place and these regions have made significant progress in curbing air pollution. In poor societies—especially in cities—air pollution remains at unhealthy levels because of the burning of "dirty" fuels.

11. Acid rain, the product of pollutants entering the atmosphere, often contaminates land and water thousands of miles away.

12. Tropical rain forests play a vital role in removing carbon dioxide from the atmosphere. Under pressure from commercial interests, rain forests the world over are now half their original size and are shrinking by about 1 percent annually.

13. Global warming refers to predictions that the average temperature of the earth will rise because

of increasing levels of carbon dioxide in the atmosphere. Both carbon emissions from factories and automobiles and the shrinking tropical rain forests, which consume carbon dioxide, aggravate this problem.

14. The elimination of rain forests is also reducing the planet's biodiversity, since these tropical regions are home to about half of all living species. Biodiversity, a source of natural beauty, is also critical to agricultural and medical research.

15. Structural-functional theory points out that cultural values underlie a society's orientation to the natural environment, that many dimensions of social organization have environmental consequences, and that societies will likely respond to environmental problems that endanger them.

16. Social-conflict analysis blames environmental decay on the selfishness of elites. It also places responsibility for the declining state of the world's natural environment primarily on rich societies, which consume the most resources.

17. A sustainable environment is one that does not threaten the well-being of future generations. Achieving this goal will require conservation of finite resources, reducing waste, and controlling the size of the world's population.

KEY CONCEPTS

acid rain precipitation made acidic by air pollution that destroys plant and animal life

ecology the study of the interaction of living organisms and their natural environment

ecosystem the system composed of the interaction of all living organisms and their natural environment

environmental deficit the situation in which negative, long-term consequences of decisions about the natural environment outweigh whatever short-term benefits people derive

greenhouse effect a rise in the earth's average temperature ("global warming") due to an increasing concentration of carbon dioxide in the atmosphere

natural environment the earth's surface and atmosphere, including various living organisms as well as the air, water, soil, and other resources necessary to sustain life

rain forests regions of dense forestation that circle the globe close to the equator

recycling programs to reuse resources that we would otherwise discard as "waste"

sustainable ecosystem the human use of the natural environment to meet the needs of the present generation without threatening the prospects of future generations

CRITICAL-THINKING QUESTIONS

1. Why do human beings have such a great impact on the natural environment? How has our capacity to manipulate the environment changed over the course of human history?

2. Why are problems of the natural environment global in scope?

3. What is the current state of the natural environment with regard to solid waste? The quality of the air? The supply and quality of water?

4. How would life in your local community change if we were to establish an environmentally sustainable society?

Social Change: Modernity and Postmodernity

The firelight flickers in the gathering darkness. Chief Kanhonk sits, as he has every evening for many years, to begin an evening of animated talk and storytelling (Simons, 1995). This is the hour when the Kaiapo, a small society in Brazil's lush Amazon region, celebrate their heritage. Because the Kaiapo are a traditional people with no written language, the elders rely on evenings by the fire to teach their culture and instruct the grandchildren. In the past, nights like this have been filled with tales of brave Kaiapo warriors fighting off Portuguese traders in pursuit of slaves and gold.

But as the minutes pass, only a few older villagers assemble for the evening ritual. None of the children is drawn to the chief's storytelling. "It is the Big Ghost," one man grumbles, explaining the poor turnout. The "Big Ghost" has indeed descended upon them, its bluish glow spilling from windows of homes throughout the village. The Kaiapo children—and many adults as well—are watching television. The consequences of installing a satellite dish three years ago have turned out to be greater than anyone imagined. In the end, what their enemies failed to do to the Kaiapo with weapons, they may do to themselves with prime-time programming.

The Kaiapo are some of the 230,000 native peoples who inhabit the country we call Brazil. They stand out because of their striking body paint and ornate ceremonial dress. Recently, they have acquired wealth, as profits from gold mining and harvesting mahogany trees have enriched the settlement. Now the Kaiapo must decide whether their new-found fortune is a blessing or a curse. To some, affluence means the opportunity to learn about the outside world through travel and television. Others, like Chief Kanhonk, have their doubts. Sitting by the fire, he muses aloud, "I have been saying that people must buy useful things like knives and fishing hooks. Television does not fill the stomach. It only shows our children and grandchildren white people's things." Bebtopup, the oldest priest, agrees: "The night is the time the old people teach the young people. Television has stolen the night" (Simons, 1995:471).

The transformation of the Kaiapo raises profound questions about the causes of change and whether change—even toward a higher standard of living—is always for the better. Moreover, the dilemma of the Kaiapo is being played out around the globe as more and more traditional societies are lured away from their heritage by the materialism and affluence of the rich societies.

This chapter examines social change as a process with both positive and negative consequences. Of particular interest to people in the United States is what sociologists call *modernity*, changes brought on by the Industrial Revolution, and *postmodernity*, more recent transformations sparked by the Information Revolution and the postindustrial economy.

What is Social Change?

Earlier chapters have explored human societies in terms of both stability and change. Relatively *static* social patterns include status and role, social stratification, and the various social institutions including the economy and the family. The *dynamic* forces that have recast humanity's consciousness, behavior, and needs range from innovations in technology to the growth of bureaucracy and the expansion of cities. These are all dimensions of **social change**, *the transformation of culture and social institutions over time*. This complex process has four key characteristics.

1. **Social change happens everywhere; however, the rate of change varies from place to place.** "Nothing is certain except death and taxes," goes the old saying. But social patterns related to death have changed dramatically as life expectancy in the United States has doubled since 1850. Taxes, meanwhile, unknown through most of human history, emerged only with complex social organization several thousand years ago. In short, one is hard pressed to identify anything not subject to the twists and turns of change.

   Still, some societies change faster than others. As Chapter 2 ("Culture") explained, hunting and gathering societies change quite slowly; members of technologically sophisticated societies, on the other hand, witness significant change even within a single lifetime.

   Moreover, some cultural elements within a society change faster than others. William Ogburn's (1964) theory of *cultural lag* (see Chapter 2) holds that material culture (that is,

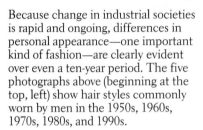

Because change in industrial societies is rapid and ongoing, differences in personal appearance—one important kind of fashion—are clearly evident over even a ten-year period. The five photographs above (beginning at the top, left) show hair styles commonly worn by men in the 1950s, 1960s, 1970s, 1980s, and 1990s.

things) usually changes faster than nonmaterial culture (ideas and attitudes). For example, medical devices that prolong life have developed more rapidly than have ethical standards for deciding when and how to use them.

2. **Social change is sometimes intentional but often unplanned.** Industrial societies actively promote many kinds of change. For example, scientists seek more efficient forms of energy, and advertisers try to convince consumers that life is incomplete without some new gadget. Yet even the experts rarely envision all the consequences of the changes they propose.

   Early automobile manufacturers understood that cars would allow people to travel in a single day distances that had required weeks or months a century before. But no one foresaw

how profoundly automobiles would reshape U.S. society, scattering family members, threatening the environment, and reconfiguring cities and suburbs. In addition, automotive pioneers could hardly have predicted the fifty thousand deaths each year caused by car accidents in the United States alone.

3. **Social change often generates controversy.** As the history of the automobile demonstrates, most social change yields both good and bad consequences. Capitalists welcomed the Industrial Revolution because advancing technology increased productivity and profits. Many workers, however, fearing that machines would make their skills obsolete, strongly resisted "progress." In the United States, changing social interaction between black people and white people, between

women and men, and between gays and hetero-sexuals give rise to misunderstandings, tensions, and, sometimes, outright hostility.

4. **Some changes matter more than others do.** Some changes have only passing significance, whereas other transformations resonate for generations. At one extreme, clothing fads among the young burst on the scene and dissipate quickly. At the other, we are still adjusting to powerful technological advances such as television half a century after its introduction. Looking ahead, who can predict with certainty how computers will transform the world during the coming century? Will the Information Revolution turn out to be as pivotal as the Industrial Revolution? Like the automobile and television, computers will have both positive and negative effects, opening the way to new kinds of jobs while eliminating old ones, linking people in ever-expanding electronic networks while threatening personal privacy.

Causes of Social Change

Social change has many causes. And in a world made smaller by sophisticated communication and transportation technology, change in one place often begets change elsewhere.

Culture and Change

Culture is a dynamic, ever-changing system. Chapter 2 ("Culture") identified three pivotal sources of cultural change. First, *invention* produces new objects, ideas, and social patterns. Through rocket propulsion research, which began in the 1940s, we have engineered high-tech vehicles for space flight. Today, we take such technology for granted; during the next century, a significant number of people may well travel in space.

Second, *discovery* occurs as people first notice particular elements of the world or learn to see them in a new way. For example, medical advances offer a growing understanding of the human body. Beyond benefits for human health, medical discoveries have extended life expectancy, setting in motion the "graying of the United States" (see Chapter 3, "Socialization: From Infancy to Old Age").

Third, *diffusion* creates change as trade, migration, and mass communication spread cultural elements from one society to another. Ralph Linton (1937)

recognized that many familiar aspects of our culture came from other lands, often as a result of immigration. For example, cloth (developed in Asia), clocks (invented in Europe), and coins (devised in Turkey) are all creations of other societies. In general, material things diffuse more easily than nonmaterial cultural traits. The Kaiapo, described at the beginning of this chapter, have been quick to adopt television, but they have been reluctant to embrace the materialism and individualism that sometimes seize those who spend hours watching Western commercial programming.

Conflict and Change

Tension and conflict within a society also produce change. Karl Marx heralded class conflict as the engine that drives societies from one historical era to another. In industrial-capitalist societies, he maintained, the struggle between capitalists and workers propels society toward a socialist system of production.

In the century since Marx's death, this model has proven simplistic; yet, he correctly foresaw that conflict arising from inequality (involving race and gender as well as class) would force changes in every society, including ours.

Ideas and Change

Max Weber, too, contributed to our understanding of social change. While Weber acknowledged the importance of conflict based on material production, he traced the roots of social change to the world of ideas. He illustrated his argument by showing how people who display charisma (described in Chapter 11, "Economics and Politics," and Chapter 12, "Family and Religion") can convey a message that sometimes changes the world.

Weber also highlighted ideas as instruments of change by revealing how the world view of early Protestants drove them to embrace industrial capitalism (see Chapter 12). Industrial capitalism developed primarily in areas of Western Europe influenced by Calvinism, Weber (1958; orig. 1904–5) noted. From this observation, he concluded that the disciplined rationality of Calvinist Protestants played a key role in this change.

Furthermore, as Chapter 15 ("The Natural Environment") detailed, European settlement of North America began with the cutting of forests, the founding of towns, and the construction of roadways in every

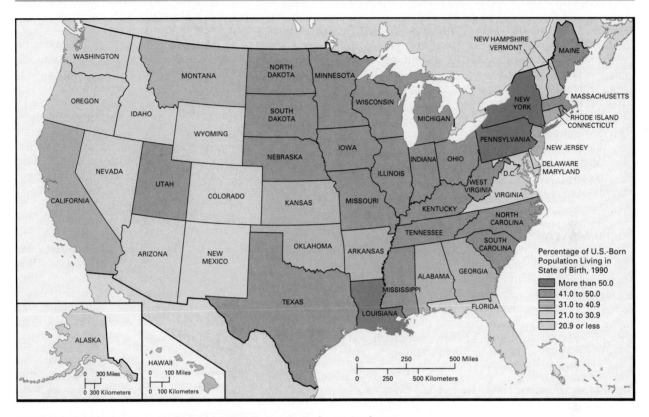

NATIONAL MAP 16–1   Moving On: Migration Across the United States

One in six households packs up and moves each year, making the United States one of the most geographically mobile societies on earth. The map indicates what percentage of each state's population is made up of migrants—people who were born somewhere else. Generally speaking, in the Snowbelt region (the Northeast and Midwest), migrants represent less than 30 percent of the people. By contrast, the western half of the United States includes the largest share of migrants, with "movers" making up absolute majorities in Oregon, Wyoming, Nevada, Colorado, and Arizona. Florida and Vermont are also home to a majority from elsewhere. Why, in each case, do you think this is so?

Source: Prepared by the author using data from the 1990 decennial census.

direction. Such human manipulation of nature reflects not only our cultural determination to master the natural environment, but also the primacy we confer on material things as a measure of "the good life."

Demographic Change

Population growth not only places escalating demands on the natural environment but it also alters cultural patterns. The Netherlands is a high-density nation.

Homes in Amsterdam are small and narrow compared to those in the United States, and staircases are extremely steep to make efficient use of space. In Tokyo, Japan, commuters routinely endure fierce crowding on subways that would challenge a lifelong New Yorker.

Throughout our long history, the United States has enjoyed a bounty of physical space, which, no doubt, has affected our notions about personal freedom. Moreover, the fast-paced and anonymous way of life that is typical of populous cities barely resembles that found in the rural villages and small towns common to our past.

Migration within and among societies is another demographic factor that promotes change. Between 1870 and 1930, tens of millions of immigrants swelled the industrial cities in the United States. Millions of rural people joined them. As a result, farm communities declined in population, metropolises expanded, and the United States became for the first time a predominantly urban society. Similar changes are taking place today as people moving from Snowbelt to Sunbelt states mingle with new immigrants from Latin America and Asia.

Demographic changes typically transform some parts of the country more than others. National Map 16–1 on page 415 identifies the states whose population contains the greatest share of migrants.

Social Movements and Change

A final cause of social change lies in people's own initiatives. People commonly band together to form **social movements,** *organized efforts encouraging or opposing some dimension of change.* Our national history is replete with social movements of all kinds, from the colonial drive for independence to contemporary movements that advocate various positions on feminism, gay rights, and the environment.

Types of social movements. Researchers classify social movements according to the kind of change they envision

FIGURE 16–1 Four Types of Social Movements
Source: Based on Aberle (1966).

How extensive is the change?

	Affecting only certain people	Affecting the whole society
Limited	Alternative social movement	Reformative social movement
Radical	Redemptive social movement	Revolutionary social movement

How intensive is the change?

(Aberle, 1966; Cameron, 1966; Blumer, 1969). One variable is *breadth*, with some movements limiting their efforts to changing only a specific category of people, while others strive to transform an entire society. A second variable is *depth*. Some crusades seek only superficial change, while others aspire to remake society in a fundamental way. Combining these variables produces four types of social movements, shown in Figure 16–1.

Alternative social movements pursue limited change in only certain individuals. For example, Planned Parenthood focuses on educating individuals of childbearing age about the consequences of sexual activity. *Redemptive social movements* also aim selectively, but they pursue radical transformation. Fundamentalist Christian organizations exemplify this type, inviting new members to be "born again." *Reformative social movements* try to change the entire society, generally working within the existing political system. The "Buy American" movement, for instance, teams manufacturers and workers in an effort to persuade consumers to purchase products made in the United States. Finally, *revolutionary social movements* advocate sweeping transformation of society. Sometimes advancing specific plans, sometimes spinning utopian dreams, such movements reject existing social institutions in favor of radical change.

Understanding social movements. Sociologists have devised several ways of looking at social movements. According to one analysis, *deprivation theory,* advocates of social change are people who see themselves as deprived of something they deserve. Research points to no absolute level of deprivation that triggers activism. Rather people react to **relative deprivation,** *a perceived disadvantage relative to some standard of comparison.* With deprivation theory in mind, we can see why revolutionary movements have surfaced in both good and bad times: It is not people's absolute standing that counts but how they subjectively perceive their situation (Tocqueville, 1955, orig. 1856; Davies, 1962; Merton, 1968).

Mass-society theory, a second approach, locates organized efforts toward change among rootless individuals who seek, through collective activity, a sense of membership and purpose. From this point of view, social movements have a personal as well as a political agenda (Kornhauser, 1959; Melucci, 1989).

Resource-mobilization theory, a third theoretical scheme, ties the success of any social movement to available resources—including money, human labor, access to the mass media, and even moral confidence. Most social movements are small, at least at the outset, and must look beyond themselves to mobilize the resources needed to increase their chances for success (McCarthy & Zald, 1977; Killian, 1984; Snow, Rochford, Jr., Worden, & Benford, 1986).

Fourth, and finally, *new social movements theory* points out that recent social movements tend to be national or international in scope, with a focus on quality-of-life issues—including the natural environment, world peace, or animal rights—rather than economic concerns. This broader scope of contemporary social movements stems from closer ties among governments and among ordinary people around the world who are now linked by the mass media and advanced communications technology (Melucci, 1980; McAdam, McCarthy, & Zald, 1988; Kriesi, 1989).

Stages in social movements. We can discern patterns even in the process of change. The *emergence* of social movements typically parallels the perception that society is flawed in some significant way. In certain cases (the women's movement), activism may be rooted in the everyday experiences of countless people; in others (the AIDS crisis), a small vanguard may seek to mobilize the public.

The *coalescence* of a social movement takes place as a newly formed group clearly defines its purpose, recruits new members, and devises policies and tactics. Leaders must also gain access to the mass media and forge alliances with other organizations.

As it marshals resources, a social movement may undergo *bureaucratization*. This means that it grows more established, depending less on the charisma and talents of a few leaders and more on a professional staff. As movements mature and become more bureaucratic, members may lose some of their initial fervor, but the movement as a whole stands a better chance of long-term survival.

Finally, social movements *decline* for a variety of reasons. Resources may dry up, the group may face overwhelming opposition, or members may become victims of their own success. Some well-established organizations outlive their original causes, moving on to new crusades; others abandon the idea of changing society and choose, instead, to work within the "system" (Piven & Cloward, 1977; Miller, 1983).

Modernity

A central concept in the study of social change is **modernity,** *social patterns linked to industrialization.* In everyday usage, modernity (its Latin root means

Although women's absolute social standing has improved markedly in recent decades, many women continue to experience a sense of deprivation relative to their growing expectation of full social equality with men.

"lately") refers to the present in relation to the past. Sociologists include within this catch-all concept the many social patterns set in motion by the Industrial Revolution, which began in Western Europe in the mid-eighteenth century. **Modernization,** then, is *the process of social change initiated by industrialization.* Peter Berger (1977) notes four major characteristics of modernization.

1. **The decline of small, traditional communities.** Modernity involves "the progressive weakening, if not destruction, of the . . . relatively cohesive communities in which human beings have found solidarity and meaning throughout most of history" (Berger, 1977:72). For thousands of years, in the camps of hunters and gatherers and in the rural villages of early North American settlers, people lived in small-scale communities based on family and neighborhood. Such traditional worlds afforded each individual a well-defined place, and while such small primary groups limited the range of personal experience, they provided a strong sense of personal identity, belonging, and purpose.

   Small, isolated communities still exist in the United States, of course, but they are now home to only a tiny fraction of our nation's people. Even for rural families, advanced communications technology and rapid transportation have brought individuals into the mainstream of the larger society and, to some extent, the entire world.

2. **The expansion of personal choice.** To people in traditional, preindustrial societies, life is shaped by forces beyond human control—gods, spirits, or, simply, fate. As the power of tradition diminishes, people come to see their lives as an unending series of options, a process Berger calls *individualization*. Recognizing alternatives in everyday life, for example, many people in the United States adopt one "lifestyle" or another, actively embracing change.

3. **Increasing social diversity.** In preindustrial societies, strong family ties and powerful religious beliefs enforce conformity while discouraging diversity and change. Modernization promotes a more rational, scientific world view in which tradition loses its hold and morality becomes a matter of individual attitude. The growth of cities, the expansion of impersonal organizations, and the social interaction of people from various backgrounds combine to foster a tolerance for a diversity of beliefs and behavior.

4. **Future orientation and growing awareness of time.** People in modern societies think more about the future, while premodern people focus more on the past. Modern people are not only forward-looking but optimistic that new inventions and discoveries will enhance their lives.

In addition, modern societies organize daily routines according to precise units of time. With the introduction of clocks in Europe in the late Middle Ages, sunlight and seasons faded in importance as measures of time's forward march in favor of hours and minutes. Preoccupied with personal gain, modern people calculate time to the moment and generally believe that "time is money." Berger points out that one key indicator of a society's degree of industrialization is the proportion of people wearing wristwatches.

Finally, recall that modernization touched off the development of sociology itself. As Chapter 1 ("Sociology: Perspective, Theory, and Method") explained, the discipline originated in the wake of the Industrial Revolution in Western Europe, as social change was proceeding most intensely. Early European and U.S. sociologists set their sights on understanding the rise of modern society and its consequences—both good and bad—for human beings.

Ferdinand Toennies: The Loss of Community

The German sociologist Ferdinand Toennies (1963; orig. 1887) produced a highly influential account of modernization, detailed in Chapter 14 ("Population and Urbanization"). Like Peter Berger, whose work he influenced, Toennies viewed modernization as the

In response to the accelerated pace of change in the late nineteenth century, Paul Gauguin (1848–1903) left his native France for the South Seas where he was captivated by a simpler and seemingly timeless way of life. He romanticized this environment in his 1894 painting *Mahana no Atua (Day of the Gods)*.

George Tooker's 1950 painting *The Subway* depicts a common problem of modern life: Weakening social ties and eroding traditions create a generic humanity in which everyone is alike yet each person is an anxious stranger in the midst of others.

progressive loss of *Gemeinschaft* or human community. As Toennies saw it, the Industrial Revolution undermined the strong social fabric of family and tradition by introducing a business-like emphasis on facts and efficiency. European and North American societies gradually became rootless and impersonal as people came to associate mostly on the basis of self-interest—the state Toennies termed *Gesellschaft*.

Early in this century, at least some of the United States approximated Toennies's concept of *Gemeinschaft*. Families that had lived in small villages and towns for many generations forged a hard-working, slow-moving way of life. Telephones (invented in 1876) were rare, and the first coast-to-coast call was placed only in 1915. Living without television (introduced in 1939, and widespread after 1950), families entertained themselves, often gathering with friends in the evening—much like Brazil's Kaiapo—to share stories, sorrows, or song. Without rapid transportation (although Henry Ford's assembly line began in 1908, cars became commonplace only after World War II), many people viewed their town as their entire world.

Inevitable tensions and conflicts—sometimes based on race, ethnicity, and religion—did erupt in these tightly knit communities. According to Toennies, however, the traditional ties of *Gemeinschaft* bound people together as a community "essentially united in spite of all separating factors" (1963:65).

Modernity turns society inside out so that, as Toennies put it, people are "essentially separated in spite of uniting factors" (1963:65). This is the world of *Gesellschaft* where, especially in large cities, most people live among strangers and ignore those they pass on the street. Trust is hard to come by in a mobile and anonymous society in which, according to researchers, people tend to put their personal needs ahead of group loyalty and a majority of adults claim that "you can't be too careful" in dealing with people (NORC, 1993:203; Russell, 1993). No wonder, as one recent news report indicated, 15 million men and women attend weekly support groups (also made up of strangers) in which they establish temporary emotional ties and find someone who is willing simply to *listen* (Leerhsen, 1990).

Critical evaluation. Toennies's theory of *Gemeinschaft* and *Gesellschaft* stands as the most widely used model for describing modernization. The theory's strength lies in its synthesis of various dimensions of change—growing population, the rise of cities, increasing impersonality. However, Toennies's theory says little about which factors are cause and which are effect. Critics also assert that Toennies favored—perhaps even romanticized—traditional societies.

Emile Durkheim: The Division of Labor

The French sociologist Emile Durkheim shared Toennies's interest in the profound social changes wrought by the Industrial Revolution. For Durkheim, the rise of modernity is marked by increasing **division of labor,** or *specialized economic activity* (1964b; orig. 1893). Whereas everyone in traditional societies performs more or less the same daily round of activities, modern societies function by having people carry out highly distinctive roles.

As Chapter 14 ("Population and Urbanization") explained, Durkheim claimed that preindustrial societies were held together by *mechanical solidarity*, social bonds resting on shared moral sentiments. Thus members of such societies have a sense that everyone is basically alike and belongs together. Mechanical

Max Weber maintained that the distinctive character of modern society was its rational world view. Virtually all of Weber's work on modernity centered on types of people he considered typical of their age: the scientist, the capitalist, and the bureaucrat. Each is rational to the core: The scientist is committed to the orderly discovery of truth, the capitalist to the orderly pursuit of profit, and the bureaucrat to orderly conformity to a rational system of rules.

solidarity—or what Toennies called *Gemeinschaft*—depends on a minimal division of labor, so that every person's life follows much the same path.

With modernization, the division of labor becomes more and more pronounced. Modern societies, then, are held together by *organic solidarity,* bonds of mutual dependency among people who engage in specialized work. Put simply, modern societies are held together not by likeness but by difference: All of us must rely on others to meet our needs. Organic solidarity corresponds to Toennies's concept of *Gesellschaft.*

Despite obvious similarities, Durkheim and Toennies interpreted modernity somewhat differently. To Toennies, modern *Gesellschaft* amounts to the loss of social solidarity—the result of the gradual erosion of "natural" and "organic" bonds of the rural past, leaving only "artificial" and "mechanical" ties of the present. Durkheim disagreed and even reversed Toennies's language: He labeled modern social life as "organic," suggesting that today's world is no less natural than before, and he described traditional societies as "mechanical" because they are so regimented. Thus Durkheim viewed modernization not so much as a loss of community as a change in the basis of community—from bonds of likeness (kinship and neighborhood) to ties of economic interdependence (the division of labor). Durkheim's view of modernity is thus both more complex and more optimistic than that of Toennies.

Critical evaluation. Durkheim's work stands alongside that of Toennies, which it closely resembles, as a highly influential analysis of modernity. Of the two, Durkheim is clearly the more hopeful; still, he feared that modern societies might become so internally diverse that they would collapse into **anomie,** *a condition in which society provides little moral guidance to individuals.* In the midst of weak moral claims from society, modern people tend to be egocentric, placing our own needs above those of others.

The suicide rate—which Durkheim considered a good index of anomie—has, in fact, increased in the United States over the course of this century. Moreover, the vast majority of U.S. adults report that they see moral questions not in clear terms of right and wrong but as confusing "shades of gray" (NORC, 1993:411). Even so, shared norms and values are still strong enough to give most people a sense of meaning and purpose. Additionally, whatever the hazards of anomie, most people value the personal autonomy modern society affords.

Max Weber: Rationalization

For Max Weber, modernity amounts to the progressive replacement of a traditional world view with a rational way of thinking. In preindustrial societies, tradition acts as a constant brake on change. To traditional people, "truth" is roughly synonymous with "what has always been" (1978:36; orig. 1921). In modern societies, by contrast, people see truth as the product of deliberate calculation. Because they value efficiency more than reverence for the past, individuals adopt whatever social patterns allow them to achieve their goals.

Echoing the claim by Toennies and Durkheim that industrialization weakens tradition, Weber declared that modern society had become "disenchanted." What were once unquestioned truths are now subject to matter-of-fact assessments. Embracing rational, scientific thought, in short, modern society turns away from the gods. Throughout his life, Weber examined modern "types"—the capitalist, the scientist, the bureaucrat—all of whom share the detached world view that he believed was coming to dominate humanity.

Critical evaluation. Compared with Toennies, and especially Durkheim, Weber was a profound critic of modern society. He recognized that science could produce technological and organizational wonders, yet he worried that the scientific approach was carrying us away from more basic questions about the meaning and purpose of human existence. Weber feared that rationalization, especially in bureaucracies, would erode the human spirit with endless rules and regulations.

Finally, some of Weber's critics think that the alienation that he attributed to bureaucracy actually stemmed from social inequality. This leads us to the work of Karl Marx.

Karl Marx: Capitalism

While other analysts of modernity spotlighted shifting patterns of social order, Karl Marx focused on social conflict. For Marx, modern society was synonymous with capitalism; he saw the Industrial Revolution primarily as a *capitalist revolution*, which prompted the bourgeoisie in medieval Europe to wrest control of society from the feudal nobility. The bourgeoisie succeeded in that mission when the Industrial Revolution placed a powerful new productive system under their control.

Marx agreed that modernity weakened small-scale communities (as described by Toennies), increased the division of labor (as noted by Durkheim), and fostered a rational world view (as asserted by Weber). But he saw these factors simply as conditions necessary for capitalism to flourish. Capitalism, according to Marx, draws people from farms and small towns into an ever-expanding market system centered

in the cities; specialization underlies efficient factories; and rationality is exemplified by the capitalists' relentless quest for profits.

Earlier chapters have painted Marx as a spirited critic of capitalist society, but his vision of modernity also incorporates a considerable measure of optimism. Unlike Weber, who viewed modern society as an "iron cage" of bureaucracy, Marx believed that social conflict in capitalist societies would sow the seeds of revolutionary change, leading to an egalitarian socialism. Such a society, as he envisioned it, would harness the wonders of industrial technology to enrich people's lives and also rid the world of social classes, the prime source of conflict and dehumanization. While Marx's evaluation of modern capitalist society was highly negative, then, he imagined a future of greater human freedom, blossoming human creativity, and renewed human community.

Critical evaluation. Marx's theory of modernization draws together many threads in a fabric dominated by capitalism. Yet Marx underestimated the dominance of bureaucracy in modern societies. And in a twist never imagined by Marx, the bloated government apparatus in socialist societies actually stifled the human spirit even more than capitalism. The recent upheavals in Eastern Europe and the former Soviet Union reveal the depth of popular opposition to rigid state bureaucracies.

Structural-Functional Analysis: The Theory of Mass Society

The rise of modernity is a complex process involving many dimensions of change, described in previous chapters and summarized in Table 16–1. How is one to make sense of so many changes going on at once? One broad approach—guided by the structural-functional paradigm and drawing on the ideas of Toennies, Durkheim, and Weber—understands modernity as the emergence of *mass society* (Dahrendorf, 1959; Kornhauser, 1959; Nisbet, 1966, 1969; Baltzell, 1968; Stein, 1972; Berger, Berger, & Kellner, 1974).

A **mass society** is *a society in which industry and bureaucracy have eroded traditional social ties.* A mass society is marked by weak kinship and neighborhood ties so that individuals are socially atomized. In their isolation, members of mass societies typically experience feelings of moral uncertainty and personal powerlessness.

TABLE 16–1 Traditional and Modern Societies: Dimensions of Difference

Elements of Society	Traditional Societies	Modern Societies
Cultural Patterns		
Values	Homogeneous; sacred character; few subcultures and countercultures	Heterogeneous; secular character; many subcultures and countercultures
Norms	Great moral significance; little tolerance of diversity	Variable moral significance; high tolerance of diversity
Time orientation	Present linked to past	Present linked to future
Technology	Preindustrial; human and animal energy	Industrial; advanced energy sources
Social Structure		
Status and role	Few statuses, most ascribed; few specialized roles	Many statuses, some ascribed and some achieved; many specialized roles
Relationships	Typically primary; little anonymity and privacy	Typically secondary; considerable anonymity and privacy
Communication	Face to face	Face-to-face communication supplemented by mass media
Social control	Informal gossip	Formal police and legal system
Social stratification	Rigid patterns of social inequality; little mobility	Fluid patterns of social inequality; considerable mobility
Gender patterns	Pronounced patriarchy; women's lives centered on the home	Declining patriarchy; increasing number of women in the paid labor force
Economy	Based on agriculture; some manufacturing in the home; little white-collar work	Based on industrial mass production; factories become centers of production; increasing white-collar work
State	Small-scale government; little state intervention in society	Large-scale government, considerable state intervention in society
Family	Extended family as the primary means of socialization and economic production	Nuclear family retains some socialization functions but is more a unit of consumption than of production
Religion	Religion guides world view; little religious pluralism	Religion weakens with the rise of science; extensive religious pluralism
Education	Formal schooling limited to elites	Basic schooling becomes universal, with growing proportion receiving advanced education
Health	High birth and death rates; brief life expectancy because of low standard of living and simple medical technology	Low birth and death rates; longer life expectancy because of higher standard of living and sophisticated medical technology
Settlement patterns	Small scale; population typically small and widely dispersed in rural villages and small towns	Large scale; population typically large and concentrated in cities
Social Change	Slow; change evident over many generations	Rapid; change evident within a single generation

The Mass Scale of Life

Mass-society theory argues, first, that the scale of modern life has increased astronomically. Before the Industrial Revolution, Europe and North America formed an intricate mosaic of countless rural villages and small towns. In these small communities, which inspired Toennies's concept of *Gemeinschaft*, people lived out their lives surrounded by kin and guided by a shared heritage. Gossip was an informal, yet highly effective, means of maintaining rigid conformity to community standards. Limited community size, coupled with strong moral values, combined to stifle social

diversity—the mechanical solidarity described by Durkheim.

For example, in England before 1690, law and local custom demanded that everyone regularly participate in the Christian ritual of Holy Communion (Laslett, 1984). Similarly, only Rhode Island among the New England colonies offered any support for the notion of religious dissent. Because social differences were repressed, subcultures and countercultures rarely flourished, change proceeded slowly, and there was little social mobility.

A surge in population, the growth of cities, and specialized economic activity during the Industrial

Revolution gradually changed all this. People came to be known by their function (for example, as the "doctor" or the "bank clerk") rather than by their kinship group or home town. People looked on most others simply as strangers. The face-to-face communication of the village was eventually replaced by the mass media—newspapers, radio, and television—that furthered social atomization. Large organizations steadily assumed more and more responsibility for daily needs that had once been fulfilled by family, friends, and neighbors; universal public education enlarged the scope of learning; police, lawyers, and courts supervised a formal criminal justice system. Even charity became the work of faceless bureaucrats employed by social welfare agencies.

Geographical mobility, mass communications, and exposure to diverse ways of life undermine traditional values. People become more tolerant of social diversity, trumpeting the merits of individual rights and freedom of choice. Subcultures and countercultures multiply. Making categorical distinctions among people—that is, treating people according to their race, sex, or religion—comes to be defined as unjust. In the process, minorities who had long lived at the margins of society gain greater power and broader participation in public life. Yet, mass-society theorists fear, transforming people of different backgrounds into a generic mass may end up dehumanizing everyone.

The Ever-Expanding State

In the small-scale, preindustrial societies of Europe, government amounted to little more than a local noble. A royal family formally reigned over an entire nation, but lacking swift transportation and efficient communication, the power of even absolute monarchs fell far short of that wielded by today's political leaders.

As technological innovation propelled the expansion of government, the centralized state grew in size and importance. At the time the United States gained independence from Great Britain, the federal government was a tiny organization whose prime function was national defense. Since then, government has entered more and more areas of social life—regulating wages and working conditions, establishing standards for products of all sorts, schooling the population, and providing financial assistance to the ill and the unemployed. Taxes have correspondingly soared, so that today's average worker labors four months a year to pay for all sorts of government services.

In a mass society, power resides in large bureaucracies, leaving people in local communities with little control over their lives. For example, state officials mandate a standardized educational program for local schools, products manufactured locally must earn state or federal government certification, and every citizen must maintain extensive records for purposes of taxation. While such regulations may protect people and enhance uniformity of treatment, they force us to deal more and more with nameless officials in unresponsive bureaucracies, and they sap the autonomy of families and neighborhoods.

Critical evaluation. The theory of mass society concedes that the transformation of small-scale societies has positive aspects, but tends to see in historical change the loss of an irreplaceable heritage. Modern societies expand individual rights, magnify tolerance of social differences, and raise living standards. But they seem prone to what Max Weber feared most—excessive bureaucracy—as well as to Toennies's self-centeredness and Emile Durkheim's anomie. The size, complexity, and tolerance of diversity in modern societies all but doom traditional values and family patterns, leaving individuals isolated, powerless, and materialistic. As Chapter 11 ("Economics and Politics") noted, voter apathy has become a serious problem in the United States. But should we be surprised that individuals in vast, impersonal societies end up thinking that no one person can make a difference?

Critics of mass-society theory contend that it romanticizes the past. They remind us that many people in the small towns of our past were actually quite eager to set out for cities in search of a better standard of living and more personal freedom. Critics also point out that this approach pays little attention to problems of social inequality. Mass-society analysis, these critics conclude, attracts social and economic conservatives who defend conventional morality and often seem indifferent to the historical plight of women and minorities.

Social-Conflict Analysis: The Theory of Class Society

A second interpretation of modernity reflects the social-conflict paradigm and, especially, the ideas of Karl Marx. From this point of view, modernity takes the form of a **class society**, *a capitalist society with pronounced social stratification.* This theory holds that inequality underlies

Mass-society theory explains the collapse of the social fabric in U.S. cities as the result of rapid social change and the erosion of tradition. Class-society theory, by contrast, suggests that social inequality diminishes the likelihood of meaningful human community.

widespread feelings of powerlessness. While acknowledging that modern societies have grown to a mass scale, this approach views the heart of modernization as an expanding capitalist economy and the inequality inherent in it (Miliband, 1969; Habermas, 1970; Polenberg, 1980; Blumberg, 1981; Harrington, 1984).

Capitalism

Class-society theory follows Marx in claiming that the growing scale of social life in modern times stems from the insatiable appetite of capitalism. Because a capitalist economy pursues ever-higher profits, both production and consumption increase.

According to Marx, capitalism rests on "naked self-interest" (1972:337; orig. 1848). This self-centeredness erodes the social ties that once cemented small-scale communities. Capitalism also fosters impersonality and anonymity by transforming people into commodities, as both a source of labor and a market for goods produced by capitalist enterprise. The net result is that

capitalism reduces human beings to cogs in the machinery of material production.

Capitalism also touts science, not just as the key to greater productivity, but also as an ideology that justifies the status quo. In modern societies, people view their own well-being as a *technical* puzzle to be solved by engineers and other experts rather than through the pursuit of *social* justice (Habermas, 1970). A capitalist culture, for example, seeks to improve health through scientific medicine rather than by eliminating poverty, which undermines many people's health in the first place.

Businesses also raise the banner of scientific logic, claiming to achieve efficiency only through continual growth. As Chapter 11 ("Economics and Politics") explained, capitalist corporations have reached gargantuan size by "going global," that is, by becoming multinationals that operate around the world. From the class-society point of view, then, the expanding scale of life is less a function of *Gesellschaft* than the inevitable and destructive consequence of capitalism.

Persistent Inequality

Modernity has gradually worn away some of the rigid categorical distinctions that divided preindustrial societies. Class-society theorists maintain, however, that elites persist albeit in a different form—as capitalist millionaires rather than nobles who inherited their status. In the United States, we may have no hereditary monarchy, but the richest 5 percent of the population nevertheless controls half of all property.

How does the state figure in reducing social inequality? While mass-society theorists believe that government has an expanding role in combating social problems, Marx was skeptical that the state could accomplish more than superficial reforms because, as he saw it, government mostly defends the wealth of capitalists. Other class-society theorists add that, while working people and minorities enjoy greater political rights and a higher standard of living today, these changes are the fruits of political struggle, not expressions of government benevolence. And, they continue, despite our claims of being a democracy, power still rests primarily in the hands of those with wealth.

Critical evaluation. As Table 16–2 summarizes, mass-society theory focuses on the increasing scale of social life and the growth of government while class-society theory stresses the expansion of capitalism and the persistence of inequality. Class-society analysts also dismiss Durkheim's argument that people in modern societies suffer from anomie; instead, they claim that people contend with alienation and powerlessness. Not surprisingly, then, the class-society interpretation of modernity enjoys widespread support among liberals (and radicals) who favor greater social equality and seek extensive regulation (or abolition) of the capitalist marketplace.

A core criticism of class-society theory holds that this analysis overlooks the many ways in which modern societies have grown more egalitarian. After all, although discrimination based on race, ethnicity, religion, and sex still persists, such practices are now illegal and widely viewed as social problems. Furthermore, most people in the United States favor unequal rewards, at least insofar as they reflect individual differences in talent and effort.

In addition, few observers believe that a centralized, socialist economy would cure the ills of modernity in light of socialism's failure to generate a high overall standard of living. Many social problems in the United States—from unemployment, homelessness, and industrial pollution to unresponsive government—have also plagued socialist nations like the former Soviet Union (Young, 1990).

There are, of course, areas of agreement. For example, both the mass- and class-society approaches underscore the world's diminishing cultural diversity. The box on page 426 takes a closer look at this trend.

Modernity and the Individual

Both mass- and class-society theories paint in broad strokes patterns of change since the Industrial Revolution. From each "macro-level" approach we can also draw "micro-level" insights into how modernity shapes individual lives.

Mass Society: Problems of Identity

Modernity liberated individuals from small, tightly knit communities of the past. Most members of modern societies possess unprecedented privacy and freedom to express their individuality. Mass-society theory suggests, however, that extensive social diversity, atomization, and rapid social change make it difficult for many people to establish any coherent identity at all (Wheelis, 1958; Riesman, 1970; Berger, Berger, & Kellner, 1974).

TABLE 16–2 Two Interpretations of Modernity: A Summary

	Key Process of Modernization	Key Effects of Modernization
Mass-society theory	Industrialization; growth of bureaucracy	Increasing scale of life; rise of the state and other formal organizations
Class-society theory	Rise of capitalism	Expansion of capitalist economy; persistence of social inequality

Chapter 3 ("Socialization: From Infancy to Old Age") explained that people forge distinctive personalities based on their social experience. The small, homogeneous, and slowly changing societies of the past provided a firm (if narrow) foundation for building meaningful personal identity. Even today, Amish communities that flourish in the United States teach young men and women "correct" ways to think and behave. Not everyone born into an Amish community can tolerate such rigid demands for conformity, but most members develop a well-integrated and satisfying personal identity (cf. Hostetler, 1980; Kraybill & Olshan, 1994).

Mass societies, with their characteristic diversity and rapid change, offer only shifting sands on which to build a personal identity. Left to make most of our own life decisions, many of us—especially those with greater affluence—confront a bewildering range of options. Autonomy has little value without standards for making choices, however, and in a tolerant mass society, people may find one path no more compelling than the next. Not surprisingly, many people shuttle from one identity to another, changing their lifestyle, relationships, and even religion in search of an elusive "true self." Beset by the widespread "relativism" of modern societies, people without a moral compass have lost the security and certainty once provided by tradition.

To David Riesman (1970; orig. 1950) modernization brings on changes in **social character,** *personality patterns common to members of a particular society.* Preindustrial societies promote what Riesman calls **tradition-directedness,** *rigid conformity to time-honored ways of living.* Members of such societies model their lives on the past: To them, what constitutes moral "good" is equivalent to "what has always been."

Tradition-directedness, then, carries to the level of individual experience Toennies's *Gemeinschaft* and Durkheim's mechanical solidarity. Culturally

The World's Disappearing Cultures: A Report From the Philippines

Eighty-six-year old Chief Tula-lang Maway sat below cloud-covered Mount Apo in the Philippines. "Our Christian brothers are enjoying life here on the plains," he declared, pointing away from the mountain to the lands his tribe, the Lumad people, long ago surrendered to outsiders. Then, turning to the sacred mountain, he continued, "We only ask them to leave us our last sanctuary" (Durning, 1993:80).

Based on the number of languages anthropologists have identified, the 5.7 billion people on earth have fashioned almost six thousand distinctive cultures. Of these, between four and five thousand are found in small and localized societies. But indigenous peoples everywhere are facing the same problem as the Lumad: Their land and way of life are in danger of disappearing.

According to mass-society theory, this trend means that a generic "mass culture" is sweeping through the entire world—a sign of global economic development. As more of the world's people gain the benefits of industrial production, they leave many traditional ways of life behind. To class-society theorists, however, the spread of "McCulture" exemplifies the relentless and exploitative march of global capitalism.

Whichever interpretation one accepts, there is no question that our world has less and less cultural diversity. Several hundred million men and women (perhaps 10 percent of the total world population) think of themselves as indigenous people. But few remain "culturally pristine," that is, free from the influence of outsiders. Even a decade ago, some 100 million isolated hunters and gatherers thrived across the Americas, Africa, and Asia. Now, as the next century approaches, the last of the indigenous peoples untouched by the materialism and high technology of industrial societies will soon disappear.

What is becoming of tribal peoples? Their cultural integrity is being compromised by the spread of Western mass media (such as the television that threatens the traditional culture of the Kaiapo, as noted at the beginning of this chapter). At the same time, many others are being driven from traditional lands by outside economic interests.

In Brazil, the Yanomamö continue to fend off mining companies just as the Gogol of New Guinea are under assault by timber interests. In these indigenous societies, meanwhile, progressive teachers are encouraging young people to abandon tribal customs, to wear Western dress, to learn English, and to look for nine-to-five jobs in cities.

Willingly or not, most tribal people are giving up their traditional ways. But is aspiring to a life based on automobiles, refrigerators, and televisions necessarily "better"? To many poor people in the world, Western materialism is synonymous with prosperity. Yet critics bemoan the loss of invaluable human diversity. Tribal people have amassed knowledge that can never be replaced. They rely on the medicinal powers of countless plants that are unknown to Westerners. Such so-called "primitive" people in the Philippines and elsewhere have discovered natural ways to fertilize their crops, to control pests, and to nurture animal life. Generally speaking, their diets are more healthful than that of the typical North American. Perhaps, then, we should be emulating—rather than working to eradicate—the tribal cultures that remain.

Sources: Based on Durning (1993) and Myers (1984c).

conservative, tradition-directed people think and act alike because everyone draws on the same solid, cultural foundation. Amish women and men exemplify tradition-direction; in the Amish culture, conformity ties everyone to ancestors and descendants in an unbroken chain of righteous living.

Members of diverse and rapidly changing societies define a tradition-directed personality as deviant because it seems so rigid. Modern people, by and large, prize personal flexibility, the capacity to adapt, and sensitivity to others. Riesman calls this type of social character **other-directedness,** *a receptiveness to the latest trends and fashions, often seen in the practice of imitating others.* Because their socialization occurs within societies that are constantly in flux, other-directed people develop fluid identities marked by superficiality, inconsistency, and change. They try on different "selves," almost like so many pieces of new clothing, seek out "role models," and engage in changing "performances" from setting to setting (Goffman, 1959). In a traditional society, such "shiftiness" marks a person as untrustworthy; but in a changing, modern society, the chameleon-like ability to fit in virtually anywhere stands as a valued personal trait (Wheelis, 1958).

In societies that value the up-to-date rather than the traditional, people look to members of their own generation, rather than elders, as significant role models. Following the same reasoning, "peer pressure" can sometimes seem irresistible to people with no enduring standards to guide them. Our society urges people to be true to themselves. But when social surroundings change so rapidly, how can people determine to which self they should be true? This problem lies at the root of the identity crisis so widespread in industrial societies today. "Who am I?" is a nagging question that many of us struggle to answer. In sociological terms, this personal problem reflects the inherent instability of modern mass society.

Class Society: Problems of Powerlessness

Class-society theory takes a different tack in explaining modernity's impact on individuals. This approach maintains that persistent inequality undermines modern society's promise of individual freedom. Modernity delivers great privilege for some, but the majority find themselves coping with a gnawing sense of powerlessness in everyday life.

For minorities, the problem of relative disadvantage looms even larger. Similarly, although women enjoy increasing participation in modern societies, they continue to run up against traditional barriers of sexism. In short, this approach rejects mass-society theory's claim that people suffer from too much freedom. Instead, class-society theory holds, our society still denies a majority of people full participation in social life.

On a global scale, as Chapter 8 ("Global Stratification") explained, the expanding scope of world capitalism has placed more of the earth's population under the influence of multinational corporations. As a result, about two-thirds of the world's income is concentrated in the richest societies, where only about 15 percent of its people live. Is it any wonder, class-society theorists ask, that people in poor nations also seek greater power to shape their own lives?

Such disparities in social power led Herbert Marcuse (1964) to challenge Max Weber's contention that modern society is rational. Marcuse condemned modern society as irrational because, he maintained, it fails to meet the needs of so many people. While modern capitalist societies produce unparalleled wealth, poverty remains the daily plight of more than a billion people. Moreover, Marcuse argued, technological advances reduce people's control over their own lives. The advent of high technology has conferred unprecedented power on a core of specialists—not the majority of people—who now control events and dominate the public agenda, whether the issue is energy production or health care. Countering the popular view that technology *solves* the world's problems, Marcuse contended that technology actually *causes* them. In sum, class-society theory asserts that people suffer because modern societies have concentrated both wealth and power in the hands of a privileged few.

The Idea of Progress

In modern societies, most people expect—and applaud—social change. People think of modernity as synonymous with the idea of *progress* (from Latin, meaning "a moving forward"), a state of continual improvement. By contrast, we denigrate stability as stagnation.

This chapter began by describing the Kaiapo of Brazil, for whom affluence has broadened opportunities but weakened traditional heritage. In examining the Kaiapo, we see that social change, with all its beneficial and detrimental consequences, is too complex to simply equate with progress.

Whether or not we view a given change as progress depends on our underlying values. A rising standard of living among the Kaiapo—or, historically, among people in the United States—has helped make our lives longer and more comfortable. As Global Map 16–1 reveals, the societies that we consider the most progressive are those with the greatest longevity.

Even so, affluence has also fueled materialism at the expense of spiritual life, rendering any simplistic notions of "progress" suspect. In a recent survey, most U.S. adults expressed mixed feelings on the subject of scientific change; aware of its benefits, many nonetheless think that science "makes our way of life change too fast" (NORC, 1993:396).

Social change, as we noted at the outset, is inherently both complex and controversial. We in the United States are proud of our commitment to basic human rights, for example. Yet, as Chapter 2 ("Culture") explained, we now have something of a "culture of rights" that tends to overlook our obligations to one another.

New technology, too, sparks controversy. More rapid transportation or more efficient communication may improve our lives in some respects. However, complex technology has also eroded traditional attachments to hometowns and even to family. Industrial technology has also unleashed an unprecedented threat to the natural environment. In sum, we know that social change is accelerating over time, but views may differ sharply on whether any particular change amounts to "progress."

Postmodernity

If modernity was the product of the Industrial Revolution, has the Information Revolution and the development of a postindustrial society unleashed the *postmodern* era? A number of scholars, answering affirmatively, use the term **postmodernity** to refer to *social patterns typical of a postindustrial society.*

Looking more closely, however, we find disagreement about precisely what constitues postmodernism. This term—long used in literary, philosophical, and even architectural circles—has edged into sociology on a wave of social criticism that has been building since the explosion of left-leaning politics in the 1960s. Although there are many variants of postmodern thinking, the following five themes run through them all (Bernstein, 1992; Borgmann, 1992; Crook, Pakulski, & Waters, 1992; Hall & Neitz, 1993):

1. **In important respects, modernity has failed.** The promise of modernity was a life free from want. As many postmodernist critics see it, however, the twentieth century was unsuccessful in

eradicating social problems like poverty or even ensuring financial security for most people.

2. **The bright light of "progress" is fading.** Modern people typically look to the future expecting that their lives will improve in significant ways. Members (including leaders) of a postmodern society, however, have less confidence about what the future holds. Furthermore, the buoyant optimism that carried society into the modern era more than a century ago has given way to stark pessimism on the part of most U.S. adults, who believe that life is getting worse (NORC, 1993:235).

3. **Science no longer holds the answers.** The defining trait of the modern era was a scientific outlook and a confident belief that technology would make human life better. But the postmodern critics charge that science has created as many problems (such as degrading the environment) as it has solved.

   More generally, postmodernist thinkers discredit the foundation of science—the assertion that there exists objective reality and truth. All reality amounts to so much social construction, they claim; moreover, "deconstructing" science shows that this system of ideas has been widely used for political purposes, especially by powerful segments of society.

4. **Cultural debates are intensifying.** As we have already explained, modernity came wrapped in the promise of enhanced individuality and expanding tolerance. Critics claim, however, that the emerging postmodern society falls short of that promise. Feminism is unmasking the extent to which patriarchy still shapes society today just as multiculturalism strives to empower minorities long pushed to the margins of social life.

5. **Social institutions are changing.** Just as industrialization brought sweeping transformations to social institutions, the rise of a postindustrial economy is remaking society once again. For example, the Industrial Revolution placed *material things* at the center of productive life in the same way that the Information Revolution has now elevated the importance of *ideas.* Similarly, the postmodern family no longer conforms to any singular model; on the contrary, individuals in family settings are devising alternative ways of relating to one another.

Critical evaluation. Postmodernist critics contend that the United States (and other rich societies) are entering

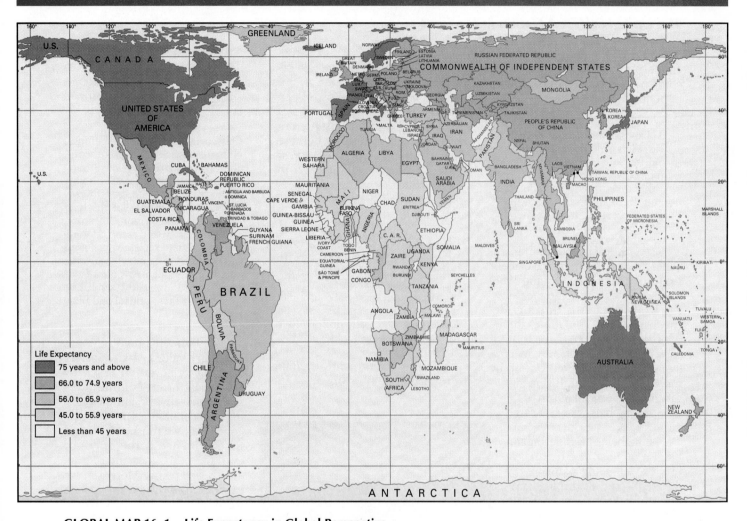

GLOBAL MAP 16–1   Life Expectancy in Global Perspective

Average life expectancy has shot upward over the course of this century in industrialized countries including Canada, the United States, the nations of Western Europe, Japan, and Australia. A newborn in the United States can expect to live about seventy-six years, and our life expectancy would be higher still were it not for the substantial risk of death among infants born into poverty. Since poverty is the rule in much of the world, lives are correspondingly shorter, especially in parts of Africa where life expectancy may be as low as forty years.

Source: *Peters Atlas of the World* (1990).

a postmodern era because modernity's bright promise remains unfulfilled. Yet few would argue that modernity has failed completely; after all, we have seen increases in the length and quality of life over the course of this century. Moreover, even if one accepts postmodernist

criticism that science and traditional notions about progress are bankrupt, what are the alternatives?

Then, too, many voices offer very different understandings of recent social trends. The box provides one case in point.

The United States: A Nation in Decline?

Asked what was his greatest concern about the future of his country, U.S. writer Walker Percy responded:

> Probably the fear of seeing America, with all its great strength and beauty and freedom . . . gradually subside into decay and be defeated . . . from within by weariness, boredom, cynicism, greed and in the end helplessness before its great problems.

Are we, in fact, a nation in decline? William Bennett (Secretary of Education between 1985 and 1988) points out that, by some measures, the United States is thriving. Between 1960 and 1990, for example, the economic output of the country tripled and median family income (controlled for inflation) was up by more than one-third. Just as significant, the official poverty rate dropped by half over the same period.

Nonetheless, Bennett maintains, a number of other indicators of well-being paint a very different—and disturbing—picture of life in the United States as we near the end of this century. Violent crime shot up by 560 percent; the number of children born to single mothers rose more than 400 percent; the number of children supported by welfare increased just as fast; the divorce rate jumped 300 percent; and teen suicide was up more than 200 percent. Since 1960, as television viewing has increased by 35 percent, the average student's College Board scores have tumbled downward by 75 points.

Government spending (in constant 1990 dollars) rose five-fold between 1960 and 1990, even as our population increased by just 41 percent. Clearly, then, a wide range of serious social problems plague our society despite (or, perhaps, because of) government efforts to address them. This fact leads Bennett to conclude that our nation's decline is primarily moral—a matter of weakening individual character:

> Our society now places less value than before on what we owe to others as a matter of moral obligation; less value on sacrifice as a moral good; less value on social conformity and respectability; and less value on correctness and restraint in matters of physical pleasure and sexuality.

Because government—even as it grows bigger and bigger—can

do little to build individual character, Bennett contends that efforts to address social problems through government programs are destined to fail. He continues:

> Our social institutions—families, churches, schools, neighborhoods, and civic associations—have traditionally taken on the responsibility of providing our children with love, order, and discipline—of teaching self-control, compassion, tolerance, civility, honesty, and respect for authority . . . The social regression of the past thirty years is due in large part to the enfeebled state of our social institutions and their failure to carry out these critical and time-honored tasks.

From Bennett's point of view, the primary values of any society are set not by government but by people living in communities and, especially, by families raising their children. In effect, he concludes, we must not assume that affluence is the only—or even the best—measure of a society's well-being. Moreover, we cannot afford to ignore—nor can we hand over to the government—our basic responsibility to sustain the social fabric that we call civilization.

Source: Based on Bennett (1993).

Postmodern culture lambasts the state of the world as we near the beginning of a new century. While the modern world was confident that orderly living would result in progress and prosperity, critics of the emerging postmodern world see little sense of meaning and security in contemporary social arrangements. Postmodern art, such as William Haney's *In Over Our Heads*, captures this sense of confusion, anxiety, and uncertainty.

Looking Ahead: Modernization and Our Global Future

This book opened by asking readers to imagine a village of one thousand people that represented all of humanity. About 175 residents of this "global village" live in the most economically developed countries, while about half of the people endure daily hunger. Most seriously, 200 people are so poor that they are at risk for their lives.

The tragic plight of the world's poor shows that some desperately needed change has not occurred at all. Chapter 8 ("Global Stratification") detailed two competing views of why 1 billion people the world over are poor. *Modernization theory* claims that in the past the entire world was poor and that technological change, especially the Industrial Revolution, enhanced human productivity and raised living standards. From this point of view, the solution to global poverty is to encourage technological development in poor nations.

For reasons outlined earlier, however, global modernization may be difficult. Recall that David Riesman portrayed preindustrial people as *tradition-directed* and resistant to change. So modernization theorists call on the world's rich societies to offer assistance to poor countries in need of productive innovation. Industrial nations can speed development by exporting technology to poor regions, welcoming students from abroad, and providing foreign aid to stimulate economic growth.

The review of modernization theory in Chapter 8 points to some limited success for these policies in Latin America and, especially, in the small Asian countries of Taiwan, South Korea, Singapore, and Hong Kong. But jump-starting development in the poorest countries of the world poses the greatest challenges. And even where dramatic change has occurred, modernization entails a tradeoff. Traditional people, such as Brazil's Kaiapo, may gain wealth through economic development, but only at the cost of losing their cultural identity and values as they are drawn into the "global village." Speaking about the Kaiapo, one Brazilian anthropologist expressed only cautious optimism about the future: "At least they quickly understood the consequences of watching television . . . . Now [they] can make a choice" (Simons, 1995:xx). Indeed, the "McDonaldization" of the United States, detailed in Chapter 5 ("Groups and Organizations"), is also proceeding on a world scale. Yet, this sacrifice of cultural distinctiveness for material plenty has not always won over the people. Some societies—including Algeria, Ethiopia, and Iran—have started on a path toward modernization only to run head on into a powerful backlash from segments of the population (often religious) who insist on restoring traditional culture.

But not everyone thinks that modernization is really an option. According to a second approach to global stratification, *dependency theory*, today's poor societies have little ability to modernize, even if they wanted to. From this point of view, the major barrier to economic development is not traditionalism but global domination by rich, capitalist societies. Initially, as Chapter 8 explains, this system took the form of colonialism, whereby European societies seized much of Latin America, Africa, and Asia. Trading relationships soon enriched England, Spain, and other colonial powers while their colonies simultaneously became poor. Almost all societies once subjected to this form of domination are now politically independent, but colonial-style ties persist in the form of multinational corporations operating around the world. Locked in a disadvantageous economic relationship with rich nations, poor countries sell their cheap raw materials to rich countries and buy whatever expensive manufactured products they can afford. Overall, dependency theorists conclude, the global economy perpetuates longstanding global stratification.

Whichever approach one finds more convincing, we can no longer isolate the study of the United States from the rest of the world. At the beginning of the twentieth century, a majority of people in even the richest nations lived in relatively small settlements with limited awareness of the larger world. Now, at the threshold of the twenty-first century, people everywhere participate in a far larger human drama. The world is smaller and the lives of all its people are increasingly interconnected. We now discuss the relationships among countries in the same way that people a mere hundred years ago talked about the expanding ties among towns and cities.

The century now coming to a close has witnessed unprecedented human achievement. Yet solutions to many problems of human existence—including finding meaning in life, resolving conflicts among societies, and eradicating poverty—remain elusive. To this list of pressing matters, we have added new concerns from controlling population growth to establishing a sustainable natural environment. As the twenty-first century nears, we are called on to tackle such problems with imagination, compassion, and determination. Our wide-ranging understanding of human society gives us reason to look to the task with optimism.

SUMMARY

1. Societies change continuously, intentionally or not, and at varying speeds.

2. Social change occurs as a result of invention, discovery, and cultural diffusion as well as social conflict.

3. Through social movements, people work to promote or resist change. Social movements gain strength because of relative deprivation, the rootlessness of mass society, and an organization's ability to muster resources.

4. Modernity refers to the social consequences of industrialization, which, according to Peter Berger, include the erosion of traditional communities, expanding personal choice, increasingly diverse beliefs, and a keen awareness of time, especially the future.

5. Ferdinand Toennies described modernization as the transition from *Gemeinschaft* to *Gesellschaft*,

which signifies the progressive loss of community amid growing individualism.

6. Emile Durkheim saw modernization as a function of society's expanding division of labor. Mechanical solidarity, based on shared activities and beliefs, gradually gives way to organic solidarity, in which specialization makes people interdependent.

7. According to Max Weber, modernity replaces tradition with a rational world view. He feared the dehumanizing effects of rational organization.

8. In Karl Marx's view, modernity emerged in the triumph of capitalism over feudalism. Because capitalist societies are fraught with conflict, Marx advocated revolutionary change leading to a more egalitarian, socialist system.

9. Mass-society theory claims that modernity increases the scale of life, enlarging the role of

government and other formal organizations in carrying out tasks previously performed by family members and neighbors. Cultural diversity and rapid social change make it difficult for people in modern societies to develop a stable identity.

10. Class-society theory states that capitalism is central to Western modernization. This approach charges that by concentrating wealth, capitalism generates widespread feelings of powerlessness.

11. Social change is too complex and controversial to be simply equated with progress.

12. Postmodernity refers to cultural traits typical of postindustrial societies. Postmodernist criticism of society centers on the failure of modernity (and, especially, science) to fulfill its promise of widespread prosperity and well-being.

KEY CONCEPTS

anomie a condition in which society provides little moral guidance to individuals

class society a capitalist society with pronounced social stratification

division of labor specialized economic activity

mass society a society in which industry and bureaucracy erode traditional social ties

modernity social patterns linked to industrialization

modernization the process of social change initiated by industrialization

other-directedness a receptiveness to the latest trends and fashions, often seen in the practice of imitating others

postmodernity social patterns typical of a postindustrial society

relative deprivation a perceived disadvantage relative to some standard of comparison

social change the transformation of culture and social institutions over time

social character personality patterns common to members of a society

social movement an organized effort to encourage or oppose some dimension of change

tradition-directedness rigid conformity to time-honored ways of living

CRITICAL-THINKING QUESTIONS

1. Identify points of agreement among Toennies, Durkheim, Weber, and Marx regarding the character of modernity. What are several important differences?

2. What traits make the United States a "mass society"? How does this affect the individual experience of living in such a society?

3. What is the difference between *anomie* (a trait of mass society) and *alienation* (a characteristic of class society)? Among which categories of the U.S. population would you expect each trait to be more pronounced?

4. In what ways has the United States become a postmodern society?

Glossary

absolute poverty a deprivation of resources that is life-threatening

achieved status a social position that a person assumes voluntarily and that reflects a significant measure of personal ability and choice

acid rain precipitation made acidic by air pollution that destroys plant and animal life

Afrocentrism the dominance of African cultural patterns

ageism prejudice and discrimination against the elderly

age-sex pyramid a graphic representation of the age and sex of a population

agriculture large-scale cultivation using plows first drawn by animals

alienation the experience of powerlessness in social life

animism the belief that natural objects are conscious forms of life that affect humanity

anomie a condition in which society provides little moral guidance to individuals

anticipatory socialization social learning directed toward gaining a desired position

ascribed status a social position a person receives at birth or assumes involuntarily later in the life course

assimilation the process by which minorities gradually adopt patterns of the dominant culture

authoritarianism a political system that denies popular participation in government

authority power that people perceive as legitimate rather than coercive

beliefs specific statements that people hold to be true

blue-collar occupation lower-prestige work that involves mostly manual labor

bureaucracy an organizational model designed to perform tasks efficiently

bureaucratic inertia the tendency of bureaucratic organizations to perpetuate themselves

bureaucratic ritualism a preoccupation with rules and regulations to the point of obstructing organizational goals

capitalism an economic system in which natural resources and the means of producing goods and services are privately owned

capitalist one who owns a factory or other productive enterprise

caste system social stratification based on ascription

cause and effect a relationship between two variables in which change in one (the independent variable) causes change in another (the dependent variable)

charisma extraordinary personal qualities that can turn an audience into followers

church a formal religious organization well integrated into the larger society

civil religion a quasi-religious loyalty based on citizenship

class society a capitalist society with pronounced social stratification

class system social stratification based on individual achievement

cohabitation the sharing of a household by an unmarried couple

cohort a category of people with a common characteristic, usually their age

colonialism the process by which some nations enrich themselves through political and economic control of other nations

concept an abstract idea that represents some aspect of the world, inevitably in a somewhat simplified form

concrete operational stage Piaget's term for the level of development at which individuals perceive causal connections in their surroundings

corporation an organization with a legal existence, including rights and liabilities, apart from those of its members

correlation a relationship between two (or more) variables

counterculture cultural patterns that strongly oppose conventional culture

credentialism evaluating people on the basis of educational degrees

crime the violation of norms formally enacted into criminal law

crimes against the person (violent crimes) crimes against people that involve violence or the threat of violence

crimes against property (property crimes) crimes that involve theft of property belonging to others

criminal justice system the lawful response to alleged crimes using police, courts, and state-sanctioned punishment

criminal recidivism subsequent offenses committed by people previously convicted of crimes

crude birth rate the number of live births in a given year for every thousand people in a population

crude death rate the number of deaths in a given year for every thousand people in a population

cult a religious organization that is substantially outside the cultural traditions of a society

cultural ecology a theoretical paradigm that explores the relationship between human culture and the physical environment

cultural integration the close relationship among various elements of a cultural system

cultural lag the fact that some cultural elements change more quickly than others, with potentially disruptive consequences

cultural relativism the practice of evaluating any culture by its own standards

cultural transmission the process by which culture is passed from one generation to the next

cultural universals traits found in every culture

culture the beliefs, values, behavior, and material objects shared by a particular people

culture shock the personal disorientation accompanying exposure to an unfamiliar way of life

democracy a type of political system giving power to the people as a whole

democratic socialism an economic and political system that combines significant government control of the economy with free elections

demographic transition theory a thesis linking population patterns to a society's level of technological development

demography the study of human population

denomination a church, not linked to the state, that recognizes religious pluralism

dependency theory a model of economic development that explains global inequality in terms of the historical exploitation of poor societies by rich societies

descent the system by which members of a society trace kinship over generations

deterrence the attempt to discourage criminality through punishment

deviance the recognized violation of cultural norms

direct-fee system a medical-care system in which patients pay directly for the services of physicians and hospitals

discrimination treating various categories of people unequally

division of labor specialized economic activity

dramaturgical analysis the investigation of social interaction in terms of theatrical performance

dyad a social group with two members

ecclesia a church that is formally allied with the state

ecology the study of the interaction of living organisms and their natural environment

economy the social institution that organizes a society's production, distribution, and consumption of goods and services

ecosystem the system composed of the interaction of all living organisms and their natural environment

education the social institution through which society provides its members with important knowledge, including facts, skills, and values

ego Freud's designation of a person's conscious attempts to balance the pleasure-seeking drives of the human organism and the demands of society

endogamy marriage between people of the same social category

environmental deficit the situation in which negative, long-term consequences of decisions about the natural environment outweigh whatever short-term benefits people derive

ethnicity a shared cultural heritage

ethnocentrism the practice of judging another culture by the standards of our own culture

ethnomethodology the study of the way people make sense of their everyday surroundings

Eurocentrism the dominance of European (especially English) cultural patterns

euthanasia (mercy killing) assisting in the death of a person suffering from an incurable illness

exogamy marriage between people of different social categories

experiment a research method that investigates cause-and-effect relationships under highly controlled conditions

expressive leaders group leaders who emphasize collective well-being

extended family (consanguine family)   a social unit including parents, children, and other kin

faith   belief anchored in conviction rather than scientific evidence

family   a relatively permanent group of two or more people, who are related by blood, marriage, or adoption and who usually live together

feminism   the advocacy of social equality for the sexes, in opposition to patriarchy and sexism

feminization of poverty   the trend by which women represent an increasing proportion of the poor

fertility   the incidence of childbearing in a society's population

folkways   norms about which people allow one another considerable personal discretion

formal operational stage   Piaget's term for the level of development at which individuals think abstractly and imagine

formal organization   a large secondary group that is organized to achieve specific goals

functional illiteracy   reading and writing skills inadequate for everyday living

Gemeinschaft   a type of social organization by which people are bound together by kinship and tradition

gender   the significance a society attaches to the biological categories of female and male

gender roles (sex roles)   attitudes and activities that a society links to each sex

gender stratification   the unequal distribution of wealth, power, and privilege between the two sexes

genocide   the systematic killing of one category of people by another

gerontocracy   a form of social organization in which the elderly have the most wealth, power, and privileges

gerontology   the study of aging and the elderly

Gesellschaft   a type of social organization by which people stand apart due to self-interest

global economy   economic activity across national borders

global perspective   a view of the larger world and our society's place in it

government   a formal organization that directs the political life of a nation

greenhouse effect   a rise in the earth's average temperature (global warming) due to an increasing concentration of carbon dioxide in the atmosphere

groupthink   group conformity that limits understanding of an issue

hate crime   a crime motivated by racial or other bias

health   a state of complete physical, mental, and social well-being

health maintenance organization (HMO)   an organization that provides comprehensive medical care for a fixed fee

hermaphrodite   a human being with some combination of female and male internal and external genitalia

high culture   cultural patterns that distinguish a society's elite

holistic medicine   an approach to health care that emphasizes prevention of illness and takes account of a person's entire physical and social environment

homogamy   marriage between people with the same social characteristics

horticulture   the use of hand tools to raise crops

hunting and gathering   the use of simple tools to hunt animals and gather vegetation

id   Freud's designation of the human being's basic drives

ideology   cultural beliefs that justify particular social arrangements

incest taboo   a norm forbidding sexual relations or marriage between certain kin

income   wages or salary from work and earnings from investments

industry   the production of goods using sophisticated fuels and machinery

infant mortality rate   the number of deaths among infants under one year of age for each thousand live births in a given year

ingroup   an esteemed social group commanding a member's loyalty

institutional discrimination   discrimination that is a normative and routine part of the economy, educational system, or some other social institution

instrumental leaders   group leaders who emphasize the completion of tasks

intergenerational social mobility   the social standing of children in relation to their parents

intragenerational social mobility   a change in social position occurring during a person's lifetime

kinship   a social bond, based on blood, marriage, or adoption, that joins people into families

labeling theory   the assertion that deviance and conformity result, not so much from what people do, as from the response of others to those actions

language   a system of symbols that allows people to communicate with one another

latent functions   the unrecognized and unintended consequences of any social pattern

least-developed countries   nations with little industrialization in which severe poverty is the rule

less-developed countries   nations characterized by limited industrialization and moderate-to-low personal income

liberation theology   a fusion of Christian principles with political (often Marxist) activism

life expectancy   the average life span of a society's population

looking-glass self   Cooley's term referring to a conception of self derived from the responses of others

macro-level orientation   a concern with large-scale patterns that characterize society as a whole

manifest functions   the recognized and intended consequences of any social pattern

marriage   a legally sanctioned relationship, involving economic cooperation as well as normative sexual activity and childbearing, that people expect to be enduring

mass media   impersonal communications directed to a vast audience

mass society   a society in which industry and bureaucracy erode traditional social ties

master status   a social position with exceptional importance for identity, often shaping a person's entire life

matriarchy   a form of social organization in which females dominate males

measurement   the process of determining the value of a variable in a specific case

mechanical solidarity   social bonds based on collective conformity to tradition

medicalization of deviance   the transformation of moral and legal issues into medical matters

medicine   the social institution that focuses on combating disease and improving health

meritocracy   social stratification based on personal merit

micro-level orientation   a concern with small-scale patterns of social interaction in specific settings

migration   the movement of people into and out of a specified territory

military-industrial complex   a close association among the government, the military, and defense industries

minority   a category of people, distinguished by physical or cultural traits, that is socially disadvantaged

miscegenation   the biological process of interbreeding among racial categories

modernity   social patterns linked to industrialization

modernization   the process of social change initiated by industrialization

modernization theory   a model of economic development that explains global inequality in terms of technological and cultural differences among societies

monarchy   a type of political system that transfers power from generation to generation within a single family

monogamy   marriage involving two partners

monopoly   domination of a market by a single producer

mores   norms that are widely observed and have great moral significance

mortality   the incidence of death in a society's population

most-developed countries   industrial nations that are relatively rich

multiculturalism   an educational program recognizing the cultural diversity of the United States and promoting the equality of all cultural traditions

multinational corporation   a large business that operates in many countries

natural environment   the earth's surface and atmosphere, including various living organisms as well as the air, water, soil, and other resources necessary to sustain life

neocolonialism   a new form of economic exploitation involving not formal political control but the operation of multinational corporations

network   a web of weak social ties

nonverbal communication   communication using body movements, gestures, and facial expressions rather than speech

norms   rules by which a society guides the behavior of its members

nuclear family (conjugal family)   a social unit containing one or, more commonly, two adults and any children

oligarchy   the rule of the many by the few

oligopoly   domination of a market by a few producers

organic solidarity   social bonds based on specialization and interdependence

other-directedness   a receptiveness to the latest trends and fashions, often seen in the practice of imitating others

outgroup   a scorned social group toward which one feels competition or opposition

participant observation   a research method in which investigators systematically observe people while joining in their routine activities

pastoralism   the domestication of animals

patriarchy   a form of social organization in which males dominate females

peer group a group whose members have interests, social position, and age in common

personality a person's fairly consistent patterns of acting, thinking, and feeling

personal space the surrounding area over which a person makes some claim to privacy

plea bargaining a legal negotiation in which the prosecution reduces a charge in exchange for a defendant's guilty plea

pluralism a state in which people of all races and ethnicities are distinct but have social parity

pluralist model an analysis of politics that views power as dispersed among many competing interest groups

political revolution the overthrow of one political system in order to establish another

politics the social institution that distributes power and makes decisions

polygamy marriage that unites three or more people

popular culture cultural patterns widespread among a society's people

positivism a path to understanding based on science

postindustrial economy a productive system based on service work and high technology

postmodernity social patterns typical of a postindustrial society

power the ability to achieve desired ends despite opposition

power-elite model an analysis of politics that views power as concentrated among the rich

prejudice a rigid and irrational generalization about a category of people

preoperational stage Piaget's term for the level of development at which individuals first use language and other symbols

presentation of self Goffman's term for the ways in which individuals, in various settings, try to create specific impressions in the minds of others

primary group a small social group in which relationships are personal and enduring

primary sector the part of the economy that generates raw materials directly from the natural environment

profane that which people define as an ordinary element of everyday life

profession a prestigious, white-collar occupation that requires extensive formal education

proletariat people who sell their productive labor

public opinion the attitudes of people throughout a society about one or more controversial issues

race a category composed of men and women who share biologically transmitted traits that members of a society deem socially significant

racism the belief that one racial category is innately superior or inferior to another

rain forests regions of dense forestation that circle the globe close to the equator

rationality deliberate, matter-of-fact calculation of the most efficient means to accomplish any particular task

rationalization Max Weber's term for the change from tradition to rationality as the dominant mode of human thought

recycling programs to reuse resources that we would otherwise discard as "waste"

reference group a social group that serves as a point of reference for making evaluations and decisions

rehabilitation reforming the offender to preclude further offenses

relative deprivation a perceived disadvantage relative to some standard of comparison

relative poverty the deprivation of some people in relation to others who have more

reliability the quality of consistency in measurement

religion a social institution, involving beliefs and practices, that distinguishes the sacred from the profane

religiosity the importance of religion in a person's life

religious fundamentalism a conservative religious doctrine that opposes intellectualism and worldly accommodation in favor of restoring traditional, other-worldly religion

research method a strategy for systematically carrying out research

resocialization deliberate socialization intended to radically alter an individual's personality

retribution inflicting on an offender suffering comparable to that caused by the offense

retrospective labeling the interpretation of someone's past consistent with present deviance

role normative patterns of behavior for those holding a particular status

role conflict incompatibility among roles corresponding to two or more statuses

role set a number of roles attached to a single status

role strain incompatibility among roles corresponding to a single status

routinization of charisma the transformation of charismatic authority into some combination of traditional and bureaucratic authority

sacred that which people define as extraordinary, inspiring a sense of awe and reverence

Sapir-Whorf hypothesis the assertion that people perceive the world only in terms of the symbols provided by their language

scapegoat a person or category of people, typically with little power, whom others unfairly blame for their own troubles

schooling formal instruction under the direction of specially trained teachers

science a logical system that derives knowledge from direct, systematic observation

secondary group a large and impersonal social group based on some special interest or activity

secondary sector the part of the economy that transforms raw materials into manufactured goods

sect a type of religious organization that stands apart from the larger society

secularization the historical decline in the influence of religion

segregation the physical and social separation of categories of people

self George Herbert Mead's term for the dimension of personality composed of an individual's self-awareness and self-image

sensorimotor stage Piaget's term for the level of development at which individuals experience the world only through sensory contact

sex the biological distinction between females and males

sexism the belief that one sex is innately superior to the other

sex ratio the number of males for every hundred females in a given population

sexual harassment comments, gestures, or physical contact of a sexual nature that are deliberate, repeated, and unwelcome

sexual orientation the manner in which people experience sexual arousal and achieve sexual pleasure

sick role patterns of behavior defined as appropriate for those who are ill

social change the transformation of culture and social institutions over time

social character personality patterns common to members of a society

social-conflict paradigm a framework for building theory based on the assumption that society is a complex system characterized by inequality and conflict that generate social change

social construction of reality the process by which individuals creatively build reality through social interaction

social control attempts by society to regulate the thought and behavior of individuals

social dysfunction the undesirable consequences of any social pattern for the operation of society

social epidemiology the study of how health and disease are distributed throughout a society's population

social function the consequences of any social pattern for the operation of society as a whole

social group two or more people who identify and interact with one another

social institution an organized sphere of social life such as the economy or the family

social interaction the process by which people act and react in relation to others

socialism an economic system in which natural resources and the means of producing goods and services are collectively owned

socialization the lifelong social experience by which individuals develop their human potential and learn culture

socialized medicine a medical-care system in which the government owns most medical facilities and employs most physicians

social mobility a change of position in a stratification system

social movement an organized effort to encourage or oppose some dimension of change

social stratification a system by which a society ranks categories of people in a hierarchy

social structure any relatively stable pattern of social behavior

societal protection rendering an offender incapable of further offenses either temporarily through incarceration or permanently by execution

society people interacting within a limited territory guided by their culture

sociobiology a theoretical paradigm that explains cultural patterns in terms of biological forces

socioeconomic status (SES) a composite social ranking based on various dimensions of inequality

sociology the scientific study of human social activity

status a recognized social position that an individual occupies

status consistency the degree of consistency in a person's social standing across various dimensions of inequality

status set   all the statuses a person holds at a particular time

stereotype   a prejudiced description of a category of people

stigma   a powerfully negative label that radically changes a person's self-concept and social identity

structural-functional paradigm   a framework for building theory based on the assumption that society is a complex system whose parts work together to promote stability

structural social mobility   a shift in the social position of large numbers of people due less to individual efforts than to changes in society itself

subculture   cultural patterns that distinguish some segment of a society's population

suburbs   urban areas beyond the political boundaries of a city

superego   Freud's designation of the presence of culture within the individual in the form of internalized values and norms

survey   a research method in which subjects respond to a series of statements or questions in a questionnaire or interview

sustainable ecosystem   the human use of the natural environment to meet the needs of the present generation without threatening the prospects of future generations

symbol   anything that carries a particular meaning recognized by people who share culture

symbolic-interaction paradigm   a framework for building theory based on the view that society is the product of the everyday interactions of individuals

technology   the application of knowledge to the practical tasks of living

terrorism   violence or the threat of violence by an individual or a group as a political strategy

tertiary sector   the part of the economy involving services rather than goods

theoretical paradigm   a set of fundamental assumptions that guides thinking and research

theory   a statement of how and why specific facts are related

Thomas theorem   the assertion that situations that are defined as real become real in their consequences

total institution   a setting in which individuals are isolated from the rest of society and manipulated by an administrative staff

totalitarianism   a highly centralized political system that extensively regulates people's lives

totem   an object collectively defined as sacred

tracking   the division of a school's students into different educational programs

tradition   sentiments and beliefs about the world that are passed from generation to generation

tradition-directedness   rigid conformity to time-honored ways of living

transsexuals   people who feel they are one sex though biologically they are the other

triad   a social group with three members

urban ecology   study of the link between the physical and social dimensions of cities

urbanization   the concentration of humanity into cities

validity   the quality of measurement gained by measuring exactly what one intends to measure

values   culturally defined standards of desirability, goodness, and beauty that serve as broad guidelines for social life

variable   a concept whose value changes from case to case

victimless crime   violation of law in which there is no readily apparent victim

war   armed conflict among the people of various countries, directed by their governments

wealth   an individual's or family's total financial assets

white-collar crime   crimes committed by people of high social position in the course of their occupations

white-collar occupation   higher-prestige work that involves mostly mental activity

References

ABERLE, DAVID F. *The Peyote Religion Among the Navaho.* Chicago: Aldine, 1966.

ADLER, JERRY. "When Harry Called Sally...." *Newsweek* (October 1, 1990):74.

ADORNO, T. W., et al. *The Authoritarian Personality.* New York: Harper & Brothers, 1950.

ALAM, SULTANA. "Women and Poverty in Bangladesh." *Women's Studies International Forum.* Vol. 8, No. 4 (1985):361–71.

ALBON, JOAN. "Retention of Cultural Values and Differential Urban Adaptation: Samoans and American Indians in a West Coast City." *Social Forces.* Vol. 49, No. 3 (March 1971):385–93.

ALLAN, EMILIE ANDERSEN, and DARRELL J. STEFFENSMEIER. "Youth, Underemployment, and Property Crime: Differential Effects of Job Availability and Job Quality on Juvenile and Young Adult Arrest Rates." *American Sociological Review.* Vol. 54, No. 1 (February 1989):107–23.

ALLEN, MICHAEL PATRICK, and PHILIP BROYLES. "Campaign Finance Reforms and the Presidential Campaign Contributions of Wealthy Capitalist Families." *Social Science Quarterly.* Vol. 72, No. 4 (December 1991):738–50.

AMERICAN SOCIOLOGICAL ASSOCIATION. "Code of Ethics." Washington, D.C.:1984.

ANDERS, GEORGE. "Doctors Lobby Patients in a Campaign to Shape Clinton Health-Care Package." *Wall Street Journal* (July 26, 1993):B1, B4.

ANDERSON, DANIEL R., and ELIZABETH PUGZLES LORCH. "Look at Television: Action or Reaction?" In Jennings Bryant and Daniel R. Anderson, eds., *Children's Understanding of Television: Research on Attention and Comprehension.* New York: Academic Press, 1983:1–33.

ANDERSON, JOHN WARD, and MOLLY MOORE. "World's Poorest Women Suffer in Common." *Columbus Dispatch* (April 11, 1993):4G.

ANDO, FAITH H. "Women in Business." In Sara E. Rix, ed., *The American Woman: A Status Report 1990–91.* New York: Norton, 1990:222–30.

ANG, IEN. *Watching Dallas: Soap Opera and the Melodramatic Imagination.* London: Methuen, 1985.

ANGIER, NATALIE. "Scientists, Finding Second Idiosyncracy in Homosexuals' Brains, Suggest Orientation is Physiological." *New York Times* (August 1, 1992):A7.

ARCHER, DANE, and ROSEMARY GARTNER. *Violence and Crime in Cross-National Perspective.* New Haven, Conn.: Yale University Press, 1987.

ARENDT, HANNAH. *The Origins of Totalitarianism.* Cleveland, Ohio: Meridian Books, 1958.

ARIÈS, PHILIPPE. *Centuries of Childhood: A Social History of Family Life.* New York: Vintage Books, 1965.

———. *Western Attitudes Toward Death: From the Middle Ages to the Present.* Baltimore, Md.: The Johns Hopkins University Press, 1974.

ASANTE, MOLEFI KETE. *Afrocentricity.* Trenton, N.J.: Africa World Press, 1988.

ASCH, SOLOMON. *Social Psychology.* Englewood Cliffs, N.J.: Prentice Hall, 1952.

ASTONE, NAN MARIE, and SARA S. MCLANAHAN. "Family Structure, Parental Practices and High School Completion." *American Sociological Review.* Vol. 56, No. 3 (June 1991):309–20.

AXTELL, ROGER E. *Gestures: The DO's and TABOOs of Body Language Around the World.* New York: Wiley, 1991.

BACHMAN, RONET. *Violence Against Women.* U.S. Bureau of Justice Statistics. Washington, D.C.: U.S. Government Printing Office, 1994.

BACHRACH, PETER, and MORTON S. BARATZ. *Power and Poverty.* New York: Oxford University Press, 1970.

BAHL, VINAY. "Caste and Class in India." Paper presented to the Southern Sociological Society, Atlanta, April, 1991.

BAILEY, WILLIAM C. "Murder, Capital Punishment, and Television: Execution Publicity and Homicide Rates." *American Sociological Review.* Vol. 55, No. 5 (October 1990):628–33.

BAILEY, WILLIAM C., and RUTH D. PETERSON. "Murder and Capital Punishment: A Monthly Time-Series Analysis of Execution Publicity." *American Sociological Review.* Vol. 54, No. 5 (October 1989):722–43.

BAKER, MARY ANNE, CATHERINE WHITE BERHEIDE, FAY ROSS GRECKEL, LINDA CARSTARPHEN GUGIN, MARCIA J. LIPETZ, and MARCIA TEXLER SEGAL. *Women Today: A Multidisciplinary Approach to Women's Studies.* Monterey, Calif.: Brooks/Cole, 1980.

BALES, ROBERT F. "The Equilibrium Problem in Small Groups." In Talcott Parsons et al., eds., *Working Papers in the Theory of Action.* New York: Free Press, 1953:111–15.

441

BALES, ROBERT F., and PHILIP E. SLATER. "Role Differentiation in Small Decision-Making Groups." In Talcott Parsons and Robert F. Bales, eds., *Family, Socialization and Interaction Process*. New York: Free Press, 1955:259–306.

BALTZELL, E. DIGBY. *The Protestant Establishment: Aristocracy and Caste in America*. New York: Vintage Books, 1964.

———, ed. *The Search for Community in Modern America*. New York: Harper & Row, 1968.

———. "The Protestant Establishment Revisited." *The American Scholar*. Vol. 45, No. 4 (Autumn 1976):499–518.

———. *Philadelphia Gentlemen: The Making of a National Upper Class*. Philadelphia: University of Pennsylvania Press, 1979; orig. 1958.

———. *Puritan Boston and Quaker Philadelphia*. New York: Free Press, 1979.

———. "The WASP's Last Gasp." *Philadelphia Magazine*. Vol. 79 (September 1988):104–7, 184, 186, 188.

BANFIELD, EDWARD C. *The Unheavenly City Revisited*. Boston: Little, Brown, 1974.

BARASH, DAVID. *The Whispering Within*. New York: Penguin Books, 1981.

BARKER, EILEEN. "Who'd Be a Moonie? A Comparative Study of Those Who Join the Unification Church in Britain." In Bryan Wilson, ed., *The Social Impact of New Religious Movements*. New York: The Rose of Sharon Press, 1981:59–96.

———. *New Religious Movements: A Practical Introduction*. London: Her Majesty's Stationery Office, 1989.

BARRY, KATHLEEN. "Feminist Theory: The Meaning of Women's Liberation." In Barbara Haber, ed., *The Women's Annual 1982–1983*. Boston: G. K. Hall, 1983:35–78.

BASSUK, ELLEN J. "The Homelessness Problem." *Scientific American*. Vol. 251, No. 1 (July 1984):40–45.

BATESON, C. DANIEL, and W. LARRY VENTIS. *The Religious Experience: A Social-Psychological Perspective*. New York: Oxford, 1982.

BAUER, P. T. *Equality, the Third World, and Economic Delusion*. Cambridge, Mass.: Harvard University Press, 1981.

BECKER, HOWARD S. *Outside: Studies in the Sociology of Deviance*. New York: Free Press, 1966.

BEEGHLEY, LEONARD. *The Structure of Social Stratification in the United States*. Needham Heights, Mass.: Allyn & Bacon, 1989.

BELL, ALAN P., MARTIN S. WEINBERG, and SUE KIEFER-HAMMERSMITH. *Sexual Preference: Its Development in Men and Women*. Bloomington: Indiana University Press, 1981.

BELLAH, ROBERT N. *The Broken Covenant*. New York: Seabury Press, 1975.

BELLAH, ROBERT N., RICHARD MADSEN, WILLIAM M. SULLIVAN, ANN SWIDLER, and STEVEN M. TIPTON. *Habits of the Heart: Individualism and Commitment in American Life*. New York: Harper & Row, 1985.

BELSKY, JAY, RICHARD M. LERNER, and GRAHAM B. SPANIER. *The Child in the Family*. Reading, Mass.: Addison-Wesley, 1984.

BEM, SANDRA LIPSITZ. "Gender Schema Theory: A Cognitive Account of Sex-Typing." *Psychological Review*. Vol. 88, No. 4 (July 1981):354–64.

BENEDICT, RUTH. "Continuities and Discontinuities in Cultural Conditioning." *Psychiatry*. Vol. 1 (May 1938):161–67.

———. *The Chrysanthemum and the Sword: Patterns of Japanese Culture*. New York: New American Library, 1974; orig. 1946.

BENJAMIN, LOIS. *The Black Elite: Facing the Color Line in the Twilight of the Twentieth Century*. Chicago: Nelson-Hall, 1991.

BENNETT, NEIL G., DAVID E. BLOOM, and PATRICIA H. CRAIG. "The Divergence of Black and White Marriage Patterns." *American Journal of Sociology*. Vol. 95, No. 3 (November 1989):692–722.

BENNETT, WILLIAM J. "Quantifying America's Decline." *Wall Street Journal* (March 15, 1993).

BENOKRAITIS, NIJOLE, and JOE FEAGIN. *Modern Sexism: Blatant, Subtle, and Overt Discrimination*. Englewood Cliffs, N.J.: Prentice Hall, 1986; 2d ed., 1994.

BERARDO, F. M. "Survivorship and Social Isolation: The Case of the Aged Widower." *The Family Coordinator*. Vol. 19 (January 1970):11–25.

BERGER, PETER L. *Invitation to Sociology*. New York: Anchor Books, 1963.

———. *The Sacred Canopy: Elements of a Sociological Theory of Religion*. Garden City, N.Y.: Doubleday, 1967.

———. *Facing Up to Modernity: Excursions in Society, Politics, and Religion*. New York: Basic Books, 1977.

———. *The Capitalist Revolution: Fifty Propositions About Prosperity, Equality, and Liberty*. New York: Basic Books, 1986.

BERGER, PETER, BRIGITTE BERGER, and HANSFRIED KELLNER. *The Homeless Mind: Modernization and Consciousness*. New York: Vintage Books, 1974.

BERGER, PETER L., and THOMAS LUCKMANN. *The Social Construction of Reality: A Treatise in the Sociology of Knowledge*. Garden City, N.Y.: Anchor Books, 1967.

BERGESEN, ALBERT, ED. *Crises in the World-System*. Beverly Hills, Calif.: Sage, 1983.

BERNARD, JESSIE. *The Female World*. New York: Free Press, 1981.

———. *The Future of Marriage*. New Haven, Conn.: Yale University Press, 1982; orig. 1973.

BERNARD, LARRY CRAIG. "Multivariate Analysis of New Sex Role Formulations and Personality." *Journal of Personality and Social Psychology*. Vol. 38, No. 2 (February 1980):323–36.

BERNSTEIN, RICHARD J. *The New Constellation: The Ethical-Political Horizons of Modernity/Postmodernity*. Cambridge, Mass.: MIT Press, 1992.

BERRILL, KEVIN T. "Anti-Gay Violence and Victimization in the United States: An Overview." In Gregory M. Herek and Kevin T. Berrill, *Hate Crimes: Confronting Violence*

Against Lesbians and Gay Men. Newbury Park, Calif.: Sage, 1992:19–45.

BERRY, BRIAN L., and PHILIP H. REES. "The Factorial Ecology of Calcutta." *American Journal of Sociology*. Vol. 74, No. 5 (March 1969):445–91.

BERSCHEID, ELLEN, and ELAINE HATFIELD. *Interpersonal Attraction*. 2d ed. Reading, Mass.: Addison-Wesley, 1983.

BEST, RAPHAELA. *We've All Got Scars: What Boys and Girls Learn in Elementary School*. Bloomington: Indiana University Press, 1983.

BIBLARZ, TIMOTHY J., and ADRIAN E. RAFTERY. "The Effects of Family Disruption on Social Mobility." *American Sociological Review*. Vol. 58, No. 1 (February 1993):97–109.

BLAU, JUDITH R., and PETER M. BLAU. "The Cost of Inequality: Metropolitan Structure and Violent Crime." *American Sociological Review*. Vol. 47, No. 1 (February 1982):114–29.

BLAU, PETER M. *Exchange and Power in Social Life*. New York: Wiley, 1964.

——. *Inequality and Heterogeneity: A Primitive Theory of Social Structure*. New York: Free Press, 1977.

BLAU, PETER M., TERRY C. BLUM, and JOSEPH E. SCHWARTZ. "Heterogeneity and Intermarriage." *American Sociological Review*. Vol. 47, No. 1 (February 1982):45–62.

BLAU, PETER M., and OTIS DUDLEY DUNCAN. *The American Occupational Structure*. New York: Wiley, 1967.

BLAUSTEIN, ALBERT P., and ROBERT L. ZANGRANDO. *Civil Rights and the Black American*. New York: Washington Square Press, 1968.

BLOOM, LEONARD. "Familial Adjustments of Japanese-Americans to Relocation: First Phase." In Thomas F. Pettigrew, ed., *The Sociology of Race Relations*. New York: Free Press, 1980:163–67.

BLUM, LINDA M. *Between Feminism and Labor: The Significance of the Comparable Worth Movement*. Berkeley: University of California Press, 1991.

BLUMBERG, PAUL. *Inequality in an Age of Decline*. New York: Oxford University Press, 1981.

BLUMER, HERBERT G. "Collective Behavior." In Alfred McClung Lee, ed., *Principles of Sociology*. 3d ed. New York: Barnes & Noble Books, 1969:65–121.

BLUMSTEIN, PHILIP, and PEPPER SCHWARTZ. *American Couples*. New York: William Morrow, 1983.

BOFF, LEONARD and CLODOVIS. *Salvation and Liberation: In Search of a Balance Between Faith and Politics*. Maryknoll, N.Y.: Orbis Books, 1984.

BOGARDUS, EMORY S. "Comparing Racial Distance in Ethiopia, South Africa, and the United States." *Sociology and Social Research*. Vol. 52, No. 2 (January 1968):149–56.

BOHM, ROBERT M. "American Death Penalty Opinion, 1936–1986: A Critical Examination of the Gallup Polls." In Robert M. Bohm, ed., *The Death Penalty in America: Current Research*. Cincinnati: Anderson Publishing Co., 1991:113–45.

BONILLA-SANTIAGO, GLORIA. "A Portrait of Hispanic Women in the United States." In Sara E. Rix, ed., *The American Woman 1990–91: A Status Report*. New York: Norton, 1990:249–57.

BONNER, JANE. Research presented in "The Two Brains." Public Broadcasting System telecast, 1984.

BOOTH, ALAN, and LYNN WHITE. "Thinking About Divorce." *Journal of Marriage and the Family*. Vol. 42, No. 3 (August 1980):605–16.

BORGMANN, ALBERT. *Crossing the Postmodern Divide*. Chicago: University of Chicago Press, 1992.

BORMANN, F. HERBERT. "The Global Environmental Deficit." *Bioscience*. Vol. 40 (1990):74.

BORMANN, F. HERBERT, and STEPHEN R. KELLERT. "The Global Environmental Deficit." In Herbert F. Bohrmann and Stephen R. Kellert, eds., *Ecology, Economics, and Ethics: The Broken Circle*. New Haven, Conn.: Yale University Press, 1991:ix–xviii.

BOSWELL, TERRY E. "A Split Labor Market Analysis of Discrimination Against Chinese Immigrants, 1850–1882." *American Sociological Review*. Vol. 51, No. 3 (June 1986):352–71.

BOTT, ELIZABETH. *Family and Social Network*. New York: Free Press, 1971; orig. 1957.

BOWLES, SAMUEL, and HERBERT GINTIS. *Schooling in Capitalist America: Educational Reform and the Contradictions of Economic Life*. New York: Basic Books, 1976.

BOYER, ERNEST L. *College: The Undergraduate Experience in America*. Prepared by The Carnegie Foundation for the Advancement of Teaching. New York: Harper & Row, 1987.

BRAITHWAITE, JOHN. "The Myth of Social Class and Criminality Reconsidered." *American Sociological Review*. Vol. 46, No. 1 (February 1981):36–57.

BRANEGAN, JAY. "Is Singapore a Model for the West?" *Time*. Vol. 141, No. 3 (January 18, 1993):36–37.

BRINTON, CRANE. *The Anatomy of Revolution*. New York: Vintage Books, 1965.

BRINTON, MARY C. "The Social-Institutional Bases of Gender Stratification: Japan as an Illustrative Case." *American Journal of Sociology*. Vol. 94, No. 2 (September 1988):300–34.

BROPHY, GWENDA. "China: Part I." *Population Today*. Vol. 17, No. 3 (March 1989a):12.

——. "China: Part II." *Population Today*. Vol. 17. No. 4 (April 1989b):12.

BROWN, E. RICHARD. *Rockefeller Medicine Men: Medicine and Capitalism in America*. Berkeley: University of California Press, 1979.

BROWN, LESTER R., et al., eds. *State of the World 1993: A Worldwatch Institute Report on Progress Toward a Sustainable Society*. New York: Norton, 1993.

BROWN, MARY ELLEN, ed. *Television and Women's Culture: The Politics of the Popular*. Newbury Park, Calif.: Sage, 1990.

BROWNMILLER, SUSAN. *Against Our Will: Men, Women and Rape*. New York: Simon and Schuster, 1975.

BROWNMILLER, SUSAN. *Femininity*. New York: Linden Press/ Simon and Schuster, 1984.

BROWNSTEIN, RONALD, and NINA EASTON. *Reagan's Ruling Class: Portraits of the President's Top One Hundred Officials*. New York: Pantheon Books, 1983.

BURCH, ROBERT. Testimony to House of Representatives Hearing in "Review: The World Hunger Problem." October 25, 1983, Serial 98–38.

BUREAU OF NATIONAL AFFAIRS. "The Challenge of Diversity: Equal Employment and Managing Difference in the 1990s." Summary report. Washington, D.C.: The Bureau of National Affairs, 1990.

BURKE, TOM. "The Future." In Sir Edmund Hillary, ed., *Ecology 2000: The Changing Face of the Earth*. New York: Beaufort Books, 1984:227–41.

BURNS, JAMES A. "Discipline: Why Does It Continue To Be a Problem? Solution Is in Changing School Culture." *National Association of Secondary School Principals Bulletin*. Vol. 69, No. 479 (March 1985):1–47.

BUSBY, LINDA J. "Sex Role Research on the Mass Media." *Journal of Communications*. Vol. 25 (Autumn 1975):107–13.

CALLAHAN, DANIEL. *Setting Limits: Medical Goals in an Aging Society*. New York: Simon and Schuster, 1987.

CAMERON, WILLIAM BRUCE. *Modern Social Movements: A Sociological Outline*. New York: Random House, 1966.

CANTOR, MURIAL G., and SUZANNE PINGREE. *The Soap Opera*. Beverly Hills, Calif.: Sage, 1983.

CAPLOW, THEODORE, et al. *Middletown Families*. Minneapolis: University of Minnesota Press, 1982.

CAPLOW, THEODORE, HOWARD M. BAHR, JOHN MODELL, and BRUCE A. CHADWICK. *Recent Social Trends in the United States, 1960–1990*. Montreal: McGill-Queen's University Press, 1991.

CARLSON, NORMAN A. "Corrections in the United States Today: A Balance Has Been Struck." *The American Criminal Law Review*. Vol. 13, No. 4 (Spring 1976):615–47.

CARMICHAEL, STOKELY, and CHARLES V. HAMILTON. *Black Power: The Politics of Liberation in America*. New York: Vintage Books, 1967.

CARROLL, GINNY. "Who Foots the Bill?" *Newsweek*. Special Issue (Fall-Winter, 1990):81–85.

CENTER FOR MEDIA AND PUBLIC AFFAIRS. 1991 report by Robert Lichter, Linda Lichter, and Stanley Rothman.

CENTER FOR THE STUDY OF SPORT IN SOCIETY. *1991 Racial Report Card: A Study in the NBA, NFL, and Major League Baseball*. Boston: Northeastern University, 1993.

CHAGNON, NAPOLEON A. *Yanomamö: The Fierce People*. 3d ed. New York: Holt, Rinehart & Winston, 1983; 4th ed., 1992.

CHANDLER, TERTIUS, and GERALD FOX. *3000 Years of Urban History*. New York: Academic Press, 1974.

CHANGE, KWANG-CHIH. *The Archaeology of Ancient China*. New Haven, Conn.: Yale University Press, 1977.

CHERLIN, ANDREW, and FRANK F. FURSTENBERG, JR. "The American Family in the Year 2000." *The Futurist*. Vol. 17, No. 3 (June 1983):7–14.

———. *The New American Grandparent: A Place in the Family, a Life Apart*. New York: Basic Books, 1986.

CHILDREN'S DEFENSE FUND. *Child Poverty in America*. Washington, D.C.: 1991.

———. *The State of America's Children, 1992*. Washington, D.C.: 1992.

CHURCH, GEORGE J. "Please Help Us." *Time*. Vol. 142, No. 19 (November 8, 1993):36–38.

CLARK, THOMAS A. *Blacks in Suburbs*. New Brunswick, N.J.: Rutgers University Center for Urban Policy Research, 1979.

CLARKE, ROBIN. "Atmospheric Pollution." In Sir Edmund Hillary, ed., *Ecology 2000: The Changing Face of the Earth*. New York: Beaufort Books, 1984a:130–48.

———. "What's Happening to Our Water?" In Sir Edmund Hillary, ed., *Ecology 2000: The Changing Face of the Earth*. New York: Beaufort Books, 1984b:108–29.

CLINARD, MARSHALL, and DANIEL ABBOTT. *Crime in Developing Countries*. New York: Wiley, 1973.

CLOWARD, RICHARD A., and LLOYD E. OHLIN. *Delinquency and Opportunity: A Theory of Delinquent Gangs*. New York: Free Press, 1966.

COAKLEY, JAY J. *Sport in Society: Issues and Controversies*. 3d ed. St. Louis, Mo.: Mosby, 1986; 4th ed., 1990.

COE, MICHAEL D., and RICHARD A. DIEHL. *In the Land of the Olmec*. Austin: University of Texas Press, 1980.

COHEN, ALBERT K. *Delinquent Boys: The Culture of the Gang*. New York: Free Press, 1971; orig. 1955.

COHEN, LLOYD R. "Sexual Harassment and the Law." *Society*. Vol. 28, No. 4 (May-June 1991):8–13.

COHEN, MICHAEL. "Restructuring the System." *Transaction*. Vol. 26, No. 4 (May-June 1989):40–48.

COLEMAN, JAMES S., and THOMAS HOFFER. *Public and Private High Schools: The Impact of Communities*. New York: Basic Books, 1987.

COLEMAN, JAMES, THOMAS HOFFER, and SALLY KILGORE. *Public and Private Schools: An Analysis of Public Schools and Beyond*. Washington, D.C.: National Center for Education Statistics, 1981.

COLEMAN, RICHARD P., and BERNICE L. NEUGARTEN. *Social Status in the City*. San Francisco: Jossey-Bass, 1971.

COLEMAN, RICHARD P., and LEE RAINWATER. *Social Standing in America*. New York: Basic Books, 1978.

COLLINS, RANDALL. "A Conflict Theory of Sexual Stratification." *Social Problems*. Vol. 19, No. 1 (Summer 1971):3–21.

———. *The Credential Society: An Historical Sociology of Education and Stratification*. New York: Academic Press, 1979.

———. *Sociological Insight: An Introduction to Nonobvious Sociology*. New York: Oxford University Press, 1982.

COLLOWAY, N. O., and PAULA L. DOLLEVOET. "Selected Tabular Material on Aging." In Caleb Finch and Leonard Hayflick, eds., *Handbook of the Biology of Aging*. New York: Van Nostrand Reinhold, 1977:666–708.

COMTE, AUGUSTE. *Auguste Comte and Positivism: The Essential Writings*. Gertrud Lenzer, ed. New York: Harper Torchbooks, 1975.

CONNETT, PAUL H. "The Disposable Society." In F. Herbert Bormann and Stephen R. Kellert, eds., *Ecology, Economics, and Ethics: The Broken Circle*. New Haven, Conn.: Yale University Press, 1991:99–122.

CONTRERAS, JOSEPH. "A New Day Dawns." *Newsweek* (March 30, 1992):40–41.

COOK, RHODES. "House Republicans Scored a Quiet Victory in '92." *Congressional Quarterly Weekly Report*. Vol. 51, No. 16 (April 17, 1993):965–68.

COOLEY, CHARLES HORTON. *Human Nature and the Social Order*. New York: Schocken Books, 1964; orig. 1902.

CORLEY, ROBERT N., O. LEE REED, PETER J. SHEDD, and JERE W. MOREHEAD. *The Legal and Regulatory Environment of Business*. 9th ed. New York: McGraw-Hill, 1993.

COUNCIL ON INTERNATIONAL EDUCATIONAL EXCHANGE. *Educating for Global Competence: The Report of the Advisory Committee for International Educational Exchange*. New York: The Council, 1988.

COUNTS, G. S. "The Social Status of Occupations: A Problem in Vocational Guidance." *School Review*. Vol. 33 (January 1925):16–27.

COURTNEY, ALICE E., and THOMAS W. WHIPPLE. *Sex Stereotyping in Advertising*. Lexington, Mass.: D.C. Heath, 1983.

COWAN, CAROLYN POPE. *When Partners Become Parents*. New York: Basic Books, 1992.

COX, HARVEY. *The Secular City*. Rev. ed. New York: Macmillan, 1971; orig. 1965.

———. *Turning East: The Promise and Peril of the New Orientalism*. New York: Simon and Schuster, 1977.

CRISPELL, DIANE. "Working in 2000." *American Demographics*. Vol. 12, No. 3 (March 1990):36–40.

———. "Sex Surveys: Does Anyone Tell the Truth?" *American Demographics*. Vol. 15, No. 7 (July 1993):9–10.

———. "Grandparents Galore." *American Demographics*. Vol. 15, No. 10 (October 1993):63.

CROOK, STEPHAN, JAN PAKULSKI, and MALCOLM WATERS. *Postmodernity: Change in Advanced Society*. Newbury Park, Calif.: Sage, 1992.

CROUSE, JAMES, and DALE TRUSHEIM. *The Case Against the SAT*. Chicago: University of Chicago Press, 1988.

CURRIE, ELLIOTT. *Confronting Crime: An American Challenge*. New York: Pantheon Books, 1985.

DAHL, ROBERT A. *Who Governs?* New Haven, Conn.: Yale University Press, 1961.

———. *Dilemmas of Pluralist Democracy: Autonomy vs. Control*. New Haven, Conn.: Yale University Press, 1982.

DAHRENDORF, RALF. *Class and Class Conflict in Industrial Society*. Stanford, Calif.: Stanford University Press, 1959.

DALY, MARTIN, and MARGO WILSON. *Homicide*. New York: Aldine, 1988.

DANIELS, ROGER. "The Issei Generation." In Amy Tachiki et al., eds., *Roots: An Asian American Reader*. Los Angeles: UCLA Asian American Studies Center, 1971:138–49.

DANNEFER, DALE. "Adult Development and Social Theory: A Reappraisal." *American Sociological Review*. Vol. 49, No. 1 (February 1984):100–16.

DAVIES, CHRISTIE. *Ethnic Humor Around the World: A Comparative Analysis*. Bloomington: Indiana University Press, 1990.

DAVIES, JAMES C. "Toward a Theory of Revolution." *American Sociological Review*. Vol. 27, No. 1 (February 1962):5–19.

DAVIES, MARK, and DENISE B. KANDEL. "Parental and Peer Influences on Adolescents' Educational Plans: Some Further Evidence." *American Journal of Sociology*. Vol. 87, No. 2 (September 1981):363–87.

DAVIS, CHARLES L. "Lifting the Gay Ban." *Society*. Vol. 31, No. 1 (November-December 1993):24–36.

DAVIS, KINGSLEY. "Extreme Social Isolation of a Child." *American Journal of Sociology*. Vol. 45, No. 4 (January 1940):554–65.

———. "Final Note on a Case of Extreme Isolation." *American Journal of Sociology*. Vol. 52, No. 5 (March 1947):432–37.

DAVIS, KINGSLEY, and WILBERT MOORE. "Some Principles of Stratification." *American Sociological Review*. Vol. 10, No. 2 (April 1945):242–49.

DAVIS, SHARON A., and EMIL J. HALLER. "Tracking, Ability, and SES: Further Evidence on the 'Revisionist-Meritocratic Debate.'" *American Journal of Education*. Vol. 89 (May 1981):283–304.

DECKARD, BARBARA SINCLAIR. *The Women's Movement: Political, Socioeconomic, and Psychological Issues*. 2d ed. New York: Harper & Row, 1979.

DEDRICK, DENNIS K., and RICHARD E. YINGER. "MAD, SDI, and the Nuclear Arms Race." Manuscript in development. Georgetown, Ky.: Georgetown College, 1990.

DELACROIX, JACQUES, and CHARLES C. RAGIN. "Structural Blockage: A Crossnational Study of Economic Dependency, State Efficacy, and Underdevelopment." *American Journal of Sociology*. Vol. 86, No. 6 (May 1981):1311–47.

DEMO, DAVID. Cited in "Women Still Chained to Housework." *USA Today Magazine*. Vol. 122 (January 1994):10.

DEPARLE, JASON. "Painted by Numbers, 1980s are Rosy to GOP, While Democrats See Red." *New York Times* (September 26, 1991a):B10.

———. "Poverty Rate Rose Sharply Last Year as Incomes Slipped." *New York Times* (September 27, 1991b):A1, A11.

DER SPIEGEL. "Third World Metropolises Are Becoming Monsters; Rural Poverty Drives Millions to the Slums." In *World Press Review* (October 1989).

DEVINE, JOEL A. "State and State Expenditure: Determinants of Social Investment and Social Consumption Spending in the Postwar United States." *American Sociological Review.* Vol. 50, No. 2 (April 1985):150–65.

DEWEY, JOHN. *Experience and Education.* New York: Collier Books, 1968; orig. 1938.

DIZARD, JAN E., and HOWARD GADLIN. *The Minimal Family.* Amherst: The University of Massachusetts Press, 1990.

DOBYNS, HENRY F. "An Appraisal of Techniques with a New Hemispheric Estimate." *Current Anthropology.* Vol. 7, No. 4 (October 1966):395–446.

DOLLARD, JOHN, et al. *Frustration and Aggression.* New Haven, Conn.: Yale University Press, 1939.

DOMHOFF, G. WILLIAM. *Who Rules America Now? A View of the '80s.* Englewood Cliffs, N.J.: Prentice Hall, 1983.

DONOVAN, VIRGINIA K., and RONNIE LITTENBERG. "Psychology of Women: Feminist Therapy." In Barbara Haber, ed., *The Women's Annual 1981: The Year in Review.* Boston: G. K. Hall, 1982:211–35.

DOYLE, JAMES A. *The Male Experience.* Dubuque, Iowa: Wm. C. Brown, 1983.

DUBOS, RENÉ. *Man Adapting.* New Haven, Conn.: Yale University Press, 1980; orig. 1965.

DUNLAP, RILEY E., GEORGE H. GALLUP, JR., and ALEC M. GALLUP. *The Health of the Planet Survey.* Princeton, N.J.: The George H. Gallup International Institute, 1992.

DUNN, JOHN. "Peddling Big Brother." *Time.* Vol. 137, No. 25 (June 24, 1991):62.

DURKHEIM, EMILE. *The Division of Labor in Society.* New York: Free Press, 1964a; orig. 1895.

———. *The Rules of Sociological Method.* New York: Free Press, 1964b; orig. 1893.

———. *The Elementary Forms of Religious Life.* New York: Free Press, 1965; orig. 1915.

DURNING, ALAN THEIN. "Supporting Indigenous Peoples." In Lester R. Brown et al., eds., *State of the World 1993: A Worldwatch Institute Report on Progress Toward a Sustainable Society.* New York: Norton, 1993:80–100.

DWORKIN, ANDREA. *Intercourse.* New York: Free Press, 1987.

EBAUGH, HELEN ROSE FUCHS. *Becoming an EX: The Process of Role Exit.* Chicago: University of Chicago Press, 1988.

ECKHOLM, ERIK, and JOHN TIERNEY. "AIDS in Africa: A Killer Rages On." *New York Times* (September 16, 1990):A1, 14.

THE ECONOMIST. "Worship Moves in Mysterious Ways." Vol. 326, No. 7802 (March 13, 1993):65, 70.

———. "Taiwan's Little Problem." Vol. 327, No. 7814 (June 5, 1993b):41.

EDMONSTON, BARRY, and THOMAS M. GUTERBOCK. "Is Suburbanization Slowing Down? Recent Trends in Population Deconcentration in U.S. Metropolitan Areas." *Social Forces.* Vol. 62, No. 4 (June 1984):905–25.

EDWARDS, DAVID V. *The American Political Experience.* 3d ed. Englewood Cliffs, N.J.: Prentice Hall, 1985.

EDWARDS, RICHARD. *Contested Terrain: The Transformation of the Workplace in the Twentieth Century.* New York: Basic Books, 1979.

EGGEBEEN, DAVID J., and DANIEL T. LICHTER. "Race, Family Structure and Changing Poverty Among American Children." *American Sociological Review.* Vol. 56, No. 6 (December 1991):801–17.

EHRENREICH, BARBARA. *The Hearts of Men: American Dreams and the Flight from Commitment.* Garden City, N.Y.: Anchor Books, 1983.

EHRENREICH, JOHN. "Introduction." In John Ehrenreich, ed., *The Cultural Crisis of Modern Medicine.* New York: Monthly Review Press, 1978:1–35.

EHRLICH, PAUL R. *The Population Bomb.* New York: Ballantine Books, 1978.

EICHLER, MARGRIT. *Nonsexist Research Methods: A Practical Guide.* Winchester, Mass.: Unwin Hyman, 1988.

EISENSTEIN, ZILLAH R., ed. *Capitalist Patriarchy and the Case for Socialist Feminism.* New York: Monthly Review Press, 1979.

EKMAN, PAUL. "Biological and Cultural Contributions to Body and Facial Movements in the Expression of Emotions." In A. Rorty, ed., *Explaining Emotions.* Berkeley: University of California Press, 1980a:73–101.

———. *Face of Man: Universal Expression in a New Guinea Village.* New York: Garland Press, 1980b.

———. *Telling Lies: Clues to Deceit in the Marketplace, Politics, and Marriage.* New York: Norton, 1985.

EKMAN, PAUL, WALLACE V. FRIESEN, and JOHN BEAR. "The International Language of Gestures." *Psychology Today* (May 1984):64–69.

ELLIOTT, DELBERT S., and SUZANNE S. AGETON. "Reconciling Race and Class Differences in Self-Reported and Official Estimates of Delinquency." *American Sociological Review.* Vol. 45, No. 1 (February 1980):95–110.

ELLISON, CHRISTOPHER G., and DARREN E. SHERKAT. "Conservative Protestantism and Support for Corporal Punishment." *American Sociological Review.* Vol. 58, No. 1 (February 1993):131–44.

EMBER, MELVIN, and CAROL R. EMBER. "The Conditions Favoring Matrilocal versus Patrilocal Residence." *American Anthropologist.* Vol. 73, No. 3 (June 1971):571–94.

EMBER, MELVIN M., and CAROL R. EMBER. *Anthropology.* 6th ed. Englewood Cliffs, N.J.: Prentice Hall, 1991.

EMERSON, JOAN P. "Behavior in Private Places: Sustaining Definitions of Reality in Gynecological Examinations." In H. P. Dreitzel, ed., *Recent Sociology.* Vol. 2. New York: Collier, 1970:74–97.

ENGELS, FRIEDRICH. *The Origin of the Family.* Chicago: Charles H. Kerr & Company, 1902; orig. 1884.

ENGLAND, PAULA. *Comparable Worth: Theories and Evidence.* Hawthorne, N.Y.: Aldine, 1992.

ERIKSON, ROBERT S., NORMAN R. LUTTBEG, and KENT L. TEDIN. *American Public Opinion: Its Origins, Content, and Impact.* 2d ed. New York: Wiley, 1980.

ETZIONI, AMITAI. *A Comparative Analysis of Complex Organization: On Power, Involvement, and Their Correlates.* Rev. and enlarged ed. New York: Free Press, 1975.

———. "Too Many Rights, Too Few Responsibilities." *Society.* Vol. 28, No. 2 (January-February 1991):41–48.

ETZIONI-HALEVY, EVA. *Bureaucracy and Democracy: A Political Dilemma.* Rev. ed. Boston: Routledge & Kegan Paul, 1985.

FALK, GERHARD. Personal communication, 1987.

FALKENMARK, MALIN, and CARL WIDSTRAND. "Population and Water Resources: A Delicate Balance." *Population Bulletin.* Vol. 47, No. 3 (November 1992). Washington, D.C.: Population Reference Bureau.

FALLON, A. E., and P. ROZIN. "Sex Differences in Perception of Desirable Body Shape." *Journal of Abnormal Psychology.* Vol. 94, No. 1 (1985):100–105.

FALLOWS, JAMES. "Immigration: How It's Affecting Us." *The Atlantic Monthly.* Vol. 252 (November 1983):45–52, 55–62, 66–68, 85–90, 94, 96, 99–106.

FARRELL, MICHAEL P., and STANLEY D. ROSENBERG. *Men at Midlife.* Boston: Auburn House, 1981.

FEAGIN, JOE. *The Urban Real Estate Game.* Englewood Cliffs, N.J.: Prentice Hall, 1983.

FEATHERMAN, DAVID L., and ROBERT M. HAUSER. *Opportunity and Change.* New York: Academic Press, 1978.

FEATHERSTONE, MIKE, ed. *Global Culture: Nationalism, Globalization, and Modernity.* London: Sage, 1990.

FERGUSON, TOM. "Medical Self-Care: Self Responsibility for Health." In Arthur C. Hastings et al., eds., *Health for the Whole Person: The Complete Guide to Holistic Medicine.* Boulder, Colo.: Westview Press, 1980:87–109.

FINKELSTEIN, NEAL W., and RON HASKINS. "Kindergarten Children Prefer Same-Color Peers." *Child Development.* Vol. 54, No. 2 (April 1983):502–8.

FIREBAUGH, GLENN. "Growth Effects of Foreign and Domestic Investment." *American Journal of Sociology.* Vol. 98, No. 1 (July 1992):105–30.

FISHER, ELIZABETH. *Woman's Creation: Sexual Evolution and the Shaping of Society.* Garden City, N.Y.: Anchor/Doubleday, 1979.

FISHER, ROGER, and WILLIAM URY. "Getting to YES." In William M. Evan and Stephen Hilgartner, eds., *The Arms Race and Nuclear War.* Englewood Cliffs, N.J.: Prentice Hall, 1988:261–68.

FITZPATRICK, JOSEPH P. *Puerto Rican Americans: The Meaning of Migration to the Mainland.* Englewood Cliffs, N.J.: Prentice Hall, 1971.

———. "Puerto Ricans." In *Harvard Encyclopedia of American Ethnic Groups.* Cambridge, Mass.: Harvard University Press, 1980:858–67.

FLAHERTY, MICHAEL G. "A Formal Approach to the Study of Amusement in Social Interaction." *Studies in Symbolic Interaction.* Vol. 5. New York: JAI Press, 1984:71–82.

———. "Two Conceptions of the Social Situation: Some Implications of Humor." *The Sociological Quarterly.* Vol. 31, No. 1 (Spring 1990).

FLORIDA, RICHARD, and MARTIN KENNEY. "Transplanted Organizations: The Transfer of Japanese Industrial Organization to the U.S." *American Sociological Review.* Vol. 56, No. 3 (June 1991):381–98.

FORD, CLELLAN S., and FRANK A. BEACH. *Patterns of Sexual Behavior.* New York: Harper & Row, 1951.

FOST, DAN. "American Indians in the 1990s." *American Demographics.* Vol. 13, No. 12 (December 1991):26–34.

FRANK, ANDRÉ GUNDER. *On Capitalist Underdevelopment.* Bombay: Oxford University Press, 1975.

———. *Crisis: In the World Economy.* New York: Holmes & Meier, 1980.

———. *Reflections on the World Economic Crisis.* New York: Monthly Review Press, 1981.

FRANKLIN ASSOCIATES. *Characterization of Municipal Solid Waste in the United States, 1960–2000.* Prairie Village, Kans.: Franklin Associates, 1986.

FRANKLIN, JOHN HOPE. *From Slavery to Freedom: A History of Negro Americans.* 3d ed. New York: Vintage Books, 1967.

FRAZIER, E. FRANKLIN. *Black Bourgeoisie: The Rise of a New Middle Class.* New York: Free Press, 1965.

FREDRICKSON, GEORGE M. *White Supremacy: A Comparative Study in American and South African History.* New York: Oxford University Press, 1981.

FRENCH, MARILYN. *Beyond Power: On Women, Men, and Morals.* New York: Summit Books, 1985.

FRIEDRICH, CARL J., and ZBIGNIEW BRZEZINSKI. *Totalitarian Dictatorship and Autocracy.* 2d ed. Cambridge, Mass.: Harvard University Press, 1965.

FRIEDRICH, OTTO. "A Proud Capital's Distress." *Time.* Vol. 124, No. 6 (August 6, 1984):26–30, 33–35.

FRUM, DAVID, and FRANK WOLFE. "If You Gotta Get Sued, Get Sued in Utah." *Forbes.* Vol. 153, No. 2 (January 1994):70–73.

FUCHS, VICTOR R. *Who Shall Live?* New York: Basic Books, 1974.

———. "Sex Differences in Economic Well-Being." *Science.* Vol. 232 (April 25, 1986):459–64.

FUGITA, STEPHEN S., and DAVID J. O'BRIEN. "Structural Assimilation, Ethnic Group Membership, and Political Participation among Japanese Americans: A Research Note." *Social Forces.* Vol. 63, No. 4 (June 1985):986–95.

FUJIMOTO, ISAO. "The Failure of Democracy in a Time of Crisis." In Amy Tachiki et al., eds., *Roots: An Asian American Reader.* Los Angeles: UCLA Asian American Studies Center, 1971:207–14.

FULLERTON, HOWARD N., JR. "Another Look at the Labor Force." *Monthly Labor Review* (November 1993):34.

FURSTENBERG, FRANK F., JR. "The New Extended Family: The Experience of Parents and Children after Remarriage." Paper presented to the Changing Family Conference XIII: The Blended Family. University of Iowa, 1984.

FURSTENBERG, FRANK F., JR., and ANDREW CHERLIN. *Divided Families: What Happens to Children When Parents Part.* Cambridge, Mass.: Harvard University Press, 1991.

GAGLIANI, GIORGIO. "How Many Working Classes?" *American Journal of Sociology.* Vol. 87, No. 2 (September 1981):259–85.

GALLUP, GEORGE, JR. *Religion in America.* Princeton, N.J.: Princeton Religion Research Center, 1982.

GALSTER, GEORGE. "Black Suburbanization: Has It Changed the Relative Location of Races?" *Urban Affairs Quarterly.* Vol. 26, No. 4 (June 1991):621–28.

GAMBLE, ANDREW, STEVE LUDLAM, and DAVID BAKER. "Britain's Ruling Class." *The Economist.* Vol. 326, No. 7795 (January 23, 1993):10.

GANS, HERBERT J. *People and Plans: Essays on Urban Problems and Solutions.* New York: Basic Books, 1968.

———. *Popular Culture and High Culture.* New York: Basic Books, 1974.

———. *Deciding What's News: A Study of CBS Evening News, NBC Nightly News, Newsweek and Time.* New York: Vintage Books, 1980.

———. *The Urban Villagers: Group and Class in the Life of Italian-Americans.* New York: Free Press, 1982; orig. 1962.

GARFINKEL, HAROLD. "Conditions of Successful Degradation Ceremonies." *American Journal of Sociology.* Vol. 61, No. 2 (March 1956):420–24.

———. *Studies in Ethnomethodology.* Cambridge: Polity Press, 1967.

GEERTZ, CLIFFORD. "Common Sense as a Cultural System." *The Antioch Review.* Vol. 33, No. 1 (Spring 1975):5–26.

GEIST, WILLIAM. *Toward a Safe and Sane Halloween and Other Tales of Suburbia.* New York: Times Books, 1985.

GELLES, RICHARD J., and CLAIRE PEDRICK CORNELL. *Intimate Violence in Families.* 2d ed. Newbury Park, Calif.: Sage, 1990.

GELMAN, DAVID. "Who's Taking Care of Our Parents?" *Newsweek* (May 6, 1985):61–64, 67–68.

———. "Born or Bred?" *Newsweek* (February 24, 1992):46–53.

GEORGE, SUSAN. *How the Other Half Dies: The Real Reasons for World Hunger.* Totowa, N.J.: Rowman & Allanheld, 1977.

GERSTEL, NAOMI. "Divorce and Stigma." *Social Problems.* Vol. 43, No. 2 (April 1987):172–86.

GESCHWENDER, JAMES A. *Racial Stratification in America.* Dubuque, Iowa: Wm. C. Brown, 1978.

GIBBONS, DON C., and MARVIN D. KROHN. *Delinquent Behavior.* 4th ed. Englewood Cliffs, N.J.: Prentice Hall, 1986.

GIBBS, NANCY. "When Is It Rape?" *Time.* Vol. 137, No. 22 (June 3, 1991a):48–54.

———. "The Clamor on Campus." *Time.* Vol. 137, No. 22 (June 3, 1991b):54–55.

GIDDENS, ANTHONY. *Sociology: A Brief but Critical Introduction.* New York: Harcourt Brace Jovanovich, 1982.

GIELE, JANET Z. "Gender and Sex Roles." In Neil J. Smelser, ed., *Handbook of Sociology.* Newbury Park, Calif.: Sage, 1988:291–323.

GILBERT, DENNIS, and JOSEPH A. KAHL. *The American Class Structure: A New Synthesis.* 4th ed. Belmont, Calif.: Wadsworth, 1993.

GILLIGAN, CAROL. *In a Different Voice: Psychological Theory and Women's Development.* Cambridge, Mass.: Harvard University Press, 1982.

GIMENEZ, MARTHA E. "Silence in the Classroom: Some Thoughts about Teaching in the 1980s." *Teaching Sociology.* Vol. 17, No. 2 (April 1989):184–91.

GINSBURG, PAUL B. "Market-Oriented Options in Medicare and Medicaid." In Jack B. Meyer, ed., *Market Reforms in Health Care: Current Issues, New Directions, Strategic Decisions.* Washington, D.C.: American Enterprise Institute for Public Policy Research, 1983:103–18.

GIOVANNINI, MAUREEN. "Female Anthropologist and Male Informant: Gender Conflict in a Sicilian Town." In John J. Macionis and Nijole V. Benokraitis, eds., *Seeing Ourselves: Classic, Contemporary, and Cross-Cultural Readings in Sociology.* 2d ed. Englewood Cliffs, N.J.: Prentice Hall, 1992:27–32.

GLAAB, CHARLES N. *The American City: A Documentary History.* Homewood, Ill.: Dorsey Press, 1963.

GLADUE, BRIAN A., RICHARD GREEN, and RONALD E. HELLMAN. "Neuroendocrine Response to Estrogen and Sexual Orientation." *Science.* Vol. 225, No. 4669 (September 28, 1984):1496–99.

GLENMARY RESEARCH CENTER. 1990 map series: Major Denominational Families, by Counties of the United States. Atlanta, Ga.: Glenmary Research Center, 1990.

GLENN, NORVAL D., and BETH ANN SHELTON. "Regional Differences in Divorce in the United States." *Journal of Marriage and the Family.* Vol. 47, No. 3 (August 1985):641–52.

GLUCK, PETER R., and RICHARD J. MEISTER. *Cities in Transition.* New York: New Viewpoints, 1979.

GLUECK, SHELDON, and ELEANOR GLUECK. *Unraveling Juvenile Delinquency.* New York: Commonwealth Fund, 1950.

GOETTING, ANN. Personal communication, 1989.

GOFFMAN, ERVING. *The Presentation of Self in Everyday Life.* Garden City, N.Y.: Anchor Books, 1959.

———. *Asylums: Essays on the Social Situation of Mental Patients and Other Inmates.* Garden City, N.Y.: Anchor Books, 1961.

———. *Stigma: Notes on the Management of Spoiled Identity.* Englewood Cliffs, N.J.: Prentice Hall, 1963.

———. *Interactional Ritual: Essays on Face to Face Behavior.* Garden City, N.Y.: Anchor Books, 1967.

GOLD, ALLAN R. "Increasingly, Prison Term is the Price for Polluters." *New York Times* (February 15, 1991):B6.

GOLDBERG, STEVEN. *The Inevitability of Patriarchy.* New York: William Morrow, 1974.

———. Personal communication, 1987.

GOLDFARB, JEFFREY C. *Beyond Glasnost: The Post-Totalitarian Mind.* Chicago: University of Chicago Press, 1989.

GOLDFARB, WILLIAM. "Groundwater: The Buried Life." In F. Herbert Bormann and Stephen R. Kellert, eds., *Ecology, Economics, and Ethics: The Broken Circle.* New Haven, Conn.: Yale University Press, 1991:123–35.

GOLDFIELD, MICHAEL. *The Decline of Organized Labor in the United States.* Chicago and London: University of Chicago Press, 1987.

GOLDSMITH, H. H. "Genetic Influences on Personality from Infancy." *Child Development.* Vol. 54, No. 2 (April 1983):331–35.

GOODE, WILLIAM J. "The Theoretical Importance of Love." *American Sociological Review.* Vol. 24, No. 1 (February 1959):38–47.

———. "Encroachment, Charlatanism, and the Emerging Profession: Psychology, Sociology and Medicine." *American Sociological Review.* Vol. 25, No. 6 (December 1960):902–14.

GOODGAME, DAN. "Ready to Operate." *Time.* Vol. 142, No. 12 (September 20, 1993):54–58.

GORDON, JAMES S. "The Paradigm of Holistic Medicine." In Arthur C. Hastings et al., eds., *Health for the Whole Person: The Complete Guide to Holistic Medicine.* Boulder, Colo.: Westview Press, 1980:3–27.

GORING, CHARLES BUCKMAN. *The English Convict: A Statistical Study.* Montclair, N.J.: Patterson Smith, 1972; orig. 1913.

GORMAN, CHRISTINE. "Mexico City's Menacing Air." *Time.* Vol. 137, No. 13 (April 1, 1991):61.

GORTMAKER, STEVEN L. "Poverty and Infant Mortality in the United States." *American Journal of Sociology.* Vol. 44, No. 2 (April 1979):280–97.

GOTTMANN, JEAN. *Megalopolis.* New York: Twentieth Century Fund, 1961.

GOUGH, KATHLEEN. "The Origin of the Family." *Journal of Marriage and the Family.* Vol. 33, No. 4 (November 1971):760–71.

GOULDNER, ALVIN. *Enter Plato.* New York: Free Press, 1965.

———. "The Sociologist as Partisan: Sociology and the Welfare State." In Larry T. Reynolds and Janice M. Reynolds, eds., *The Sociology of Sociology.* New York: David McKay, 1970a:218–55.

———. *The Coming Crisis of Western Sociology.* New York: Avon Books, 1970b.

GRANOVETTER, MARK. "The Strength of Weak Ties." *American Journal of Sociology.* Vol. 78, No. 6 (May 1973):1360–80.

GRANT, KAREN R. "The Inverse Care Law in the Context of Universal Free Health Insurance in Canada: Toward Meeting Health Needs Through Public Policy." *Sociological Focus.* Vol. 17, No. 2 (April 1984):137–55.

GREELEY, ANDREW M. *Religious Change in America.* Cambridge, Mass.: Harvard University Press, 1989.

———. "Because of the Stories." *The New York Times Magazine* (July 10, 1994):38–41.

GREEN, JOHN C. "Pat Robertson and the Latest Crusade: Resources and the 1988 Presidential Campaign." *Social Sciences Quarterly.* Vol. 74, No. 1 (March 1993):156–68.

GREENBERG, DAVID F. *The Construction of Homosexuality.* Chicago: University of Chicago Press, 1988.

GREENBERG, PAM. "Hate Crimes." *NCSL Legisbrief.* Vol. 2, No. 8 (February 1994).

GREENHOUSE, LINDA. "Justices Uphold Stiffer Sentences for Hate Crimes." *New York Times* (June 12, 1993):1, 8.

GREER, SCOTT. *Urban Renewal and American Cities.* Indianapolis, Ind.: Bobbs-Merrill, 1965.

GREGORY, PAUL R., and ROBERT C. STUART. *Comparative Economic Systems.* 2d ed. Boston: Houghton Mifflin, 1985.

GROSS, JANE. "New Challenge of Youth: Growing Up in a Gay Home." *New York Times* (February 11, 1991):A1, B7.

GUP, TED. "What Makes This School Work?" *Time.* Vol. 140, No. 25 (December 21, 1992):63–65.

GUPTE, PRANAY. *The Crowded Earth: People and the Politics of Population.* New York: Norton, 1984.

GURAK, DOUGLAS T., and JOSEPH P. FITZPATRICK. "Intermarriage Among Hispanic Ethnic Groups in New York City." *American Journal of Sociology.* Vol. 87, No. 4 (January 1982):921–34.

GUTFELD, ROSE. "Enforcing Recycling Laws is a Dirty Job." *Wall Street Journal* (July 29, 1991b):B1.

———. "Eight of Ten Americans are Environmentalists." *Wall Street Journal* (August 2, 1991a):A1.

GWARTNEY-GIBBS, PATRICIA A., JEAN STOCKARD, and SUSANNE BOHMER. "Learning Courtship Aggression: The Influence of Parents, Peers, and Personal Experiences." *Family Relations.* Vol. 36, No. 3 (July 1987):276–82.

HAAS, LINDA. "Domestic Role Sharing in Sweden." *Journal of Marriage and the Family.* Vol. 43, No. 4 (November 1981):957–67.

HABERMAS, JÜRGEN. *Toward a Rational Society: Student Protest, Science, and Politics.* Jeremy J. Shapiro, trans. Boston: Beacon Press, 1970.

HACKER, HELEN MAYER. "Women as a Minority Group." *Social Forces.* Vol. 30 (October 1951):60–69.

———. "Women as a Minority Group: 20 Years Later." In Florence Denmark, ed., *Who Discriminates Against Women?* Beverly Hills, Calif.: Sage, 1974:124–34.

HADAWAY, C. KIRK, PENNY LONG MARLER, and MARK CHAVES. "What the Polls Don't Show: A Closer Look at U.S. Church Attendance." *American Sociological Review.* Vol. 58, No. 6 (December 1993):741–52.

HADDEN, JEFFREY K., and CHARLES E. SWAIN. *Prime Time Preachers: The Rising Power of Televangelism.* Reading, Mass.: Addison-Wesley, 1981.

HAIG, ROBIN ANDREW. *The Anatomy of Humor: Biopsychosocial and Therapeutic Perspectives.* Springfield, Ill.: Charles C. Thomas, 1988.

HALBERSTAM, DAVID. *The Reckoning.* New York: Avon Books, 1986.

HALL, JOHN R., and MARY JO NEITZ. *Culture: Sociological Perspectives*. Englewood Cliffs, N.J.: Prentice Hall, 1993.

HALLINAN, MAUREEN T., and RICHARD A. WILLIAMS. "Interracial Friendship Choices in Secondary Schools." *American Sociological Review*. Vol. 54, No. 1 (February 1989):67–78.

HAMBLIN, DORA JANE. *The First Cities*. New York: Time-Life Books, 1973.

HAMMOND, PHILIP E. "Introduction." In Philip E. Hammond, ed., *The Sacred in a Secular Age: Toward Revision in the Scientific Study of Religion*. Berkeley: University of California Press, 1985:1–6.

HAMRICK, MICHAEL H., DAVID J. ANSPAUGH, and GENE EZELL. *Health*. Columbus, Ohio: Merrill, 1986.

HANDLER, JOEL F., and YEHESKEL HASENFELD. *The Moral Construction of Poverty: Welfare Reform in America*. Newbury Park, Calif.: Sage, 1991.

HANDLIN, OSCAR. *Boston's Immigrants 1790–1865: A Study in Acculturation*. Cambridge, Mass.: Harvard University Press, 1941.

HAREVEN, TAMARA K. "The Life Course and Aging in Historical Perspective." In Tamara K. Hareven and Kathleen J. Adams, eds., *Aging and Life Course Transitions: An Interdisciplinary Perspective*. New York: Guilford Press, 1982:1–26.

HARLOW, HARRY F., and MARGARET KUENNE HARLOW. "Social Deprivation in Monkeys." *Scientific American*. Vol. 207 (November 1962):137–46.

HARRIES, KEITH D. *Serious Violence: Patterns of Homicide and Assault in America*. Springfield, Ill.: Charles C. Thomas, 1990.

HARRINGTON, MICHAEL. *The New American Poverty*. New York: Penguin Books, 1984.

HARRIS, CHAUNCEY D., and EDWARD L. ULLMAN. "The Nature of Cities." *The Annals*. Vol. 242 (November 1945):7–17.

HARRIS, MARVIN. *Cows, Pigs, Wars and Witches: The Riddles of Culture*. New York: Vintage Books, 1975.

———. "Why Men Dominate Women." *New York Times Magazine* (November 13, 1977):46, 115–23.

———. *Good to Eat: Riddle of Food and Culture*. New York: Simon and Schuster, 1985.

———. *Cultural Anthropology*. 2d ed. New York: Harper & Row, 1987.

HARTMANN, BETSY, and JAMES BOYCE. *Needless Hunger: Voices from a Bangladesh Village*. San Francisco: Institute for Food and Development Policy, 1982.

HAVILAND, WILLIAM A. *Anthropology*. 4th ed. New York: Holt, Rinehart & Winston, 1985.

HAYNEMAN, STEPHEN P., and WILLIAM A. LOXLEY. "The Effect of Primary-School Quality on Academic Achievement Across Twenty-nine High- and Low-Income Countries." *American Journal of Sociology*. Vol. 88, No. 6 (May 1983):1162–94.

HELIN, DAVID W. "When Slogans Go Wrong." *American Demographics*. Vol. 14, No. 2 (February 1992):14.

HELMUTH, JOHN W. "World Hunger Amidst Plenty." *USA Today*. Vol. 117, No. 2526 (March 1989):48–50.

HENLEY, NANCY, MYKOL HAMILTON, and BARRIE THORNE. "Womanspeak and Manspeak: Sex Differences in Communication, Verbal and Nonverbal." In John J. Macionis and Nijole V. Benokraitis, eds., *Seeing Ourselves: Classic, Contemporary, and Cross-Cultural Readings in Sociology*, 2d ed. Englewood Cliffs, N.J.: Prentice Hall, 1992:10–15.

HERMAN, DIANNE F. "The Rape Culture." In John J. Macionis and Nijole V. Benokraitis, eds., *Seeing Ourselves: Classic, Contemporary, and Cross-Cultural Readings in Sociology*. 3d ed. Englewood Cliffs, N.J.: Prentice Hall, 1995.

HERMAN, EDWARD S. *Corporate Control, Corporate Power: A Twentieth Century Fund Study*. New York: Cambridge University Press, 1981.

HIRSCHI, TRAVIS. *Causes of Delinquency*. Berkeley: University of California Press, 1969.

HOCHSCHILD, ARLIE, WITH ANNE MACHUNG. *The Second Shift: Working Parents and the Revolution at Home*. New York: Viking Books, 1989.

HODGE, ROBERT W., DONALD J. TREIMAN, and PETER H. ROSSI. "A Comparative Study of Occupational Prestige." In Reinhard Bendix and Seymour Martin Lipset, eds., *Class, Status, and Power: Social Stratification in Comparative Perspective*. 2d ed. New York: Free Press, 1966:309–21.

HOERR, JOHN. "The Payoff from Teamwork." *Business Week*. No. 3114 (July 10, 1989):56–62.

HOGAN, DENNIS P., and EVELYN M. KITAGAWA. "The Impact of Social Status and Neighborhood on the Fertility of Black Adolescents." *American Journal of Sociology*. Vol. 90, No. 4 (January 1985):825–55.

HONEYWELL, ROY J. *The Educational Work of Thomas Jefferson*. Cambridge, Mass.: Harvard University Press, 1931.

HOOK, ERNEST B. "Behavioral Implications of the XYY Genotype." *Science*. Vol. 179 (January 12, 1973):139–50.

HOROWITZ, IRVING LOUIS, et al. "Realities and Fallacies of Homosexuality." *Society*. Vol. 30, No. 5 (July-August 1993):2–3.

HOSTETLER, JOHN A. *Amish Society*. 3d ed. Baltimore: The Johns Hopkins University Press, 1980.

HOWE, NEIL, and WILLIAM STRAUSS. "America's 13th Generation." *New York Times* (April 16, 1991).

HOWLETT, DEBBIE. "Cruzan's Struggle Left Imprint: 10,000 Others in Similar State." *USA Today* (December 27, 1990):3A.

HOYT, HOMER. *The Structure and Growth of Residential Neighborhoods in American Cities*. Washington, D.C.: Federal Housing Administration, 1939.

HSU, FRANCIS L. K. *The Challenge of the American Dream: The Chinese in the United States*. Belmont, Calif.: Wadsworth, 1971.

HUBER, JOAN, and GLENNA SPITZE. "Considering Divorce: An Expansion of Becker's Theory of Marital Instability." *American Journal of Sociology*. Vol. 86, No. 1 (July 1980):75–89.

HUET-COX, ROCIO. "Medical Education: New Wine in Old Wine Skins." In Victor W. Sidel and Ruth Sidel, eds., *Reforming Medicine: Lessons of the Last Quarter Century*. New York: Pantheon Books, 1984:129-49.

HULS, GLENNA. Personal communication, 1987.

HUMPHREY, CRAIG R., and FREDERICK R. BUTTEL. *Environment, Energy, and Society*. Belmont, Calif.: Wadsworth, 1982.

HUMPHRIES, HARRY LEROY. *The Structure and Politics of Intermediary Class Positions: An Empirical Examination of Recent Theories of Class*. Unpublished Ph.D. dissertation. Eugene: University of Oregon, 1984.

HUNT, MORTON. *Sexual Behavior in the 1970s*. Chicago: Playboy Press, 1974.

HUNTER, JAMES DAVISON. *American Evangelicalism: Conservative Religion and the Quandary of Modernity*. New Brunswick, N.J.: Rutgers University Press, 1983.

———. "Conservative Protestantism." In Philip E. Hammond, ed., *The Sacred in a Secular Age*. Berkeley: University of California Press, 1985:50-66.

———. *Evangelicalism: The Coming Generation*. Chicago: University of Chicago Press, 1987.

HURN, CHRISTOPHER. *The Limits and Possibilities of Schooling*. Needham Heights, Mass.: Allyn & Bacon, 1978.

ILLICH, IVAN. *Medical Nemesis: The Expropriation of Health*. New York: Pantheon Books, 1976.

INSTITUTE FOR PHILOSOPHY AND PUBLIC POLICY. "The Graying of America." Vol. 8, No. 2 (Spring 1988):1-5.

ISAY, RICHARD A. *Being Homosexual: Gay Men and Their Development*. New York: Farrar, Straus, & Giroux, 1989.

JACOB, JOHN E. "An Overview of Black America in 1985." In James D. Williams, ed., *The State of Black America 1986*. New York: National Urban League, 1986:i-xi.

JACOBS, JANE. *The Death and Life of Great American Cities*. New York: Random House, 1961.

———. *The Economy of Cities*. New York: Vintage Books, 1970.

JACQUET, CONSTANT H., and ALICE M. JONES. *Yearbook of American and Canadian Churches 1993*. Nashville, Tenn.: Abingdon Press, 1993.

JAGGER, ALISON. "Political Philosophies of Women's Liberation." In Laurel Richardson and Verta Taylor, eds., *Feminist Frontiers: Rethinking Sex, Gender, and Society*. Reading, Mass.: Addison-Wesley, 1983.

JAMES, DAVID R. "City Limits on Racial Equality: The Effects of City-Suburb Boundaries on Public-School Desegregation, 1968-1976." *American Sociological Review*. Vol. 54, No. 6 (December 1989):963-85.

JANIS, IRVING. *Victims of Groupthink*. Boston: Houghton Mifflin, 1972.

———. *Crucial Decisions: Leadership in Policymaking and Crisis Management*. New York: Free Press, 1989.

JENCKS, CHRISTOPHER. "Genes and Crime." *The New York Review* (February 12, 1987):33-41.

JENCKS, CHRISTOPHER, et al. *Inequality: A Reassessment of the Effect of Family and Schooling in America*. New York: Basic Books, 1972.

JENKINS, HOLMAN, JR. "The 'Poverty' Lobby's Inflated Numbers." *Wall Street Journal* (December 14, 1992):A10.

JOHNSON, DIRK. "Census Finds Many Claiming New Identity: Indian." *New York Times* (March 5, 1991):A1, A16.

JOHNSON, PAUL. "The Seven Deadly Sins of Terrorism." In Benjamin Netanyahu, ed., *International Terrorism*. New Brunswick, N.J.: Transaction Books, 1981:12-22.

JOHNSTON, R. J. "Residential Area Characteristics." In D. T. Herbert and R. J. Johnston, eds., *Social Areas in Cities. Vol. 1: Spatial Processes and Form*. New York: Wiley, 1976:193-235.

JOINT ECONOMIC COMMITTEE. *The Concentration of Wealth in the United States: Trends in the Distribution of Wealth Among American Families*. Washington, D.C.: United States Congress, 1986.

JOSEPHY, ALVIN M., JR. *Now That the Buffalo's Gone: A Study of Today's American Indians*. New York: Alfred A. Knopf, 1982.

KAIN, EDWARD L. "A Note on the Integration of AIDS Into the Sociology of Human Sexuality." *Teaching Sociology*. Vol. 15, No. 4 (July 1987):320-23.

———. *The Myth of Family Decline: Understanding Families in a World of Rapid Social Change*. Lexington, Mass.: Lexington Books, 1990.

KAIN, EDWARD L., and SHANNON HART. "AIDS and the Family: A Content Analysis of Media Coverage." Presented to National Council on Family Relations, Atlanta, 1987.

KALISH, RICHARD A. *Late Adulthood: Perspectives on Human Development*. 2d ed. Monterey, Calif.: Brooks/Cole, 1982.

KAMINER, WENDY. "Volunteers: Who Knows What's in It for Them." *Ms.* (December 1984):93-94, 96, 126-28.

KANTER, ROSABETH MOSS. *Men and Women of the Corporation*. New York: Basic Books, 1977.

———. *The Change Masters: Innovation and Entrepreneurship in the American Corporation*. New York: Simon and Schuster, 1983.

———. *When Giants Learn to Dance: Mastering the Challenges of Strategy, Management, and Careers in the 1990s*. New York: Simon and Schuster, 1989.

KANTER, ROSABETH MOSS, and BARRY A. STEIN. "The Gender Pioneers: Women in an Industrial Sales Force." In R. M. Kanter and B. A. Stein, eds., *Life in Organizations*. New York: Basic Books, 1979:134-60.

KANTER, ROSABETH MOSS, and BARRY STEIN. *A Tale of "O": On Being Different in an Organization*. New York: Harper & Row, 1980.

KAPLAN, ERIC B., et al. "The Usefulness of Preoperative Laboratory Screening." *Journal of the American Medical Association*. Vol. 253, No. 24 (June 28, 1985):3576-81.

KAPTCHUK, TED. "The Holistic Logic of Chinese Medicine." In Shepard Bliss et al., eds., *The New Holistic Health*

Handbook. Lexington, Mass.: The Steven Greene Press/Penguin Books, 1985:41.

KARP, DAVID A., and WILLIAM C. YOELS. "The College Classroom: Some Observations on the Meaning of Student Participation." *Sociology and Social Research*. Vol. 60, No. 4 (July 1976):421–39.

KAUFMAN, POLLY WELTS. "Women and Education." In Barbara Haber, ed., *The Women's Annual, 1981: The Year in Review*. Boston: G. K. Hall, 1982:24–55.

KAUFMAN, WALTER. *Religions in Four Dimensions: Existential, Aesthetic, Historical and Comparative*. New York: Reader's Digest Press, 1976.

KELLER, SUZANNE. *The Urban Neighborhood*. New York: Random House, 1968.

KELLERT, STEPHEN R., and F. HERBERT BORMANN. "Closing the Circle: Weaving Strands Among Ecology, Economics, and Ethics." In F. Herbert Bormann and Stephen R. Kellert, eds., *Ecology, Economics, and Ethics: The Broken Circle*. New Haven, Conn.: Yale University Press, 1991:205–10.

KEMP, ALICE ABEL, and SHELLEY COVERMAN. "Marginal Jobs or Marginal Workers: Identifying Sex Differences in Low-Skill Occupations." *Sociological Focus*. Vol. 22, No. 1 (February 1989):19–37.

KENNICKELL, ARTHUR, and JANICE SHACK-MARQUEZ. "Changes in Family Finances from 1983 to 1989: Evidence from the Survey of Consumer Finances." *Federal Reserve Bulletin*. (January 1992):1–18.

KENYON, KATHLEEN. *Digging Up Jericho*. London: Ernest Benn, 1957.

KERCKHOFF, ALAN C., RICHARD T. CAMPBELL, and IDEE WINFIELD-LAIRD. "Social Mobility in Great Britain and the United States." *American Journal of Sociology*. Vol. 91, No. 2 (September 1985):281–308.

KIDRON, MICHAEL, and RONALD SEGAL. *The New State of the World Atlas*. New York: Simon and Schuster, 1991.

KILBOURNE, BROCK K. "The Conway and Siegelman Claims Against Religious Cults: An Assessment of Their Data." *Journal for the Scientific Study of Religion*. Vol. 22, No. 4 (December 1983):380–85.

KILGORE, SALLY B. "The Organizational Context of Tracking in Schools." *American Sociological Review*. Vol. 56, No. 2 (April 1991):189–203.

KING, KATHLEEN PIKER, and DENNIS E. CLAYSON. "The Differential Perceptions of Male and Female Deviants." *Sociological Focus*. Vol. 21, No. 2 (April 1988):153–64.

KING, MARTIN LUTHER, JR. "The Montgomery Bus Boycott." In Walt Anderson, ed., *The Age of Protest*. Pacific Palisades, Calif.: Goodyear, 1969:81–91.

KINKEAD, GWEN. *Chinatown: A Portrait of a Closed Society*. New York: HarperCollins, 1992.

KINSEY, ALFRED, et al. *Sexual Behavior in the Human Male*. Philadelphia: Saunders, 1948.

———. *Sexual Behavior in the Human Female*. Philadelphia: Saunders, 1953.

KIPP, RITA SMITH. "Have Women Always Been Unequal?" In Beth Reed, ed., *Towards a Feminist Transformation of the Academy: Proceedings of the Fifth Annual Women's Studies Conference*. Ann Arbor, Mich.: Great Lakes Colleges Association, 1980:12–18.

KITSON, GAY C., and HELEN J. RASCHKE. "Divorce Research: What We Know, What We Need to Know." *Journal of Divorce*. Vol. 4, No. 3 (Spring 1981):1–37.

KITTRIE, NICHOLAS N. *The Right To Be Different: Deviance and Enforced Therapy*. Baltimore: The Johns Hopkins University Press, 1971.

KLEIN, SUSAN SHURBERG. "Education." In Sarah M. Pritchard, ed., *The Women's Annual, Number 4, 1983–1984*. Boston: G. K. Hall, 1984:9–30.

KLUCKHOHN, CLYDE. "As an Anthropologist Views It." In Albert Deuth, ed., *Sex Habits of American Men*. New York: Prentice Hall, 1948.

KOHLBERG, LAWRENCE. *The Psychology of Moral Development: The Nature and Validity of Moral Stages*. New York: Harper & Row, 1981.

KOHLBERG, LAWRENCE, and CAROL GILLIGAN. "The Adolescent as Philosopher: The Discovery of Self in a Postconventional World." *Daedalus*. Vol. 100 (Fall 1971):1051–86.

KOHN, MELVIN L. *Class and Conformity: A Study in Values*. 2d ed. Homewood, Ill.: Dorsey Press, 1977.

KOMAROVSKY, MIRRA. *Blue Collar Marriage*. New York: Vintage Books, 1967.

———. "Cultural Contradictions and Sex Roles: The Masculine Case." *American Journal of Sociology*. Vol. 78, No. 4 (January 1973):873–84.

KORNHAUSER, WILLIAM. *The Politics of Mass Society*. New York: Free Press, 1959.

KOZOL, JONATHAN. *Prisoners of Silence: Breaking the Bonds of Adult Illiteracy in the United States*. New York: Continuum, 1980.

———. "A Nation's Wealth." *Publisher's Weekly* (May 24, 1985a):28–30.

———. *Illiterate America*. Garden City, N.Y.: Doubleday, 1985b.

———. *Rachel and Her Children: Homeless Families in America*. New York: Crown Publishers, 1988.

KRAFFT, SUSAN. "¿Quién es Numero Uno?" *American Demographics*. Vol. 15, No. 7 (July 1993):16–17.

KRAYBILL, DONALD B., and MARC A. OLSHAN, eds. *The Amish Struggle with Modernity*. Hanover, N.H.: University Press of New England, 1994.

KRIESI, HANSPETER. "New Social Movements and the New Class in the Netherlands." *American Journal of Sociology*. Vol. 94, No. 5 (March 1989):1078–116.

KÜBLER-ROSS, ELISABETH. *On Death and Dying*. New York: Macmillan, 1969.

KUHN, THOMAS. *The Structure of Scientific Revolutions*. 2d ed. Chicago: University of Chicago Press, 1970.

KUZNETS, SIMON. "Economic Growth and Income Inequality." *The American Economic Review*. Vol. XLV, No. 1 (March 1955):1–28.

——. *Modern Economic Growth: Rate, Structure, and Spread.* New Haven, Conn.: Yale University Press, 1966.

LADD, JOHN. "The Definition of Death and the Right to Die." In John Ladd, ed., *Ethical Issues Relating to Life and Death*. New York: Oxford University Press, 1979:118–45.

LAI, H. M. "Chinese." In *Harvard Encyclopedia of American Ethnic Groups*. Cambridge, Mass.: Harvard University Press, 1980:217–33.

LAMBERG-KARLOVSKY, C. C., and MARTHA LAMBERG-KARLOVSKY. "An Early City in Iran." In *Cities: Their Origin, Growth, and Human Impact*. San Francisco: Freeman, 1973:28–37.

LANDERS, RENE M. "Gender, Race, and the State Courts." *Radcliffe Quarterly*. Vol. 76, No. 4 (December 1990):6–9.

LAPPÉ, FRANCES MOORE, and JOSEPH COLLINS. *World Hunger: Twelve Myths*. New York: Grove Press/Food First Books, 1986.

LAPPÉ, FRANCES MOORE, JOSEPH COLLINS, and DAVID KINLEY. *Aid as Obstacle: Twenty Questions about Our Foreign Policy and the Hungry*. San Francisco: Institute for Food and Development Policy, 1981.

LARMER, BROOK. "Dead End Kids." *Newsweek* (May 25, 1992):38–40.

LASLETT, PETER. *The World We Have Lost: England Before the Industrial Age*. 3d ed. New York: Charles Scribner's Sons, 1984.

LAUMANN, EDWARD O., JOHN H. GAGNON, ROBERT T. MICHAEL, and STUART MICHAELS. *The Social Organization of Sexuality: Sexual Practices in the United States*. Chicago: University of Chicago Press, 1994.

LEACOCK, ELEANOR. "Women's Status in Egalitarian Societies: Implications for Social Evolution." *Current Anthropology*. Vol. 19, No. 2 (June 1978):247–75.

LEAVITT, JUDITH WALZER. "Women and Health in America: An Overview." In Judith Walzer Leavitt, ed., *Women and Health in America*. Madison: University of Wisconsin Press, 1984:3–7.

LEE, BARRETT A., R. S. OROPESA, BARBARA J. METCH, and AVERY M. GUEST. "Testing the Decline of Community Thesis: Neighborhood Organization in Seattle, 1929 and 1979." *American Journal of Sociology*. Vol. 89, No. 5 (March 1984):1161–88.

LEERHSEN, CHARLES. "Unite and Conquer." *Newsweek* (February 5, 1990):50–55.

LEMERT, EDWIN M. *Social Pathology*. New York: McGraw-Hill, 1951.

——. *Human Deviance, Social Problems, and Social Control.* 2d ed. Englewood Cliffs, N.J.: Prentice Hall, 1972.

LENGERMANN, PATRICIA MADOO, and RUTH A. WALLACE. *Gender in America: Social Control and Social Change*. Englewood Cliffs, N.J.: Prentice Hall, 1985.

LENSKI, GERHARD. *Power and Privilege: A Theory of Social Stratification*. New York: McGraw-Hill, 1966.

LENSKI, GERHARD, JEAN LENSKI, and PATRICK NOLAN. *Human Societies: An Introduction to Macrosociology*. 6th ed. New York: McGraw-Hill, 1991.

LEONARD, EILEEN B. *Women, Crime, and Society: A Critique of Theoretical Criminology*. New York: Longman, 1982.

LESTER, DAVID. *The Death Penalty: Issues and Answers*. Springfield, Ill.: Charles C. Thomas, 1987.

LEVER, JANET. "Sex Differences in the Complexity of Children's Play and Games." *American Sociological Review*. Vol. 43, No. 4 (August 1978):471–83.

LEVINE, MICHAEL P. *Student Eating Disorders: Anorexia Nervosa and Bulimia*. Washington, D.C.: National Educational Association, 1987.

LEVINE, ROBERT V. "Is Love a Luxury?" *American Demographics*. Vol. 15, No. 2 (February 1993):27–28.

LEVINSON, DANIEL J., with CHARLOTTE N. DARROW, EDWARD B. KLEIN, MARIA H. LEVINSON, and BRAXTON MCKEE. *The Seasons of a Man's Life*. New York: Alfred A. Knopf, 1978.

LEVY, FRANK. *Dollars and Dreams: The Changing American Income Distribution*. New York: Russell Sage Foundation, 1987.

LEWIS, FLORA. "The Roots of Revolution." *New York Times Magazine* (November 11, 1984):70–71, 74, 77–78, 82, 84, 86.

LEWIS, OSCAR. *The Children of Sachez*. New York: Random House, 1961.

LI, JIANG HONG, and ROGER A. WOJTKIEWICZ. "A New Look at the Effects of Family Structure on Status Attainment." *Social Science Quarterly*. Vol. 73, No. 3 (September 1992):581–95.

LIAZOS, ALEXANDER. "The Poverty of the Sociology of Deviance: Nuts, Sluts and Preverts." *Social Problems*. Vol. 20, No. 1 (Summer 1972):103–20.

LICHTER, DANIEL R. "Race, Employment Hardship, and Inequality in the American Nonmetropolitan South." *American Sociological Review*. Vol. 54, No. 3 (June 1989):436–46.

LIEBERSON, STANLEY. *A Piece of the Pie: Black and White Immigrants Since 1880*. Berkeley: University of California Press, 1980.

LIN, NAN, WALTER M. ENSEL, and JOHN C. VAUGHN. "Social Resources and Strength of Ties: Structural Factors in Occupational Status Attainment." *American Sociological Review*. Vol. 46, No. 4 (August 1981):393–405.

LIN, NAN, and WEN XIE. "Occupational Prestige in Urban China." *American Journal of Sociology*. Vol. 93, No. 4 (January 1988):793–832.

LING, PYAU. "Causes of Chinese Emigration." In Amy Tachiki et al., eds., *Roots: An Asian American Reader*. Los Angeles: UCLA Asian American Studies Center, 1971:134–38.

LINO, MARK. "Expenditures on a Child by Families, 1993." *Family Economics Review*. Vol. 7, No. 3 (1994):2–19.

LINTON, RALPH. "One Hundred Percent American." *The American Mercury*. Vol. 40, No. 160 (April 1937):427–29.

———. *The Study of Man.* New York: D. Appleton-Century, 1937.

LISKA, ALLEN E. *Perspectives on Deviance.* 3d ed. Englewood Cliffs, N.J.: Prentice Hall, 1991.

LISKA, ALLEN E., and MARK TAUSIG. "Theoretical Interpretations of Social Class and Racial Differentials in Legal Decision Making for Juveniles." *Sociological Quarterly.* Vol. 20, No. 2 (Spring 1979):197–207.

LISKA, ALLEN E., and BARBARA D. WARNER. "Functions of Crime: A Paradoxical Process." *American Journal of Sociology.* Vol. 96, No. 6 (May 1991):1441–63.

LOGAN, JOHN R., and MARK SCHNEIDER. "Racial Segregation and Racial Change in American Suburbs, 1970–1980." *American Journal of Sociology.* Vol. 89, No. 4 (January 1984):874–88.

LOHR, STEVE. "British Health Service Faces a Crisis in Funds and Delays." *New York Times* (August 7, 1988):1, 12.

LONG, EDWARD V. *The Intruders: The Invasion of Privacy by Government and Industry.* New York: Praeger, 1967.

LORD, WALTER. *A Night to Remember.* Rev. ed. New York: Holt, Rinehart & Winston, 1976.

LORENZ, KONRAD. *On Aggression.* New York: Harcourt, Brace & World, 1966.

LOY, PAMELA HEWITT, and LEA P. STEWART. "The Extent and Effects of Sexual Harassment of Working Women." *Sociological Focus.* Vol. 17, No. 1 (January 1984):31–43.

LUBENOW, GERALD C. "A Troubling Family Affair." *Newsweek* (May 14, 1984):34.

LUTZ, CATHERINE, and GEOFFREY M. WHITE. "The Anthropology of Emotions." In Bernard J. Siegel, Alan R. Beals, and Stephen A. Tyler, eds., *Annual Review of Anthropology.* Palo Alto, Calif.: Annual Reviews, Vol. 15 (1986):405–36.

LUTZ, CATHERINE A. *Unnatural Emotions: Everyday Sentiments on a Micronesia Atoll and Their Challenge to Western Theory.* Chicago: University of Chicago Press, 1988.

LYND, ROBERT S. *Knowledge For What? The Place of Social Science in American Culture.* Princeton, N.J.: Princeton University Press, 1967.

LYND, ROBERT S., and HELEN MERRELL LYND. *Middletown in Transition.* New York: Harcourt, Brace & World, 1937.

MA, LI-CHEN. Personal communication, 1987.

MABRY, MARCUS. "New Hope for Old Unions?" *Newsweek* (February 24, 1992):39.

MCADAM, DOUG, JOHN D. MCCARTHY, and MAYER N. ZALD. "Social Movements." In Neil J. Smelser, ed., *Handbook of Sociology.* Newbury Park, Calif.: Sage, 1988:695–737.

MCCARTHY, JOHN D., and MAYER N. ZALD. "Resource Mobilization and Social Movements: A Partial Theory." *American Journal of Sociology.* Vol. 82, No. 6 (May 1977):1212–41.

MACCOBY, ELEANOR EMMONS, and CAROL NAGY JACKLIN. *The Psychology of Sex Differences.* Palo Alto, Calif.: Stanford University Press, 1974.

MCCOLM, R. BRUCE, JAMES FINN, DOUGLAS W. PAYNE, JOSEPH E. RYAN, LEONARD R. SUSSMAN, and GEORGE ZARYCKY. *Freedom in the World: Political Rights & Civil Liberties, 1990–1991.* New York: Freedom House, 1991.

MACE, DAVID, and VERA MACE. *Marriage East and West.* Garden City, N.Y.: Doubleday (Dolphin), 1960.

MCGUIRE, MEREDITH B. *Religion: The Social Context.* 2d ed. Belmont, Calif.: Wadsworth, 1987.

MACIONIS, JOHN J. "Intimacy: Structure and Process in Interpersonal Relationships." *Alternative Lifestyles.* Vol. 1, No. 1 (February 1978):113–30.

———. "The Search for Community in Modern Society: An Interpretation." *Qualitative Sociology.* Vol. 1, No. 2 (September 1978):130–43.

———. "A Sociological Analysis of Humor." Presentation to the Texas Junior College Teachers Association, Houston, 1987.

———. "Making Society (and, Increasingly, the World) Visible." In Earl Babbie, ed., *The Spirit of Sociology.* Belmont, Calif.: Wadsworth, 1993:221–24.

MACKAY, DONALD G. "Prescriptive Grammar and the Pronoun Problem." In Barrie Thorne, Cheris Kramarae, and Nancy Henley, eds., *Language, Gender and Society.* Rowley, Mass.: Newbury House, 1983:38–53.

MACKINNON, CATHARINE A. *Feminism Unmodified: Discourses on Life and Law.* Cambridge, Mass.: Harvard University Press, 1987.

MACKLIN, ELEANOR D. "Nonmarital Heterosexual Cohabitation: An Overview." In Eleanor D. Macklin and Roger H. Rubin, eds., *Contemporary Families and Alternative Lifestyles: Handbook on Research and Theory.* Beverly Hills, Calif.: Sage, 1983:49–74.

MCKUSICK, LEON, et al. "Reported Changes in the Sexual Behavior of Men at Risk for AIDS, San Francisco, 1982–84—The AIDS Behavioral Research Project." *Public Health Reports.* Vol. 100, No. 6 (November-December 1985):622–29.

MCLANAHAN, SARA. "Family Structure and the Reproduction of Poverty." *American Journal of Sociology.* Vol. 90, No. 4 (January 1985):873–901.

MCLEOD, JANE D., and MICHAEL J. SHANAHAN. "Poverty, Parenting, and Children's Mental Health." *American Sociological Review.* Vol. 58, No. 3 (June 1993):351–66.

MCNEIL, DONALD G., JR. "Should Women Be Sent Into Combat?" *New York Times* (July 21, 1991):E3.

MCRAE, SUSAN. *Cross-Class Families: A Study of Wives' Occupational Superiority.* New York: Oxford University Press, 1986.

MADSEN, AXEL. *Private Power: Multinational Corporations for the Survival of Our Planet.* New York: William Morrow, 1980.

MAJKA, LINDA C. "Sexual Harassment in the Church." *Society.* Vol. 28. No. 4 (May-June 1991):14–21.

MALTHUS, THOMAS ROBERT. *First Essay on Population 1798.* London: Macmillan, 1926; orig. 1798.

MARCUSE, HERBERT. *One-Dimensional Man.* Boston: Beacon Press, 1964.

MARE, ROBERT D. "Five Decades of Educational Assortative Mating." *American Sociological Review.* Vol. 56, No. 1 (February 1991):15–32.

MARGOLICK, DAVID. "Rape in Marriage Is No Longer Within the Law." *New York Times* (December 13, 1984):6E.

MARÍN, GERARDO, and BARBARA VANOSS MARÍN. *Research With Hispanic Populations.* Newbury Park, Calif.: Sage, 1991.

MARKOFF, JOHN. "Remember Big Brother? Now He's a Company Man." *New York Times* (March 31, 1991):7.

MARLIOS, PETER. "Interlocking Directorates and the Control of Corporations: The Theory of Bank Control." *Social Science Quarterly.* Vol. 56, No. 3 (December 1975):425–39.

MARRIOTT, MICHAEL. "Fathers Find that Child Support Means Owing More Than Money." *New York Times* (July 20, 1992):A1, A13.

MARSDEN, PETER. "Core Discussion Networks of Americans." *American Sociological Review.* Vol. 52, No. 1 (February 1987):122–31.

MARSHALL, SUSAN E. "Ladies Against Women: Mobilization Dilemmas of Antifeminist Movements." *Social Problems.* Vol. 32, No. 4 (April 1985):348–62.

MARTIN, JOHN M., and ANNE T. ROMANO. *Multinational Crime: Terrorism, Espionage, Drug and Arms Trafficking.* Newbury Park, Calif.: Sage, 1992.

MARTIN, WILLIAM. "The Birth of a Media Myth." *The Atlantic.* Vol. 247, No. 6 (June 1981):7, 10, 11, 16.

MARULLO, SAM. "The Functions and Dysfunctions of Preparations for Fighting Nuclear War." *Sociological Focus.* Vol. 20, No. 2 (April 1987):135–53.

MARX, KARL. *Karl Marx: Selected Writings in Sociology and Social Philosophy.* T. B. Bottomore, trans. New York: McGraw-Hill, 1964.

———. *Capital.* Friedrich Engels, ed. New York: International Publishers, 1967; orig. 1867.

———. "Theses on Feuer." In Robert C. Tucker, ed., *The Marx-Engels Reader.* New York: Norton, 1972:107–9; orig. 1845.

MARX, KARL, and FRIEDRICH ENGELS. "Manifesto of the Communist Party." In Robert C. Tucker, ed., *The Marx-Engels Reader.* New York: Norton, 1972:331–62; orig. 1848.

———. *The Marx-Engels Reader.* Robert C. Tucker, ed. New York: Norton, 1977.

MASSEY, DOUGLAS S., and NANCY A. DENTON. "Hypersegregation in U.S. Metropolitan Areas: Black and Hispanic Segregation Along Five Dimensions." *Demography.* Vol. 26, No. 3 (August 1989):373–91.

MASTERS, WILLIAM H., VIRGINIA E. JOHNSON, and ROBERT C. KOLODNY. *Human Sexuality.* 3d ed. Glenview, Ill.: Scott, Foresman/Little, Brown, 1988.

MATTHIESSEN, PETER. *In the Spirit of Crazy Horse.* New York: Viking Press, 1983.

———. *Indian Country.* New York: Viking Press, 1984.

MAURO, TONY. "Cruzan's Struggle Left Imprint: Private Case Triggered Public Debate." *USA Today* (December 27, 1990):3A.

MAY, ELAINE TYLER. "Women in the Wild Blue Yonder." *New York Times* (August 7, 1991):21.

MAYO, KATHERINE. *Mother India.* New York: Harcourt, Brace, 1927.

MEAD, GEORGE HERBERT. *Mind, Self, and Society.* Charles W. Morris, ed. Chicago: University of Chicago Press, 1962; orig. 1934.

MEAD, MARGARET. *Sex and Temperament in Three Primitive Societies.* New York: William Morrow, 1963; orig. 1935.

MEADOWS, DONELLA H., DENNIS L. MEADOWS, JORGAN RANDERS, and WILLIAM W. BEHRENS III. *The Limits to Growth: A Report on the Club of Rome's Project on the Predicament of Mankind.* New York: Universe, 1972.

MECHANIC, DAVID. *Medical Sociology.* 2d ed. New York: Free Press, 1978.

MELTZER, BERNARD N. "Mead's Social Psychology." In Jerome G. Manis and Bernard N. Meltzer, eds., *Symbolic Interaction: A Reader in Social Psychology.* 3d ed. Needham Heights, Mass.: Allyn & Bacon, 1978.

MELUCCI, ALBERTO. "The New Social Movements: A Theoretical Approach." *Social Science Information.* Vol. 19, No. 2 (May 1980):199–226.

———. *Nomads of the Present: Social Movements and Individual Needs in Contemporary Society.* Philadelphia: Temple University Press, 1989.

MERTON, ROBERT K. "Social Structure and Anomie." *American Sociological Review.* Vol. 3, No. 6 (October 1938):672–82.

———. *Social Theory and Social Structure.* New York: Free Press, 1968.

———. "Discrimination and the American Creed." In *Sociological Ambivalence and Other Essays.* New York: Free Press, 1976:189–216.

MICHELS, ROBERT. *Political Parties.* Glencoe, Ill.: Free Press, 1949; orig. 1911.

MILBRATH, LESTER W. *Envisioning a Sustainable Society: Learning Our Way Out.* Albany: State University of New York Press, 1989.

MILGRAM, STANLEY. "Behavioral Study of Obedience." *Journal of Abnormal and Social Psychology.* Vol. 67, No. 4 (1963):371–78.

———. "Group Pressure and Action Against a Person." *Journal of Abnormal and Social Psychology.* Vol. 69, No. 2 (August 1964):137–43.

———. "Some Conditions of Obedience and Disobedience to Authority." *Human Relations.* Vol. 18 (February 1965):57–76.

MILIBAND, RALPH. *The State in Capitalist Society.* London: Weidenfield and Nicolson, 1969.

MILLER, ARTHUR G. *The Obedience Experiments: A Case of Controversy in Social Science.* New York: Praeger, 1986.

MILLER, FREDERICK D. "The End of SDS and the Emergence of Weatherman: Demise Through Success." In Jo

Freeman, ed., *Social Movements of the Sixties and Seventies*. New York: Longman, 1983:279–97.

MILLER, G. TYLER, JR. *Living in the Environment: An Introduction to Environmental Science*. Belmont, Calif.: Wadsworth, 1992.

MILLER, MICHAEL. "Lawmakers Begin to Heed Calls to Protect Privacy." *Wall Street Journal* (April 11, 1991):A16.

MILLER, WALTER B. "Lower Class Culture as a Generating Milieu of Gang Delinquency." In Marvin E. Wolfgang, Leonard Savitz, and Norman Johnston, eds., *The Sociology of Crime and Delinquency*. 2d ed. New York: Wiley, 1970:351–63; orig. 1958.

MILLET, KATE. *Sexual Politics*. Garden City, N.Y.: Doubleday, 1970.

MILLMAN, JOEL, NINA MUNK, MICHAEL SCHUMAN, and NEIL WEINBERG. "The World's Wealthiest People." *Forbes*. Vol. 152, No. 1 (July 5, 1993):66–69.

MILLS, C. WRIGHT. *The Power Elite*. New York: Oxford University Press, 1956.

———. *The Sociological Imagination*. New York: Oxford University Press, 1959.

MINK, BARBARA. "How Modernization Affects Women." *Cornell Alumni News*. Vol. III, No. 3 (April 1989):10–11.

MINTZ, BETH, and MICHAEL SCHWARTZ. "Interlocking Directorates and Interest Group Formation." *American Sociological Review*. Vol. 46, No. 6 (December 1981):851–69.

MIROWSKY, JOHN. "The Psycho-Economics of Feeling Underpaid: Distributive Justice and the Earnings of Husbands and Wives." *American Journal of Sociology*. Vol. 92, No. 6 (May 1987):1404–34.

MOLNAR, STEPHEN. *Human Variation: Races, Types, and Ethnic Groups*. 2d ed. Englewood Cliffs, N.J.: Prentice Hall, 1983.

MOLOTCH, HARVEY. "The City as a Growth Machine." *American Journal of Sociology*. Vol. 82, No. 2 (September 1976):309–33.

MOLOTCH, HARVEY L., and DEIRDRE BODEN. "Talking Social Structure: Discourse, Domination, and the Watergate Hearings." *American Sociological Review*. Vol. 50, No. 3 (June 1985):273–88.

MONTAGU, ASHLEY. *The Nature of Human Aggression*. New York: Oxford University Press, 1976.

MOORE, GWEN. "Structural Determinants of Men's and Women's Personal Networks." *American Sociological Review*. Vol. 55, No. 5 (October 1991):726–35.

———. "Gender and Informal Networks in State Government." *Social Science Quarterly*. Vol. 73, No. 1 (March 1992):46–61.

MOORE, JOAN, and HARRY PACHON. *Hispanics in the United States*. Englewood Cliffs, N.J.: Prentice Hall, 1985.

MOORE, WILBERT E. "Modernization as Rationalization: Processes and Restraints." In Manning Nash, ed., *Essays on Economic Development and Cultural Change in Honor of Bert F. Hoselitz*. Chicago: University of Chicago Press, 1977:29–42.

———. *World Modernization: The Limits of Convergence*. New York: Elsevier, 1979.

MORAN, JOHN S., S. O. ARAL, W. C. JENKINS, T. A. PETERMAN, and E. R. ALEXANDER. "The Impact of Sexually Transmitted Diseases on Minority Populations." *Public Health Reports*. Vol. 104, No. 6 (November-December 1989):560–65.

MOSLEY, W. HENRY, and PETER COWLEY. "The Challenge of World Health." *Population Bulletin*. Vol. 46, No. 4 (December 1991). Washington, D.C.: Population Reference Bureau.

MUELLER, DANIEL P., and PHILIP W. COOPER. "Children of Single Parent Families: How Do They Fare as Young Adults?" Presentation to the American Sociological Association, San Antonio, Texas, 1984.

MUMFORD, LEWIS. *The City in History: Its Origins, Its Transformations, and Its Prospects*. New York: Harcourt, Brace & World, 1961.

MURDOCK, GEORGE P. "Comparative Data on the Division of Labor by Sex." *Social Forces*. Vol. 15, No. 4 (May 1937):551–53.

———. "The Common Denominator of Cultures." In Ralph Linton, ed., *The Science of Man in World Crisis*. New York: Columbia University Press, 1945:123–42.

MURDOCK, GEORGE PETER. *Social Structure*. New York: Free Press, 1965; orig. 1949.

MURRAY, PAULI. *Proud Shoes: The History of an American Family*. New York: Harper & Row, 1978.

MYERS, NORMAN. "Disappearing Cultures." In Sir Edmund Hillary, ed., *Ecology 2000: The Changing Face of the Earth*. New York: Beaufort Books, 1984c:162–69.

———. "Humanity's Growth." In Sir Edmund Hillary, ed., *Ecology 2000: The Changing Face of the Earth*. New York: Beaufort Books, 1984a:16–35.

———. "The Mega-Extinction of Animals and Plants." In Sir Edmund Hillary, ed., *Ecology 2000: The Changing Face of the Earth*. New York: Beaufort Books, 1984b:82–107.

———. "Biological Diversity and Global Security." In F. Herbert Bormann and Stephen R. Kellert, eds., *Ecology, Economics, and Ethics: The Broken Circle*. New Haven, Conn.: Yale University Press, 1991:11–25.

MYERS, SHEILA, and HAROLD G. GRASMICK. "The Social Rights and Responsibilities of Pregnant Women: An Application of Parsons' Sick Role Model." Paper presented to Southwestern Sociological Association, Little Rock, Ark., March 1989.

MYRDAL, GUNNAR. *An American Dilemma: The Negro Problem and Modern Democracy*. New York: Harper & Brothers, 1944.

NAJAFIZADEH, MEHRANGIZ, and LEWIS A. MENNERICK. "Sociology of Education or Sociology of Ethnocentrism: The Portrayal of Education in Introductory Sociology Textbooks." *Teaching Sociology*. Vol. 20, No. 3 (July 1992):215–21.

NATIONAL CENTER FOR EDUCATION STATISTICS. *Digest of Education Statistics: 1990*. Washington, D.C.: U.S. Government Printing Office, 1991:244.

———. *Digest of Education Statistics: 1991*. Washington, D.C.: U.S. Government Printing Office, 1992.

NATIONAL CENTER ON WOMEN AND FAMILY LAW. "Marital Rape Exemption Chart: State by State Analysis." Washington, D.C.: The Center, 1991.

NATIONAL COMMISSION ON EXCELLENCE IN EDUCATION. *A Nation at Risk*. Washington, D.C.: U.S. Government Printing Office, 1983.

NEIDERT, LISA J., and REYNOLDS FARLEY. "Assimilation in the United States: An Analysis of Ethnic and Generation Differences in Status and Achievement." *American Sociological Review*. Vol. 50, No. 6 (December 1985):840–50.

NELAN, BRUCE W. "Crimes Without Punishment." *Time*. Vol. 141, No. 2 (January 11, 1993):21.

NEUHOUSER, KEVIN. "The Radicalization of the Brazilian Catholic Church in Comparative Perspective." *American Sociological Review*. Vol. 54, No. 2 (April 1989):233–44.

NEWMAN, WILLIAM M. *American Pluralism: A Study of Minority Groups and Social Theory*. New York: Harper & Row, 1973.

NIEBUHR, R. GUSTAV. "California Top Court to Wrestle With 'Sin' vs. Tenants' Rights." *The Wall Street Journal* (August 25, 1992):B1, B8.

NIELSEN, JOYCE MCCARL, ed. *Feminist Research Methods: Exemplary Readings in the Social Sciences*. Boulder, Colo.: Westview, 1990.

1991 Green Book. U.S. House of Representatives. Washington, D.C.: U.S. Government Printing Office, 1991.

NISBET, ROBERT. "Sociology as an Art Form." In *Tradition and Revolt: Historical and Sociological Essays*. New York: Vintage Books, 1970.

NISBET, ROBERT A. *The Sociological Tradition*. New York: Basic Books, 1966.

———. *The Quest for Community*. New York: Oxford University Press, 1969.

NORC. *General Social Surveys, 1972–1991: Cumulative Codebook*. Chicago: National Opinion Research Center, 1991.

———. *General Social Surveys, 1972–1992: Cumulative Codebook*. Chicago: National Opinion Research Center, 1992.

———. *General Social Surveys, 1972–1993: Cumulative Codebook*. University of Chicago: National Opinion Research Center, 1993.

NUNN, CLYDE Z., HARRY J. CROCKETT, JR., and J. ALLEN WILLIAMS, JR. *Tolerance for Nonconformity*. San Francisco: Jossey-Bass, 1978.

OAKES, JEANNIE. "Classroom Social Relationships: Exploring the Bowles and Gintis Hypothesis." *Sociology of Education*. Vol. 55, No. 4 (October 1982):197–212.

———. *Keeping Track: How High Schools Structure Inequality*. New Haven, Conn.: Yale University Press, 1985.

O'DEA, THOMAS F., and JANET O'DEA AVIAD. *The Sociology of Religion*. 2d ed. Englewood Cliffs, N.J.: Prentice Hall, 1983.

OFFIR, CAROLE WADE. *Human Sexuality*. New York: Harcourt Brace Jovanovich, 1982.

OGBURN, WILLIAM F. *On Culture and Social Change*. Chicago: University of Chicago Press, 1964.

O'HARE, WILLIAM. "In the Black." *American Demographics*. Vol. 11, No. 11 (November 1989):25–29.

———. "The Rise of Hispanic Affluence." *American Demographics*. Vol. 12, No. 8 (August 1990):40–43.

O'HARE, WILLIAM, and JAN LARSON. "Women in Business: Where, What, and Why." *American Demographics*. Vol. 13, No. 7 (July 1991):34–38.

OKIMOTO, DANIEL. "The Intolerance of Success." In Amy Tachiki et al., eds., *Roots: An Asian American Reader*. Los Angeles: UCLA Asian American Studies Center, 1971:14–19.

OLZAK, SUSAN. "Labor Unrest, Immigration, and Ethnic Conflict in Urban America, 1880–1914." *American Journal of Sociology*. Vol. 94, No. 6 (May 1989):1303–33.

ORLANSKY, MICHAEL D., and WILLIAM L. HEWARD. *Voices: Interviews with Handicapped People*. Columbus, Ohio: Merrill, 1981:85, 92, 133–34, 172.

OSTLING, RICHARD N. "Jerry Falwell's Crusade." *Time*. Vol. 126, No. 9 (September 2, 1985):48–52, 55, 57.

OSTRANDER, SUSAN A. "Upper Class Women: The Feminine Side of Privilege." *Qualitative Sociology*. Vol. 3, No. 1 (Spring 1980):23–44.

———. *Women of the Upper Class*. Philadelphia: Temple University Press, 1984.

OUCHI, WILLIAM. *Theory Z: How American Business Can Meet the Japanese Challenge*. Reading, Mass.: Addison-Wesley, 1981.

OWEN, DAVID. *None of the Above: Behind the Myth of Scholastic Aptitude*. Boston: Houghton Mifflin, 1985.

PAMPEL, FRED C., KENNETH C. LAND, and MARCUS FELSON. "A Social Indicator Model of Changes in the Occupational Structure of the United States: 1947-1974." *American Sociological Review*. Vol. 42, No. 6 (December 1977):951–64.

PARCEL, TOBY L., CHARLES W. MUELLER, and STEVEN CUVELIER. "Comparable Worth and Occupational Labor Market: Explanations of Occupational Earnings Differentials." Paper presented to the American Sociological Association, New York, 1986.

PARENTI, MICHAEL. *Inventing Reality: The Politics of the Mass Media*. New York: St. Martin's Press, 1986.

PARILLO, VINCENT N. *Strangers to These Shores*. 4th ed. New York: Macmillan, 1994.

PARK, ROBERT E. *Race and Culture*. Glencoe, Ill.: Free Press, 1950.

PARKINSON, C. NORTHCOTE. *Parkinson's Law and Other Studies in Administration*. New York: Ballantine Books, 1957.

PARSONS, TALCOTT. *Essays in Sociological Theory*. New York: Free Press, 1954.

——. *The Social System*. New York: Free Press, 1964; orig. 1951.

——. *Societies: Evolutionary and Comparative Perspectives*. Englewood Cliffs, N.J.: Prentice Hall, 1966.

PARSONS, TALCOTT, and ROBERT F. BALES, eds. *Family, Socialization and Interaction Process*. New York: Free Press, 1955.

PAUL, ELLEN FRANKEL. "Bared Buttocks and Federal Cases." *Society*. Vol. 28. No. 4 (May-June 1991):4–7.

PEAR, ROBERT, WITH ERIK ECKHOLM. "When Healers are Entrepreneurs: A Debate Over Costs and Ethics." *New York Times* (June 2, 1991):1, 17.

PENNINGS, JOHANNES M. "Organizational Birth Frequencies: An Empirical Investigation." *Administrative Science Quarterly*. Vol. 27, No. 1 (March 1982):120–44.

PERSELL, CAROLINE HODGES. *Education and Inequality: A Theoretical and Empirical Synthesis*. New York: Free Press, 1977.

PESSEN, EDWARD. *Riches, Class, and Power: America Before the Civil War*. New Brunswick, N.J.: Transaction, 1990.

PETER, LAURENCE J., and RAYMOND HULL. *The Peter Principle: Why Things Always Go Wrong*. New York: William Morrow, 1969.

Peters Atlas of the World. New York: Harper & Row, 1990.

PETERS, THOMAS J., and ROBERT H. WATERMAN, JR. *In Search of Excellence: Lessons From America's Best-Run Companies*. New York: Warner Books, 1982.

PHYSICIANS' TASK FORCE ON HUNGER IN AMERICA. "Hunger Reaches Blue-Collar America." Report issued 1987.

PIOTROW, PHYLLIS T. *World Population: The Present and Future Crisis*. Headline Series 251 (October 1980). New York: Foreign Policy Association.

PIRANDELLO, LUIGI. "The Pleasure of Honesty." In *To Clothe the Naked and Two Other Plays*. New York: Dutton, 1962:143–98.

PIVEN, FRANCES FOX, and RICHARD A. CLOWARD. *Poor People's Movements: Why They Succeed, How They Fail*. New York: Pantheon Books, 1977.

——. *Why Americans Don't Vote*. New York: Pantheon Books, 1988.

PLOMIN, ROBERT, and TERRYL T. FOCH. "A Twin Study of Objectively Assessed Personality in Childhood." *Journal of Personality and Sociology Psychology*. Vol. 39, No. 4 (October 1980):680–88.

POLENBERG, RICHARD. *One Nation Divisible: Class, Race, and Ethnicity in the United States Since 1938*. New York: Pelican Books, 1980.

POLSBY, NELSON W. "Three Problems in the Analysis of Community Power." *American Sociological Review*. Vol. 24, No. 6 (December 1959):796–803.

POMER, MARSHALL I. "Labor Market Structure, Intragenerational Mobility, and Discrimination: Black Male Advancement Out of Low-Paying Occupations, 1962–1973." *American Sociological Review*. Vol. 51, No. 5 (October 1986):650–59.

POPENOE, DAVID. *Disturbing the Nest: Family Change and Decline in Modern Societies*. New York: Aldine, 1988.

——. "Family Decline in the Swedish Welfare State." *The Public Interest*. No. 102 (Winter 1991):65–77.

——. "The Controversial Truth: Two-Parent Families are Better." *New York Times* (December 26, 1992):21.

——. "Parental Androgyny." *Society*. Vol. 30, No. 6 (September-October 1993):5–11.

POPKIN, SUSAN J. "Welfare: Views From the Bottom." *Social Problems*. Vol. 17, No. 1 (February 1990):64–79.

PORTES, ALEJANDRO, and LEIF JENSEN. "The Enclave and the Entrants: Patterns of Ethnic Enterprise in Miami Before and After Mariel." *American Sociological Review*. Vol. 54, No. 6 (December 1989):929–49.

POSTEL, SANDRA. "Facing Water Scarcity." In Lester R. Brown et al., eds., *State of the World 1993: A Worldwatch Institute Report on Progress Toward a Sustainable Society*. New York: Norton, 1993:22–41.

POWELL, CHRIS, and GEORGE E. C. PATON, eds. *Humour in Society: Resistance and Control*. New York: St. Martin's Press, 1988.

PRESSER, HARRIET B. "The Housework Gender Gap." *Population Today*. Vol. 21, No. 7/8 (July-August 1993):5.

PRESSLEY, SUE ANNE, and NANCY ANDREWS. "For Gay Couples, the Nursery Becomes the New Frontier." *Washington Post* (December 20, 1992):A1, A22–23.

PUTERBAUGH, GEOFF, ed. *Twins and Homosexuality: A Casebook*. New York: Garland, 1990.

PUTKA, GARY. "SAT To Become a Better Gauge." *Wall Street Journal* (November 1, 1990):B1.

——. "Whittle Develops Plan to Operate Schools for Profit." *Wall Street Journal* (May 15, 1991):B1.

QUEENAN, JOE. "The Many Paths to Riches." *Forbes*. Vol. 144, No. 9 (October 23, 1989):149.

QUINNEY, RICHARD. *Class, State and Crime: On the Theory and Practice of Criminal Justice*. New York: David McKay, 1977.

RANDALL, VICKI. *Women and Politics*. London: Macmillan Press, 1982.

RAPHAEL, RAY. *The Men from the Boys: Rites of Passage in Male America*. Lincoln and London: University of Nebraska Press, 1988.

RECKLESS, WALTER C. "Containment Theory." In Marvin E. Wolfgang, Leonard Savitz, and Norman Johnstone, eds., *The Sociology of Crime and Delinquency*. 2d ed. New York: Wiley, 1970:401–5.

RECKLESS, WALTER C., and SIMON DINITZ. "Pioneering with Self-Concept as a Vulnerability Factor in Delinquency." *Journal of Criminal Law, Criminology, and Police Science*. Vol. 58, No. 4 (December 1967):515–23.

REED, RODNEY J. "Administrator's Advice: Causes and Remedies of School Conflict and Violence." *National Association of Secondary School Principals Bulletin*. Vol. 67, No. 462 (April 1983):75–79.

REID, SUE TITUS. *Crime and Criminology.* 6th ed. Fort Worth, Tex.: Holt, Rinehart & Winston, 1991.

REIMERS, CORDELIA W. "Sources of the Family Income Differentials Among Hispanics, Blacks, and White Non-Hispanics." *American Journal of Sociology.* Vol. 89, No. 4 (January 1984):889–903.

REINHARZ, SHULAMIT. *Feminist Methods in Social Research.* New York: Oxford University Press, 1992.

REMOFF, HEATHER TREXLER. *Sexual Choice: A Woman's Decision.* New York: Dutton/Lewis, 1984.

RICHARDSON, JAMES T. "Definitions of Cult: From Sociological-Technical to Popular Negative." Paper presented to the American Psychological Association, Boston, August, 1990.

RIDGEWAY, CECILIA, and DAVID DIEKEMA. "Dominance and Collective Hierarchy Formation in Male and Female Task Groups." *American Sociological Review.* Vol. 54, No. 1 (February 1989):79–93.

RIDGEWAY, CECILIA L. *The Dynamics of Small Groups.* New York: St. Martin's Press, 1983.

RIESMAN, DAVID. *The Lonely Crowd: A Study of the Changing American Character.* New Haven, Conn.: Yale University Press, 1970; orig. 1950.

RILEY, MATILDA WHITE, ANNE FONER, and JOAN WARING. "Sociology of Age." In Neil J. Smelser, ed., *Handbook of Sociology.* Newbury Park, Calif.: Sage, 1988:243–90.

RITZER, GEORGE. *The McDonaldization of Society: An Investigation Into the Changing Character of Contemporary Social Life.* Thousand Oaks, Calif.: Pine Forge Press, 1993.

RITZER, GEORGE, and DAVID WALCZAK. *Working: Conflict and Change.* 4th ed. Englewood Cliffs, N.J.: Prentice Hall, 1990.

ROBERTS, J. DEOTIS. *Roots of a Black Future: Family and Church.* Philadelphia: The Westminster Press, 1980.

ROBINSON, JOYCE, and GLENNA SPITZE. "Whistle While You Work? The Effect of Household Task Performance on Women's and Men's Well-Being." *Social Science Quarterly.* Vol. 73, No. 4 (December 1992):844–61.

ROBINSON, VERA M. "Humor and Health." In Paul E. McGhee and Jeffrey H. Goldstein, eds., *Handbook of Humor Research, Vol. II, Applied Studies.* New York: Springer-Verlag, 1983:109–28.

ROESCH, ROBERTA. "Violent Families." *Parents.* Vol. 59, No. 9 (September 1984):74–76, 150–52.

ROETHLISBERGER, F. J., and WILLIAM J. DICKSON. *Management and the Worker.* Cambridge, Mass.: Harvard University Press, 1939.

ROGERS, ALISON. "The World's 101 Richest People." *Fortune.* Vol. 127, No. 13 (June 28, 1993):36–66.

ROHLEN, THOMAS P. *Japan's High Schools.* Berkeley: University of California Press, 1983.

ROOF, WADE CLARK. "Socioeconomic Differentials Among White Socioreligious Groups in the United States." *Social Forces.* Vol. 58, No. 1 (September 1979):280–89.

ROOF, WADE CLARK, and WILLIAM MCKINNEY. *American Mainline Religion: Its Changing Shape and Future.* New Brunswick, N.J.: Rutgers University Press, 1987.

ROOS, PATRICIA. "Marriage and Women's Occupational Attainment in Cross-Cultural Perspective." *American Sociological Review.* Vol. 48, No. 6 (December 1983):852–64.

ROPER CENTER FOR PUBLIC OPINION RESEARCH. *Attitudes Toward the Public Schools.* Storrs, Ct. The University of Connecticut, Storrs: The Center, 1994.

ROSENTHAL, ELIZABETH. "Canada's National Health Plan Gives Care to All, With Limits." *New York Times* (April 30, 1991):A1, A16.

ROSENTHAL, JACK. "The Rapid Growth of Suburban Employment." In Lois H. Masotti and Jeffrey K. Hadden, eds., *Suburbia in Transition.* New York: New York Times Books, 1974:95–100.

ROSKIN, MICHAEL G. *Countries and Concepts: An Introduction to Comparative Politics.* Englewood Cliffs, N.J.: Prentice Hall, 1982.

ROSS, SUSAN. "Education: A Step Ladder to Mobility." *Popline.* Vol. 7, No. 7 (July 1985):1–2.

ROSSI, ALICE S. "Gender and Parenthood." In Alice S. Rossi, ed., *Gender and the Life Course.* New York: Aldine, 1985:161–91.

ROSSIDES, DANIEL W. *Social Stratification: The American Class System in Comparative Perspective.* Englewood Cliffs, N.J.: Prentice Hall, 1990.

ROSTOW, WALT W. *The World Economy: History and Prospect.* Austin: University of Texas Press, 1978.

ROTHMAN, STANLEY, STEPHEN POWERS, and DAVID ROTHMAN. "Feminism in Films." *Society.* Vol. 30, No. 3 (March-April 1993):66–72.

ROWE, DAVID C. "Biometrical Genetic Models of Self-Reported Delinquent Behavior: A Twin Study." *Behavior Genetics.* Vol. 13, No. 5 (1983):473–89.

ROWE, DAVID C., and D. WAYNE OSGOOD. "Heredity and Sociological Theories of Delinquency: A Reconsideration." *American Sociological Review.* Vol. 49, No. 4 (August 1984):526–40.

RUBIN, LILLIAN BRESLOW. *Worlds of Pain: Life in the Working-Class Family.* New York: Basic Books, 1976.

RUDOLPH, BARBARA. "Tobacco Takes a New Road." *Time.* Vol. 126, No. 20 (November 18, 1985):70–71.

RUSSELL, CHERYL. "The Master Trend." *American Demographics.* Vol. 15, No. 10 (October 1993):28–37.

RYAN, WILLIAM. *Blaming the Victim.* Rev. ed. New York: Vintage Books, 1976.

RYTINA, JOAN HUBER, WILLIAM H. FORM, and JOHN PEASE. "Income and Stratification Ideology: Beliefs About the American Opportunity Structure." *American Journal of Sociology.* Vol. 75, No. 4 (January 1970):703–16.

SABATO, LARRY J. *PAC Power: Inside the World of Political Action Committees.* New York: Norton, 1984.

SALAS, RAFAEL M. "The State of World Population 1985: Population and Women." *Popline*. Vol. 7, No. 7 (July 1985):4–5.

SALE, KIRKPATRICK. *The Conquest of Paradise: Christopher Columbus and the Columbian Legacy*. New York: Alfred A. Knopf, 1990.

SALHOLZ, ELOISE. "The Future of Gay America." *Newsweek* (March 12, 1990):20–25.

SAMPSON, ANTHONY. *The Changing Anatomy of Britain*. New York: Random House, 1982.

SAMPSON, ROBERT J. "Urban Black Violence: The Effects of Male Joblessness and Family Disruption." *American Journal of Sociology*. Vol. 93, No. 2 (September 1987):348–82.

SAMPSON, ROBERT J., and JOHN H. LAUB. "Crime and Deviance Over the Life Course: The Salience of Adult Social Bonds." *American Sociological Review*. Vol. 55, No. 5 (October 1990):609–27.

SAPIR, EDWARD. "The Status of Linguistics as a Science." *Language*. Vol. 5 (1929):207–14.

———. *Selected Writings of Edward Sapir in Language, Culture, and Personality*. David G. Mandelbaum, ed. Berkeley: University of California Press, 1949.

SCAFF, LAWRENCE A. "Max Weber and Robert Michels." *American Journal of Sociology*. Vol. 86, No. 6 (May 1981):1269–86.

SCHEFF, THOMAS J. *Being Mentally Ill: A Sociological Theory*. 2d ed. New York: Aldine, 1984.

SCHLESINGER, ARTHUR. "The City in American Civilization." In A. B. Callow, Jr., ed., *American Urban History*. New York: Oxford University Press, 1969:25–41.

SCHLESINGER, ARTHUR, JR. "The Cult of Ethnicity: Good and Bad." *Time*. Vol. 137, No. 27 (July 8, 1991):21.

SCHOOLER, CARMI, JOANNE MILLER, KAREN A. MILLER, and CAROL N. RICHTAND. "Work for the Household: Its Nature and Consequences for Husbands and Wives." *American Journal of Sociology*. Vol. 90, No. 1 (July 1984):97–124.

SCHUTT, RUSSELL K. "Objectivity versus Outrage." *Society*. Vol. 26, No. 4 (May/June 1989):14–16.

SCHWARTZ, MARTIN D. "Gender and Injury in Spousal Assault." *Sociological Focus*. Vol. 20, No. 1 (January 1987):61–75.

SCHWARTZ-NOBEL, LORETTA. *Starving in the Shadow of Plenty*. New York: McGraw-Hill, 1981.

SCOTT, JOHN, and CATHERINE GRIFF. *Directors of Industry: The British Corporate Network, 1904–1976*. New York: Blackwell, 1985.

SCOTT, W. RICHARD. *Organizations: Rational, Natural, and Open Systems*. Englewood Cliffs, N.J.: Prentice Hall, 1981.

SEGAL, DAVID R., PAUL A. GADE, and EDGAR M. JOHNSON. "Homosexuals in Western Armed Forces." *Society*. Vol. 31, No. 1 (November-December 1993):37–42.

SEGAL, MADY WECHSLER, and AMANDA FAITH HANSEN. "Value Rationales in Policy Debates on Women in the Military: A Content Analysis of Congressional Testimony, 1941–1985." *Social Science Quarterly*. Vol. 73, No. 2 (June 1992):296–309.

SELLIN, THORSTEN. *The Penalty of Death*. Beverly Hills, Calif.: Sage, 1980.

SENNETT, RICHARD, and JONATHAN COBB. *The Hidden Injuries of Class*. New York: Vintage Books, 1973.

SHANAS, ETHEL. "Social Myth as Hypothesis: The Case of the Family Relations of Old People." *The Gerontologist*. Vol. 19, No. 1 (February 1979):3–9.

SHAPIRO, NINA. "Botswana Test Case." *Chicago Tribune* (September 15, 1991):1.

SHAWCROSS, WILLIAM. *Sideshow: Kissinger, Nixon and the Destruction of Cambodia*. New York: Pocket Books, 1979.

SHEEHAN, TOM. "Senior Esteem as a Factor in Socioeconomic Complexity." *The Gerontologist*. Vol. 16, No. 5 (October 1976):433–40.

SHELDON, WILLIAM H., EMIL M. HARTL, and EUGENE MCDERMOTT. *Varieties of Delinquent Youth*. New York: Harper, 1949.

SHEPHARD, ROY J. *The Risks of Passive Smoking*. London: Croom Helm, 1982.

SHERRID, PAMELA. "Hot Times in the City of London." *U.S. News & World Report* (October 27, 1986):45–46.

SHEVKY, ESHREF, and WENDELL BELL. *Social Area Analysis*. Stanford, Calif.: Stanford University Press, 1955.

SHIPLEY, JOSEPH T. *Dictionary of Word Origins*. Totowa, N.J.: Roman & Allanheld, 1985.

SHIVELY, JOELLEN. "Cowboys and Indians: Perceptions of Western Films Among American Indians and Anglos." *American Sociological Review*. Vol. 57, No. 6 (December 1992):725–34.

SHUPE, ANSON, WILLIAM A. STACEY, and LONNIE R. HAZLEWOOD. *Violent Men, Violent Couples: The Dynamics of Domestic Violence*. Lexington, Mass.: Lexington Books, 1987.

SIDEL, RUTH, and VICTOR W. SIDEL. *The Health Care of China*. Boston: Beacon Press, 1982b.

———. *A Healthy State: An International Perspective on the Crisis in United States Medical Care*. Rev. ed. New York: Pantheon Books, 1982a.

SILLS, DAVID L. "The Succession of Goals." In Amitai Etzioni, ed., *A Sociological Reader on Complex Organizations*. 2d ed. New York: Holt, Rinehart & Winston, 1969:175–87.

SILVERBERG, ROBERT. "The Greenhouse Effect: Apocalypse Now or Chicken Little?" *Omni* (July 1991):50–54.

SILVERSTEIN, MICHAEL. In Jon Snodgrass, ed., *A Book of Readings for Men Against Sexism*. Albion, Calif.: Times Change Press, 1977:178–79.

SIMMEL, GEORG. *The Sociology of Georg Simmel*. Kurt Wolff, ed. New York: Free Press, 1950:118–69.

———. "The Mental Life of the Metropolis." In Kurt Wolff, ed., *The Sociology of Georg Simmel*. New York: Free Press, 1964:409–24; orig. 1905.

SIMON, JULIAN. *The Ultimate Resource*. Princeton, N.J.: Princeton University Press, 1981.

SIMONS, CAROL. "Japan's *Kyoiku* Mamas." In John J. Macionis and Nijole V. Benokraitis, eds., *Seeing Ourselves: Classic,*

Contemporary, and Cross-Cultural Readings in Sociology. Englewood Cliffs, N.J.: Prentice Hall, 1989:281–86.

SIMONS, MARLISE. "The Price of Modernization: The Case of Brazil's Kaiapo Indians." In John J. Macionis and Nijole V. Benokraitis, eds., *Seeing Ourselves: Classic, Contemporary, and Cross-Cultural Readings in Sociology.* 3d ed. Englewood Cliffs, N.J.: Prentice Hall, 1995:470–76.

SIMPSON, JANICE C. "Buying Black." *Time.* Vol. 140, No. 9 (August 31, 1992):52–53.

SINGER, DOROTHY. "A Time to Reexamine the Role of Television in Our Lives." *American Psychologist.* Vol. 38, No. 7 (July 1983):815–16.

SINGER, JEROME L., and DOROTHY G. SINGER. "Psychologists Look at Television: Cognitive, Developmental, Personality, and Social Policy Implications." *American Psychologist.* Vol. 38, No. 7 (July 1983):826–34.

SIVARD, RUTH LEGER. *World Military and Social Expenditures, 1987–88.* 12th ed. Washington, D.C.: World Priorities, 1988.

———. *World Military and Social Expenditures, 1992–93.* 17th ed. Washington, D.C.: World Priorities, 1993.

SIZER, THEODORE R. *Horace's Compromise: The Dilemma of the American High School.* Boston: Houghton Mifflin, 1984.

SKOCPOL, THEDA. *States and Social Revolutions: A Comparative Analysis of France, Russia, and China.* Cambridge: Cambridge University Press, 1979.

SKOLNICK, ARLENE. *The Psychology of Human Development.* New York: Harcourt Brace Jovanovich, 1986.

SLATER, PHILIP. *The Pursuit of Loneliness.* Boston: Beacon Press, 1976.

SMITH, ADAM. *An Inquiry into the Nature and Causes of the Wealth of Nations.* New York: The Modern Library, 1937; orig. 1776.

SMITH, DOUGLAS A. "Police Response to Interpersonal Violence: Defining the Parameters of Legal Control." *Social Forces.* Vol. 65, No. 3 (March 1987):767–82.

SMITH, DOUGLAS A., and PATRICK R. GARTIN. "Specifying Specific Deterrence: The Influence of Arrest on Future Criminal Activity." *American Sociological Review.* Vol. 54, No. 1 (February 1989):94–105.

SMITH, DOUGLAS A., and CHRISTY A. VISHER. "Street-Level Justice: Situational Determinants of Police Arrest Decisions." *Social Problems.* Vol. 29, No. 2 (December 1981):167–77.

SMITH, ROBERT ELLIS. *Privacy: How to Protect What's Left of It.* Garden City, N.Y.: Anchor/Doubleday, 1979.

SMITH-LOVIN, LYNN, and CHARLES BRODY. "Interruptions in Group Discussions: The Effects of Gender and Group Composition." *American Journal of Sociology.* Vol. 54, No. 3 (June 1989):424–35.

SMOLOWE, JILL. "Land of Slaughter." *Time.* Vol. 139, No. 23 (June 8, 1992):32–36.

SNELL, MARILYN BERLIN. "The Purge of Nurture." *New Perspectives Quarterly.* Vol. 7, No. 1 (Winter 1990):1–2.

SNOW, DAVID A., E. BURKE ROCHFORD, JR., STEVEN K. WORDEN, and ROBERT D. BENFORD. "Frame Alignment Processes, Micromobilization, and Movement Participation." *American Sociological Review.* Vol. 51, No. 4 (August 1986):464–81.

SOUTH, SCOTT J., and STEVEN F. MESSNER. "Structural Determinants of Intergroup Association: Interracial Marriage and Crime." *American Journal of Sociology.* Vol. 91, No. 6 (May 1986):1409–30.

SOWELL, THOMAS. *Ethnic America.* New York: Basic Books, 1981.

SPATES, JAMES L. "Sociological Overview." In Alan Milberg, ed., *Street Games.* New York: McGraw-Hill, 1976a:286–90.

———. "Counterculture and Dominant Culture Values: A Cross-National Analysis of the Underground Press and Dominant Culture Magazines." *American Sociological Review.* Vol. 41, No. 5 (October 1976b):868–83.

———. "The Sociology of Values." In Ralph Turner, ed., *Annual Review of Sociology.* Vol. 9. Palo Alto, Calif.: Annual Reviews, 1983:27–49.

SPATES, JAMES L., and JOHN J. MACIONIS. *The Sociology of Cities.* 2d ed. Belmont, Calif.: Wadsworth, 1987.

SPECTOR, LEONARD S. "Nuclear Proliferation Today." In William M. Evan and Stephen Hilgartner, eds., *The Arms Race and Nuclear War.* Englewood Cliffs, N.J.: Prentice Hall, 1988:25–29.

SPEER, JAMES A. "The New Christian Right and Its Parent Company: A Study in Political Contrasts." In David G. Bromley and Anson Shupe, eds., *New Christian Politics.* Macon, Ga.: Mercer University Press, 1984:19–40.

SPITZER, STEVEN. "Toward a Marxian Theory of Deviance." In Delos H. Kelly, ed., *Criminal Behavior: Readings in Criminology.* New York: St. Martin's Press, 1980:175–91.

SRINIVAS, M. N. *Social Change in Modern India.* Berkeley: University of California Press, 1971.

STACEY, JUDITH. *Patriarchy and Socialist Revolution in China.* Berkeley: University of California Press, 1983.

———. *Brave New Families: Stories of Domestic Upheaval in Late Twentieth-Century America.* New York: Basic Books, 1990.

STAHURA, JOHN M. "Suburban Development, Black Suburbanization and the Black Civil Rights Movement Since World War II." *American Sociological Review.* Vol. 51, No. 1 (February 1986):131–44.

STANLEY, LIZ, ed. *Feminist Praxis: Research, Theory, and Epistemology in Feminist Sociology.* London: Routledge & Kegan Paul, 1990.

STANLEY, LIZ, and SUE WISE. *Breaking Out: Feminist Consciousness and Feminist Research.* London: Routledge & Kegan Paul, 1983.

STARK, RODNEY. *Sociology.* Belmont, Calif.: Wadsworth, 1985.

STARK, RODNEY, and WILLIAM SIMS BAINBRIDGE. "Of Churches, Sects, and Cults: Preliminary Concepts for a Theory of Religious Movements." *Journal for the Scientific Study of Religion.* Vol. 18, No. 2 (June 1979):117–31.

————. "Secularization and Cult Formation in the Jazz Age." *Journal for the Scientific Study of Religion*. Vol. 20, No. 4 (December 1981):360–73.

STARK, RODNEY, and CHARLES Y. GLOCK. *American Piety: The Nature of Religious Commitment*. Berkeley: University of California Press, 1968.

STARR, PAUL. *The Social Transformation of American Medicine*. New York: Basic Books, 1982.

Statistics of Income Bulletin. Vol. 11, No. 3 (Winter 1991–92).

STAVRIANOS, L. S. *A Global History: The Human Heritage*. 3d ed. Englewood Cliffs, N.J.: Prentice Hall, 1983.

STEELE, SHELBY. *The Content of Our Character: A New Vision of Race in America*. New York: St. Martin's Press, 1990.

STEIN, MAURICE R. *The Eclipse of Community: An Interpretation of American Studies*. Princeton, N.J.: Princeton University Press, 1972.

STEPHENS, JOHN D. *The Transition from Capitalism to Socialism*. Urbana: University of Illinois Press, 1986.

STERNLIEB, GEORGE, and JAMES W. HUGHES. "The Uncertain Future of the Central City." *Urban Affairs Quarterly*. Vol. 18, No. 4 (June 1983):455–72.

STEVENS, GILLIAN, and GRAY SWICEGOOD. "The Linguistic Context of Ethnic Endogamy." *American Sociological Review*. Vol. 52, No. 1 (February 1987):73–82.

STEVENS, ROSEMARY. *American Medicine and the Public Interest*. New Haven, Conn.: Yale University Press, 1971.

STIEHM, JUDITH HICKS. *Arms and the Enlisted Woman*. Philadelphia: Temple University Press, 1989.

STONE, LAWRENCE. *The Family, Sex and Marriage in England 1500–1800*. New York: Harper & Row, 1977.

STONE, ROBYN, GAIL LEE CAFFERATA, and JUDITH SANGL. *Caregivers of the Frail Elderly: A National Profile*. Washington, D.C.: U.S. Department of Health and Human Services, 1987.

STOUFFER, SAMUEL A., et al. *The American Soldier: Adjustment During Army Life*. Princeton, N.J.: Princeton University Press, 1949.

STRAUS, MURRAY A., and RICHARD J. GELLES. "Societal Change and Change in Family Violence from 1975 to 1985 as Revealed by Two National Surveys." *Journal of Marriage and the Family*. Vol. 48, No. 4 (August 1986):465–79.

SUDNOW, DAVID N. *Passing On: The Social Organization of Dying*. Englewood Cliffs, N.J.: Prentice Hall, 1967.

SUMNER, WILLIAM GRAHAM. *Folkways*. New York: Dover, 1959; orig. 1906.

SUNG, BETTY LEE. *Mountains of Gold: The Story of the Chinese in America*. New York: Macmillan, 1967.

SUTHERLAND, EDWIN H. "White Collar Criminality." *American Sociological Review*. Vol. 5, No. 1 (February 1940):1–12.

SUTHERLAND, EDWIN H., and DONALD R. CRESSEY. *Criminology*. 10th ed. Philadelphia: J.B. Lippincott, 1978.

SUZUKI, DAVID, and PETER KNUDTSON. *Genethics: The Clash Between the New Genetics and Human Values*. Cambridge, Mass.: Harvard University Press, 1989.

SWARTZ, STEVE. "Why Michael Milken Stands to Qualify for Guinness Book." *Wall Street Journal*. Vol. LXX, No. 117 (March 31, 1989):1, 4.

SYZMANSKI, ALBERT. *Class Structure: A Critical Perspective*. New York: Praeger, 1983.

SZASZ, THOMAS S. *The Manufacturer of Madness: A Comparative Study of the Inquisition and the Mental Health Movement*. New York: Dell, 1961.

————. *The Myth of Mental Illness: Foundations of a Theory of Personal Conduct*. New York: Harper & Row, 1970; orig. 1961.

TAJFEL, HENRI. "Social Psychology of Intergroup Relations." *Annual Review of Psychology*. Palo Alto, Calif.: Annual Reviews, 1982:1–39.

TANNEN, DEBORAH. *You Just Don't Understand Me: Women and Men in Conversation*. New York: William Morrow, 1990.

TANNENBAUM, FRANK. *Slave and Citizen: The Negro in the Americas*. New York: Vintage Books, 1946.

TAVRIS, CAROL, and SUSAN SADD. *The Redbook Report on Female Sexuality*. New York: Delacorte Press, 1977.

TAYLOR, JOHN. "Don't Blame Me: The New Culture of Victimization." *New York Magazine* (June 3, 1991):26–34.

TERRY, DON. "In Crackdown on Bias, A New Tool." *New York Times* (June 12, 1993):8.

THERNSTROM, STEPHAN. "The Minority Majority Will Never Come." *Wall Street Journal* (July 26, 1990):A16.

THOITS, PEGGY A. "Self-labeling Processes in Mental Illness: The Role of Emotional Deviance." *American Journal of Sociology*. Vol. 91, No. 2 (September 1985):221–49.

THOMAS, PIRI. *Down These Mean Streets*. New York: Signet, 1967.

THOMAS, W. I. "The Relation of Research to the Social Process." In Morris Janowitz, ed., *W. I. Thomas on Social Organization and Social Personality*. Chicago: University of Chicago Press, 1966:289–305; orig. 1931.

THORNBERRY, TERRANCE, and MARGARET FARNSWORTH. "Social Correlates of Criminal Involvement: Further Evidence on the Relationship Between Social Status and Criminal Behavior." *American Sociological Review*. Vol 47, No. 4 (August 1982):505–18.

THORNE, BARRIE, CHERIS KRAMARAE, and NANCY HENLEY, EDS. *Language, Gender and Society*. Rowley, Mass.: Newbury House, 1983.

THORNTON, ARLAND. "Changing Attitudes Toward Separation and Divorce: Causes and Consequences." *American Journal of Sociology*. Vol. 90, No. 4 (January 1985):856–72.

THUROW, LESTER C. "A Surge in Inequality." *Scientific American*. Vol. 256, No. 5 (May 1987):30–37.

TIEN, H. YUAN. "Second Thoughts on the Second Child." *Population Today*. Vol. 17, No. 4 (April 1989):6–9.

TIGER, LIONEL, and JOSEPH SHEPHER. *Women in the Kibbutz*. New York: Harcourt Brace Jovanovich, 1975.

TILLY, CHARLES. "Does Modernization Breed Revolution?" In Jack A. Goldstone, ed., *Revolutions: Theoretical*,

Comparative, and Historical Studies. New York: Harcourt Brace Jovanovich, 1986:47–57.

TOBIN, GARY. "Suburbanization and the Development of Motor Transportation: Transportation Technology and the Suburbanization Process." In Barry Schwartz, ed., *The Changing Face of the Suburbs.* Chicago: University of Chicago Press, 1976.

TOCH, THOMAS. "The Exodus." *U.S. News and World Report.* Vol. 111, No. 24 (December 9, 1991):68–77.

TOCQUEVILLE, ALEXIS DE. *The Old Regime and the French Revolution.* Stuart Gilbert, trans. Garden City, N.Y.: Anchor/Doubleday Books, 1955; orig. 1856.

TOENNIES, FERDINAND. *Community and Society (Gemeinschaft und Gesellschaft).* New York: Harper & Row, 1963; orig. 1887.

TOFANI, LORETTA. "AIDS Ravages a Continent, and Sweeps a Family." *Philadelphia Inquirer* (March 24, 1991):1, 15–A.

TROELTSCH, ERNST. *The Social Teaching of the Christian Churches.* New York: Macmillan, 1931.

TROIDEN, RICHARD R. *Gay and Lesbian Identity: A Sociological Analysis.* Dix Hills, N.Y.: General Hall, 1988.

TUMIN, MELVIN M. "Some Principles of Stratification: A Critical Analysis." *American Sociological Review.* Vol. 18, No. 4 (August 1953):387–94.

———. *Social Stratification: The Forms and Functions of Inequality.* 2d ed. Englewood Cliffs, N.J.: Prentice Hall, 1985.

TYGIEL, JULES. *Baseball's Great Experiment: Jackie Robinson and His Legacy.* New York: Oxford University Press, 1983.

TYLER, S. LYMAN. *A History of Indian Policy.* Washington, D.C.: United States Department of the Interior, Bureau of Indian Affairs, 1973.

UNITED NATIONS DEVELOPMENT PROGRAMME. *Human Development Report 1990.* New York: Oxford University Press, 1990.

———. *Human Development Report 1991.* New York: Oxford University Press, 1991.

———. *Human Development Report 1993.* New York: Oxford University Press, 1993.

UNNEVER, JAMES D., CHARLES E. FRAZIER, and JOHN C. HENRETTA. "Race Differences in Criminal Sentencing." *The Sociological Quarterly.* Vol. 21, No. 2 (Spring 1980):197–205.

UNRUH, JOHN D., JR. *The Plains Across.* Urbana, Ill.: University of Illinois Press, 1979.

U.S. BUREAU OF THE CENSUS. *Statistical Abstract of the United States 1970.* 91st ed. Washington, D.C.: U.S. Government Printing Office, 1970.

———. *Money Income of Households, Families, and Persons in the United States: 1990.* Current Population Reports, Series P-60, No. 174. Washington, D.C.: U.S. Government Printing Office, 1991.

———. *Educational Attainment in the United States: March 1991 and 1990.* Current Population Reports, Series P-20,

No. 462. Washington, D.C.: U.S. Government Printing Office, 1992.

———. *1987 Survey of Minority-Owned Business Enterprises—Summary.* Washington, D.C.: U.S. Government Printing Office, 1992.

———. *Population Projections of the United States by Age, Sex, Race, and Hispanic Origin: 1992 to 2050.* Current Population Reports, Series P-25, No. 1092. Washington, D.C.: U.S. Government Printing Office, 1992.

———. *Statistical Abstract of the United States: 1992.* 112th ed. Washington, D.C.: U.S. Government Printing Office, 1992.

———. *Money Income of Households, Families, and Persons in the United States: 1992.* Current Population Reports, Series P-60, No. 184. Washington, D.C.: U.S. Government Printing Office, 1993.

———. *Poverty in the United States: 1992.* Current Population Reports, Series P-60, No. 185. Washington, D.C.: U.S. Government Printing Office, 1993.

———. *Statistical Abstract of the United States: 1993.* 113th ed. Washington, D.C.: U.S. Government Printing Office, 1993.

———. *We the American... Asians.* Washington, D.C.: U.S. Government Printing Office, 1993.

———. *We the... First Americans.* Washington, D.C.: U.S. Government Printing Office, 1993.

———. *Educational Attainment in the United States: March 1993 and 1992.* Current Population Reports, Series P-20, No. 476. Washington, D.C.: U.S. Government Printing Office, 1994.

———. *Household and Family Characteristics: March 1993.* Current Population Reports, Series P-20, No. 477. Washington, D.C.: U.S. Government Printing Office, 1994.

———. *Marital Status and Living Arrangements: March 1993.* Current Population Reports, Series 20, No. 478. Washington, D.C.: U.S. Government Printing Office, 1994.

———. "Resident Population of the United States: Estimates by Sex, Race, and Hispanic Origin, with Median Age." Supplied by the Census Bureau, December 14, 1994.

———. *School Enrollment—Social and Economic Characteristics of Students: October 1992.* Current Population Reports, Series P-20, No. 469. Washington, D.C.: U.S. Government Printing Office, 1994.

———. *Statistical Abstract of the United States: 1994.* 114th ed. Washington, D.C.: U.S. Government Printing Office, 1994.

———. *Statistical Abstract of the United States: 1995.* 115th ed. Washington, D.C.: U.S. Government Printing Office, 1995.

U.S. BUREAU OF JUSTICE STATISTICS. *Sourcebook of Criminal Justice Statistics 1990.* Timothy J. Flanagan and Kathleen Maguire, eds. Washington, D.C.: U.S. Government Printing Office, 1991.

———. *Compendium of Federal Justice Statistics, 1989.* Washington D.C.: U.S. Government Printing Office, 1992.

————. *Survey of State Prison Inmates, 1991*. Washington, D.C.: U.S. Government Printing Office, 1993.

U.S. CENTERS FOR DISEASE CONTROL AND PREVENTION. *STD Surveillance 1992*. Washington, D.C.: U.S. Department of Human Services, National Center for Prevention Services, 1993.

————. *HIV/AIDS Surveillance Report*. Vol. 6, No. 1. Washington, D.C.: U.S. Department of Human Services, National Center for Prevention Services, 1994.

U.S. DEPARTMENT OF DEFENSE. "Secretary of Defense Perry Approves Plans to Open New Jobs for Women in the Military." News release (July 29, 1994).

U.S. DEPARTMENT OF LABOR. Bureau of Labor Statistics. *Employment and Earnings*. Vol. 41, No. 1 (January). Washington, D.C.: U.S. Government Printing Office, 1994.

U.S. EQUAL EMPLOYMENT OPPORTUNITY COMMISSION. *Job Patterns for Minorities and Women in Private Industry 1992*. Washington, D.C.: U.S. Government Printing Office, 1993.

U.S. FEDERAL BUREAU OF INVESTIGATION. *Crime in the United States 1993*. Washington, D.C.: U.S. Government Printing Office, 1994.

————. *Uniformed Crime Reports for the United States 1993*. Washington, D.C.: U.S. Government Printing Office, 1994.

U.S. HOUSE OF REPRESENTATIVES, SELECT COMMITTEE ON CHILDREN, YOUTH, AND FAMILIES. *Abused Children in America: Victims of Neglect*. Washington, D.C.: U.S. Government Printing Office, 1987.

U.S. HOUSE OF REPRESENTATIVES. "Street Children: A Global Disgrace." Hearing on November 7, 1991. Washington, D.C.: U.S. Government Printing Office, 1992.

U.S. IMMIGRATION AND NATURALIZATION SERVICE. *Statistical Yearbook*. Washington, D.C.: U.S. Government Printing Office, 1991.

U.S. NATIONAL CENTER FOR HEALTH STATISTICS. *Current Estimates from the National Health Interview Survey, 1991*. Hyattsville, Md.: The Center, 1992.

————. *Life Tables*. Hyattsville, Md.: The Center, 1993.

————. *Current Estimates from the National Health Interview Survey, 1992*. Hyattsville, Md.: The Center, 1994.

U.S. WOMEN'S BUREAU. *Employers and Child Care: Benefiting Work and Family*. Washington, D.C.: U.S. Government Printing Office, 1989.

VAN DE KAA, DIRK J. "Europe's Second Demographic Transition." *Population Bulletin*. Vol. 42, No. 1 (March 1987). Washington, D.C.: Population Reference Bureau.

VAN DEN HAAG, ERNEST, and JOHN P. CONRAD. *The Death Penalty: A Debate*. New York: Plenum Press, 1983.

VATZ, RICHARD E., and LEE S. WEINBERG. *Thomas Szasz: Primary Values and Major Contentions*. Buffalo, N.Y.: Prometheus Books, 1983.

VAUGHAN, MARY KAY. "Multinational Corporations: The World as a Company Town." In Ahamed Idris-Soven et al., eds., *The World as a Company Town: Multinational Corporations and Social Change*. The Hague: Mouton Publishers, 1978:15–35.

VAYDA, EUGENE, and RAISA B. DEBER. "The Canadian Health Care System: An Overview." *Social Science and Medicine*. Vol. 18, No. 3 (1984):191–97.

VEUM, JONATHAN R. "Accounting for Income Mobility Changes in the United States." *Social Science Quarterly*. Vol. 73, No. 4 (December 1992):773–85.

VIGUERIE, RICHARD A. *The New Right: We're Ready to Lead*. Falls Church, Va.: The Viguerie Company, 1981.

VINOVSKIS, MARIS A. "Have Social Historians Lost the Civil War? Some Preliminary Demographic Speculations." *Journal of American History*. Vol. 76, No. 1 (June 1989):34–58.

VOGEL, EZRA F. *Japan as Number One: Lessons for America*. Cambridge, Mass.: Harvard University Press, 1979.

————. *The Four Little Dragons: The Spread of Industrialization in East Asia*. Cambridge, Mass.: Harvard University Press, 1991.

VOGEL, LISE. *Marxism and the Oppression of Women: Toward a Unitary Theory*. New Brunswick, N.J.: Rutgers University Press, 1983.

VOLD, GEORGE B., and THOMAS J. BERNARD. *Theoretical Criminology*. 3d ed. New York: Oxford University Press, 1986.

VON HIRSH, ANDREW. *Past or Future Crimes: Deservedness and Dangerousness in the Sentencing of Criminals*. New Brunswick, N.J.: Rutgers University Press, 1986.

WAITE, LINDA J., GUS W. HAGGSTROM, and DAVID I. KANOUSE. "The Consequences of Parenthood for the Marital Stability of Young Adults." *American Sociological Review*. Vol. 50, No. 6 (December 1985):850–57.

WALDMAN, STEVEN. "Deadbeat Dads." *Newsweek* (May 4, 1992):46–52.

WALL, THOMAS F. *Medical Ethics: Basic Moral Issues*. Washington, D.C.: University Press of America, 1980.

WALLERSTEIN, IMMANUEL. *The Modern World-System: Capitalist Agriculture and the Origins of the European World-Economy in the Sixteenth Century*. New York: Academic Press, 1974.

————. *The Capitalist World-Economy*. New York: Cambridge University Press, 1979.

————. "Crises: The World Economy, the Movements, and the Ideologies." In Albert Bergesen, ed., *Crises in the World-System*. Beverly Hills, Calif.: Sage, 1983:21–36.

————. *The Politics of the World Economy: The States, the Movements, and the Civilizations*. Cambridge: Cambridge University Press, 1984.

WALLERSTEIN, JUDITH S., and SANDRA BLAKESLEE. *Second Chances: Men, Women, and Children a Decade after Divorce*. New York: Ticknor & Fields, 1989.

WARNER, SAM BASS, JR. *Streetcar Suburbs*. Cambridge, Mass.: Harvard University and MIT Presses, 1962.

WARNER, W. LLOYD, and PAUL S. LUNT. *The Social Life of a Modern Community*. New Haven, Conn.: Yale University Press, 1941.

WAXMAN, CHAIM I. *The Stigma of Poverty: A Critique of Poverty Theories and Policies*. 2d ed. New York: Pergamon Press, 1983.

WEBER, ADNA FERRIN. *The Growth of Cities*. New York: Columbia University Press, 1963; orig. 1899.

WEBER, MAX. *The Protestant Ethic and the Spirit of Capitalism*. New York: Charles Scribner's Sons, 1958; orig. 1904–5.

———. *Economy and Society*. G. Roth and C. Wittich, eds. Berkeley: University of California Press, 1978.

WEINBERG, GEORGE. *Society and the Healthy Homosexual*. Garden City, N.Y.: Anchor Books, 1973.

WEINRICH, JAMES D. *Sexual Landscapes: Why We Are What We Are, Why We Love Whom We Love*. New York: Charles Scribner's Sons, 1987.

WEISBURD, DAVID, STANTON WHEELER, ELIN WARING, and NANCY BODE. *Crimes of the Middle Class: White Collar Defenders in the Courts*. New Haven, Conn.: Yale University Press, 1991.

WEISNER, THOMAS S., and BERNICE T. EIDUSON. "The Children of the '60s as Parents." *Psychology Today* (January 1986):60–66.

WEITZMAN, LENORE J. *The Divorce Revolution: The Unexpected Social and Economic Consequences for Women and Children in America*. New York: Free Press, 1985.

WELLFORD, CHARLES. "Labeling Theory and Criminology: An Assessment." In Delos H. Kelly, ed., *Criminal Behavior: Readings in Criminology*. New York: St. Martin's Press, 1980:234–47.

WELLMAN, BARRY. "The Community Question: Intimate Networks of East Yorkers." *American Journal of Sociology*. Vol. 84, No. 5 (March 1979):1201–31.

WENKE, ROBERT J. *Patterns of Prehistory*. New York: Oxford University Press, 1980.

WESTERMAN, MARTY. "Death of the Frito Bandito." *American Demographics*. Vol. 11, No. 3 (March 1989):28–32.

WESTERN, BRUCE. "Postwar Unionization in Eighteen Advanced Capitalist Countries." *American Sociological Review*. Vol. 58, No. 2 (April 1993):266–82.

WESTOFF, CHARLES F., and ELISE F. JONES. "The Secularization of U.S. Catholic Birth Control Practices." *Family Planning Perspective*. Vol. X, No. 5 (September-October 1977):203–7.

WHEELIS, ALLEN. *The Quest for Identity*. New York: Norton, 1958.

WHITAKER, MARK. "Ten Ways to Fight Terrorism." *Newsweek* (July 1, 1985):26–29.

WHITE, RALPH, and RONALD LIPPITT. "Leader Behavior and Member Reaction in Three 'Social Climates.'" In Dorwin Cartwright and Alvin Zander, eds., *Group Dynamics*. Evanston, Ill.: Row, Peterson, 1953:586–611.

WHITMAN, DAVID. "Shattering Myths about the Homeless." *U.S. News & World Report* (March 20, 1989):26, 28.

WHORF, BENJAMIN LEE. "The Relation of Habitual Thought and Behavior to Language." In *Language, Thought, and Reality*. Cambridge, Mass.: The Technology Press of MIT/New York: Wiley, 1956:134–59; orig. 1941.

WHYTE, WILLIAM H., JR. *The Organization Man*. Garden City, N.Y.: Anchor Books, 1957.

WIARDA, HOWARD J. "Ethnocentrism and Third World Development." *Society*. Vol. 24, No. 6 (September-October 1987):55–64.

WIATROWSKI, MICHAEL A., DAVID B. GRISWOLD, and MARY K. ROBERTS. "Social Control Theory and Delinquency." *American Sociological Review*. Vol. 46, No. 5 (October 1981):525–41.

WILCOX, CLYDE. "Race, Gender, and Support for Women in the Military." *Social Science Quarterly*. Vol. 73, No. 2 (June 1992):310–23.

WILES, P. J. D. *Economic Institutions Compared*. New York: Halsted Press, 1977.

WILLIAMS, RHYS H., and N. J. DEMERATH III. "Religion and Political Process in an American City." *American Sociological Review*. Vol. 56, No. 4 (August 1991):417–31.

WILLIAMS, ROBIN M., JR. *American Society: A Sociological Interpretation*. 3d ed. New York: Alfred A. Knopf, 1970.

WILLIAMSON, JEFFREY G., and PETER H. LINDERT. *American Inequality: A Macroeconomic History*. New York: Academic Press, 1980.

WILSON, CLINT C., II, and FELIX GUTIERREZ. *Minorities and Media: Diversity and the End of Mass Communication*. Beverly Hills, Calif.: Sage, 1985.

WILSON, EDWARD O. "Biodiversity, Prosperity, and Value." In F. Herbert Bormann and Stephen R. Kellert, eds., *Ecology, Economics, and Ethics: The Broken Circle*. New Haven, Conn.: Yale University Press, 1991:3–10.

WILSON, JAMES Q. *Bureaucracy: What Government Agencies Do and Why They Do It*. New York: Basic Books, 1991.

WILSON, JAMES Q., and RICHARD J. HERRNSTEIN. *Crime and Human Nature*. New York: Simon and Schuster, 1985.

WILSON, THOMAS C. "Urbanism and Tolerance: A Test of Some Hypotheses Drawn from Wirth and Stouffer." *American Sociological Review*. Vol. 50, No. 1 (February 1985):117–23.

WILSON, WILLIAM JULIUS. "The Black Underclass." *The Wilson Quarterly*. Vol. 8 (Spring 1984):88–99.

WINNICK, LOUIS. "America's 'Model Minority'." *Commentary*. Vol. 90, No. 2 (August 1990):22–29.

WIRTH, LOUIS. "Urbanism as a Way of Life." *American Journal of Sociology*. Vol. 44, No. 1 (July 1938):1–24.

WITKIN-LANOIL, GEORGIA. *The Female Stress Syndrome: How to Recognize and Live With It*. New York: Newmarket Press, 1984.

WOLF, NAOMI. *The Beauty Myth: How Images of Beauty Are Used Against Women*. New York: William Morrow, 1990.

WOLFE, DAVID B. "Killing the Messenger." *American Demographics*. Vol. 13, No. 7 (July 1991):40–43.

WOLFGANG, MARVIN E., ROBERT M. FIGLIO, and THORSTEN SELLIN. *Delinquency in a Birth Cohort*. Chicago: University of Chicago Press, 1972.

WOLFGANG, MARVIN E., TERRENCE P. THORNBERRY, and ROBERT M. FIGLIO. *From Boy to Man, From Delinquency to Crime*. Chicago: University of Chicago Press, 1987.

WONG, BUCK. "Need for Awareness: An Essay on Chinatown, San Francisco." In Amy Tachiki et al., eds., *Roots: An Asian Studies Center*, 1971:265–73.

WOODWARD, C. VANN. *The Strange Career of Jim Crow*. 3d rev. ed. New York: Oxford University Press, 1974.

WOODWARD, KENNETH L. "Feminism and the Churches." *Newsweek*. Vol. 13, No. 7 (February 13, 1989):58–61.

———. "The Elite, and How to Avoid It." *Newsweek* (July 20, 1992):55.

THE WORLD BANK. *World Development Report 1984*. New York: Oxford University Press, 1984.

———. *World Development Report 1991: The Challenge of Development*. New York: Oxford University Press, 1991.

———. *World Development Report 1993: Investing in Health*. New York: Oxford University Press, 1993.

———. *World Development Report 1994: Infrastructure for Development*. New York: Oxford University Press, 1994.

WORLD HEALTH ORGANIZATION. *Constitution of the World Health Organization*. New York: World Health Organization Interim Commission, 1946.

WREN, CHRISTOPHER S. "In Soweto-by-the-Sea, Misery Lives on as Apartheid Fades." *New York Times* (June 9, 1991):1, 7.

WRIGHT, ERIK OLIN, and BILL MARTIN. "The Transformation of the American Class Structure, 1960–1980." *American Journal of Sociology*. Vol. 93, No. 1 (July 1987):1–29.

WRIGHT, JAMES D. "Address Unknown: Homelessness in Contemporary America." *Society*. Vol. 26, No. 6 (September-October 1989):45–53.

WRIGHT, QUINCY. "Causes of War in the Atomic Age." In William M. Evan and Stephen Hilgartner, eds., *The Arms Race and Nuclear War*. Englewood Cliffs, N.J.: Prentice Hall, 1987:7–10.

WRONG, DENNIS H. "The Oversocialized Conception of Man in Modern Sociology." *American Sociological Review*. Vol. 26, No. 2 (April 1961):183–93.

YODER, JAN D., and ROBERT C. NICHOLS. "A Life Perspective: Comparison of Married and Divorced Persons." *Journal of Marriage and the Family*. Vol. 42, No. 2 (May 1980):413–19.

YOUNG, CATHY. "Notes From the Underclass: 'Bomzh' Away." *The New Republic*. Vol. 202, No. 5 (January 29, 1990): 18–20.

ZHOU, MIN, and JOHN R. LOGAN. "Returns of Human Capital in Ethnic Enclaves: New York City's Chinatown." *American Sociological Review*. Vol. 54, No. 5 (October 1989):809–20.

ZIPP, JOHN F. "Perceived Representativeness and Voting: An Assessment of the Impact of 'Choices' vs. 'Echoes.'" *The American Political Science Review*. Vol. 79, No. 1 (March 1985):50–61.

ZIPP, JOHN F., and JOEL SMITH. "A Structural Analysis of Class Voting." *Social Forces*. Vol. 60, No. 3 (March 1982):738–59.

ZOLA, IRVING KENNETH. "Medicine as an Institution of Social Control." In John Ehrenreich, ed., *The Cultural Crisis of Modern Medicine*. New York: Monthly Review Press, 1978:80–100.

ZUBOFF, SHOSHANA. "New Worlds of Computer-Mediated Work." *Harvard Business Review*. Vol. 60, No. 5 (September-October 1982):142–52.

Photo Credits

CHAPTER 1: Neal Simpson/Epic Ltd./Woodfin Camp & Associates, xxviii; Paul Liebhardt, 3; Alexandra Avakian/ Contact Press Images, 7; Bettmann, 9; Marc Chagall, *I and the Village*, 1911. Oil on canvas, 6'3⅝ inches. The Museum of Modern Art, New York. Mrs. Simon Guggenheim Fund, 12; Martineau: Mrs. Harriet, 1802–1876. Author of *Society in America*, 1837. Retrospect of Western Travel, 1837, 13(left); Brown Brothers, 13(center, right); Jacob Lawrence, *Strike*, 1949, Tempera on masonite, 20 x 24 inches. The Howard University Gallery of Art (Permanent Collection), Washington, D.C., 16; Roxanne Swentzell, The Emergence of the Clowns, 1988. Coiled and scraped clay: 48 x 48 x 23 inches. The Collection of The Heard Museum, Phoenix, Arizona, 18; Paul Liebhardt, 19; Jeffrey Mark Dunn/Stock Boston, 21; Nubar Alexanian/ Woodfin Camp & Associates, 22; Luis Villota/The Stock Market, 23.

CHAPTER 2: Eric Meola, 28; Paul Liebhardt, 31(top, left; top, center; top, right; middle, left; middle, right; bottom, left); David Austen/Stock Boston, 31(middle, center); Jack Fields/Photo Researchers, 31(bottom, right); Les Stone/Sygma, 33; Jeff Greenberg/Picture Cube, 34(left); Alex Webb/Magnum Photos, 34(center); Pedrick/The Image Works, 34(right); Sabina Dowell, 35(left); CLEO Photo/Jeroboam, 35(center); David Young-Wolff/Photoedit, 35(right); Sally Swain/*Great House-wives of Art*, 37; Karen Hofer/Actuality, 38; Grandma Moses, Joy Ride, 1953. Copyright 1991, Grandma Moses Properties Co., NY, 40; Four to Five, 41(top, left); James R. Holland/Stock Boston, 41(top, right); Paul Liebhardt, 41(bottom, left and right); Keith Dannemiller/SABA, 46; Jesse Levine, Laguna Sales, Palo Alto, 49; Paul Liebhardt, 51; Peter Menzel, 53.

CHAPTER 3: Hale Woodruff, *Girls Skipping*, 1949. Oil on canvas, 24 x 32 inches. Courtesy of Michael Rosenfield Gallery, New York, 56; Ted Horowitz/Stock Market, 59(left); Henley & Savage/ Stock Market, 59(center); Tom Pollack/Monkmeyer Press, 59(right); Alon Reininger/Woodfin Camp & Associates, 60; Elizabeth Crews, 62; Keith Carter, 63; Fateh Al-Moudarres(Syrian), *Les Refugies*. Institut du Monde Arabe, Paris. Photo © *Phillipe Maillard*, 64; Henry Ossawa Tanner, *The Banjo Lesson*, 1893. Oil on canvas. Hampton University Museum, Hampton, Virginia, 66; Laura Dwight/Peter Arnold, 67(top); Paul Liebhardt, 67(bottom); Brown Brothers, 69; Dana Fineman/Sygma, 74; The Stanley Burns, M. D., Collection, 76; Danny Lyon/Magnum Photos, 77.

CHAPTER 4: Junebug Clark/Photo Researchers, Inc., 80; Winslow Homer, A *Visit From the Old Mistress*, 1876. National Museum of American Art [National Museum of American Art/Art Resource, New York] [Consignment: S0025392], 83; John Focht, 84; Paul Liebhardt, 88; David Cooper/Gamma-Liaison, 91(top, left); Alan Weiner/Gamma-Liaison, 91(top, center); Lynn McLaren/Picture Cube, 91(top, right); Ellis Herwig/Picture Cube, 91(bottom, left); Richard Pan/The Image Bank, 91(bottom, center); Erik Leigh Simmone/The Image Works, 91(bottom, right); Jacob Lawrence, Theatre Series, No. 8: *Vaudeville*, 1951. Tempera on fiberboard, 29⅞ x 19¹⁵⁄₁₆ inches. Hirshhorn Museum and Sculpture Garden, Smithsonian Institution, Gift of Joseph H. Hirshhorn, 1966, 92; Bob Daemmrich/The Image Works, 93; Ruth Orkin/Ruth Orkin Photo Archive, 94; Paul Liebhardt, 95; Tony Freeman/ Photoedit, 97; Emile Ardolino/Sygma, 99.

CHAPTER 5: Michael O'Neill, 102; Frank Siteman/ Picture Cube, 105; Douglas Kirkland/The Image Bank, 109; Joseph Decker/Private Collection, 110; Ann States/SABA, 112; Bibliotheque Nationale, Paris. From "The Horizon History of China," by the editors of *Horizon* Magazine, American Heritage Publishing Co., Inc., 551 5th Avenue, New York, NY 10017 © 1969, 113; Paul Liebhardt, 117; Peter Charlesworth/JB Pictures, 118; George Tooker, *Government Bureau*, 1956. Egg tempera on gesso panel, 19⅝ x 29⅝ inches. The Metropolitan Museum of Art, George A. Hearn Fund, 1956 (56.78), 119; AP/Wide World Photos, 121; Karen Kasmauski/Woodfin Camp & Associates, 123.

CHAPTER 6: Billy E. Barnes/Stock Boston, 127; Sipa Press, 129; Jacques Chenet/Woodfin Camp & Associates, 131; Stephen Shames/Matrix International, Inc., 133; Gerry Gropp/Sipa Press, 134; Edward Gargan/*New York Times* Pictures, 135; Frank Romero, *The Closing of Whittier Boulevard*, 1984. Oil on canvas. 6 x 10 feet, 137; Pool/Saba Press Photos, Inc., 138; Sipa Press, 140; Schoenrock/Action Press/SABA, 142; Courtesy of Bennetton, 146; Najlah Feanny/SABA, 147; Vincent Van Gogh, 1853–1890. *Prisoners Round*. Dutch. Pushkin State Museum, Moscow, Superstock, 150.

CHAPTER 7: Burt Glinn/Magnum Photos, Inc., 154; Sebastiao Salgado/Magnum Photos, 157; Paula Bronstein/Impact Visuals, 158; Katie Arkell/Gamma-Liaison, 160; Limbourg Brothers, *Le Duc de Berry à Table, Tres Riches Heures du Duc de Berry*, January, folio iv. Chantilly, Musée Conde, 161; Granger Collection, 163; John George Brown/Art Resource, 164(left); Jacob A. Riis/Museum of the City of New York, 164(right); Michael Grecco/Stock Boston, 172; Miguel Fairbanks, 174; Dennis Brack/Black Star, 175; Henry O. Tanner/Philadelphia Museum of Art, 181; Mary Ellen Mark, 182.

CHAPTER 8: Betty Press/Woodfin Camp & Associates, 186; Ira Block/The Image Bank, 190(top, left); Peter Turnley/Black Star, 190(top, right); Thomas Hoepker/Magnum Photos, 190(bottom, left); Christopher Morris/Time/Black Star, 192; Patrick Aventurier/Gamma Liaison, 196; Eric Vaudeville/Gamma-Liaison, 197; Rick Smolan/Stock Boston, 198; ARCHIV/Photo Researchers, 200; Betty Press/Woodfin Camp & Associates, 201; Diego Rivera/Granger Collection, 203; Radhi/Chalasani/Gamma-Liaison, 205.

CHAPTER 9: Norman Prince, 210; Paul Liebhardt, 213(top, left; top, center; bottom, left; bottom, center); Robert Caputo/Stock Boston, 213(top, right); Lisl Dennis/The Image Bank, 213(bottom, right); Raveendran/Agence France, 217; The Bettmann Archive/Bettmann, 218(top, left); Culver Pictures, 218(bottom, left); Schomburg Center/New York Public Library, 218(bottom, center); UPI/Bettmann, 218(bottom, right); Chester Higgins, Jr./Photo Researchers, 220; Bettmann, 221; Steve Lehman/SABA, 222; Jacob Lawrence, The cruelty of the planters led to the slaves' revolt, 1776. These revolts kept on cropping up from time to time and finally came to a head in the rebellion, from Toussaint L'Ouverture Series, 1937–38. Tempera on paper, 11 x 19 inches. The Amistad Research Center's Aaron Douglas Collection, New Orleans, 224; UPI/Bettmann, 225; Hardy A. Saffold/ ipa Press, 228; Erich Hartmann/Magnum Photos, 230; Randy Taylor/Sygma, 233.

CHAPTER 10: Michael O'Neill, 236; Michel Tcherevkoff/The Image Bank, 239; Aspect Picture Library/Stock Market, 241; Jacky Gucia/The Image Bank, 242; Jacques M. Chenet/Gamma-Liaison, Inc., 245; Jacob Lawrence, Ironers, 1943. Gouache on paper, 21 x 30 inches. Private Collection Francine Seders Gallery, 249; Shepard Sherbell/SABA Press Photos, Inc., 252; John Coletti/Stock Boston, 253; Natsuko Utsumi/Gamma-Liaison, Inc., 254; Courtesy NOW, 256; Carlson © 1993 Milwaukee Sentinel. Reprinted with permission of Universal Press Syndicate. All Rights Reserved, 255; UPI/Bettmann, 257; Maggie Steber/Stock Market, 259.

CHAPTER 11: C. Hires-G. Merrillon/Gamma-Liaison, Inc., 262; Bellavia/REA/SABA, 267(left); John Bryson/Sygma, 267(right); Carlo Brogi/Contrasto/SABA, 269; Geoffrey Clements/Collection of Whitney Museum of American Art, New York. Issac Soyer 1907–1981. Employment Agency, 1937. Oil on canvas. 34¼ x 45 in. (87 x 114.3 cm.), 273; Mayer/Gamma-Liaison, 277; © Smith Georges, 278; David Ball/Picture Cube, 281; Francisco Goya (1746–1828), Third of May, Prado, Madrid, Scala/Art Resource, 282; John Duricka/AP/Worldwide Photos, 283; John Marmaras/Woodfin Camp & Associates, 284; T. W. Wood Art Gallery, Vermont, 286; Barry Iverson/Time/Life, 288; Peter Northall/Black Star, 290; Porter Gifford/Gamma-Liaison, 291.

CHAPTER 12: Louinés Mentor, 296; Farrell Grehan/Photo Researchers, 299; M. Chagall/New York artist's rights, 302; Kitagawa Utamaro/British Library, 304; Carmen Lomas Garza, Tamalada. Medium: Oil on linen mounted on wood, size: 24 x

32". © 1988. Collection of Paula Maciel-Benecke and Norbert Benecke, 308; James Skovmand/San Diego Union, 312; James D. Wilson/Gamma-Liaison, Inc., 313; Stern (Ullal)/Black Star, 315; R. Rai/Magnum Photos, 316; Ira Wyman/Sygma, 317; William Campbell/Time Magazine, 318; Gilles Peress/Magnum Photos, Inc., 320; Thomas Hart Benton, Arts of the South. Tempera w/oil glaze, 8 x 13 feet, Harriet Russell Stanley, 326.

CHAPTER 13: Robert Burke/Gamma-Liaison, Inc., 331; Hans Neleman/The Image Bank, 335; Davis Young Wolff/Photoedit, 336; Bob Daemmrich/The Image Works, 337(left); Charles Gupton/Stock Boston, 337(right); Michael Newman/Photoedit, 341; Literacy Volunteers of America, 343; The Granger Collection, 345; W. Campbell/Sygma, 347(left); Peter Magubane/Black Star, 347(right); Marty Katz, 350; D. Michael Cheers from Songs of My People, © New African Visions, Inc., 354; Howard Sochurek/Woodfin Camp & Associates, 359.

CHAPTER 14: Red Grooms, Taxi to the Terminal, 1993. Color Lithograph, 22 x 30". Courtesy of Marlborough Gallery, New York, 362; Jacob Lawrence, The Migration of the Negro, Panel 1: During the World War There Was a Great Migration North by Southern Negroes, 11½ x 17½, The Phillips Collection, 366; N. Maceschal/The Image Bank, 370; Owen Franken/Stock Boston, 372; Forum Against Sex Discrimination and Sex Pre-Selection Techniques in Bombay, 373; Leonard Von Matt/Photo Researchers, 374; Pieter Brueghel the Elder, Peasant Dance, c. 1565, Kunsthistorisches Museum, Vienna, Superstock., 381(left); Fernand Léger, The City, 1919, Oil on canvas, 90 3.4 x 117¼", Philadelphia Museum of Art, A. E. Gallatin Collection, 381(right); University of Chicago Library, 382.

CHAPTER 15: Louie Psihoyos/Matrix International, 388; Tony Freeman/Photoedit, 391(left); Gregory G. Dimijian/Photo Researchers, 391(right); Michael Nichols/Magnum Photos, 392; Peter Martens/Magnum Photos, 393; Gordon/Rea/SABA, 397; Utarbekov Nabihan/Press Studio/Lehtikuva/SABA, 399; Stephanie Stokes/Stock Market, 403; Paul Liebhardt, 405; Claus Meyer/Black Star, 407.

CHAPTER 16: James Willis/Tony Stone Images, 410; Lambert/Archive Photos, 413(top, left); Owen Franken/Stock Boston, 413(top, center); Charles Harbutt/Actuality, 413(top, right); Terje Rakke/The Image Bank, 413(bottom, center); G & M. David de Lossy/The Image Bank, 413(bottom, right); Sylvia Johnson, 417; Paul Ganguin, The Day of the God (Mahana no Atua), 1894, Oil on canvas, 68.3 x 91.5 cm., Helen Birch Bartlett Memorial Collection, 1926. 198, Photograph © 1994, The Art Institute of Chicago. All Rights Reserved, 418; George Tooker, The Subway, 1950, Egg tempera on composition board, 18⅛ x 36⅛", Whitney Museum of American Art, New York, Purchase, with funds from the Juliana Force Purchase Award, 50.23, 419; Andrew Holbrooke/Black Star, 424; Mauri Rautkari/WWF Photo Library, 426; Rafael Macia/Photo Researchers, 430; William L. Haney, In Over Our Heads, 1984, Oil on canvas, 58 x 74", Courtesy Sherry French Gallery, New York, 431.

Index

Name Index

Abbott, Daniel, 147
Aberle, David F., 416
Abernathy, Ralph, 323
Addams, Jane, 13
Adler, Jerry, 97
Adorno, T. W., 217
Ageton, Suzanne S., 146
Alam, Sultana, 201
Albon, Joan, 223
Allan, Emilie Andersen, 134
Allen, Michael Patrick, 285
Al-Moudarres, Fateh, 64
Amman, Jost, 345
Anders, George, 357
Anderson, Daniel R., 69
Anderson, John Ward, 196
Anderson, Marian, 218
Ando, Faith H., 248
Andrews, Nancy, 314
Ang, Ien, 69
Angier, Natalie, 240
Anspaugh, David J., 357
Aral, S. O., 350
Archer, Dane, 151
Arendt, Hannah, 282
Ariès, Philippe, 70, 75
Aristide, Jean-Bertrand, 278
Aristotle, 46, 332
Asante, Molefi Kete, 44
Asch, Solomon, 108
Astin, Alexander W., 47
Astone, Nan Marie, 313
Astor, John Jacob, 163
Aviad, Janet O'Dea, 319, 324
Axtell, Roger E., 35

Bachman, Ronet, 311
Bachrach, Peter, 286
Bahl, Vinay, 157
Bahr, Howard M., 283, 359
Bailey, William C., 151
Bainbridge, William Sims, 320, 325, 327
Baker, David, 334
Baker, Mary Anne, 240
Bales, Robert F., 106, 301

Baltzell, E. Digby, 163, 172, 174, 223, 233, 377, 421
Banfield, Edward, 181
Barash, David, 52
Baratz, Morton S., 286
Barker, Eileen, 321, 325, 327
Barry, Kathleen, 52, 197, 256, 257
Bassuk, Ellen J., 182
Bateson, C. Daniel, 327
Bauer, P. T., 199, 202
Beach, Frank A., 239
Bear, John, 35, 93
Becker, Howard S., 128, 134
Beeghley, Leonard, 167
Behrens, William W., III, 395
Bell, Alan P., 314
Bell, Wendell, 382
Bellah, Robert N., 39, 53, 324
Belsky, Jay, 66
Bem, Sandra Lipsitz, 243
Benedict, Ruth, 71–72, 334
Benford, Robert D., 417
Benjamin, Lois, 215
Bennett, William, 430
Benokraitis, Nijole, 99, 248, 250
Benton, Thomas Hart, 326
Berardo, F. M., 306
Berger, Brigitte, 421, 425
Berger, Peter L., 2, 53, 77, 86, 167, 199, 201, 276, 317, 417, 418, 421, 425
Bergesen, Albert, 203, 276
Berheide, Catherine White, 240
Bernard, Jessie, 244, 248, 252, 257, 308
Bernard, Larry Craig, 243
Bernard, Thomas J., 129, 136
Bernstein, Richard J., 428
Berrill, Kevin T., 142
Berry, Brian, 382
Berscheid, Ellen, 304
Best, Raphaela, 66
Biblarz, Timothy J., 313
Blakeslee, Sandra, 313
Blau, Judith R., 146

Blau, Peter M., 14, 111, 146, 175, 303
Blaustein, Albert P., 224
Bloom, Leonard, 229
Blum, Linda M., 249
Blum, Terry M., 111
Blumberg, Paul, 176, 424
Blumer, Herbert G., 416
Blumstein, Philip, 24, 304, 313
Bode, Nancy, 139
Boden, Deidre, 87
Boff, Leonard, 319
Bogardus, Emory S., 218
Bohm, Robert M., 151
Bohmer, Susanne, 312
Bonilla-Santiago, Gloria, 251
Bonner, Jane, 244
Booth, Alan, 310
Borgmann, Albert, 428
Bormann, F. Herbert, 393, 407
Boswell, Terry E., 226
Bott, Elizabeth, 306
Bowles, Samuel, 13, 336
Boyce, James, 197
Boyer, Ernest L., 342
Brady, James, 147
Braithwaite, John, 146
Branegan, Jay, 281
Braungart, Margaret M., 47
Braungart, Richard G., 47
Brinton, Crane, 287
Brinton, Mary C., 334
Brody, Charles, 93
Brophy, Gwenda, 372
Brown, E. Richard, 358
Brown, John George, 164
Brown, Lester R., 404, 407
Brown, Louise, 314
Brown, Mary Ellen, 69
Brownmiller, Susan, 141, 238
Brownstein, Ronald, 286
Broyles, Philip, 285
Brzezinski, Zbigniew, 282
Burch, Robert, 194
Burgess, Ernest W., 381–82
Burke, Tom, 407, 408
Burns, James A., 340

Busby, Linda J., 245
Buttel, Frederick R., 407

Cafferata, Gail Lee, 74
Callahan, Daniel, 74
Calvin, John, 318
Cameron, William Bruce, 416
Campbell, Richard T., 159
Cantor, Murial G., 69
Caplow, Theodore, 283, 359
Capone, Al, 132, 138
Carlson, Norman A., 151
Carmichael, Stokely, 217
Carnegie, Andrew, 163
Carroll, Ginny, 337
Castro, Fidel, 232
Chadwick, Bruce A., 283
Chagall, Marc, 12, 302
Chagnon, Napoleon, 30, 32, 35, 42, 47, 50
Chandler, Tertius, 375
Change, Kwang-Chih, 374
Chaves, Mark, 322
Cheers, Michael, 354
Cherlin, Andrew, 306, 309, 315
Church, George J., 357
Clark, Thomas A., 378
Clarke, Robin, 391, 399, 401
Clayson, Dennis E., 141
Clinard, Marshall B., 147
Clinton, Bill, 160, 162, 284, 292, 356
Clinton, Hillary Rodham, 255
Cloward, Richard A., 132, 134, 285, 418
Coakley, Jay J., 16, 17
Cobb, Jonathan, 183, 340
Coe, Michael D., 374
Cohen, Albert, 133, 134
Cohen, Lloyd R., 253
Cohen, Michael, 338
Coleman, James S., 337, 341
Coleman, Richard P., 171, 172
Collins, Joseph, 205
Collins, Randall, 255, 322, 339, 340
Colloway, N. O., 73

Martin, John M., 148
Martin, William, 327
Martineau, Harriet, 13
Marullo, Sam, 291
Marx, Karl, 10, 13, 19, 51, 98,
    131, 137, 160, 161,
    163–66, 257, 258, 270,
    287, 317, 318, 369, 414,
    421, 423, 424
Massey, Douglas S., 221
Masters, William H., 350
Matthiessen, Peter, 221–23
Mauro, Tony, 353
May, Elaine Tyler, 292
Mayo, Katherine, 303
Mead, George Herbert, 14,
    63–65, 77
Mead, Margaret, 241
Meadows, Dennis L., 395
Meadows, Donella H., 395
Mechanic, David, 346
Meister, Richard J., 378
Meltzer, Bernard N., 65
Melucci, Alberto, 416, 417
Mennerick, Lewis A., 332
Merton, Robert K., 11–12, 84,
    109, 116, 132, 138, 140,
    219, 416
Messner, Steven F., 111
Metch, Barbara J., 381
Michael, Robert T., 240, 304
Michaels, Stuart, 240, 304
Michels, Robert, 118
Milbrath, Lester W., 390, 393,
    394
Milgram, Stanley, 108
Miliband, Ralph, 165, 424
Milken, Michael, 138–39
Miller, Arthur G., 108
Miller, G. Tyler, Jr., 392, 396, 418
Miller, Joanne, 248, 302
Miller, Karen A., 248, 302
Miller, Michael, 118
Miller, Walter B., 133, 134
Millet, Kate, 257
Millman, Joel, 169
Mills, C. Wright, 5, 286
Mink, Barbara, 201
Mintz, Beth, 276
Mirowsky, John, 109
Modell, John, 283, 359
Molnar, Stephen, 212
Molotch, Harvey, 382
Molotch, Harvey L., 87
Montague, Ashley, 289
Moore, Gwen, 112
Moore, Joan, 308, 370
Moore, Molly, 196
Moore, Wilbert E., 161–62, 164,
    202
Moran, John S., 350
Morehead, Jere W., 398
Morgan, J. P., 163

Moses, Anna Mary Robertson
    (Grandma), 40
Mosley, W. Henry, 349, 359
Mott, Lucretia, 256
Mueller, Charles W., 249
Mueller, Daniel P., 313
Mumford, Lewis, 346, 374, 375
Munk, Nina, 169
Murdock, George Peter, 50, 241,
    299, 301
Murray, Pauli, 224
Myers, Norman, 392, 394, 397,
    399, 401, 404, 426
Myers, Sheila, 357
Myrdal, Gunnar, 224

Najafizadeh, Mehrangiz, 332
Neidert, Lisa J., 223
Neitz, Mary Jo, 39, 50, 428
Nelan, Bruce W., 290
Neugarten, Bernice L., 172
Neuhouser, Kevin, 319
Newman, William M., 220, 234
Newton, Isaac, 9
Nichols, Robert C., 310
Niebuhr, R. Gustav, 298
Nielsen, Joyce McCarl, 20
Nisbet, Robert A., 19, 282, 421
Nolan, Patrick, 40, 42, 166, 241,
    373, 374
Nunn, Clyde Z., 174, 284

Oakes, Jeannie, 13, 336
O'Brien, David J., 229
O'Dea, Thomas F., 319, 324
Offir, Carole Wade, 239
Ogburn, William F., 47, 412
O'Hare, William, 171, 172, 248,
    308
Ohlin, Lloyd E., 132
Okimoto, Daniel, 230
Olshan, Marc A., 319, 425
Olzak, Susan, 218
Orkin, Ruth, 94
Orlansky, Michael D., 84
Oropesa, R. S., 381
Osgood, D. Wayne, 130
Ostling, Richard N., 326
Ostrander, Susan A., 173
Ouchi, William, 122
Owen, David, 336

Pachon, Harry, 308, 370
Pampel, Fred C., 176
Parcel, Toby L., 249
Parenti, Michael, 69
Parillo, Vincent N., 230
Park, Robert E., 380–82
Parkinson, C. Northcote, 117
Parks, Rosa, 84, 221
Parsons, Talcott, 50, 106, 202,
    254, 255, 301
Pasteur, Louis, 359
Paton, George E. C., 99

Paul, Ellen Frankel, 253
Payne, Douglas W., 268, 280
Pear, Robert, 250, 358
Pease, John, 183
Pennings, Johannes M., 120
Percy, Walker, 431
Persell, Caroline Hodges, 336
Pessen, Edward, 163
Peter, Laurence J., 117
Peterman, T. A., 350
Peters, Thomas J., 119
Peterson, Ruth D., 151
Piaget, Jean, 61–62, 64, 65
Pingree, Suzanne, 69
Piotrow, Phyllis T., 371
Pirandello, Luigi, 85–86
Piven, Frances Fox, 285, 418
Plato, 161, 332
Plomin, Robert, 59
Polenberg, Richard, 424
Polsby, Nelson W., 286
Pomer, Marshall I., 176
Popenoe, David, 243, 259, 313
Portes, Alejandro, 228
Postel, Sandra, 397–99
Powell, Chris, 99
Powers, Stephen, 70
Presser, Harriet B., 248
Pressley, Sue Anne, 314
Puterbaugh, Geoff, 240
Putka, Gary, 336, 344

Queenan, Joe, 171
Quinney, Richard, 137

Raftery, Adrian E., 313
Ragin, Charles C., 203, 276
Rainwater, Lee, 171
Randall, Vicki, 256
Randers, Jorgan, 395
Raphael, Ray, 243
Raschke, Helen J., 309
Reckless, Walter, 130
Reed, O. Lee, 398
Reed, Rodney J., 340
Rees, Philip, 382
Reid, Sue Titus, 149
Reimers, Cordelia W., 232
Reinharz, Shulamit, 20
Remoff, Heather Trexler, 52
Richardson, James T., 321
Richtand, Carol N., 248, 302
Ridgeway, Cecilia L., 106, 107
Riesman, David, 425, 427, 430
Riggs, Ellyne R., 47
Riis, Jacob, 164
Riley, Matilda White, 65, 76
Ritzer, George, 104, 121, 122,
    272
Rivera, Diego, 203
Roberts, J. Deotis, 323
Roberts, Mary K., 133
Roberts, Oral, 327
Robertson, Pat, 327

Robinson, Joyce, 248
Robinson, Vera M., 99
Rochford, E. Burke, Jr., 417
Roesch, Roberta, 252, 311
Roethlisberger, F. J., 116
Rogers, Alison, 169
Rohlen, Thomas P., 332, 334
Romano, Anne T., 148
Romero, Frank, 137
Roof, Wade Clark, 322, 325
Roos, Patricia, 248
Roosevelt, Franklin, 228
Rosenberg, Stanley D., 72
Rosenthal, Elizabeth, 355
Rosenthal, Jack, 377
Roskin, Michael G., 279
Ross, Susan, 371
Rossi, Alice S., 243
Rossi, Peter H., 170
Rossides, Daniel W., 172
Rostow, Walt W., 199, 276
Rothman, David, 70
Rowe, David C., 130
Rozin, P., 348
Rubin, Lillian Breslow, 306
Rudolph, Barbara, 349
Russell, Cheryl, 419
Ryan, Jospeh E., 268, 280
Ryan, William, 181, 182
Rytina, Joan Huber, 183

Sabato, Larry J., 285
Sadd, Susan, 304
Salas, Rafael M., 371
Sale, Kirkpatrick, 221, 222
Salholz, Eloise, 239
Salmans, Sandra, 251
Sampson, Anthony, 334
Sampson, Robert J., 133, 146
Sanger, Margaret Higgins, 257
Sangl, Judith, 74
Sansom, William, 92
Sapir, Edward, 35
Scaff, Lawrence A., 279
Scheff, Thomas J., 135, 136
Schlesinger, Arthur, Jr., 46, 109,
    376
Schneider, Mark, 378
Schoenberger, Richard, 250
Schooler, Carmi, 248, 302
Schuller, Robert, 327
Schuman, Michael, 169
Schutt, Russell K., 182
Schwartz, Joseph E., 111
Schwartz, Martin D., 311
Schwartz, Michael, 276
Schwartz, Pepper, 24, 304, 313
Schwartz-Nobel, Loretta, 178
Scott, John, 276
Scott, W. Richard, 114
Segal, David R., 292
Segal, Mady Wechsler, 292
Segal, Marcia Texler, 240
Segal, Ronald, 267

Subject Index

Lesbian, 142, 239 (*see also* Gay people; Gay rights movement; Homosexuality)
Less-developed countries, 189
  division of population and global income, 194
  economic development of, 6, 7, 191
  gross domestic product in, 6, 192, 193
  median age at death, global map, 195
Liberal feminism, 257, 326
Liberal politics, 283–85
Liberation theology, 319
Liberty, 10, 279
  in global perspective, 280
Libya, 291
Life course:
  and family, 303–4
  and socialization, 70–76
Life expectancy, 43, 306, 346, 349, 359, 365, 371, 414
  and gender, 240, 349
  global map, 195, 346, 429
  and race, 348, 349
  and social class, 174
Limits to growth thesis, 395
Literacy, 166
Lithuania, 192, 193
Lobbyists, 284
Logic of growth, 394
Looking-glass self, 64
Love, 303–5, 309
Lower class, 173–74
Lower-upper class, 173
Lumad people, 426

Machismo, 308
Macro-level orientation, 14, 15
Mainstreaming in schools, 344
Malaysia, 40, 212, 281, 289
Male sex (*see* Gender; Men)
Malthusian theory, 368–69
Mandatory education law, 332
Manifest function, 11–12
Manufacturing, 9, 265
Marginality (*see* Social marginality)
Marital rape, 312
Marriage, 298 (*see also* Family)
  arranged, 303
  divorce, 46, 309–11, 314
  endogamous, 157, 299, 302
  ideal and real, 304
  patterns, 299
  religion and social construction of, 317
  remarriage, 310
  and sexual activity, 24
  types, global map, 300
Marxist theory, 161, 163–66, 218, 255, 405, 421, 423, 424

Mass consumption, 200
Mass media:
  advertising, 69, 245, 272
  and gender, 245, 348
  and minorities, 69
  and socialization, 68–70
Mass production, 265
Mass-society theory of modernity, 416, 421–27
Master status, 83–84
  stigma as, 135
Material culture, 30, 394
Materialism, 51
Matriarchy, 242
Matrilineal descent, 301
Matrilocality, 300–301
Matrimony (*see* Marriage)
McDonaldization of society, 104, 121–22
"Me" (G. H. Mead), 64, 65
Mean, 16
Measurement, 15–16
Mechanical solidarity, 380, 419–20, 425
Media (*see* Mass media)
Median, 16
Medicaid, 356
Medicalization of deviance, 136
Medicare, 356
Medicine:
  cost of care, 356
  in global perspective, 354–55
  holistic, 354, 355, 359
  rise of scientific, 353–54
  social-conflict analysis of, 358–59
  structural-functional analysis of, 357
  symbolic-interaction analysis of, 357–58
  in U.S., 355–57
Megalopolis, 379
Melting pot, 220
Men (*see also* Family; Gay people; Gender):
  and aging, 306
  biological development, 238, 240
  and cigarette smoking, 349
  and college majors, 245
  and deviance, 140–42, 145–46
  and earnings, 249–50, 339, 340
  and education, 339, 340
  and feminism, 259
  and health, 347, 348
  and housework, 248
  masculine traits, 243
  masculinity as contest, 244
  and mass media, 245
  and networking, 111–12
  patriarchy, 242–43, 252, 302, 308, 318, 428
  sex ratio, 366

and social construction of reality, 85–89
socialization of, 243–45
and stratification, 245–54
as victims of sexism, 243
and voting frequency, 285
and work, 270, 273–75
Mental illness, labeling and, 135–36
Mercy killing, 353
Meritocracy, 162, 335
Metaphysical stage (Comte), 9
Metropolitan statistical area (MSA), 378
Mexican Americans, 230, 232, 234
Mexico, 168, 193, 365, 367, 368, 384, 396
Mexico City, 364, 381, 385
Micro-level orientation, 14, 15
Middle Ages (*see also* Agrarian society):
  cities in, 374, 418
  health during, 345, 346
  schooling during, 334
Middle class, 173, 182
Middle East, 191, 288, 293, 299, 322, 332
Migration, 48, 212, 365, 415–16
  national map, 415
Militarism, 291, 293
Military, and social diversity, 291–92
Military-industrial complex, 291
Minority:
  characteristics, 214–15
  defined, 214
  -majority interaction patterns, 220–21
  national map, 231
  women as, 251–52
"Minority-majority," 215, 216, 273
  national map, 216
Miscegenation, 220
Mobility (*see* Social mobility)
Mode, 16
"Model minority" image, 226
Modernity, 412, 417–21
  class society, 423–25, 427
  and individual, 425, 427
  mass society, 421–27
Modernization, characteristics of, 417–18
Modernization theory, 199–202, 204, 205, 207, 276, 370, 418–19, 430
Monarchy, 279, 317, 423
Mongoloid, 213
Monogamy, 299, 300
Monopoly, 276
Moral development, 62–63
Mores, 39, 197
Mortality, 365–68

Most-developed countries:
  and dependency theory, 205–6
  division of population and global income, 194
  economic development of, 5, 6, 189–91
  gross domestic product in, 6, 192, 193
  median age at death, global map, 195
  and modernization theory, 199–202
MSA (*see* Metropolitan statistical area)
Mud men, 403
Multi-centered cities, 382
Multiculturalism, 44–46, 428
Multinational corporation, 197–98, 276, 277, 281, 432
Mundugumor culture, 241
Mutually assured destruction (MAD), 293

Names, changes in, 4
Native Americans, 88, 215, 221, 222–23, 234, 275, 300, 301, 350, 374, 375
  citizenship of, 223
  and income, 223
  religion of, 321
Nativist movements, 223
Natural environment, 389–409
  acid rain, 401
  air pollution, 399–401, 404
  defined, 390
  global approach, 391
  international opinion data, 396
  and population growth, 393–95
  rain forests, 391, 401–4
  social-conflict analysis of, 405–6
  solid waste, 395–97
  structural-functional analysis of, 404–5
  sustainable ecosystem, 406–8
  and technology, 391–93, 428
  water, 397–99
Natural selection, 52
Nature versus nurture, 58–59
Navajo Indians, 238, 301
Nazi Germany, 216–17, 221, 281, 282, 290, 314
Negroid, 212–13
Neocolonialism, 197
Neolocality, 301
Netherlands, 279, 396, 415
Network, 111–12
New Guinea, 193, 403
New reproductive technology, 314, 315

New social movements theory, 417
Newspaper reading, national map, 68
New Zealand, 114
Nicaragua, 167, 332
Niger, 241
Nigerian, 365
Nile River, 397
Nisei, 229
Nonmaterial culture, 30
Nonverbal communication, 92–93
Normative organization, 112
Norms, 39
 and authority, 277–78
 and deviance, 131, 137
North Korea, 282, 291
Norway, 243, 279, 396
Nuclear family, 299
Nuclear proliferation, 291
Nuclear weapons, 291, 293
Nurture, versus nature, 58–59
Nutrition, 194, 207, 347

Objectivity, in scientific research, 18–19
Occupations:
 and gender, 246–48
 and prestige, 170
Old age (*see* Aging)
Oligarchy, 118
Oligopoly, 276
Oman, 191
One-parent family, 46, 179, 251, 312–13
Operationalizing a variable, 15
Oral tradition, 333
Organic solidarity, 380, 420
Organization (*see* Formal organization)
Organizational environment, 120
Osteopathy, 353
Other-directedness, 427
Outgroup, 109–10, 215
Overgeneralizing, 19–20
Ozone layer, 391

PAC (*see* Political action committee)
Pakistan, 291, 304
Panama, 191
Paradigm (*see* Theoretical paradigm)
Paraprofessionals, 272
Parenting, 305–6
 aging parents, 73, 74, 306
 single parents, 46, 179, 251, 312–13
Parochial schools, 336–37
Participant observation, 23, 25
Pastoralism, 42, 392 (*see also* Preindustrial society)

Patriarchy, 252, 302, 308, 428
 and feminism, 256–58
 and religion, 317–18
 and sexism, 242–43
Patrilineal descent, 301
Patrilocality, 300–301
Peace, 289, 292–93
Pearl Harbor, 229
Peer group, 67
 and gender socialization, 244–45
People's Republic of China, 148, 167, 168, 191, 193, 266, 268, 289, 291, 293
 medicine in, 355
 population of, 371, 372
Perestroika, 160
Performance, 90–94
Persian Gulf War (1991), 290, 291
Personality, 58
 and charisma, 278
 and deviant behavior, 130
 Freud's model, 60–61
Personal space, 93
Philippines, 191, 206, 232, 385, 396, 426
Physical disability:
 and education, 344
 as master status, 84
Physicians, 357
 social interaction of, 90–92
Pink-collar jobs, 247
Planned obsolescence, 406
Plant biodiversity, 402–3
Play, and gender, 244–45
"Play" stage (G. H. Mead), 65
Plea bargaining, 149
Pluralism, 220, 221, 285–87
Pokot, 238
Poland, 124, 191, 193, 396, 406
Police, 149
Political action committee (PAC), 284–85
Political change, 10
Political party, 284, 285
Political revolution, 287–88
Political spectrum, 283
Politics, 277–94
 and African Americans, 226, 284, 285
 apathy, 285, 423
 and authority, 277–78
 and economics, 279, 283–84
 and gender, 250–51
 global system, 282
 history of, 277–78
 medicine as, 358
 party identification, 284, 285
 and peace, 289, 292–93
 political freedom, global map, 280
 and religion, 316, 317
 and revolution, 287–88
 and social class, 174, 284, 286

systems of, 278–79, 281–82
 terrorism, 288–89
 theoretical analysis of, 285–87
 in twenty-first century, 293
 U.S., 283–85
Pollution, 393
 air, 399–401, 404
 water, 399
Polyandry, 299
Polygamy, 299, 300
Polygyny, 299, 301
Popular culture, 39–40
Population, 364–73, 386, 387 (*see also* Urbanization)
 composition, 366–68
 demography, 364–68
 in global perspective, 370–71
 and global poverty, 197
 growth, 366, 368–70, 371, 375, 377, 393–95, 407
 global map, 367
 history of, 368–70
 and income distribution, 194
 in survey research, 21
 in twenty-first century, 371, 373
Pornography, 253–54, 257, 281
Portugal, 190
Positivism, 9
Postconventional level (Kohlberg), 62
Postindustrial economy, 176–78, 266
Postindustrial society, 266
Postmodernity, 412, 428–30
Poverty, 178–83
 and African Americans, 178, 179
 and aging, 75
 and Asian Americans, 178, 179
 and children, 178, 179, 315
 and families, 178–80, 182, 308, 313
 and gender, 179–80, 194
 in global perspective, 188–207
 and health, 346, 347
 and Hispanics, 178, 232
 homelessness, 182–83
 and Native Americans, 223
 and population growth, 393
 and society, 180–82
 in U.S., 178–83
 and women, 308, 313
 and work, 173, 182
Power, 165–66, 279 (*see also* Politics)
 and deviance, 137
 and gender, 241–43, 254, 255
 global power relationships, 197
 in interaction, 90–92, 94, 96
Power-elite model, 286–87, 405

Powerlessness, modernity and, 425, 427
Preconventional level (Kohlberg), 62
Predestination, 318
Preindustrial society:
 and aging, 73
 and cities, 374, 381
 compared to modern, 422
 economy of, 264
 and education, 332
 and family, 299–300, 305
 and gender, 241
 and health, 346
 and patriarchy, 243
 patterns of descent, 301
 and population growth, 369
 and religion, 321
 social groups in, 105
 and tradition, 113
Prejudice, 215, 217–19, 228
Preoperational stage (Piaget), 61–62
Presentation of self, 89–90
Prestige, 166, 170
Primary deviance, 134
Primary economic sector, 266
Primary group, 104–6
Primogeniture, 159
Prison, 76–77, 150, 151
Privacy, 117, 118
Private school, 336–38
Productivity, 269
Profane, 315, 319
Professions, 272
Progress:
 and social change, 427–28
 as value, 37
Progressive education, 335
Proletariat, 163, 164
Promotion practices, 275
Property, 267
Prostitution, 147, 196, 201
 global map, 148
Protestantism, 4, 199, 223, 318–19, 322, 323, 414
Psychosomatic disorders, 357
Public opinion, 70
Public school, 336–38
Puerto Ricans, 230, 232, 307 (*see also* Hispanics)
Puerto Rico, 365
Punishment, 149–51
Purchasing power parties, 192, 193

Questionnaire, 21–22
Quid pro quo sexual harassment, 253
Quota system, 227
Qur'an, 315, 317

Race, 211–35
 composition of U.S., 214, 216

and criminal behavior, 146, 149
defined, 212–13
and education, 219, 226, 339, 342
and family life, 251, 306–9, 313
and formal organzations, 119, 120
and group dynamics, 111
and hate crimes, 142–43
ingroup vs. outgroup, 110, 215
and labor force participation, 270
and poverty, 178
and religion, 323–24
and social inequality, 171
and social mobility, 176
and sports, 17
and stratification, 171
and suicide rates, 4–5
and television programming, 69
and unemployment, 225–26, 273, 274
and voting frequency, 284, 285
workplace diversity, 273
Racism, 38, 216–17
and sexism compared, 243
Radical feminism, 258
Rain forests, 391, 401–4
global map, 402
Rape, 252, 253, 257
date, 140–41
marital, 312
Rationality, 113–14
Rationalization of society, 113–14, 420–21, 427
Rational-legal authority, 278
Real culture, 39
Reality (*see* Social construction of reality)
Rebellion, 132
Recidivism (*see* Criminal recidivism)
Recycling, 397, 398, 407
Redemptive social movements, 416–17
Red tape, 116
Reference group, 109
Reformative social movements, 416–17
Regional cities, 378–79
Rehabilitation, 150, 151
Relative deprivation, 416
Relative poverty, 178, 192, 193
Relativism (*see* Cultural relativism)
Reliability, of measurement, 16–17
Religion, 214, 298, 315–28
in changing society, 324–27
in history, 321
organization, 319–21

and social change, 318–19
social-conflict analysis of, 317–18
structural-functional analysis of, 316–17
symbolic-interaction analysis of, 317
in twenty-first century, 327
in U.S., 321–24
Religiosity, 322
Religious affiliation, 322–25
Religious diversity, national map, 323
Religious fundamentalism, 325–26
Remarriage, 310
Repression, 61
Research:
ethics in, 20–21
and gender, 19–20
methods, 21–25
objectivity in research, 18–19
Residential patterns, 299–301, 383
Resocialization, 76–77
Resource-mobilization theory, 416–17
Retirement, 306
Retreatism, 132, 133, 138
Retribution, 150, 151
Retrospective labeling, 135
Reverse discrimination, 227
Revolution:
political, 287–88
as social movement, 416–17
Rhesus monkey experiments, 59–60
Rights, 10
Ritualism, 132
bureaucratic, 116
Rodney King incident, 128, 149, 217
Role, 84
Role conflict, 85
Role exit, 85
Role set, 84
Role strain, 85, 249
Roman Catholic church (*see* Catholic church)
Romania, 191, 270, 312
Romantic love, 303–5, 309
Rome, 374
Routinization of charisma, 278
Rules and regulations, 114
Rural life (*see* Gemeinschaft; Mechanical solidarity)
Russia, 167, 365, 396, 406
Russian Federation, 193
Russian Revolution:
1917 revolution, 160, 287
recent revolution, 160, 270
Rwanda, 350

Sacred, 315, 316, 319

Samoans, 230
"Sandwich generation," 73, 74, 306
Sansei, 229
Sapir-Whorf hypothesis, 35
Saudi Arabia, 33, 140, 191, 193, 243, 279, 365
Scapegoat theory, 217
School choice, 343–44
Schooling (*see also* Education):
in Japan, 332, 333–34, 342
people with disabilities, 344
for profit, 344
and segregation, 219, 225
and social inequality, 171
and socialization, 66–67, 335
tracking, 336
in twenty-first century, 344–45
Science:
and religion, 321
and sociology, 8–9, 14–21
and theory of class society, 424
as value, 37
Scientific medicine, 353–54
Scientific stage (Comte), 9
SDI (*see* Strategic Defense Initiative)
Secondary deviance, 134–36
Secondary economic sector, 266
Secondary group, 105–6
Second World, 189
Sect, 319, 320
Secular humanism, 326
Secularization, 324
Segregation, 219, 220–21, 225
Self, 63–65
presentation of, 89–90
Self-employment, 272
Semai, 32, 34, 289
Sensorimotor stage (Piaget), 61
Serbian "ethnic cleansing," 212
Service industries, 266
SES (*see* Socioeconomic status)
Sex, 238–39 (*see also* Sociobiology)
Sexism, 52
and medicine, 354
and patriarchy, 242–43
and racism compared, 243
Sex ratio, 366
Sex role (*see* Gender role)
Sexual activity:
among U.S. couples, 24
and the family, 301–2, 304
and gender, 52
Sexual harassment, 252–53, 257, 275, 292
Sexually transmitted disease (STD), 349–52
Sexual orientation, 43, 239–40
Sexual slavery, 196
Shame, 39
Sick role, 357

Significant other, 65
Singapore, 190, 201, 202, 206, 207, 268, 279, 281, 430
Singlehood, 314, 370
Single-parent households, 46, 179, 251, 312–13
Slavery, 224–25, 318
Slovakia, 270
Smiling, 94
Smoking (*see* Cigarette smoking)
Snowbelt cities, 378, 379
Social area analysis, 382
Social behaviorism, 63
Social change, 411–32 (*see also* Class conflict; Modernity; Rationalization of society; Sociocultural evolution)
causes of, 414–17
characteristics of, 412–14
class society, 423–25, 427
and culture, 46–47
and deviance, 131
idea of progress, 427–28
mass society, 421–24
modernity, 417–21
and religion, 318–19
Social character, 425
Social class:
and conflict, 163–65
and crime, 146
and deviance, 132–33
and family life, 174, 306
in Great Britain, 159–60
and health, 174, 347–48
and life expectancy, 174
and politics, 174, 284, 286
and religion, 322
and socialization, 66
and stratification, 157, 159, 161
in United States, 171–74
and values, 174
Social conflict:
as cause of prejudice, 218–19
Marxist, 161, 163–66, 218, 255, 405, 421, 423, 424
Social-conflict paradigm, 12–15, 16 (*see also* individual topics)
Social construction of reality, 85–89, 357 (*see also* Dramaturgical analysis; Symbolic-interaction paradigm)
Social control, 128
and education, 336
medicine as, 357
and religion, 316
Social distance, 218
Social diversity, 22, 418 (*see also* Cultural diversity)
and group dynamics, 111
and the military, 291–92

inequality in, 167–71
medicine in, 355–57
occupational prestige in, 170
politics in, 283–85
poverty in, 178–83
quality of life index, 193
religion in, 321–24
social classes in, 171–74
social mobility in, 175–78
suicide rates in, 11
work in postindustrial, 270–75
Upper class, 172–73, 174
Upper-middle class, 173
Upper-upper class, 172–73, 223
Upward social mobility, 175
Urban decentralization, 376–78
Urban ecology, 381–82
Urbanism, as way of life, 379–82
Urbanization, 10, 373–87
global map, 384
growth of cities, 373–79
in poor societies, 382–85
theories of, 379–82
in twenty-first century, 385
Urban renewal, 378
Urban revolutions, 373, 374,
382–83
Uruguay, 396
USSR (*see* Commonwealth of
Independent States;
Soviet Union, former)
Utilitarian organization, 112

Validity of measurement, 16–18
Values, 35–37
and class, 174
conflict of, 39
and deviance, 131
and education, 335
and natural environment, 404
and science, 19
Variable, 15
Venereal disease, 349
Vesuvius, 374

Veto group, 285
Victimization, culture of, 38, 39,
136
Victimization survey, 144
Victimless crime, 144
Vietnam, 205, 289, 290, 365
Vietnamese Americans, 230
Violence:
in families, 257, 310–12
in schools, 340, 341
in war, 290
Violence against women,
140–41, 252–54, 257,
311–12
Voluntary association, 112
Voter apathy, 285, 423

Wage labor, 266
War, 289–93
WASP (*see* White Anglo-Saxon
Protestant)
Water pollution, 399
Water supply, 397–99
Wealth (*see also* Income):
distribution of, in U.S., 166,
169
as value, 37
Weddings (*see* Marriage)
Wedge-shaped sectors, 382
White Anglo-Saxon Protestant
(WASP), 223 (*see also*
Race)
White-collar crime, 138–39, 146,
405
White-collar occupations, 164,
270, 272
White Ethnic Americans,
233–34 (*see also* Race)
Widowhood, 306
Wodaabe, 241
Women (*see also* Family;
Feminism; Gender;
Marriage; individual
topics)

and aging, 306
Asian American, 230
and beauty myth, 238, 245,
348
biological development, 238,
240
business owners, 248
Chinese, 228
and cigarette smoking, 349
and college degrees, 245, 250
of color, 218, 251, 307–8
and deviance, 140–42, 145–46
and divorce, 46, 309–11
and earnings, 249–50, 339, 340
and eating disorders, 348
and education, 339, 340, 371
feminine traits, 243
gay, 142, 239
and health, 347, 348
Hispanic, 232
and housework, 248, 308
global map, 86
and infanticide, 196
Japanese, 228
and mass media, 245
in medical profession, 354,
355
and middle age, 72
in military, 291–92
as minority, 214, 251–52
and modernization, 201
Muslim, 317–18
and networking, 112
paid employment, global map,
247
and politics, 250–51
and poverty, 179, 308, 313
and religion, 317–18
sex ratio, 366
and sexual slavery, 196
and singlehood, 314
socialization of, 243–45
social mobility of, 176

and stratification, 245–54
violence against, 140–41,
252–54, 257, 311–12
and voting frequency, 285
and work, 246–48, 270, 273–75
Women's movement, 256–60,
417
Work (*see also* Capitalism;
Housework):
and adult education, 344
agricultural employment,
global map, 265
and alienation, 116, 163
child labor, global map, 71
earnings of workers, by sex,
250
and gender, 246–48, 271
industrial employment, global
map, 265
labor force, U.S., 246–48, 271,
272
occupational prestige, 170
in postindustrial economy,
270–74, 275
and technology, 273–74
as value, 37
women and, 246–48, 270,
273–75
Work ethic, 223, 319
Working class, 173
Working poor, 173, 182

Yąnomamö, 30, 32–34, 40, 47, 48,
289, 426
Yonsei, 229
Yugoslavia, 43–44, 212, 290

Zaire, 168, 191, 192, 193, 206,
385
Zebaleen of Egypt, 188
Zero population growth, 370
Zimbabwe, 332

About the Author

John J. Macionis (pronounced ma-SHOW-nis) grew up in Philadelphia, Pennsylvania. He received his bachelor's degree from Cornell University and a doctorate in sociology from the University of Pennsylvania. His publications are wide-ranging, focusing on community life in the United States, interpersonal intimacy in families, effective teaching, humor, and the importance of global education. He is author of *Sociology*, the leading introductory textbook in the field. He is also coauthor of *The Sociology of Cities* and has coedited the third edition of the companion volume to this text, *Seeing Ourselves: Classic, Contemporary, and Cross-Cultural Readings in Sociology*.

John Macionis is professor of sociology at Kenyon College in Gambier, Ohio. He has served as chair of the Anthropology-Sociology Department, director of Kenyon's multidisciplinary program in humane studies, and chair of the college's faculty.

Professor Macionis teaches a wide range of upper-level courses but his favorite course is Introduction to Sociology, which he teaches every semester. He enjoys extensive contact with students, making an occasional appearance on campus with his guitar and each term inviting his students to enjoy a home-cooked meal. Macionis is a frequent visitor to other campuses as well and participates regularly in teaching programs abroad. In the fall of 1994, he directed the global education course for the University of Pittsburgh's Semester at Sea program, teaching four hundred students on a floating campus that visited twelve countries as it circled the globe.

John Macionis lives on a farm in rural Ohio with his wife Amy and children McLean and Whitney. In his free time, he enjoys bicycling through the Ohio countryside and restoring an old tractor to health. The Macionis home serves as a popular bed and breakfast where they enjoy visiting with old friends and making new ones.

The author welcomes (and responds to) comments and suggestions about this edition of *Society: The Basics* from faculty and students. Write to John Macionis, Palme House, Kenyon College, Gambier, Ohio 43022. His internet address is MACIONIS@KENYON.EDU